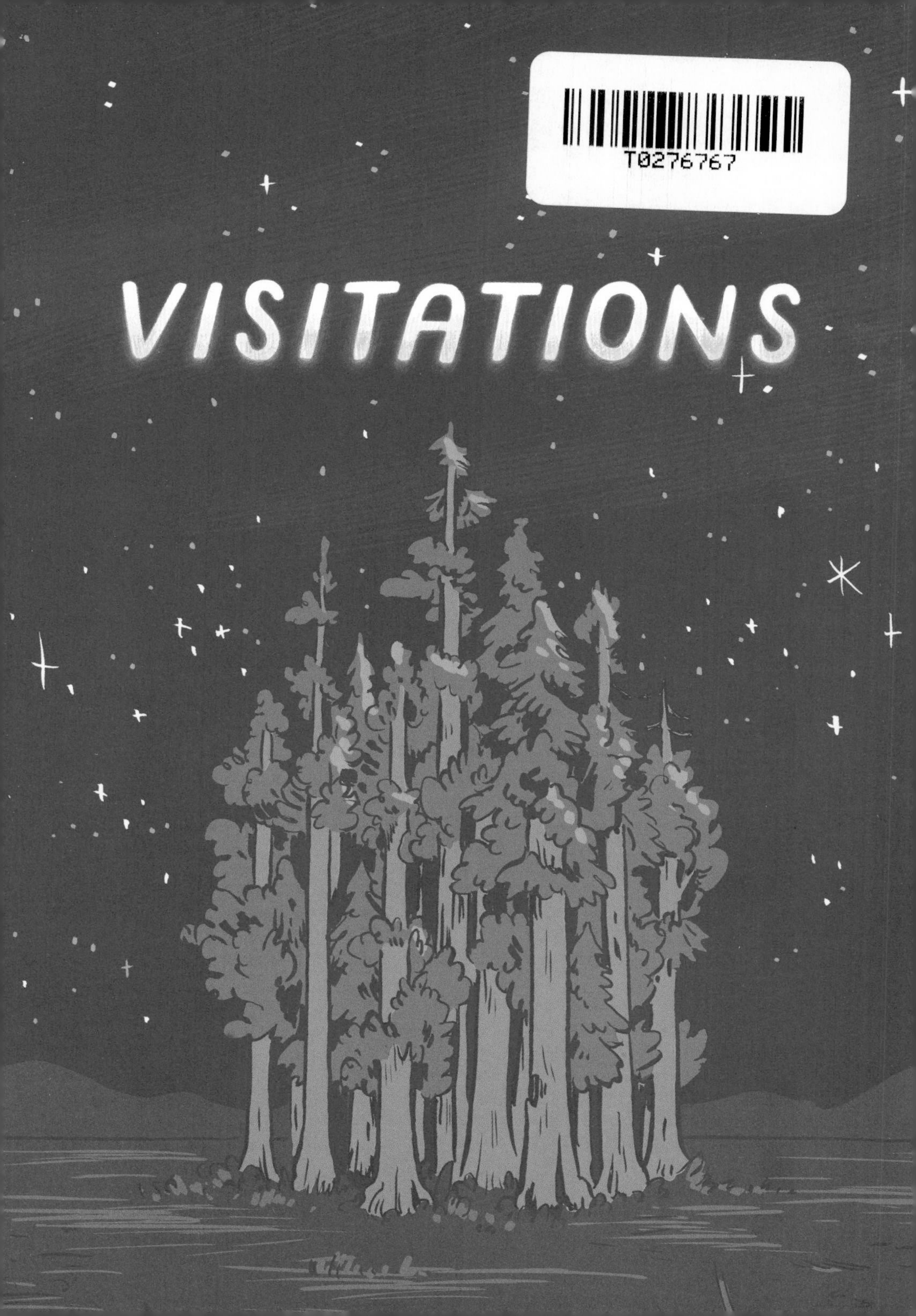
VISITATIONS

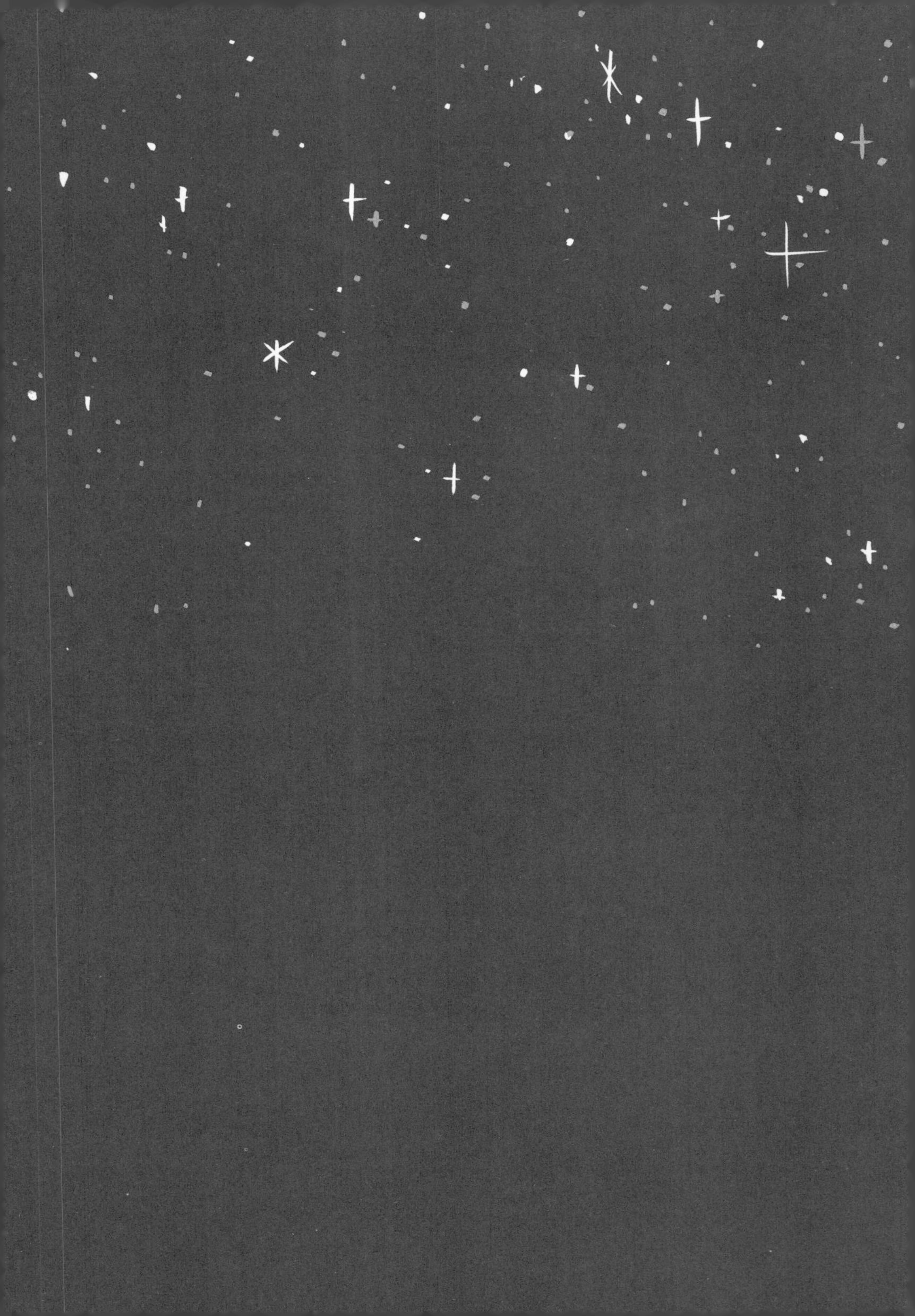

VISITATIONS

COREY EGBERT

Farrar Straus Giroux
New York

Published by Farrar Straus Giroux Books for Young Readers
An imprint of Macmillan Publishing Group, LLC
120 Broadway, New York, NY 10271 · Fiercereads.com

Our books may be purchased in bulk for promotional, educational, or business use.
Please contact your local bookseller or the Macmillan Corporate and Premium Sales Department
at (800) 221-7945 ext. 5442 or by email at MacmillanSpecialMarkets@macmillan.com.

Library of Congress Cataloging-in-Publication Data is available.

First edition, 2024
Edited by Joy Peskin
Book design by Sunny Lee and Yan L. Moy
Production editing by Helen Seachrist

The illustrations were inked with Japanese brush pens and Sharpie on paper, then scanned
and colored digitally in Photoshop. The font was created with Fontself extension for Adobe Illustrator.

Printed in China by RR Donnelley Asia Printing Solutions Ltd.,
Dongguan City, Guangdong Province

ISBN 978-0-374-30839-1 (paperback)
1 3 5 7 9 10 8 6 4 2

ISBN 978-0-374-30842-1 (hardcover)
1 3 5 7 9 10 8 6 4 2

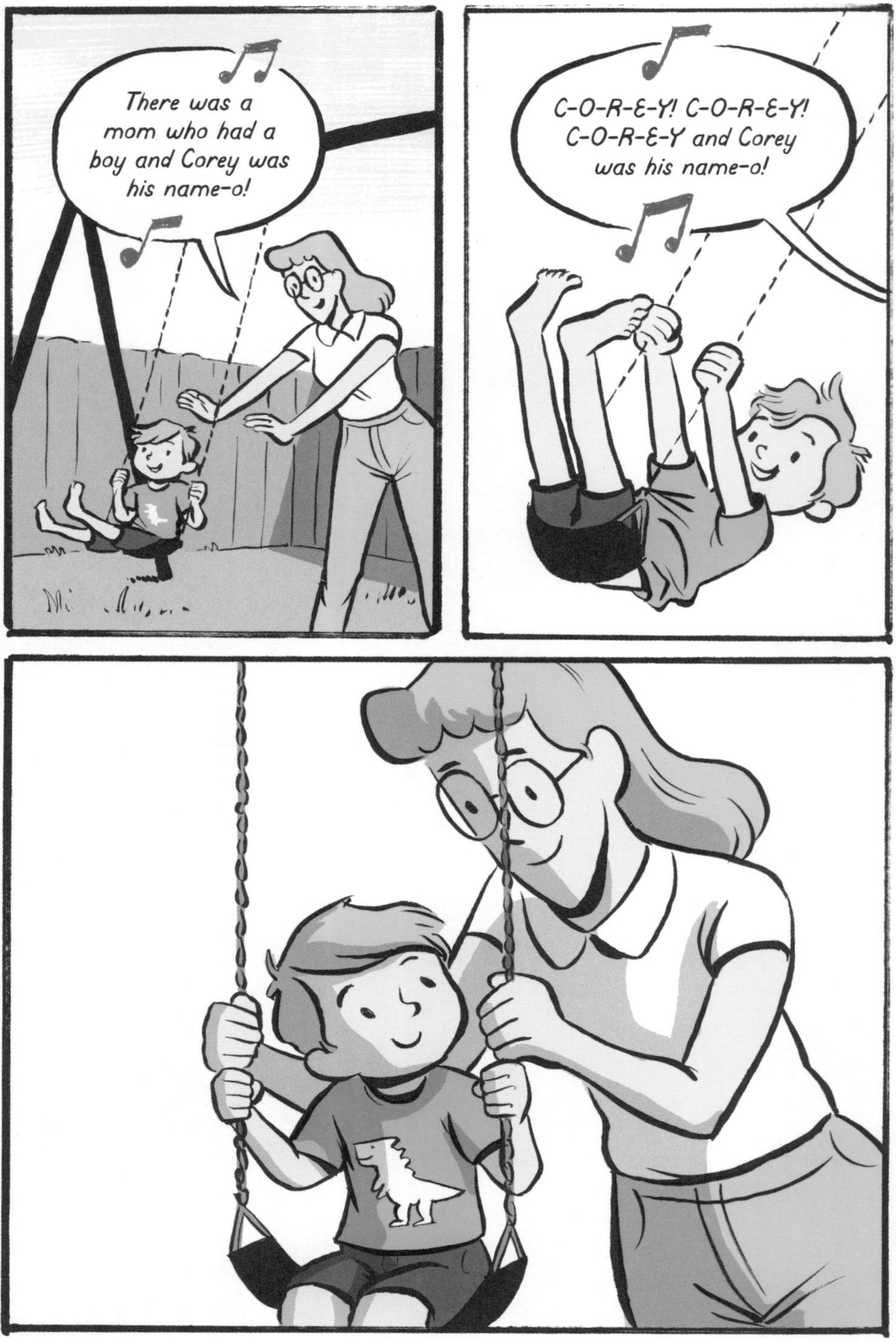
There was a mom who had a boy and Corey was his name-o!
C-O-R-E-Y! C-O-R-E-Y! C-O-R-E-Y and Corey was his name-o!

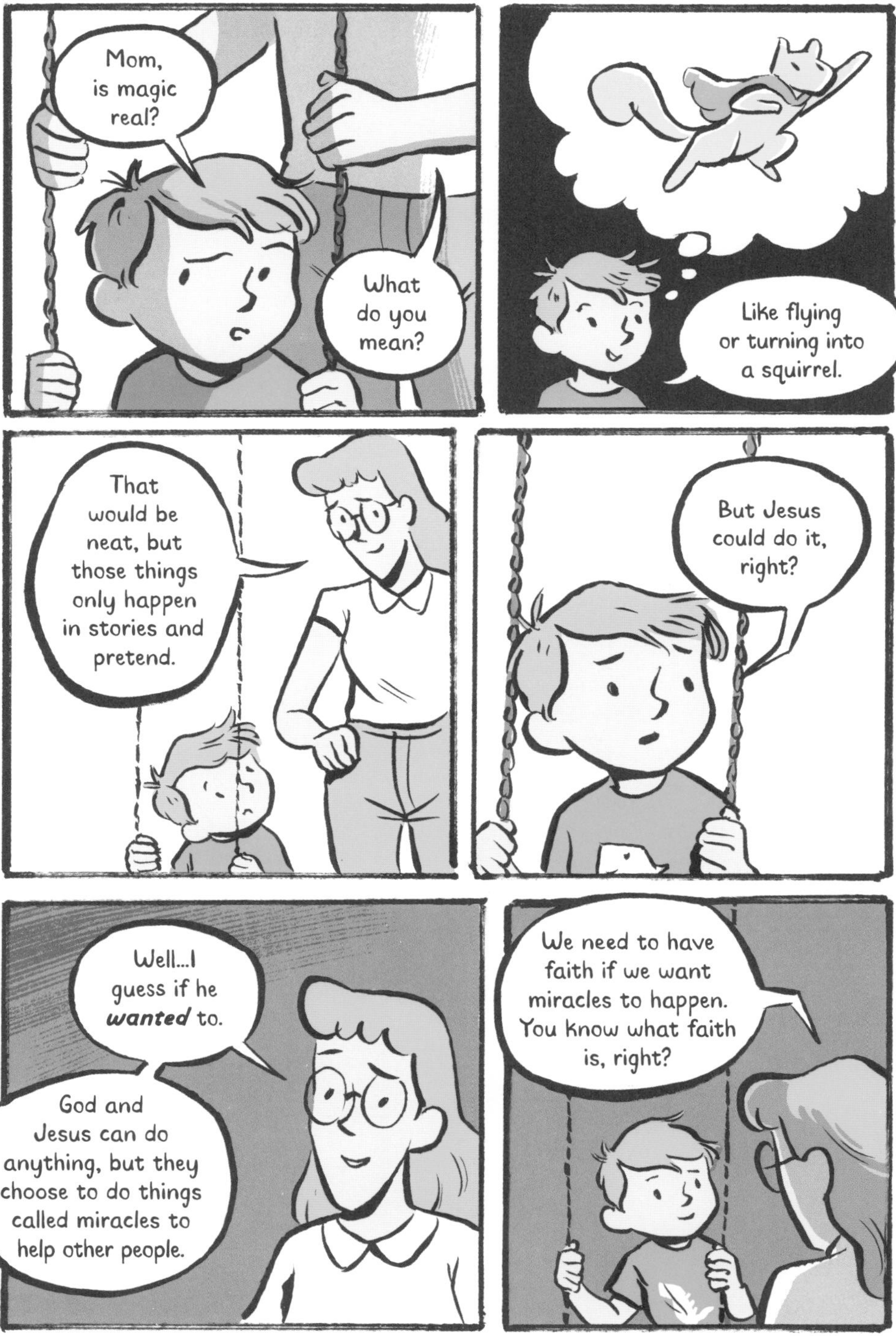
Mom, is magic real?
What do you mean?
Like flying or turning into a squirrel.
That would be neat, but those things only happen in stories and pretend.
But Jesus could do it, right?
Well...I guess if he *wanted* to.
God and Jesus can do anything, but they choose to do things called miracles to help other people.
We need to have faith if we want miracles to happen. You know what faith is, right?

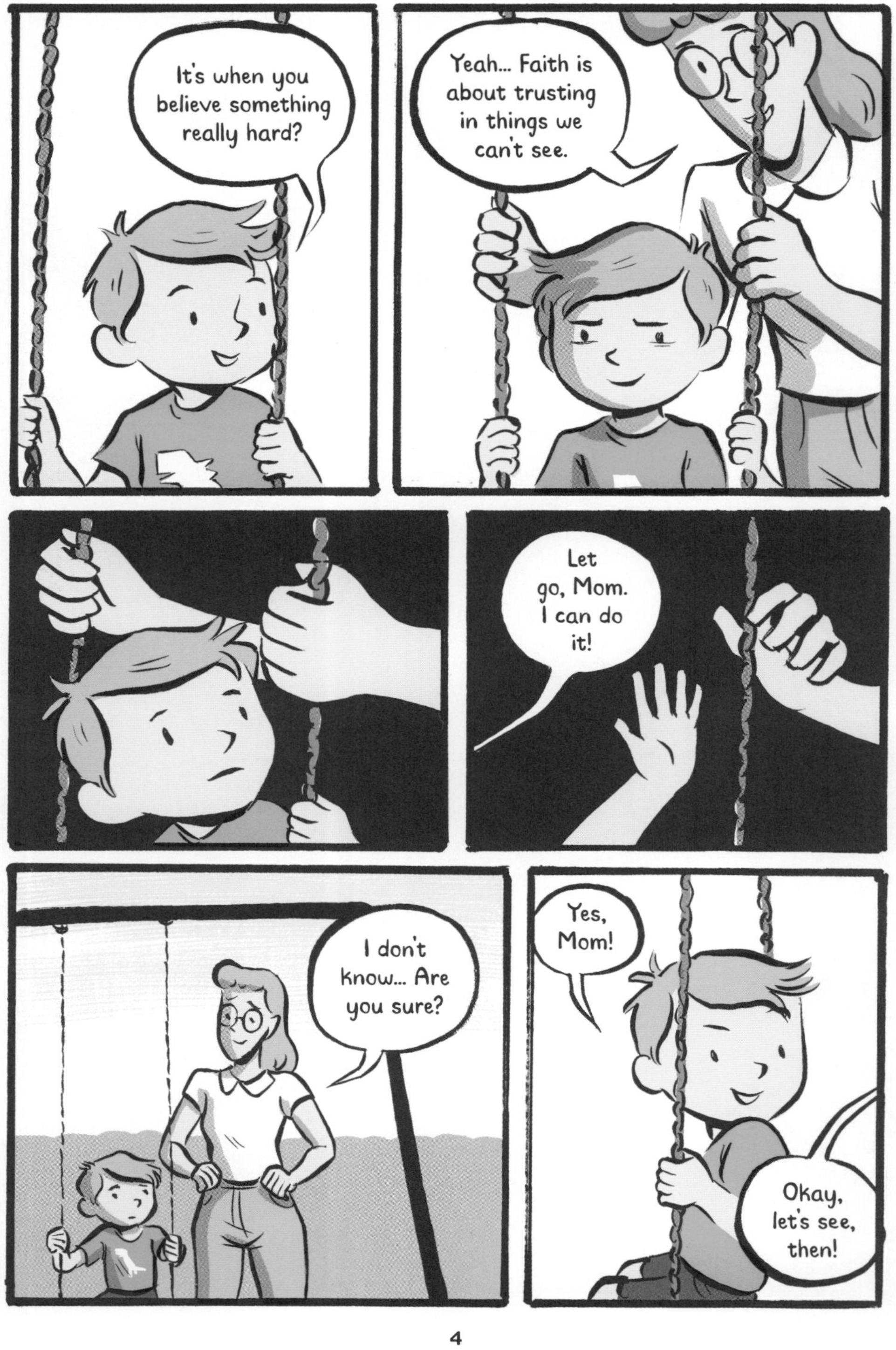

It's when you believe something really hard?
Yeah... Faith is about trusting in things we can't see.
Let go, Mom. I can do it!
I don't know... Are you sure?
Yes, Mom!
Okay, let's see, then!

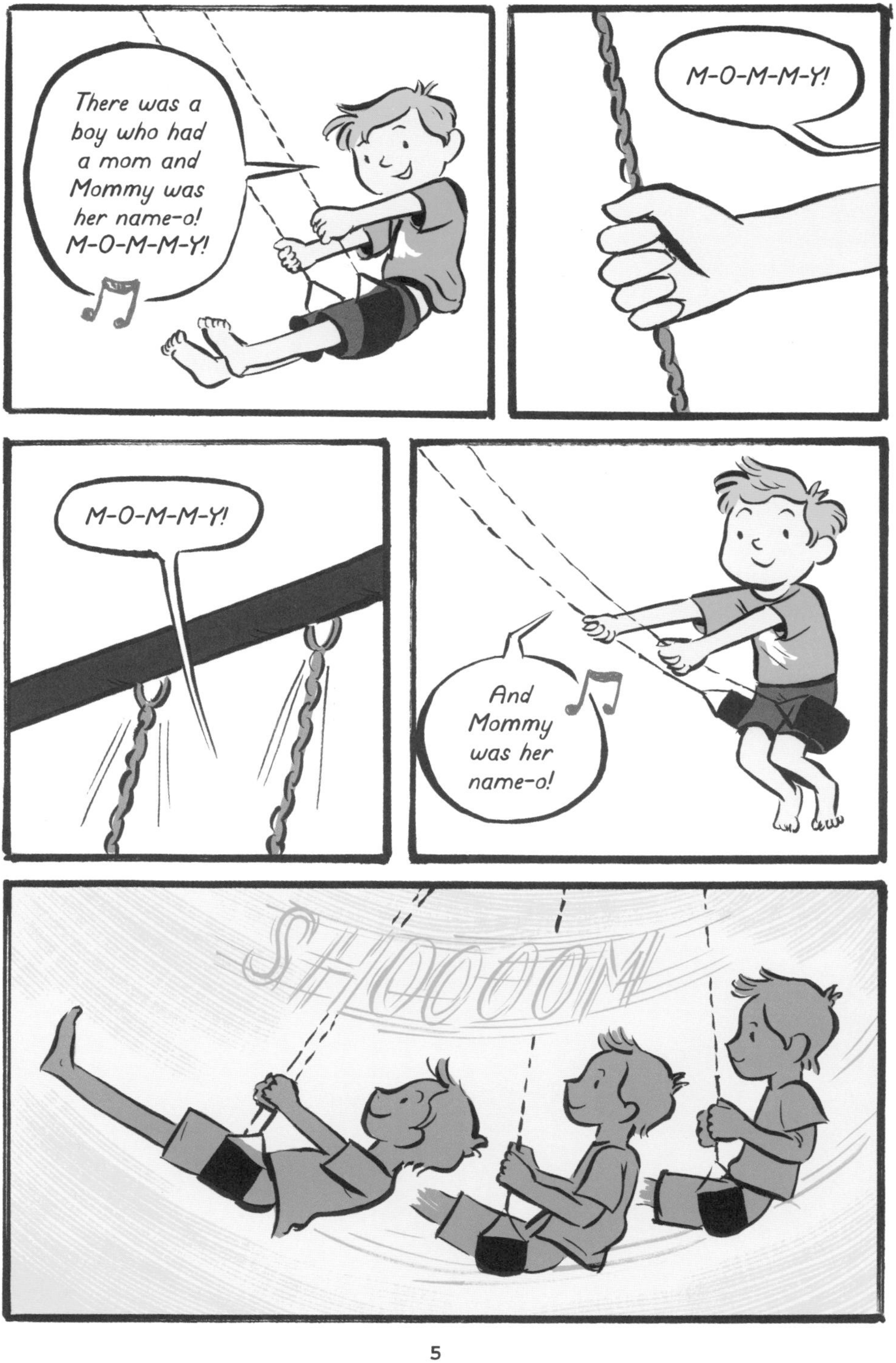
There was a boy who had a mom and Mommy was her name-o! M-O-M-M-Y!
M-O-M-M-Y!
M-O-M-M-Y!
And Mommy was her name-o!
SHOOOOM

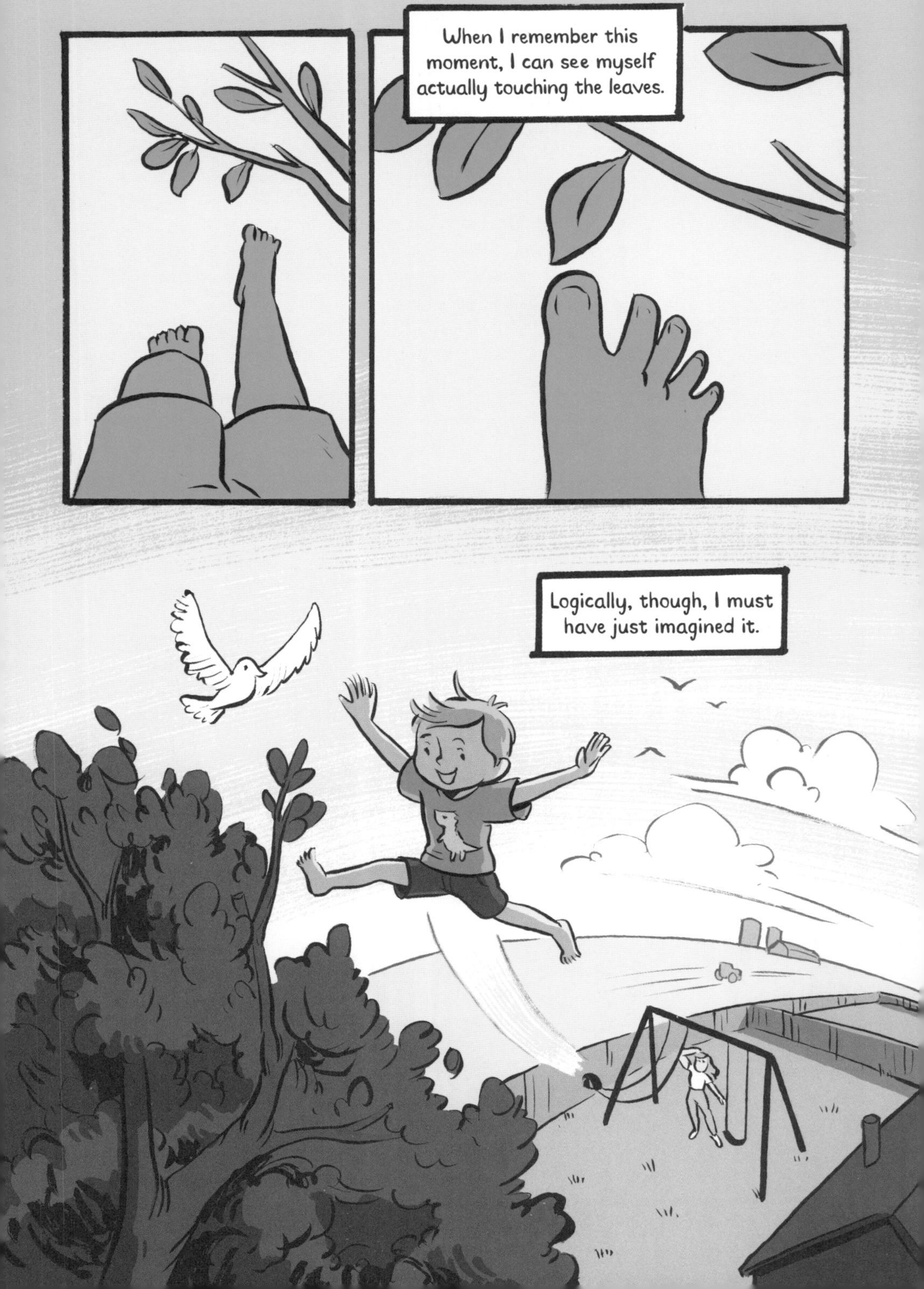
When I remember this moment, I can see myself actually touching the leaves.
Logically, though, I must have just imagined it.

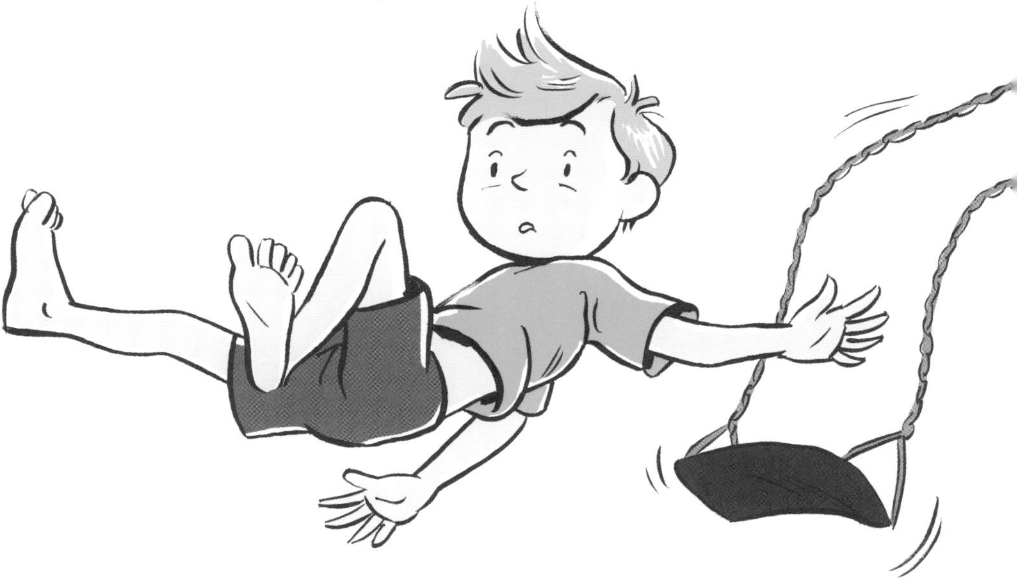

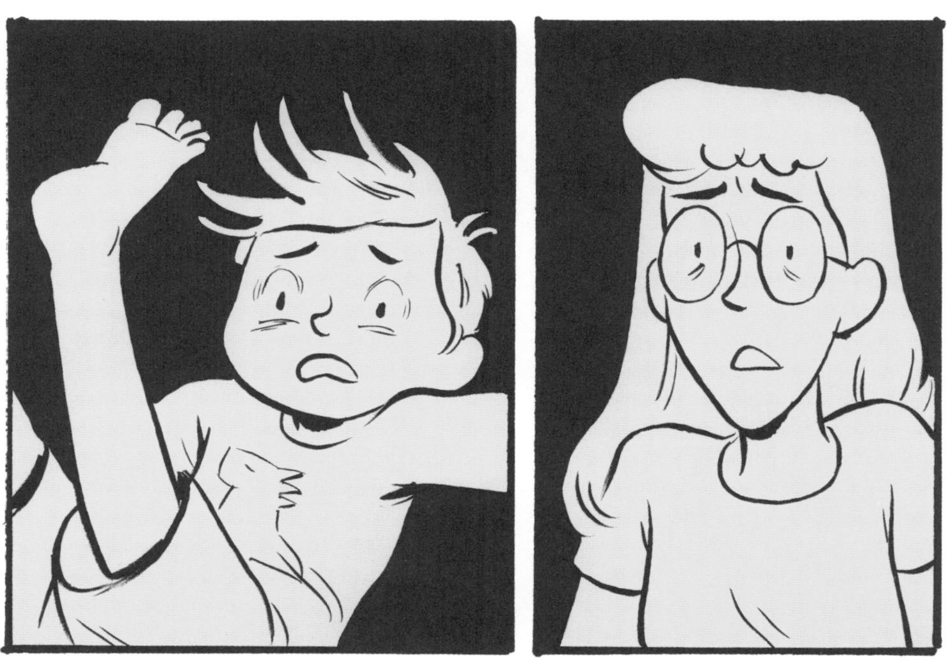

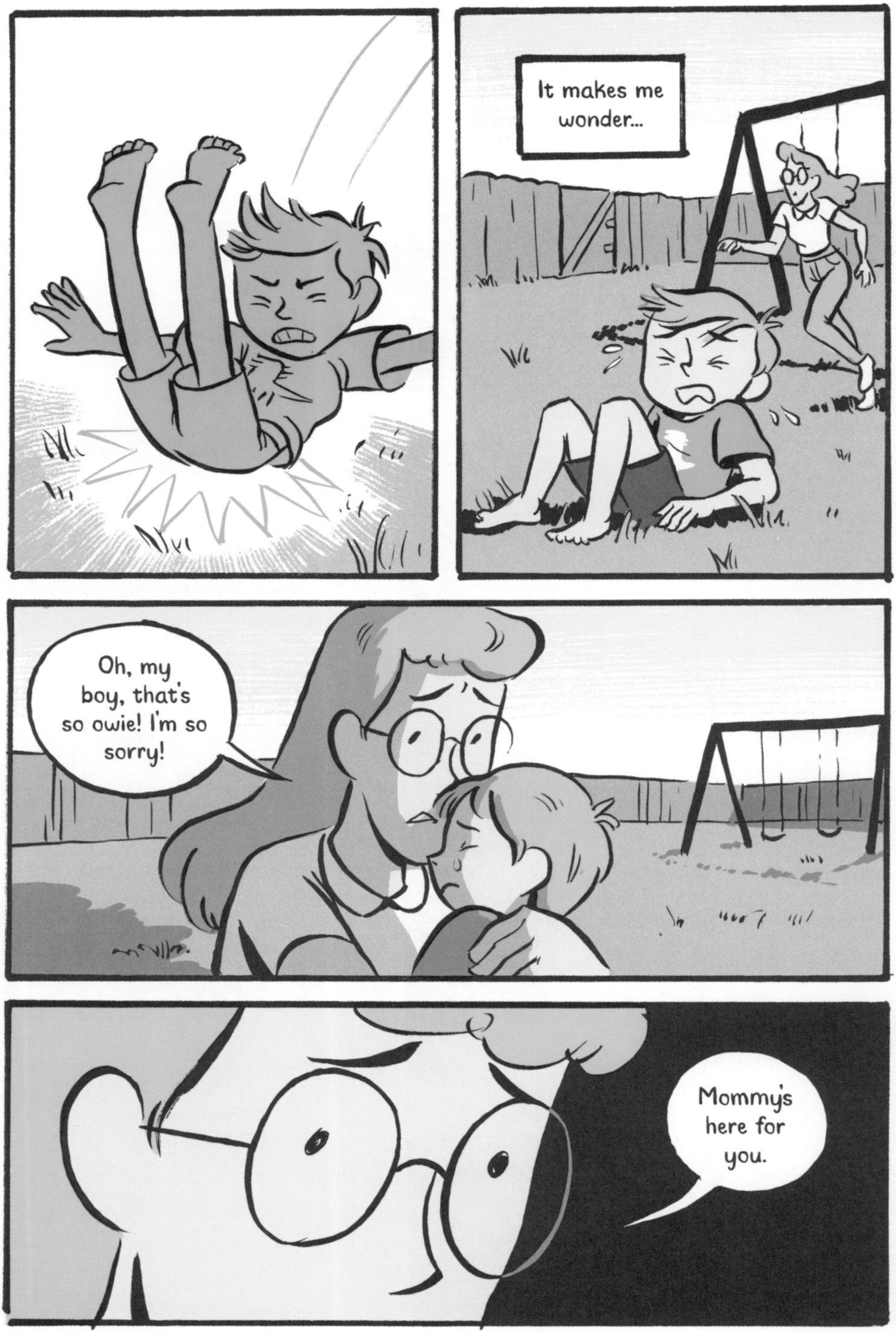
It makes me wonder...
Oh, my boy, that's so owie! I'm so sorry!
Mommy's here for you.

...how much of
my childhood
was real.

PART ONE

"And it came to pass that the Lord
commanded my father, even in
a dream, that he should take his
family and depart into
the wilderness."

1 NEPHI 2:2

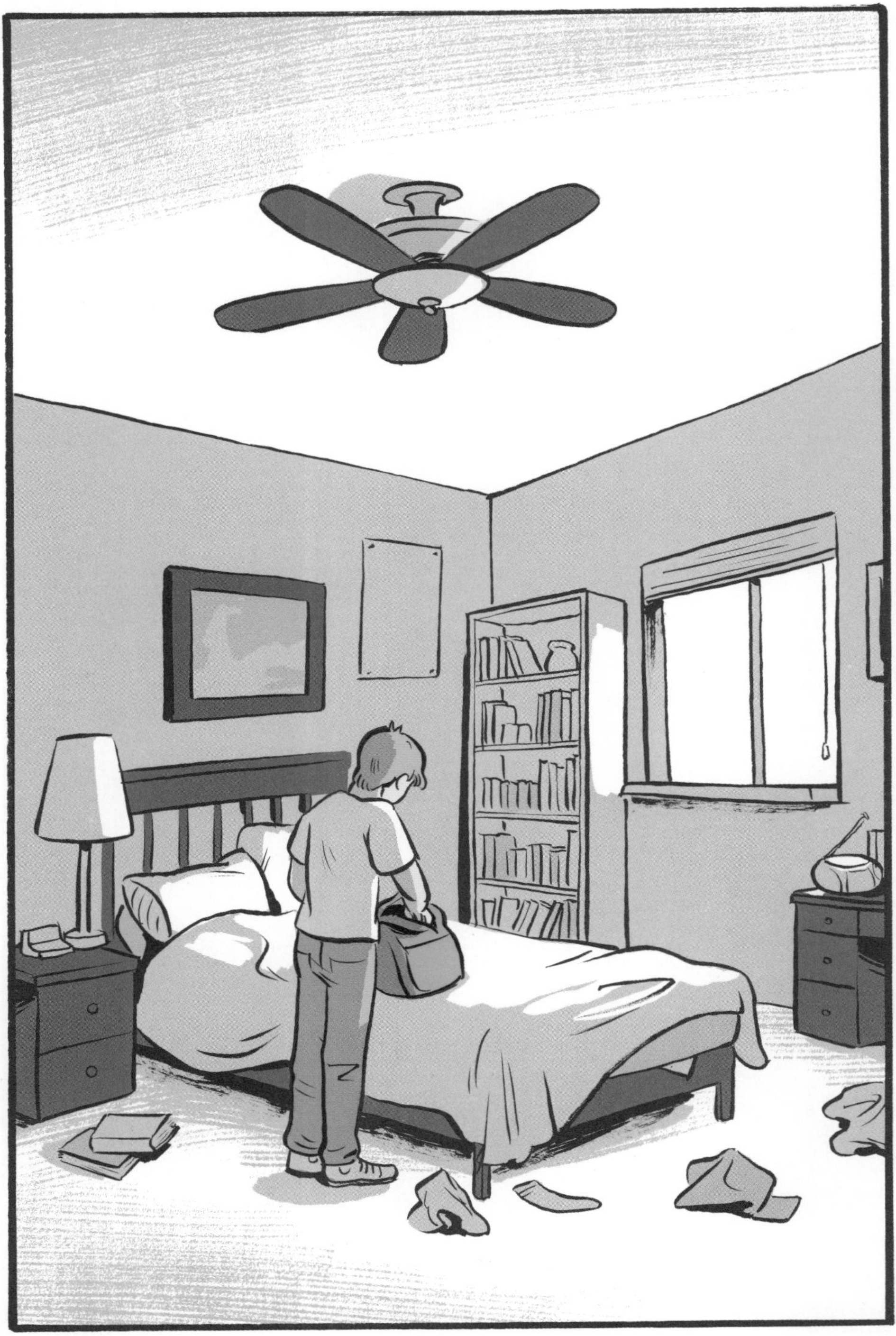

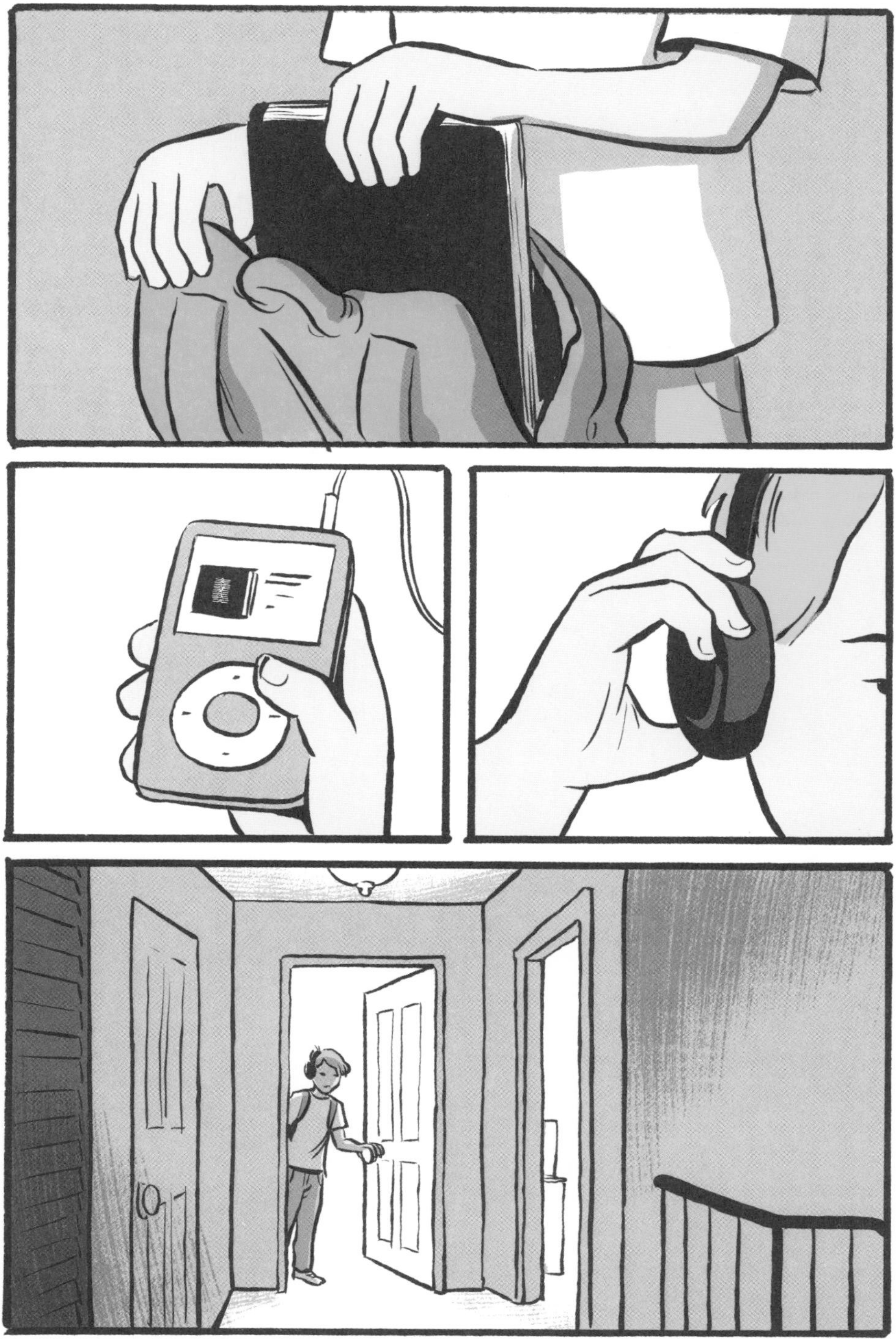

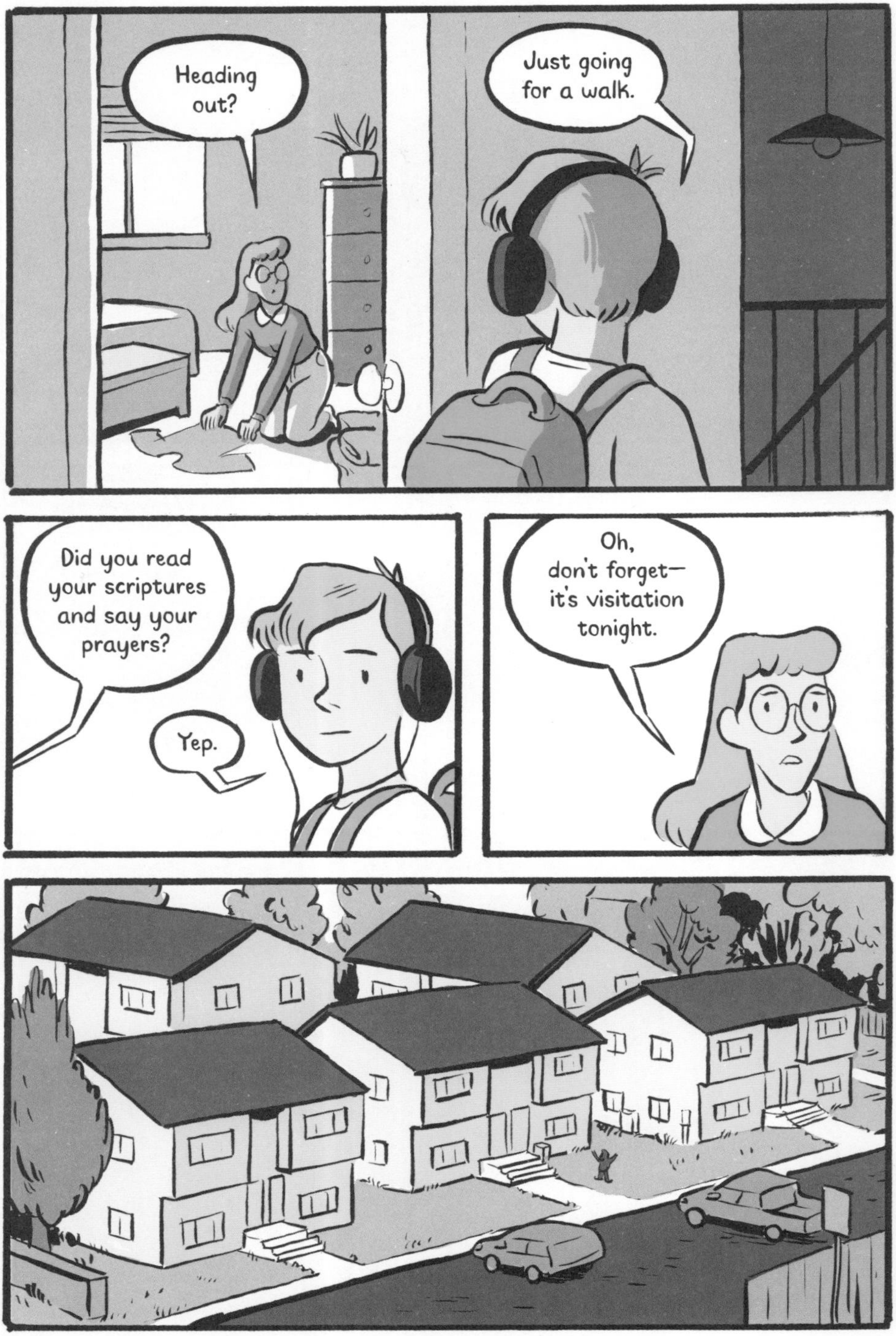
Heading out?
Just going for a walk.
Did you read your scriptures and say your prayers?
Yep.
Oh, don't forget— it's visitation tonight.

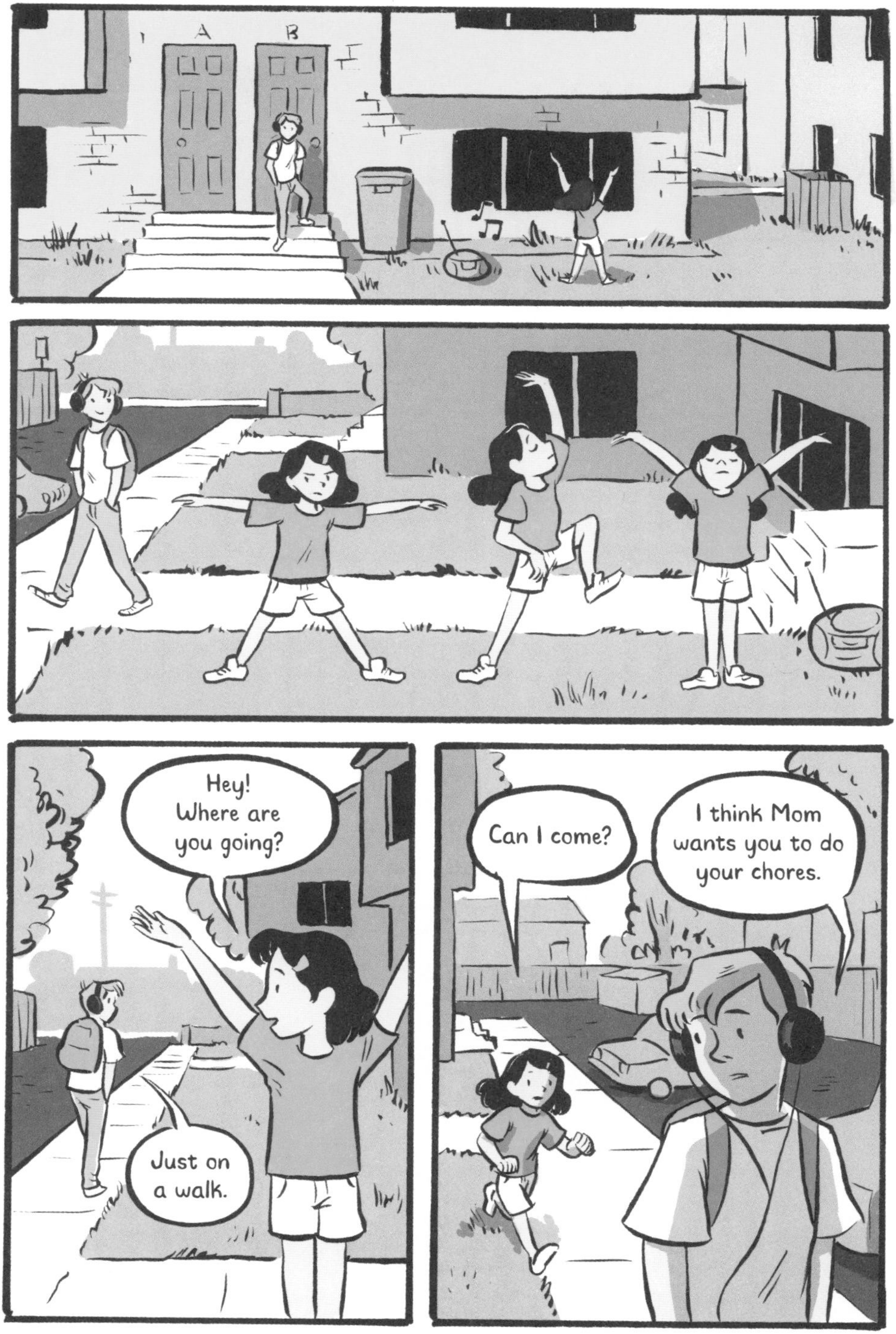
A
B
Hey! Where are you going?
Just on a walk.
Can I come?
I think Mom wants you to do your chores.

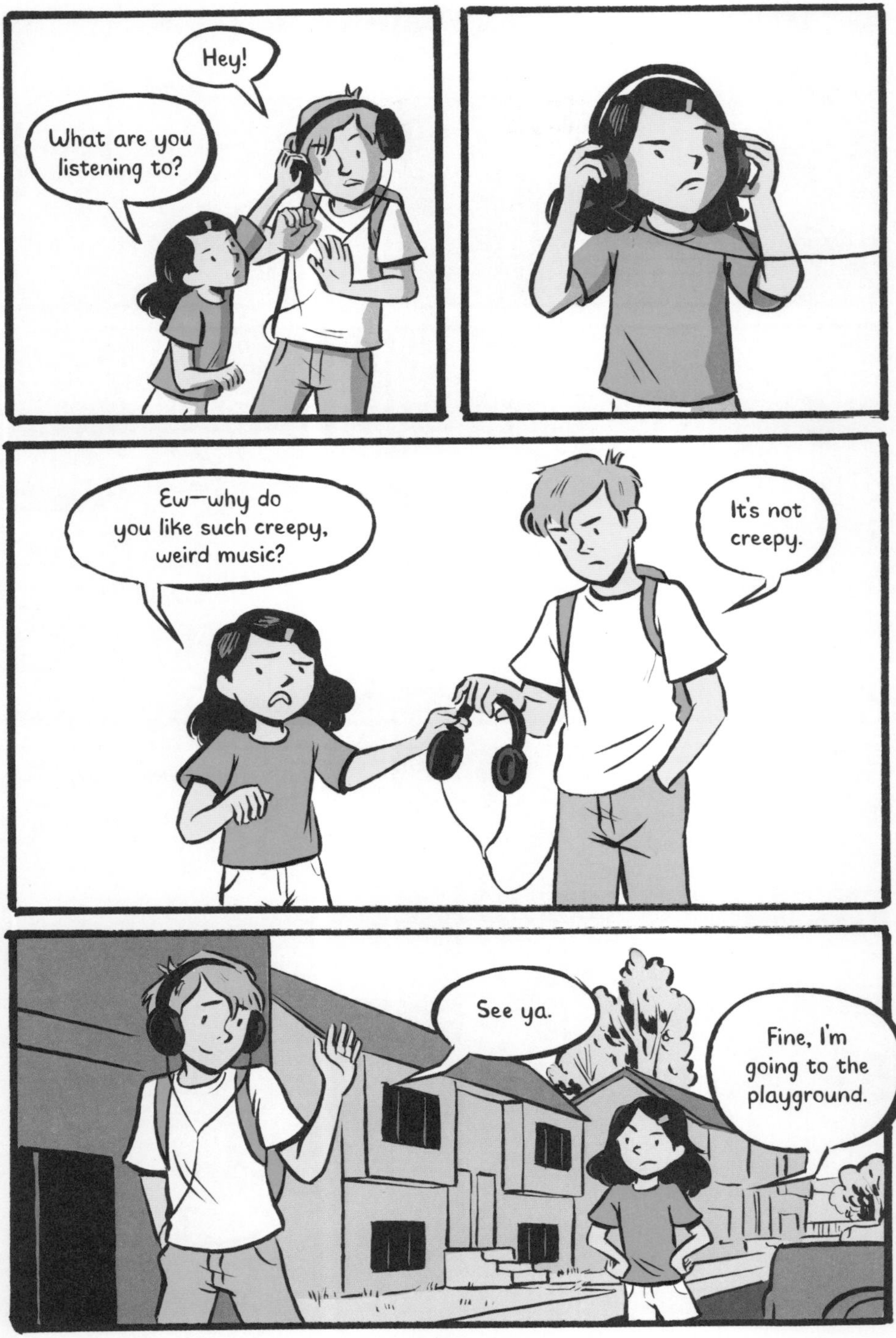
Hey!
What are you listening to?
Ew—why do you like such creepy, weird music?
It's not creepy.
See ya.
Fine, I'm going to the playground.

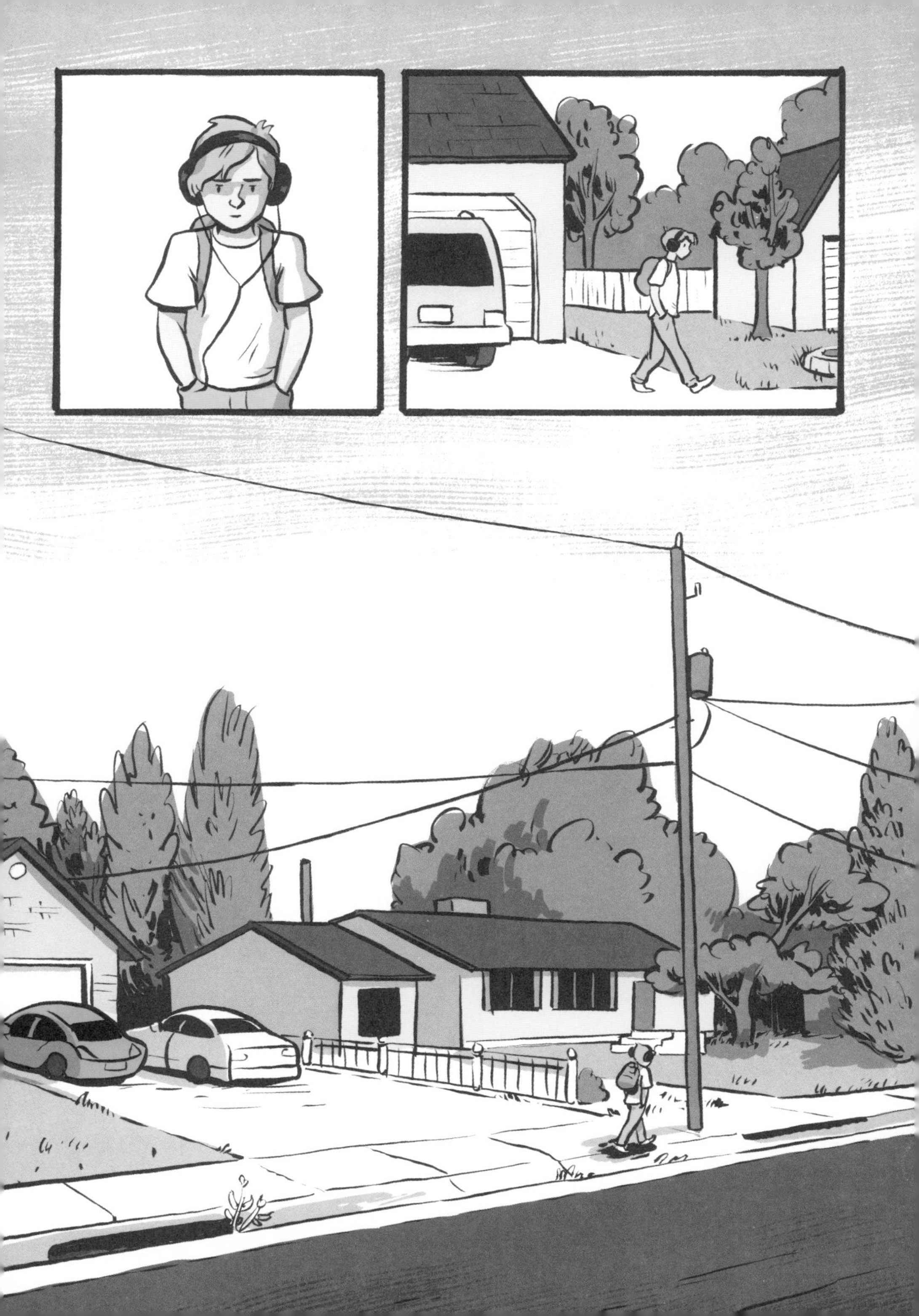

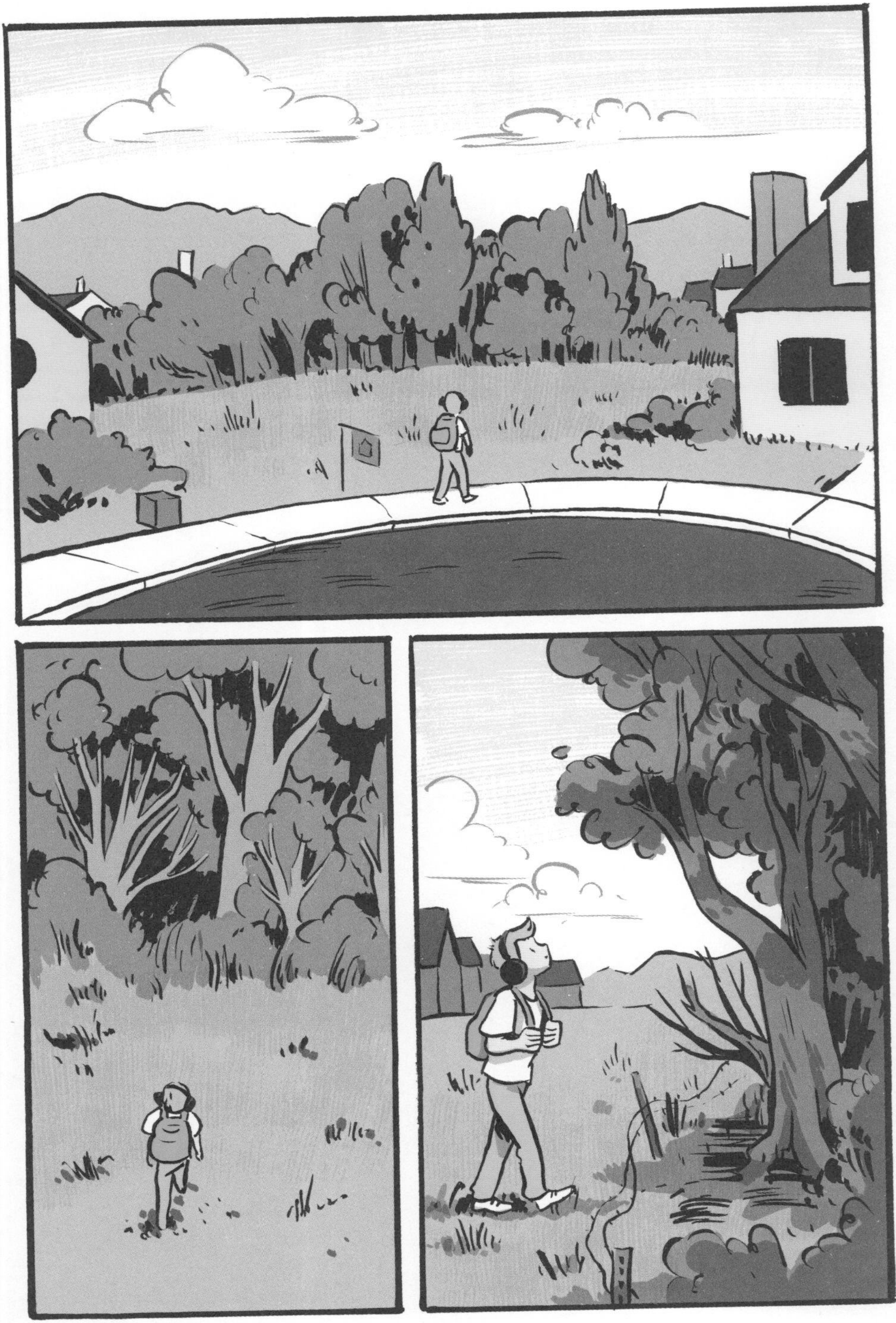

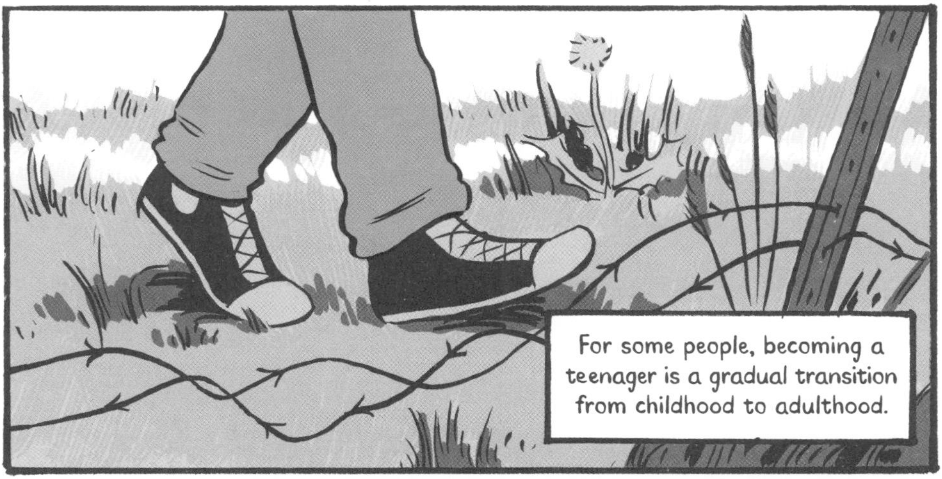
For some people, becoming a teenager is a gradual transition from childhood to adulthood.

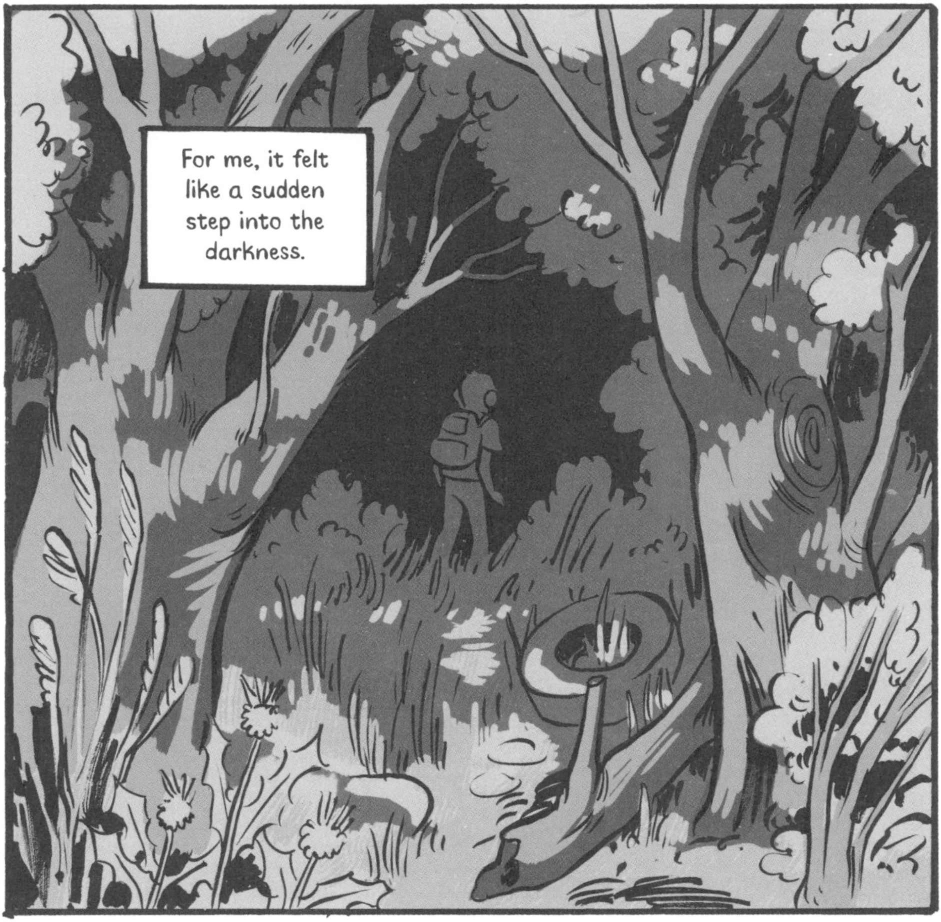
For me, it felt like a sudden step into the darkness.

When I was little, my mom, dad, and I lived in the California farming country.

Five Points Field Station

My dad worked in an agricultural research lab testing produce and fertilizers.

We were far from any town. The closest school was over two hours away.

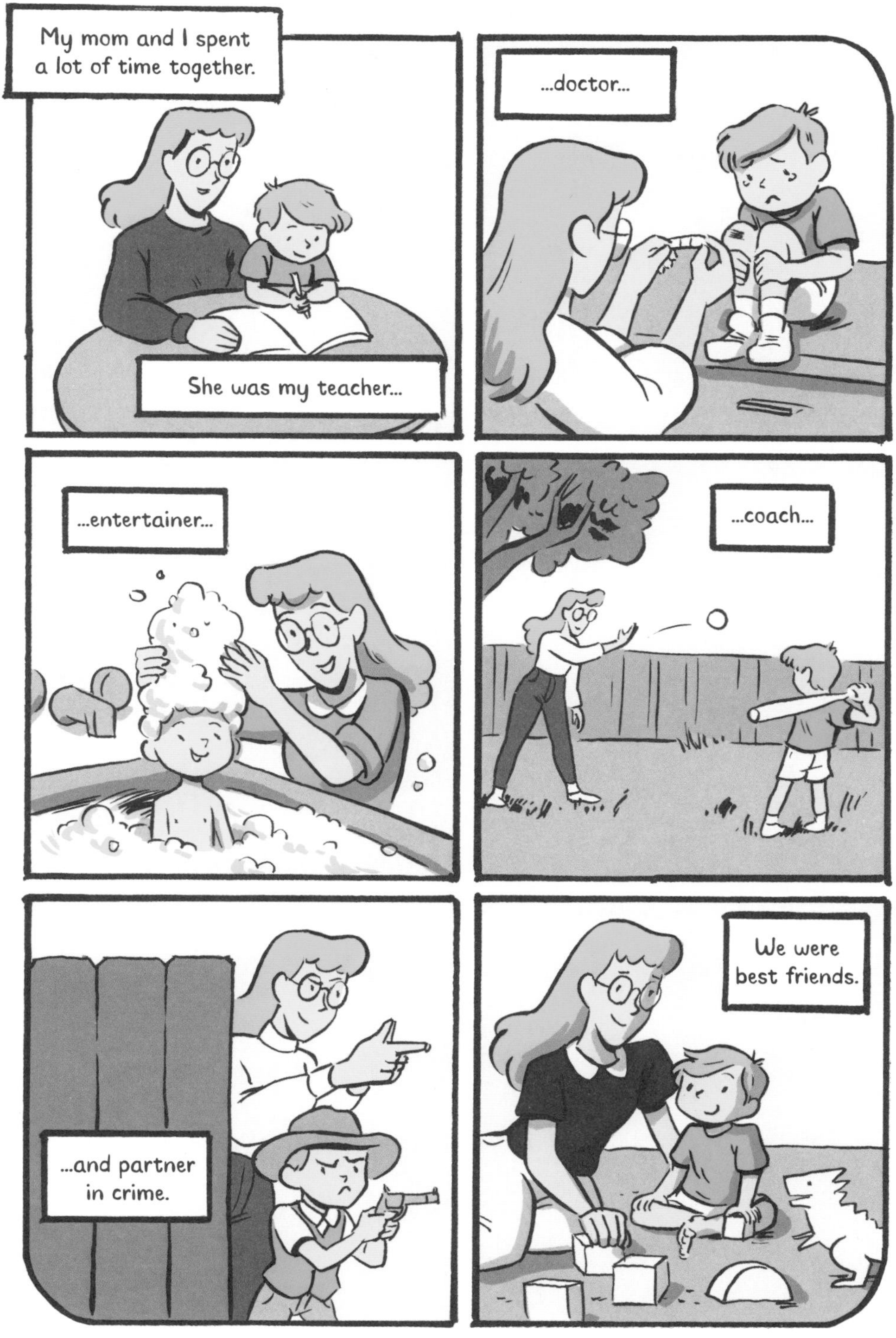
My mom and I spent a lot of time together.
She was my teacher...
...doctor...
...entertainer...
...coach...
...and partner in crime.
We were best friends.

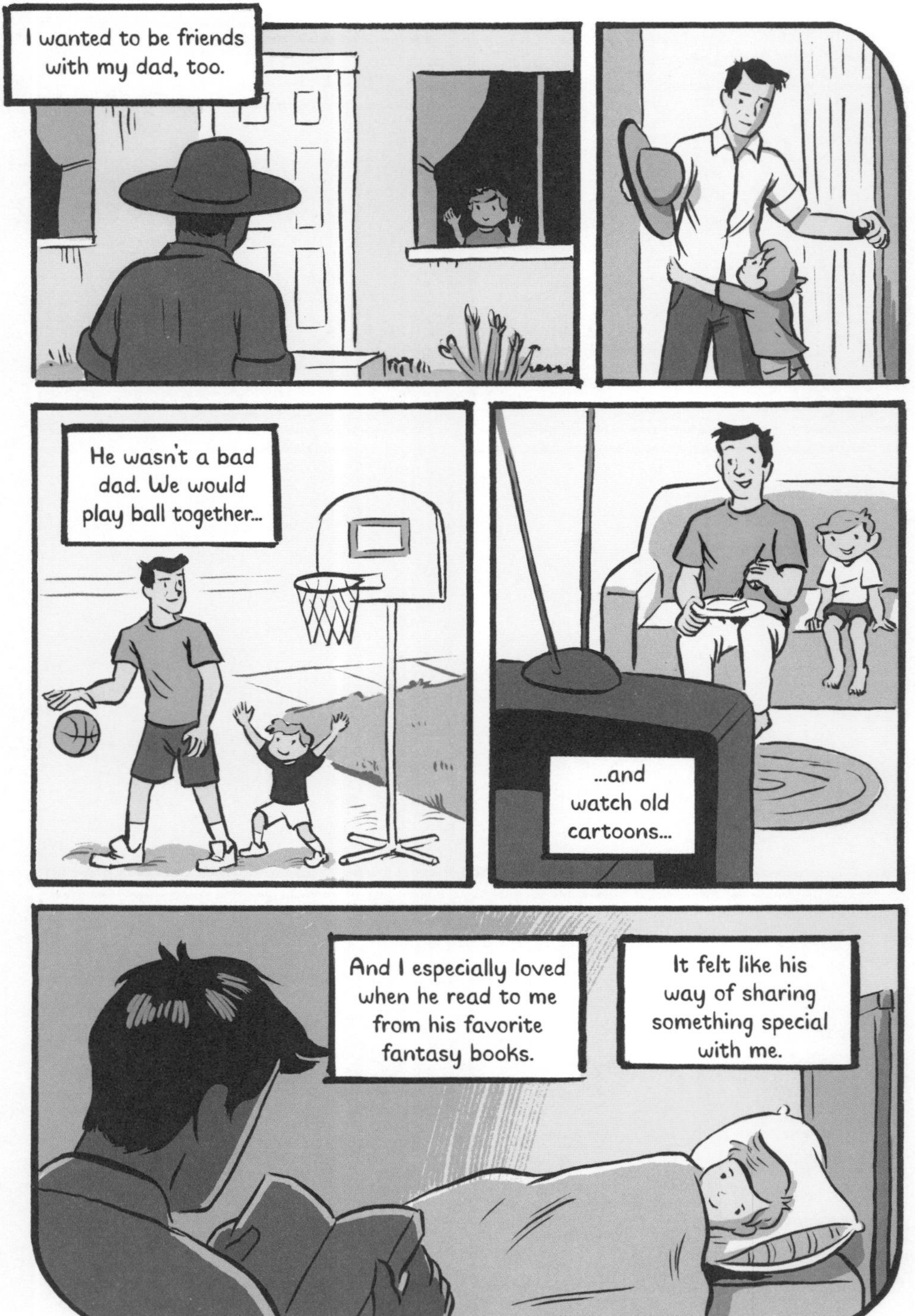
I wanted to be friends with my dad, too.
He wasn't a bad dad. We would play ball together...
...and watch old cartoons...
And I especially loved when he read to me from his favorite fantasy books.
It felt like his way of sharing something special with me.

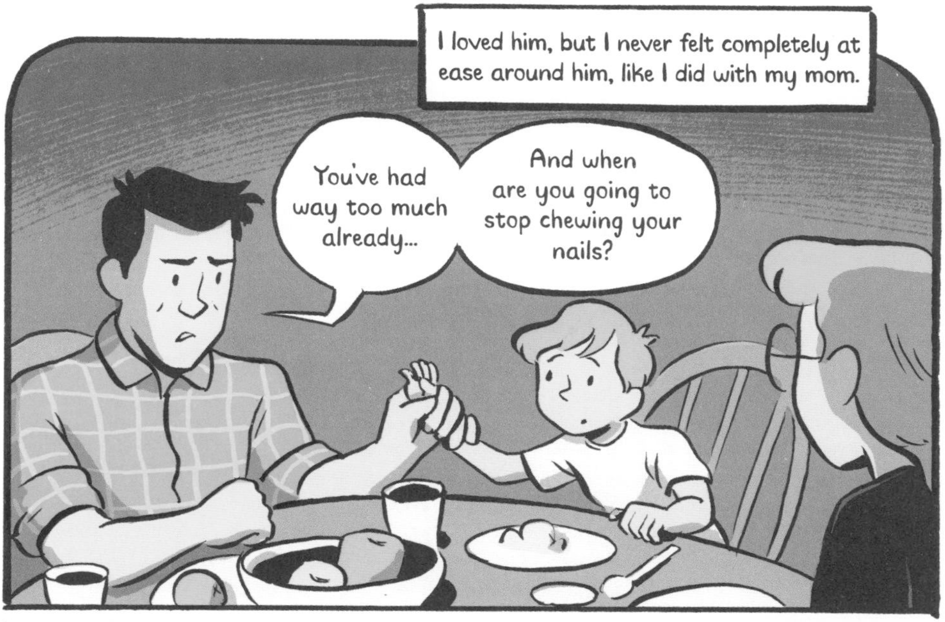
I loved him, but I never felt completely at ease around him, like I did with my mom.
You've had way too much already...
And when are you going to stop chewing your nails?

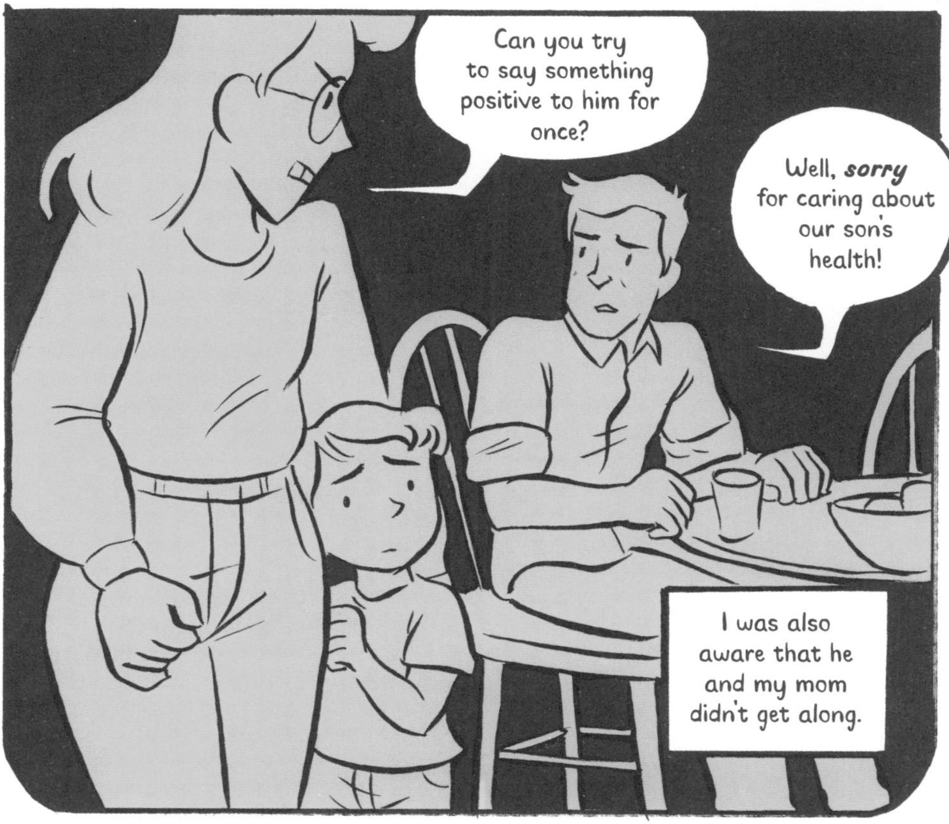
Can you try to say something positive to him for once?
Well, ***sorry*** for caring about our son's health!
I was also aware that he and my mom didn't get along.

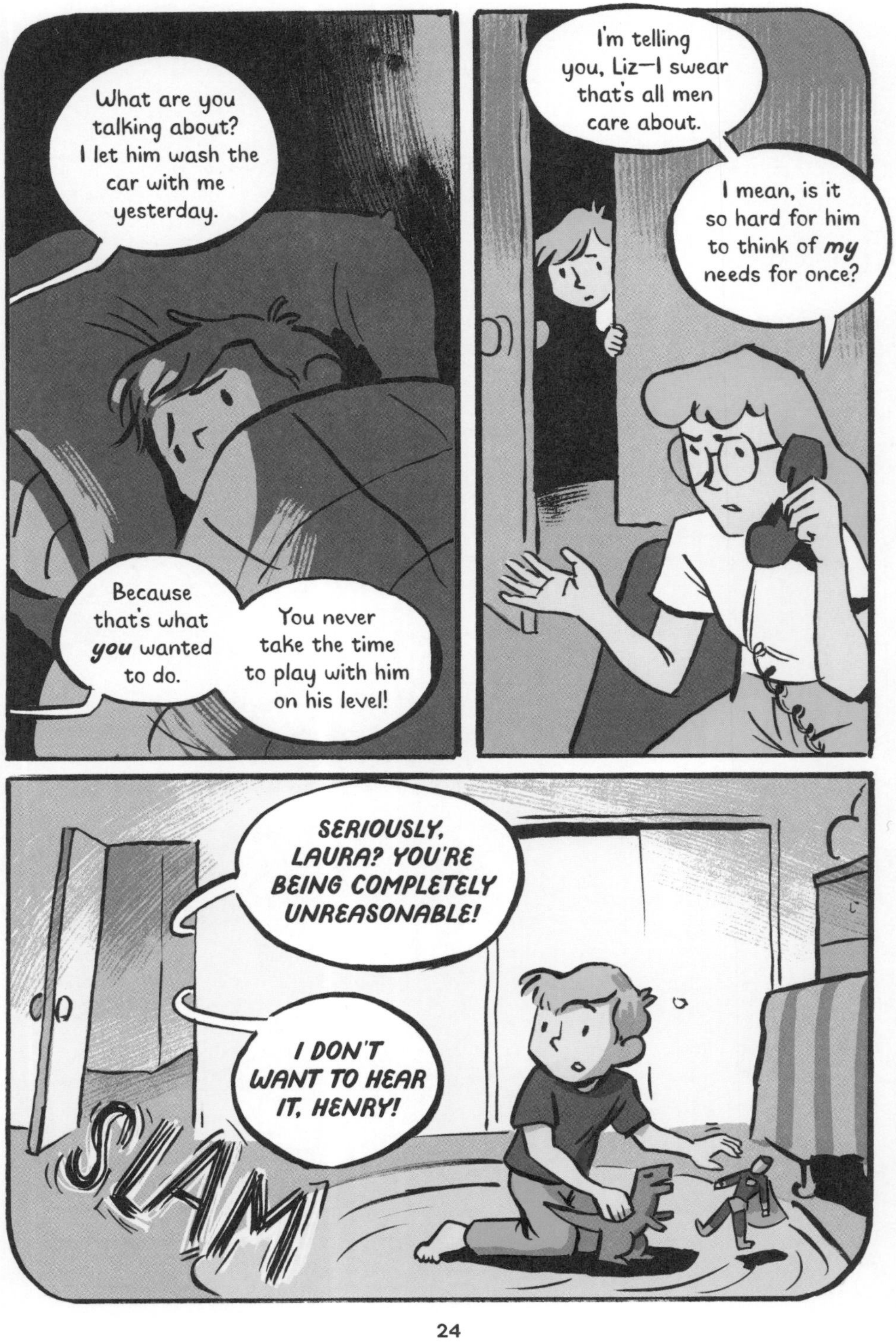
What are you talking about? I let him wash the car with me yesterday.
Because that's what *you* wanted to do.
You never take the time to play with him on his level!
I'm telling you, Liz—I swear that's all men care about.
I mean, is it so hard for him to think of *my* needs for once?
SERIOUSLY, LAURA? YOU'RE BEING COMPLETELY UNREASONABLE!
I DON'T WANT TO HEAR IT, HENRY!
SLAM

When I was six, we moved to Utah, where my sister, Sarah, was born. Soon after, we were shocked to hear that my mom's dad, my grandpa Don, had been arrested.

Mom explained to me that he had done bad things to a little girl...

Grandpa Don

...things like inappropriately touching her private parts.

It was my first encounter with the strange, dark adult world.

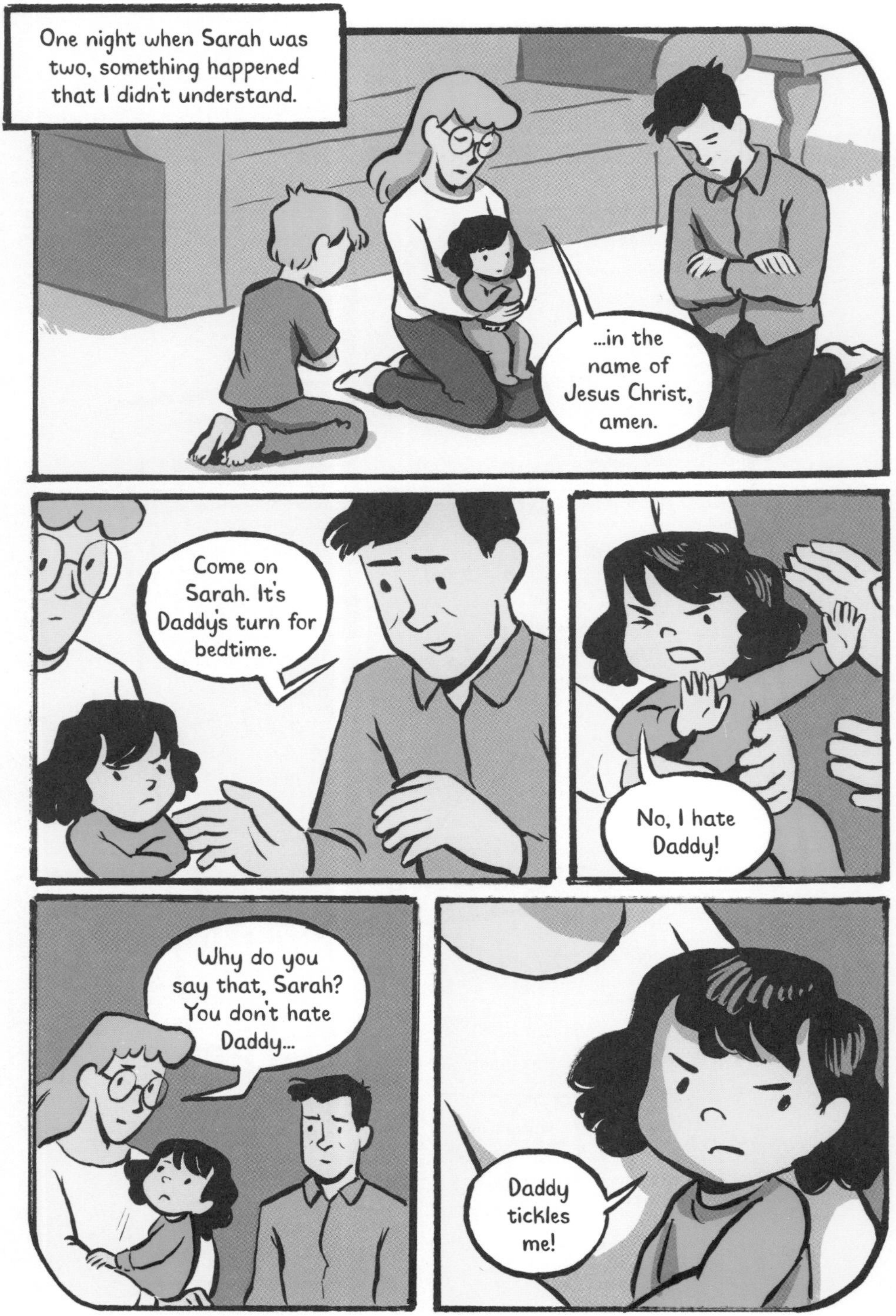
One night when Sarah was two, something happened that I didn't understand.
...in the name of Jesus Christ, amen.
Come on Sarah. It's Daddy's turn for bedtime.
No, I hate Daddy!
Why do you say that, Sarah? You don't hate Daddy...
Daddy tickles me!

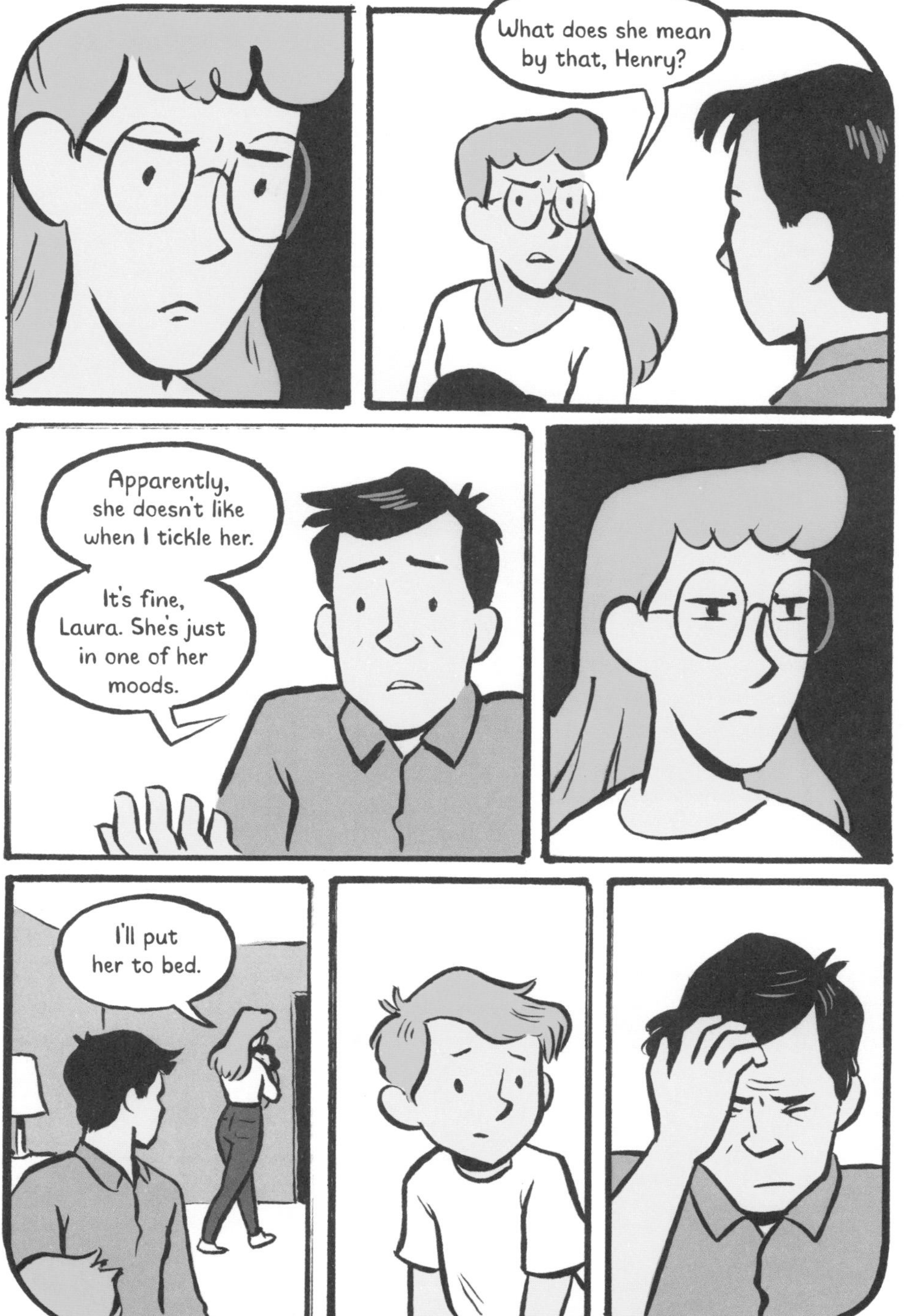
What does she mean by that, Henry?
Apparently, she doesn't like when I tickle her.
It's fine, Laura. She's just in one of her moods.
I'll put her to bed.

They separated shortly after that and eventually divorced.

Lehi Apartment

We received alimony checks from my dad and occasional money from my aunt Liz, my mom's wealthy sister. Liz also paid for me to go to a private school.

We moved to a cheap apartment so Mom could continue to be a stay-at-home mom.

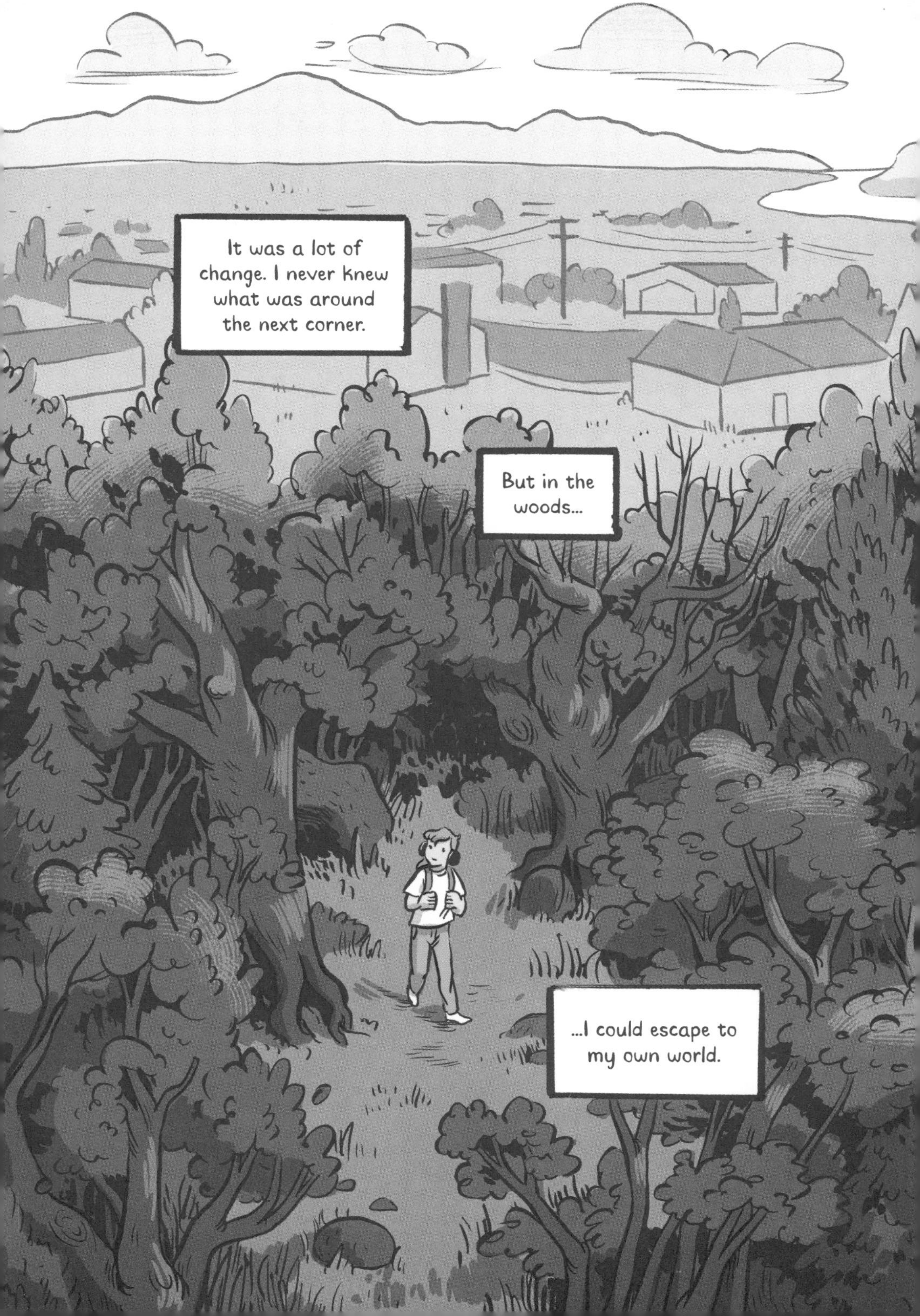
It was a lot of change. I never knew what was around the next corner.
But in the woods...
...I could escape to my own world.

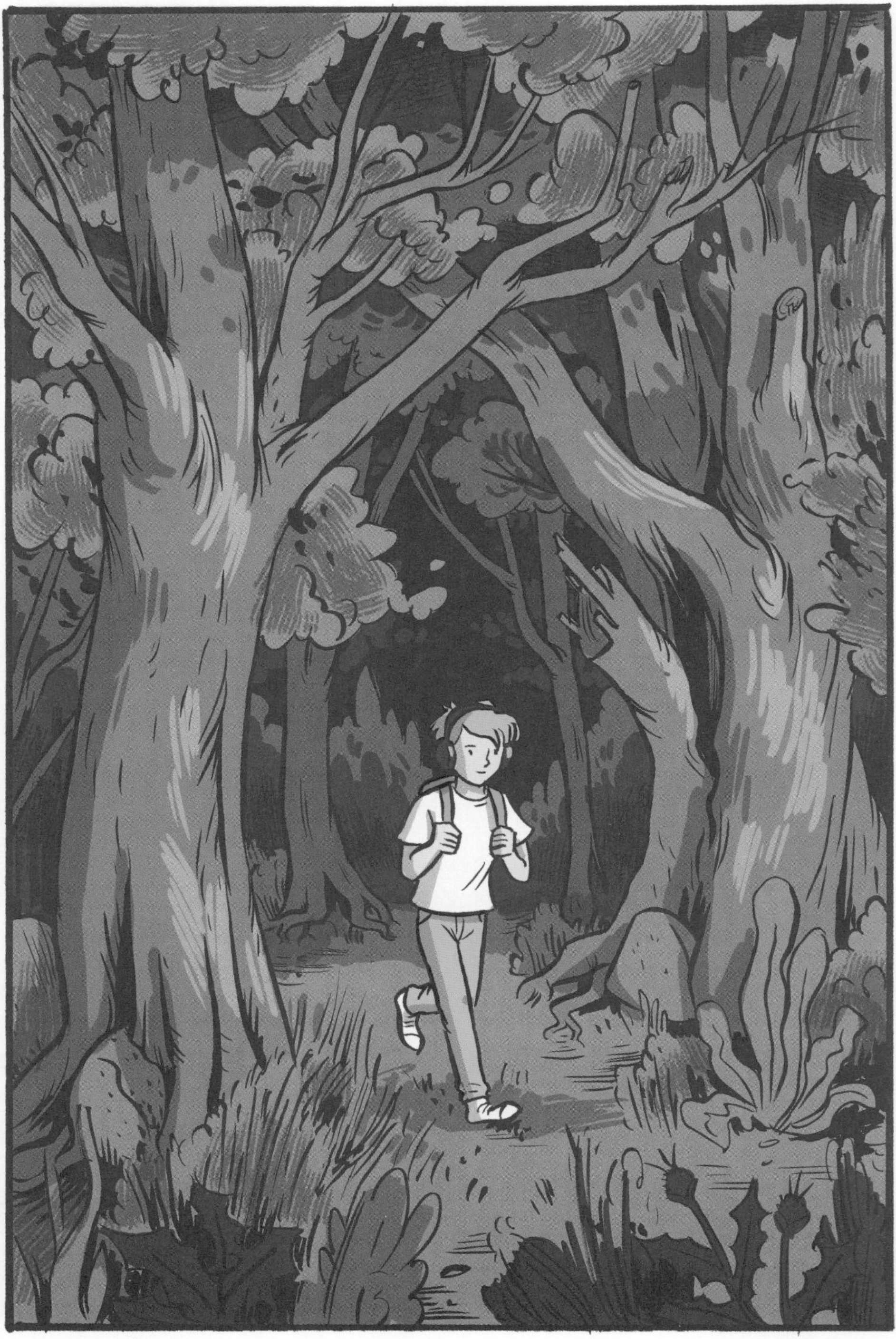

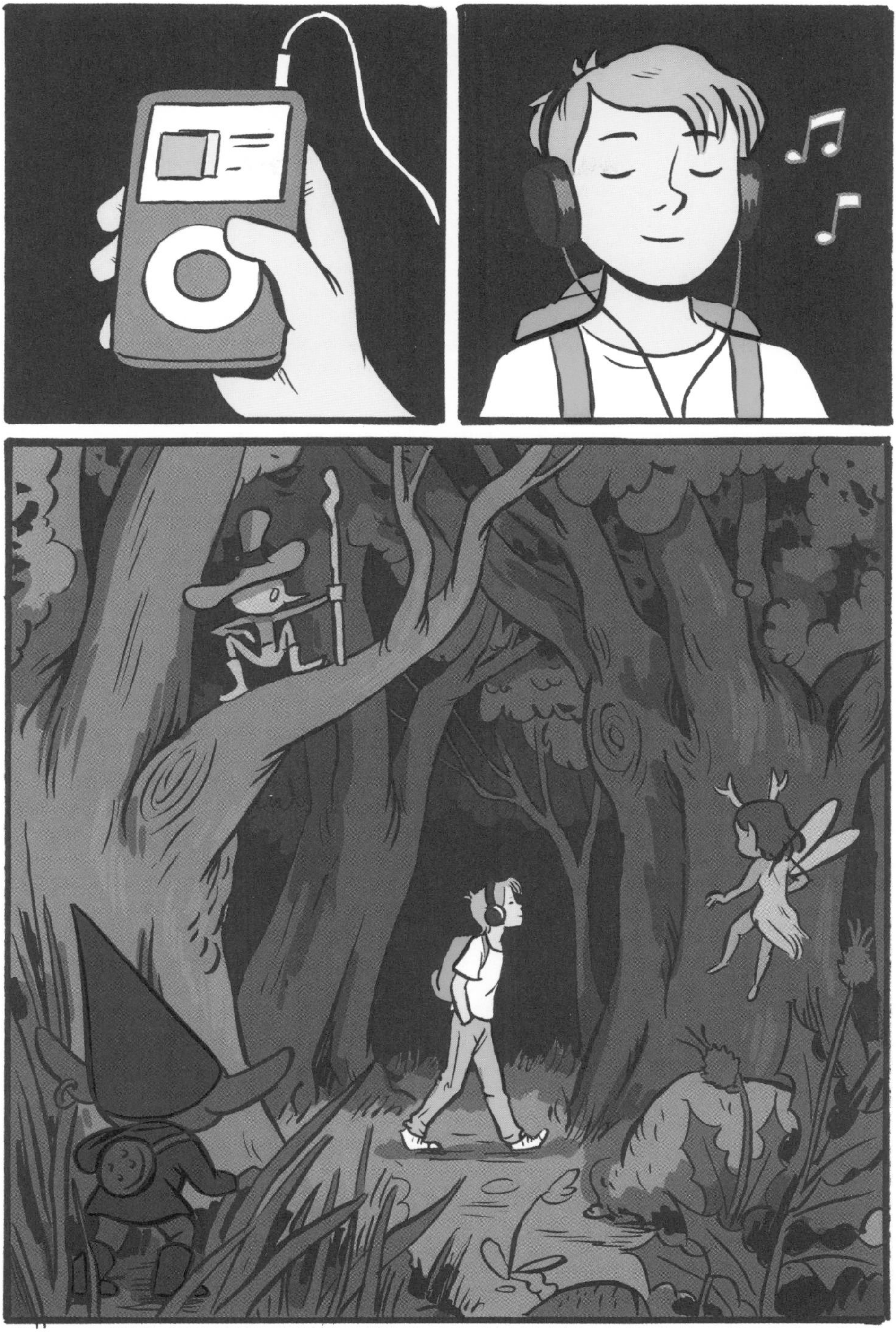

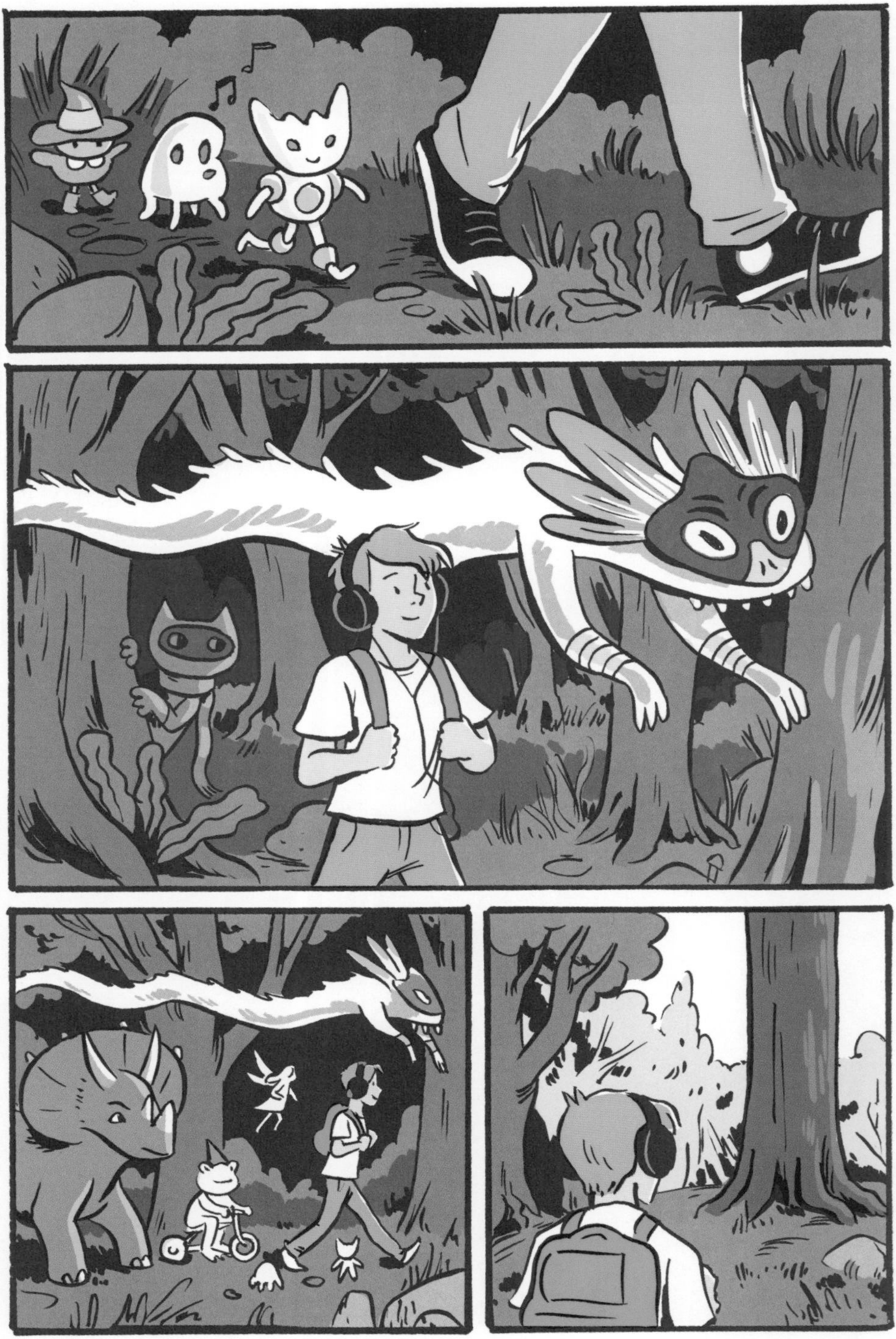

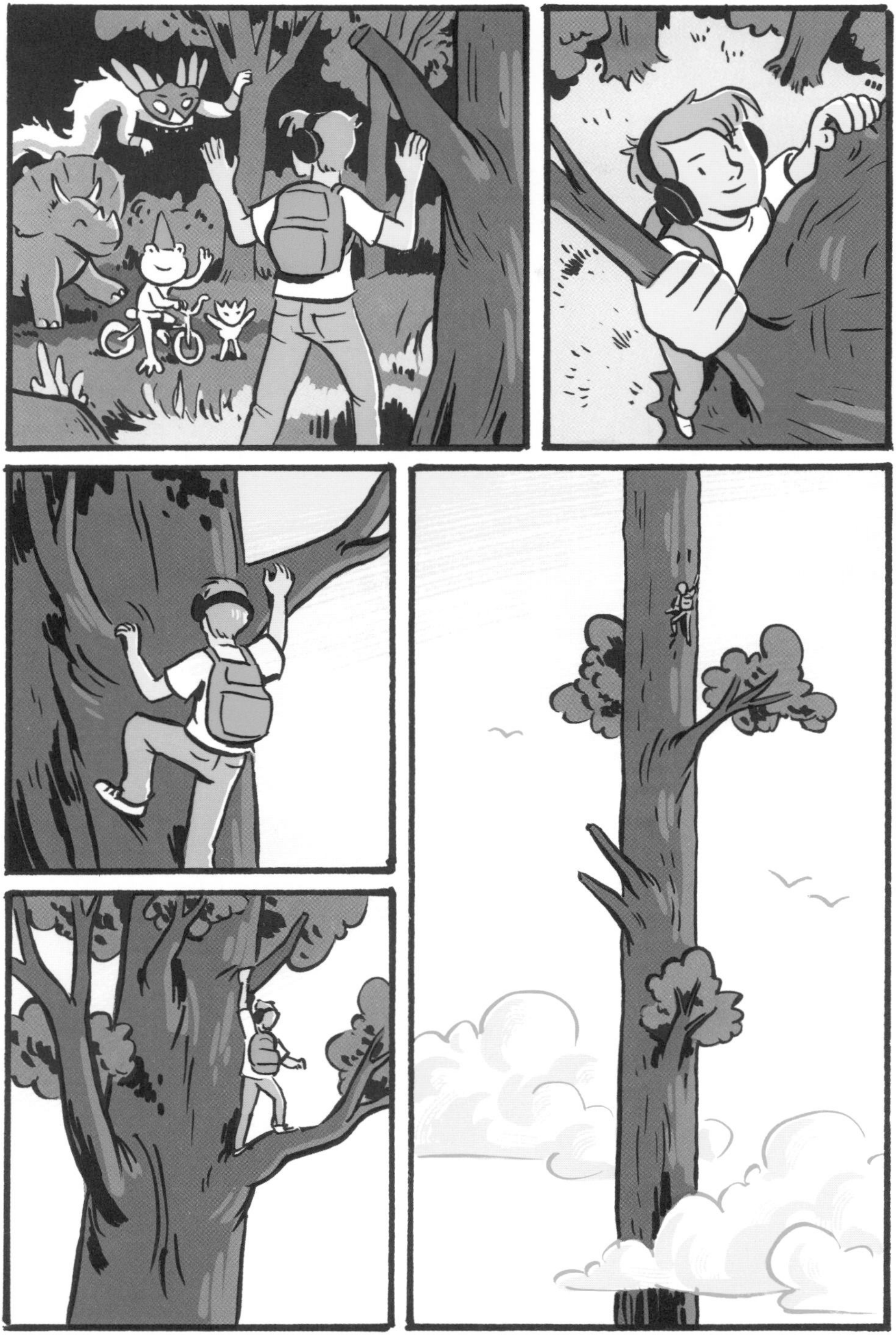

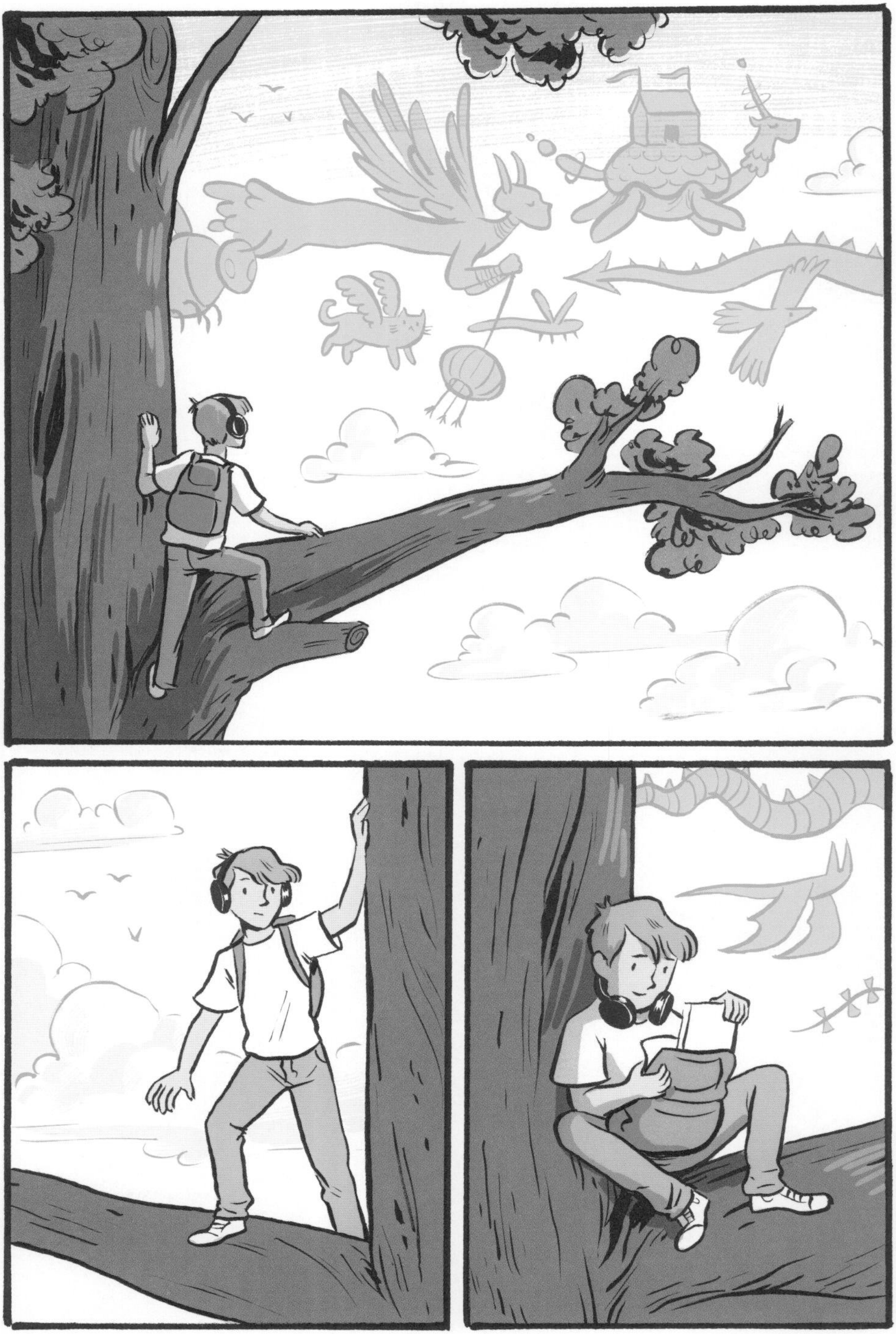

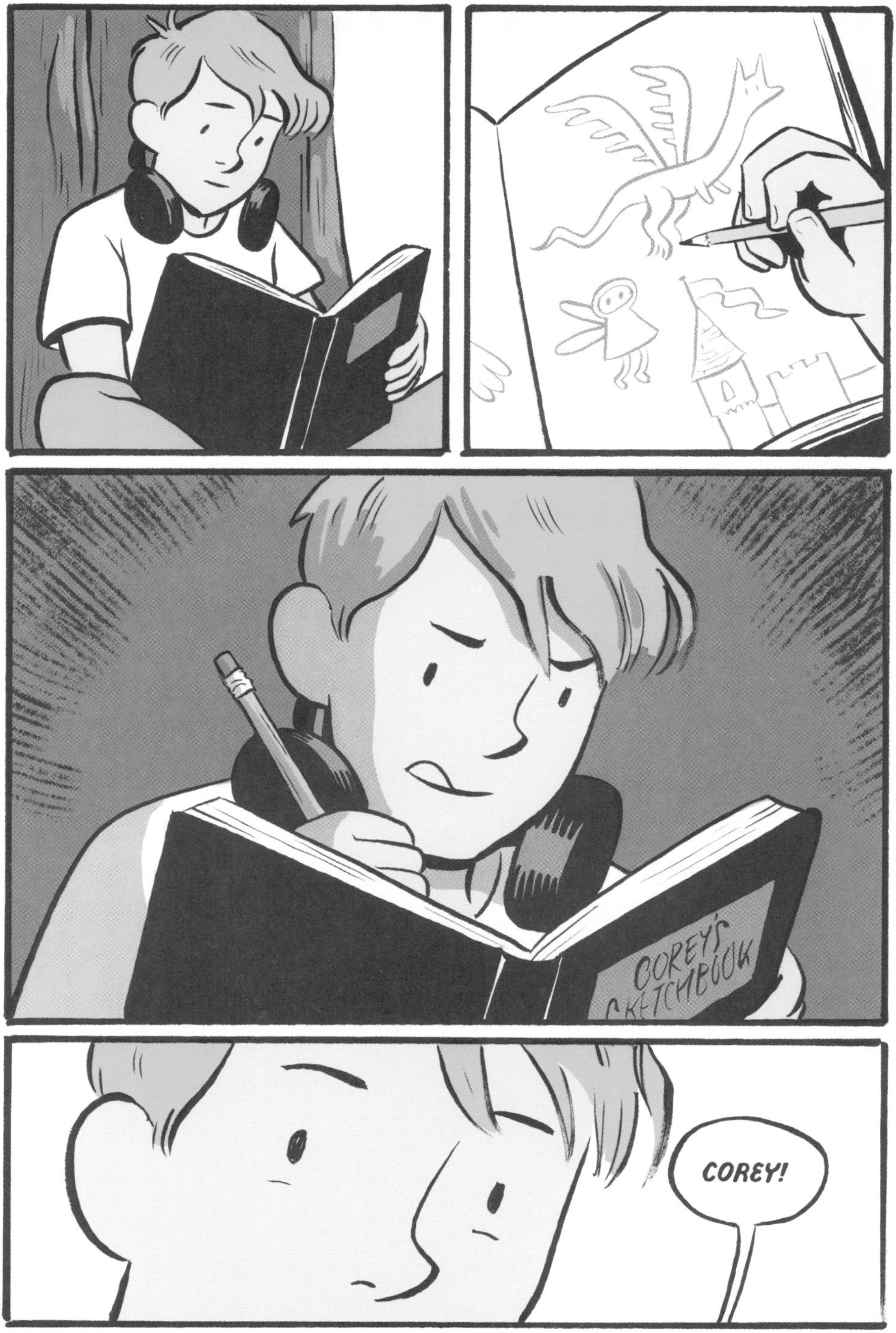
COREY'S SKETCHBOOK
COREY!

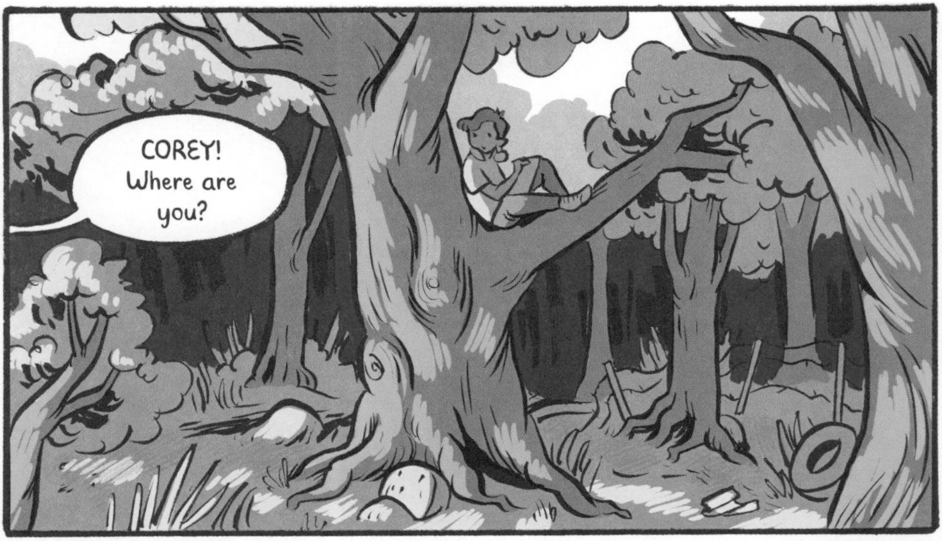
COREY!
Where are you?

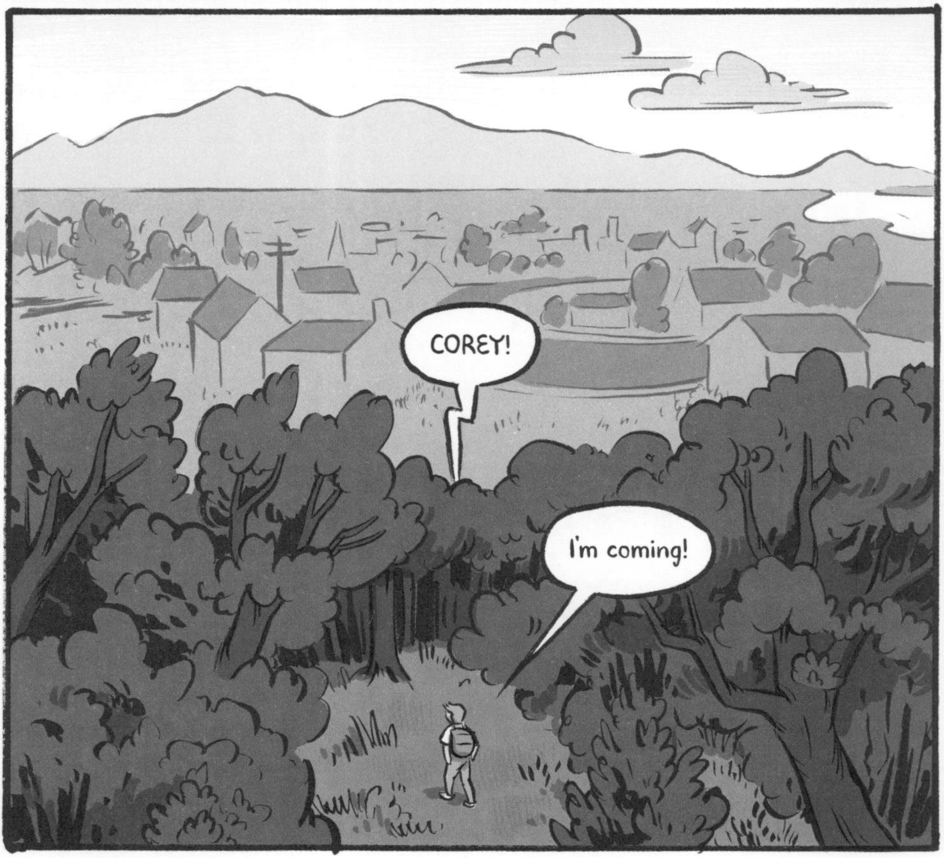
COREY!
I'm coming!

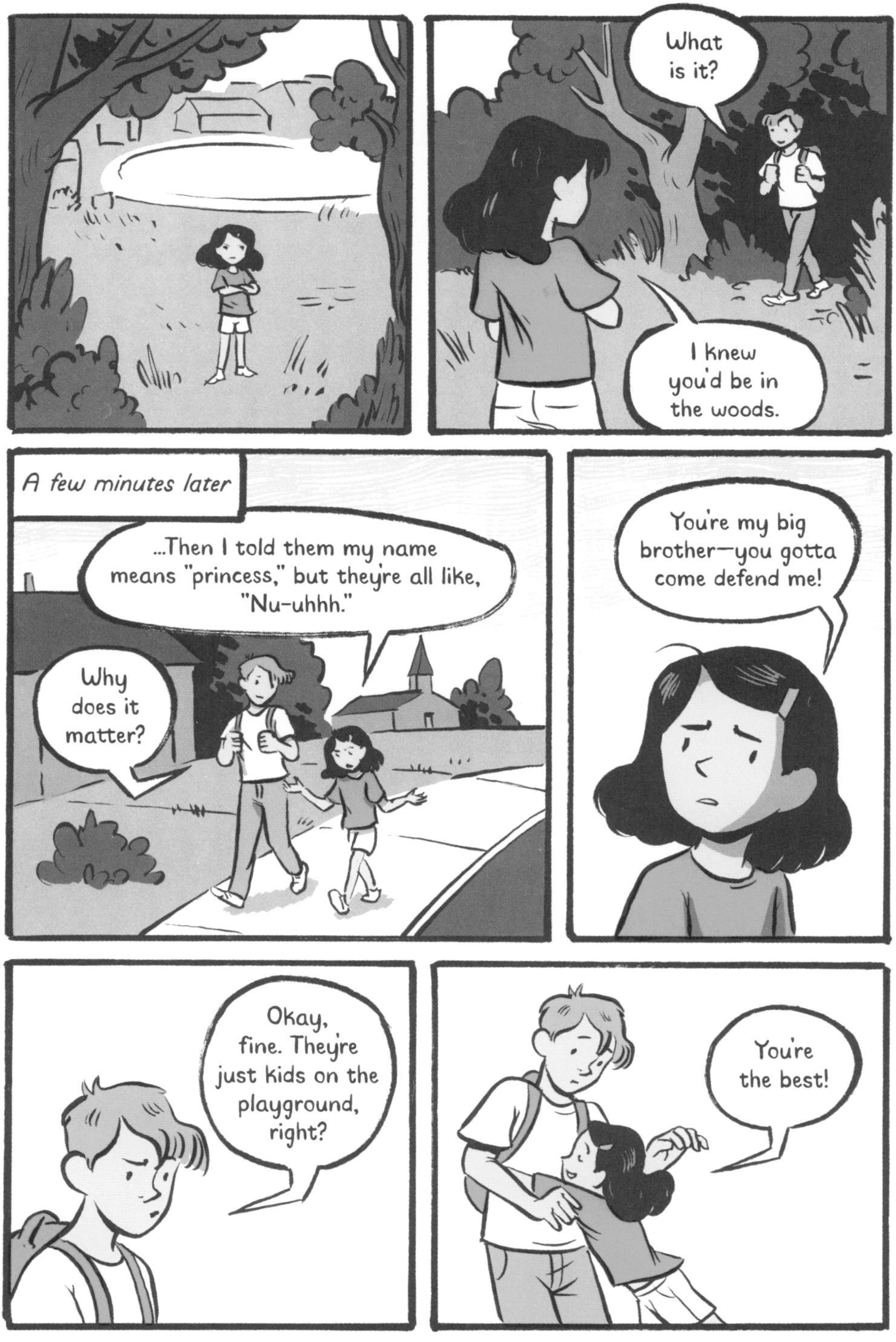

What is it?
I knew you'd be in the woods.
A few minutes later
...Then I told them my name means "princess," but they're all like, "Nu-uhhh."
Why does it matter?
You're my big brother—you gotta come defend me!
Okay, fine. They're just kids on the playground, right?
You're the best!

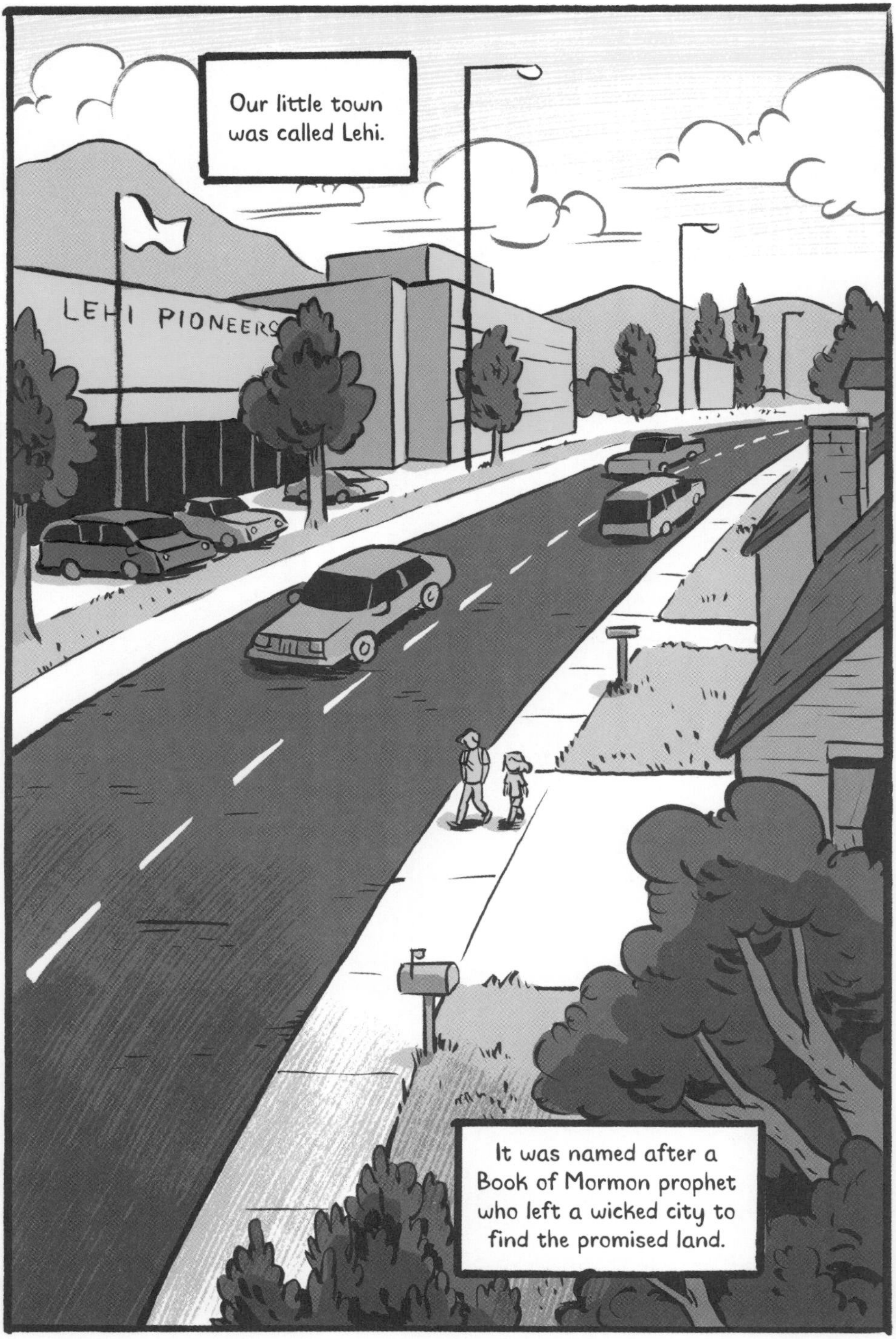
Our little town was called Lehi.
LEHI PIONEERS
It was named after a Book of Mormon prophet who left a wicked city to find the promised land.

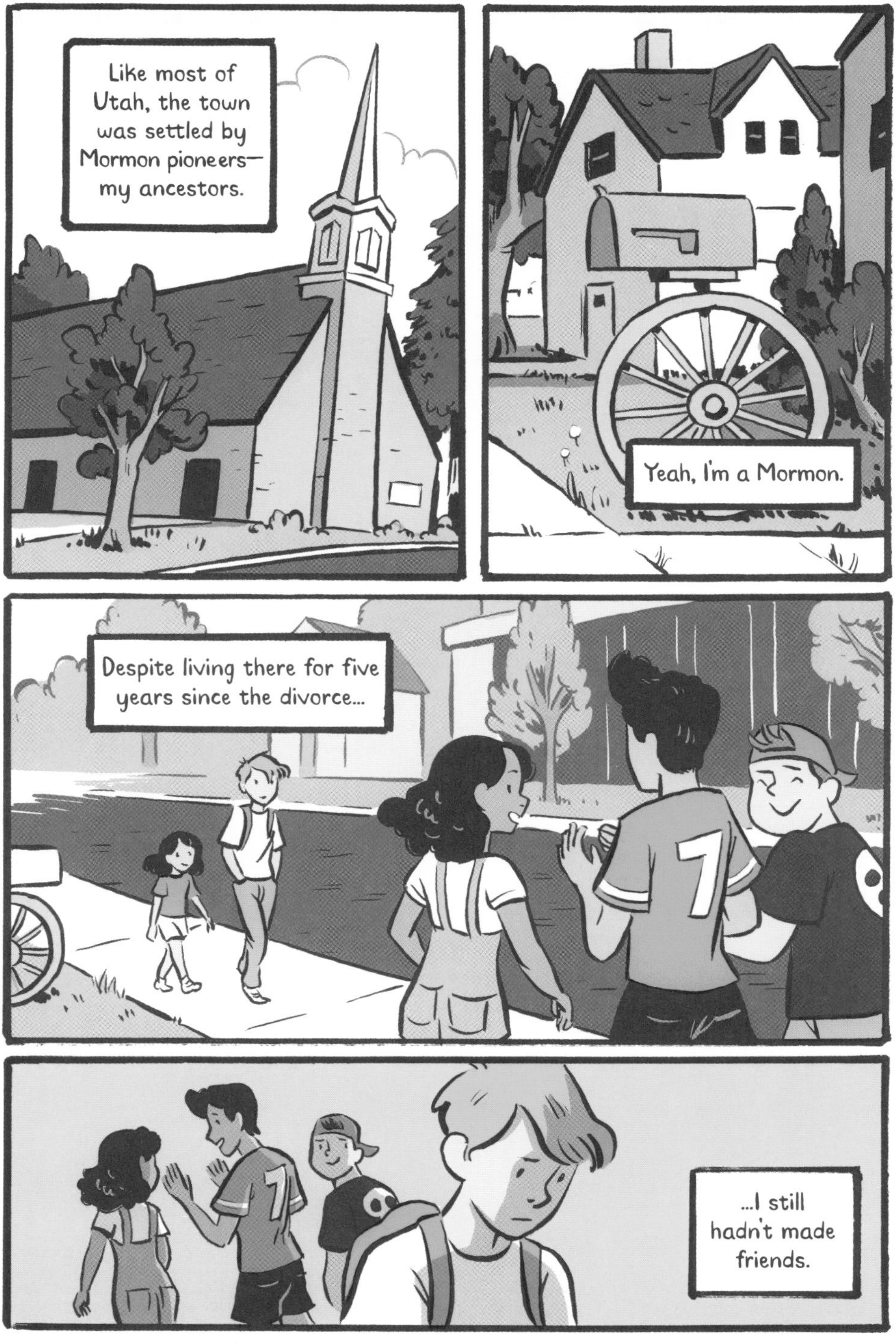
Like most of Utah, the town was settled by Mormon pioneers—my ancestors.
Yeah, I'm a Mormon.
Despite living there for five years since the divorce...
...I still hadn't made friends.

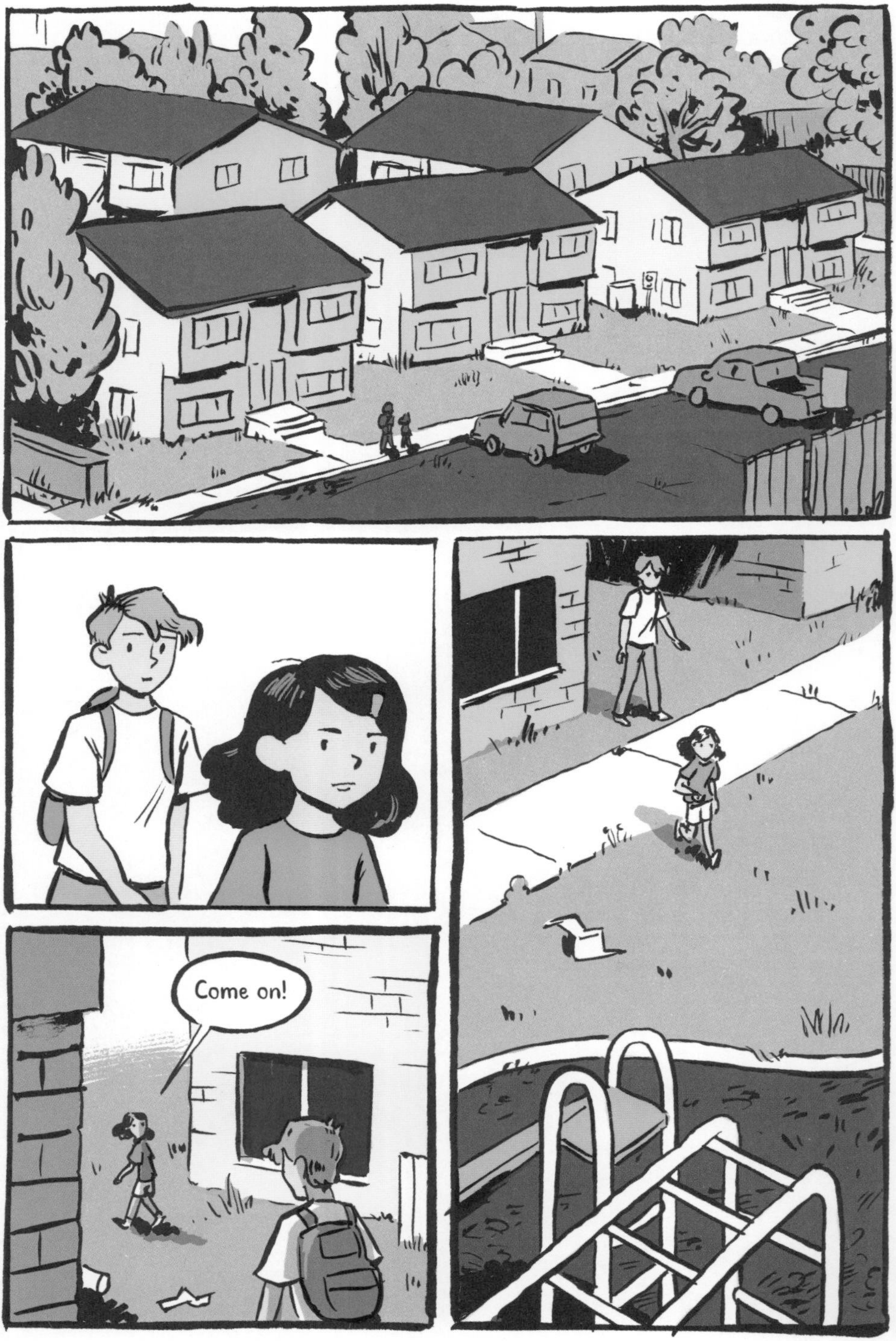
Come on!

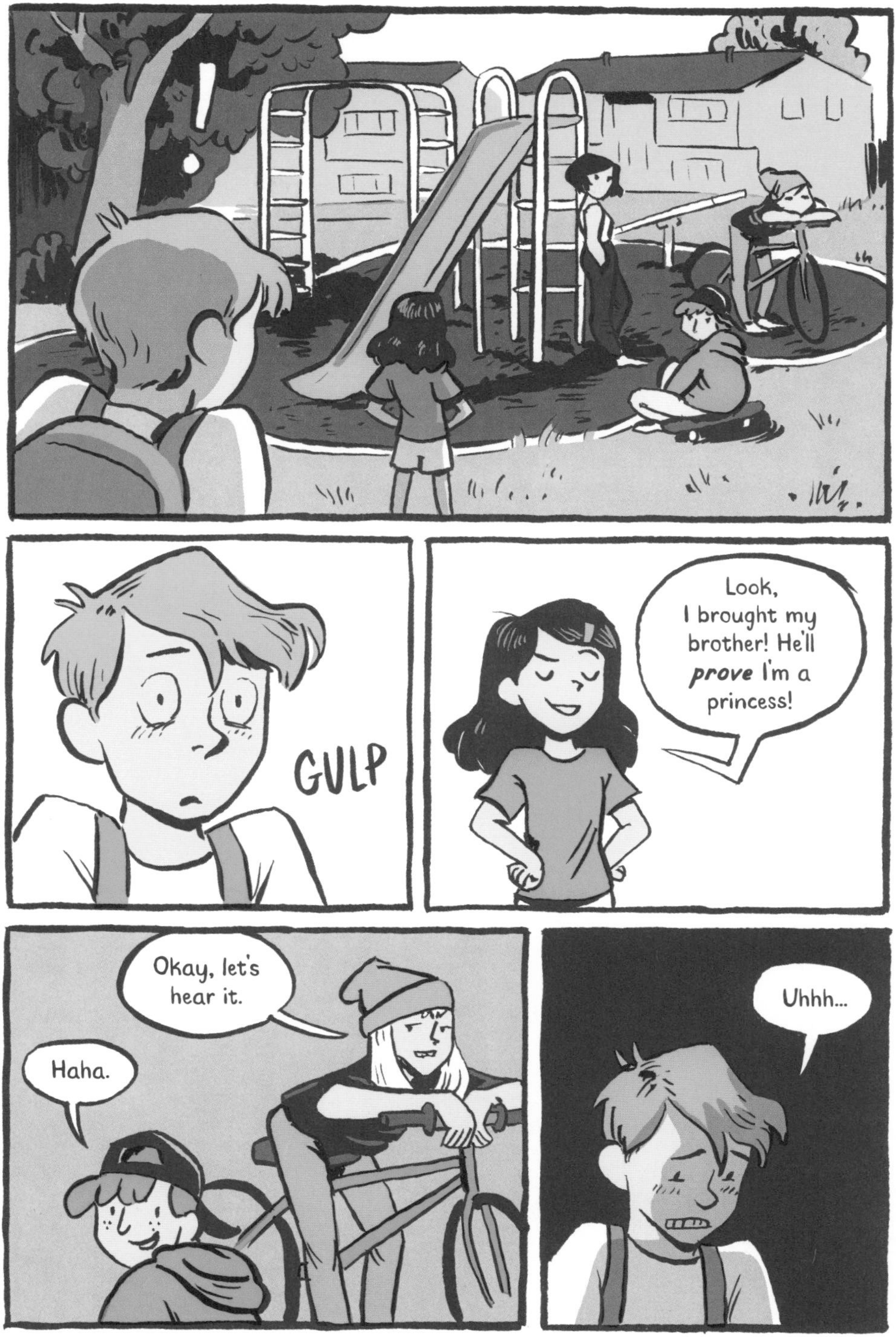
!
GULP
Look, I brought my brother! He'll **prove** I'm a princess!
Okay, let's hear it.
Haha.
Uhhh...

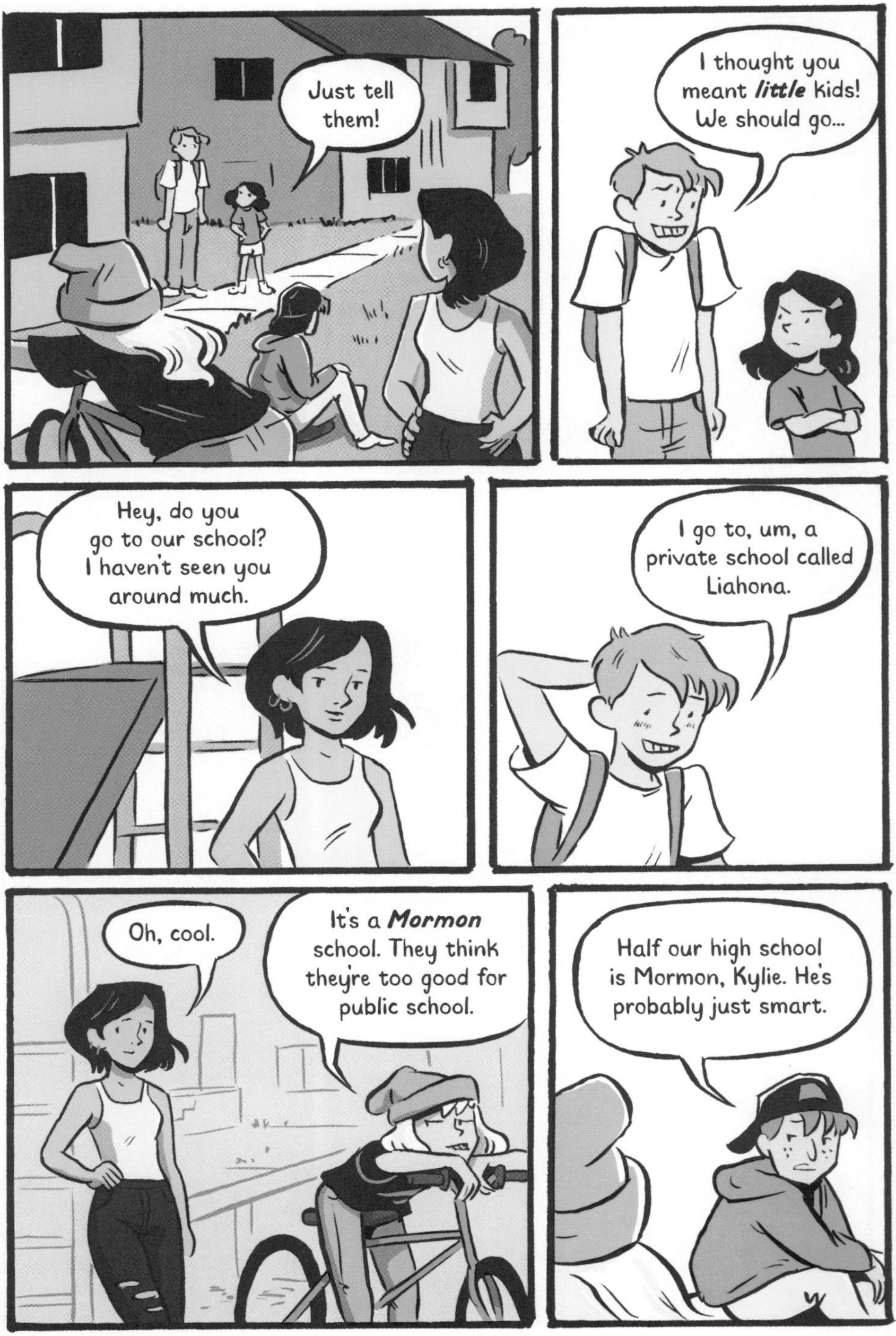
Just tell them!
I thought you meant *little* kids! We should go...
Hey, do you go to our school? I haven't seen you around much.
I go to, um, a private school called Liahona.
Oh, cool.
It's a *Mormon* school. They think they're too good for public school.
Half our high school is Mormon, Kylie. He's probably just smart.

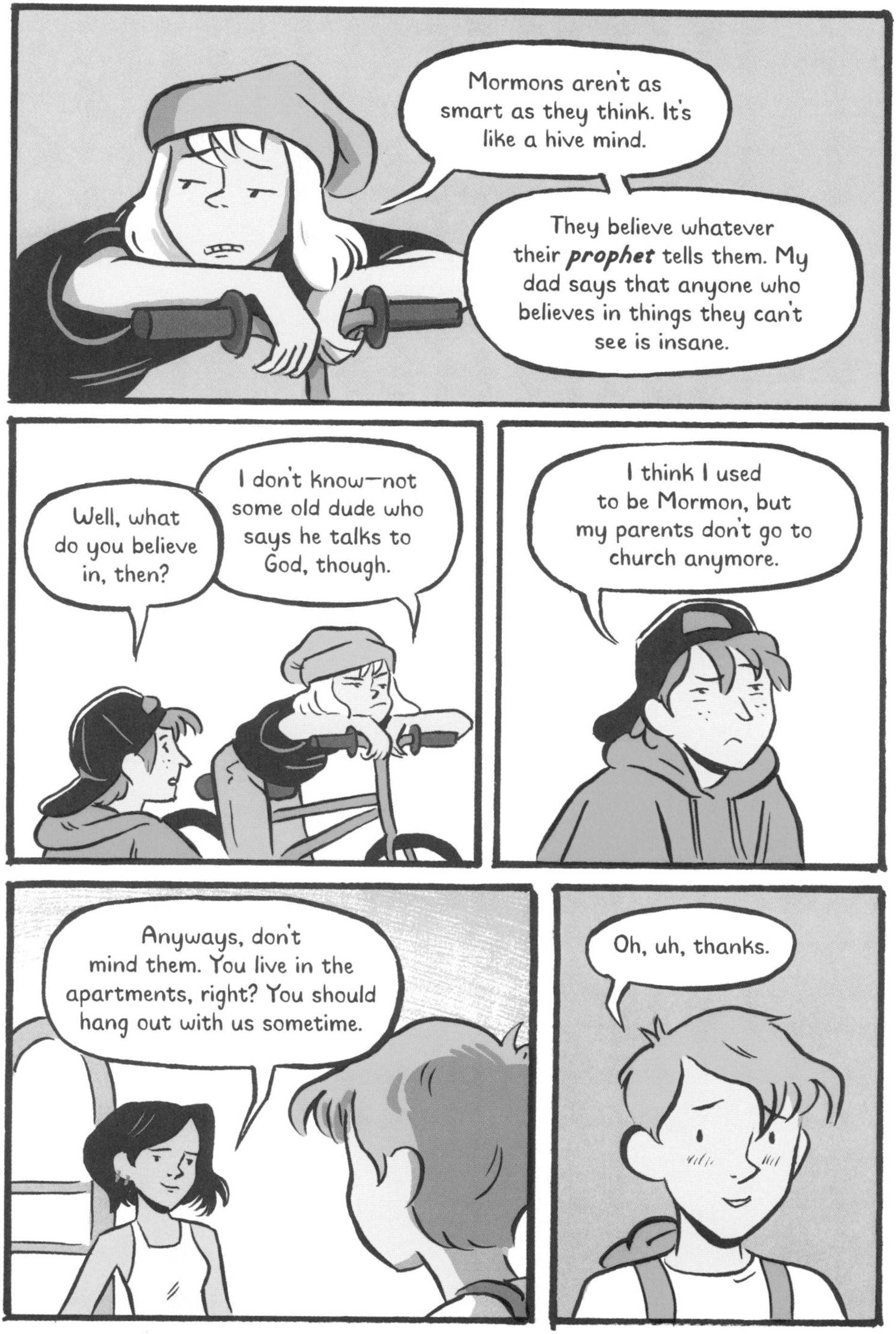
Mormons aren't as smart as they think. It's like a hive mind.
They believe whatever their ***prophet*** tells them. My dad says that anyone who believes in things they can't see is insane.
Well, what do you believe in, then?
I don't know—not some old dude who says he talks to God, though.
I think I used to be Mormon, but my parents don't go to church anymore.
Anyways, don't mind them. You live in the apartments, right? You should hang out with us sometime.
Oh, uh, thanks.

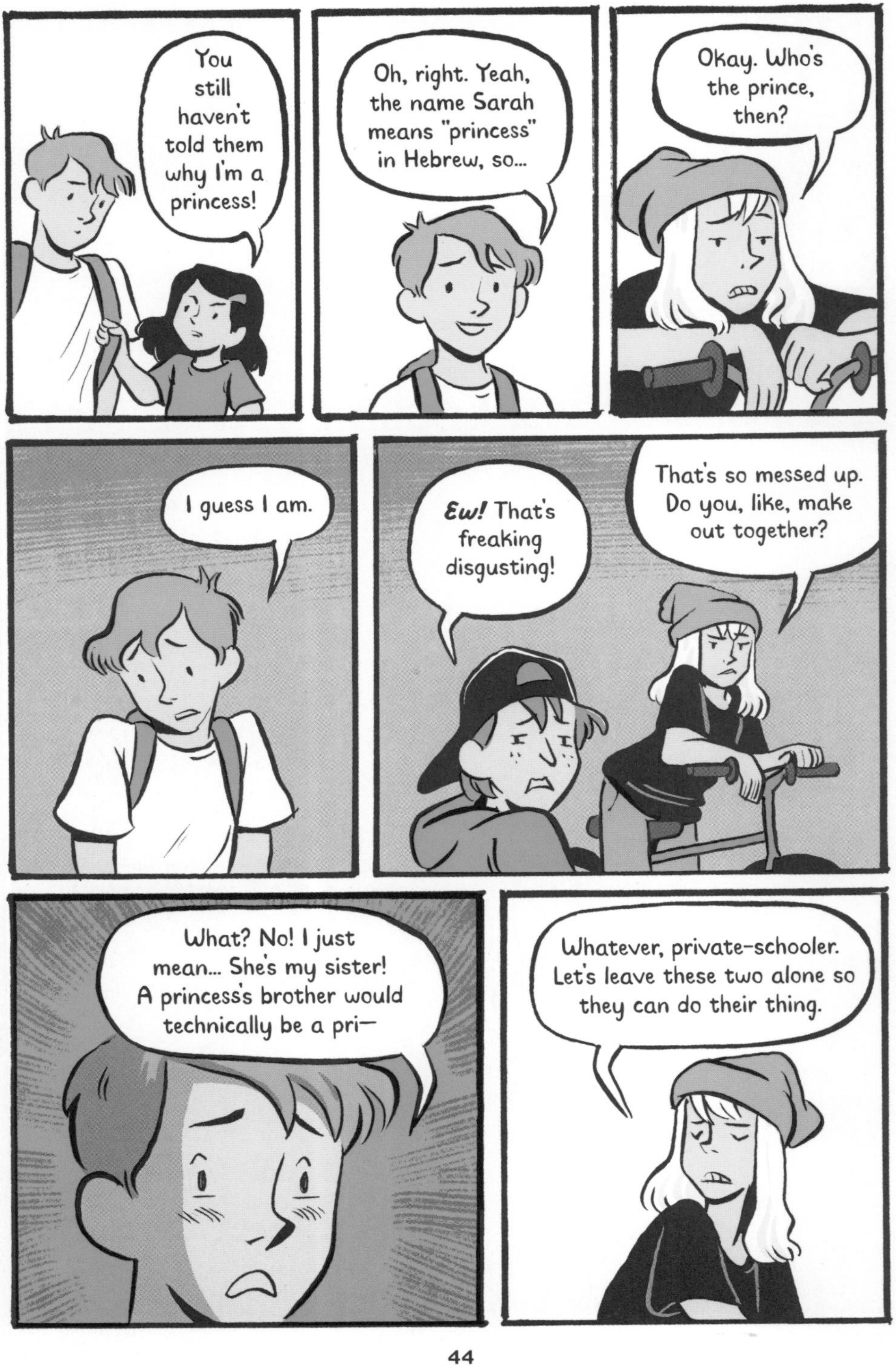
You still haven't told them why I'm a princess!
Oh, right. Yeah, the name Sarah means "princess" in Hebrew, so...
Okay. Who's the prince, then?
I guess I am.
Ew! That's freaking disgusting!
That's so messed up. Do you, like, make out together?
What? No! I just mean... She's my sister! A princess's brother would technically be a pri—
Whatever, private-schooler. Let's leave these two alone so they can do their thing.

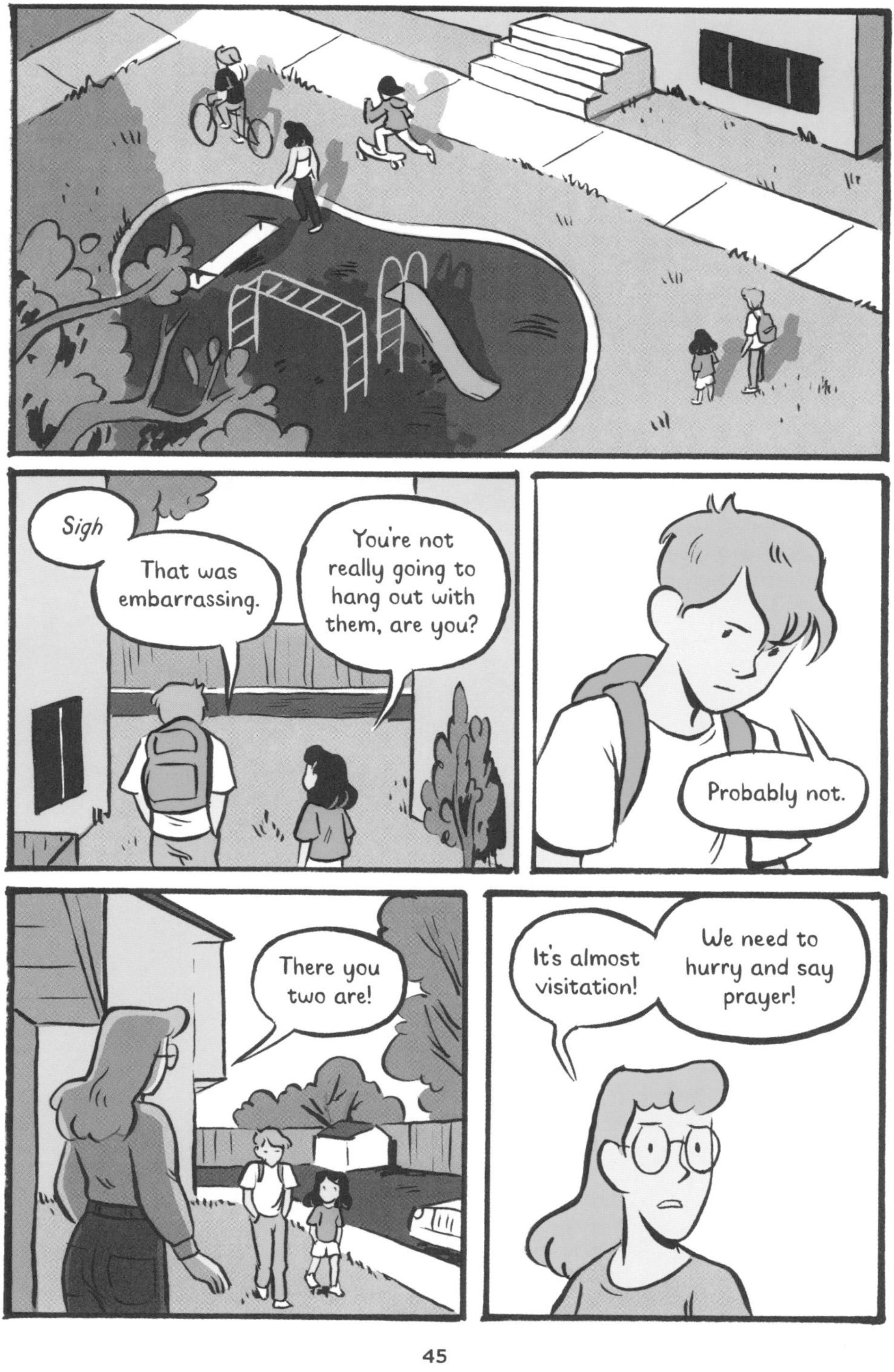
Sigh
That was embarrassing.
You're not really going to hang out with them, are you?
Probably not.
There you two are!
It's almost visitation!
We need to hurry and say prayer!

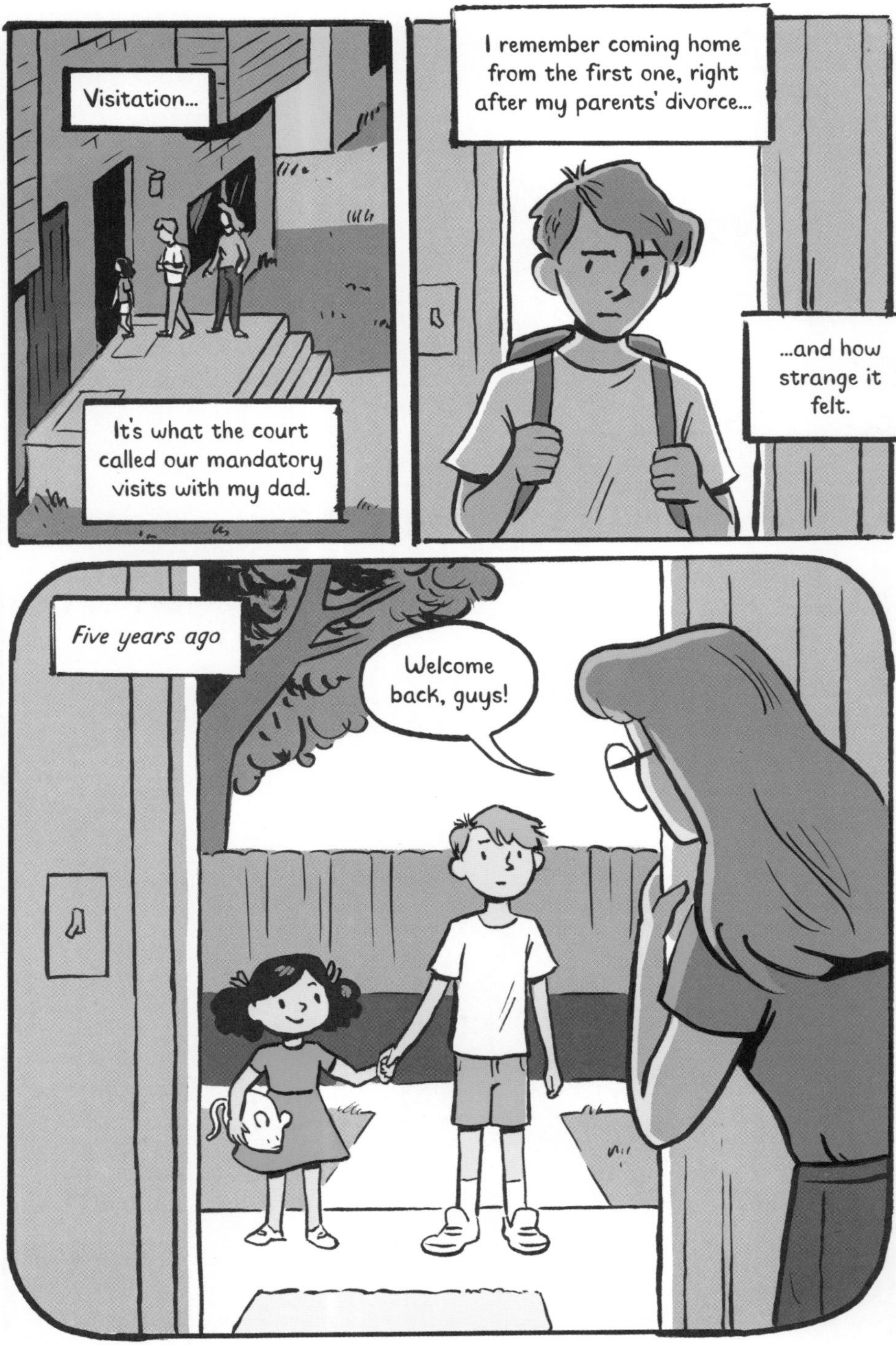

Visitation...
It's what the court called our mandatory visits with my dad.
I remember coming home from the first one, right after my parents' divorce...
...and how strange it felt.
Five years ago
Welcome back, guys!

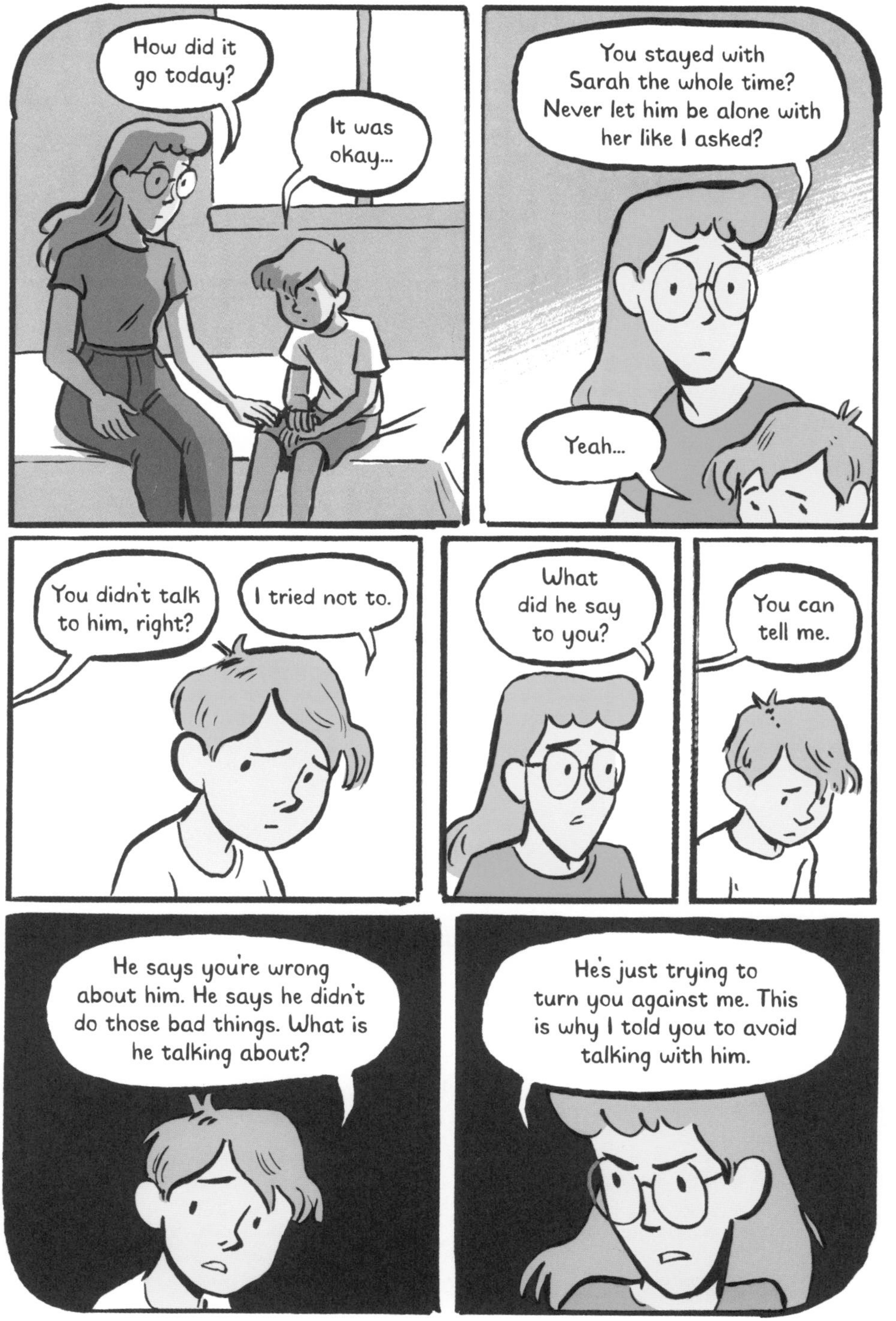
How did it go today?
It was okay...
You stayed with Sarah the whole time? Never let him be alone with her like I asked?
Yeah...
You didn't talk to him, right?
I tried not to.
What did he say to you?
You can tell me.
He says you're wrong about him. He says he didn't do those bad things. What is he talking about?
He's just trying to turn you against me. This is why I told you to avoid talking with him.

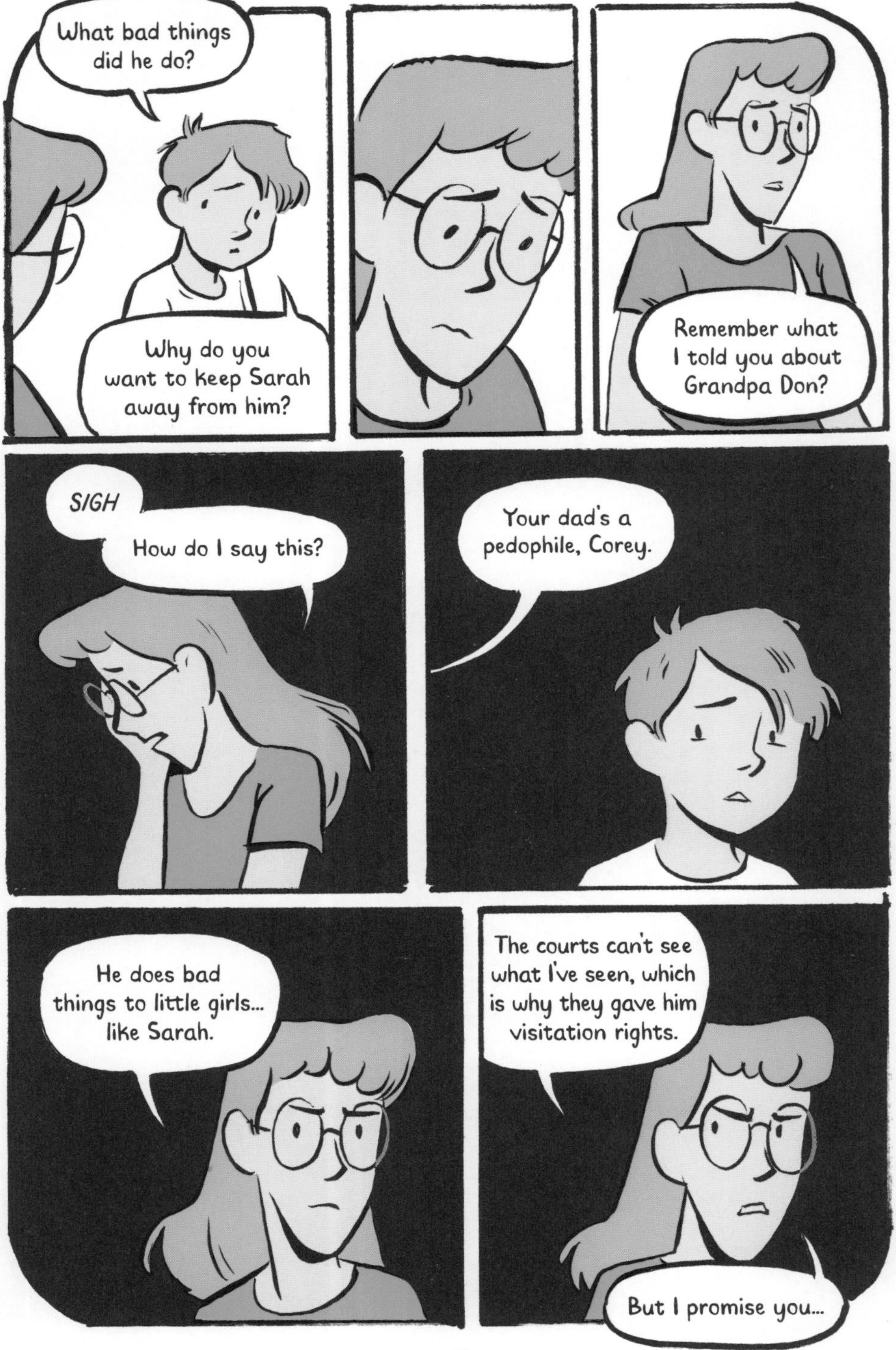
What bad things did he do?
Why do you want to keep Sarah away from him?
Remember what I told you about Grandpa Don?
SIGH
How do I say this?
Your dad's a pedophile, Corey.
He does bad things to little girls... like Sarah.
The courts can't see what I've seen, which is why they gave him visitation rights.
But I promise you...

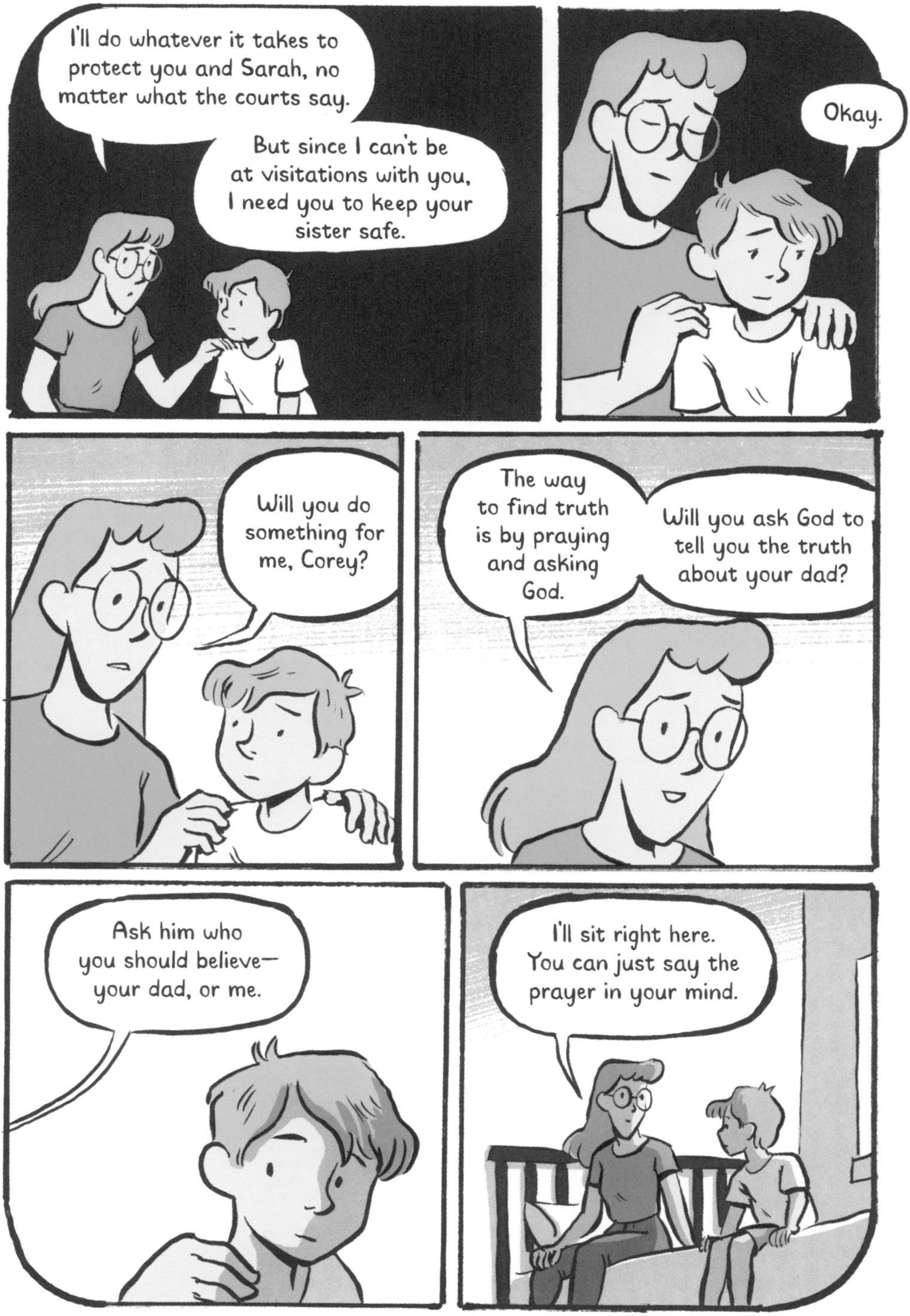
I'll do whatever it takes to protect you and Sarah, no matter what the courts say.
But since I can't be at visitations with you, I need you to keep your sister safe.
Okay.
Will you do something for me, Corey?
The way to find truth is by praying and asking God.
Will you ask God to tell you the truth about your dad?
Ask him who you should believe—your dad, or me.
I'll sit right here. You can just say the prayer in your mind.

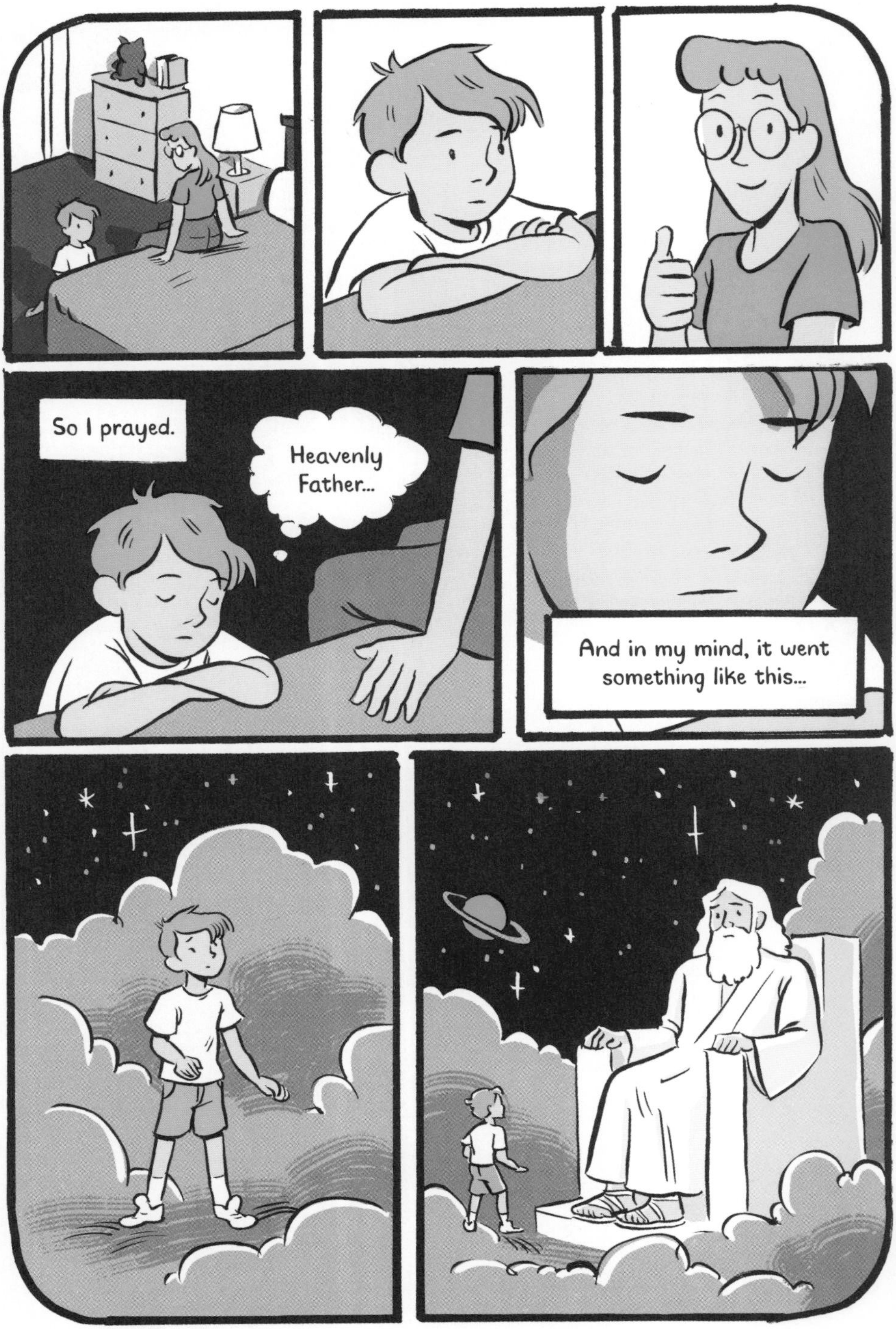
So I prayed.
Heavenly Father...
And in my mind, it went something like this...

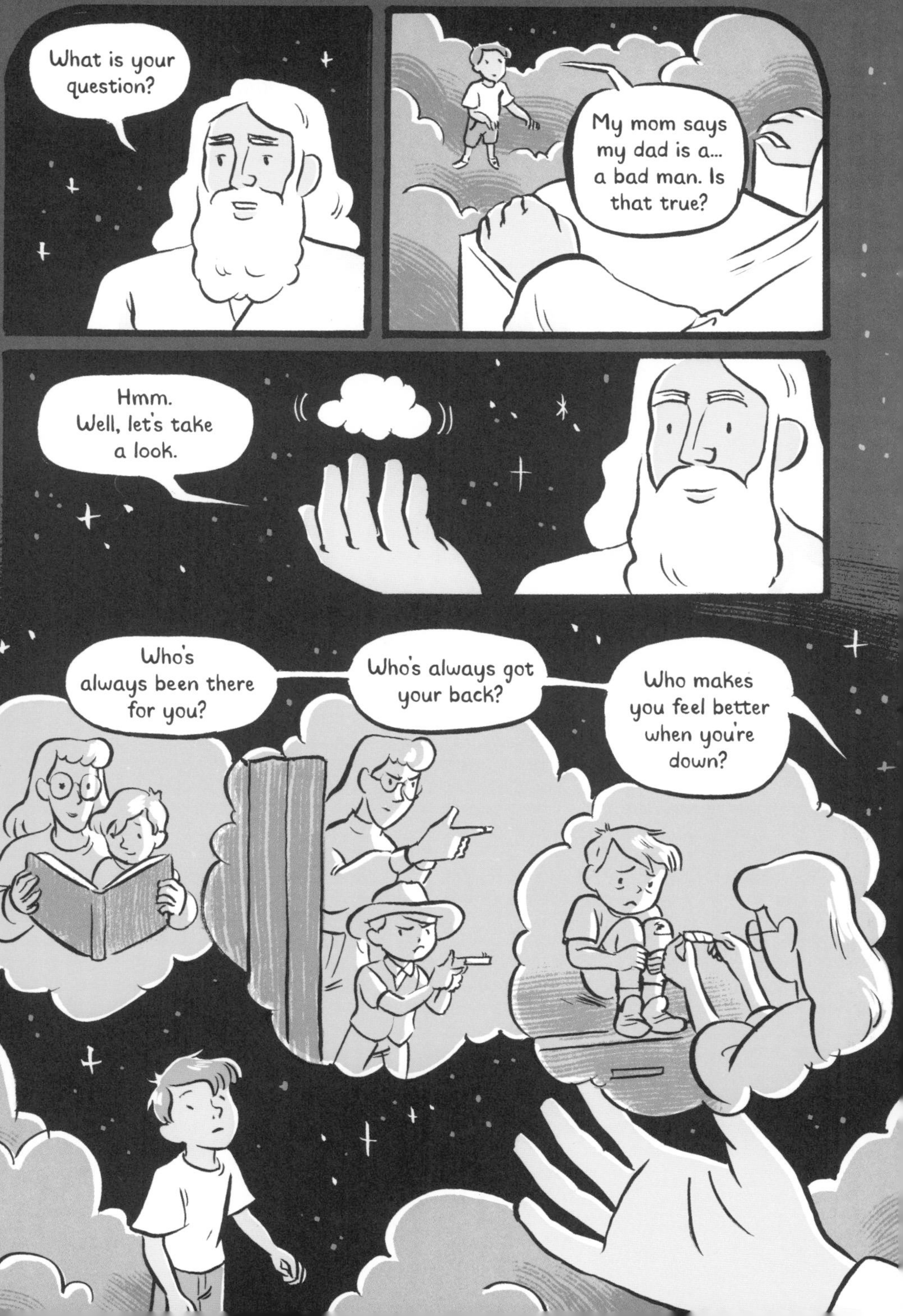
What is your question?
My mom says my dad is a... a bad man. Is that true?
Hmm. Well, let's take a look.
Who's always been there for you?
Who's always got your back?
Who makes you feel better when you're down?

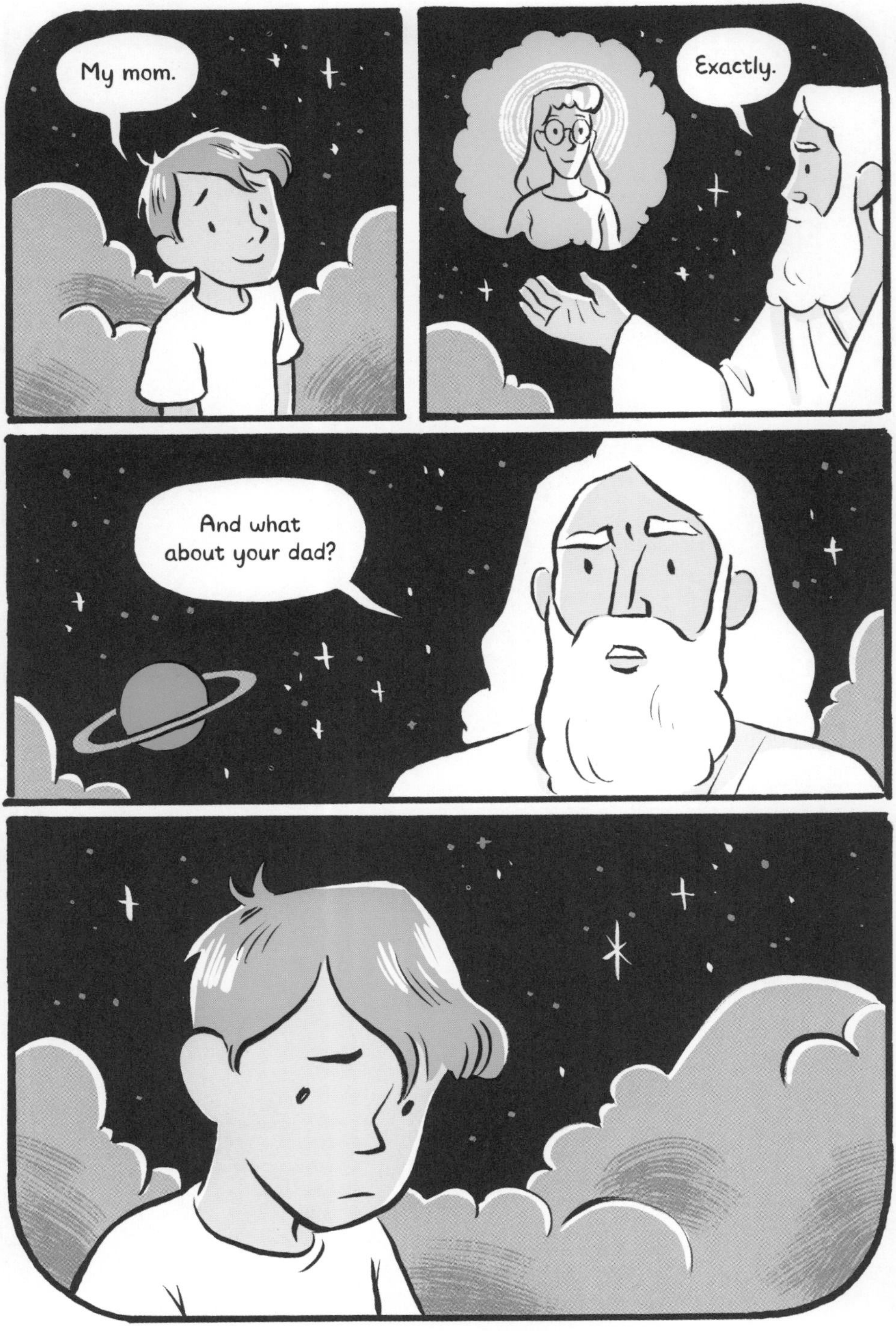
My mom.
Exactly.
And what about your dad?

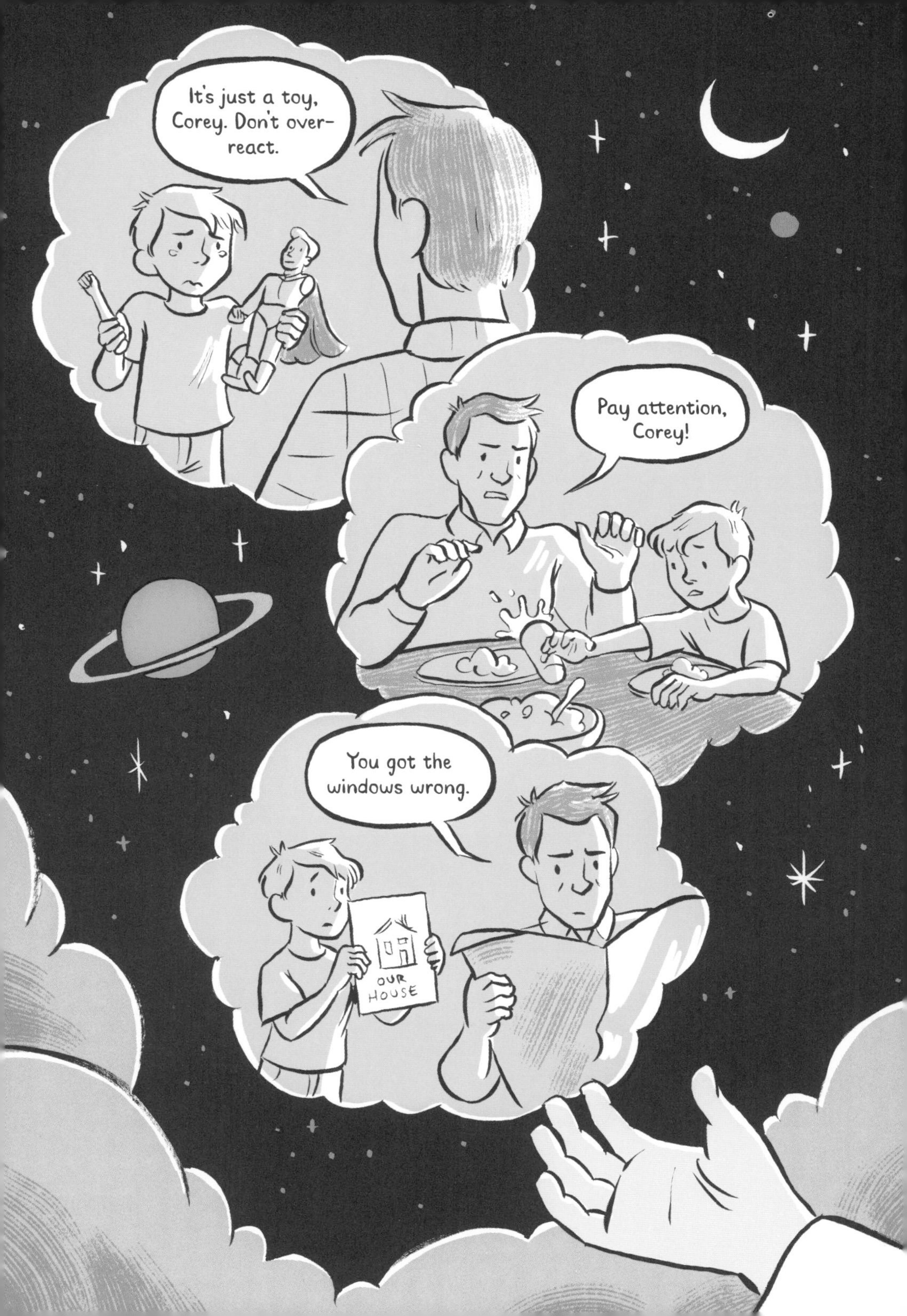
It's just a toy, Corey. Don't over-react.
Pay attention, Corey!
You got the windows wrong.
OUR HOUSE

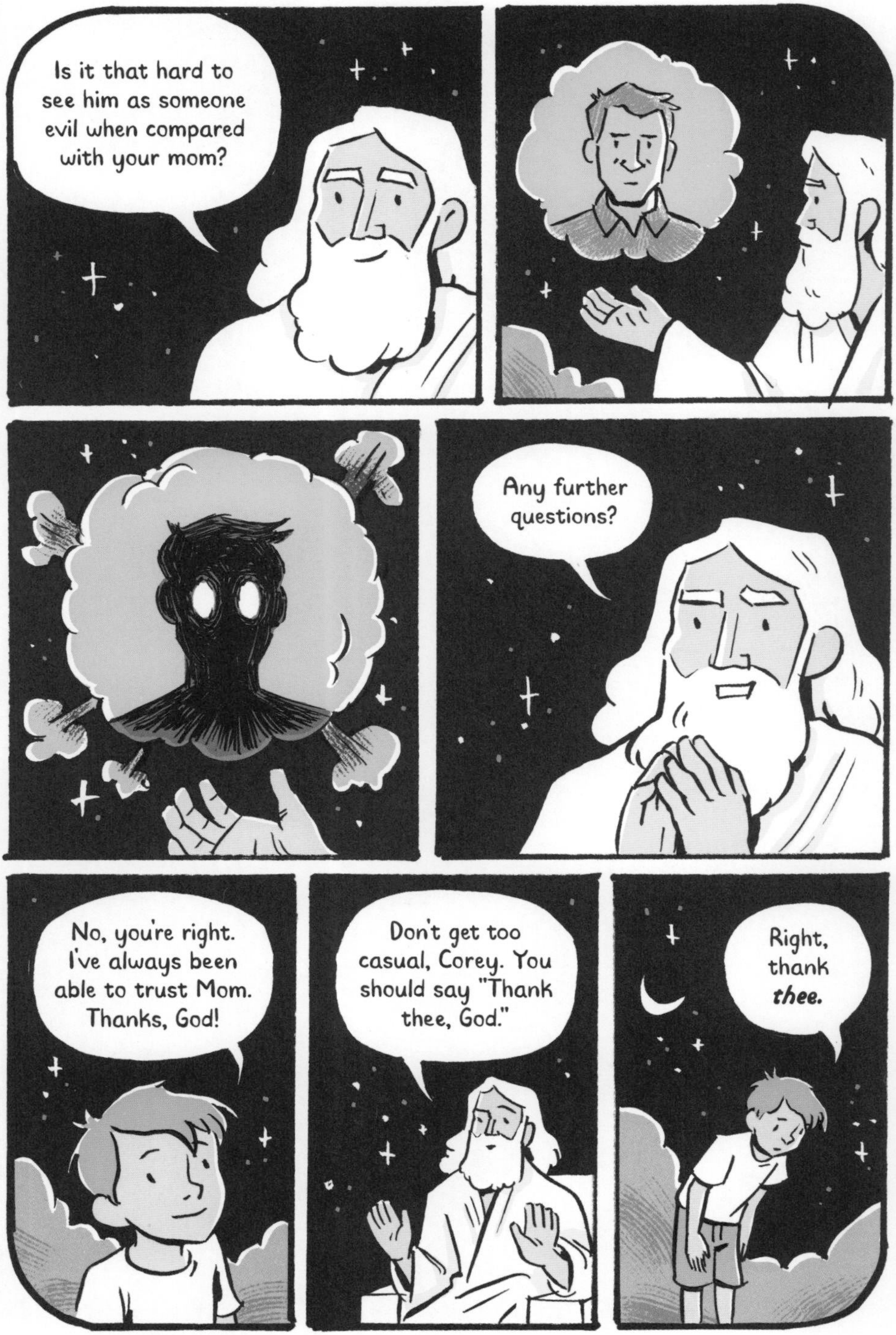
Is it that hard to see him as someone evil when compared with your mom?
Any further questions?
No, you're right. I've always been able to trust Mom. Thanks, God!
Don't get too casual, Corey. You should say "Thank thee, God."
Right, thank *thee.*

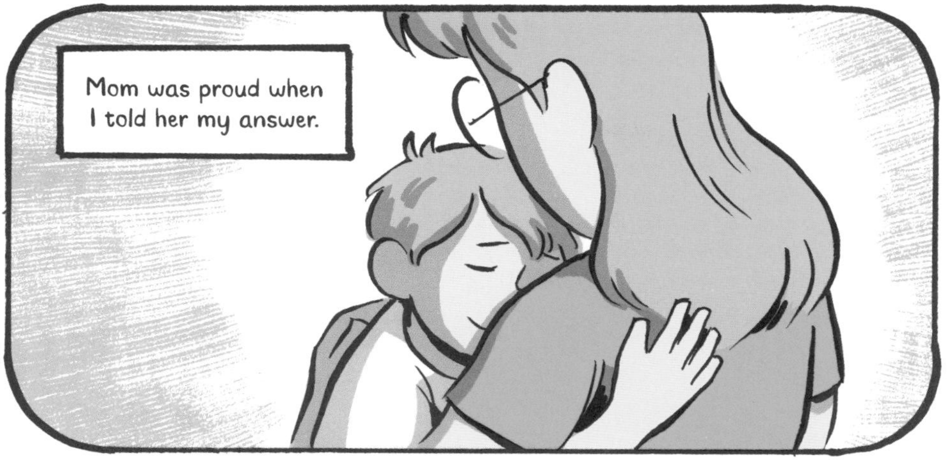
Mom was proud when I told her my answer.

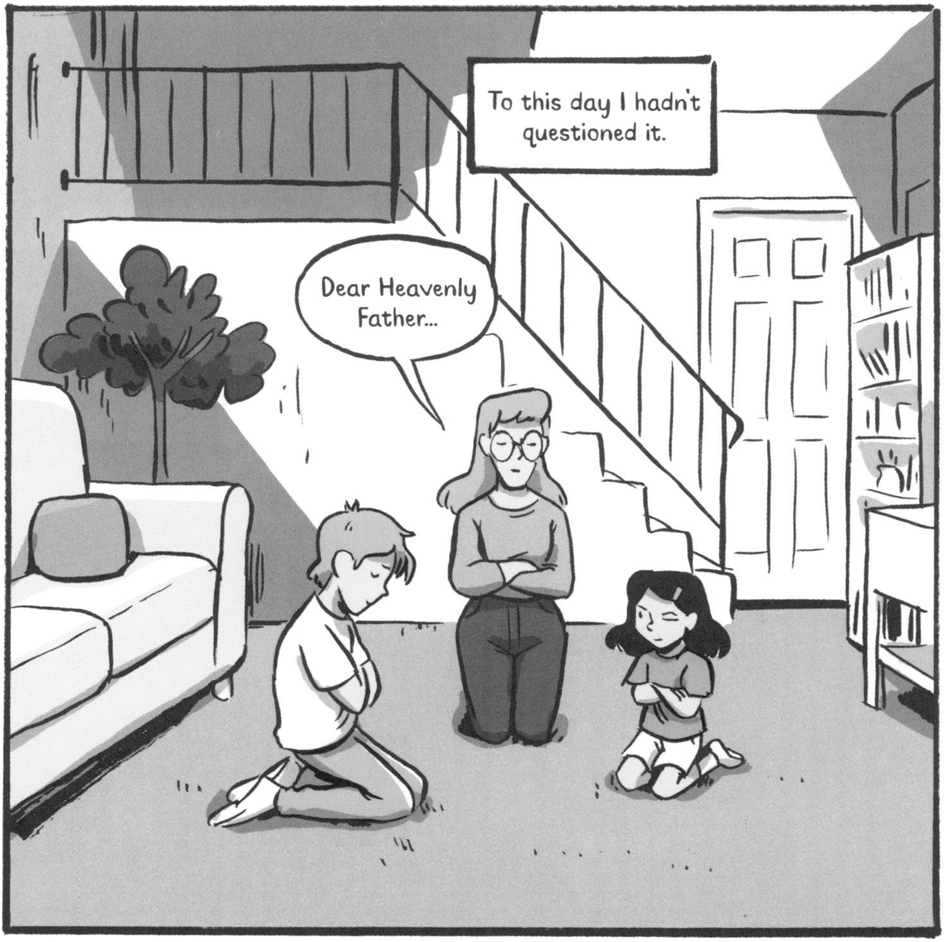
To this day I hadn't questioned it.
Dear Heavenly Father...

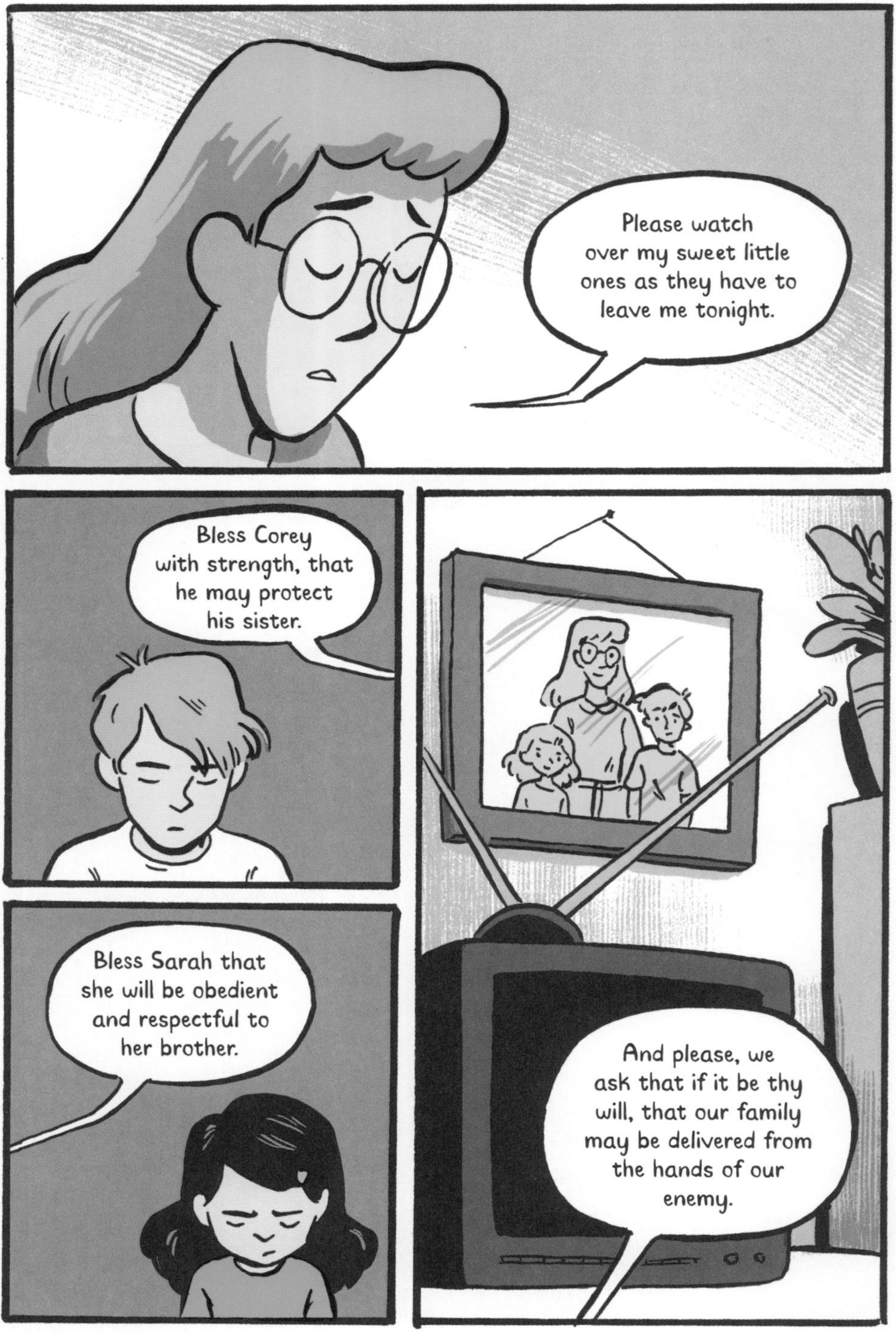
Please watch over my sweet little ones as they have to leave me tonight.
Bless Corey with strength, that he may protect his sister.
Bless Sarah that she will be obedient and respectful to her brother.
And please, we ask that if it be thy will, that our family may be delivered from the hands of our enemy.

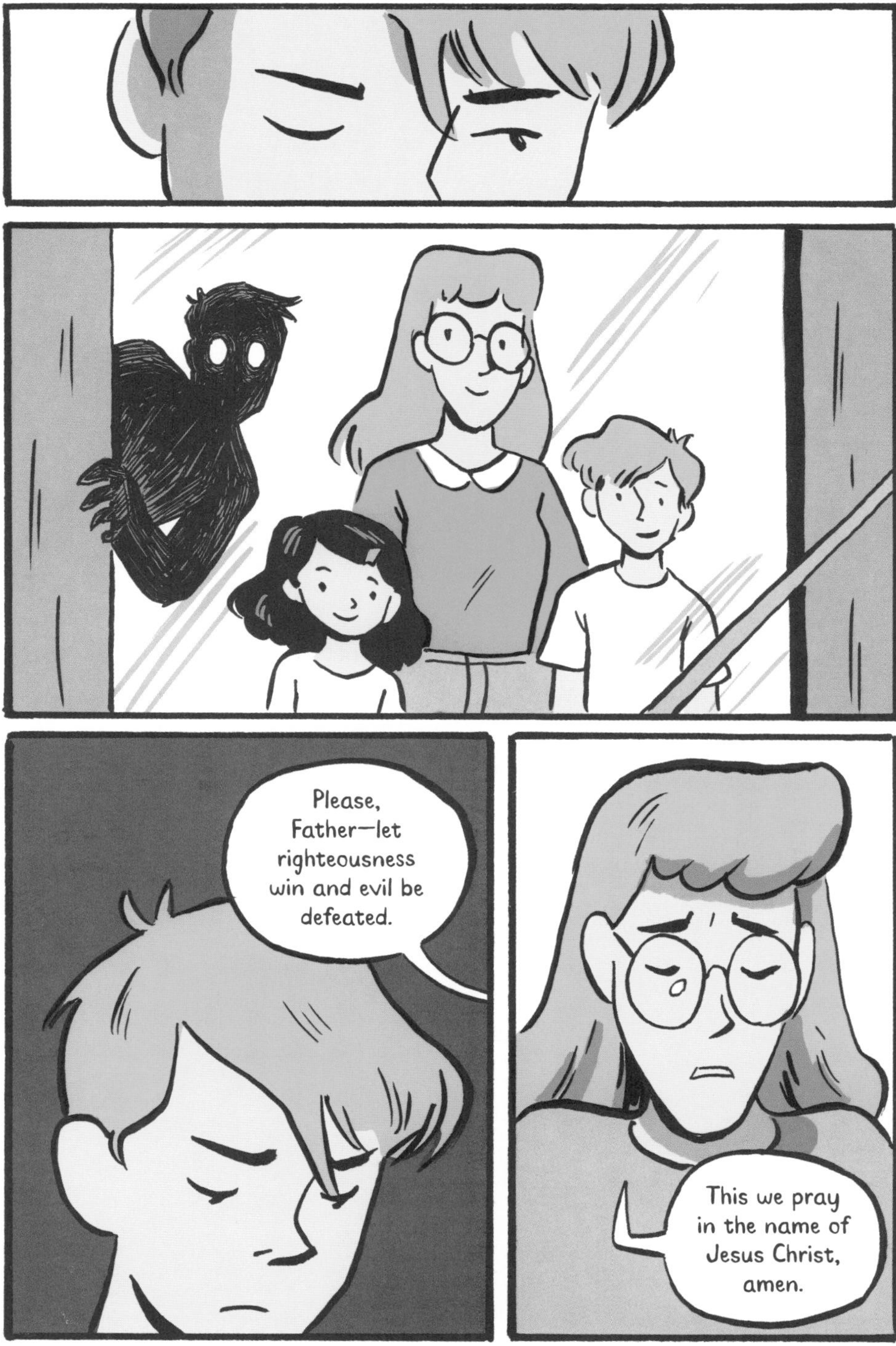
Please, Father—let righteousness win and evil be defeated.
This we pray in the name of Jesus Christ, amen.

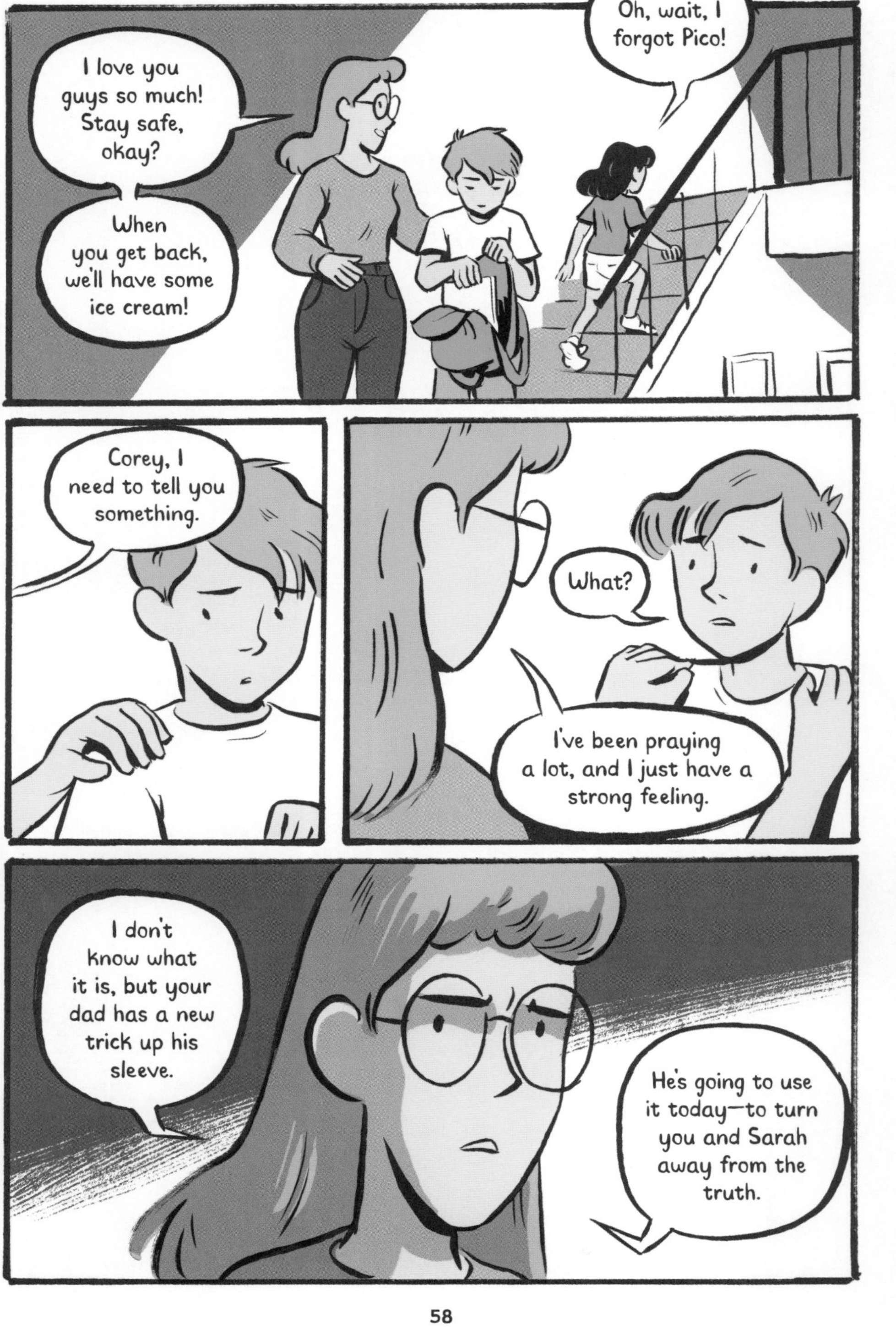

I love you guys so much! Stay safe, okay?
When you get back, we'll have some ice cream!
Oh, wait, I forgot Pico!
Corey, I need to tell you something.
What?
I've been praying a lot, and I just have a strong feeling.
I don't know what it is, but your dad has a new trick up his sleeve.
He's going to use it today—to turn you and Sarah away from the truth.

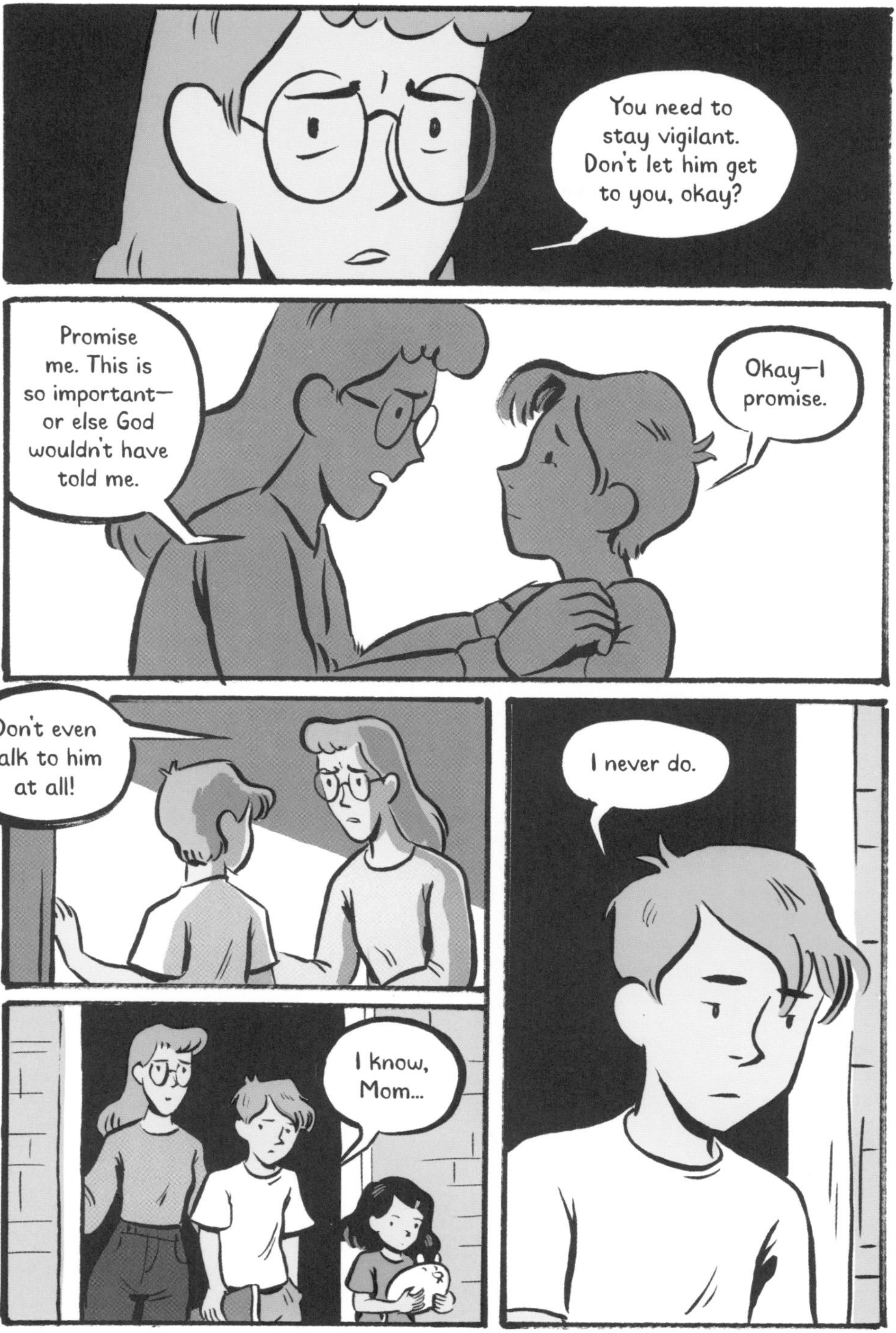
You need to stay vigilant. Don't let him get to you, okay?
Promise me. This is so important—or else God wouldn't have told me.
Okay—I promise.
Don't even talk to him at all!
I know, Mom...
I never do.

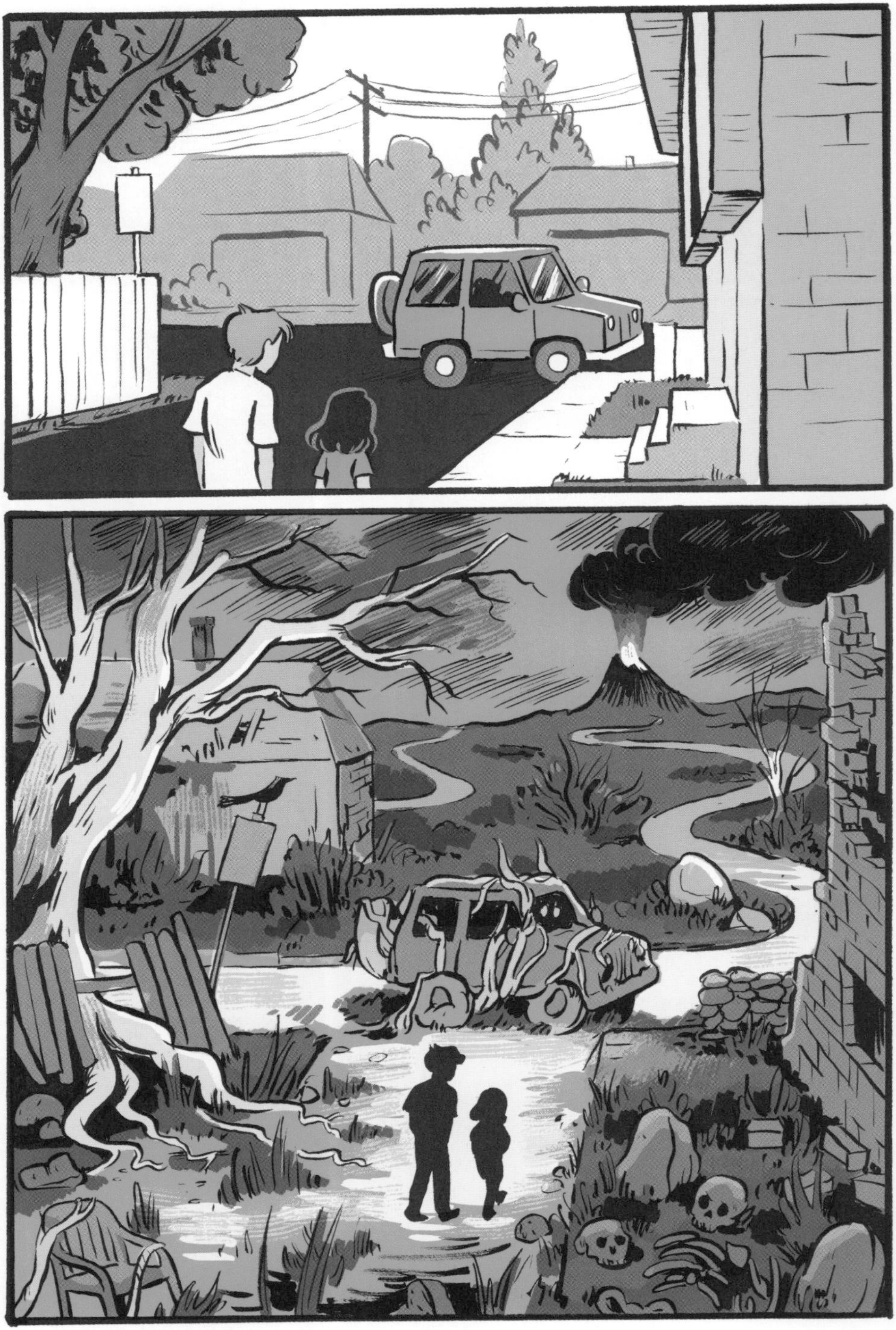

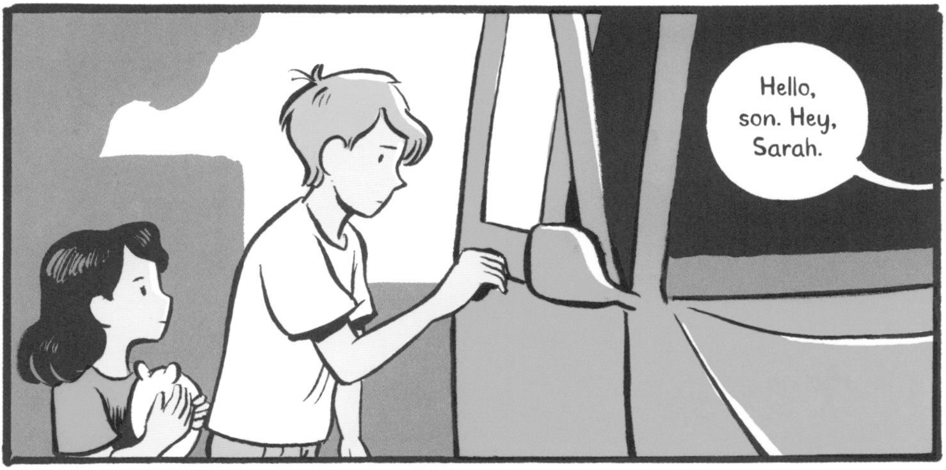
Hello, son. Hey, Sarah.

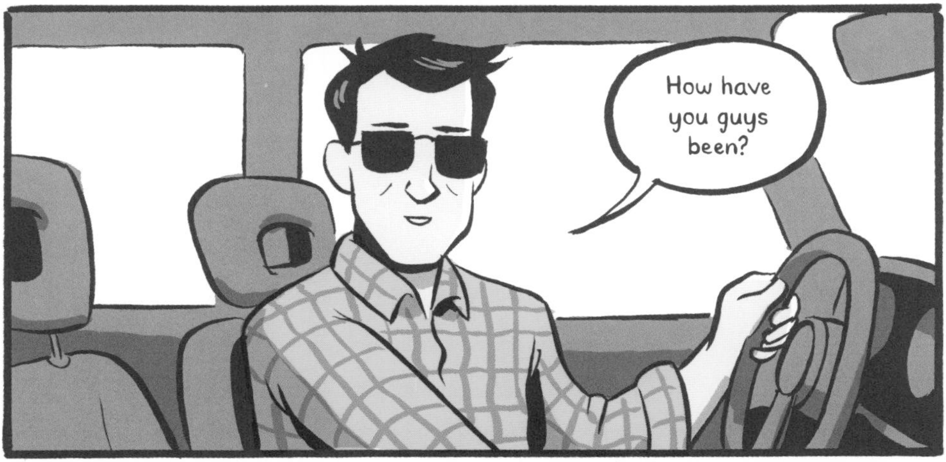
How have you guys been?

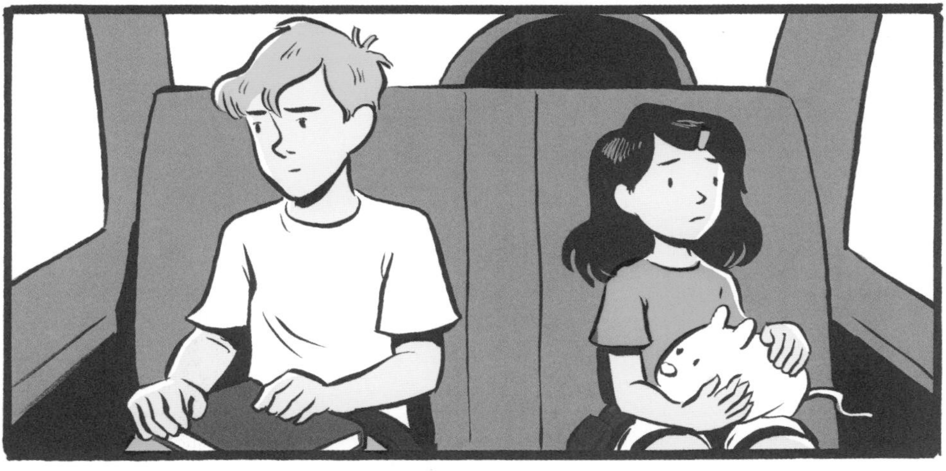

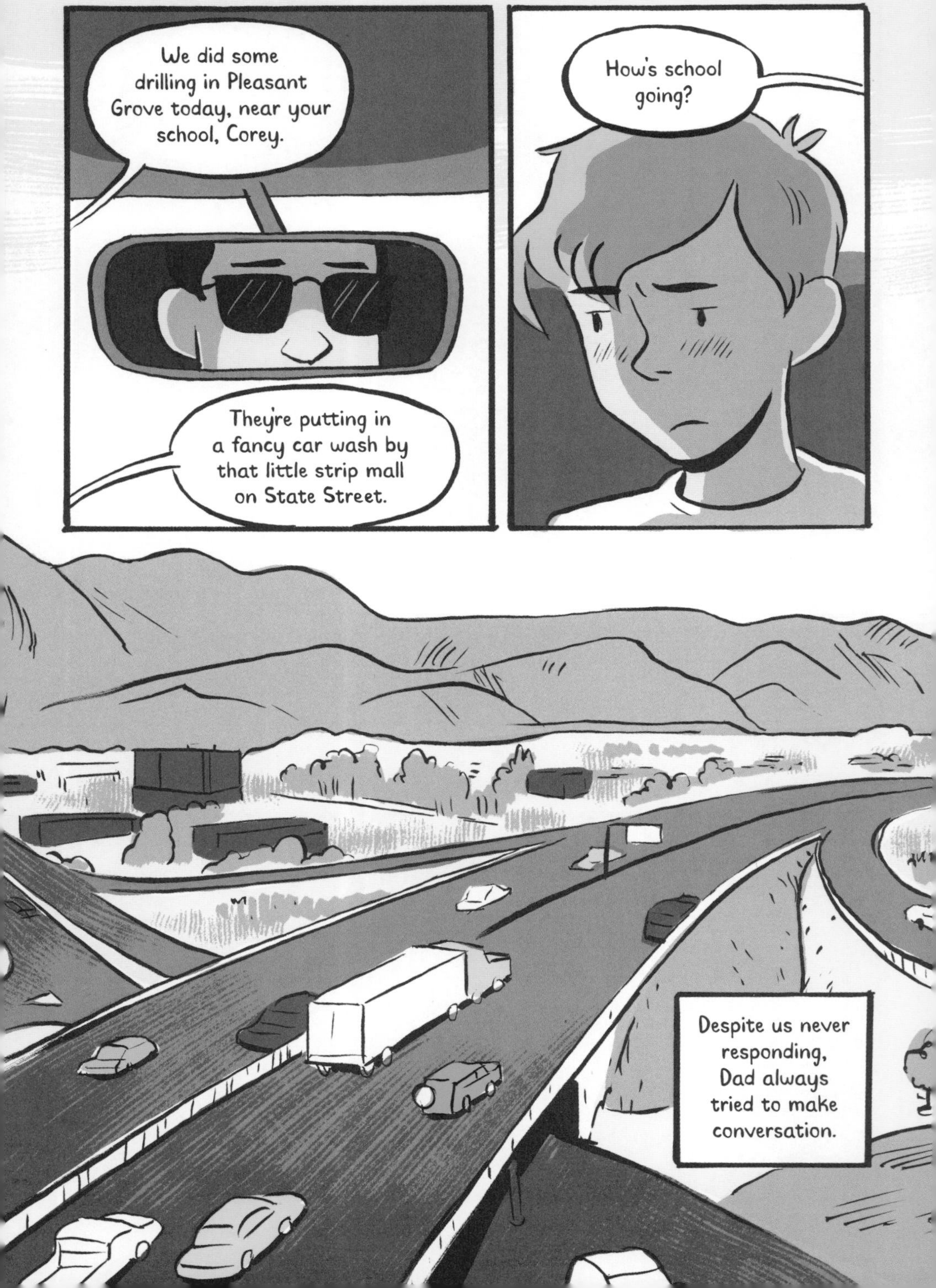
We did some drilling in Pleasant Grove today, near your school, Corey.
They're putting in a fancy car wash by that little strip mall on State Street.
How's school going?
Despite us never responding, Dad always tried to make conversation.

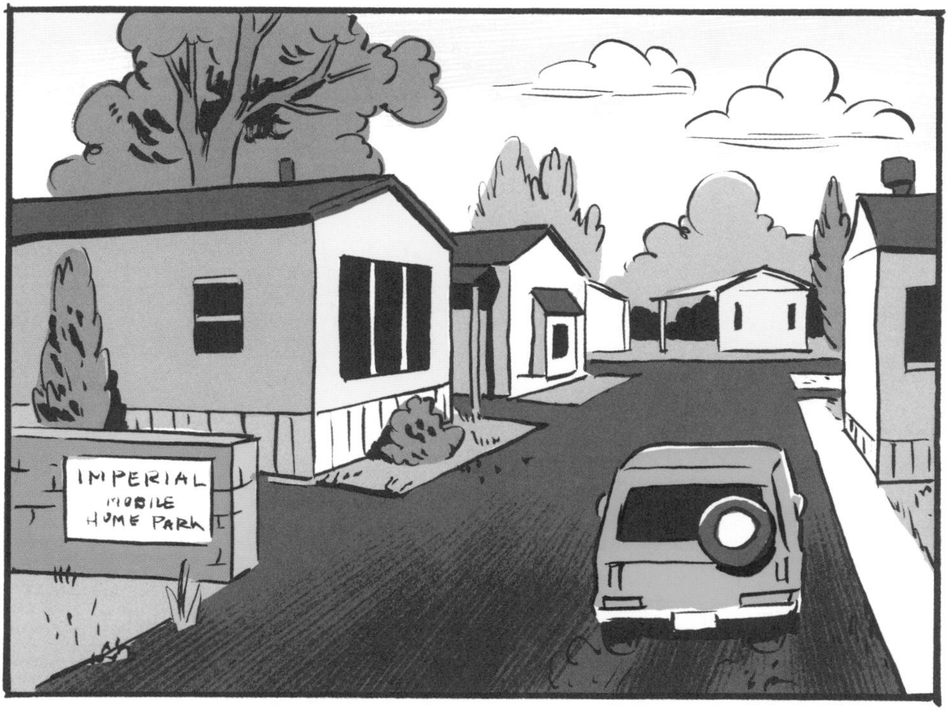
IMPERIAL
MOBILE
HOME PARK

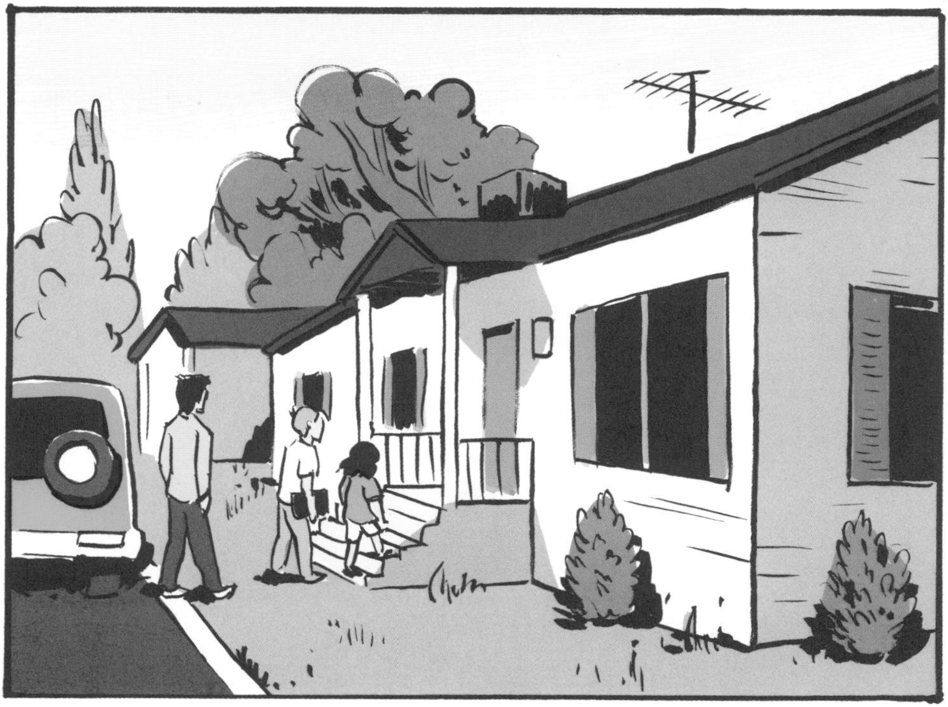

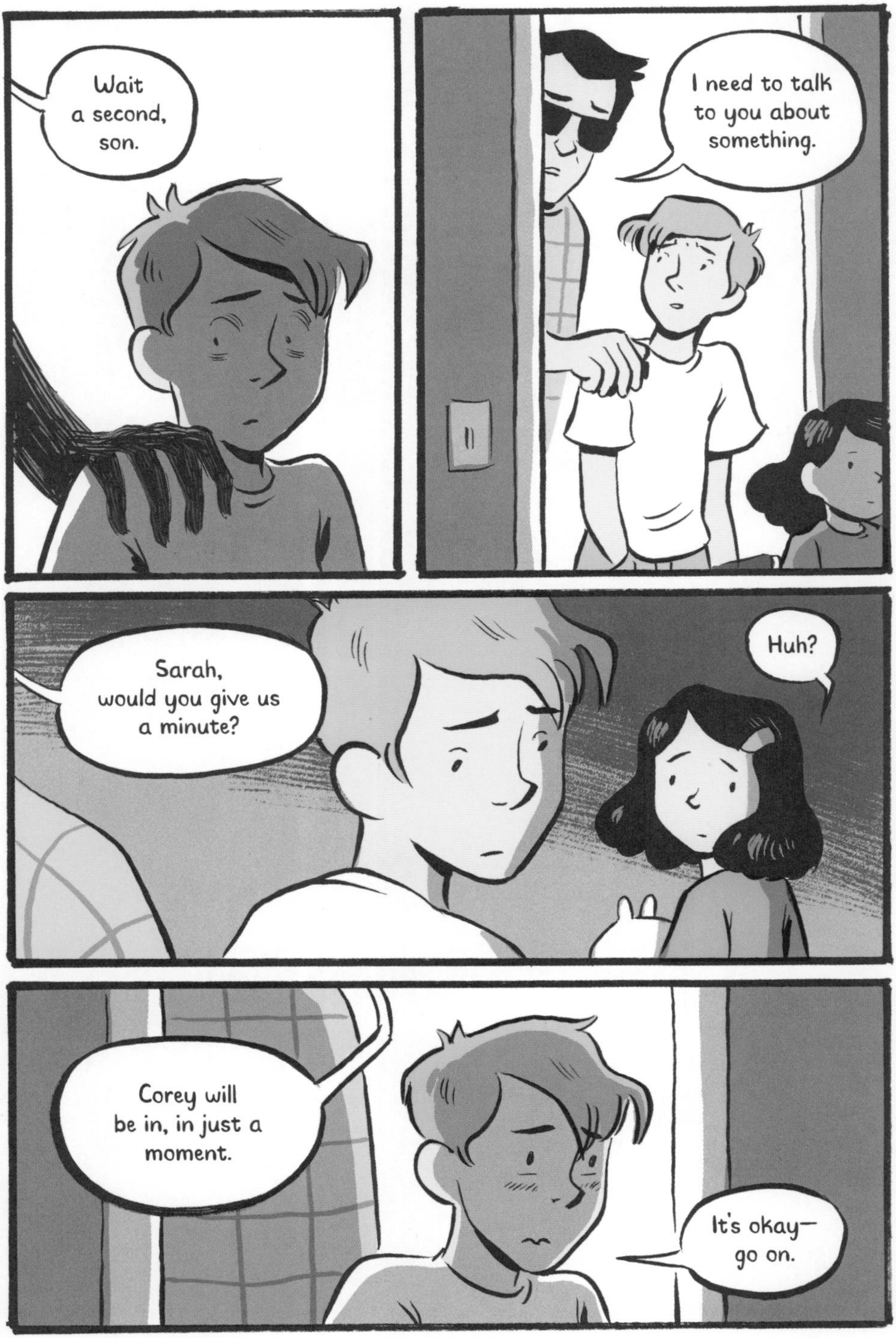
Wait a second, son.
I need to talk to you about something.
Sarah, would you give us a minute?
Huh?
Corey will be in, in just a moment.
It's okay— go on.

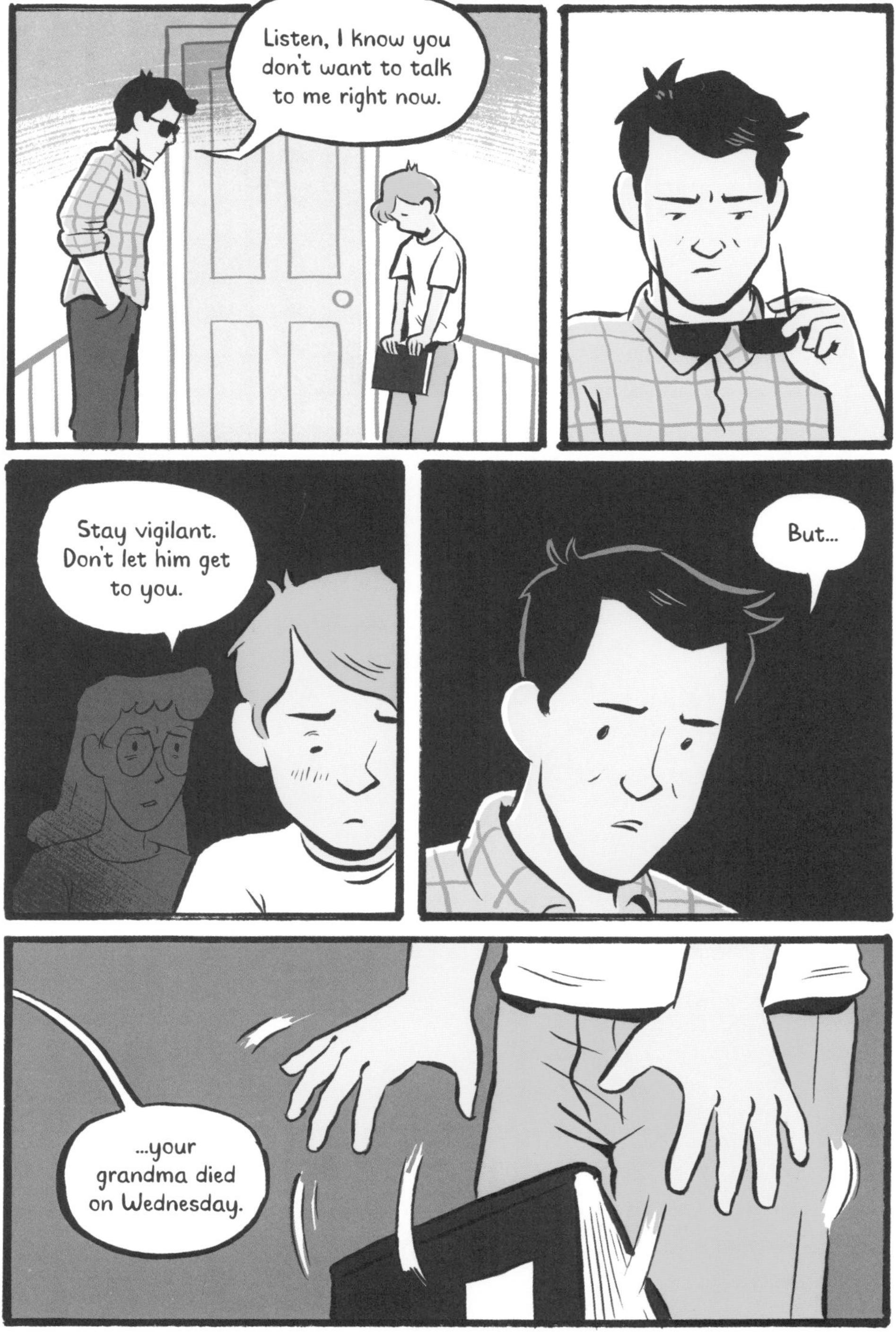
Listen, I know you don't want to talk to me right now.
Stay vigilant. Don't let him get to you.
But...
...your grandma died on Wednesday.

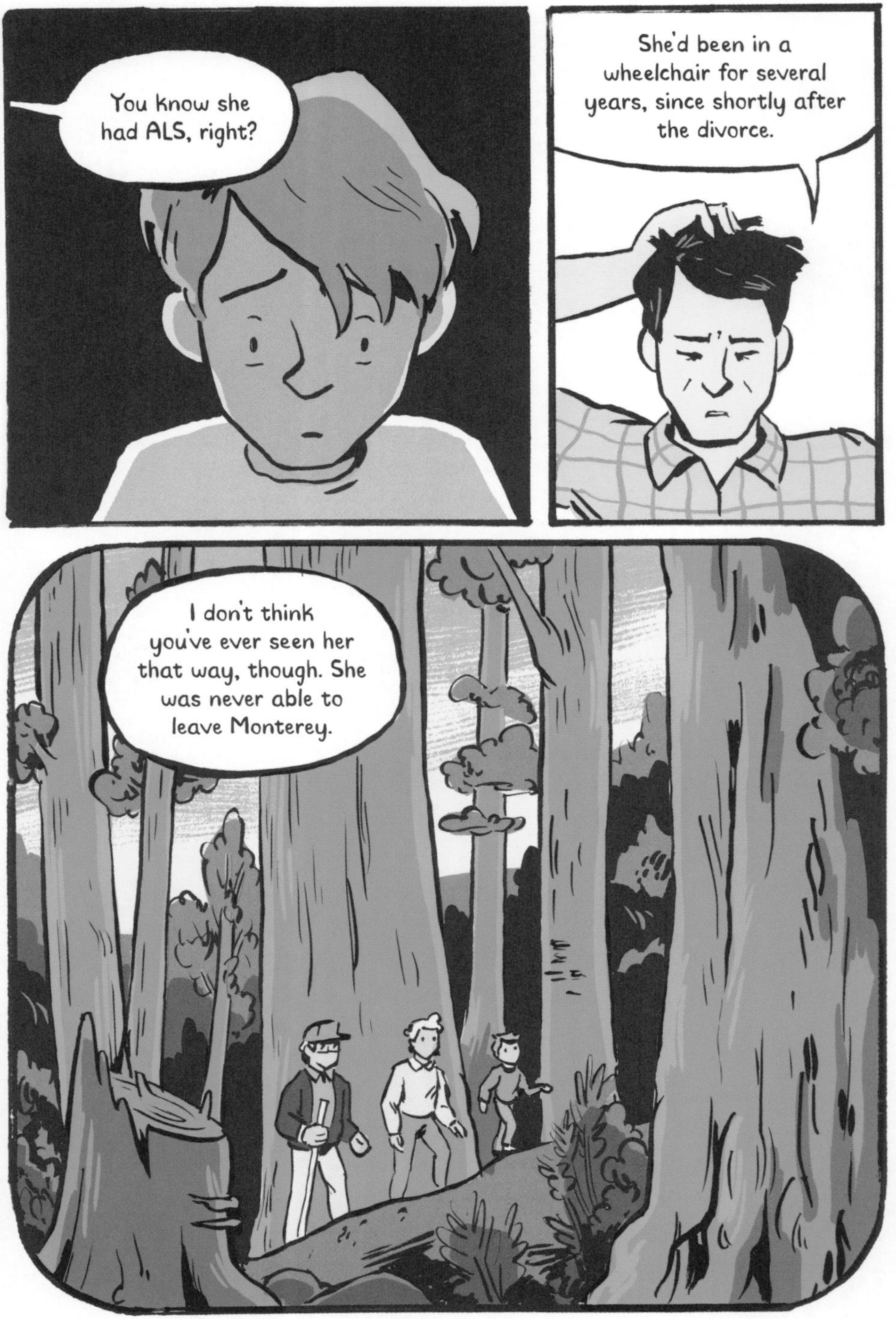
You know she had ALS, right?
She'd been in a wheelchair for several years, since shortly after the divorce.
I don't think you've ever seen her that way, though. She was never able to leave Monterey.

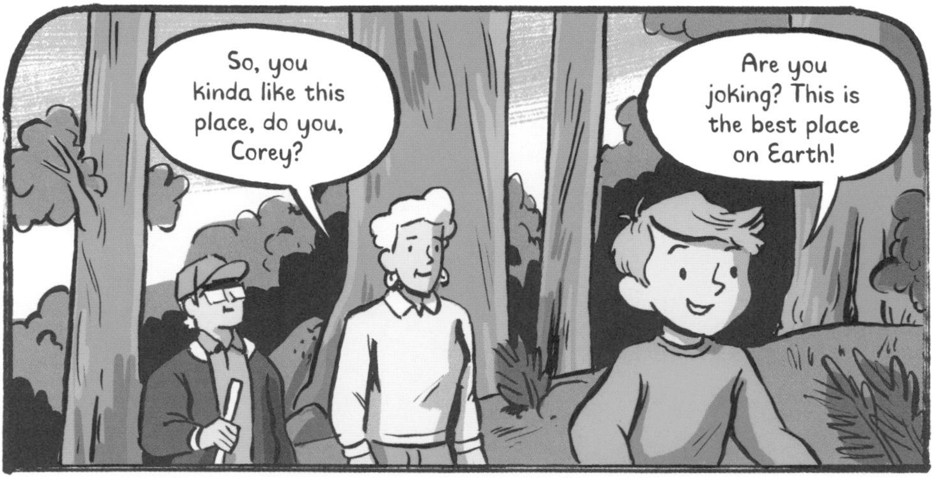
So, you kinda like this place, do you, Corey?
Are you joking? This is the best place on Earth!

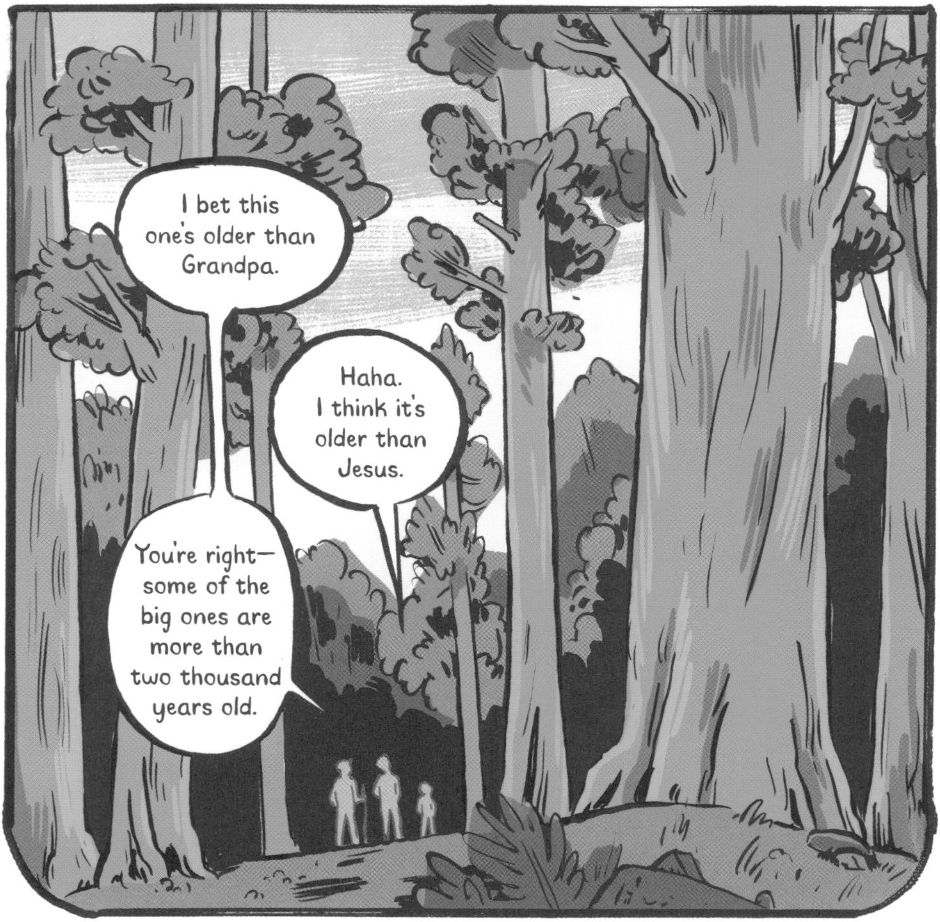
I bet this one's older than Grandpa.
Haha. I think it's older than Jesus.
You're right—some of the big ones are more than two thousand years old.

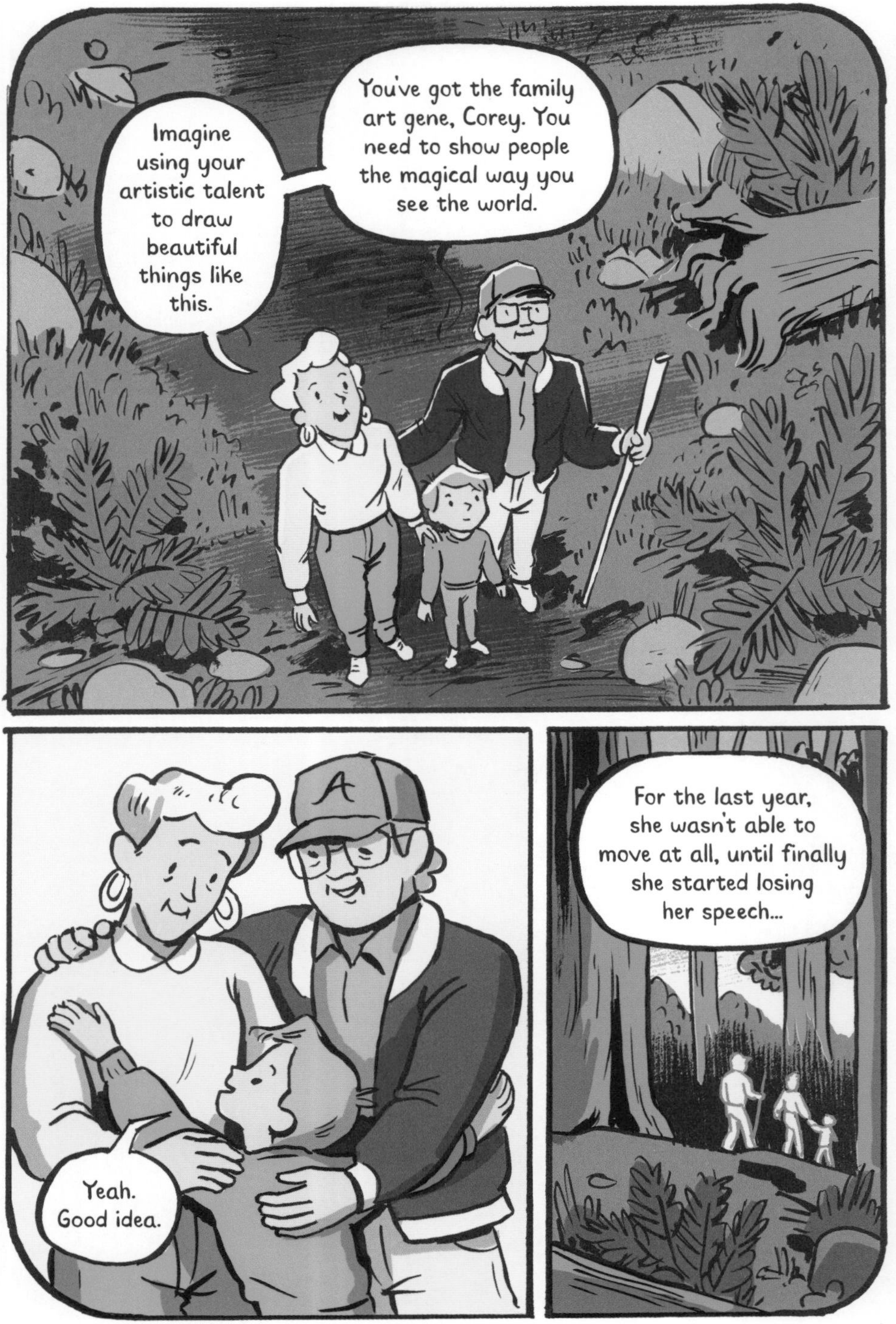
Imagine using your artistic talent to draw beautiful things like this.
You've got the family art gene, Corey. You need to show people the magical way you see the world.
Yeah. Good idea.
For the last year, she wasn't able to move at all, until finally she started losing her speech...

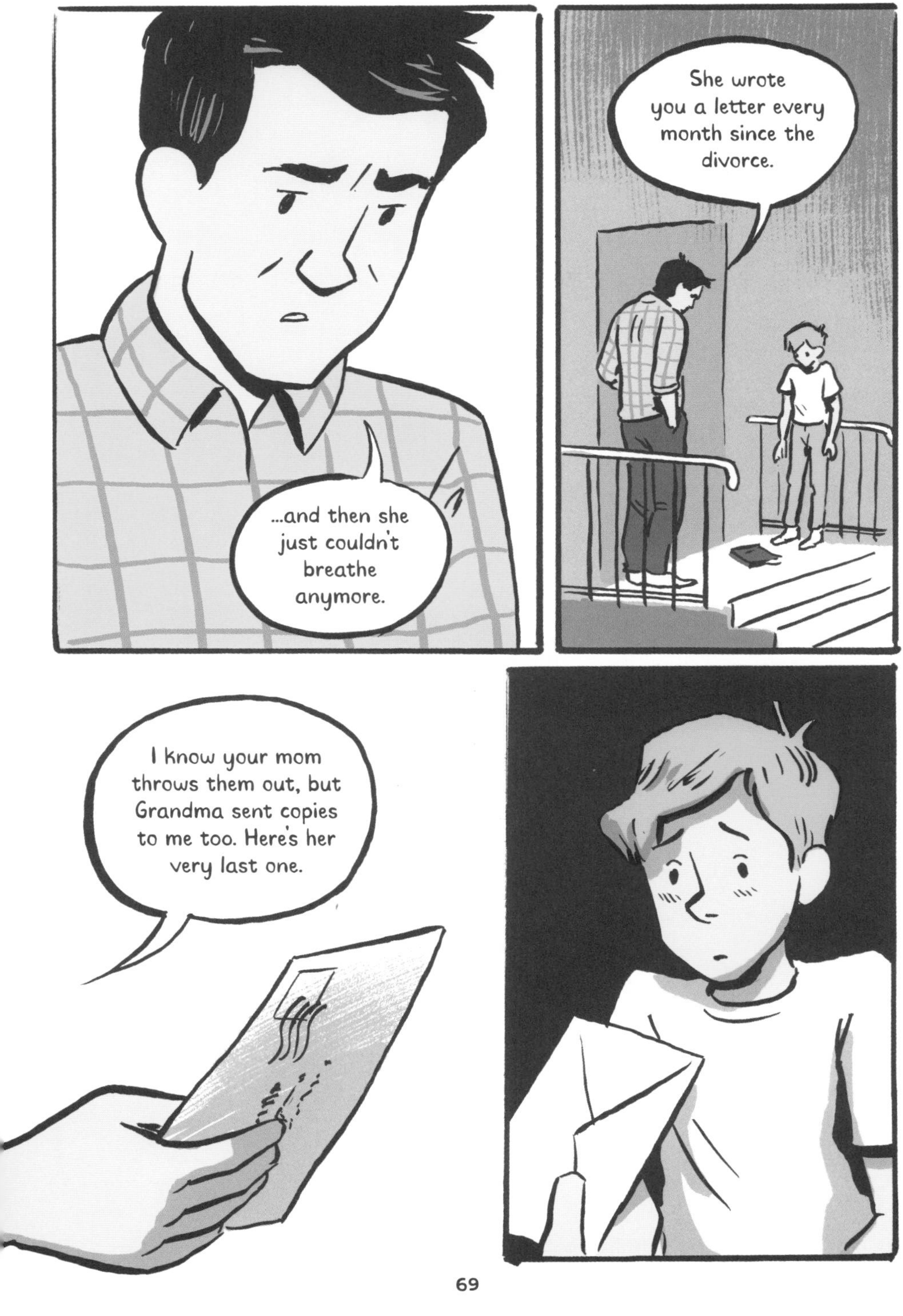
...and then she just couldn't breathe anymore.
She wrote you a letter every month since the divorce.
I know your mom throws them out, but Grandma sent copies to me too. Here's her very last one.

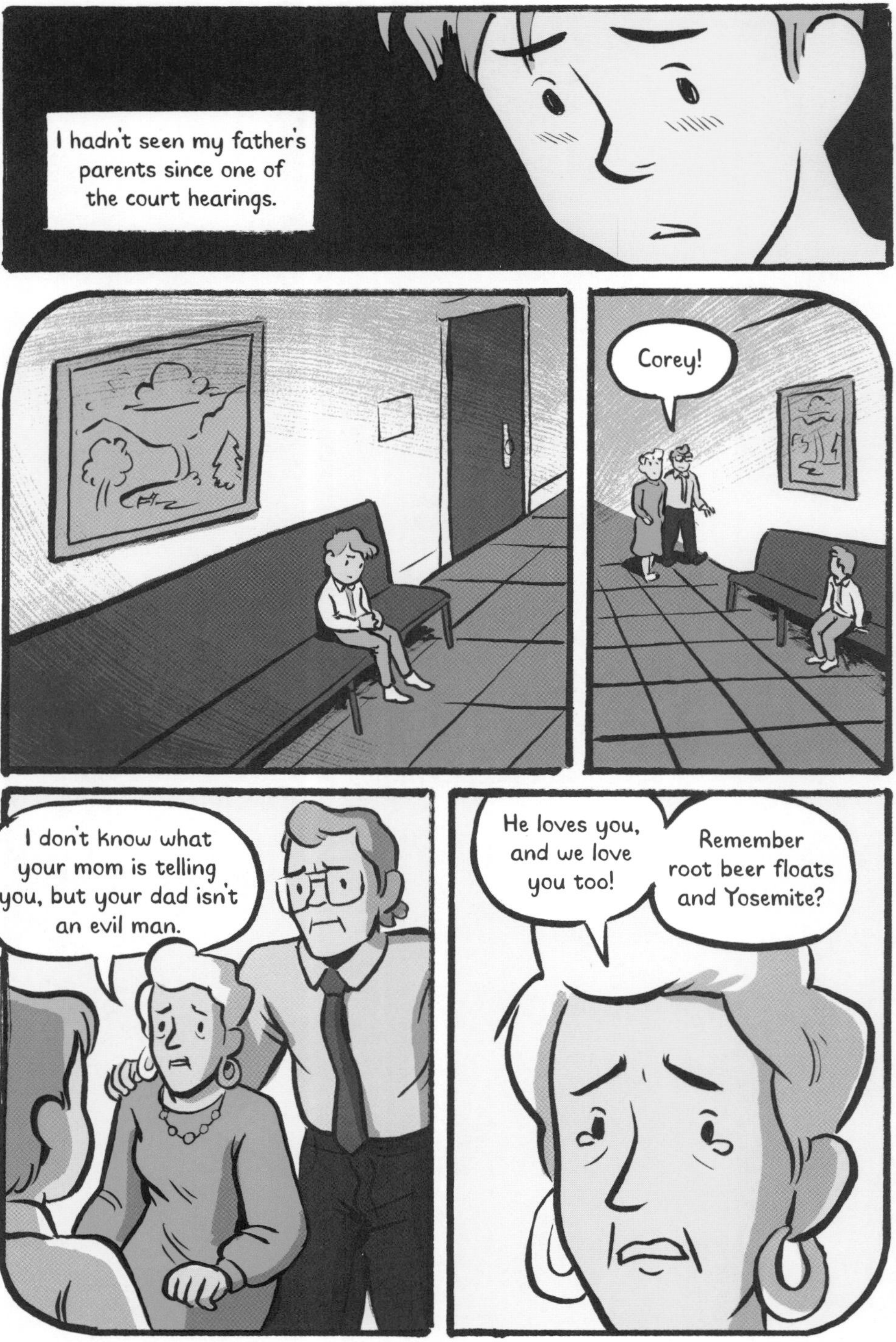
I hadn't seen my father's parents since one of the court hearings.
Corey!
I don't know what your mom is telling you, but your dad isn't an evil man.
He loves you, and we love you too!
Remember root beer floats and Yosemite?

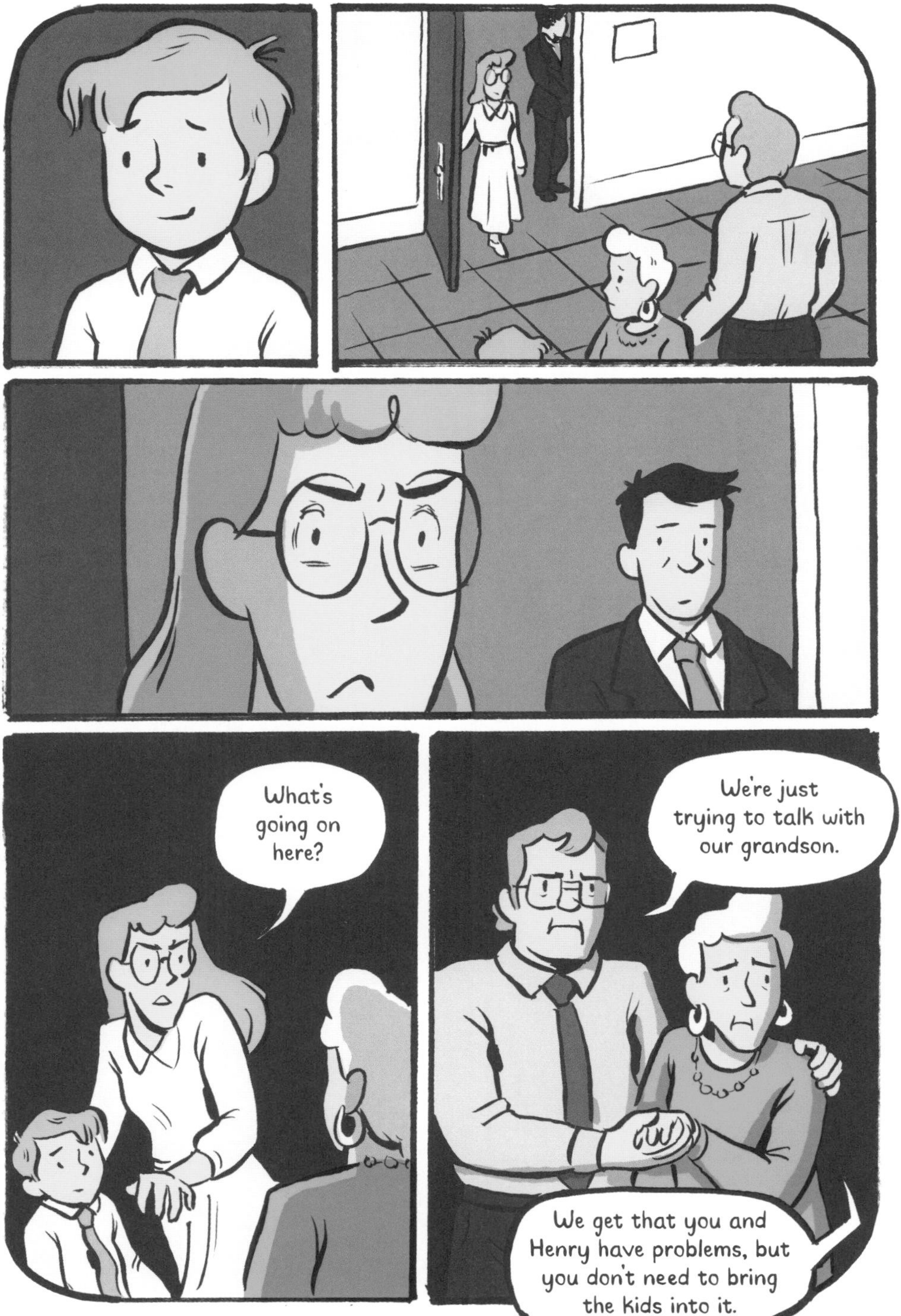
What's going on here?
We're just trying to talk with our grandson.
We get that you and Henry have problems, but you don't need to bring the kids into it.

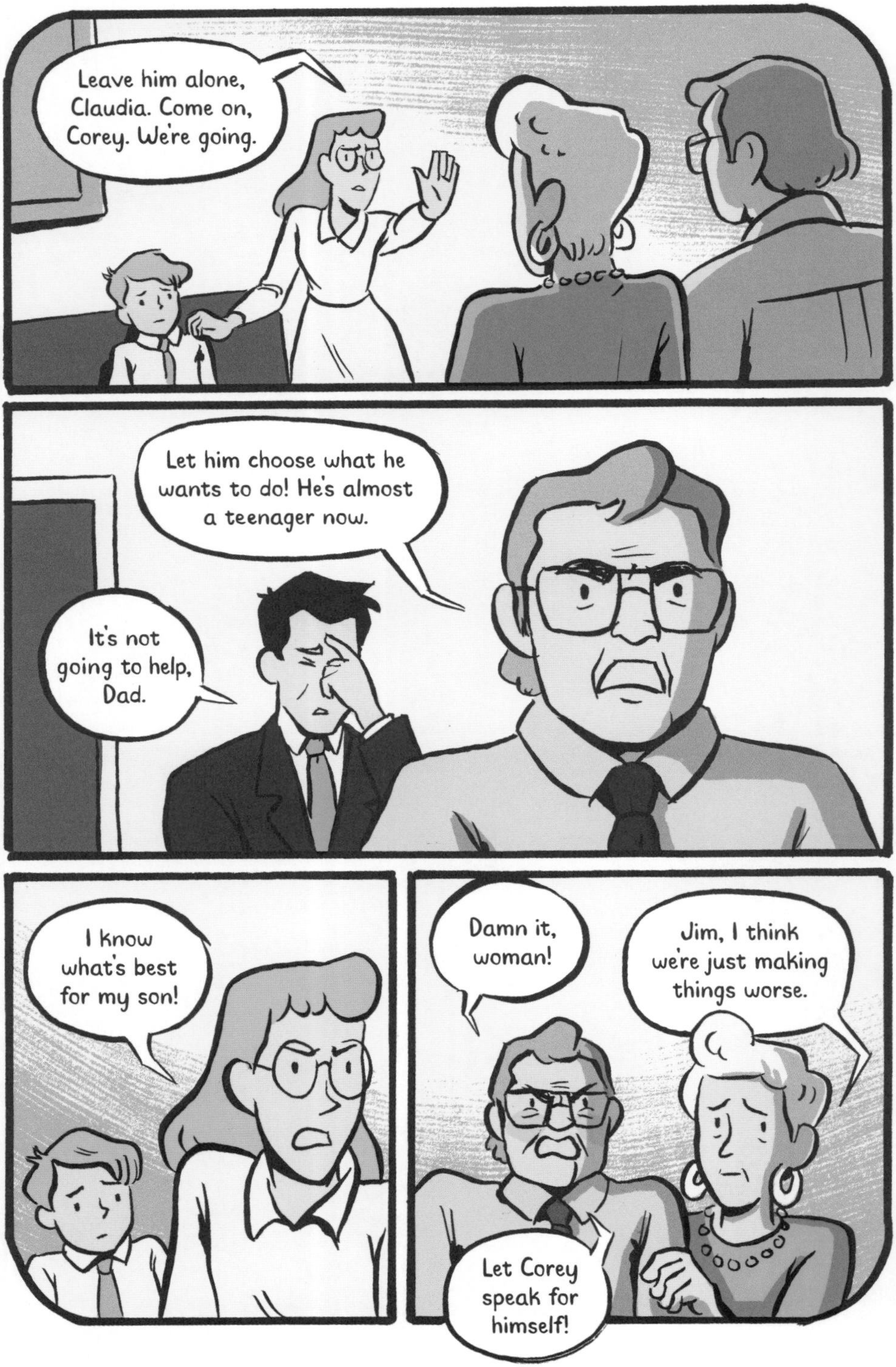
Leave him alone, Claudia. Come on, Corey. We're going.
Let him choose what he wants to do! He's almost a teenager now.
It's not going to help, Dad.
I know what's best for my son!
Damn it, woman!
Jim, I think we're just making things worse.
Let Corey speak for himself!

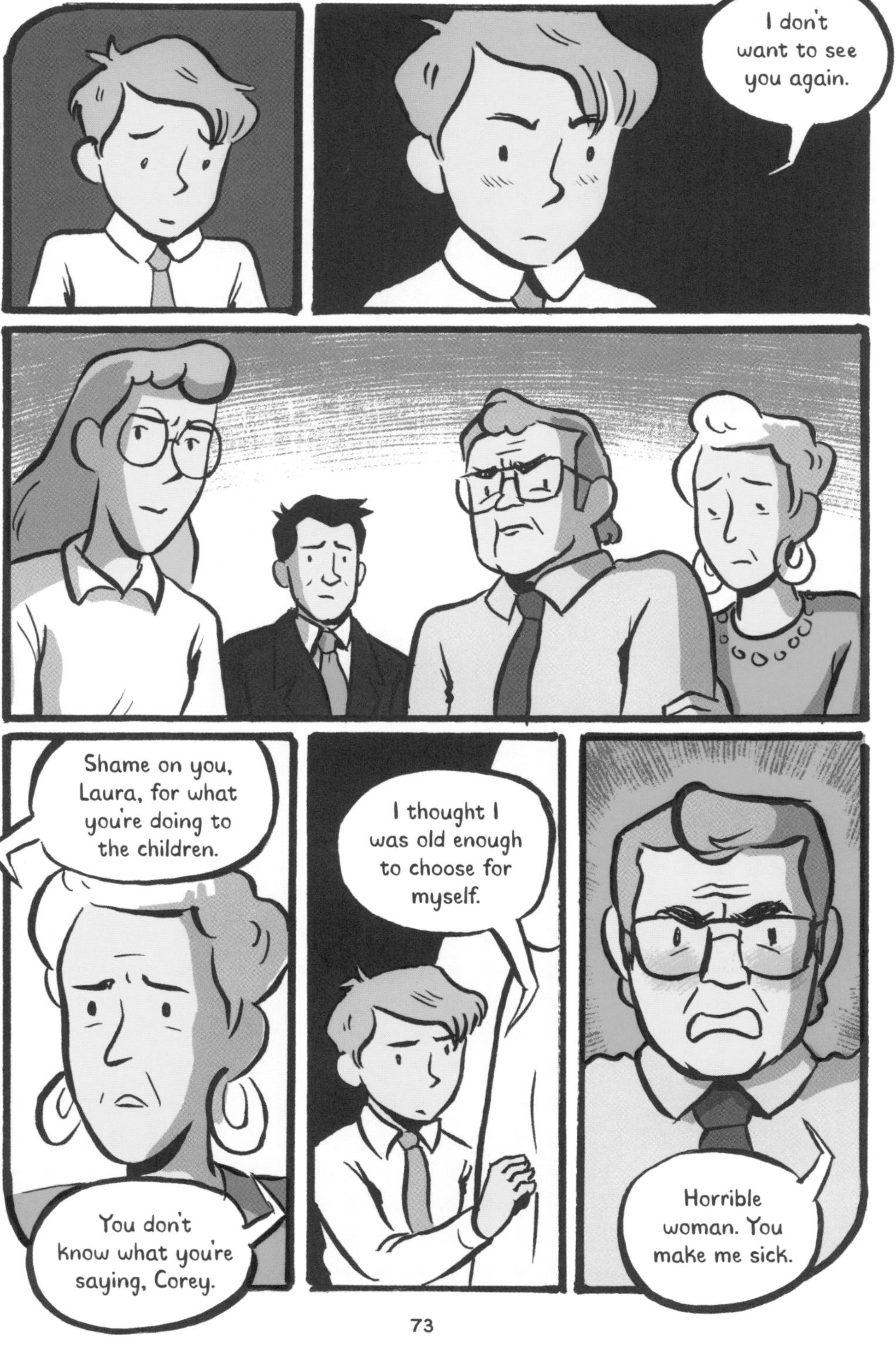
I don't want to see you again.
Shame on you, Laura, for what you're doing to the children.
You don't know what you're saying, Corey.
I thought I was old enough to choose for myself.
Horrible woman. You make me sick.

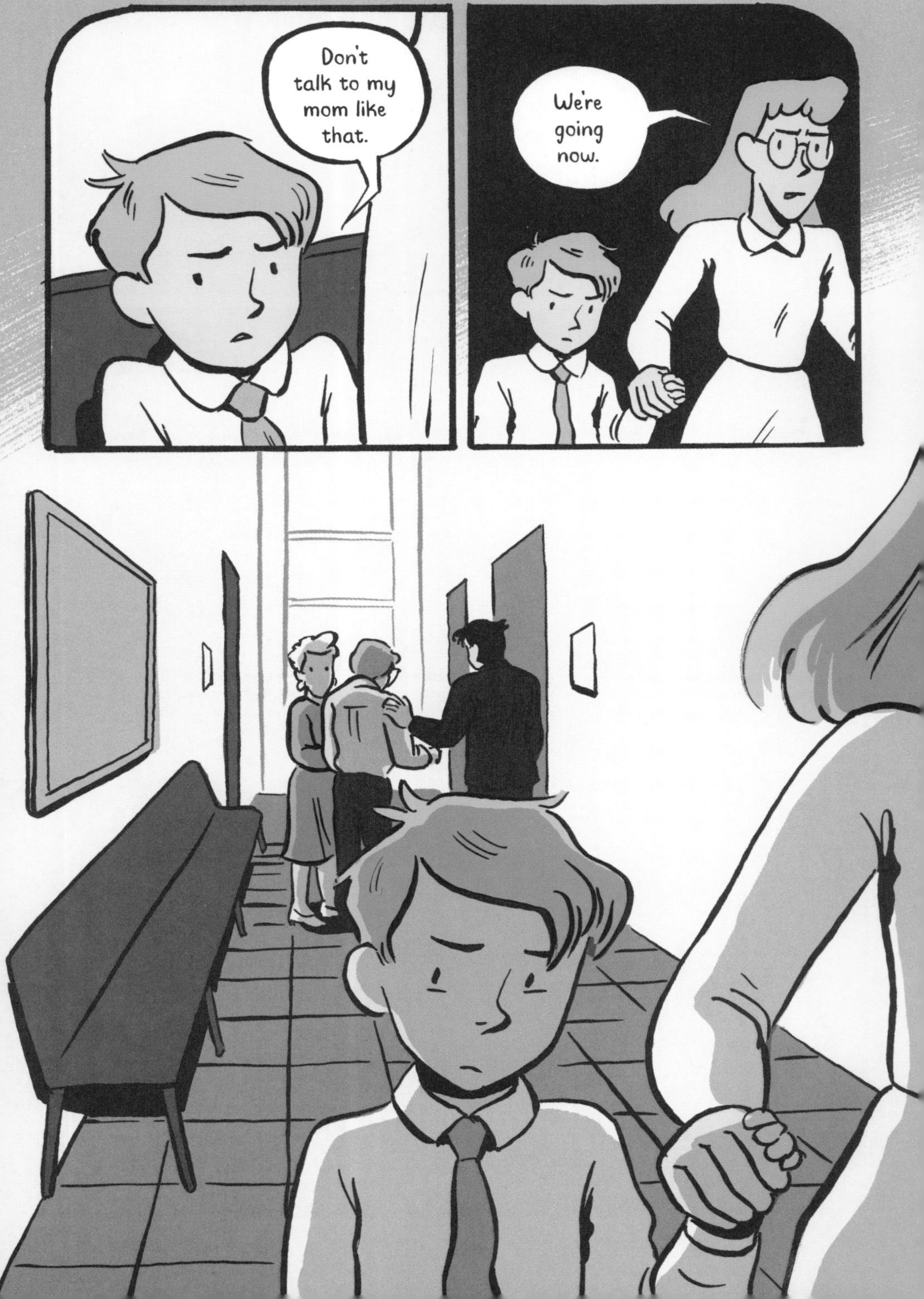
Don't talk to my mom like that.
We're going now.

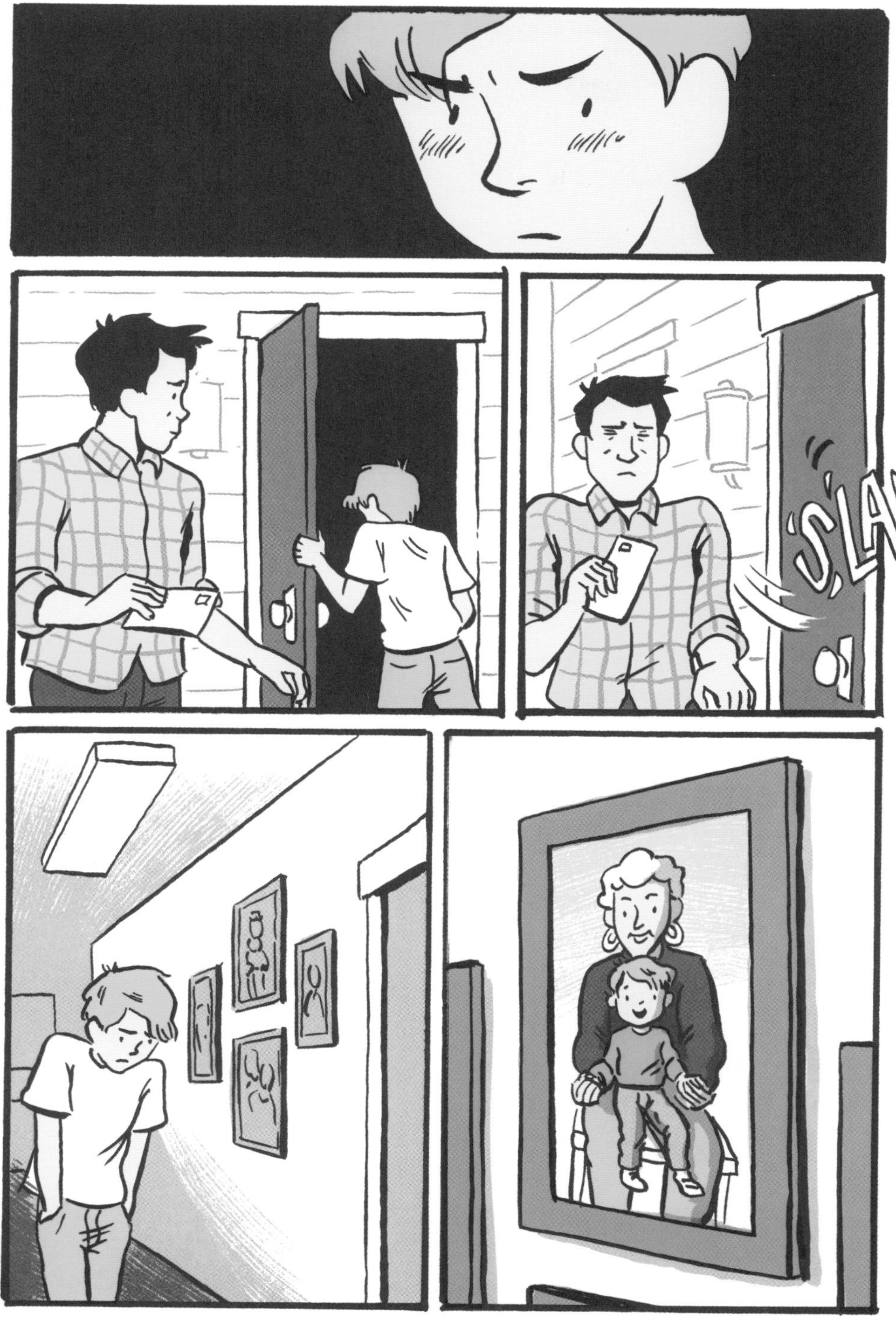
SLAM

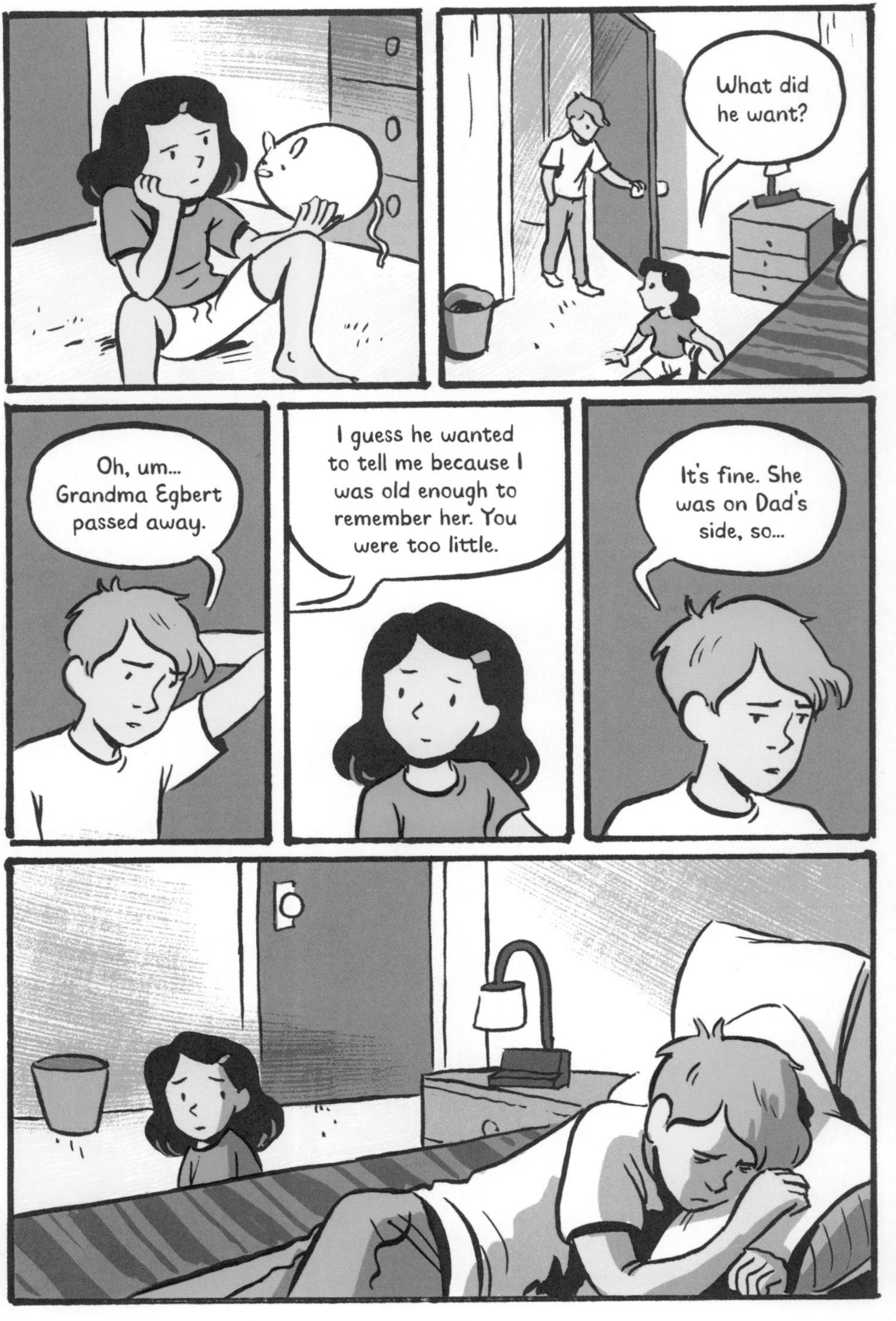
What did he want?
Oh, um... Grandma Egbert passed away.
I guess he wanted to tell me because I was old enough to remember her. You were too little.
It's fine. She was on Dad's side, so...

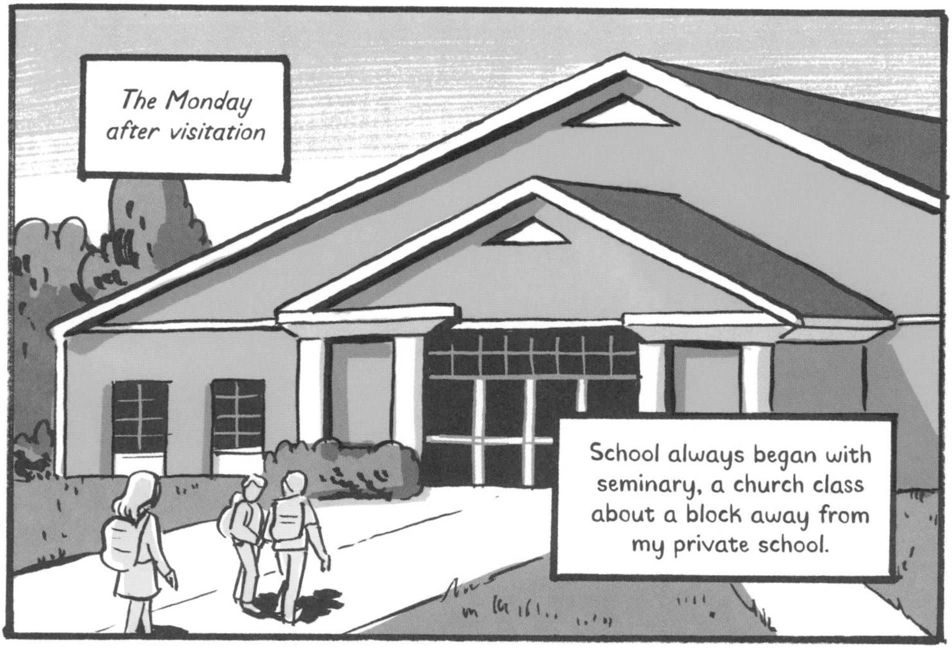
The Monday after visitation
School always began with seminary, a church class about a block away from my private school.

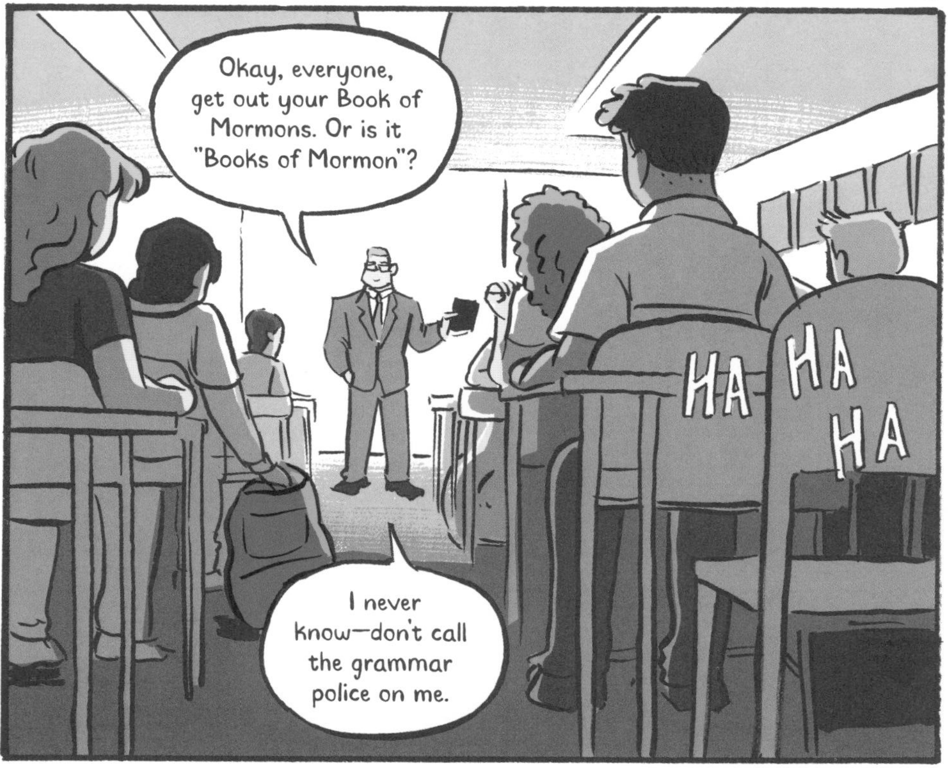
Okay, everyone, get out your Book of Mormons. Or is it "Books of Mormon"?
I never know—don't call the grammar police on me.
HA HA HA HA

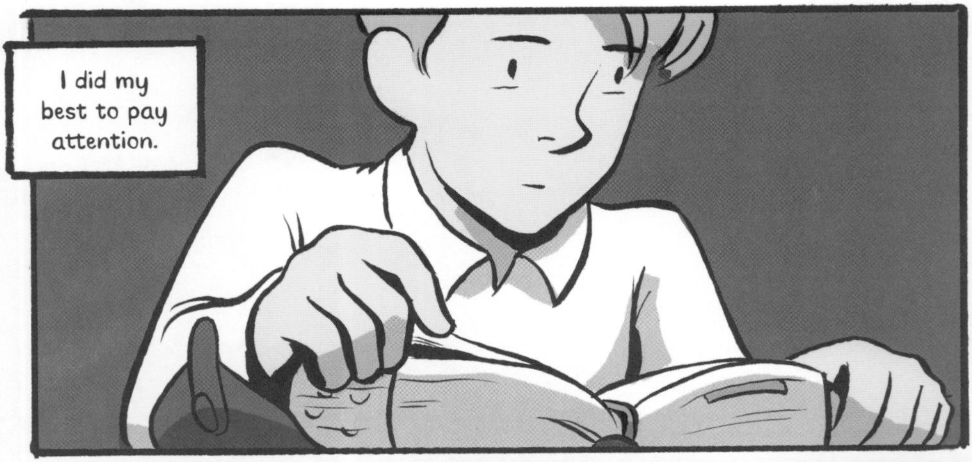
I did my best to pay attention.

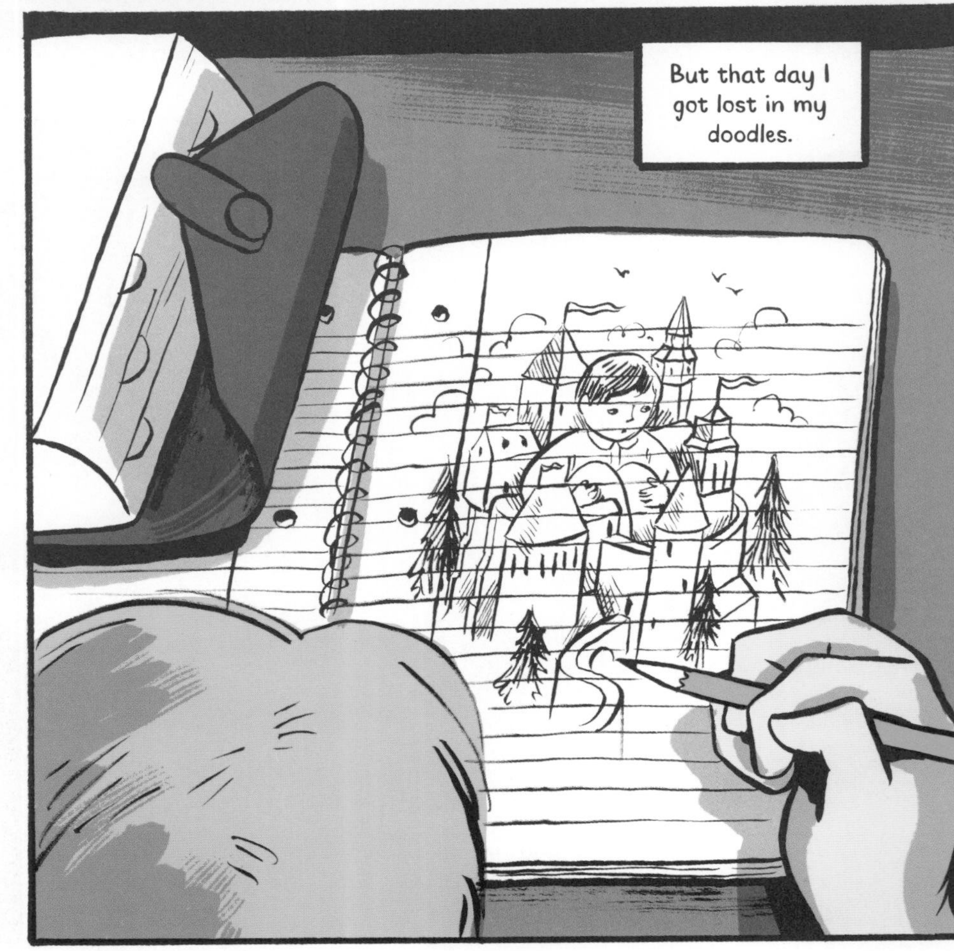
But that day I got lost in my doodles.

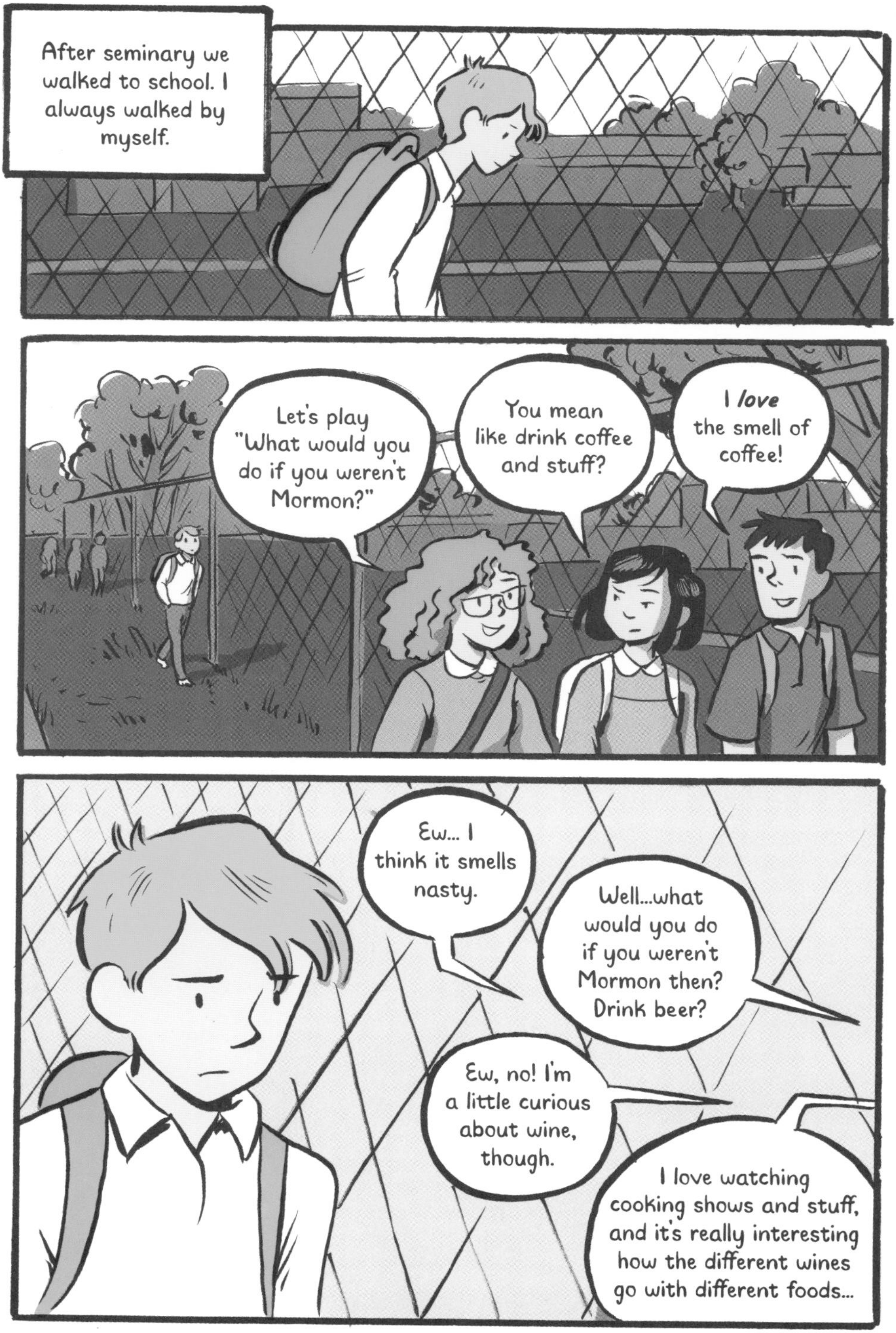
After seminary we walked to school. I always walked by myself.
Let's play "What would you do if you weren't Mormon?"
You mean like drink coffee and stuff?
I *love* the smell of coffee!
Ew... I think it smells nasty.
Well...what would you do if you weren't Mormon then? Drink beer?
Ew, no! I'm a little curious about wine, though.
I love watching cooking shows and stuff, and it's really interesting how the different wines go with different foods...

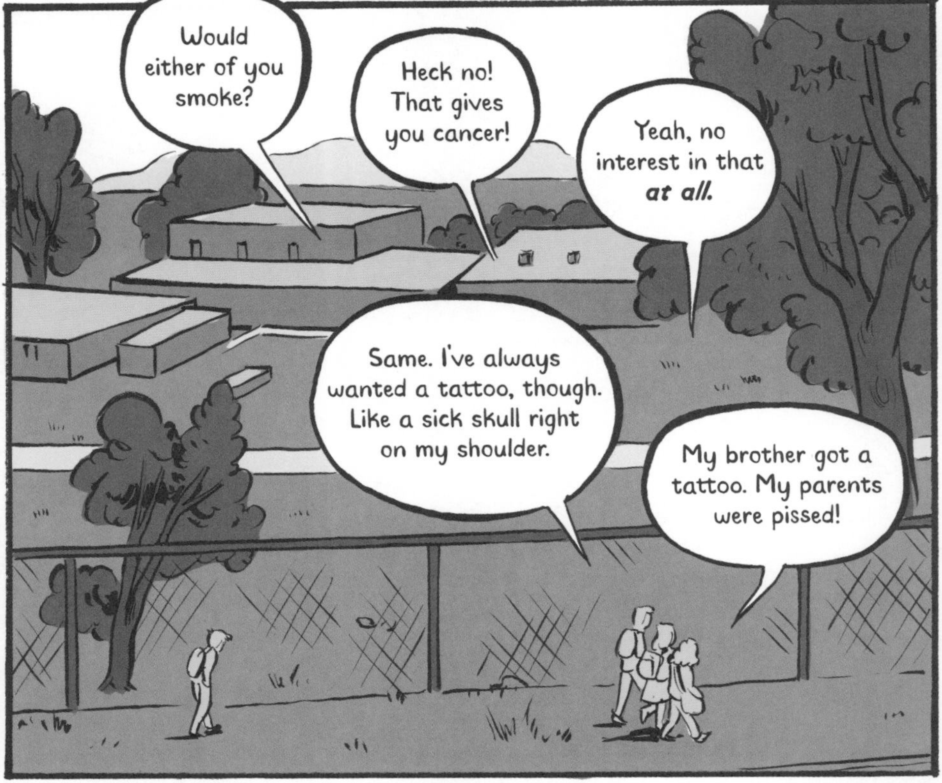
Would either of you smoke?
Heck no! That gives you cancer!
Yeah, no interest in that ***at all.***
Same. I've always wanted a tattoo, though. Like a sick skull right on my shoulder.
My brother got a tattoo. My parents were pissed!

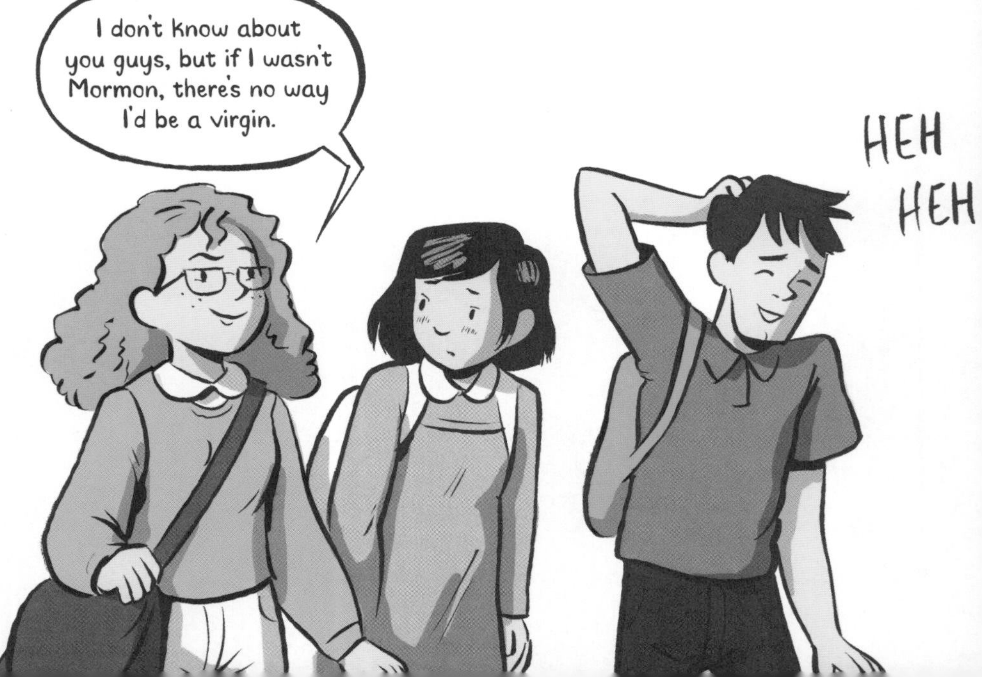
I don't know about you guys, but if I wasn't Mormon, there's no way I'd be a virgin.
HEH HEH

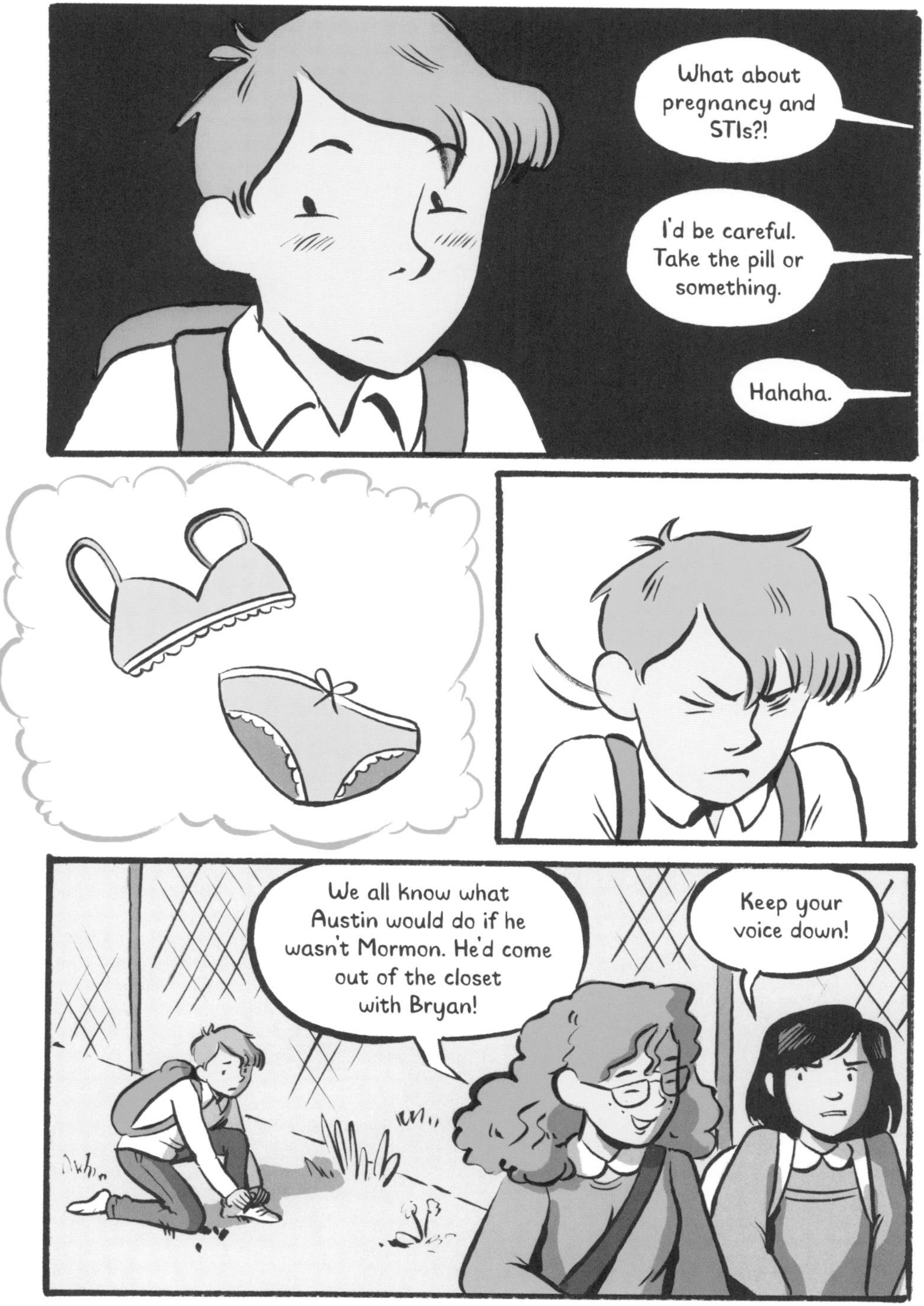
What about pregnancy and STIs?!
I'd be careful. Take the pill or something.
Hahaha.
We all know what Austin would do if he wasn't Mormon. He'd come out of the closet with Bryan!
Keep your voice down!

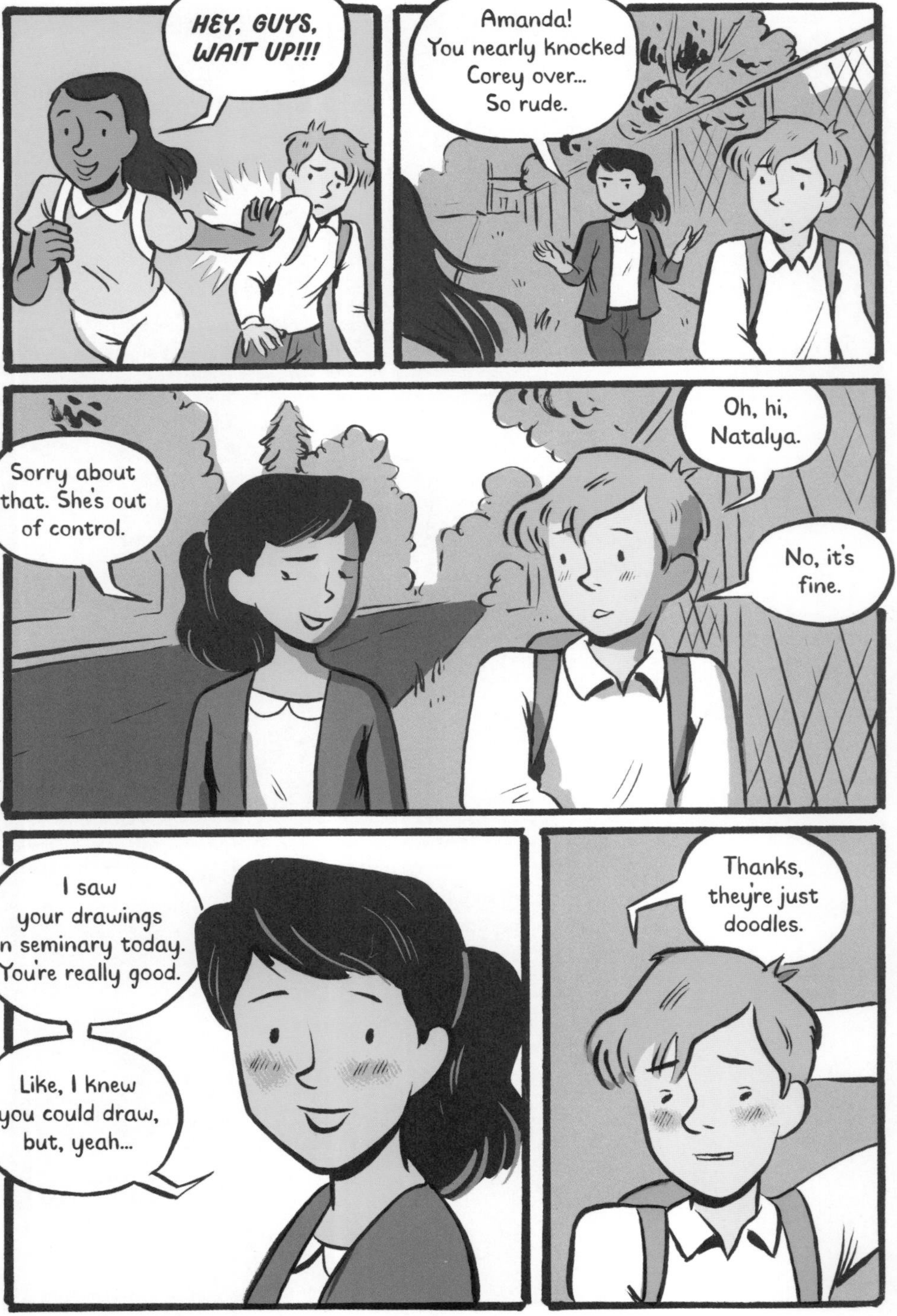
HEY, GUYS, WAIT UP!!!
Amanda! You nearly knocked Corey over... So rude.
Sorry about that. She's out of control.
Oh, hi, Natalya.
No, it's fine.
I saw your drawings in seminary today. You're really good.
Like, I knew you could draw, but, yeah...
Thanks, theyre just doodles.

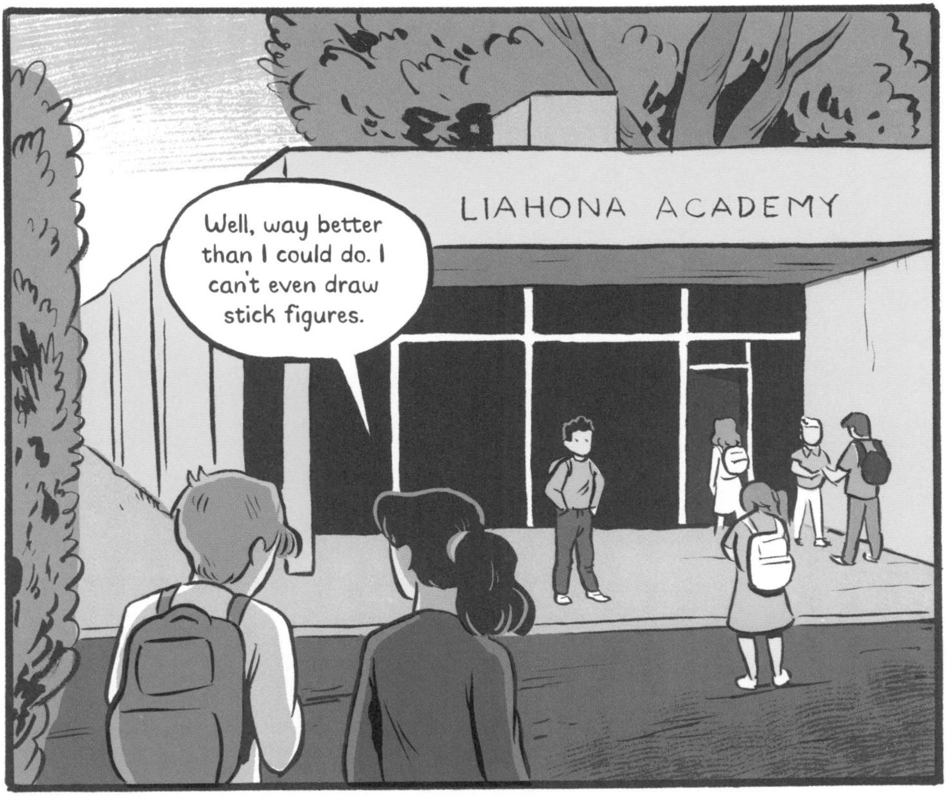
Well, way better than I could do. I can't even draw stick figures.
LIAHONA ACADEMY

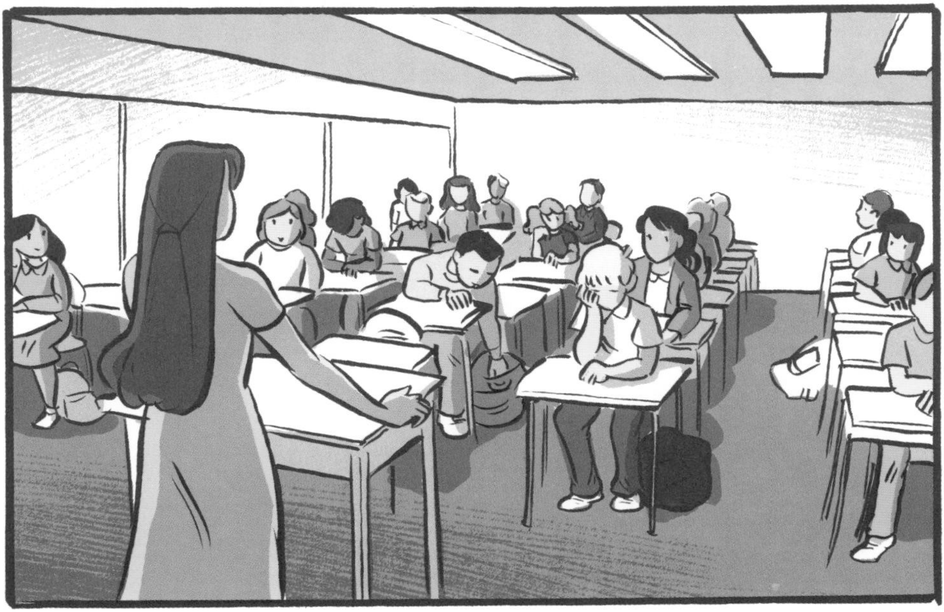

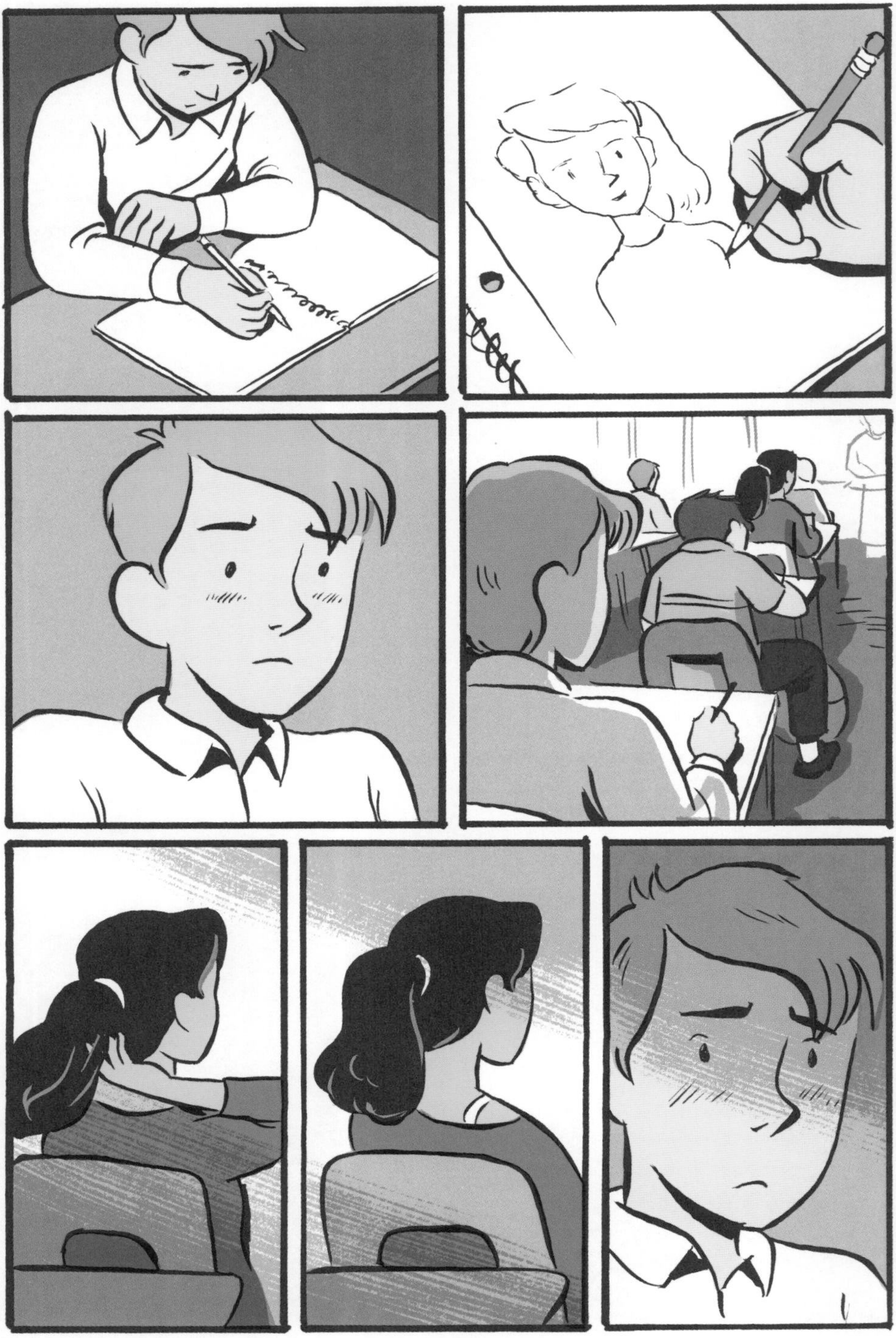

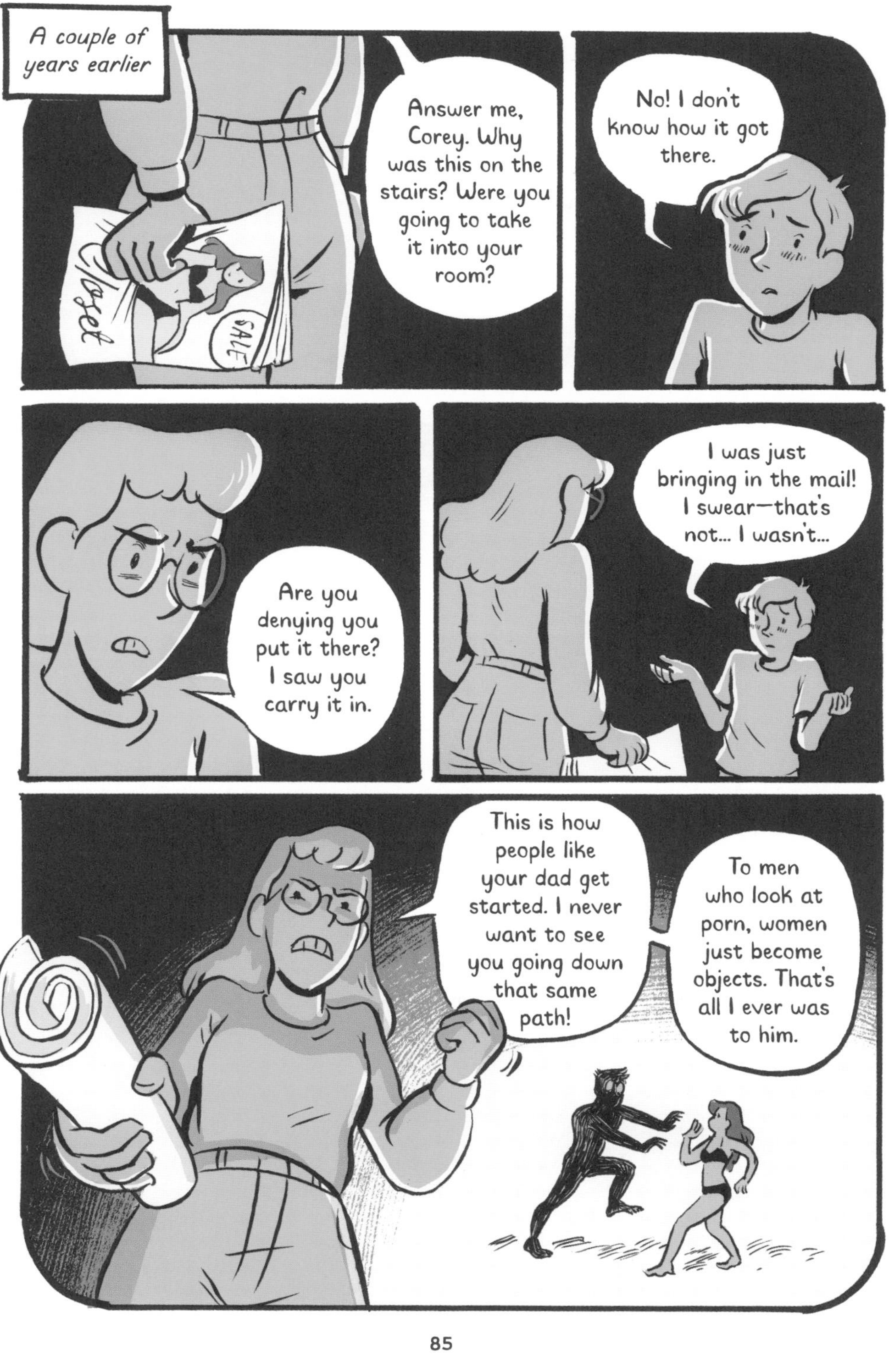
A couple of years earlier
Answer me, Corey. Why was this on the stairs? Were you going to take it into your room?
Closet
SALE
No! I don't know how it got there.
Are you denying you put it there? I saw you carry it in.
I was just bringing in the mail! I swear—that's not... I wasn't...
This is how people like your dad get started. I never want to see you going down that same path!
To men who look at porn, women just become objects. That's all I ever was to him.

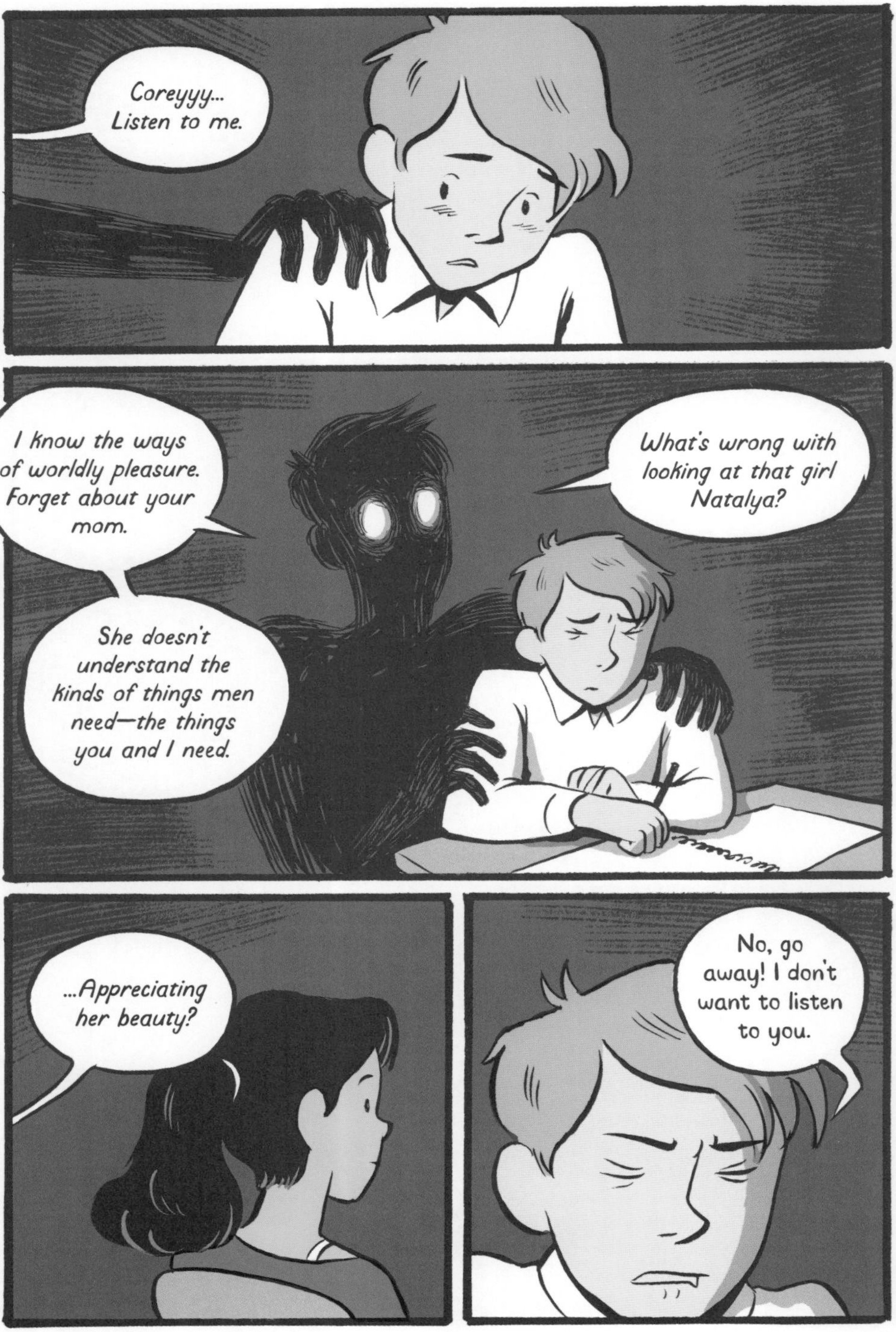
Coreyyy...
Listen to me.
I know the ways of worldly pleasure. Forget about your mom.
She doesn't understand the kinds of things men need—the things you and I need.
What's wrong with looking at that girl Natalya?
...Appreciating her beauty?
No, go away! I don't want to listen to you.

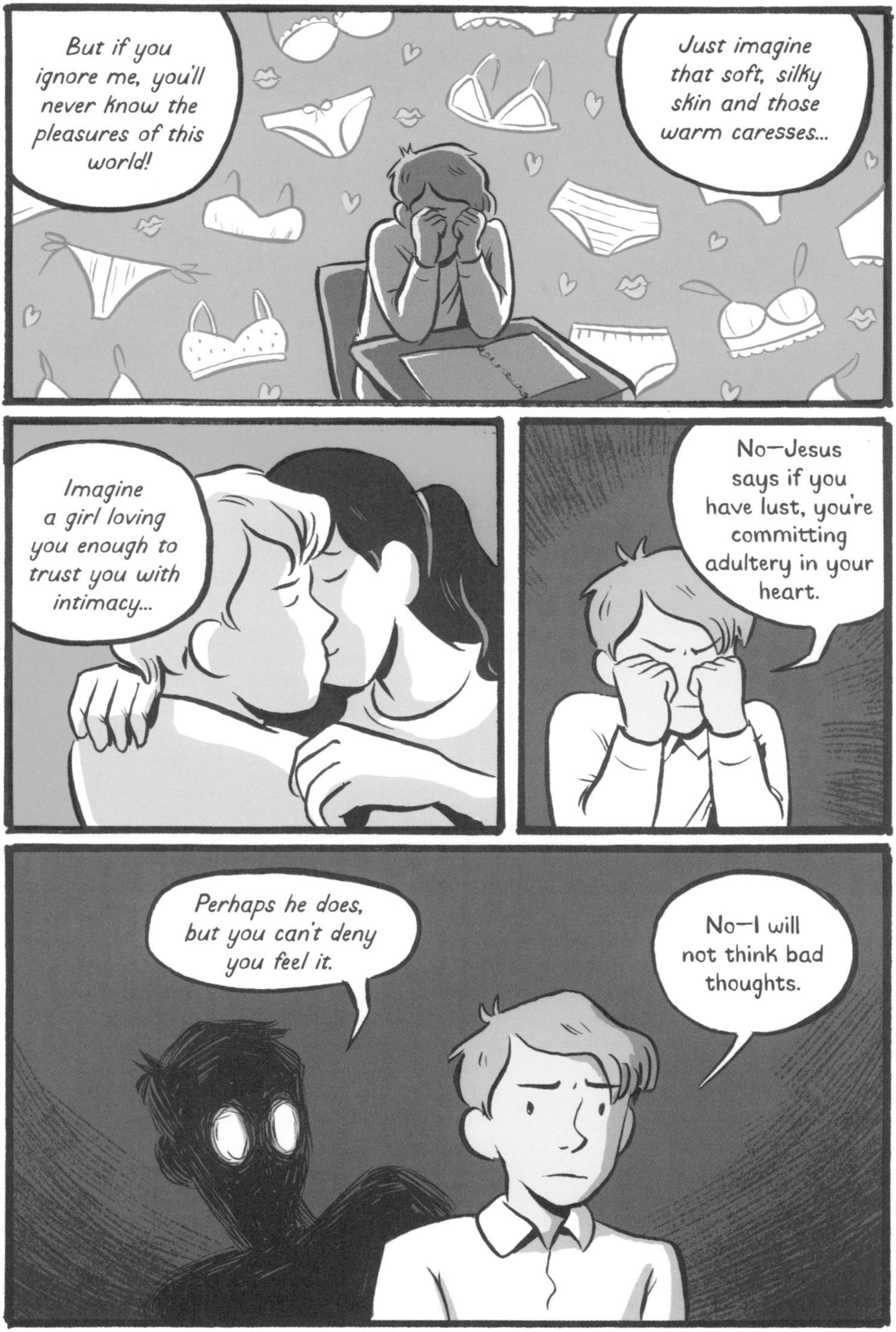
But if you ignore me, you'll never know the pleasures of this world!
Just imagine that soft, silky skin and those warm caresses...
Imagine a girl loving you enough to trust you with intimacy...
No—Jesus says if you have lust, you're committing adultery in your heart.
Perhaps he does, but you can't deny you feel it.
No—I will not think bad thoughts.

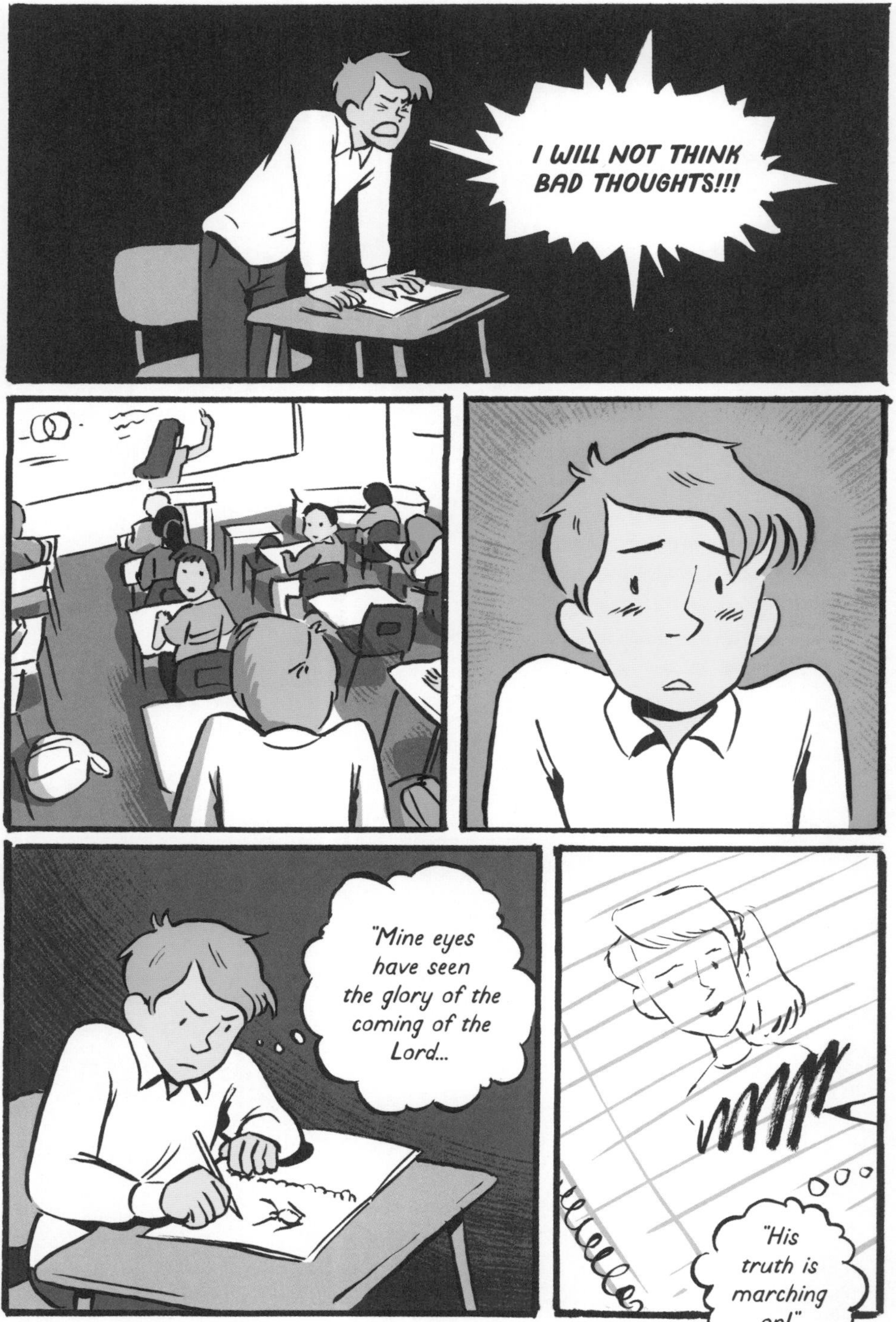
I WILL NOT THINK BAD THOUGHTS!!!
"Mine eyes have seen the glory of the coming of the Lord...
"His truth is marching on!"

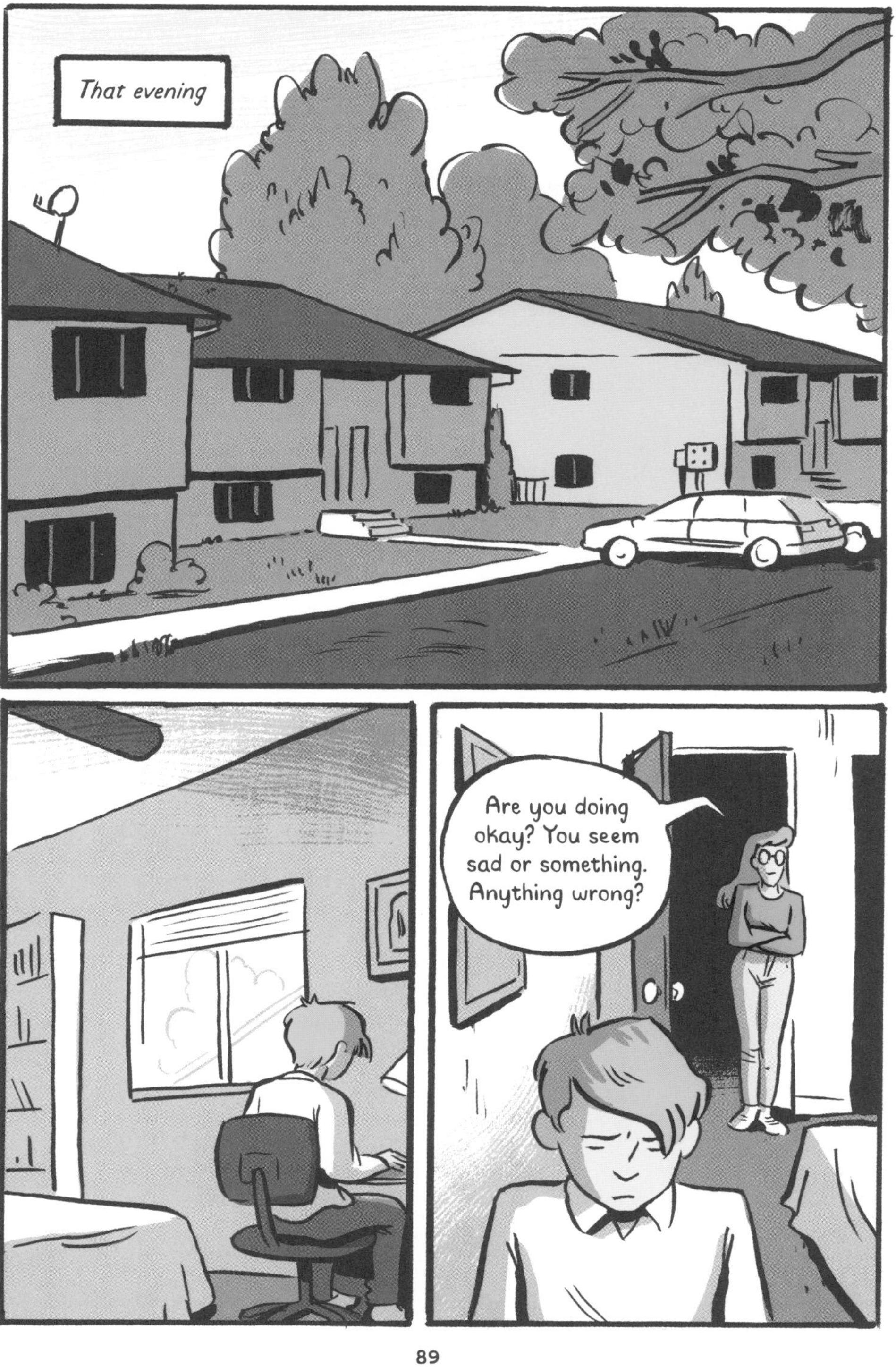
That evening
Are you doing okay? You seem sad or something. Anything wrong?

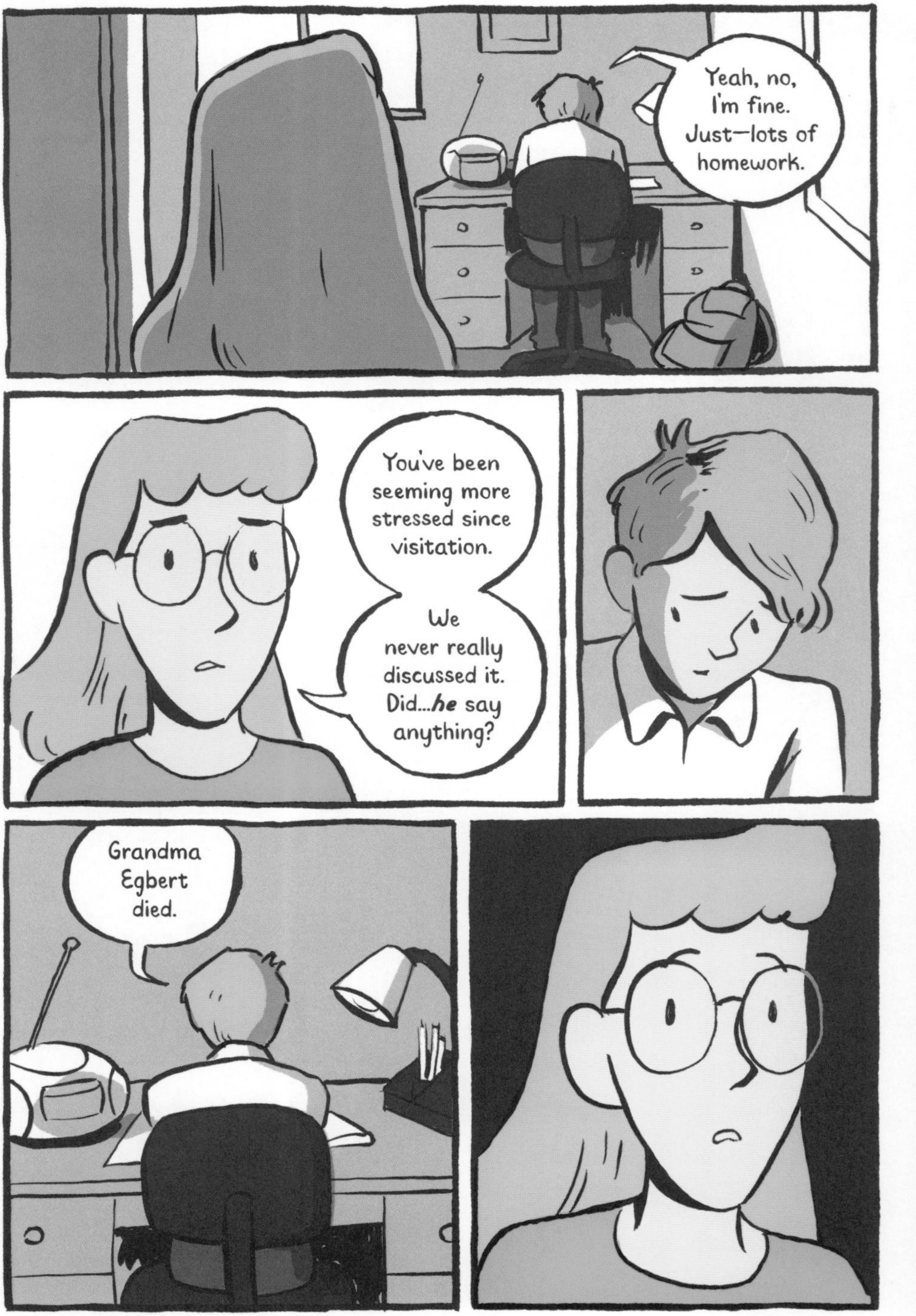

Yeah, no, I'm fine. Just—lots of homework.
You've been seeming more stressed since visitation.
We never really discussed it. Did...*he* say anything?
Grandma Egbert died.

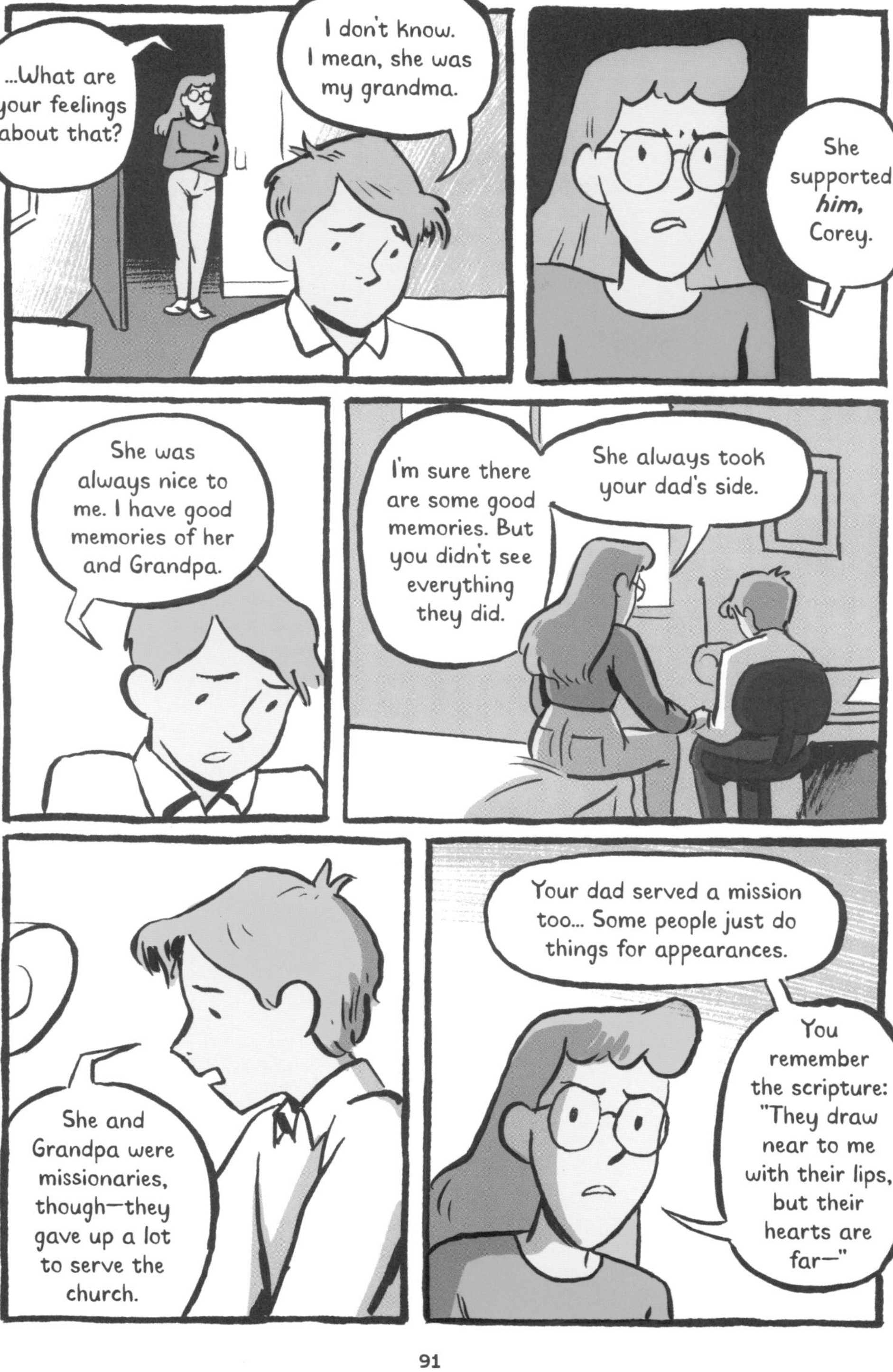
...What are your feelings about that?
I don't know. I mean, she was my grandma.
She supported *him*, Corey.
She was always nice to me. I have good memories of her and Grandpa.
I'm sure there are some good memories. But you didn't see everything they did.
She always took your dad's side.
She and Grandpa were missionaries, though—they gave up a lot to serve the church.
Your dad served a mission too... Some people just do things for appearances.
You remember the scripture: "They draw near to me with their lips, but their hearts are far—"

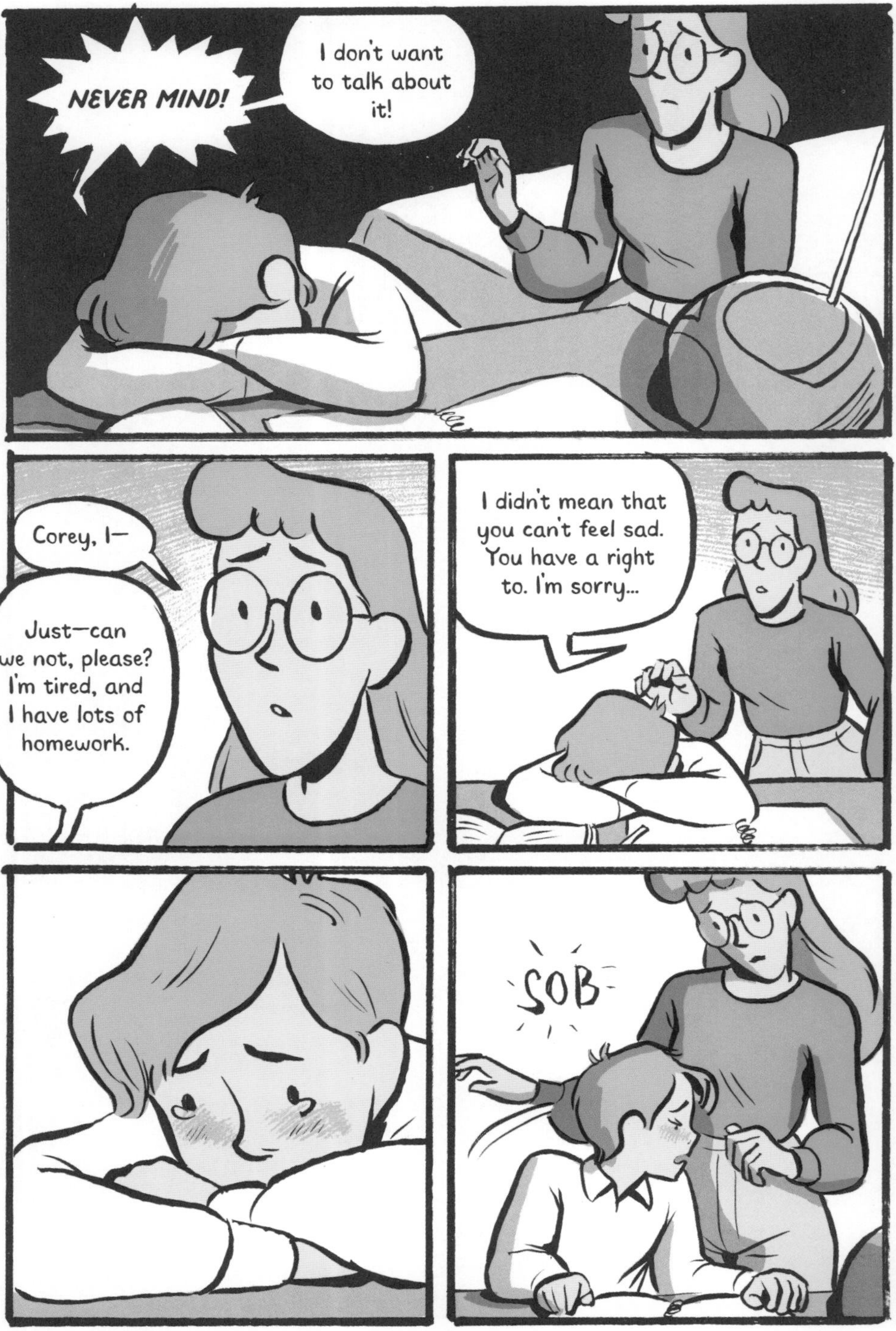
NEVER MIND!
I don't want to talk about it!
Corey, I—
Just—can we not, please? I'm tired, and I have lots of homework.
I didn't mean that you can't feel sad. You have a right to. I'm sorry...
SOB

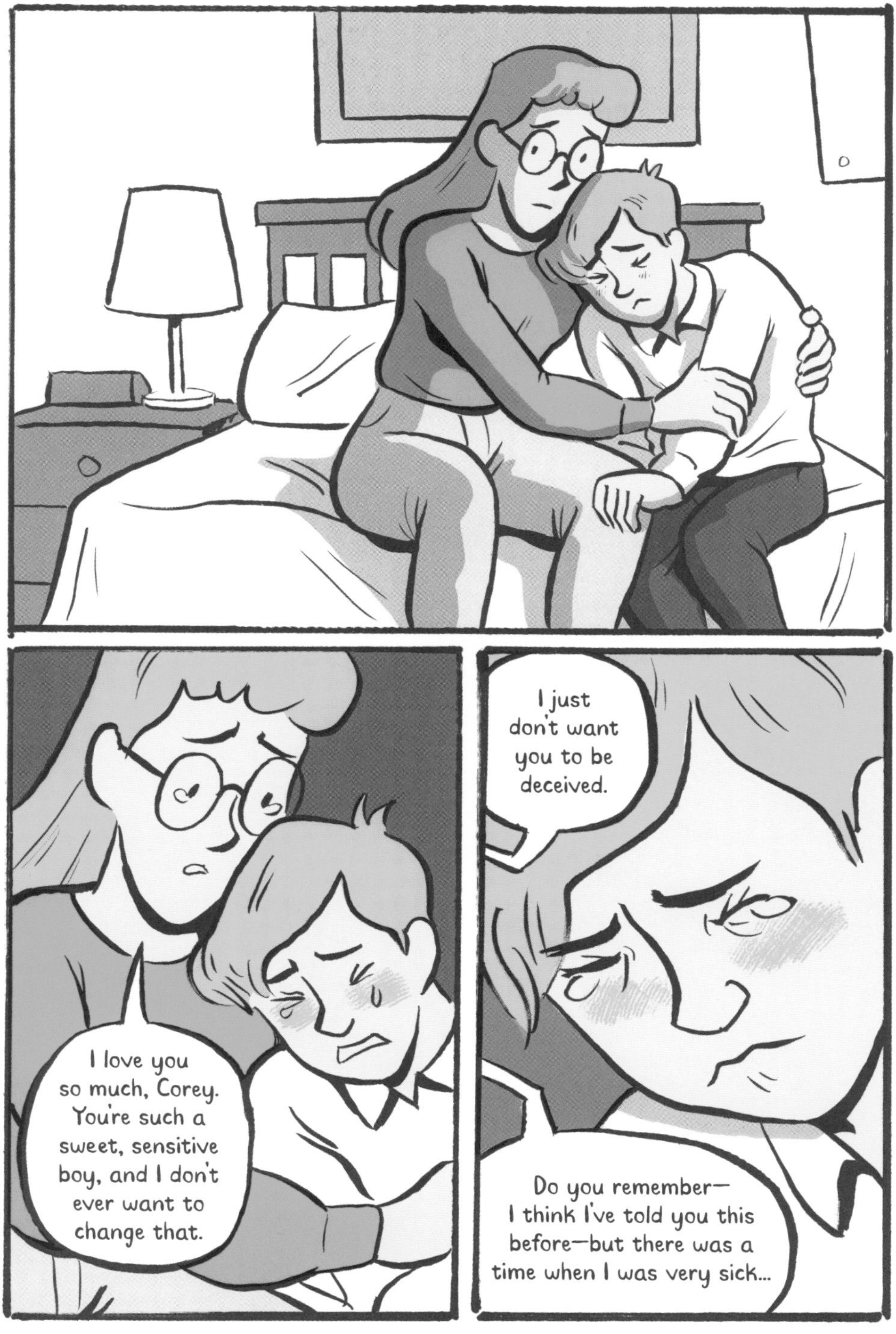
I love you so much, Corey. You're such a sweet, sensitive boy, and I don't ever want to change that.
I just don't want you to be deceived.
Do you remember— I think I've told you this before—but there was a time when I was very sick...

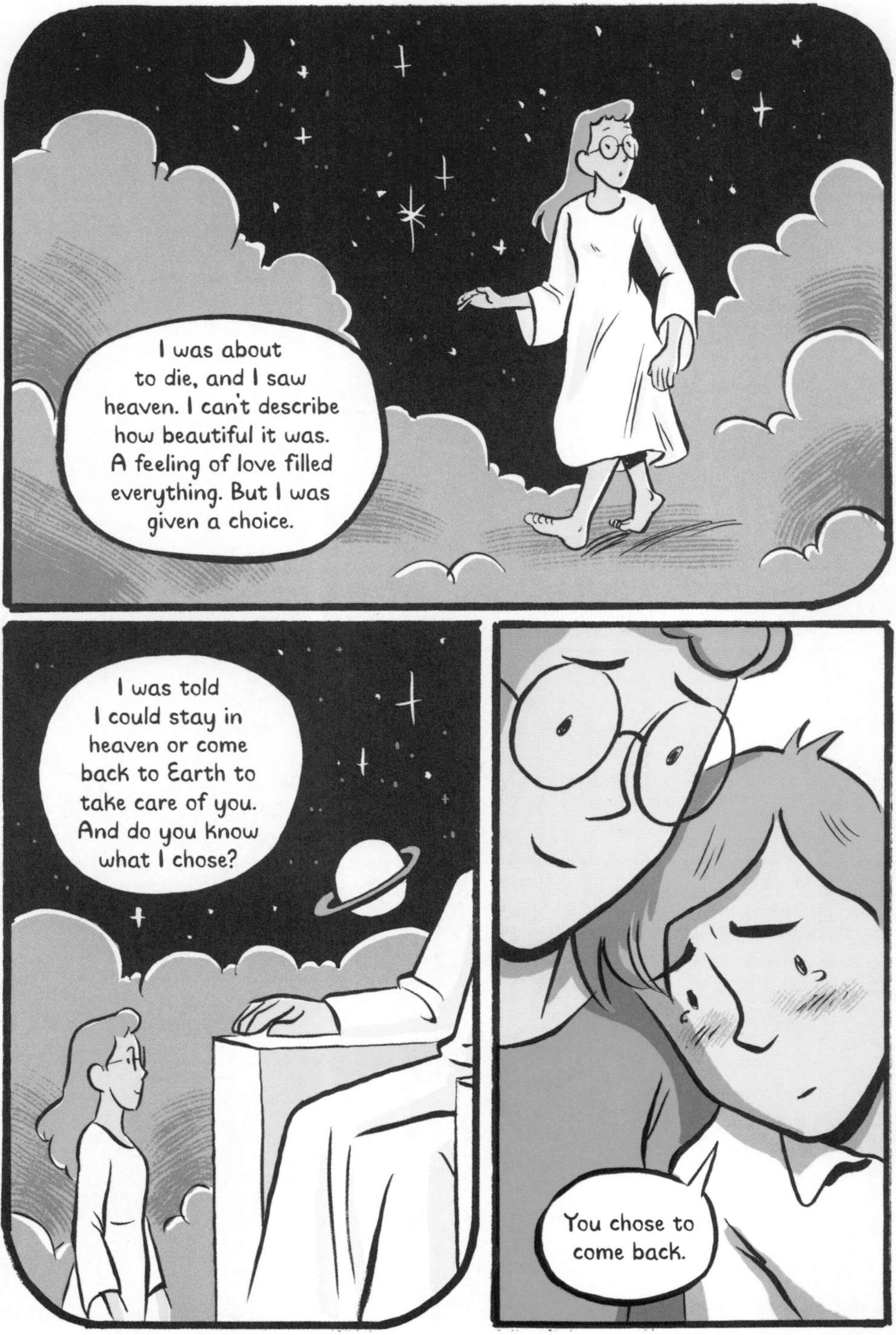
I was about to die, and I saw heaven. I can't describe how beautiful it was. A feeling of love filled everything. But I was given a choice.
I was told I could stay in heaven or come back to Earth to take care of you. And do you know what I chose?
You chose to come back.

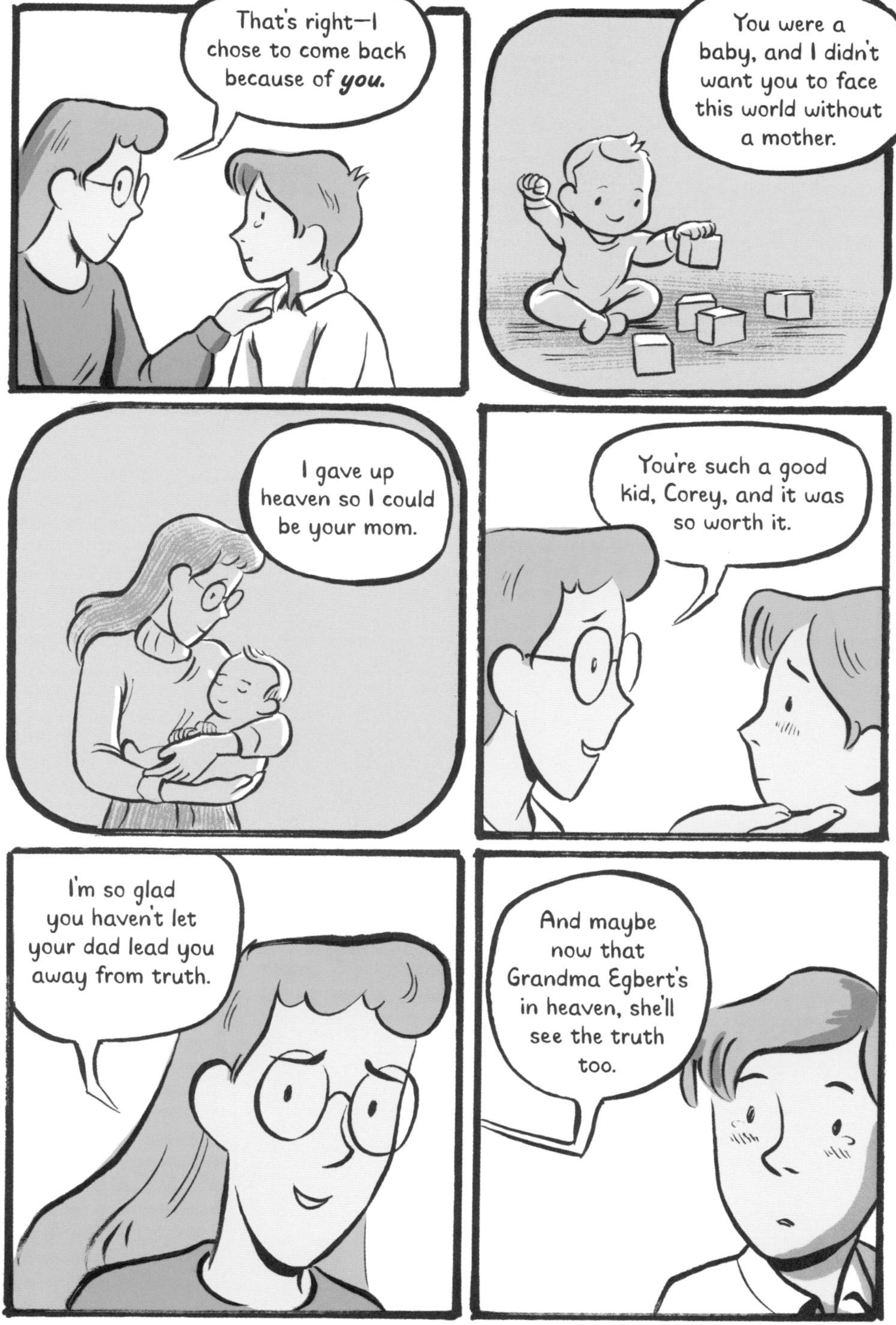
That's right—I chose to come back because of ***you.***
You were a baby, and I didn't want you to face this world without a mother.
I gave up heaven so I could be your mom.
You're such a good kid, Corey, and it was so worth it.
I'm so glad you haven't let your dad lead you away from truth.
And maybe now that Grandma Egbert's in heaven, she'll see the truth too.

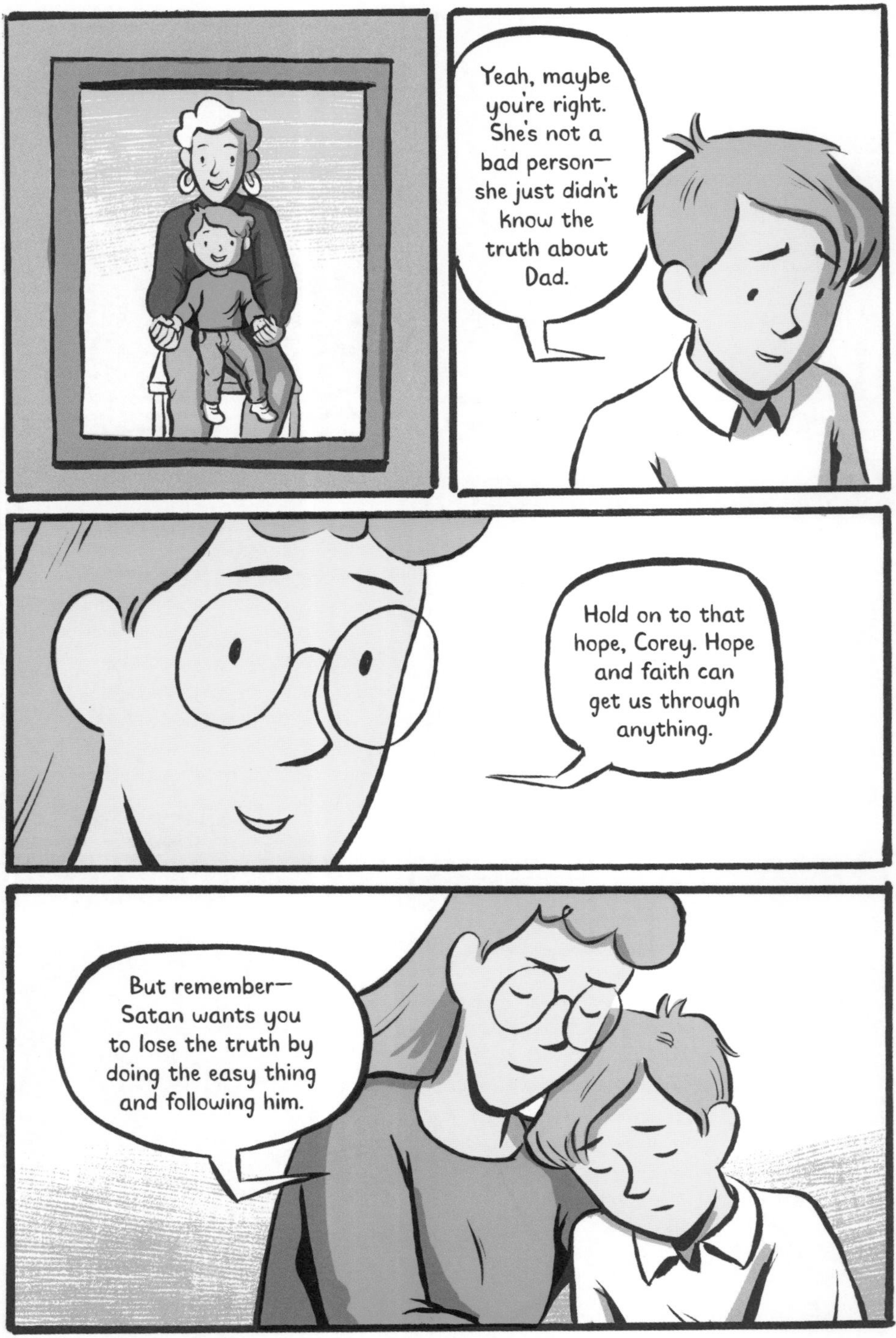
Yeah, maybe you're right. She's not a bad person—she just didn't know the truth about Dad.
Hold on to that hope, Corey. Hope and faith can get us through anything.
But remember—Satan wants you to lose the truth by doing the easy thing and following him.

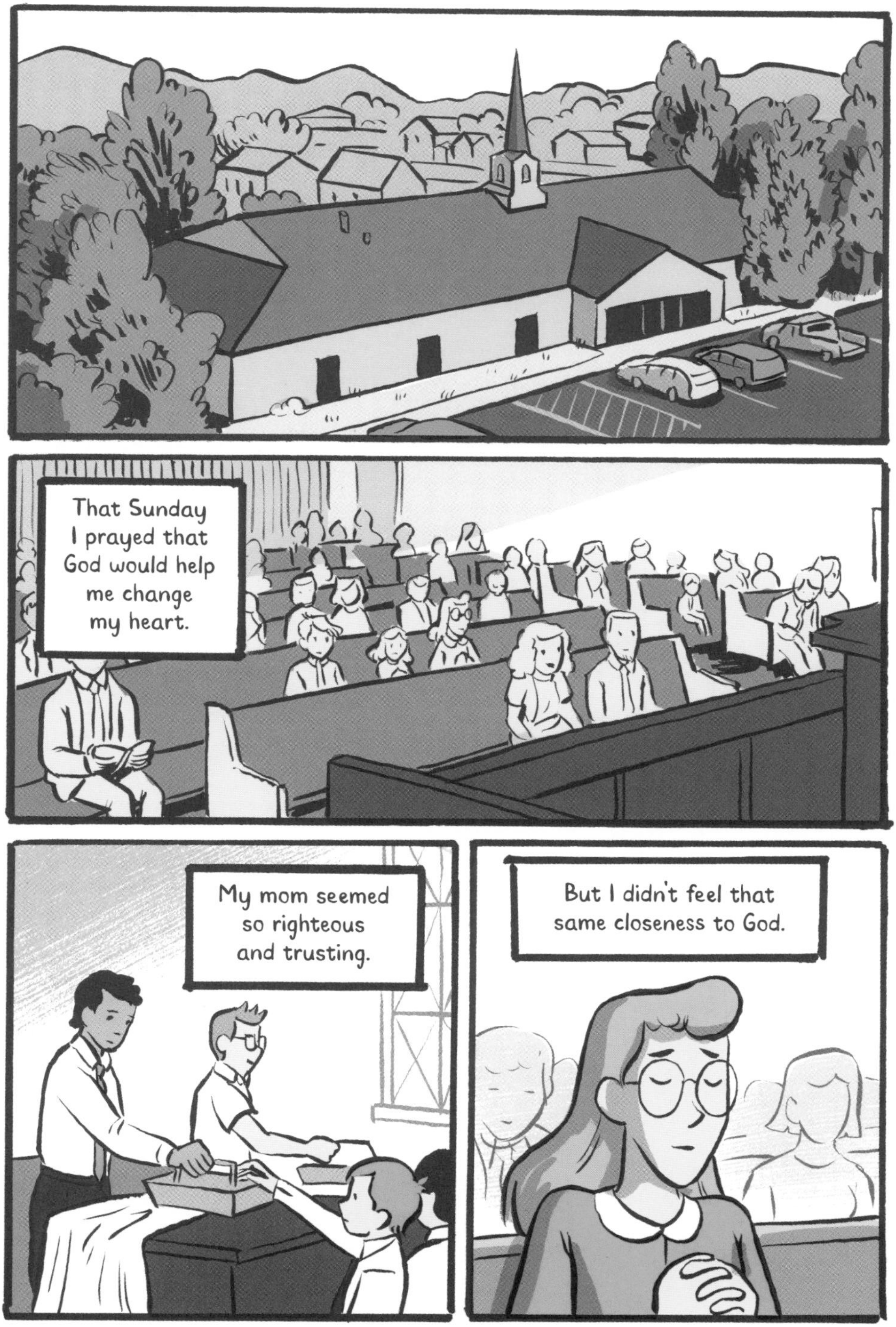
That Sunday I prayed that God would help me change my heart.
My mom seemed so righteous and trusting.
But I didn't feel that same closeness to God.

I felt guilty. Guilty for doubting my mom.

Guilty for how I treated my grandma. Guilty for my impure thoughts.

Feeling confused, huh?

No.

It's understandable. Your mom asked you to do some painful things.

My mom loves me. You're just trying to turn me away from truth.

Truth? Whose truth?

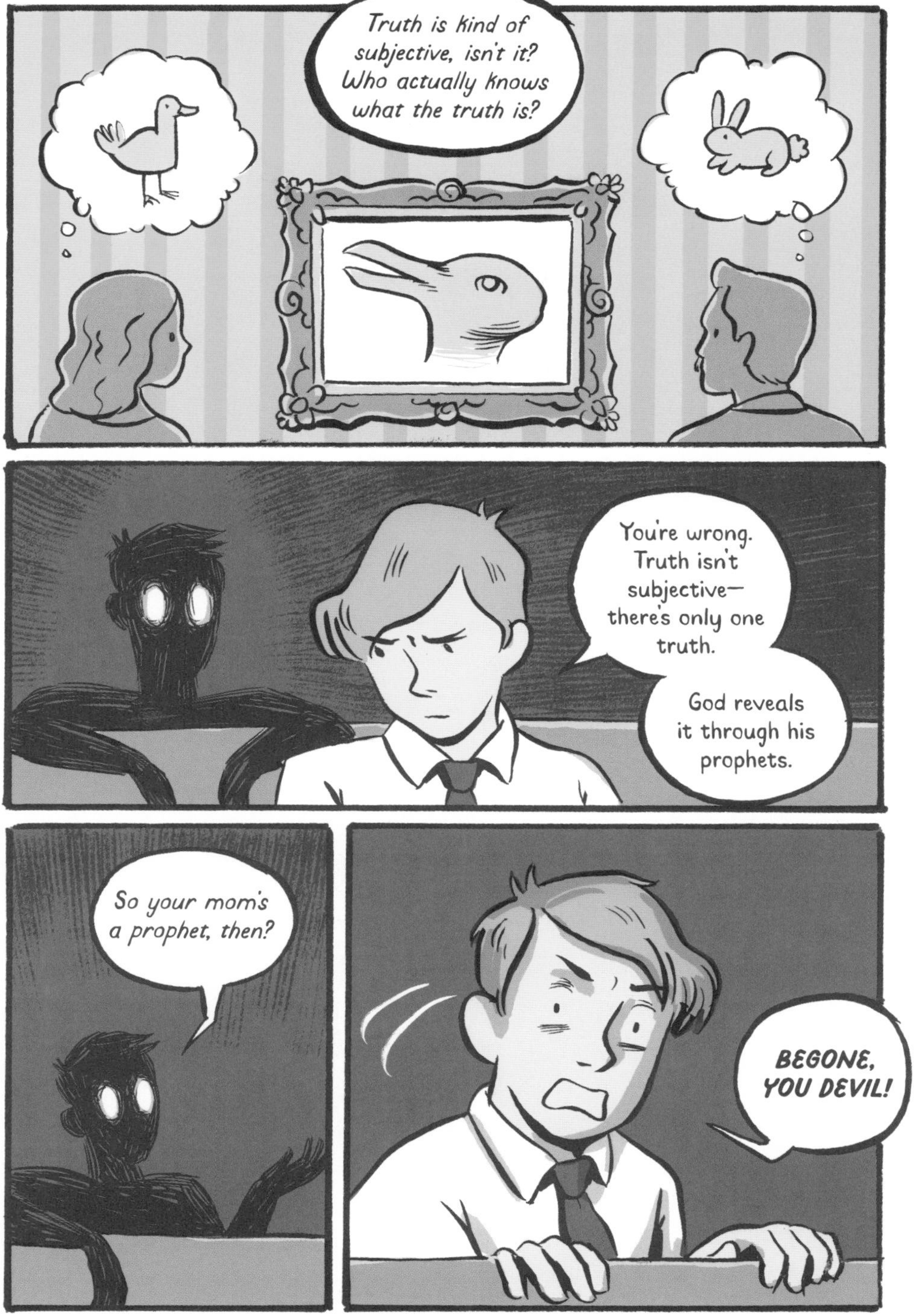
Truth is kind of subjective, isn't it? Who actually knows what the truth is?
You're wrong. Truth isn't subjective—there's only one truth.
God reveals it through his prophets.
So your mom's a prophet, then?
BEGONE, YOU DEVIL!

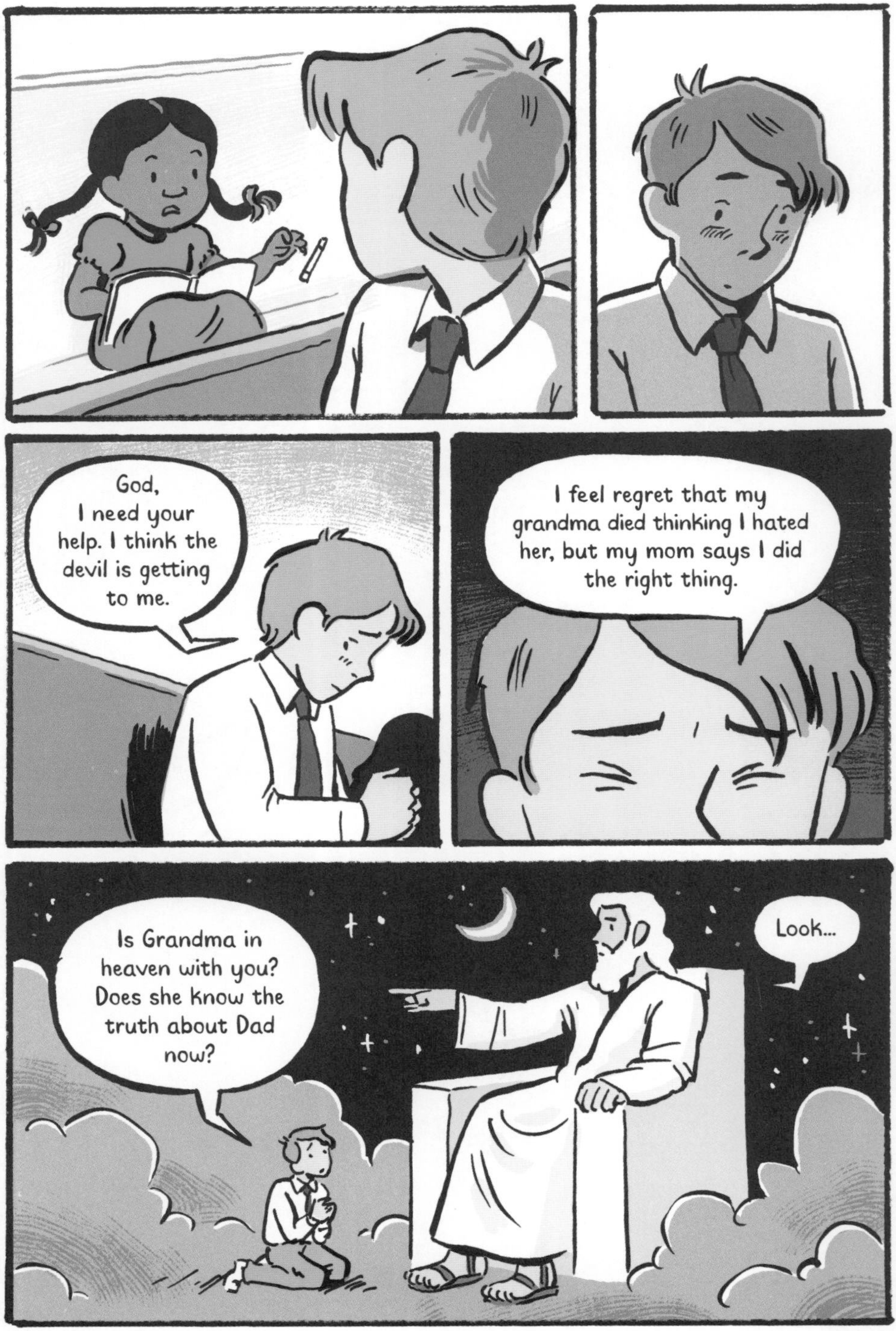
God, I need your help. I think the devil is getting to me.
I feel regret that my grandma died thinking I hated her, but my mom says I did the right thing.
Is Grandma in heaven with you? Does she know the truth about Dad now?
Look...

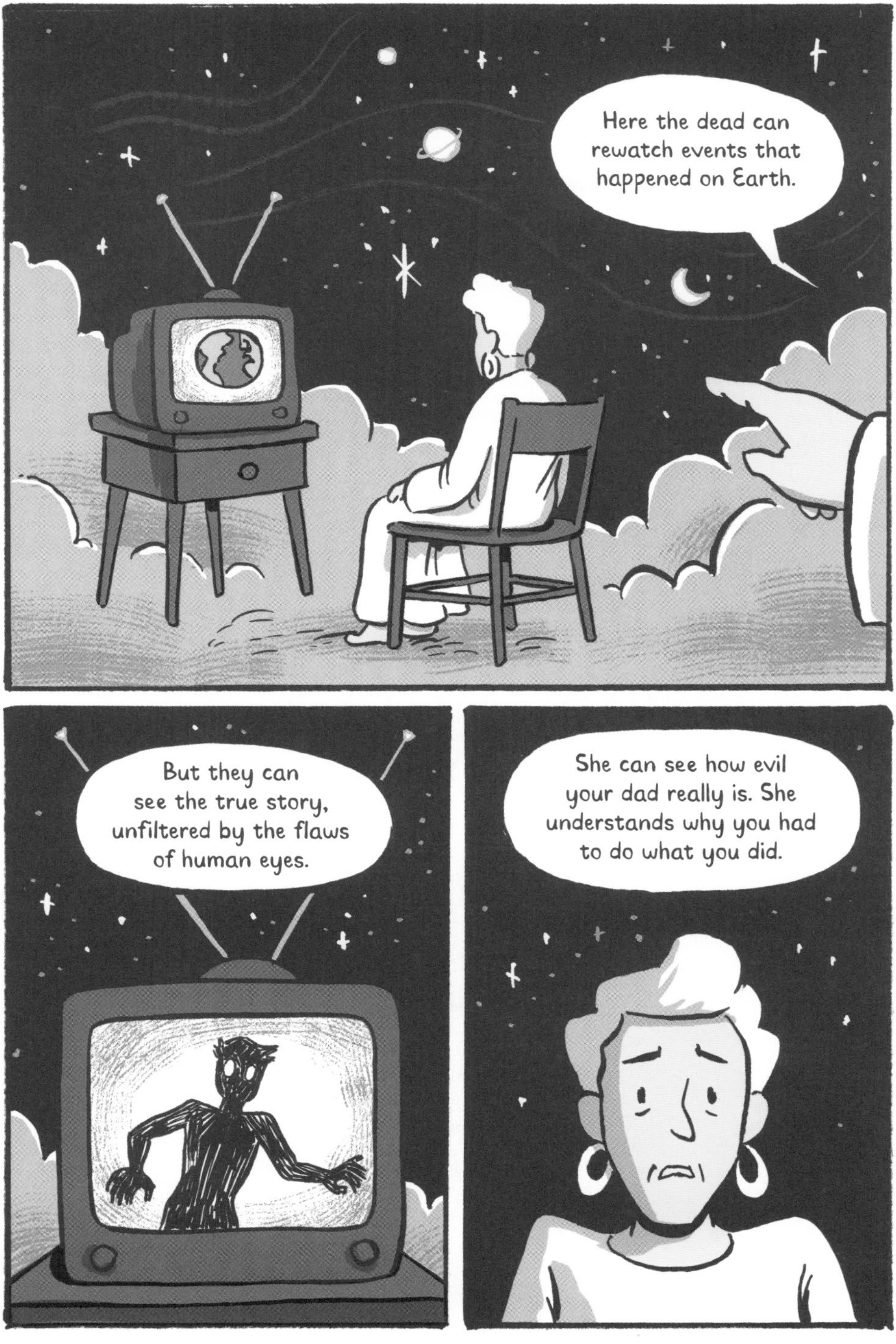
Here the dead can rewatch events that happened on Earth.
But they can see the true story, unfiltered by the flaws of human eyes.
She can see how evil your dad really is. She understands why you had to do what you did.

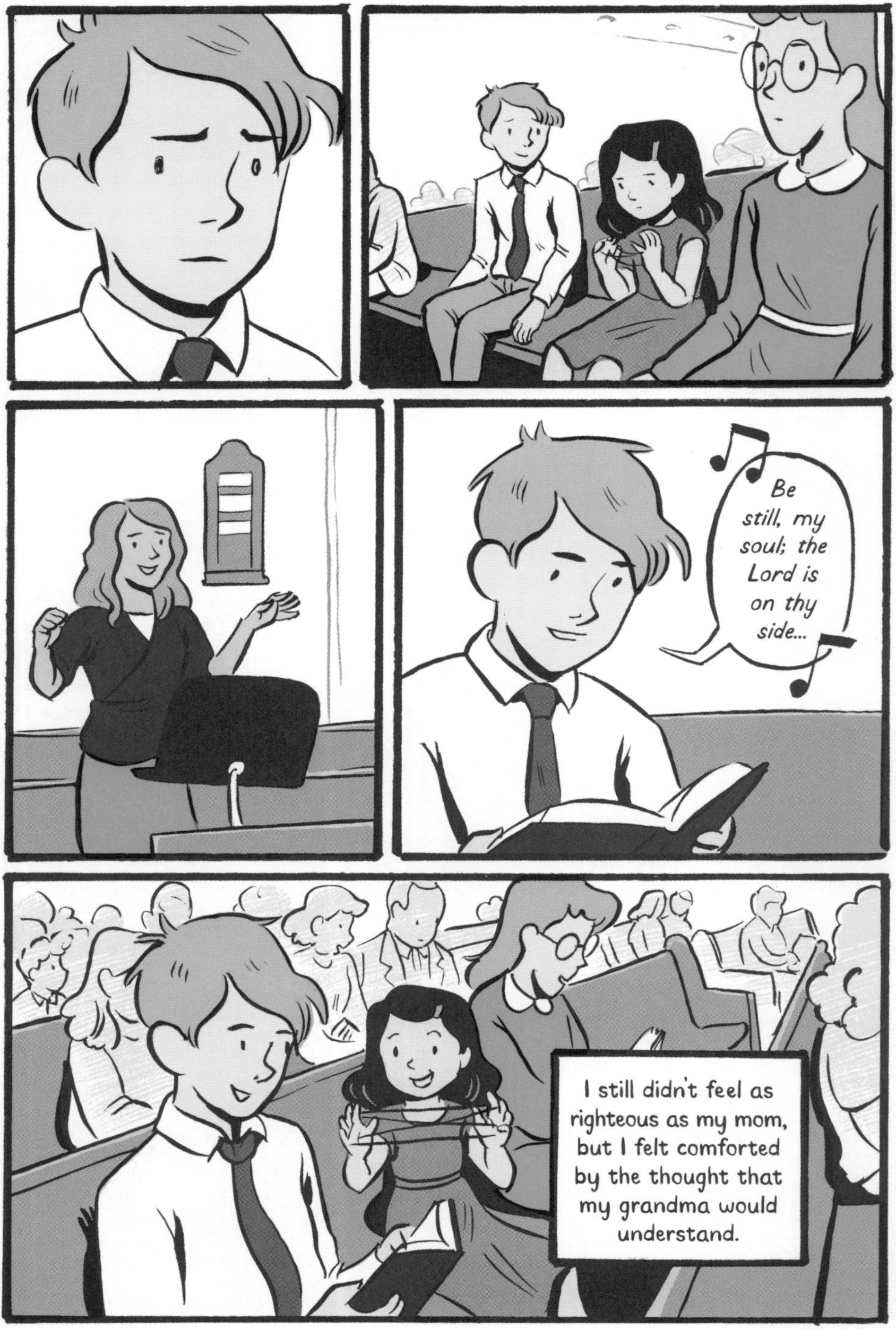
Be still, my soul; the Lord is on thy side...
I still didn't feel as righteous as my mom, but I felt comforted by the thought that my grandma would understand.

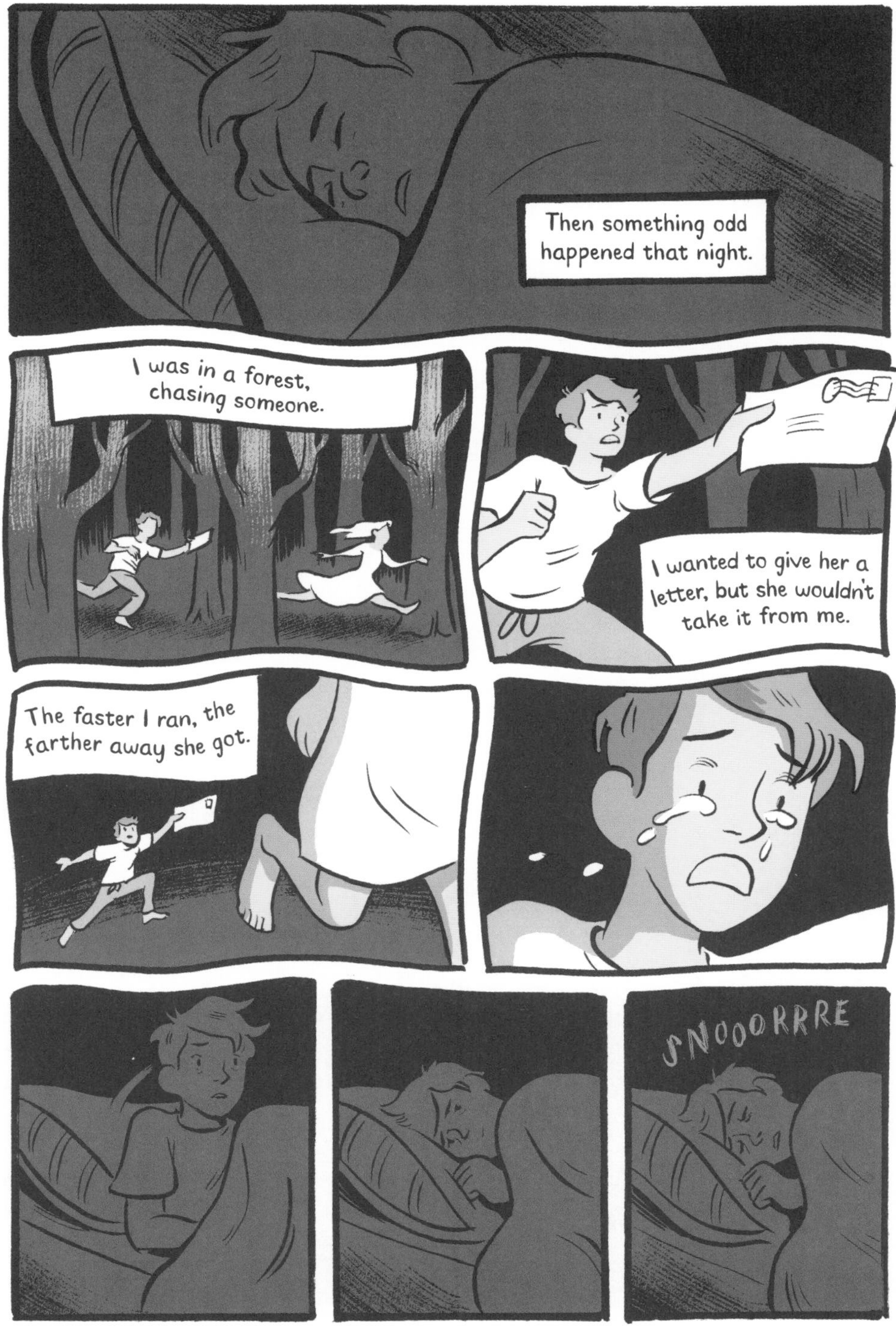
Then something odd happened that night.
I was in a forest, chasing someone.
I wanted to give her a letter, but she wouldn't take it from me.
The faster I ran, the farther away she got.
SNOOORRRE

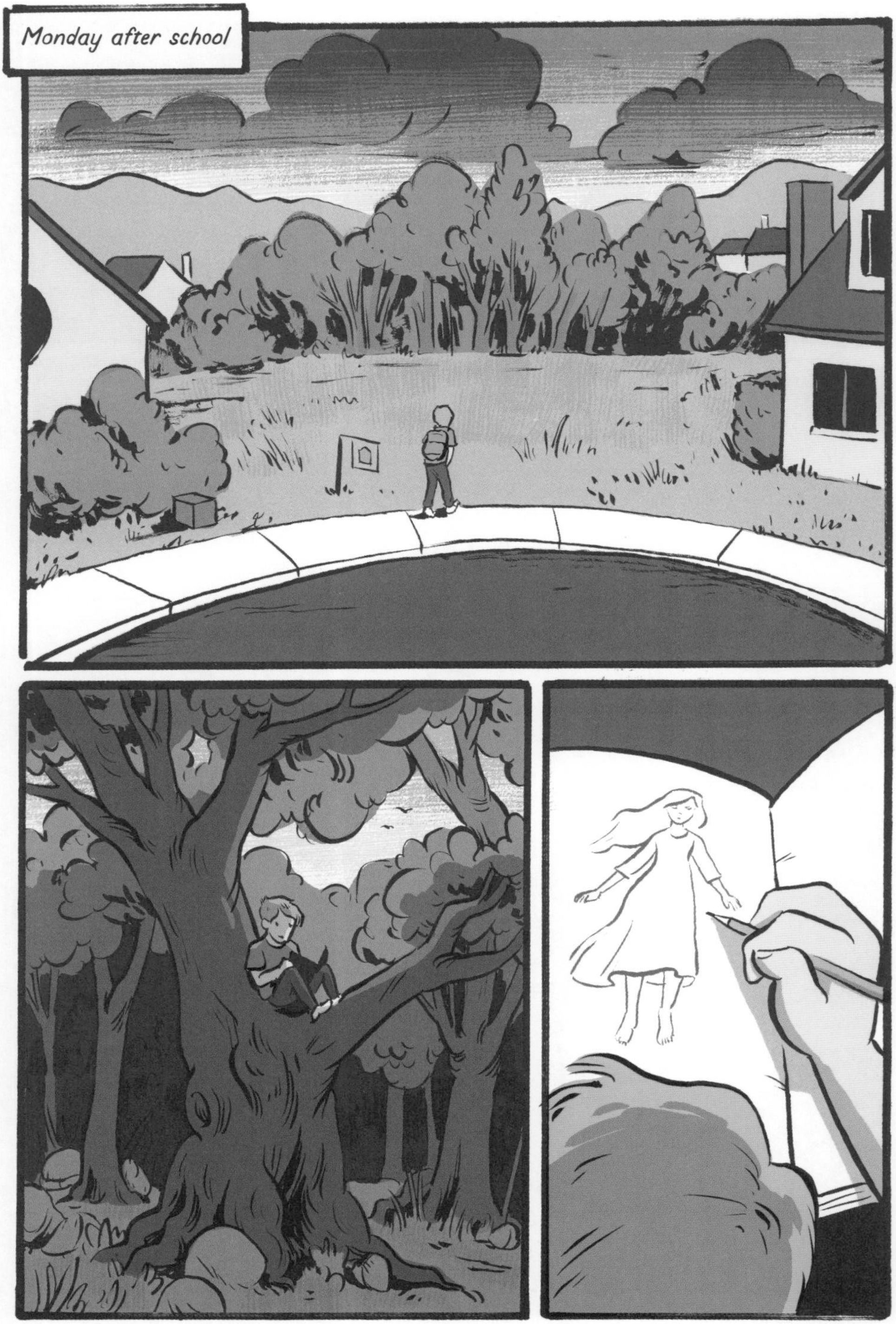
Monday after school

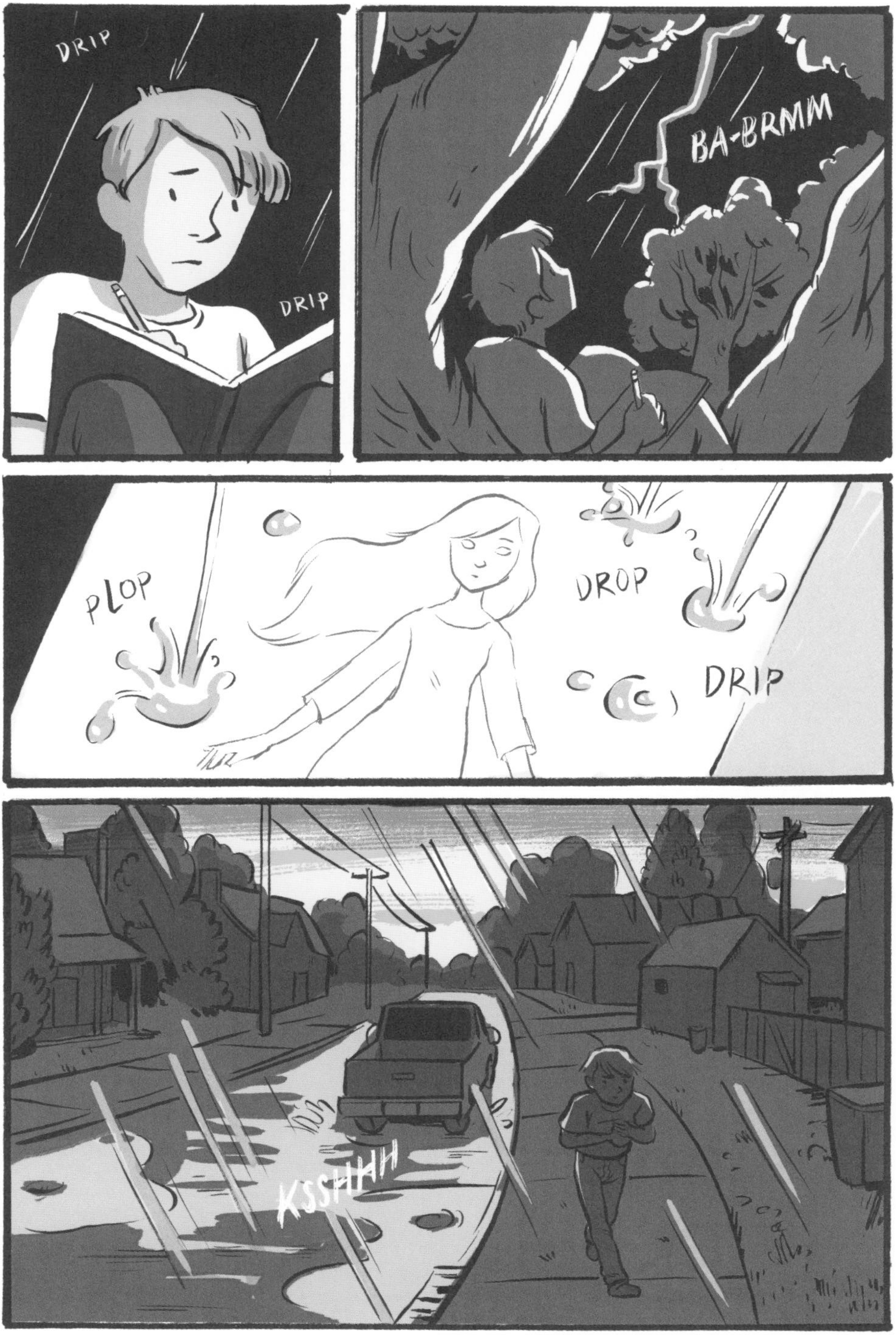
DRIP
DRIP
BA-BRMM
PLOP
DROP
DRIP
KSSHHH

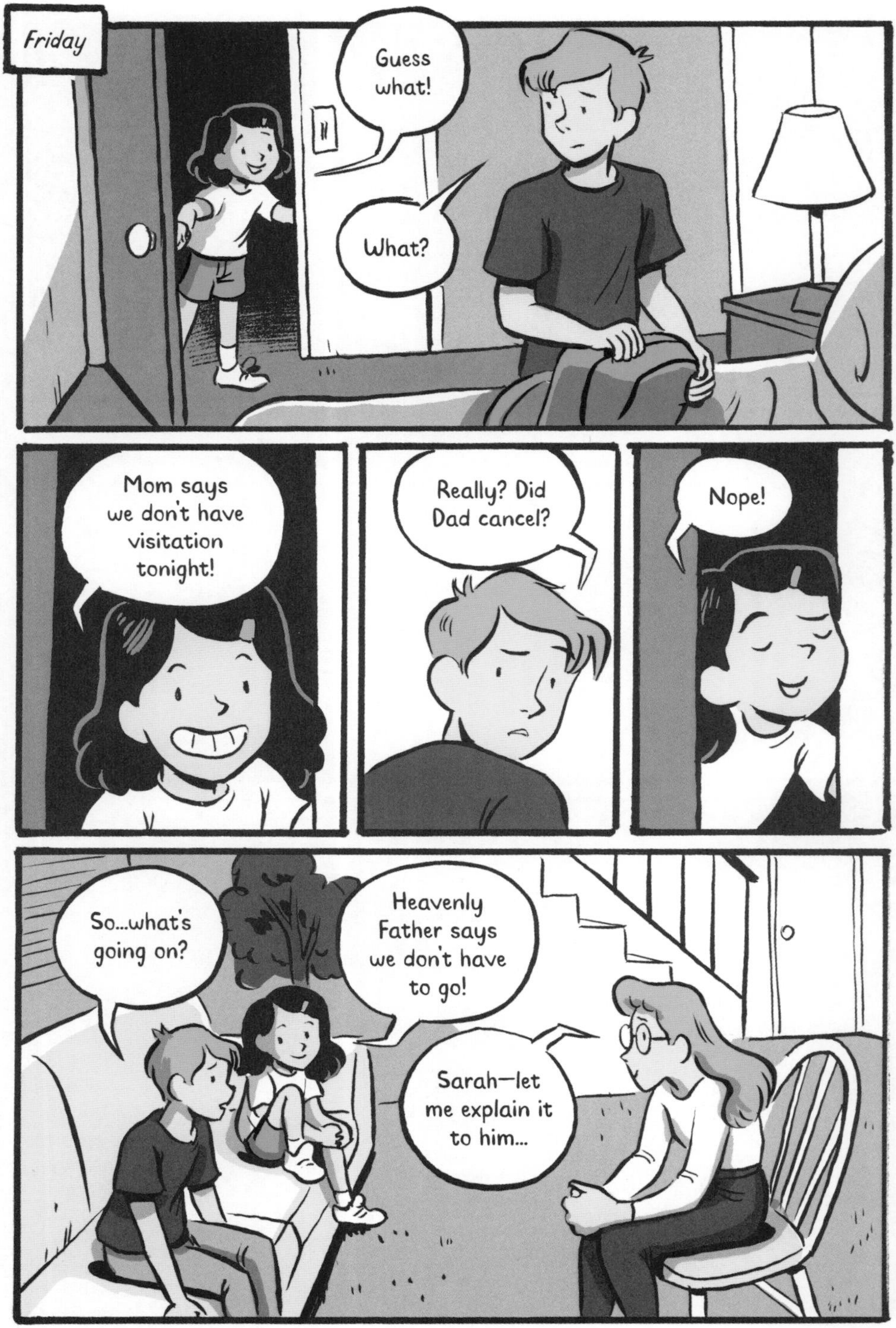
Friday
Guess what!
What?
Mom says we don't have visitation tonight!
Really? Did Dad cancel?
Nope!
So...what's going on?
Heavenly Father says we don't have to go!
Sarah—let me explain it to him...

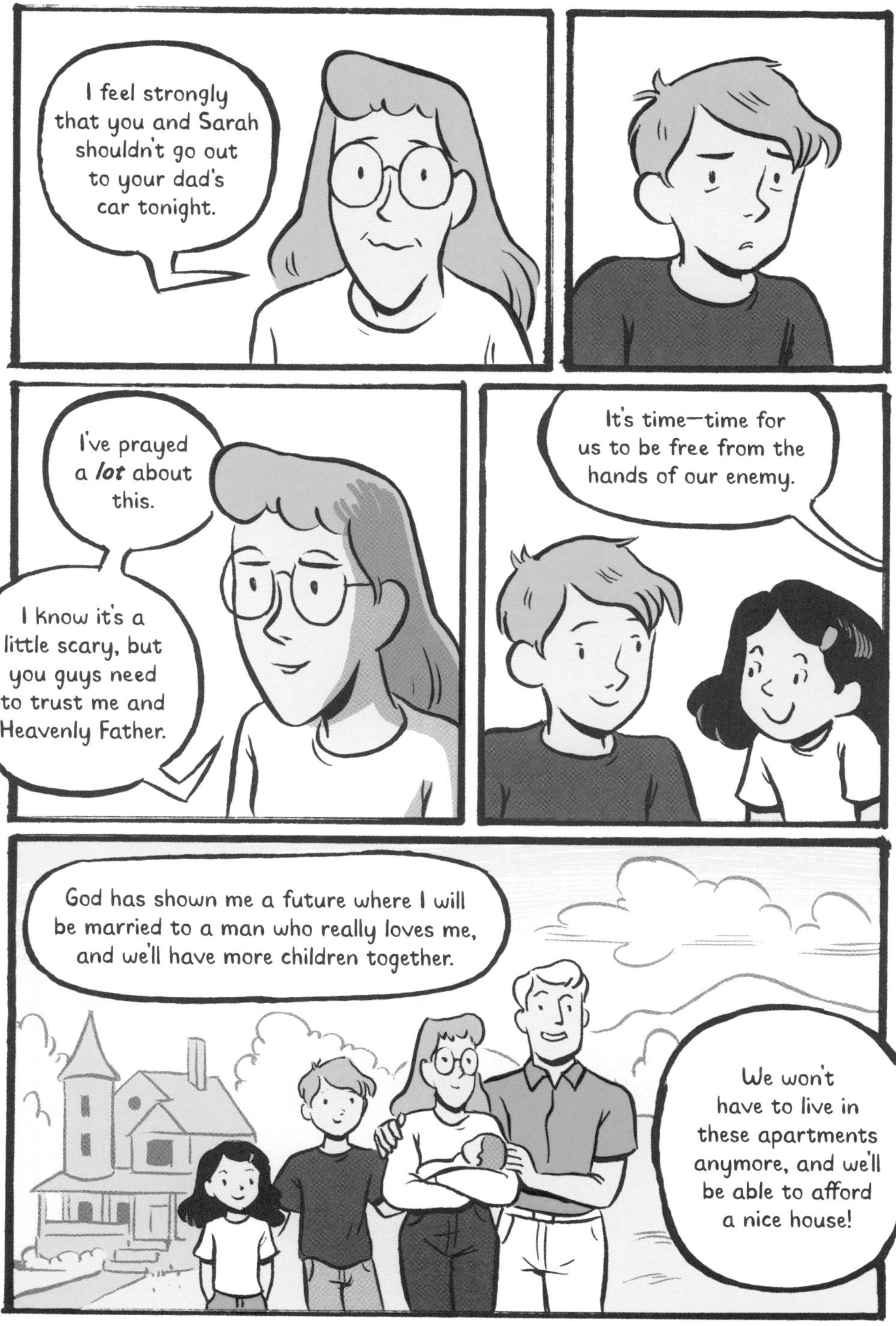
I feel strongly that you and Sarah shouldn't go out to your dad's car tonight.
I've prayed a *lot* about this.
I know it's a little scary, but you guys need to trust me and Heavenly Father.
It's time—time for us to be free from the hands of our enemy.
God has shown me a future where I will be married to a man who really loves me, and we'll have more children together.
We won't have to live in these apartments anymore, and we'll be able to afford a nice house!

What about the courts? Won't we get in trouble for missing visitation?

Don't worry—we just need to have faith in him and not fear men. God will deliver us.

I know the burden that's been on you to protect your sister.

You've been so brave, Corey. I see how hard it's been.

You want your family to be safe. So much adult responsibility has made it hard for you to be a normal kid.

Heavenly Father wants you to enjoy your teen years. Will you trust me?

Okay, I trust you.

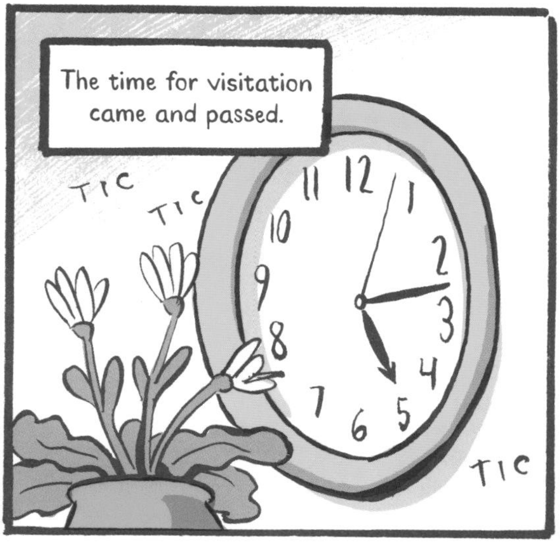
The time for visitation came and passed.
TIC
TIC
TIC

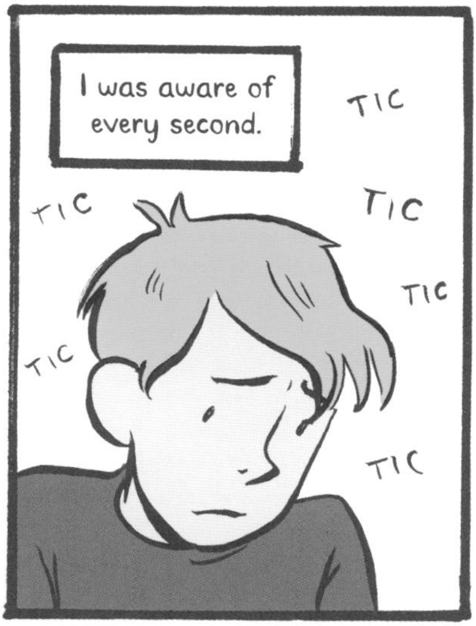
I was aware of every second.
TIC
TIC
TIC
TIC
TIC
TIC

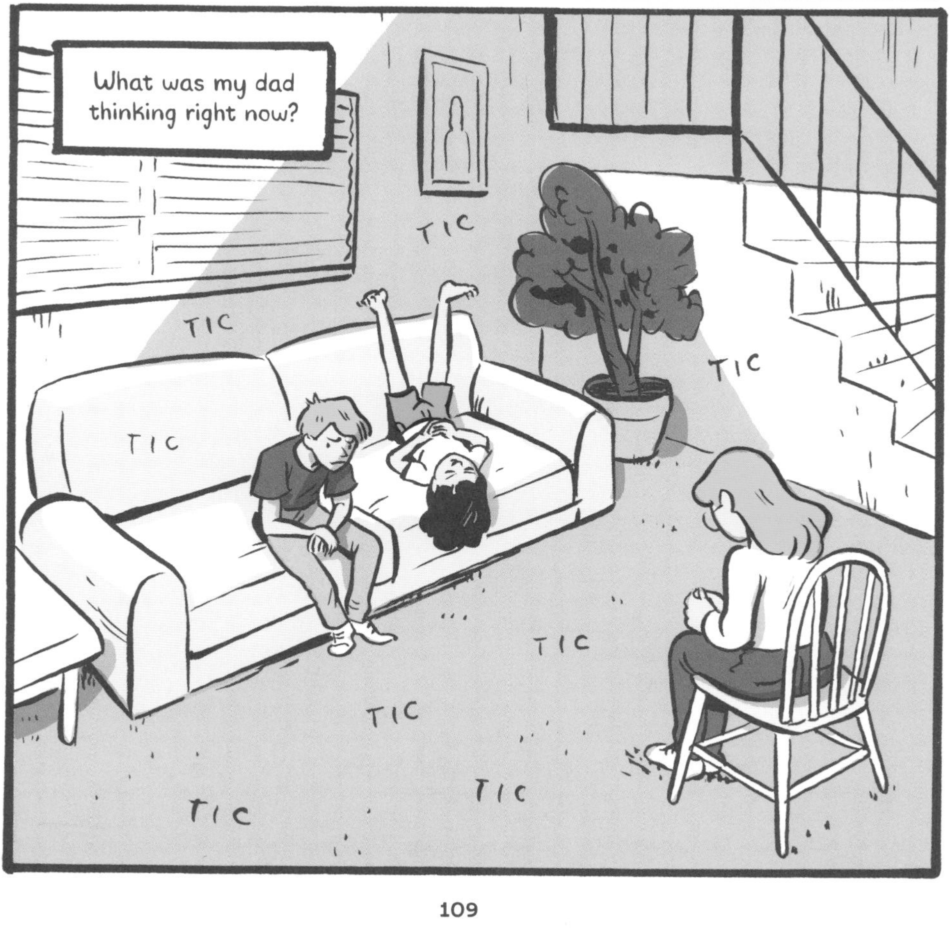
What was my dad thinking right now?
TIC
TIC
TIC
TIC
TIC
TIC
TIC
TIC

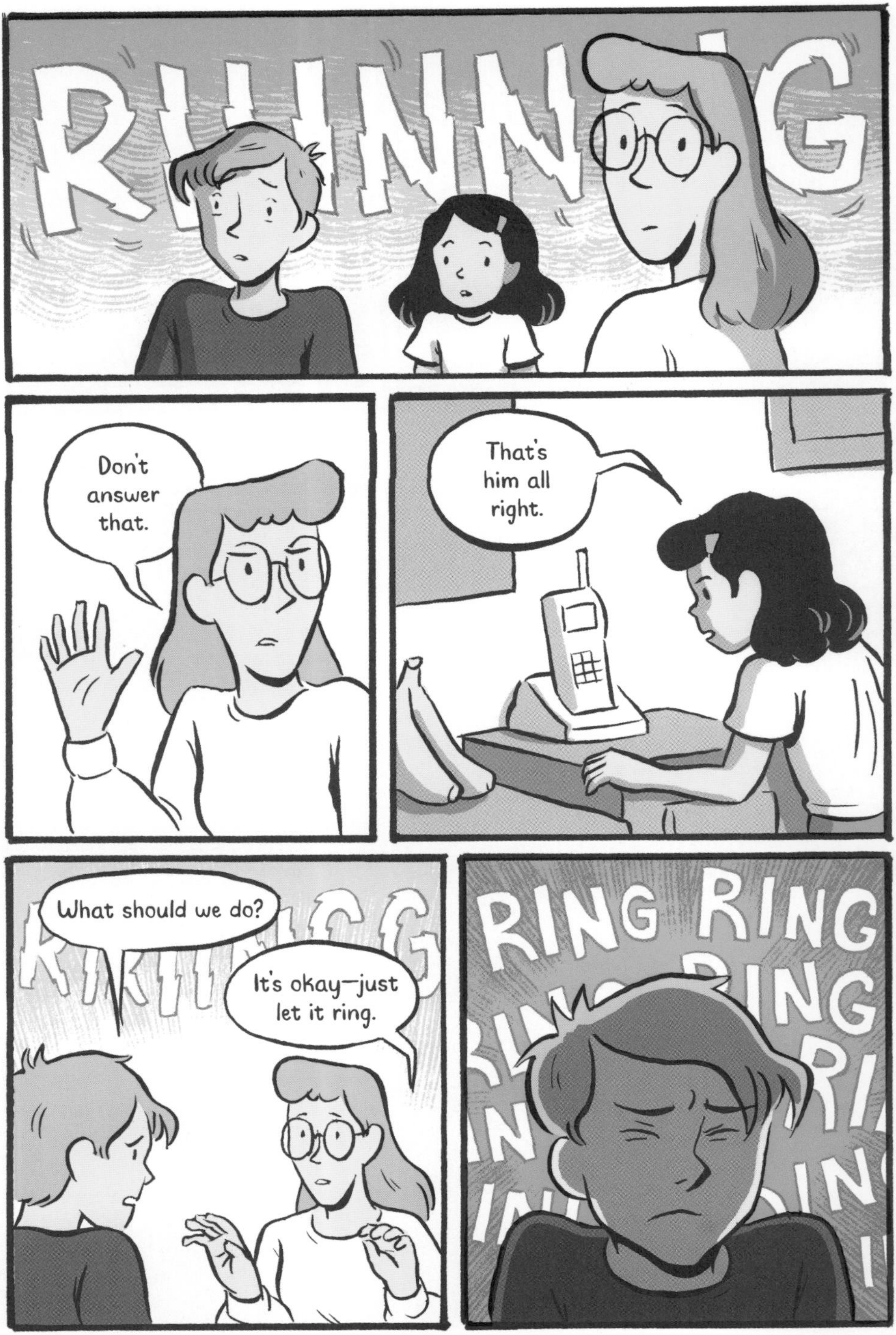

Don't answer that.
That's him all right.
What should we do?
It's okay—just let it ring.
RING RING
RING

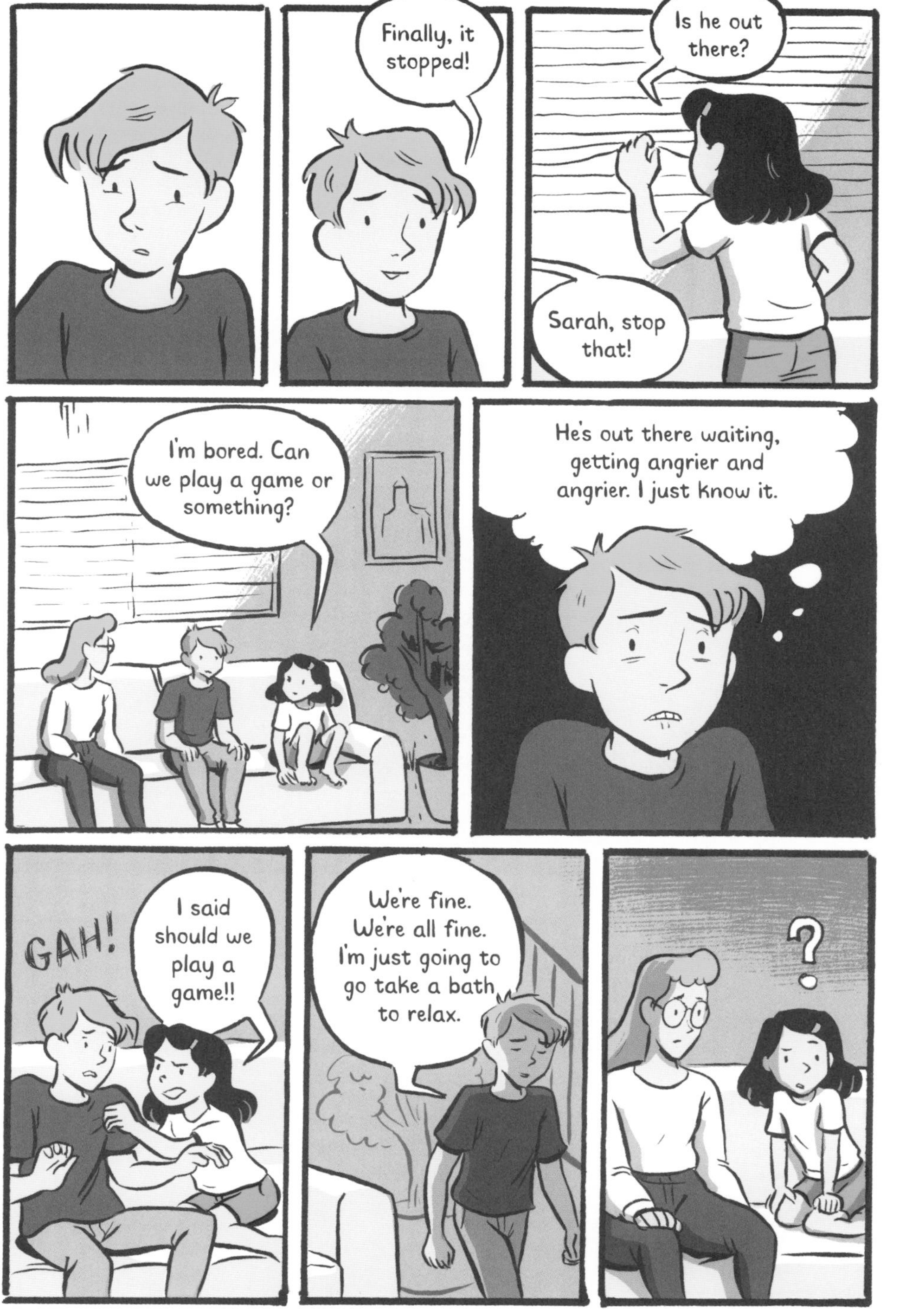
Finally, it stopped!
Is he out there?
Sarah, stop that!
I'm bored. Can we play a game or something?
He's out there waiting, getting angrier and angrier. I just know it.
GAH!
I said should we play a game!!
We're fine. We're all fine. I'm just going to go take a bath to relax.
?

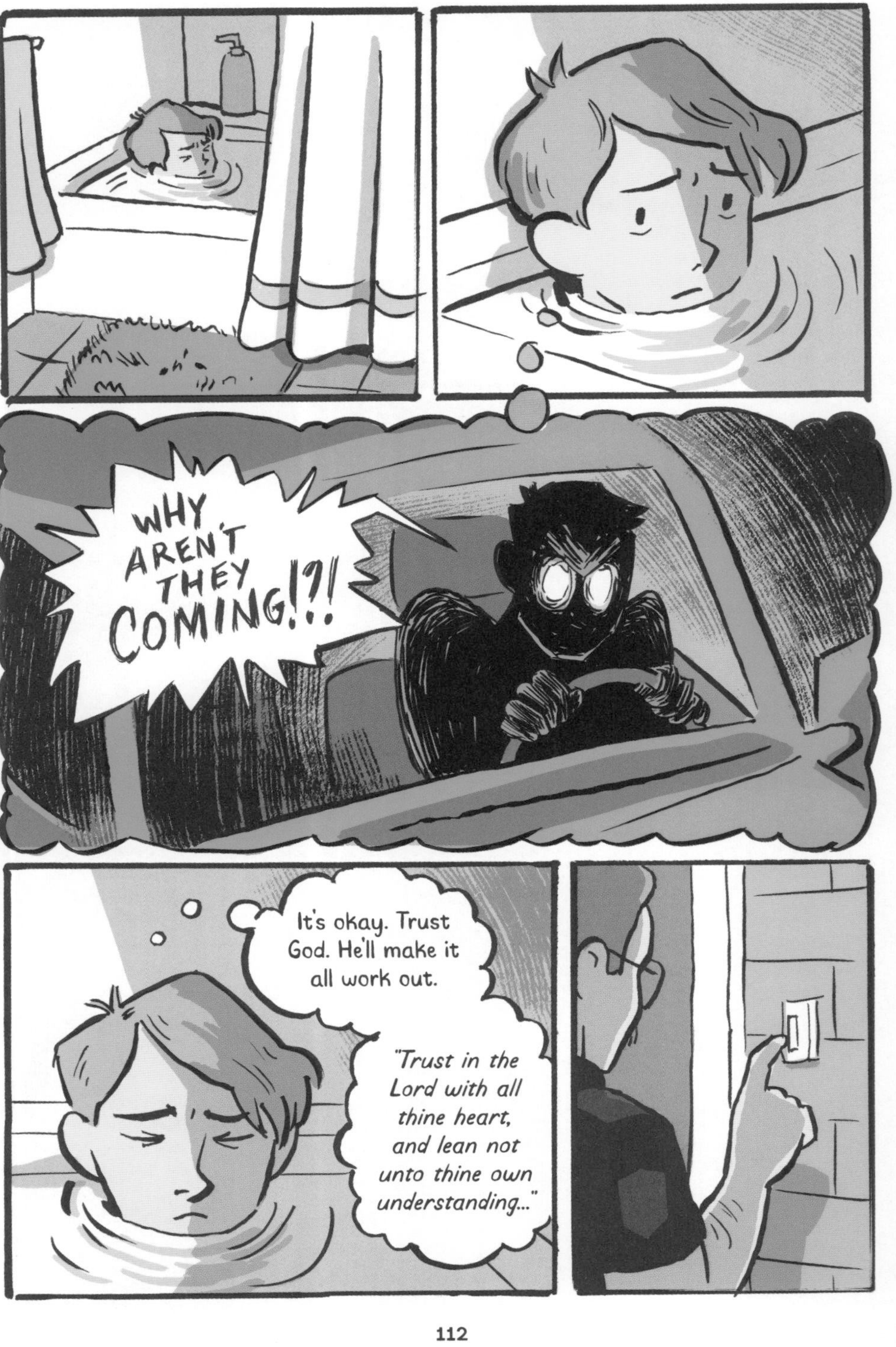
WHY AREN'T THEY COMING!?!
It's okay. Trust God. He'll make it all work out.
"Trust in the Lord with all thine heart, and lean not unto thine own understanding..."

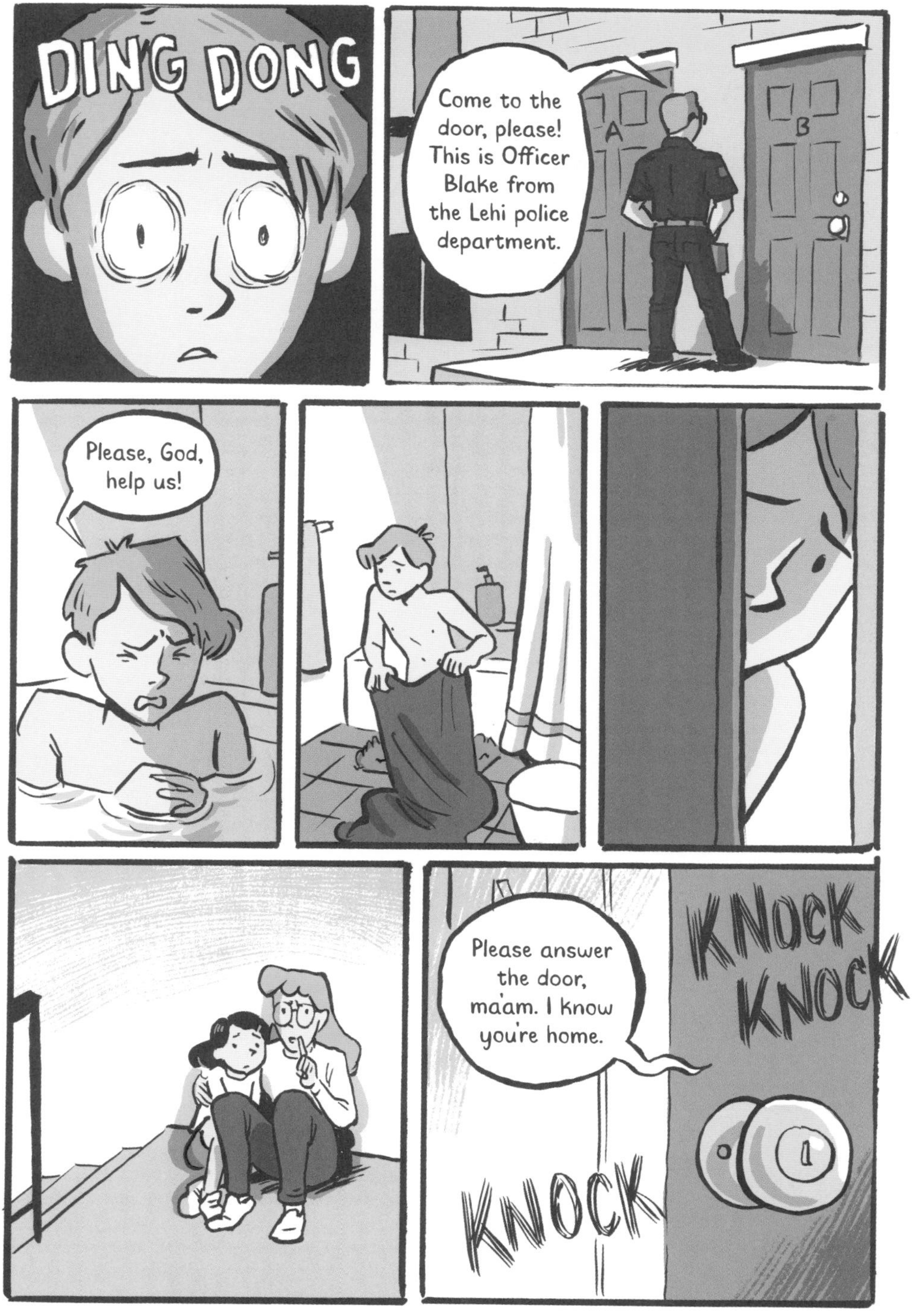
DING DONG
Come to the door, please! This is Officer Blake from the Lehi police department.
A
B
Please, God, help us!
Please answer the door, ma'am. I know you're home.
KNOCK
KNOCK
KNOCK

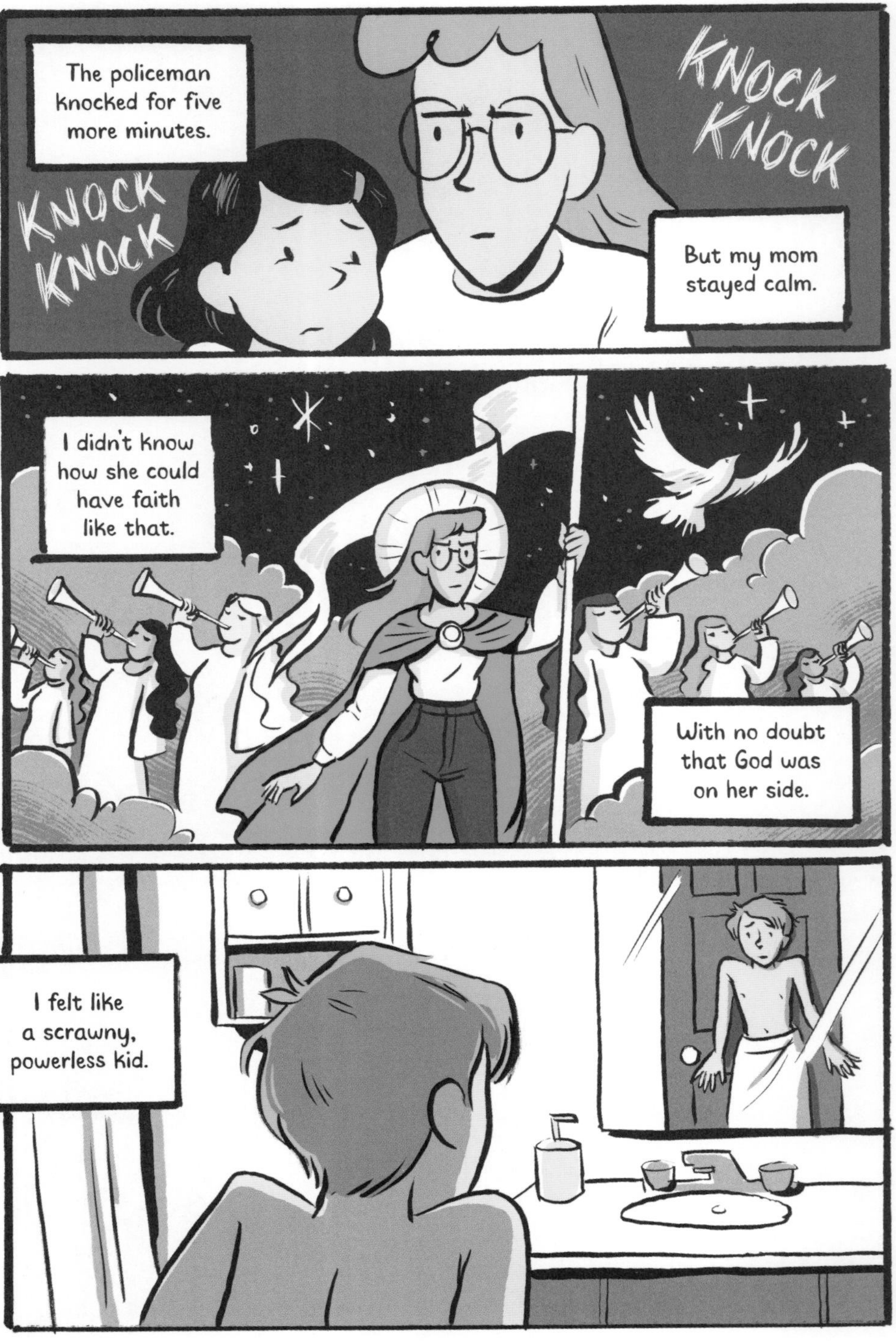
The policeman knocked for five more minutes.
KNOCK KNOCK
KNOCK KNOCK
But my mom stayed calm.
I didn't know how she could have faith like that.
With no doubt that God was on her side.
I felt like a scrawny, powerless kid.

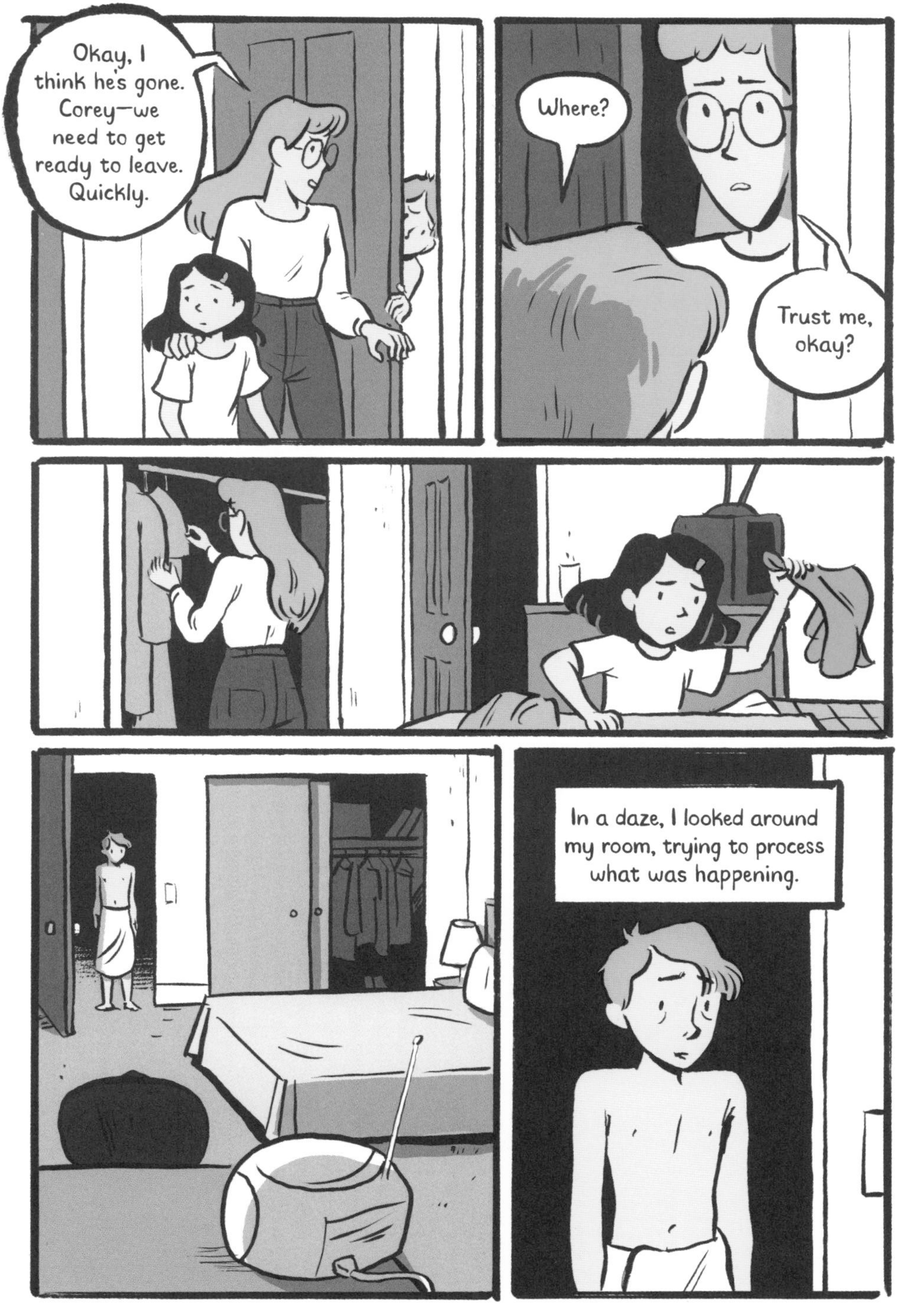
Okay, I think he's gone. Corey—we need to get ready to leave. Quickly.
Where?
Trust me, okay?
In a daze, I looked around my room, trying to process what was happening.

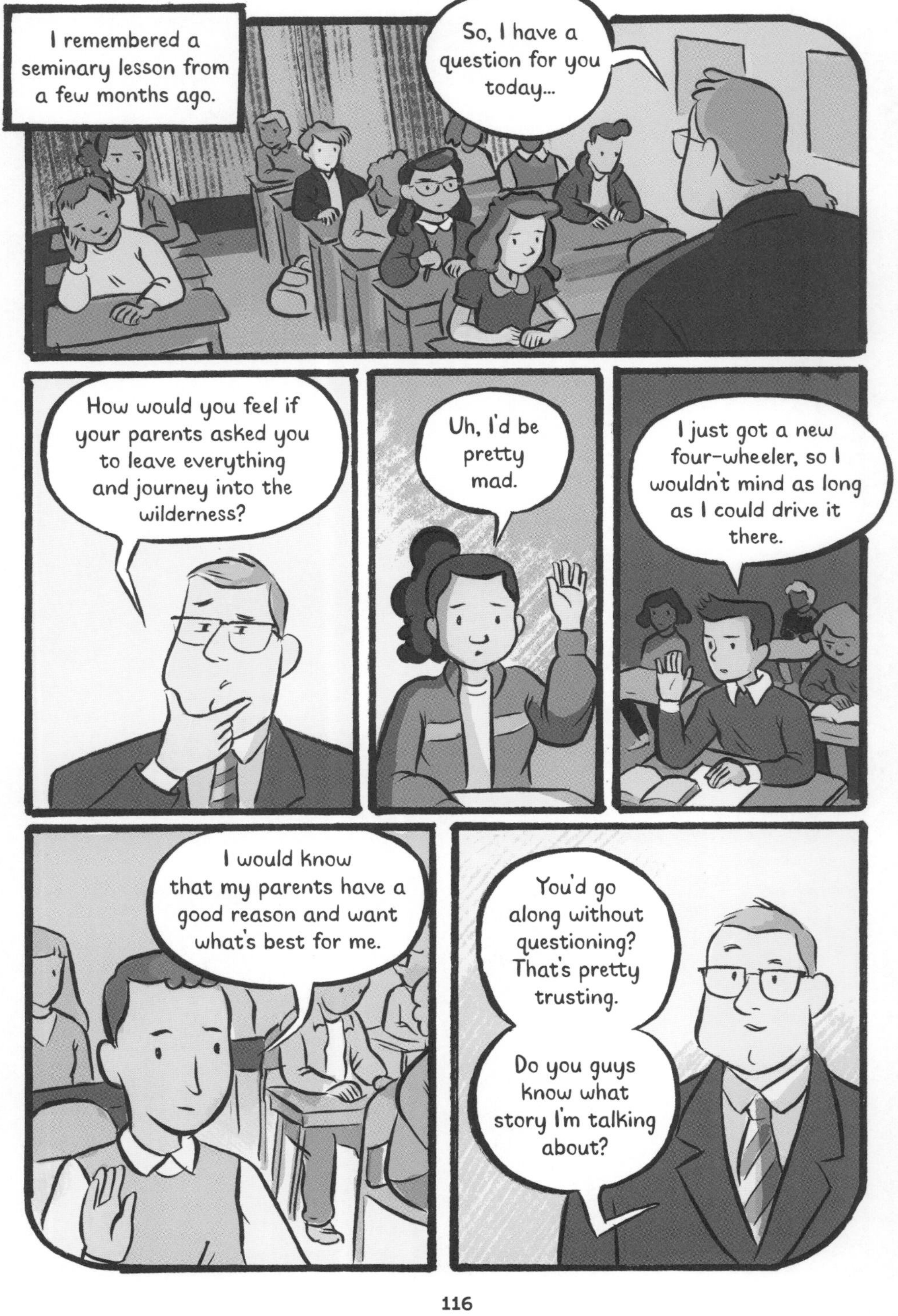

I remembered a seminary lesson from a few months ago.
So, I have a question for you today...
How would you feel if your parents asked you to leave everything and journey into the wilderness?
Uh, I'd be pretty mad.
I just got a new four-wheeler, so I wouldn't mind as long as I could drive it there.
I would know that my parents have a good reason and want what's best for me.
You'd go along without questioning? That's pretty trusting.
Do you guys know what story I'm talking about?

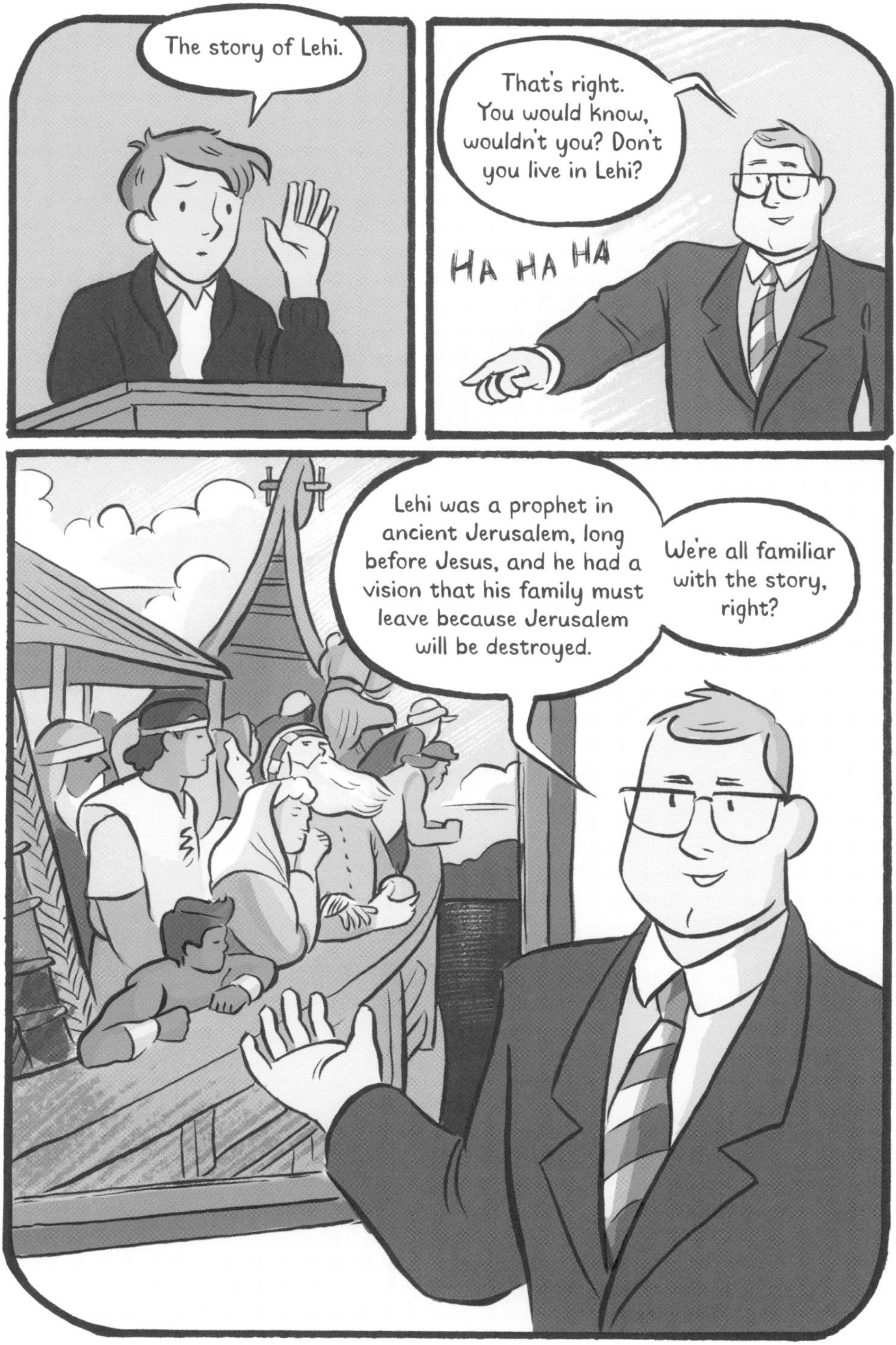
The story of Lehi.
That's right. You would know, wouldn't you? Don't you live in Lehi?
HA HA HA
Lehi was a prophet in ancient Jerusalem, long before Jesus, and he had a vision that his family must leave because Jerusalem will be destroyed.
We're all familiar with the story, right?

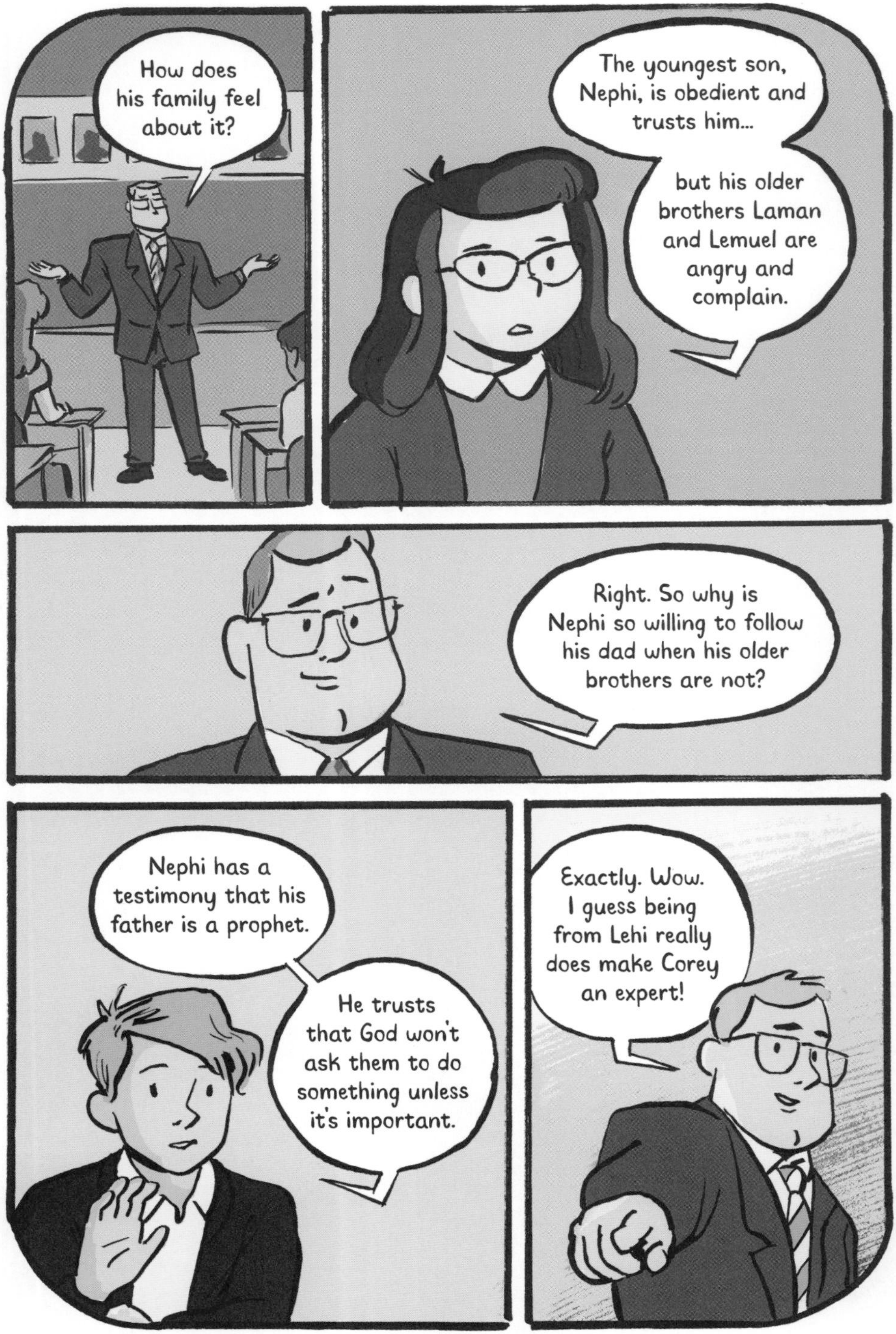
How does his family feel about it?
The youngest son, Nephi, is obedient and trusts him...
but his older brothers Laman and Lemuel are angry and complain.
Right. So why is Nephi so willing to follow his dad when his older brothers are not?
Nephi has a testimony that his father is a prophet.
He trusts that God won't ask them to do something unless it's important.
Exactly. Wow. I guess being from Lehi really does make Corey an expert!

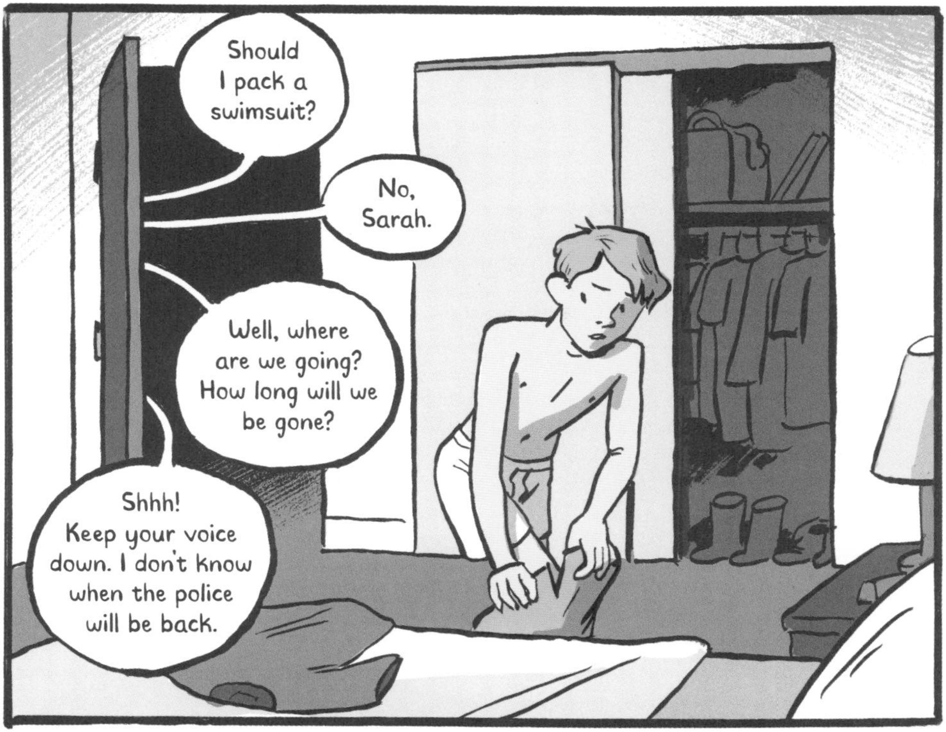
Should I pack a swimsuit?
No, Sarah.
Well, where are we going? How long will we be gone?
Shhh! Keep your voice down. I don't know when the police will be back.

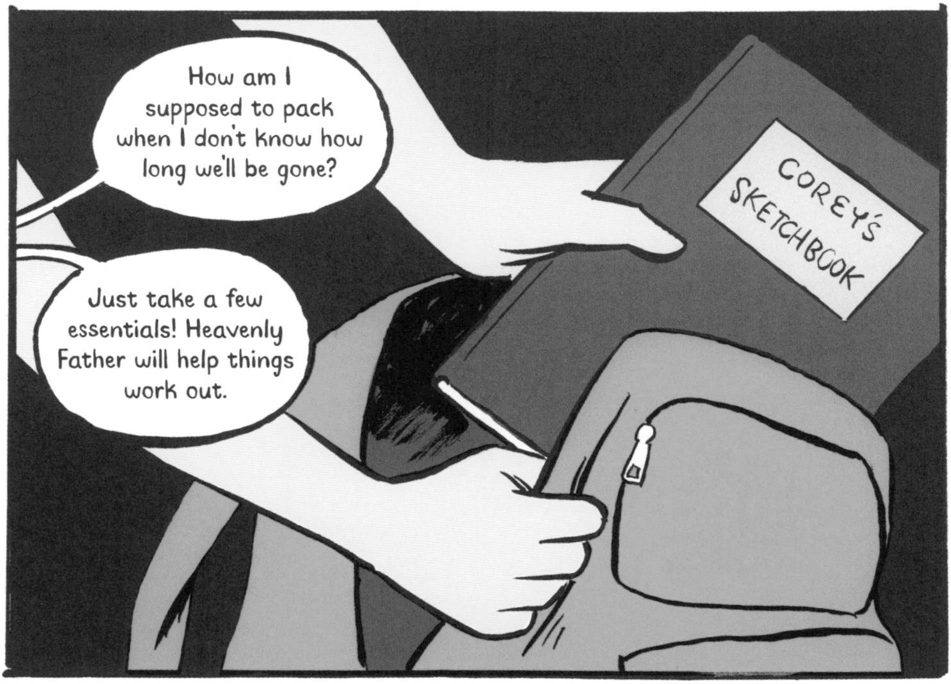
How am I supposed to pack when I don't know how long we'll be gone?
COREY'S SKETCHBOOK
Just take a few essentials! Heavenly Father will help things work out.

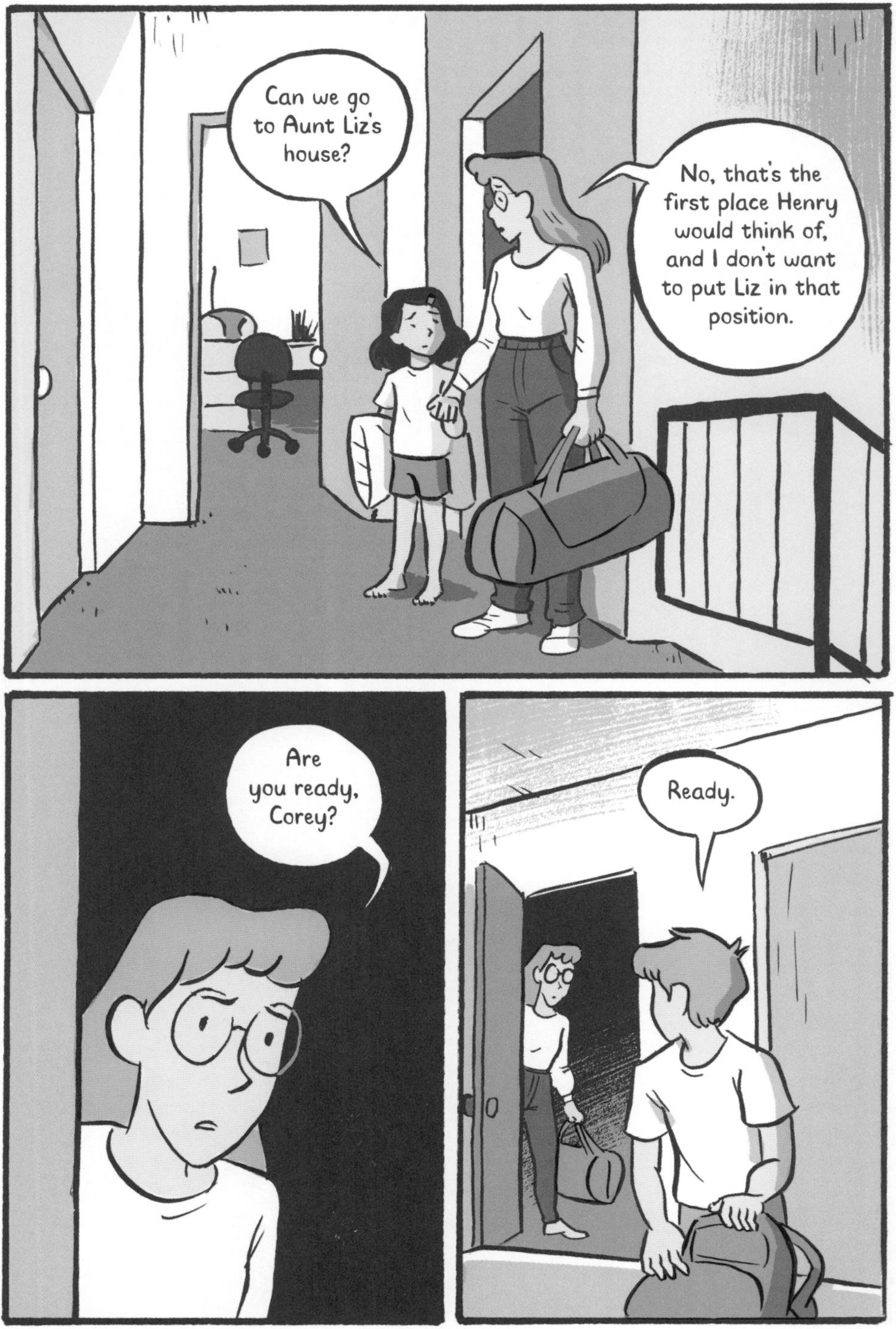
Can we go to Aunt Liz's house?
No, that's the first place Henry would think of, and I don't want to put Liz in that position.
Are you ready, Corey?
Ready.

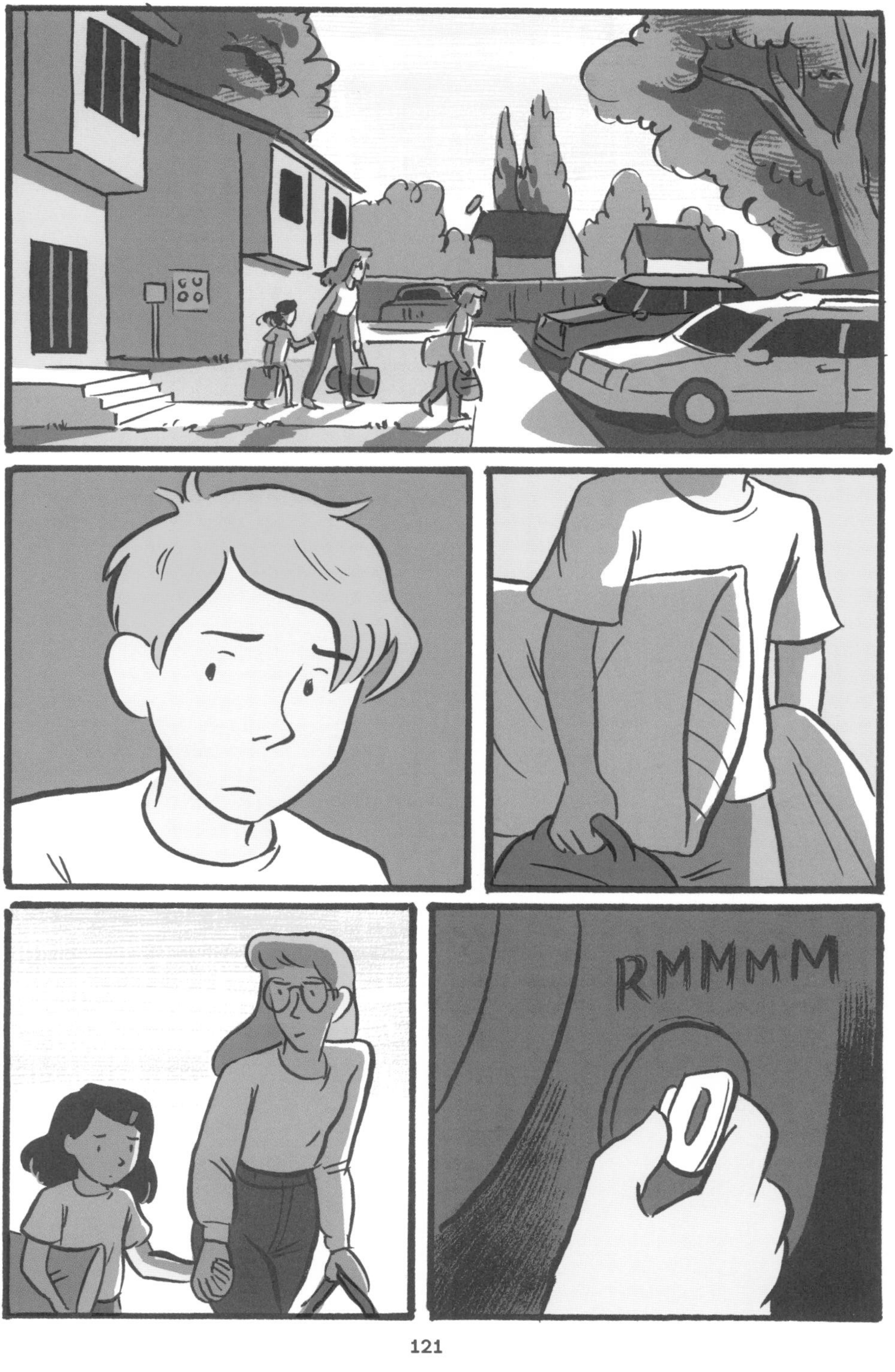
RMMMM

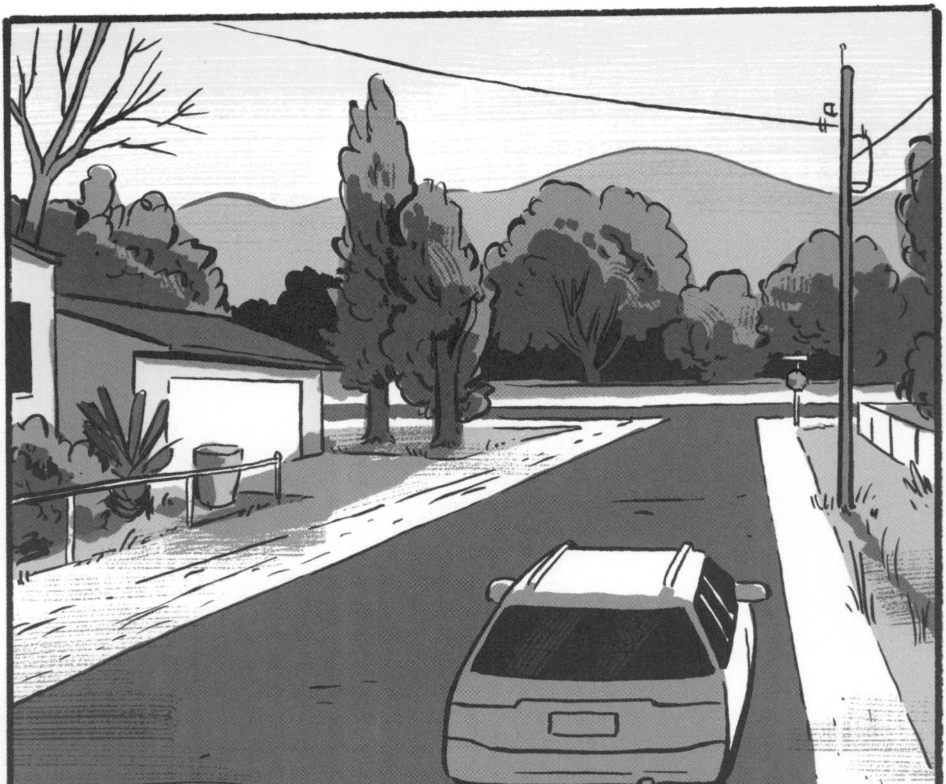

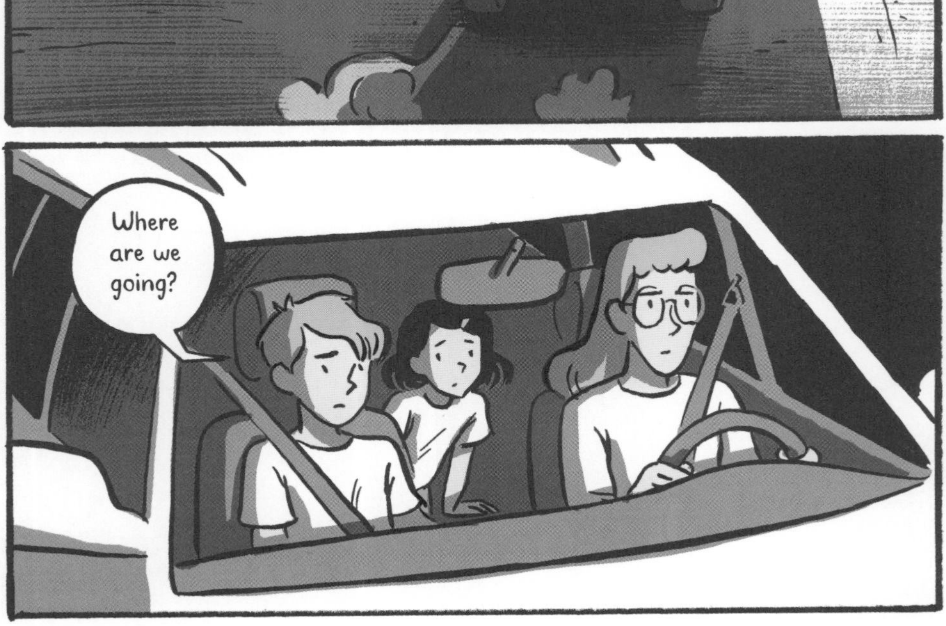
Where are we going?

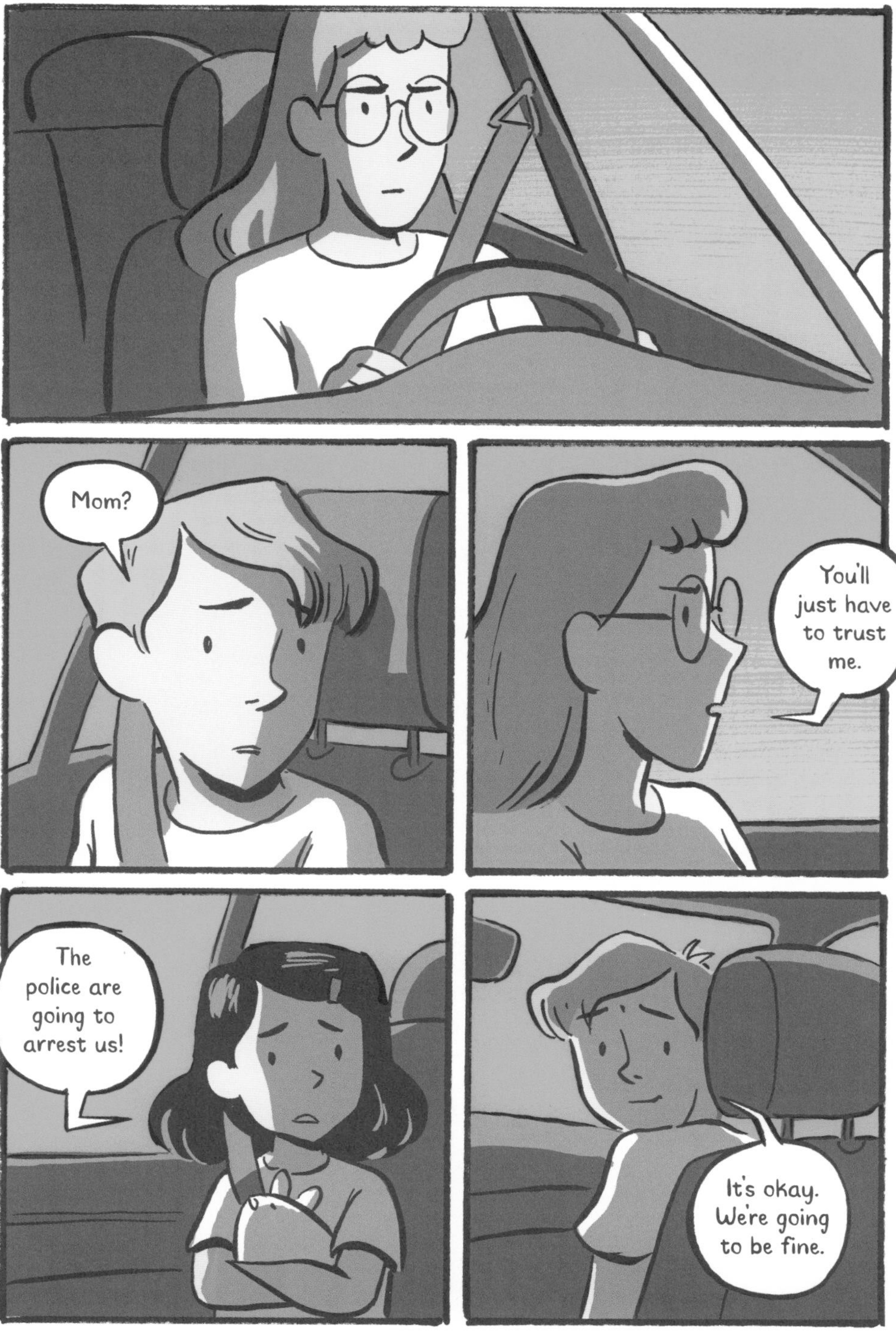
Mom?
You'll just have to trust me.
The police are going to arrest us!
It's okay. We're going to be fine.

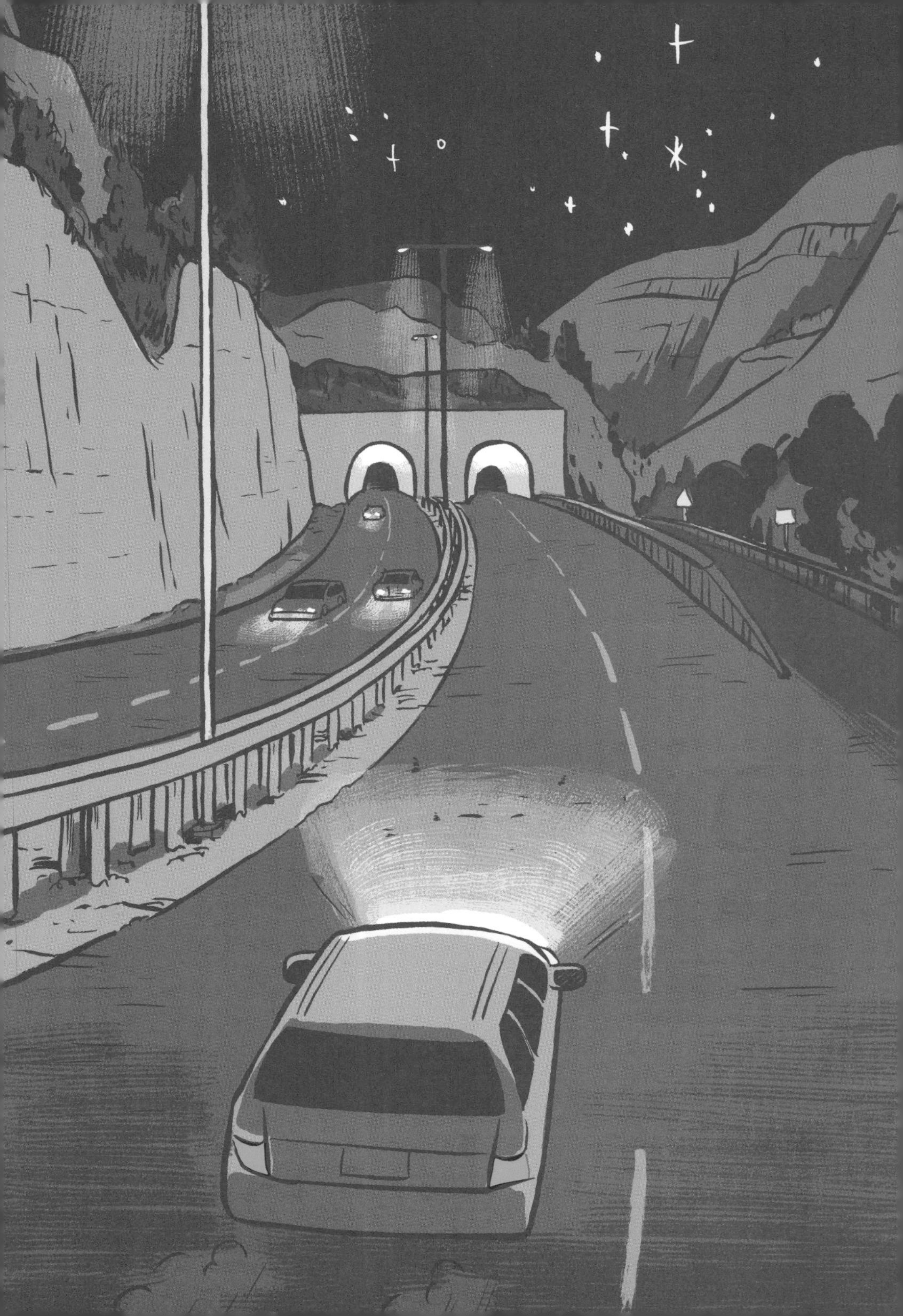

PART TWO

"And I was led by the
Spirit, not knowing
beforehand the things
which I should do."

1 NEPHI 4:6

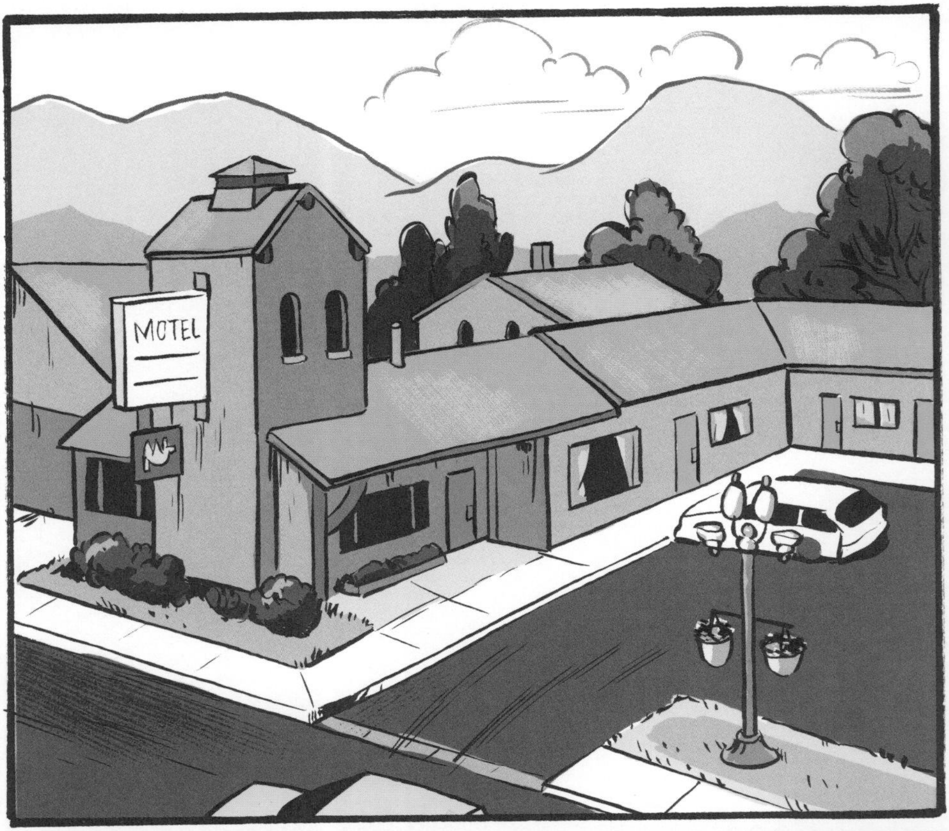
MOTEL

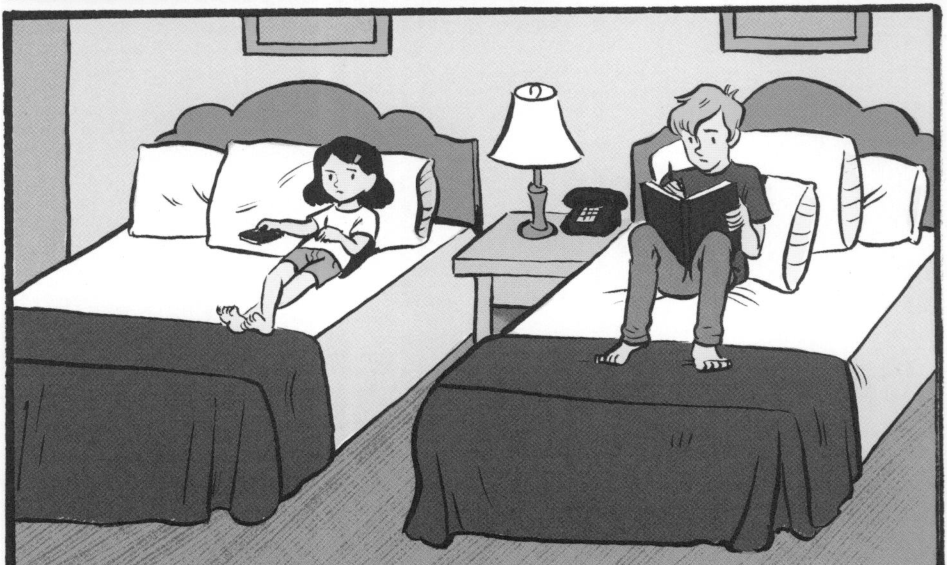

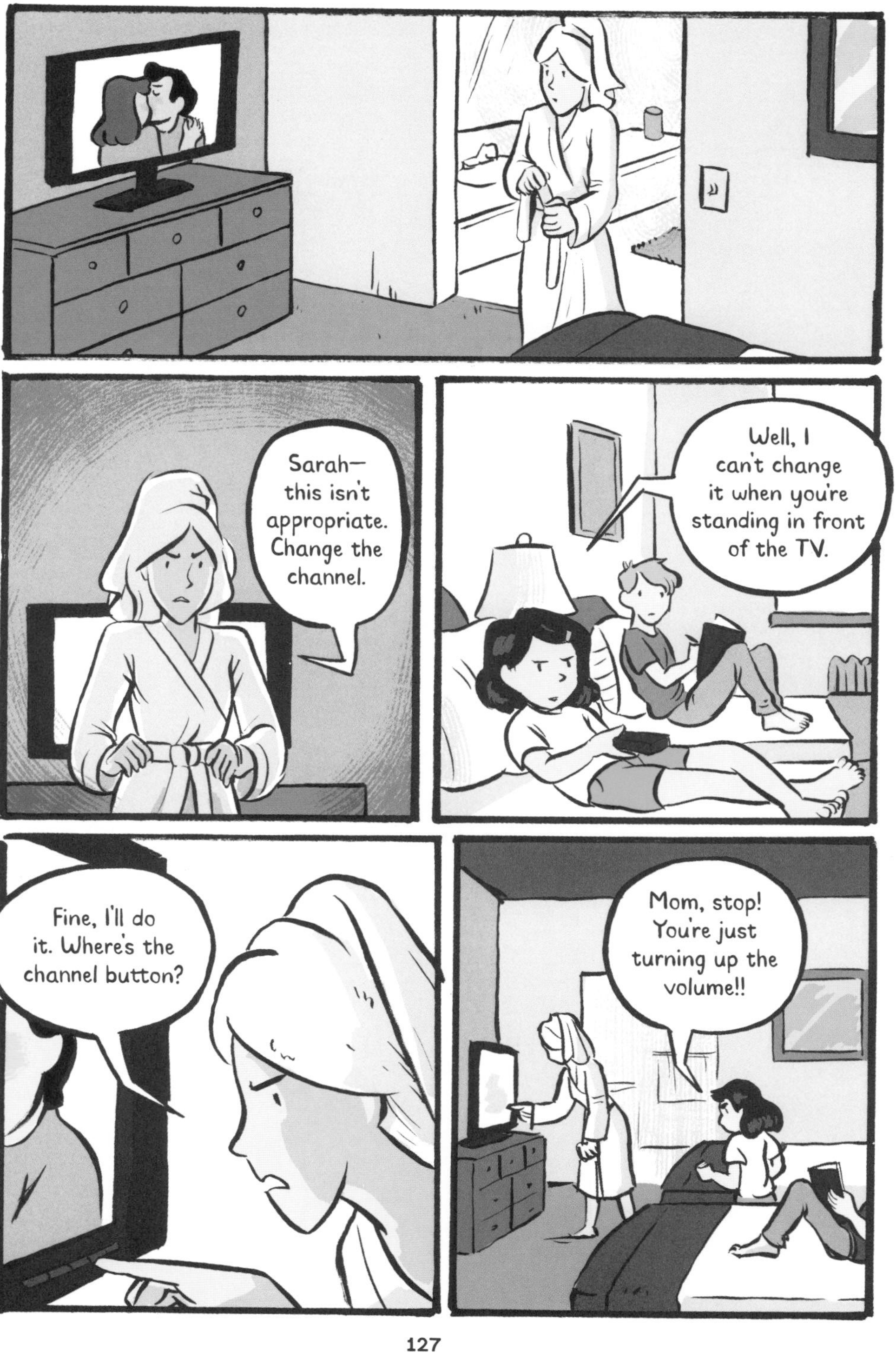
Sarah—this isn't appropriate. Change the channel.
Well, I can't change it when you're standing in front of the TV.
Fine, I'll do it. Where's the channel button?
Mom, stop! You're just turning up the volume!!

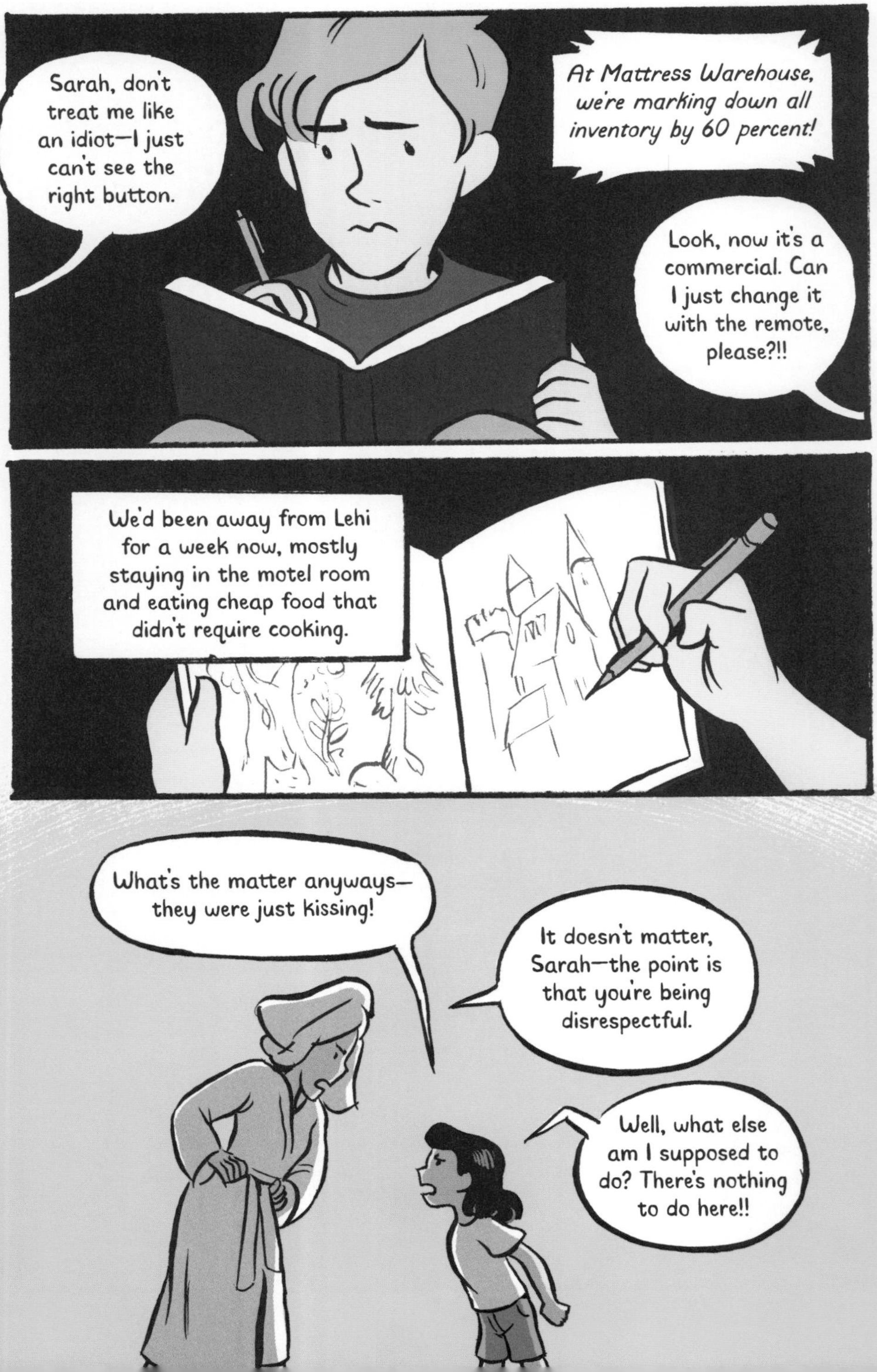
Sarah, don't treat me like an idiot—I just can't see the right button.
At Mattress Warehouse, we're marking down all inventory by 60 percent!
Look, now it's a commercial. Can I just change it with the remote, please?!!
We'd been away from Lehi for a week now, mostly staying in the motel room and eating cheap food that didn't require cooking.
What's the matter anyways—they were just kissing!
It doesn't matter, Sarah—the point is that you're being disrespectful.
Well, what else am I supposed to do? There's nothing to do here!!

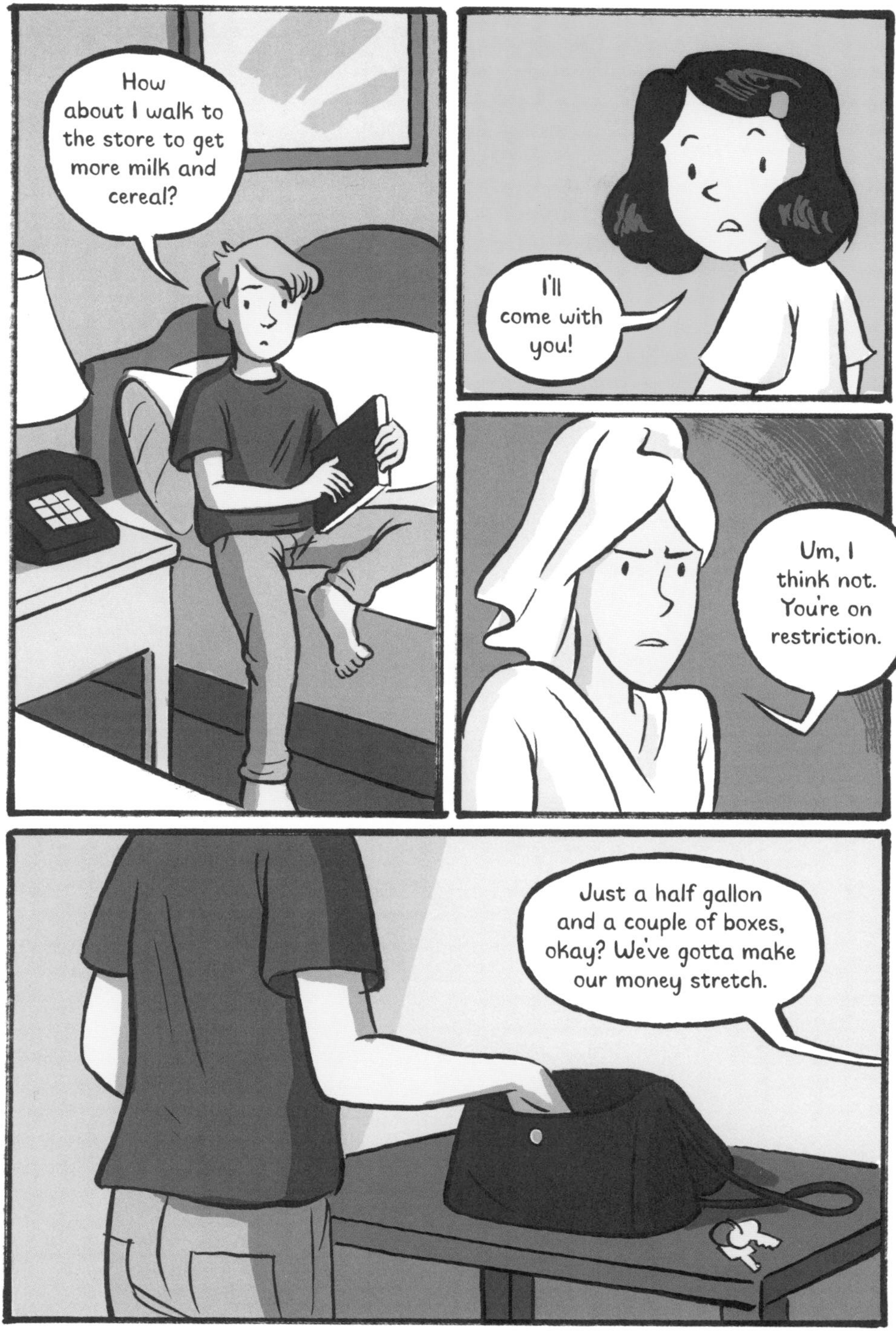
How about I walk to the store to get more milk and cereal?
I'll come with you!
Um, I think not. You're on restriction.
Just a half gallon and a couple of boxes, okay? We've gotta make our money stretch.

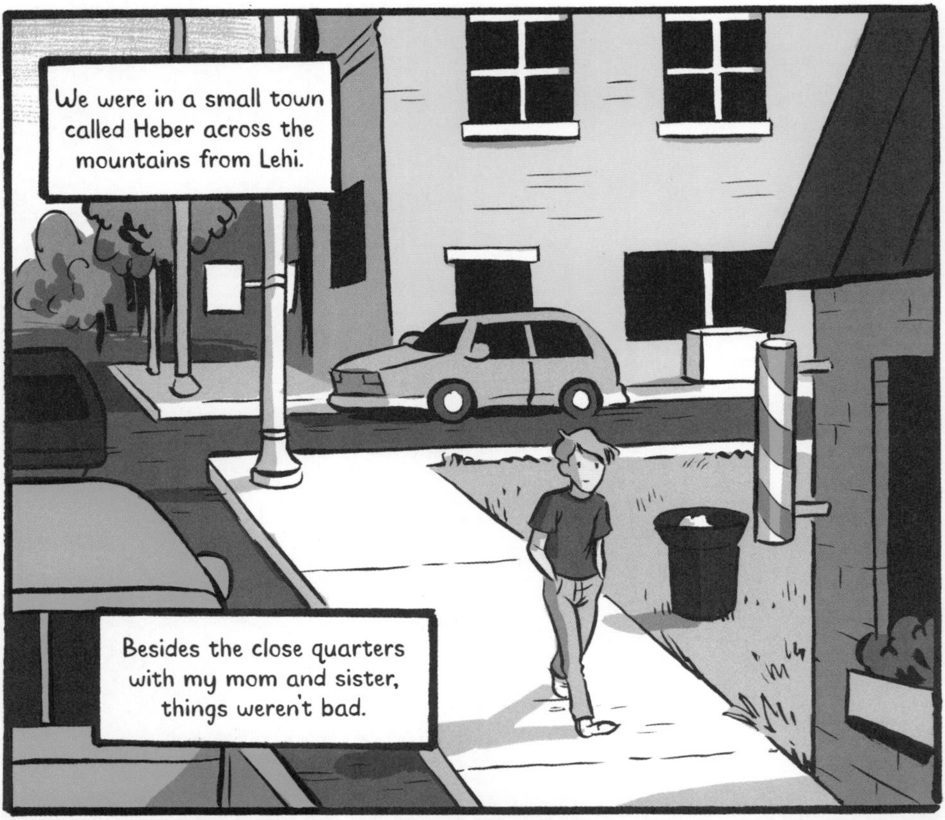
We were in a small town called Heber across the mountains from Lehi.
Besides the close quarters with my mom and sister, things weren't bad.

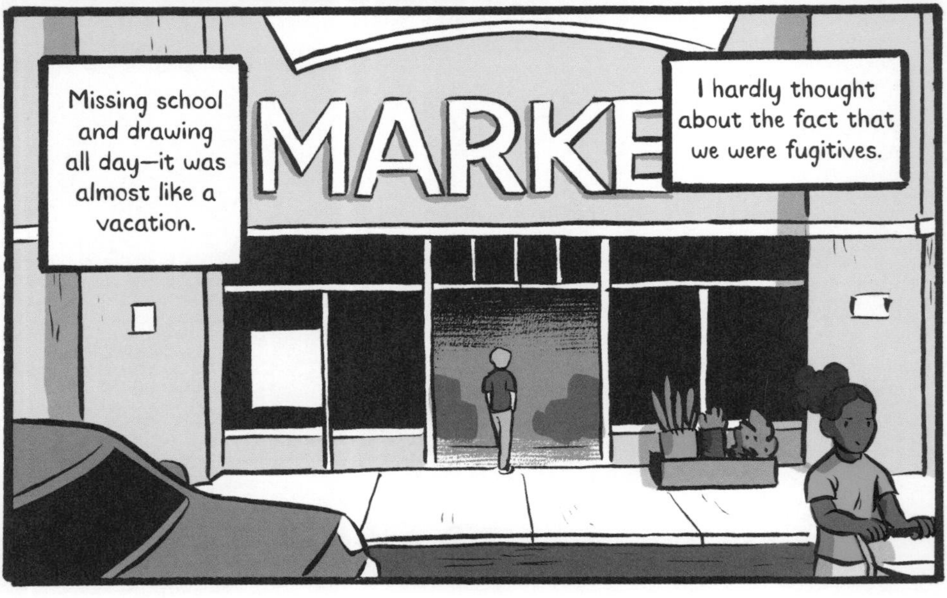
Missing school and drawing all day—it was almost like a vacation.
MARKE
I hardly thought about the fact that we were fugitives.

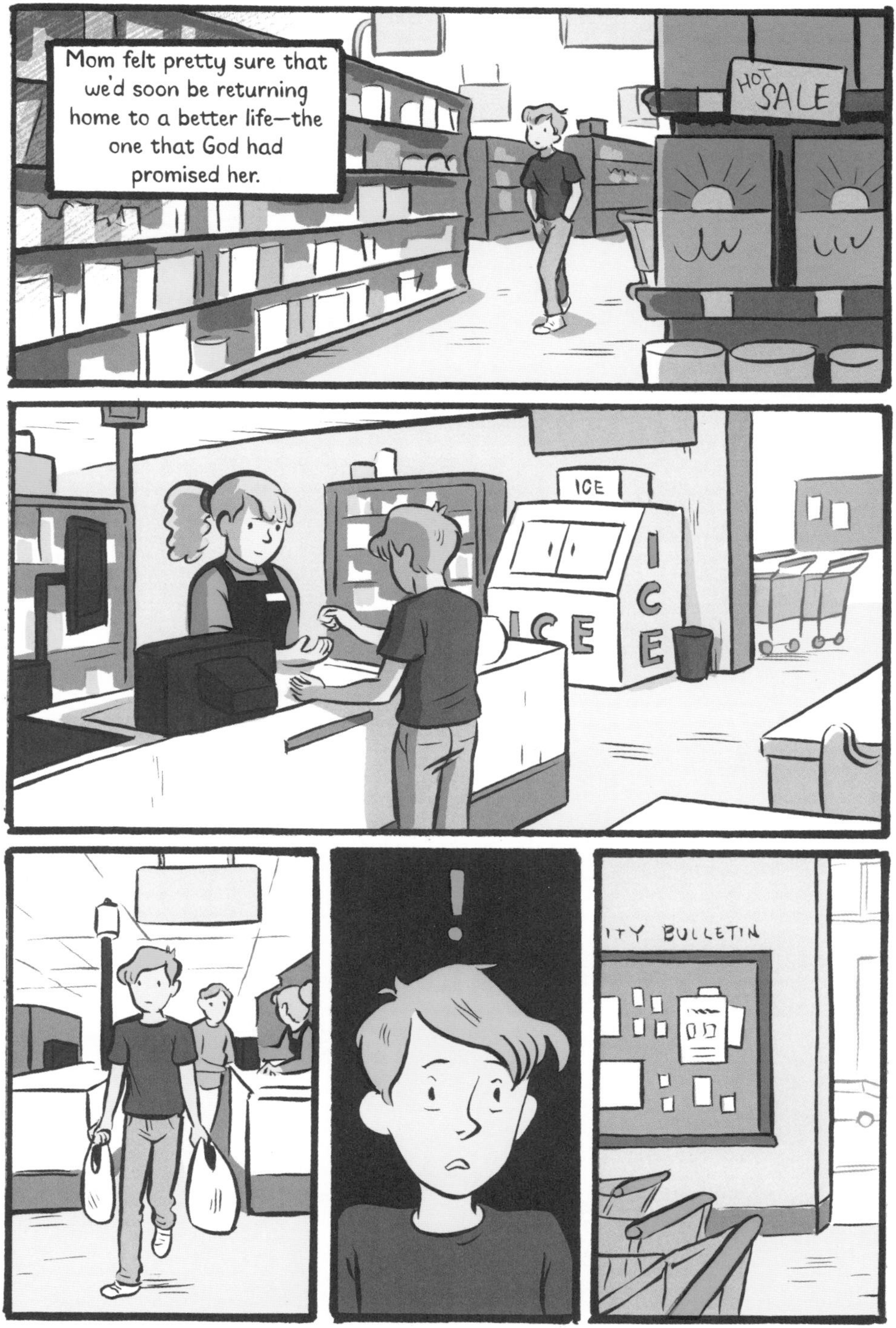
Mom felt pretty sure that we'd soon be returning home to a better life—the one that God had promised her.
HOT SALE
ICE
ICE
ICE
!
ITY BULLETIN

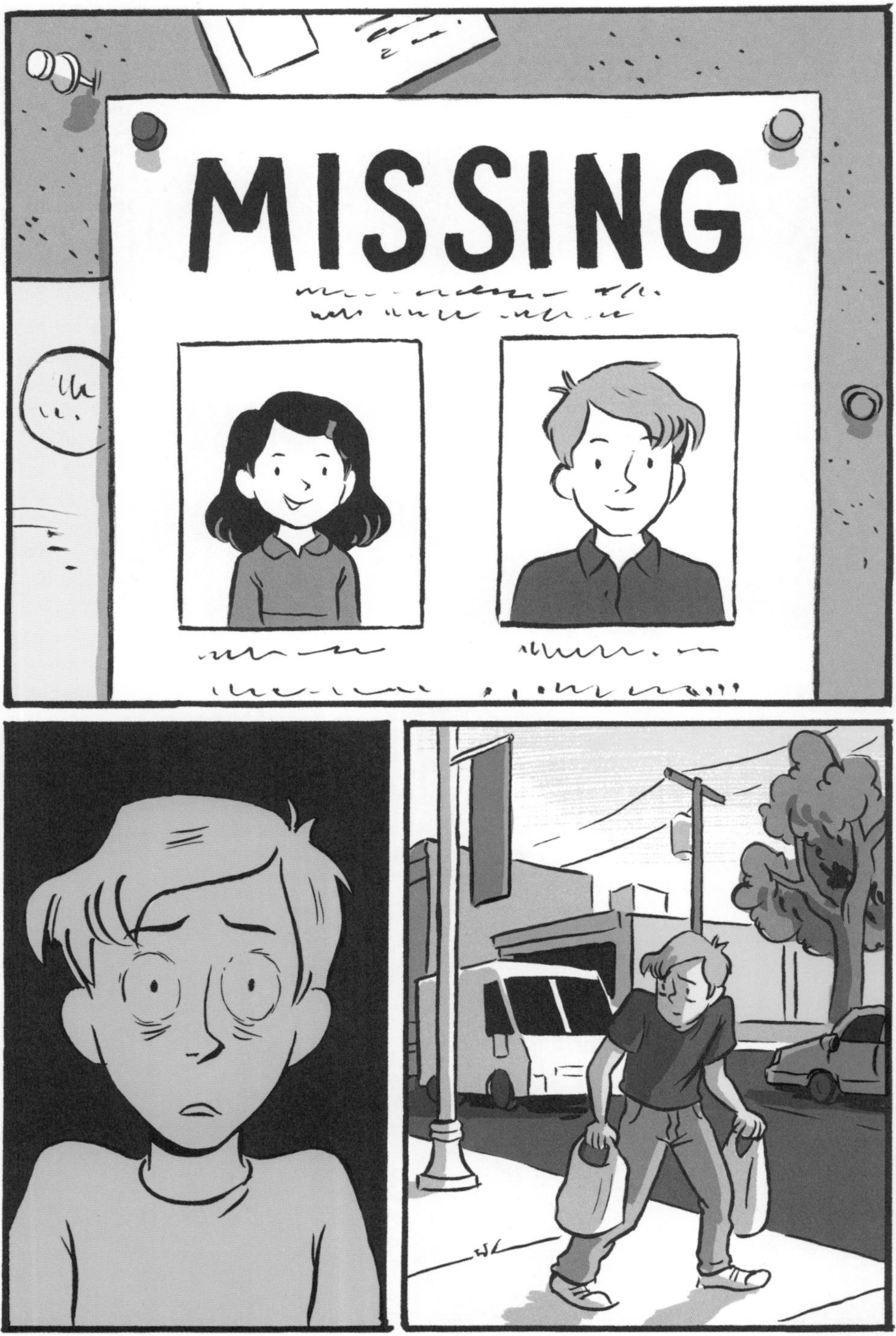
MISSING

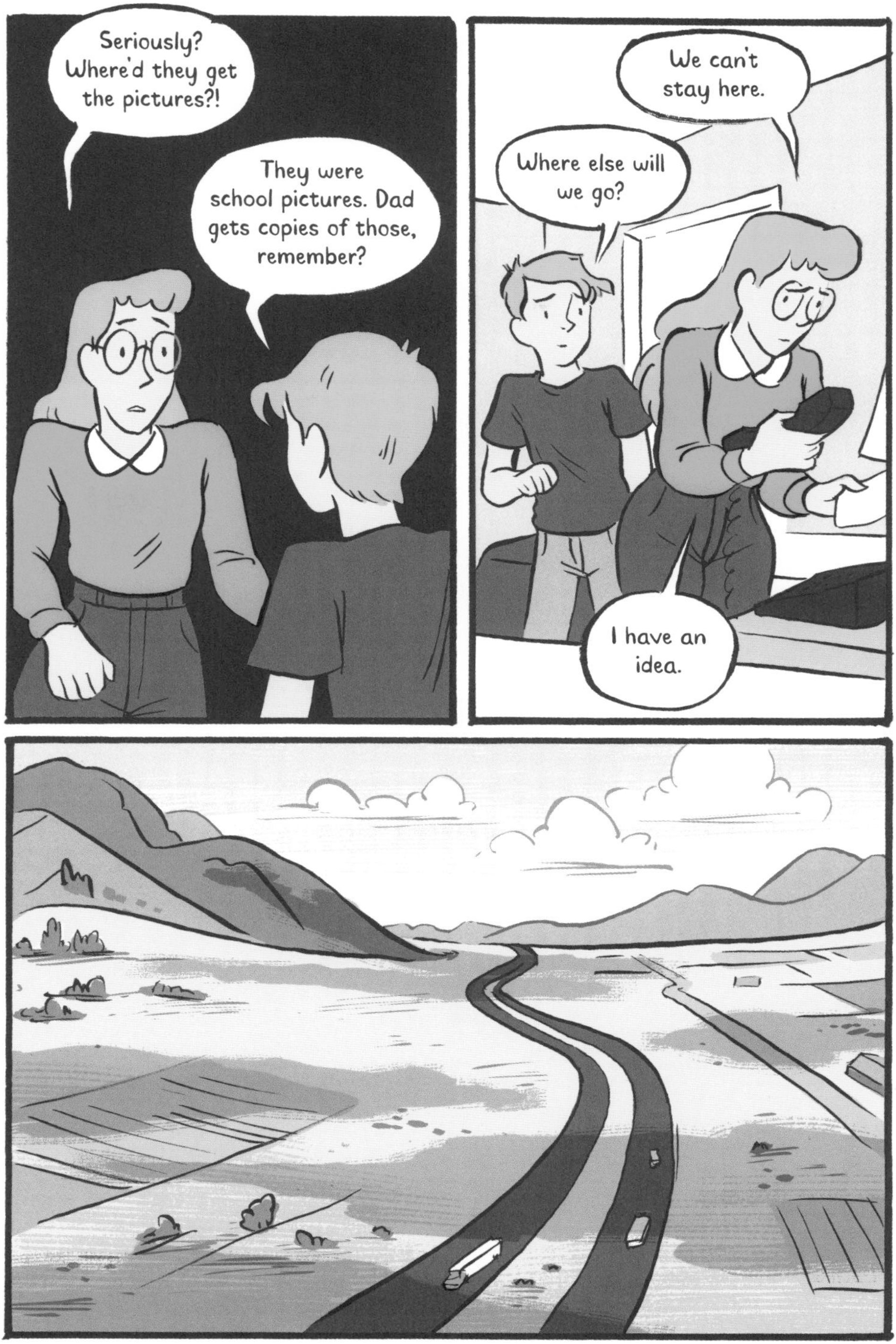
Seriously? Where'd they get the pictures?!
They were school pictures. Dad gets copies of those, remember?
We can't stay here.
Where else will we go?
I have an idea.

Hello! Oh my goodness, Corey and Sarah, you're so big!
Hi, Amber! Are you expecting again? I didn't know!
Number seven. Can you believe it? When we were neighbors, I only had the two, right?
And you always keep a spotless house. I don't know how you manage it. You're amazing, girl!
Oh no, are you kidding? My house is never clean.

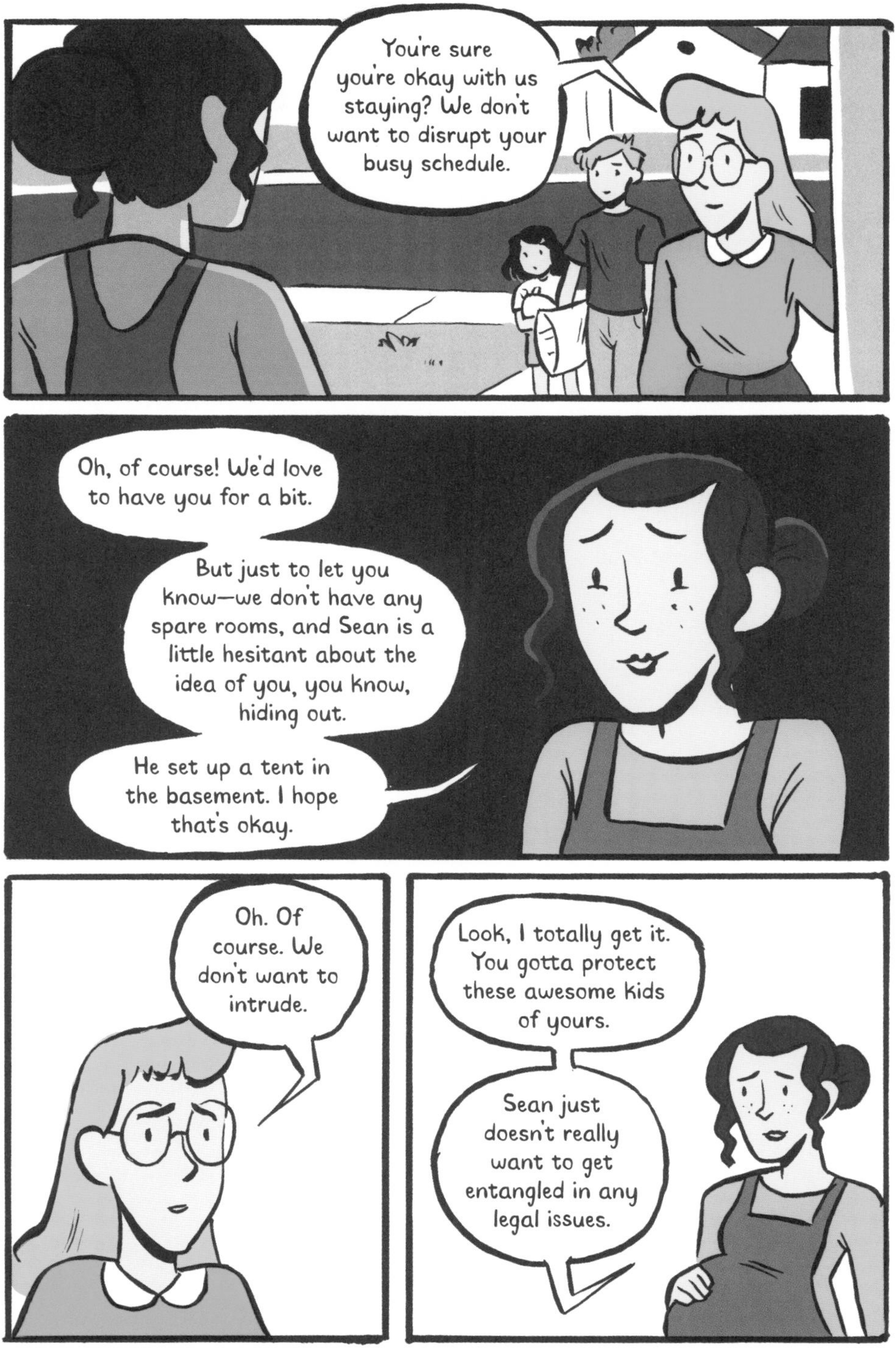
You're sure you're okay with us staying? We don't want to disrupt your busy schedule.
Oh, of course! We'd love to have you for a bit.
But just to let you know—we don't have any spare rooms, and Sean is a little hesitant about the idea of you, you know, hiding out.
He set up a tent in the basement. I hope that's okay.
Oh. Of course. We don't want to intrude.
Look, I totally get it. You gotta protect these awesome kids of yours.
Sean just doesn't really want to get entangled in any legal issues.

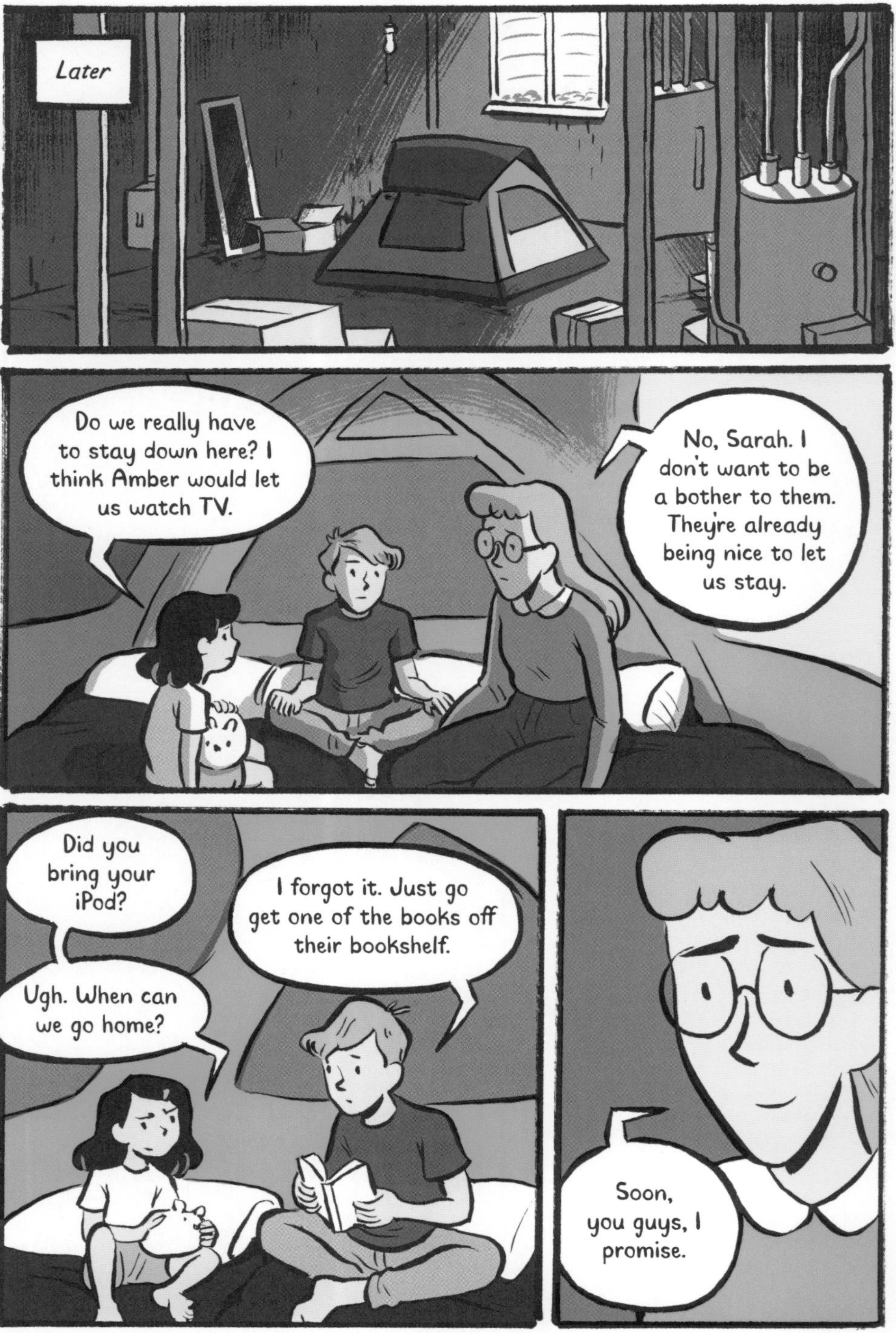
Later
Do we really have to stay down here? I think Amber would let us watch TV.
No, Sarah. I don't want to be a bother to them. They're already being nice to let us stay.
Did you bring your iPod?
Ugh. When can we go home?
I forgot it. Just go get one of the books off their bookshelf.
Soon, you guys, I promise.

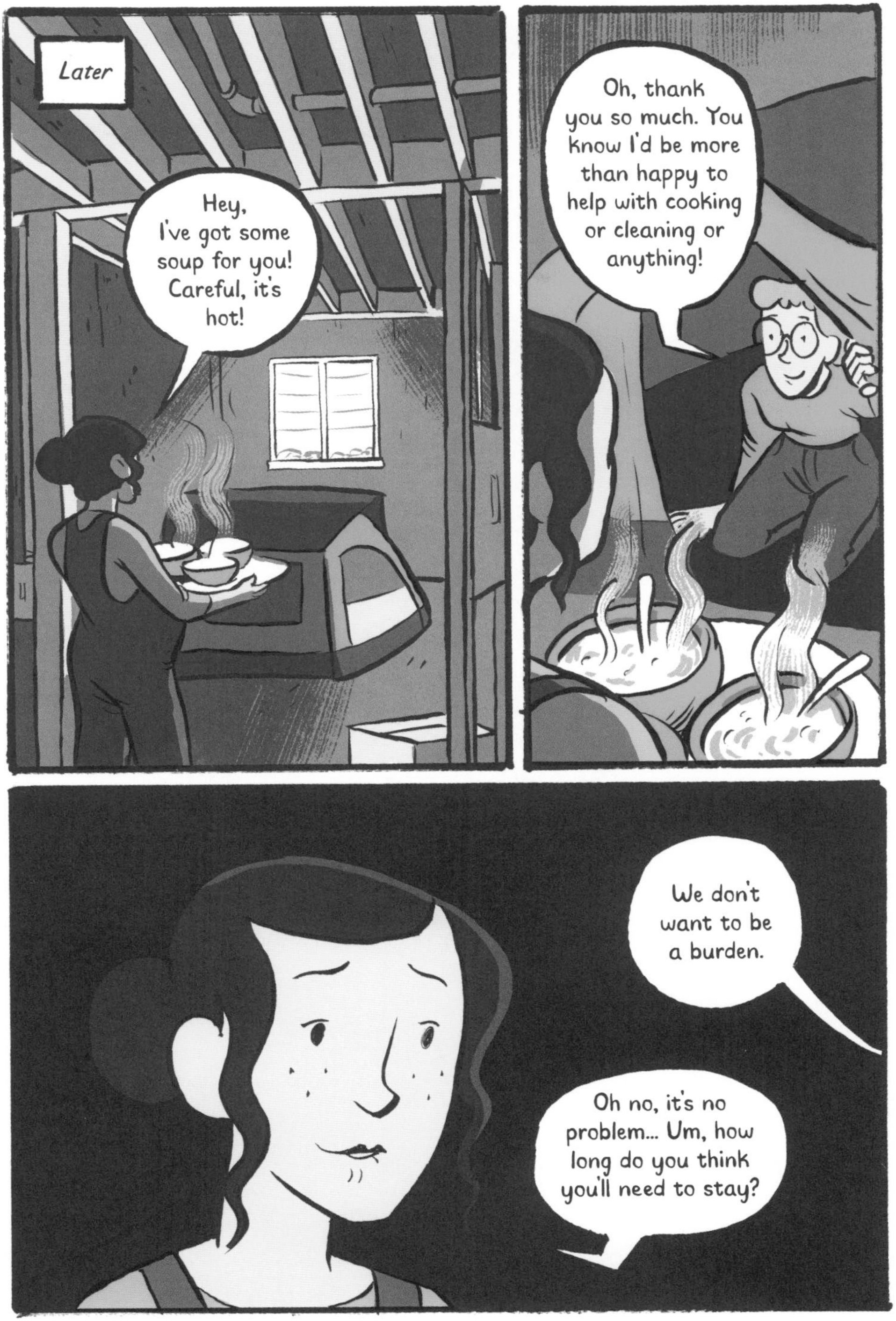
Later
Hey, I've got some soup for you! Careful, it's hot!
Oh, thank you so much. You know I'd be more than happy to help with cooking or cleaning or anything!
We don't want to be a burden.
Oh no, it's no problem... Um, how long do you think you'll need to stay?

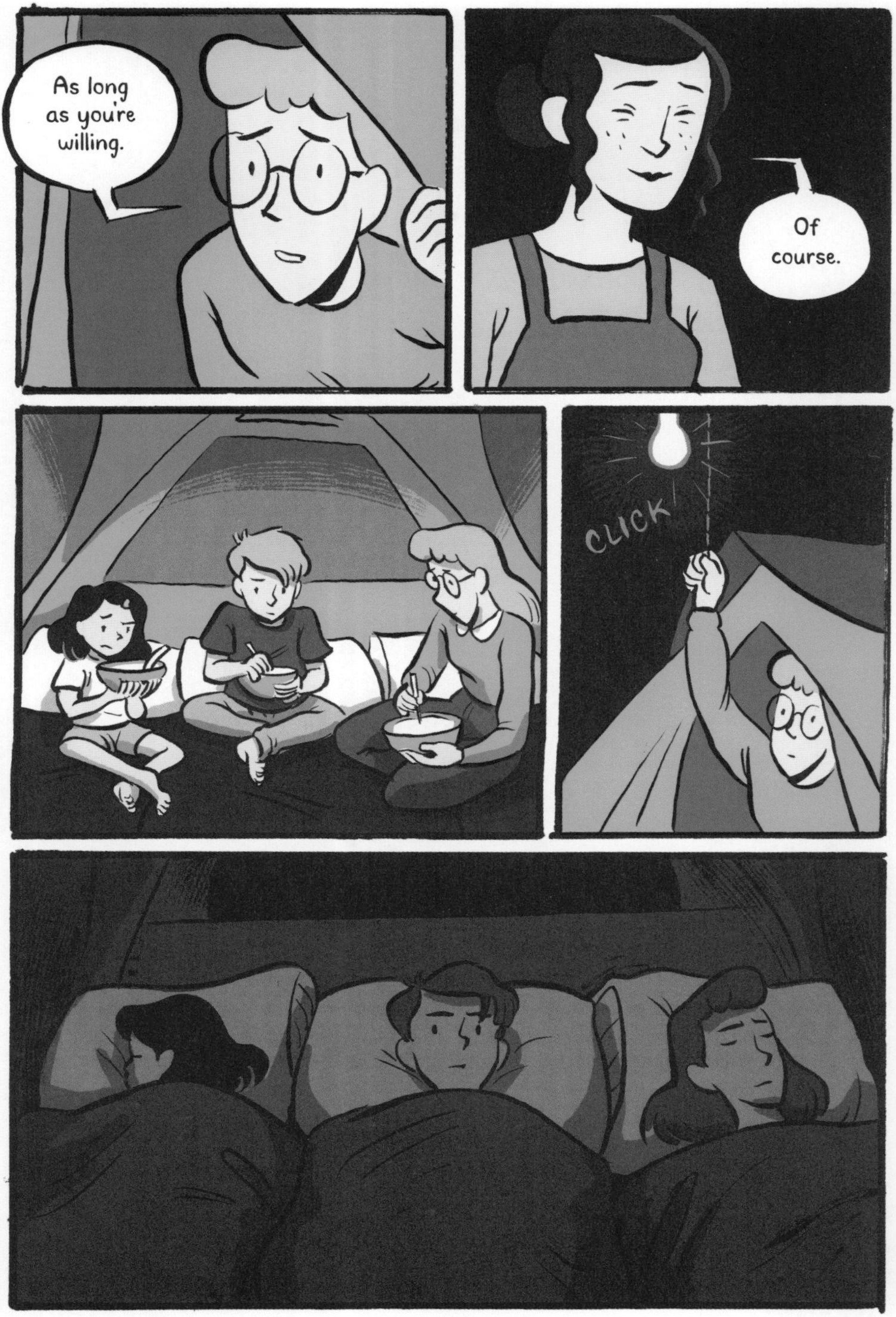
As long as you're willing.
Of course.
CLICK

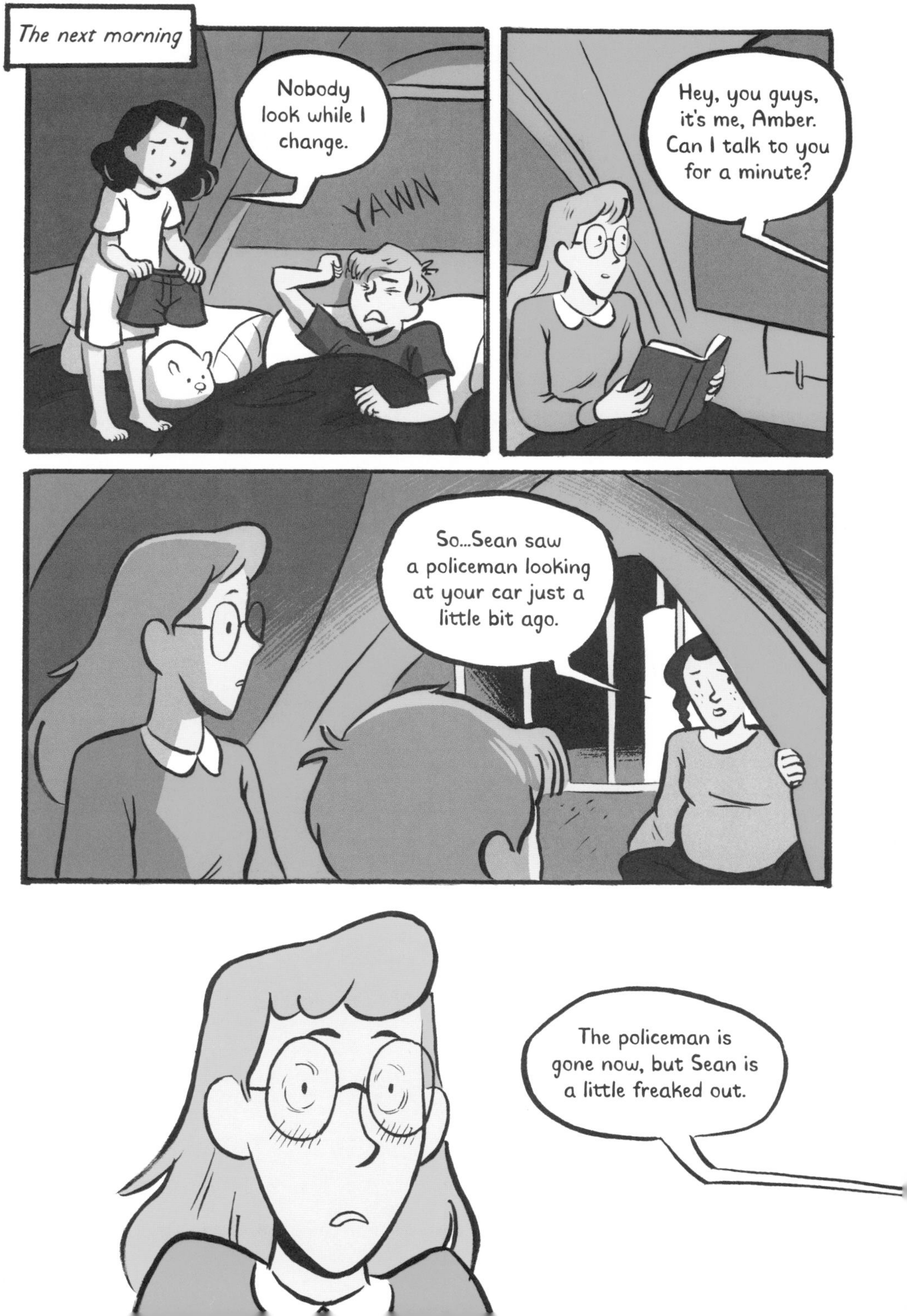
The next morning
Nobody look while I change.
YAWN
Hey, you guys, it's me, Amber. Can I talk to you for a minute?
So...Sean saw a policeman looking at your car just a little bit ago.
The policeman is gone now, but Sean is a little freaked out.

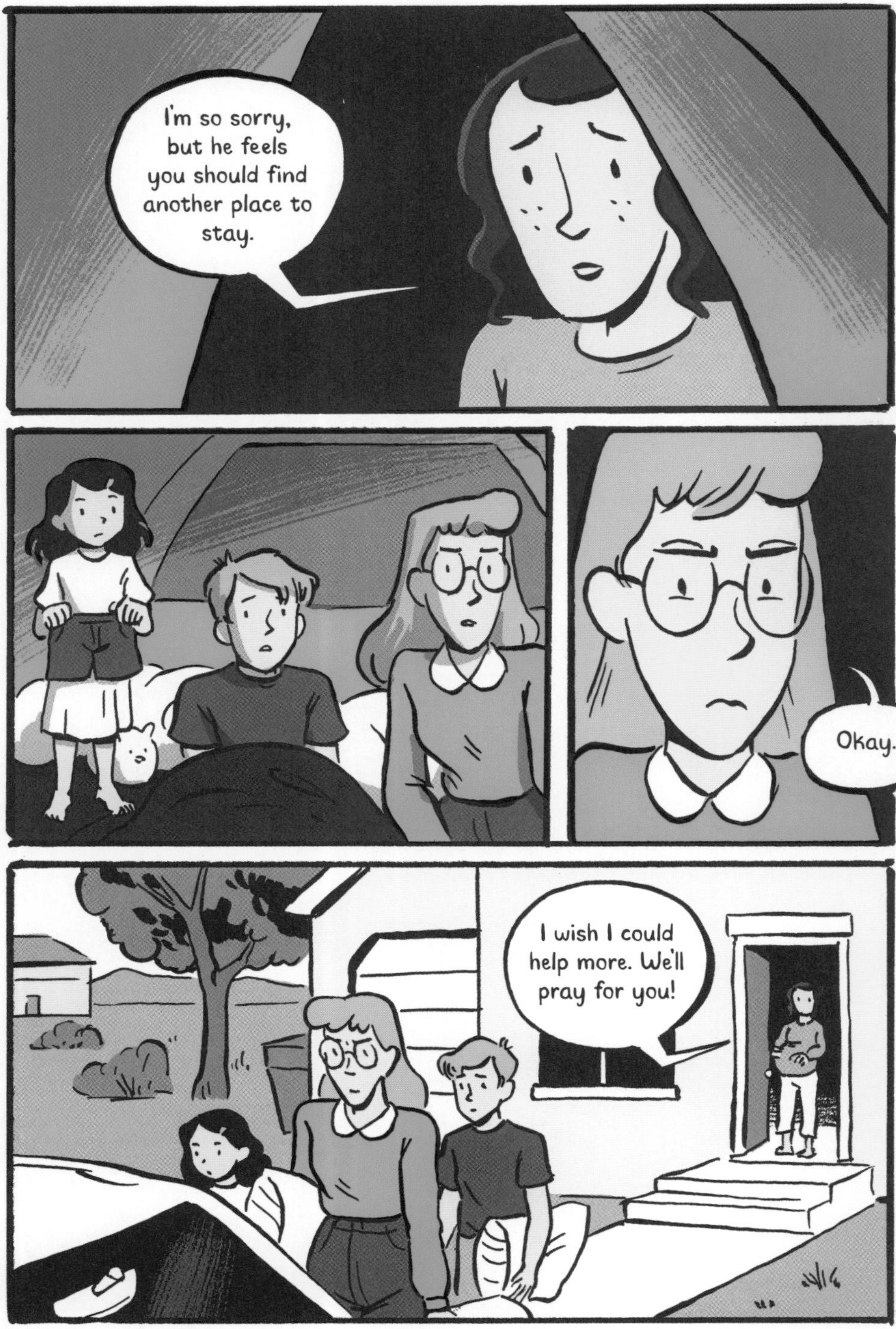
I'm so sorry, but he feels you should find another place to stay.
Okay.
I wish I could help more. We'll pray for you!

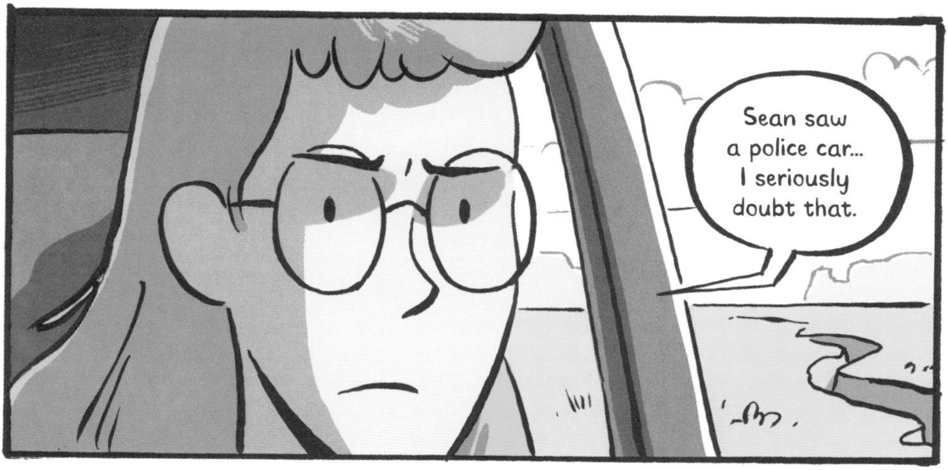
Sean saw a police car... I seriously doubt that.

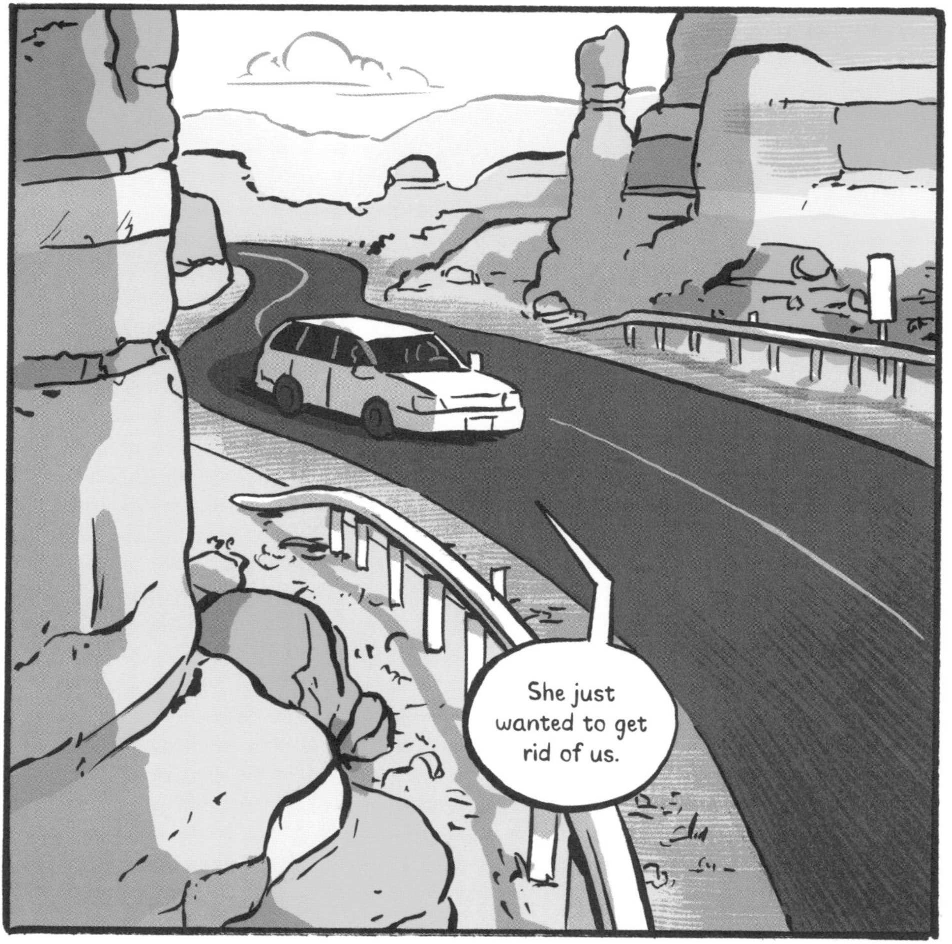
She just wanted to get rid of us.

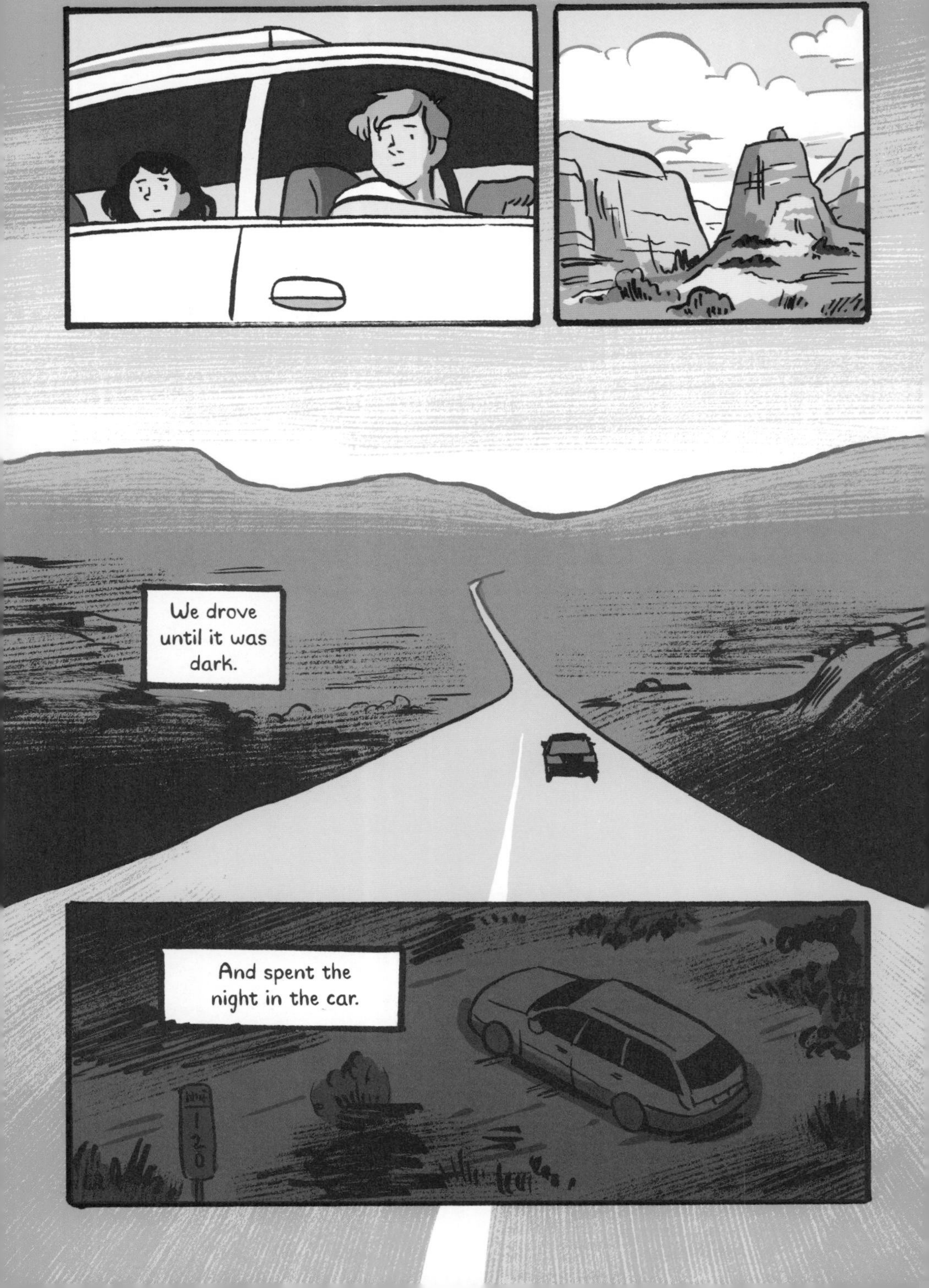
We drove until it was dark.
And spent the night in the car.

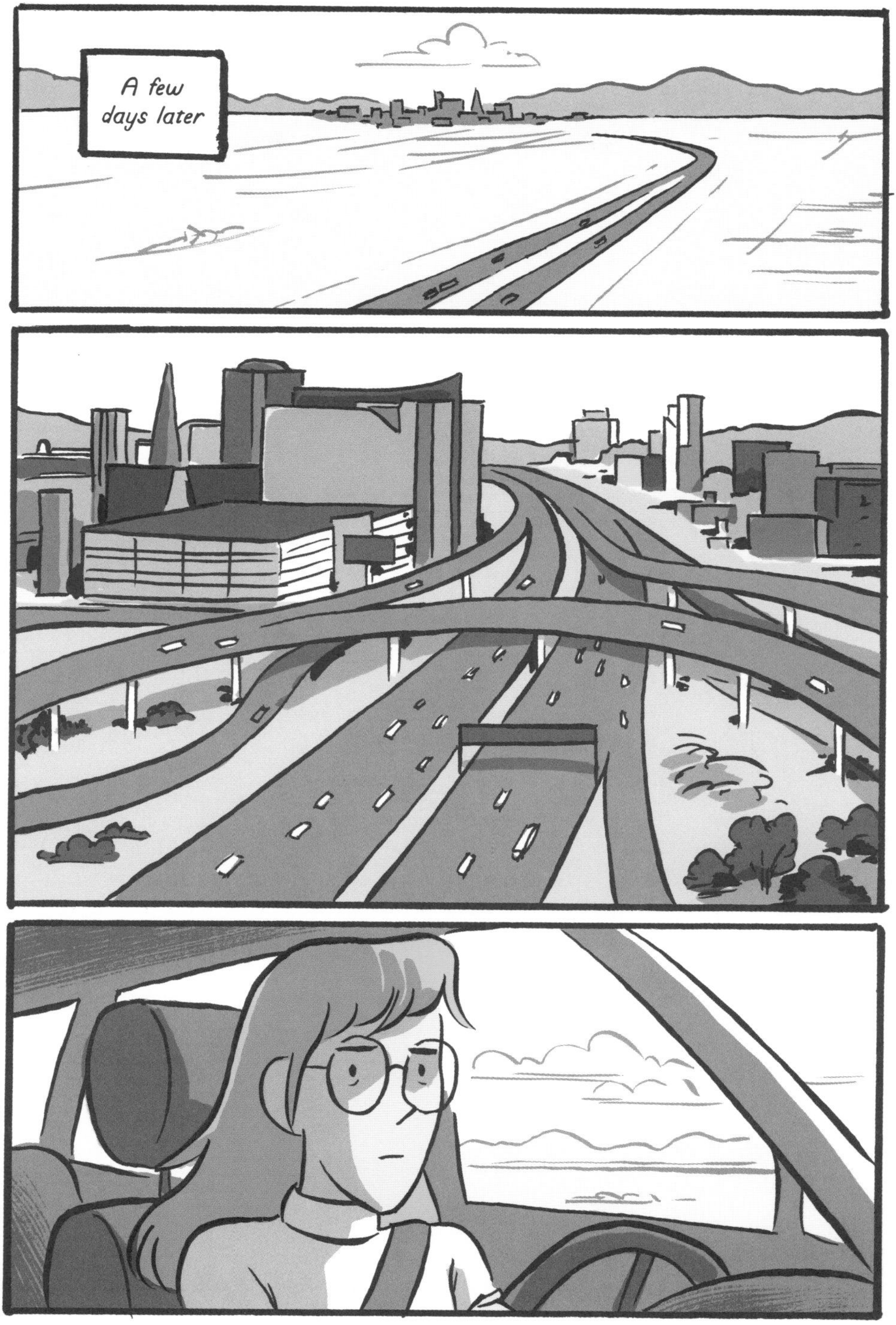
A few
days later

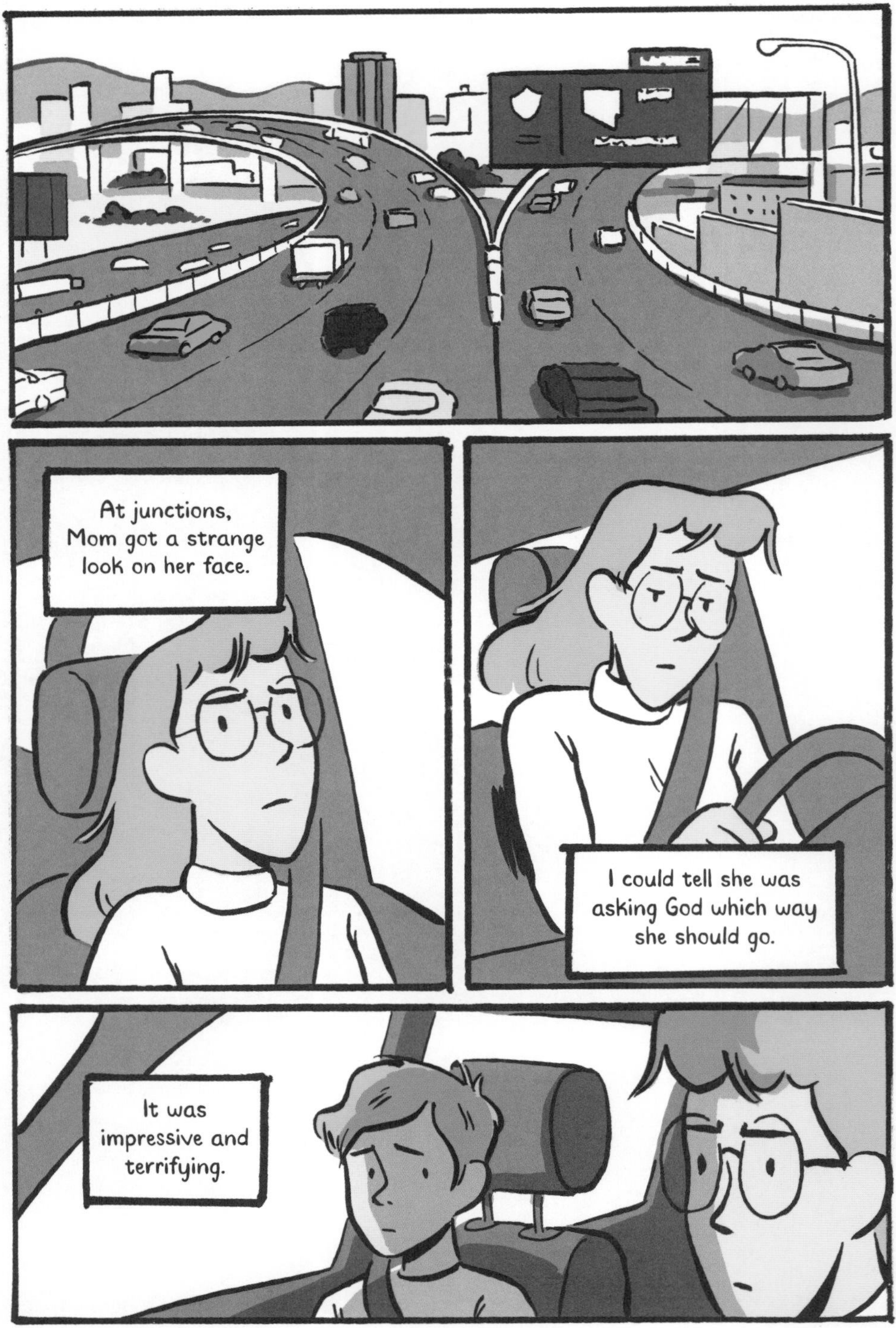
At junctions, Mom got a strange look on her face.
I could tell she was asking God which way she should go.
It was impressive and terrifying.

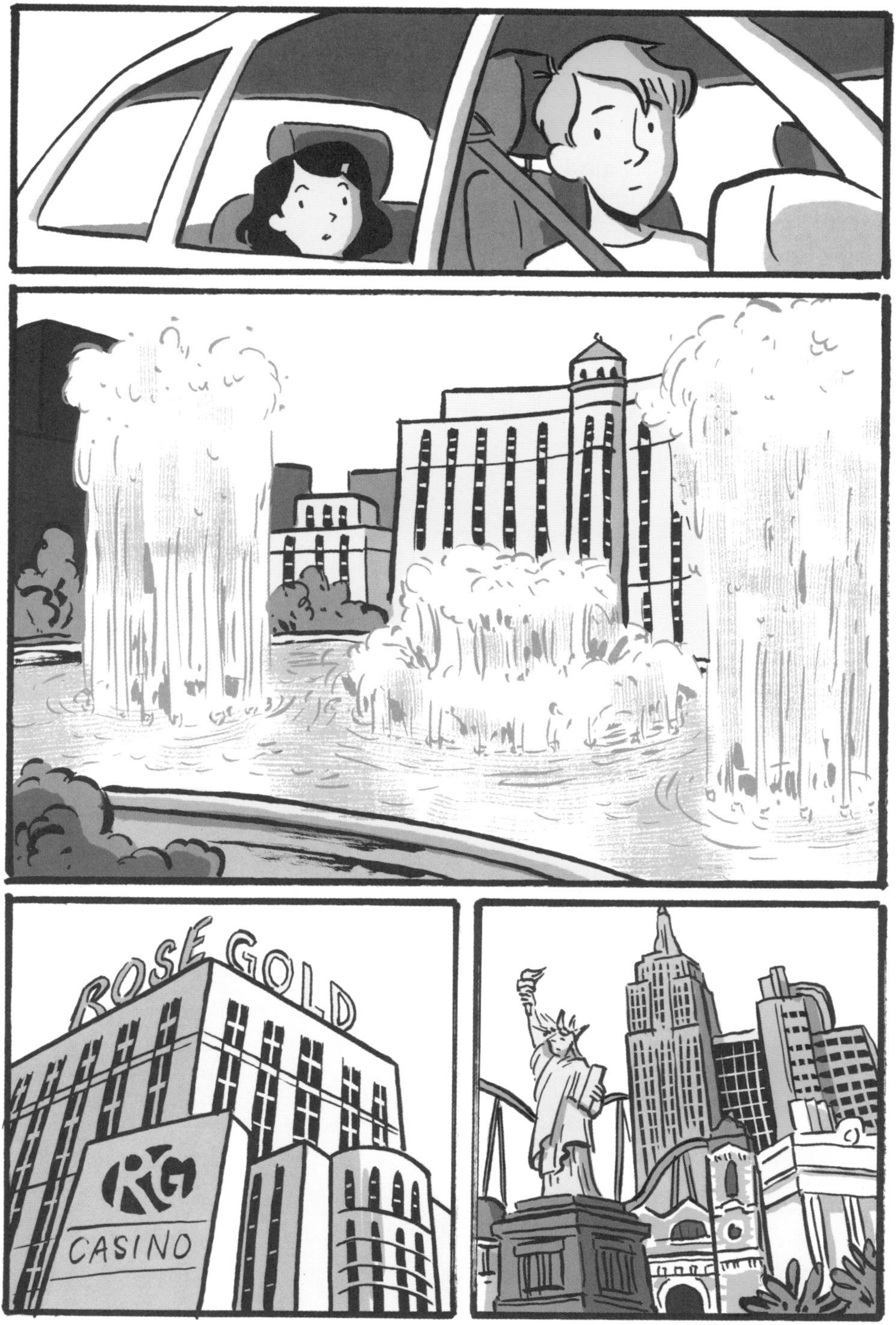
ROSE GOLD
RG
CASINO

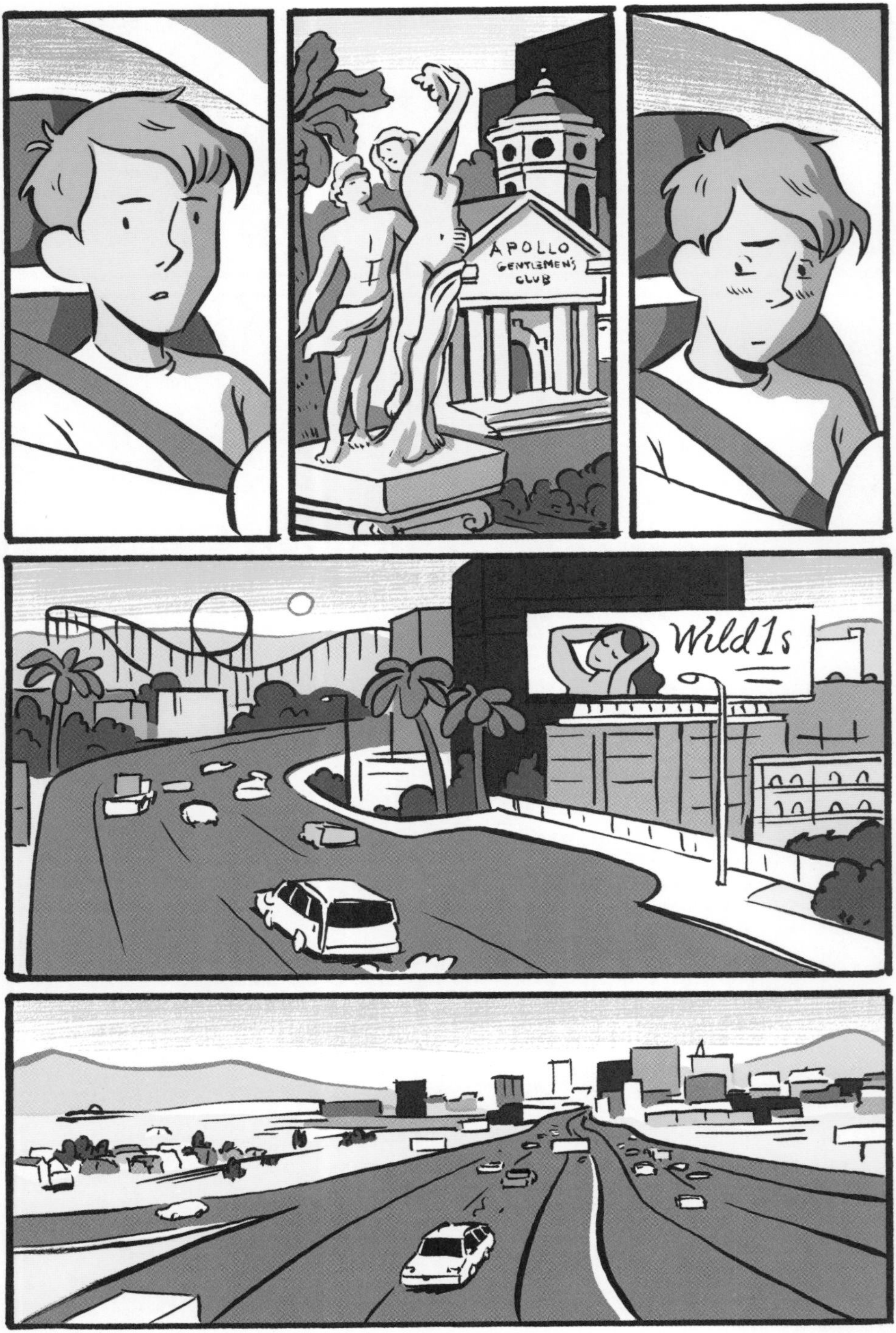
APOLLO
GENTLEMEN'S
CLUB
Wild1s

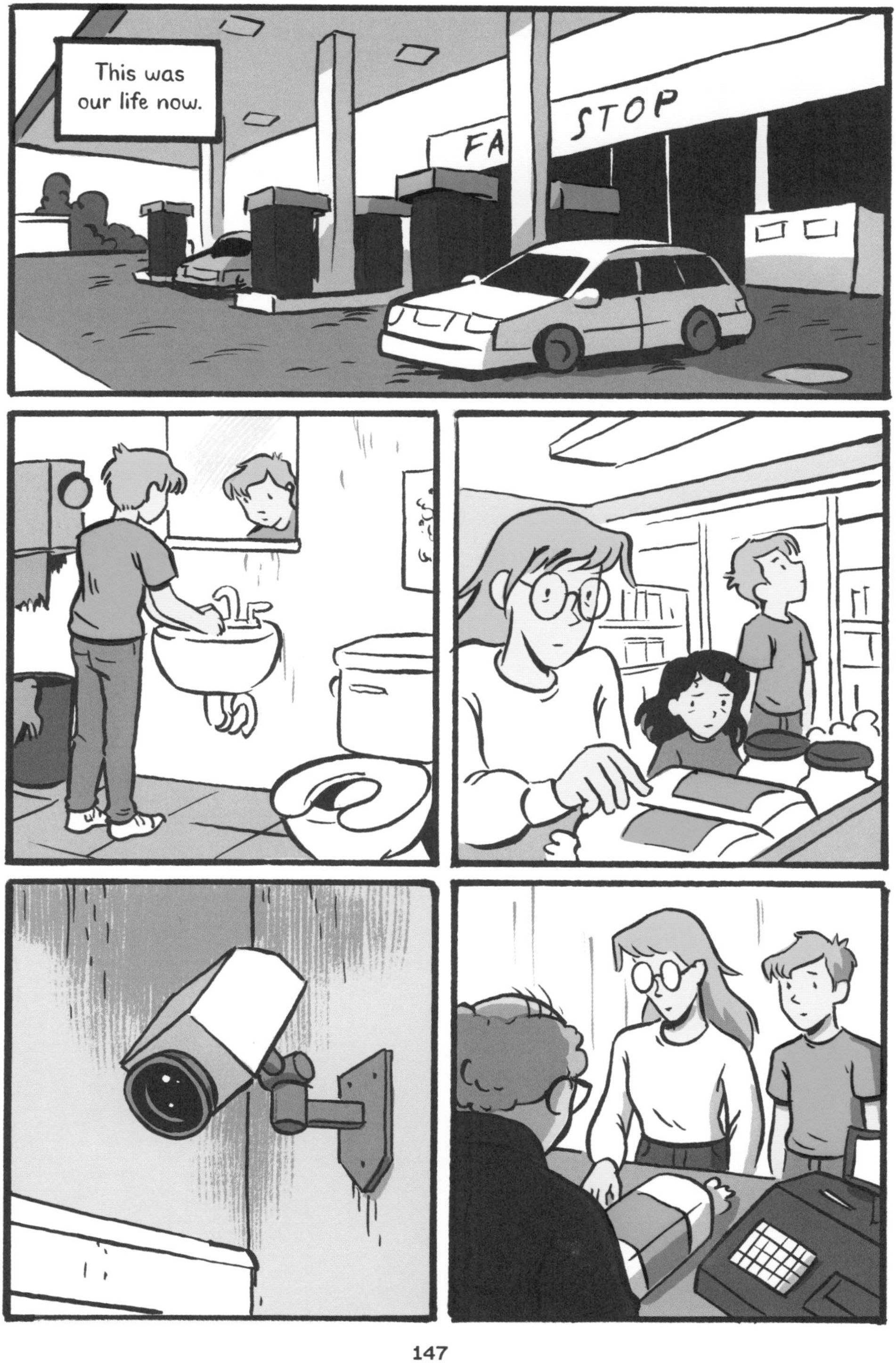
This was our life now.
FA STOP

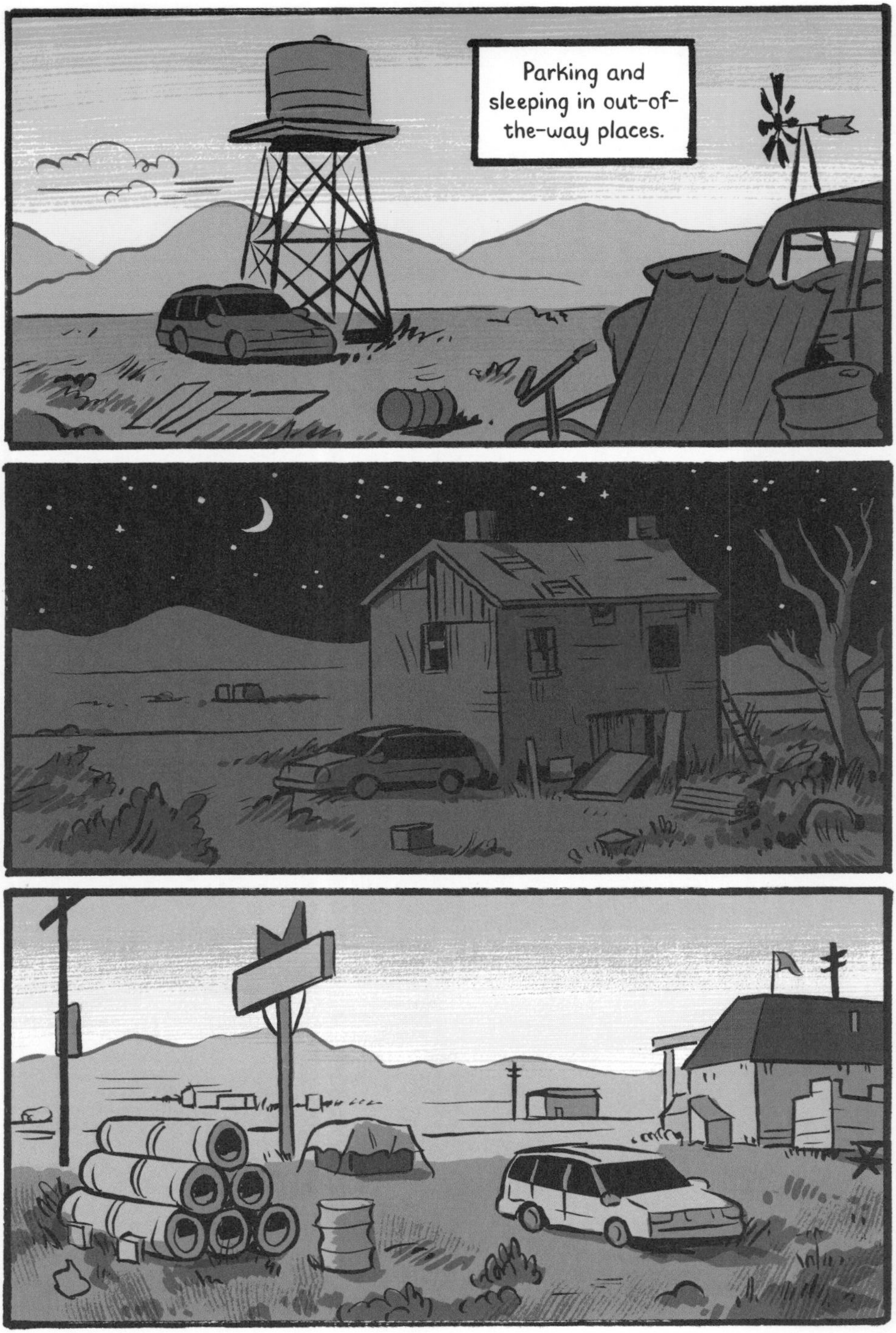
Parking and sleeping in out-of-the-way places.

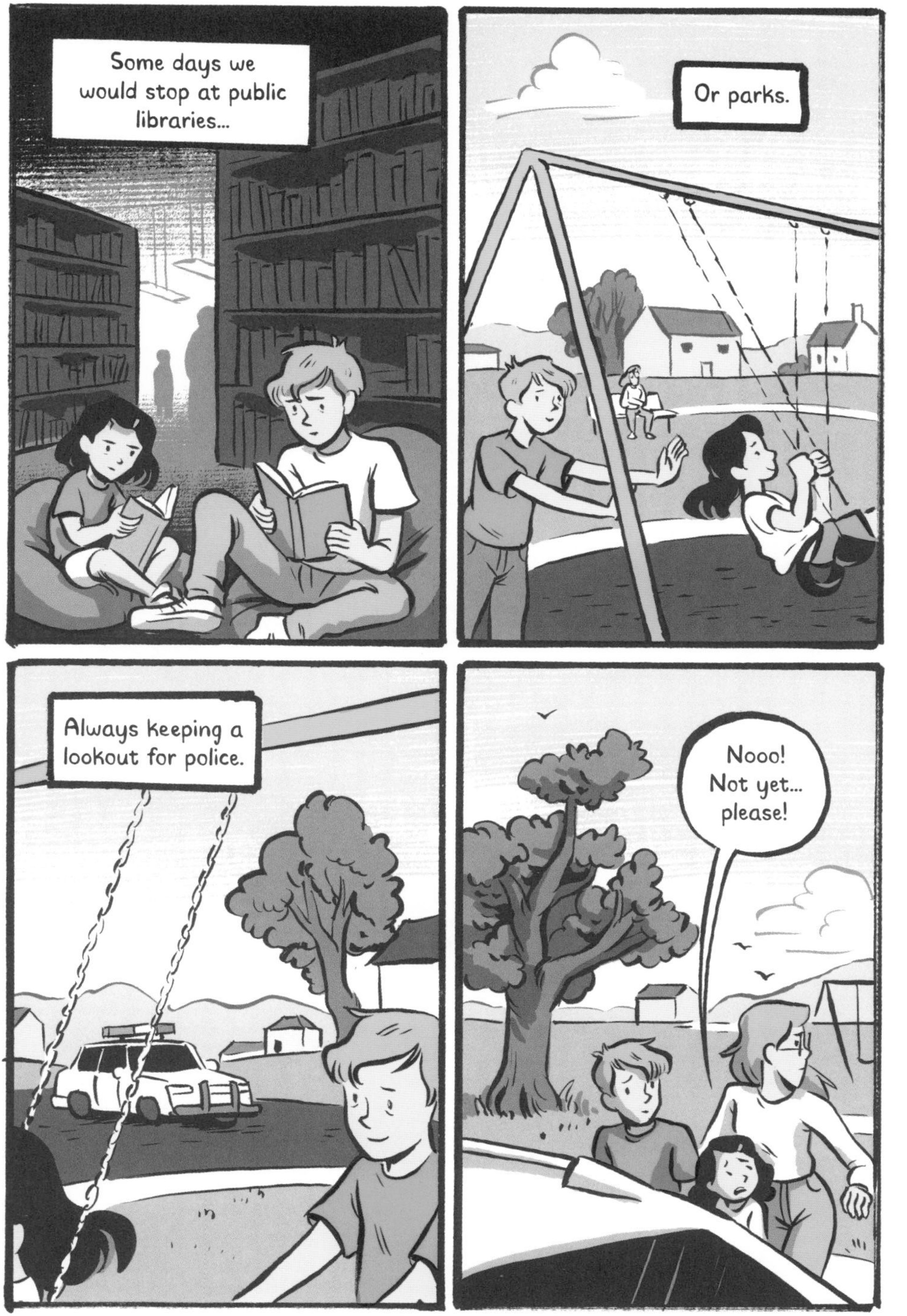
Some days we would stop at public libraries...
Or parks.
Always keeping a lookout for police.
Nooo! Not yet... please!

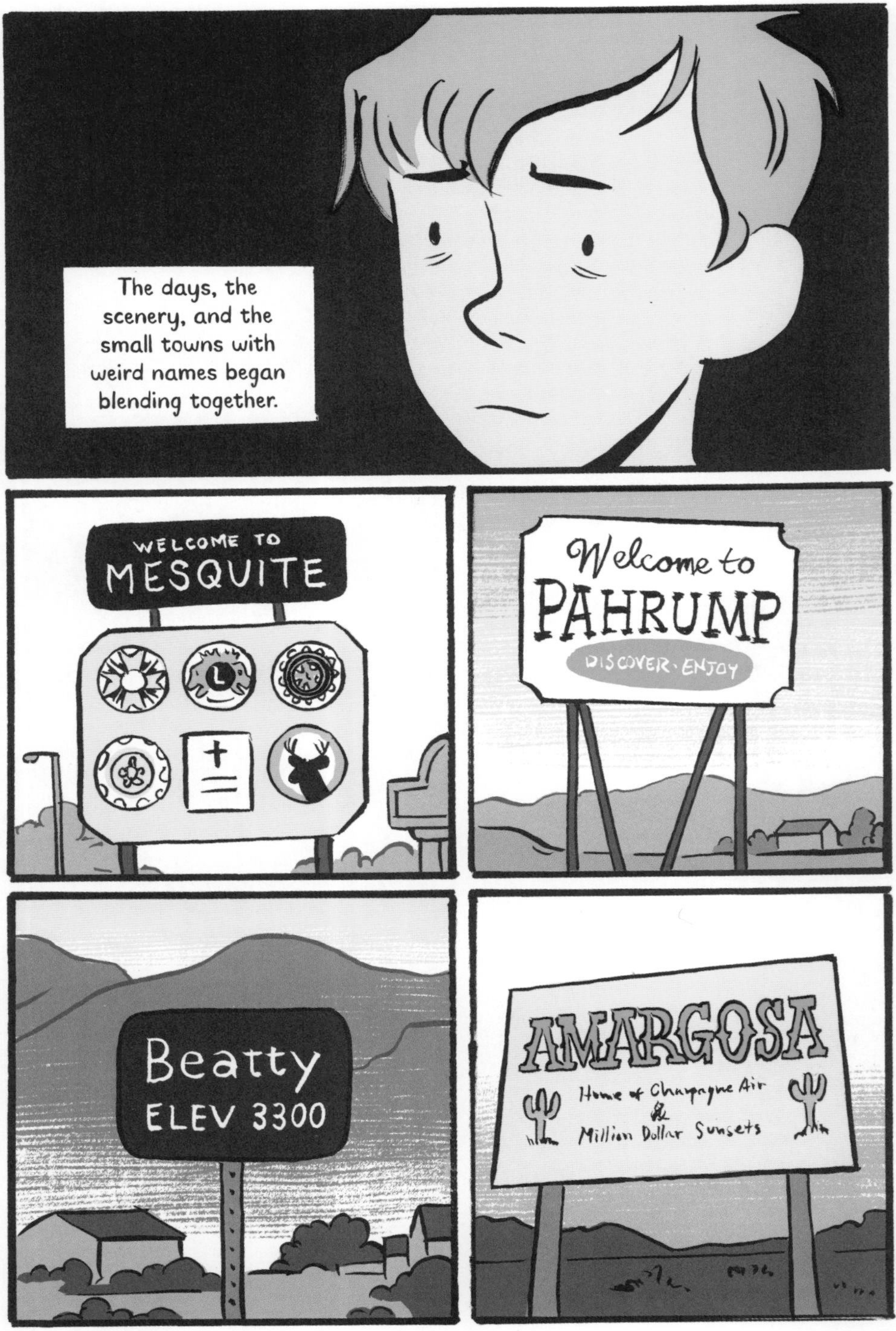
The days, the scenery, and the small towns with weird names began blending together.
WELCOME TO
MESQUITE
Welcome to
PAHRUMP
DISCOVER · ENJOY
Beatty
ELEV 3300
AMARGOSA
Home of Champagne Air
&
Million Dollar Sunsets

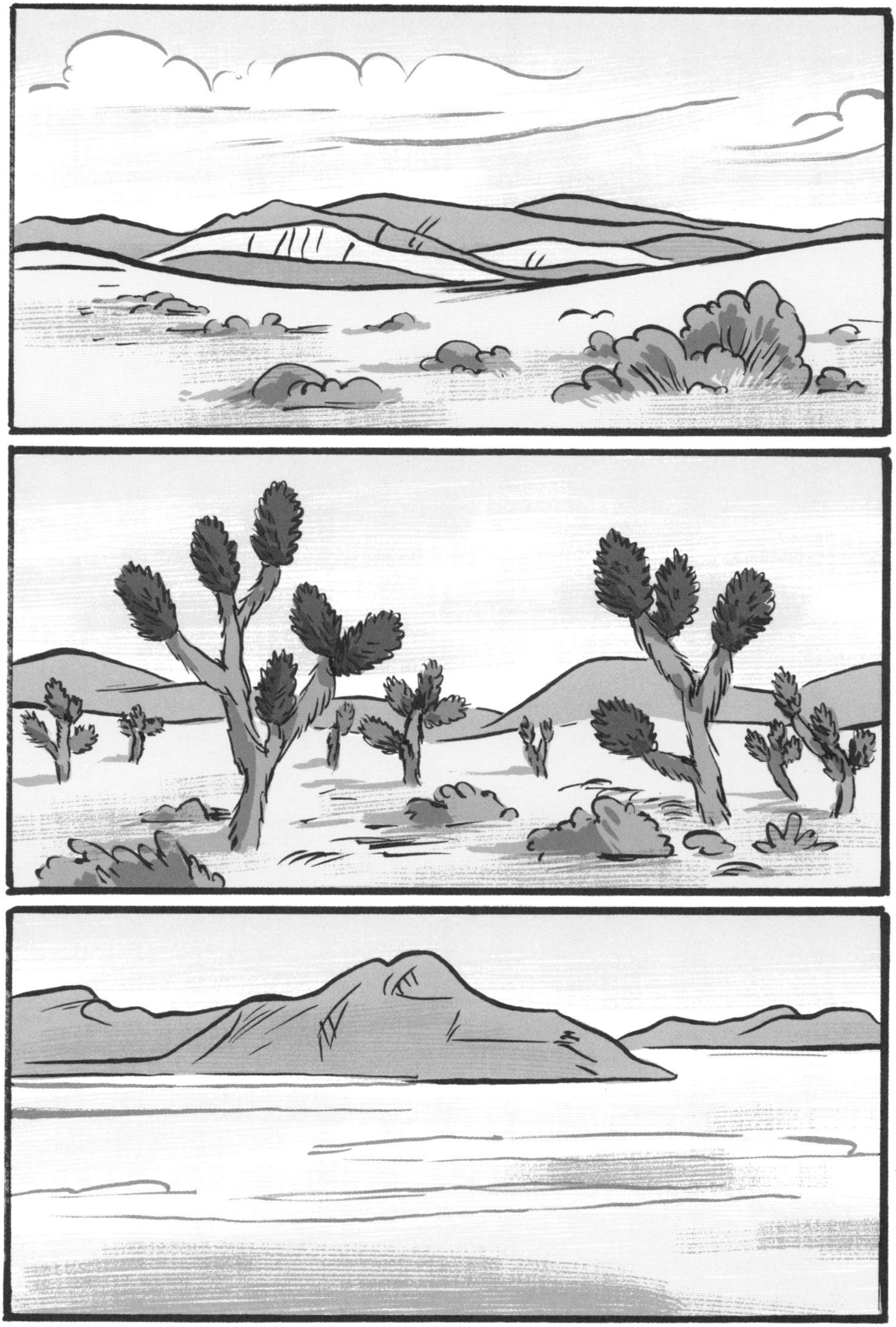

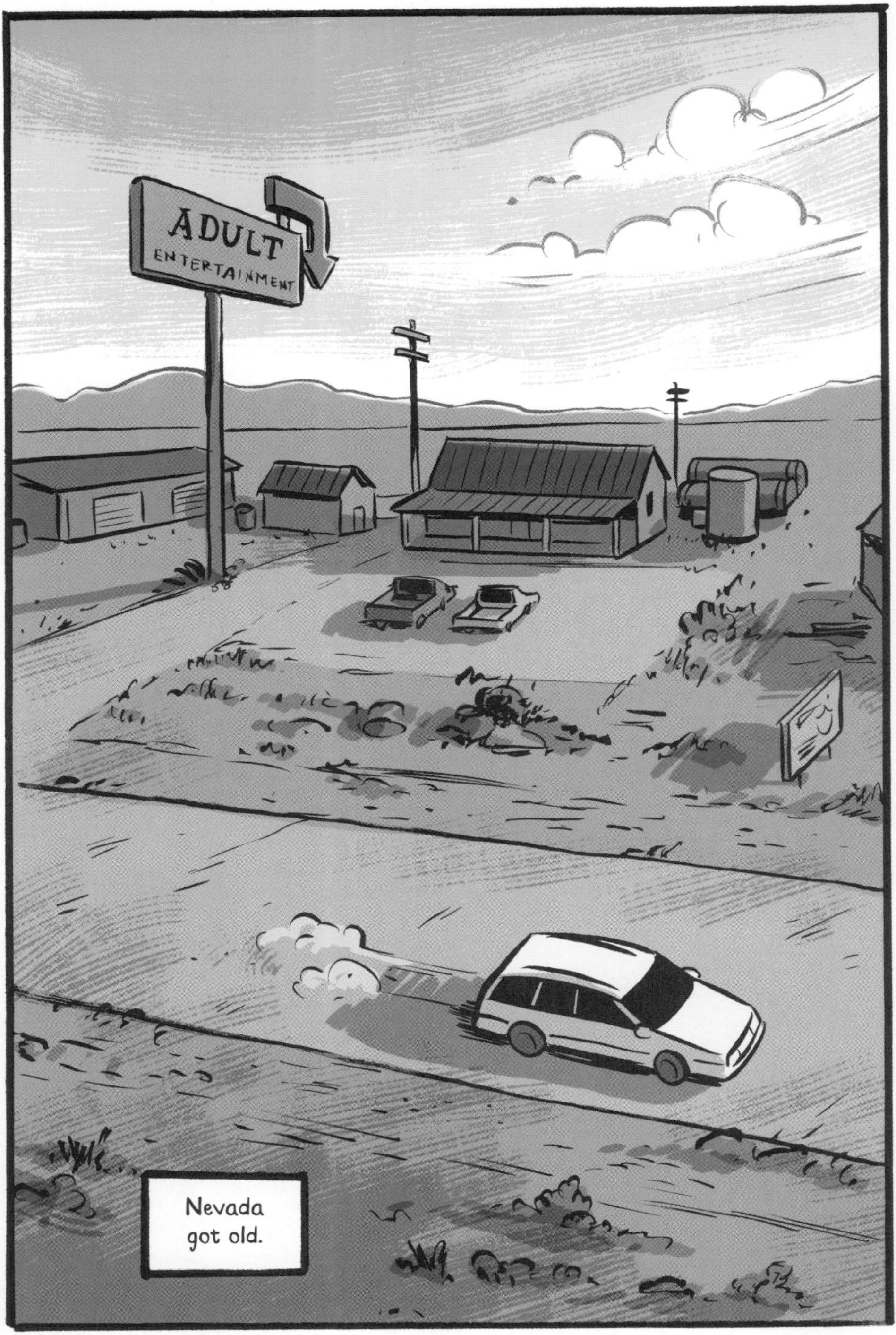
ADULT
ENTERTAINMENT
Nevada
got old.

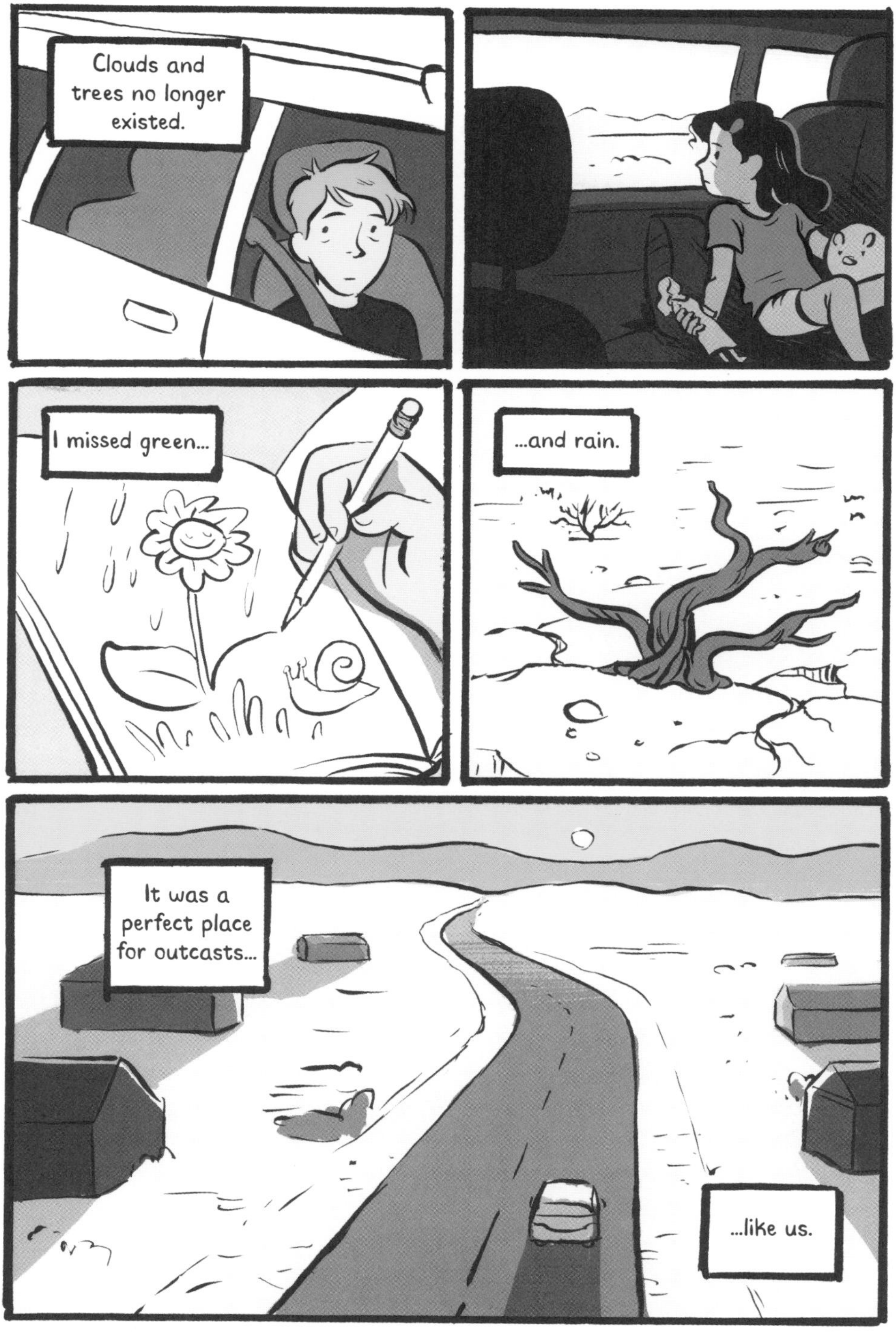
Clouds and trees no longer existed.
I missed green...
...and rain.
It was a perfect place for outcasts...
...like us.

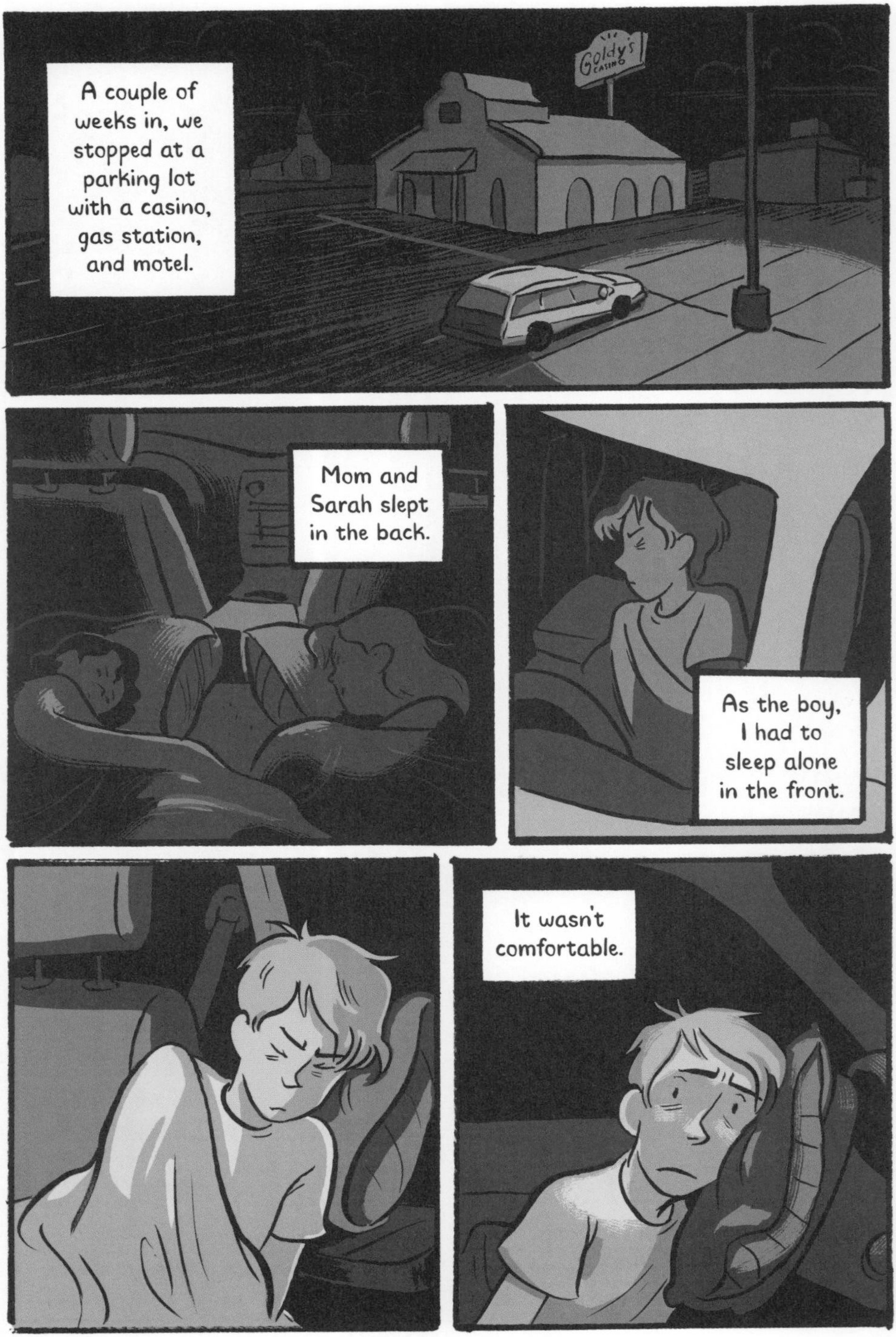
A couple of weeks in, we stopped at a parking lot with a casino, gas station, and motel.
Goldy's CASINO
Mom and Sarah slept in the back.
As the boy, I had to sleep alone in the front.
It wasn't comfortable.

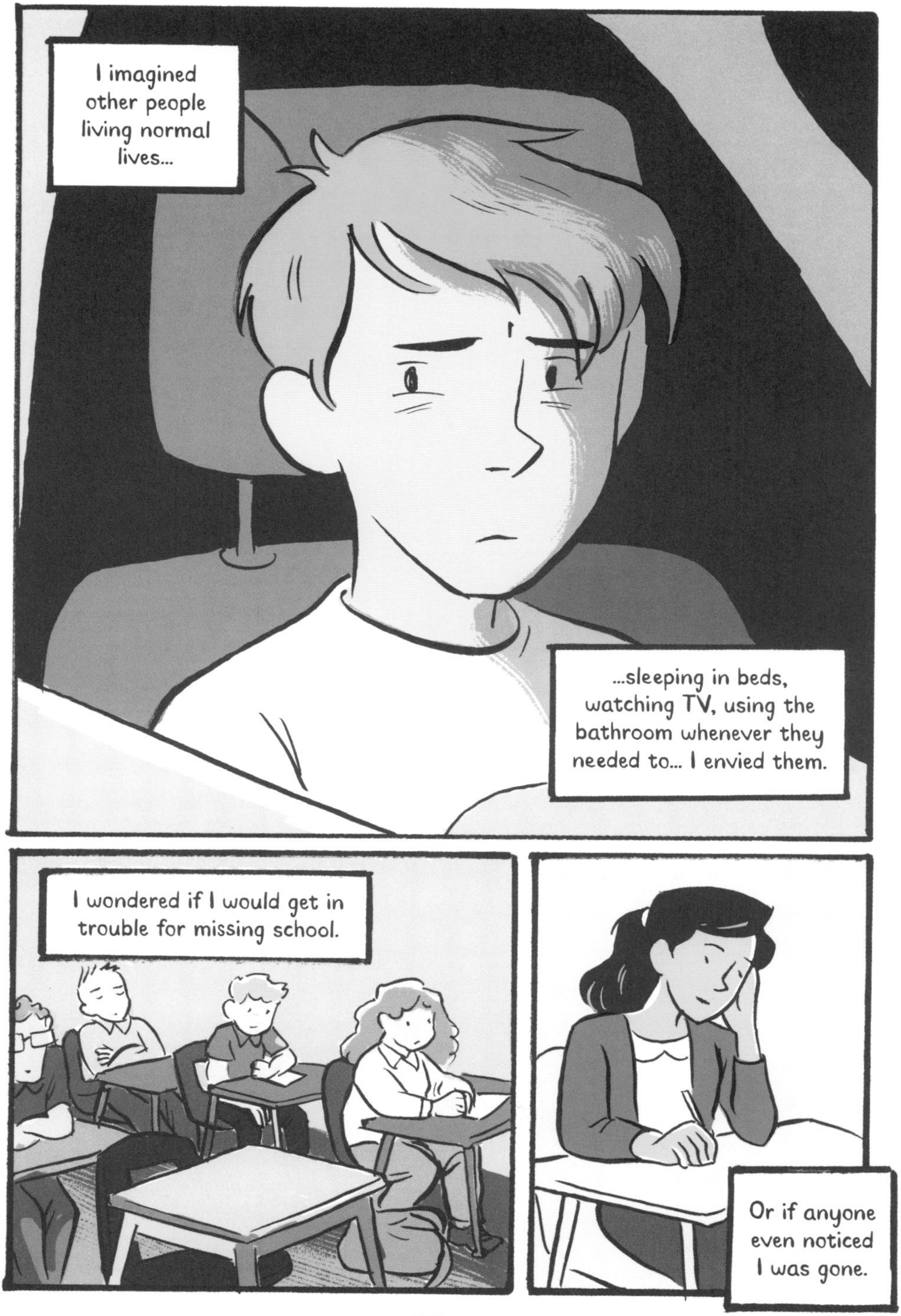
I imagined other people living normal lives...
...sleeping in beds, watching TV, using the bathroom whenever they needed to... I envied them.
I wondered if I would get in trouble for missing school.
Or if anyone even noticed I was gone.

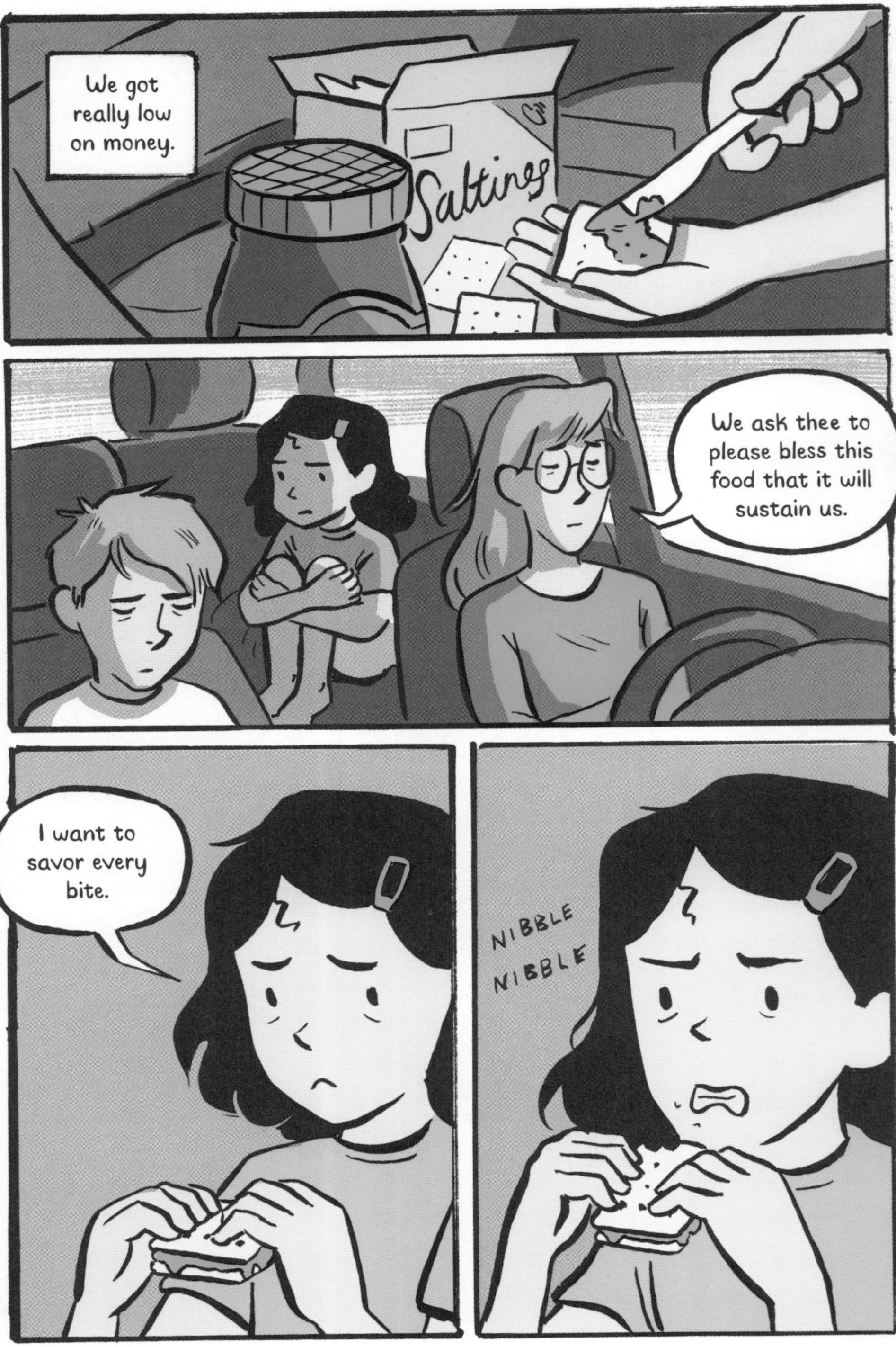
We got really low on money.
Saltines
We ask thee to please bless this food that it will sustain us.
I want to savor every bite.
NIBBLE NIBBLE

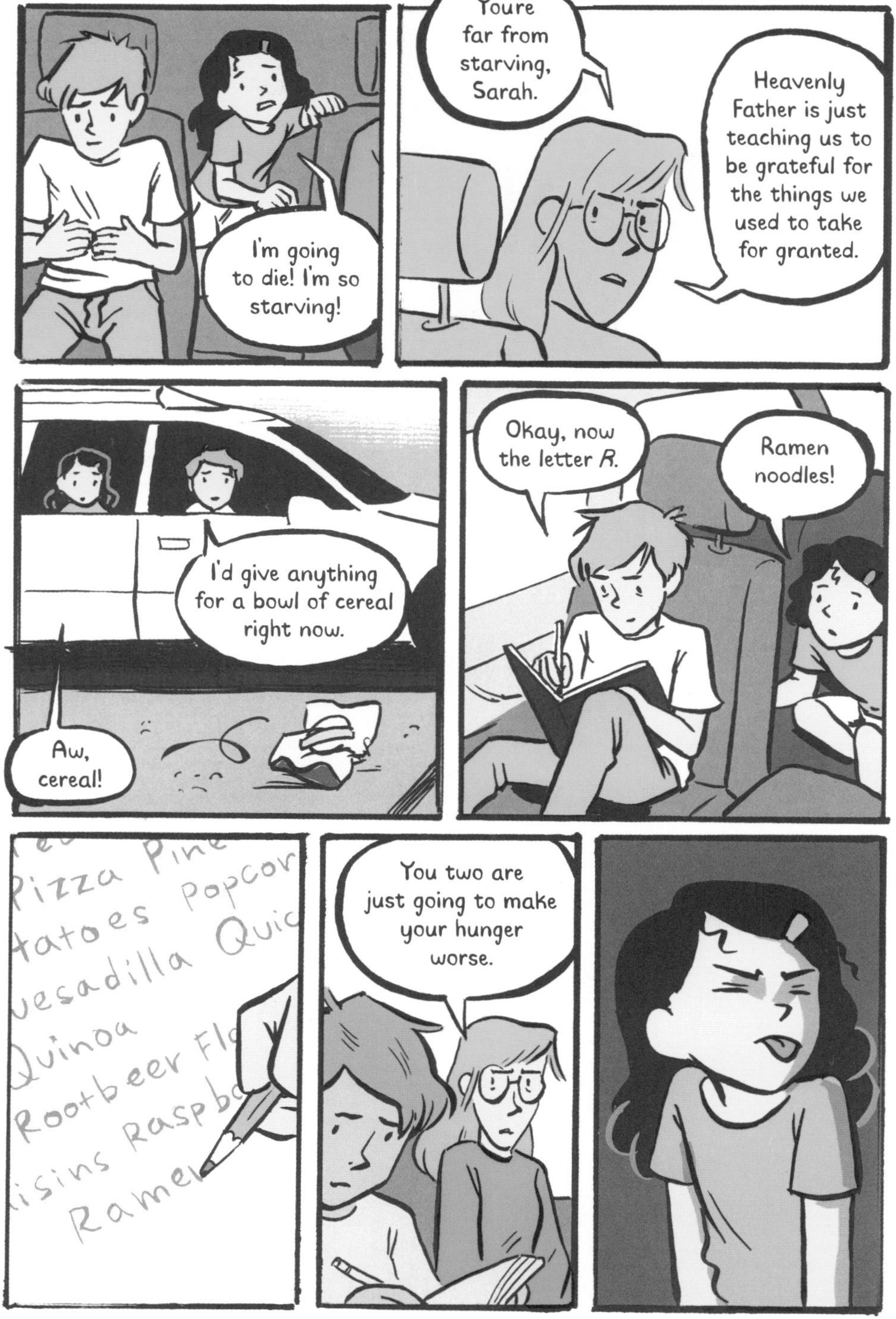
I'm going to die! I'm so starving!
You're far from starving, Sarah.
Heavenly Father is just teaching us to be grateful for the things we used to take for granted.
I'd give anything for a bowl of cereal right now.
Aw, cereal!
Okay, now the letter *R*.
Ramen noodles!
Pizza Pine
tatoes Popcor
uesadilla Quic
Quinoa
Rootbeer Flo
isins Raspb
Ramen
You two are just going to make your hunger worse.

My pants got real loose, and I developed rashes.

Turns out weeks without showering makes you incredibly itchy.

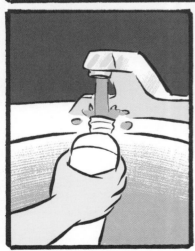

What are you doing?

Trying to wash my hair.

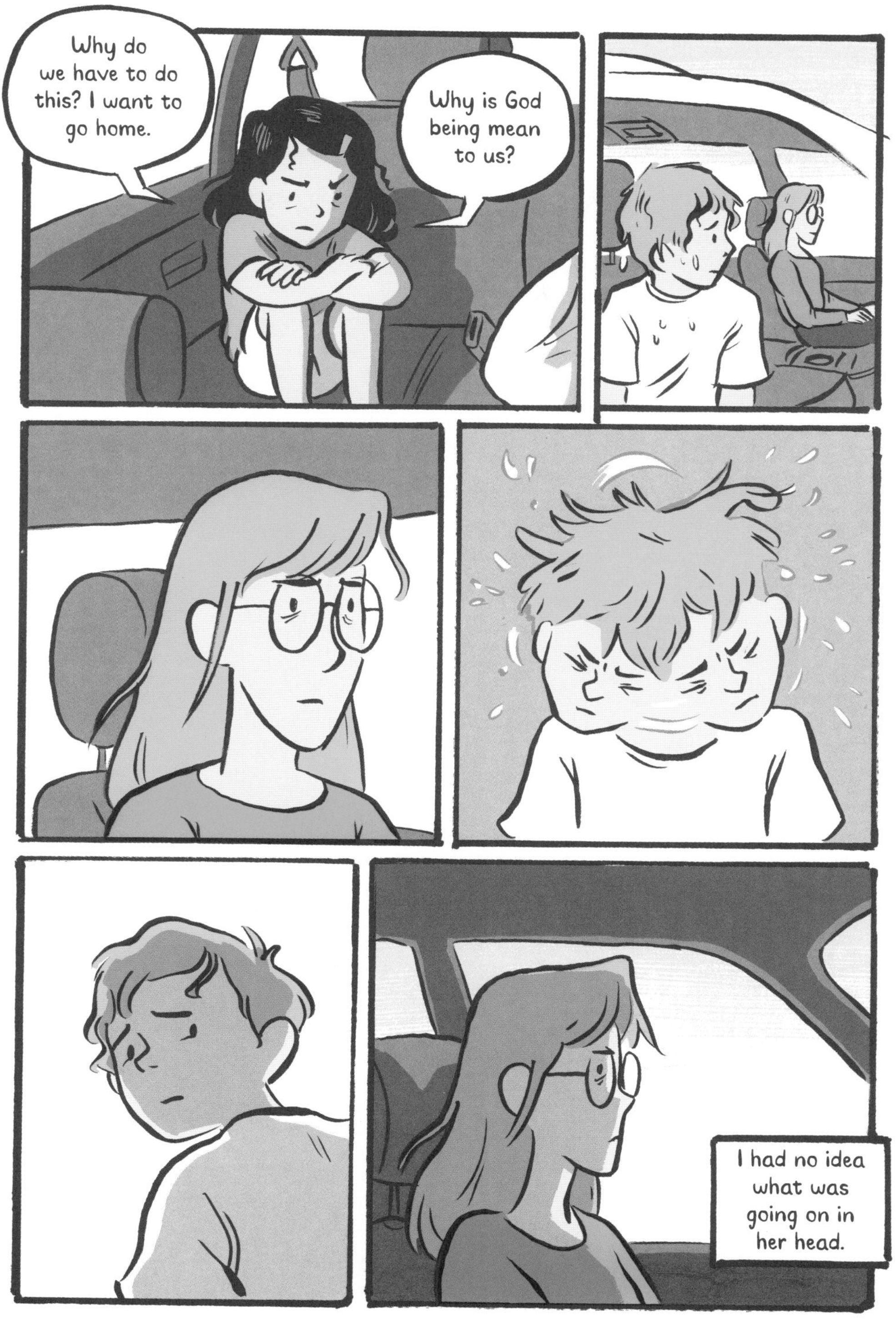
Why do we have to do this? I want to go home.
Why is God being mean to us?
I had no idea what was going on in her head.

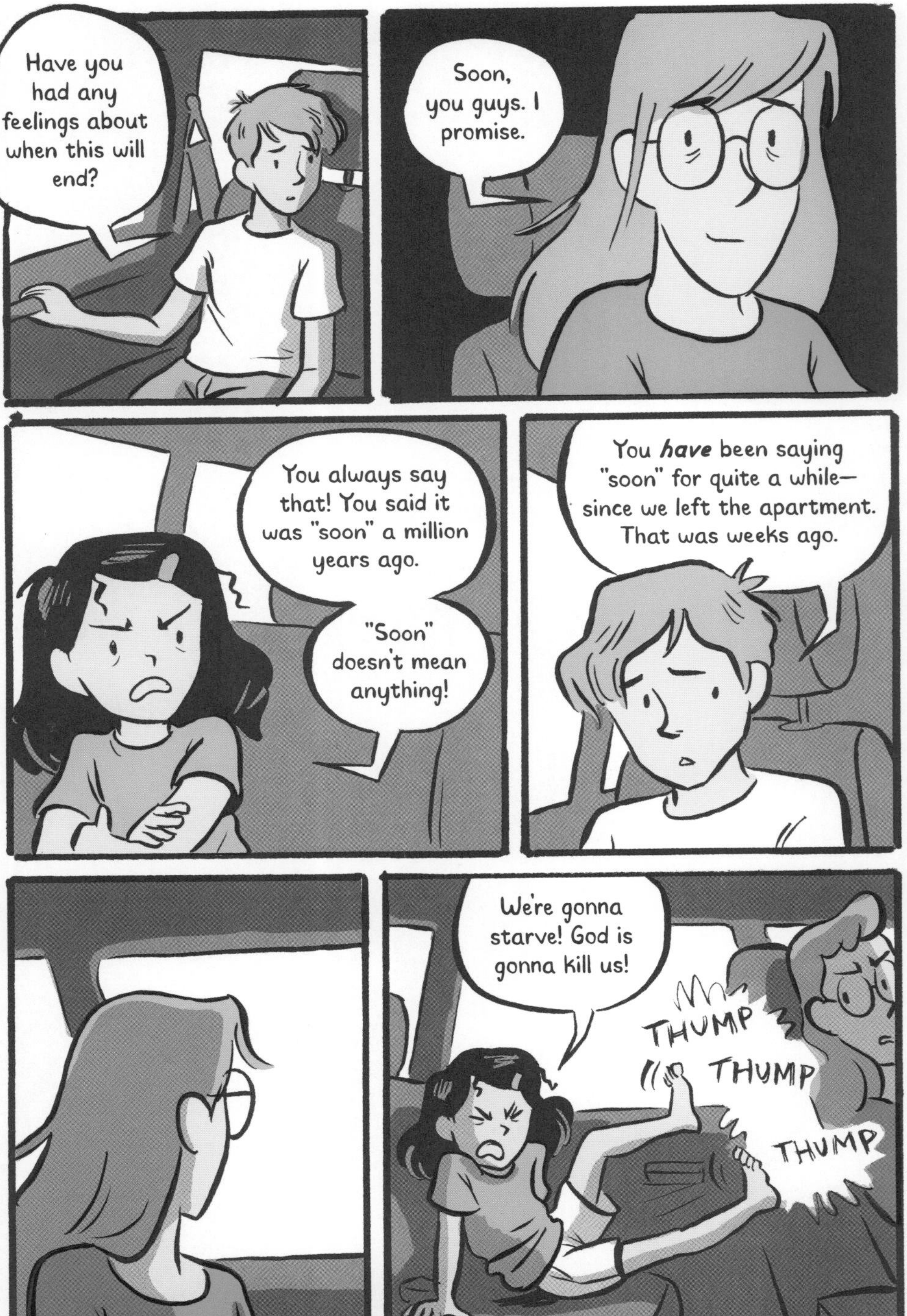

Have you had any feelings about when this will end?
Soon, you guys. I promise.
You always say that! You said it was "soon" a million years ago.
"Soon" doesn't mean anything!
You **have** been saying "soon" for quite a while— since we left the apartment. That was weeks ago.
We're gonna starve! God is gonna kill us!
THUMP
THUMP
THUMP

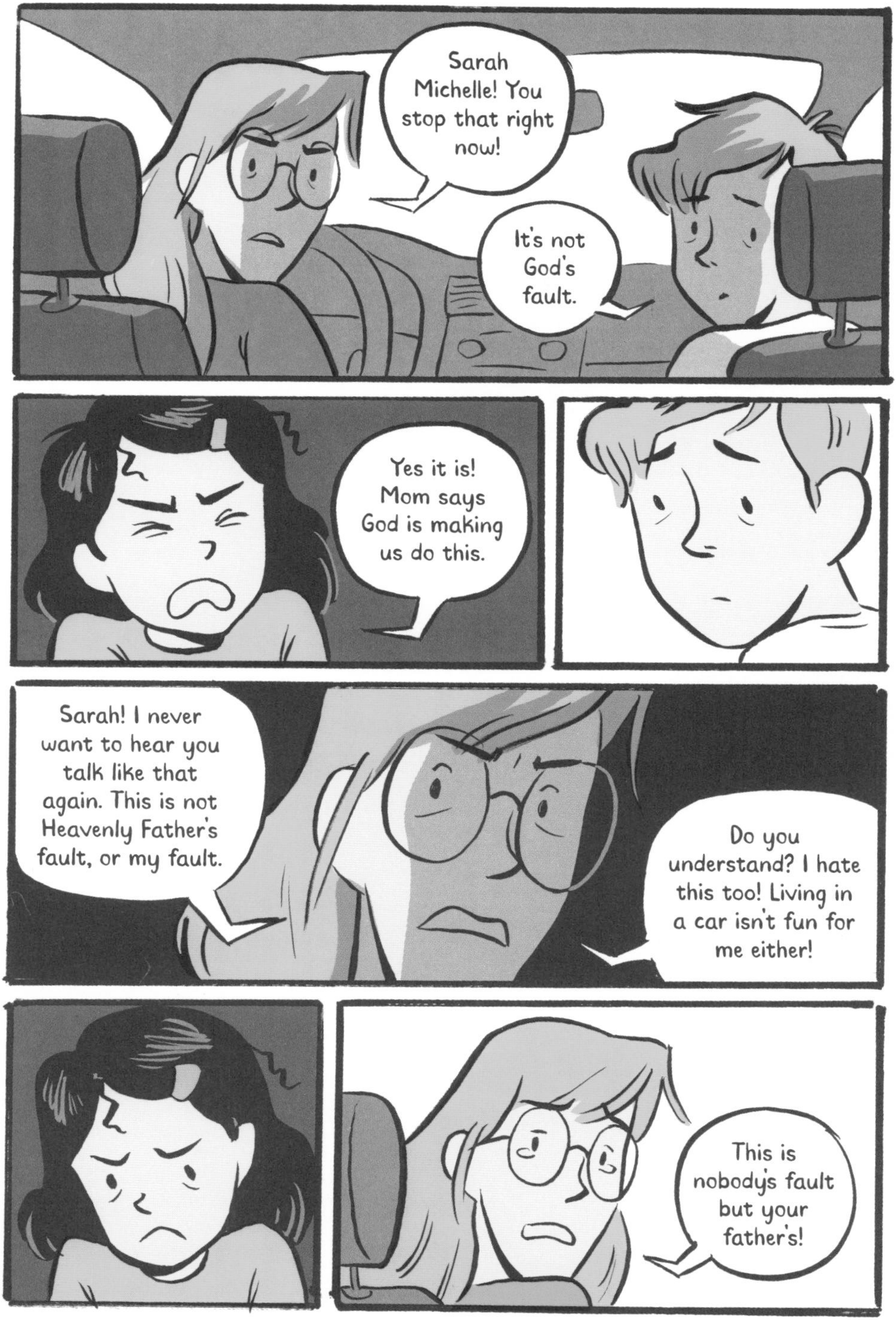

Sarah Michelle! You stop that right now!
It's not God's fault.
Yes it is! Mom says God is making us do this.
Sarah! I never want to hear you talk like that again. This is not Heavenly Father's fault, or my fault.
Do you understand? I hate this too! Living in a car isn't fun for me either!
This is nobody's fault but your father's!

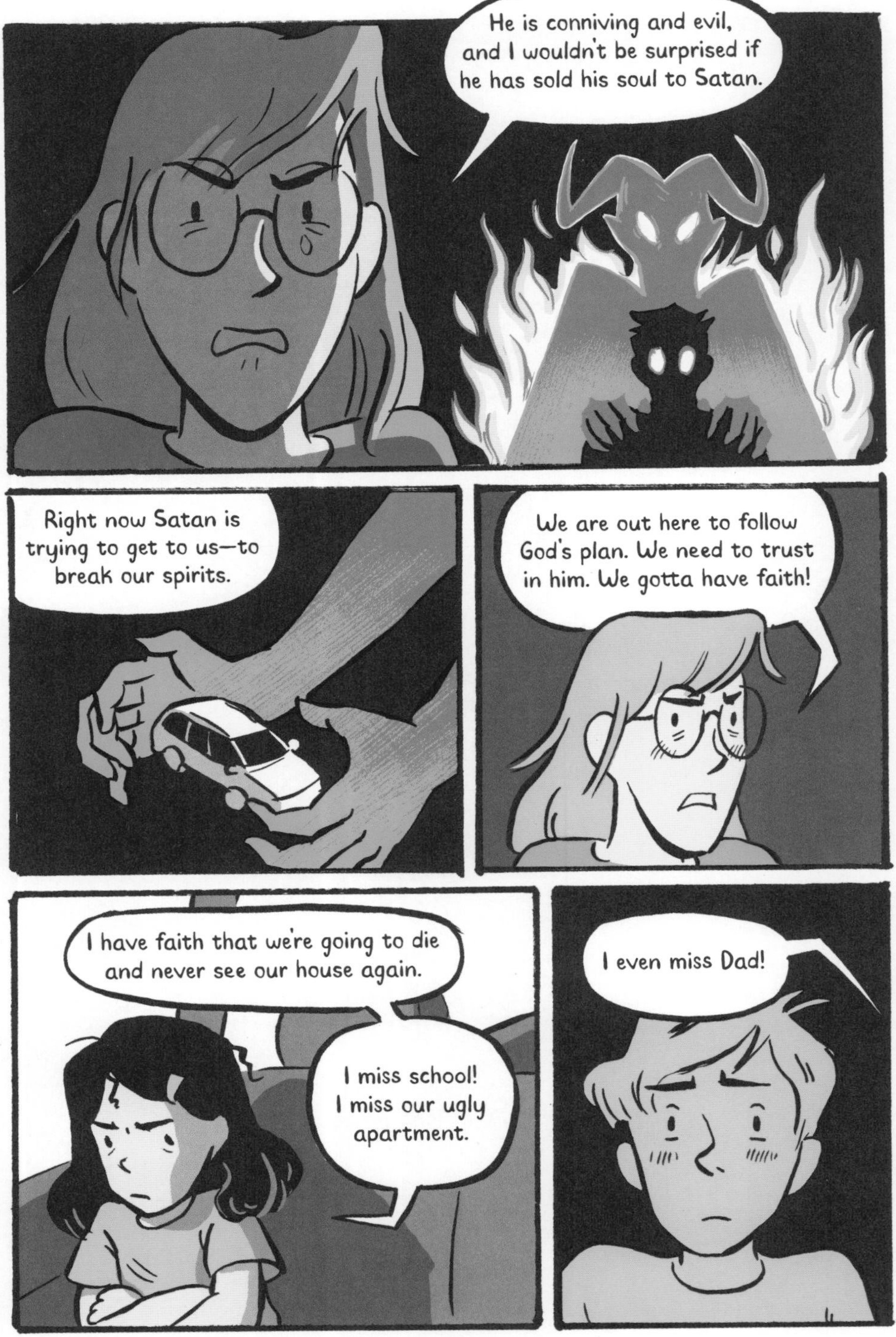
He is conniving and evil, and I wouldn't be surprised if he has sold his soul to Satan.
Right now Satan is trying to get to us—to break our spirits.
We are out here to follow God's plan. We need to trust in him. We gotta have faith!
I have faith that we're going to die and never see our house again.
I miss school! I miss our ugly apartment.
I even miss Dad!

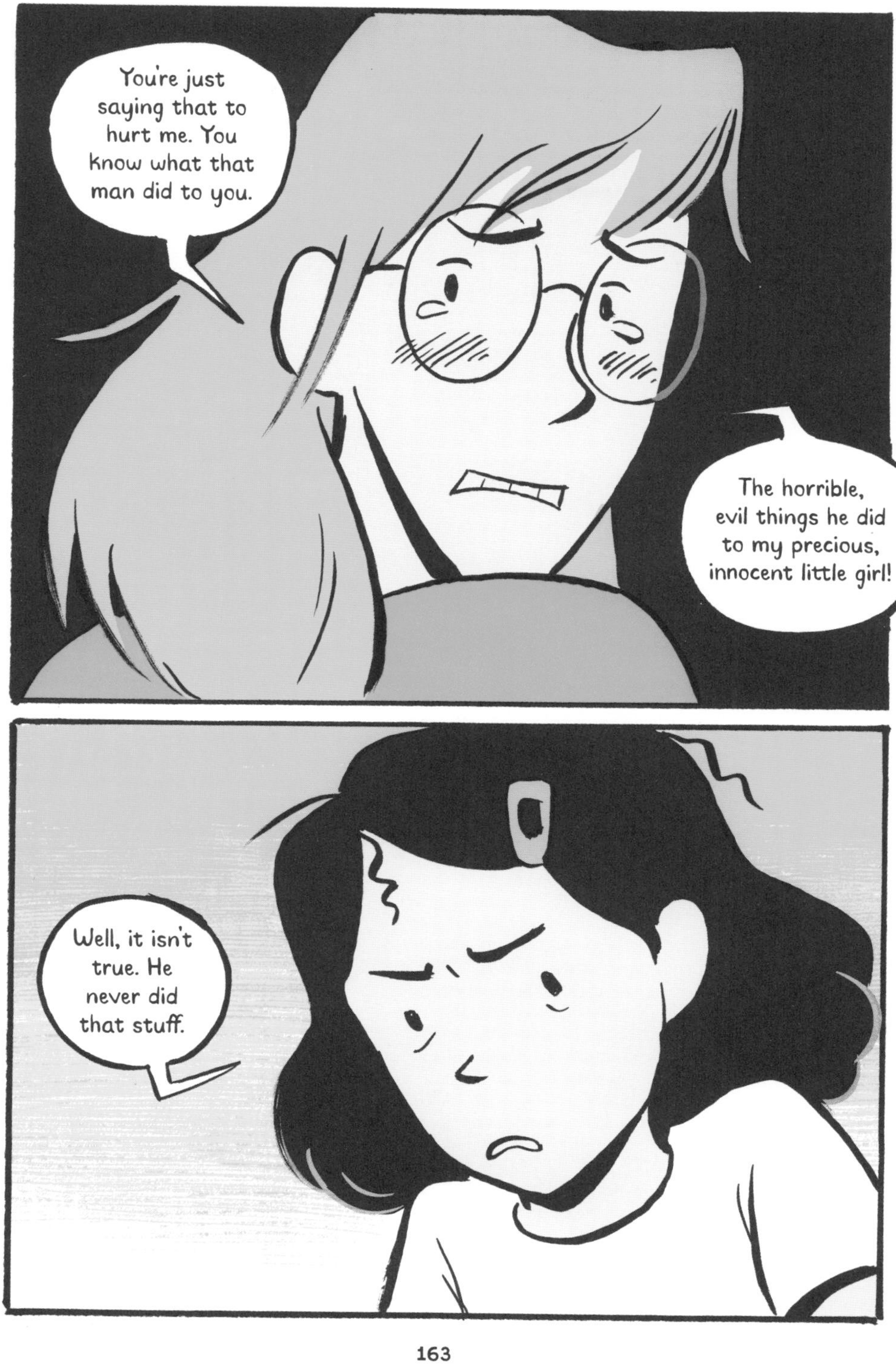
You're just saying that to hurt me. You know what that man did to you.
The horrible, evil things he did to my precious, innocent little girl!
Well, it isn't true. He never did that stuff.

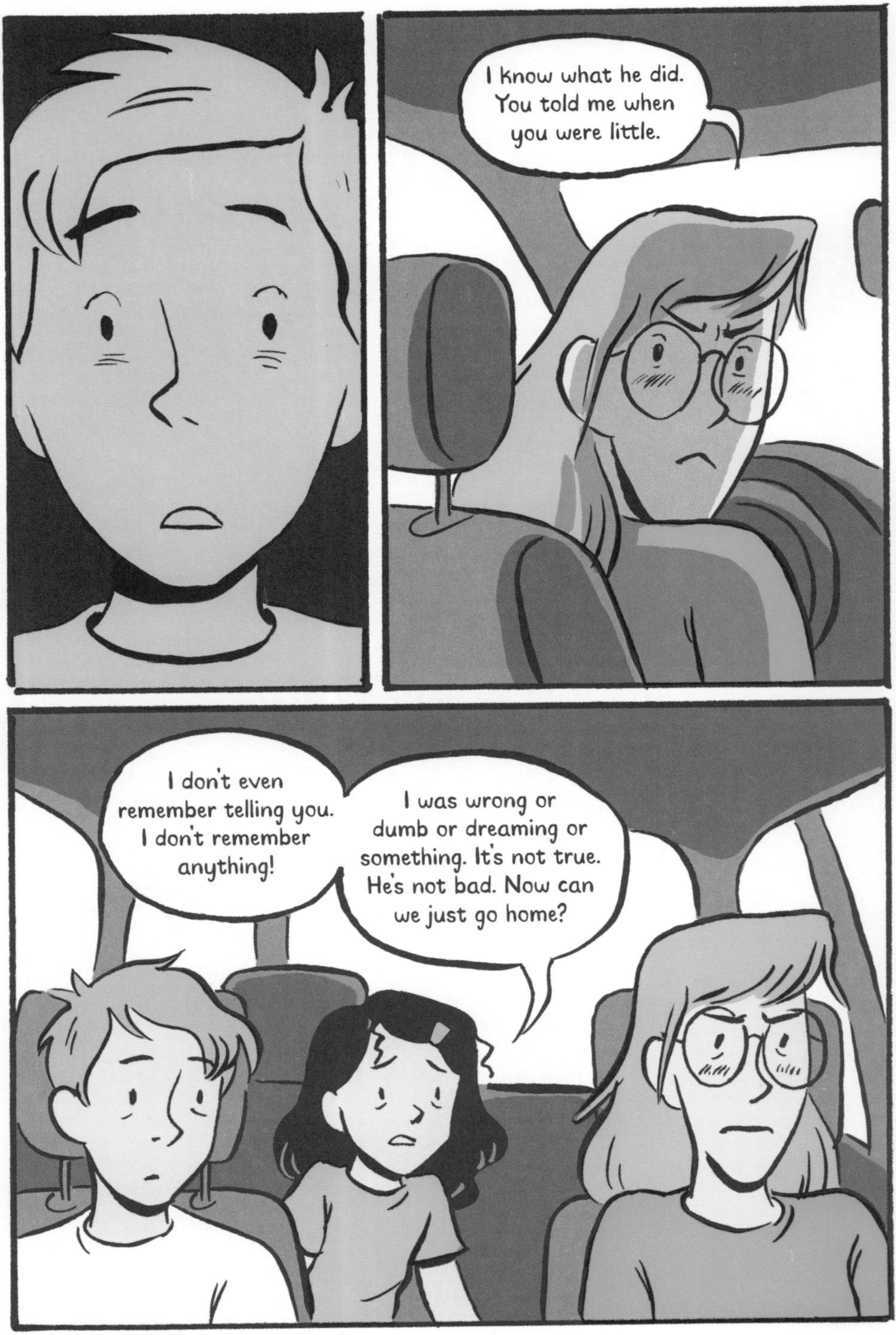
I know what he did. You told me when you were little.
I don't even remember telling you. I don't remember anything!
I was wrong or dumb or dreaming or something. It's not true. He's not bad. Now can we just go home?

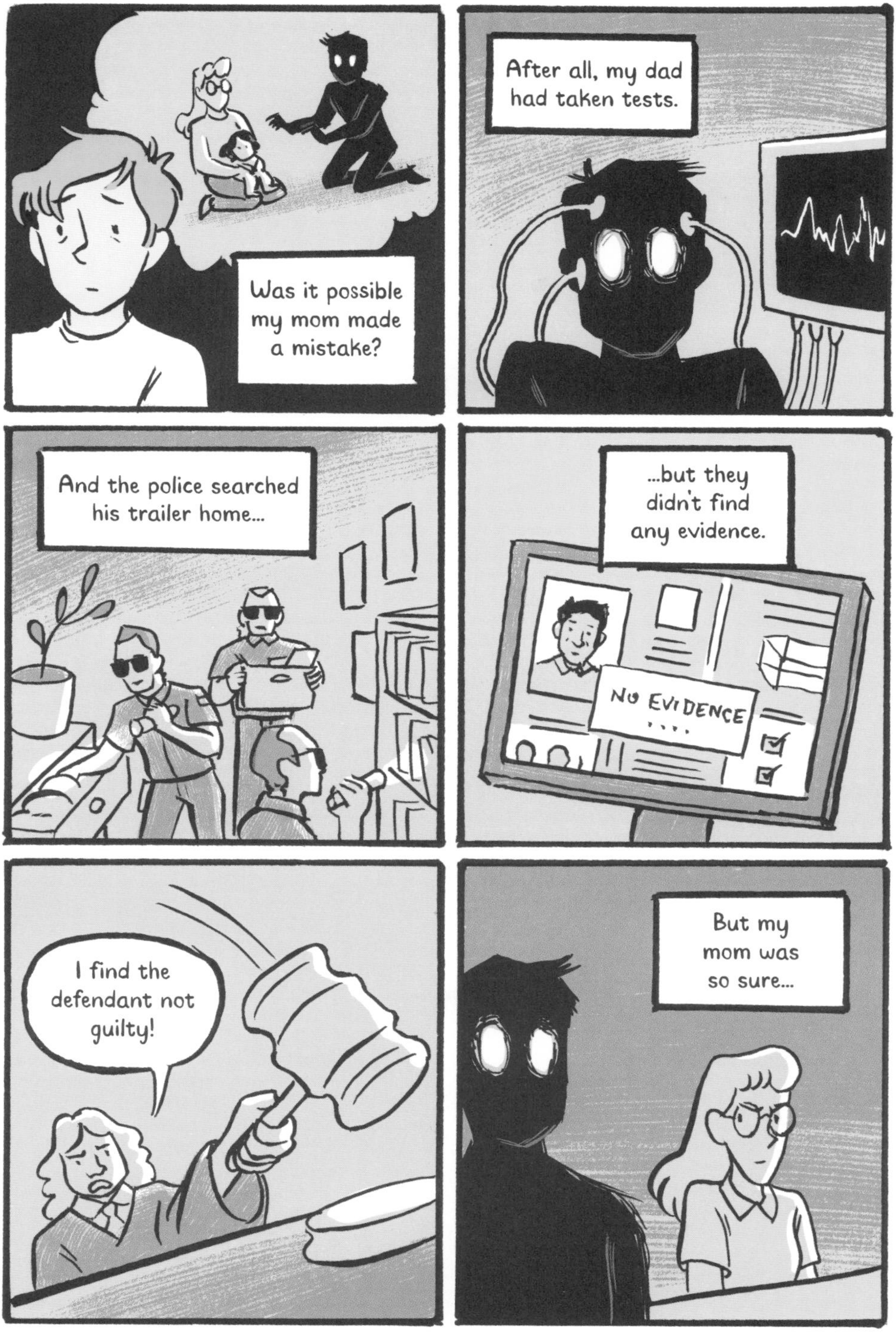
Was it possible my mom made a mistake?
After all, my dad had taken tests.
And the police searched his trailer home...
...but they didn't find any evidence.
NO EVIDENCE ....
I find the defendant not guilty!
But my mom was so sure...

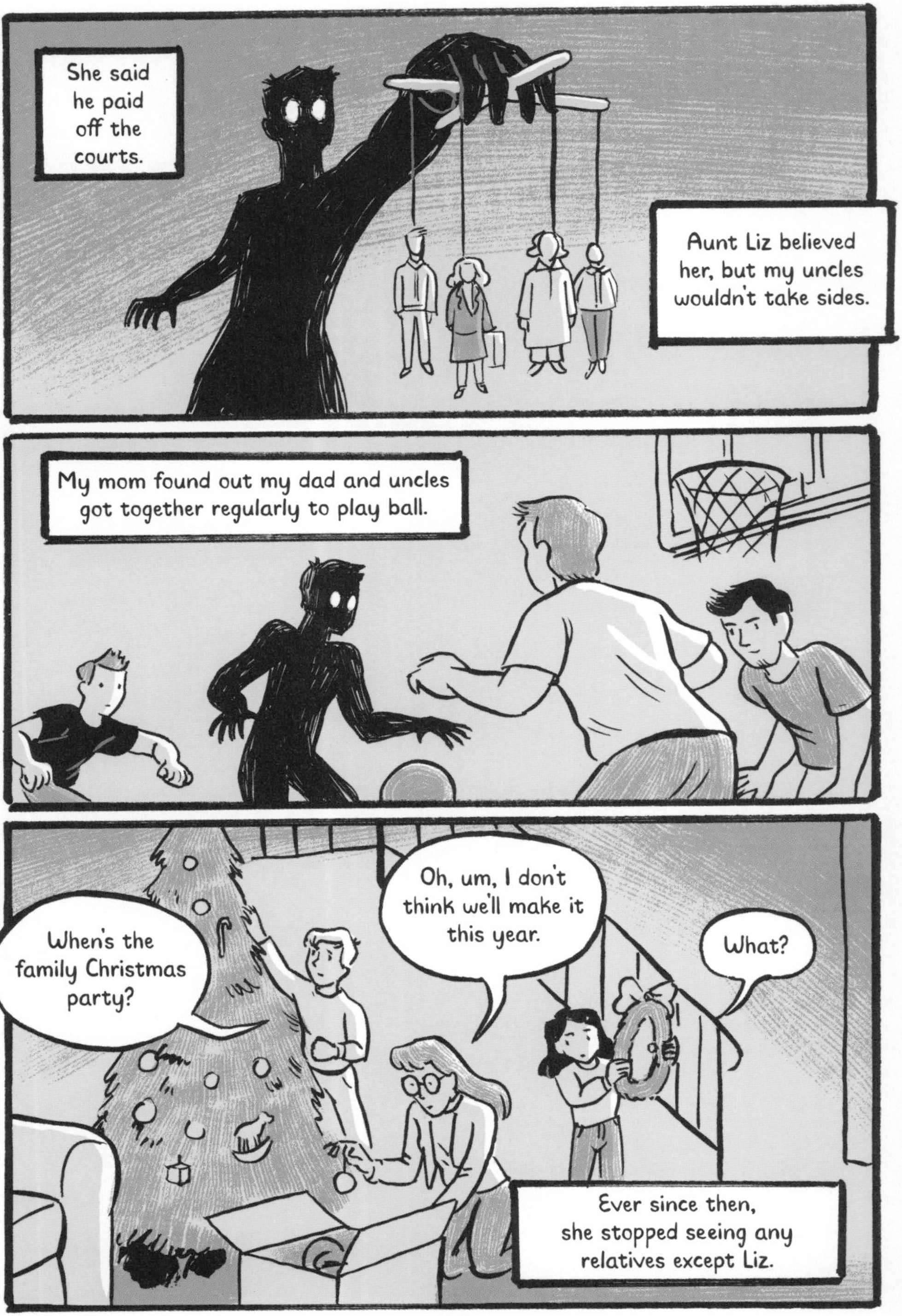
She said he paid off the courts.
Aunt Liz believed her, but my uncles wouldn't take sides.
My mom found out my dad and uncles got together regularly to play ball.
When's the family Christmas party?
Oh, um, I don't think we'll make it this year.
What?
Ever since then, she stopped seeing any relatives except Liz.

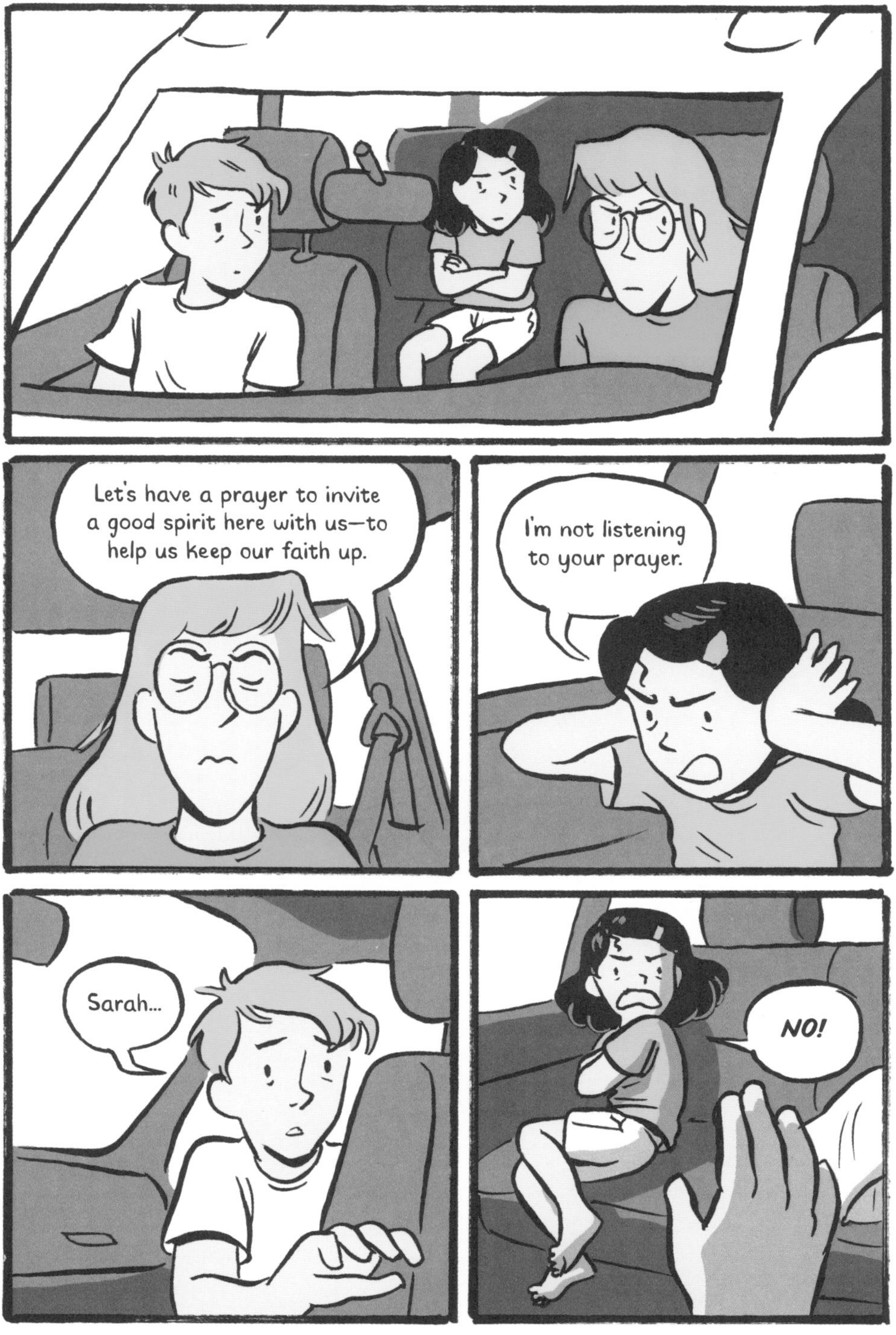
Let's have a prayer to invite a good spirit here with us—to help us keep our faith up.
I'm not listening to your prayer.
Sarah...
NO!

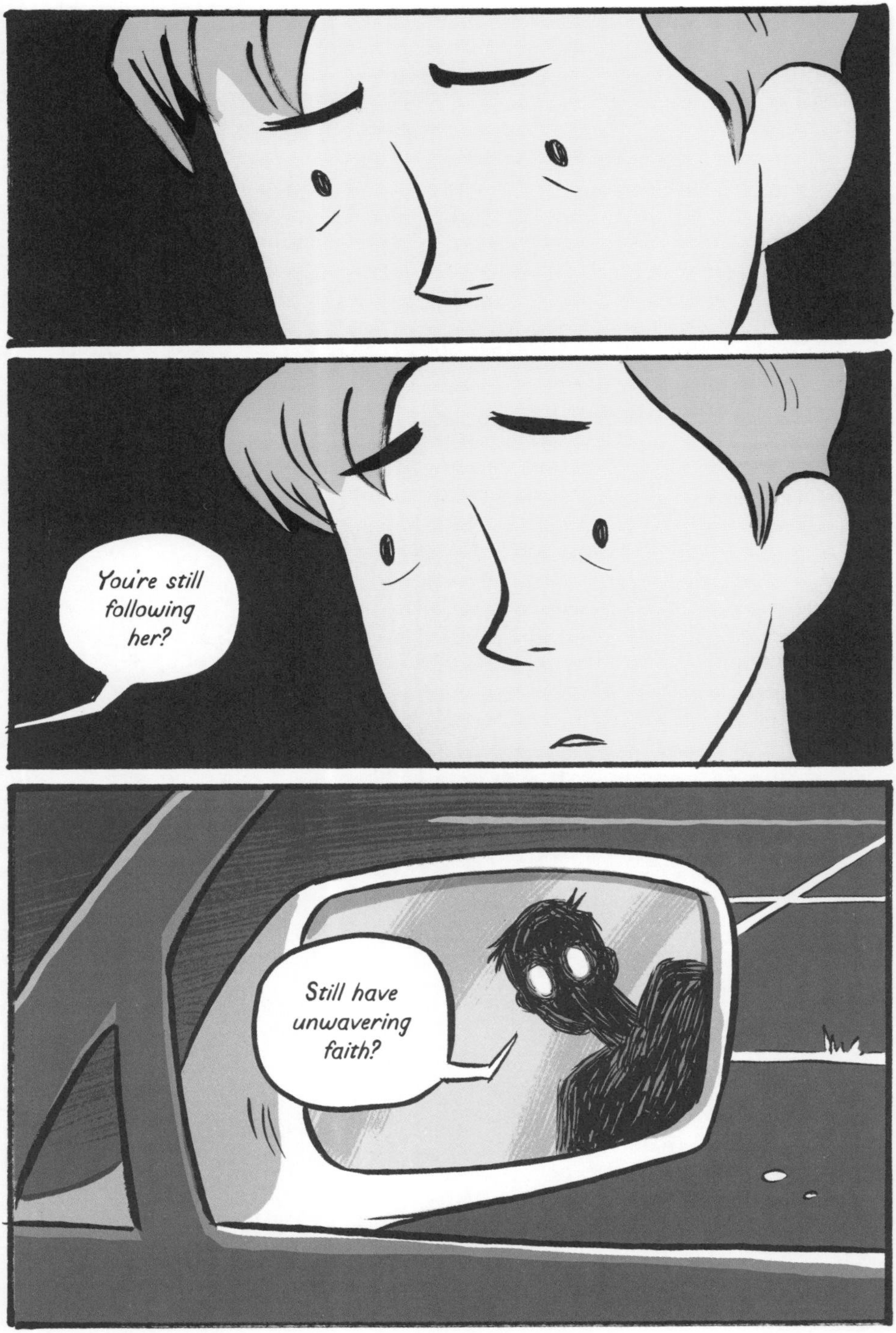
You're still following her?
Still have unwavering faith?

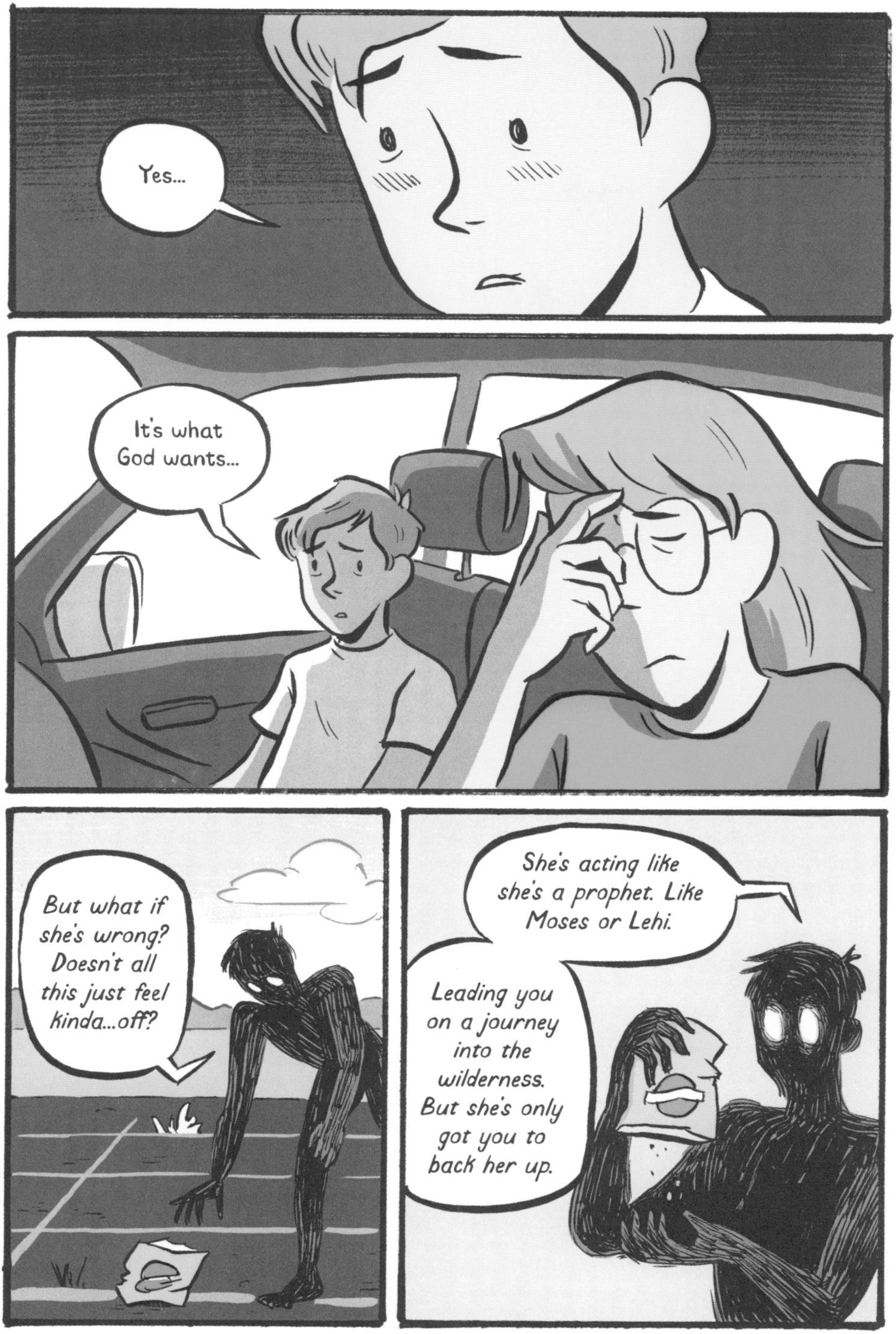
Yes...
It's what God wants...
But what if she's wrong? Doesn't all this just feel kinda...off?
She's acting like she's a prophet. Like Moses or Lehi.
Leading you on a journey into the wilderness. But she's only got you to back her up.

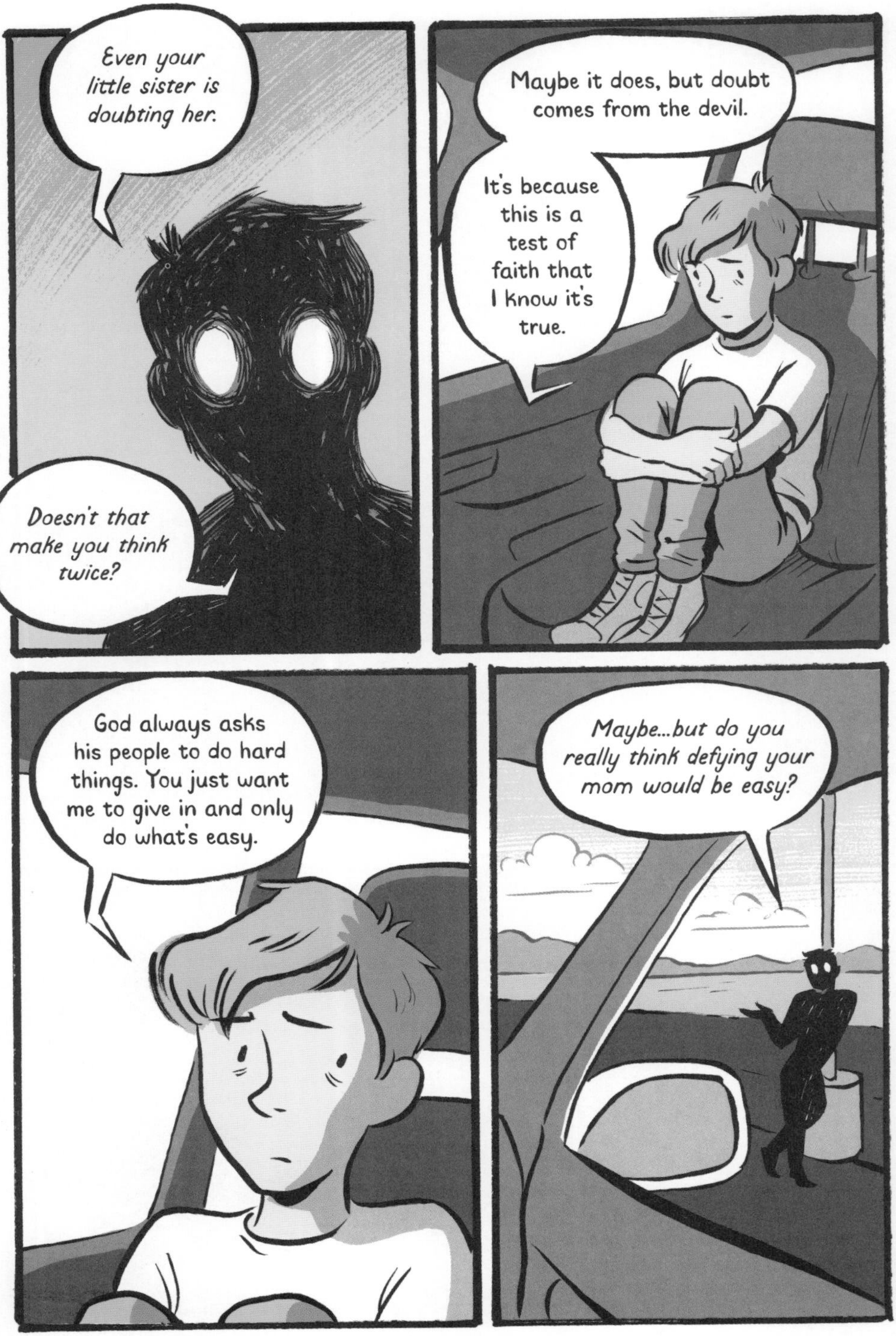
Even your little sister is doubting her.
Doesn't that make you think twice?
Maybe it does, but doubt comes from the devil.
It's because this is a test of faith that I know it's true.
God always asks his people to do hard things. You just want me to give in and only do what's easy.
Maybe...but do you really think defying your mom would be easy?

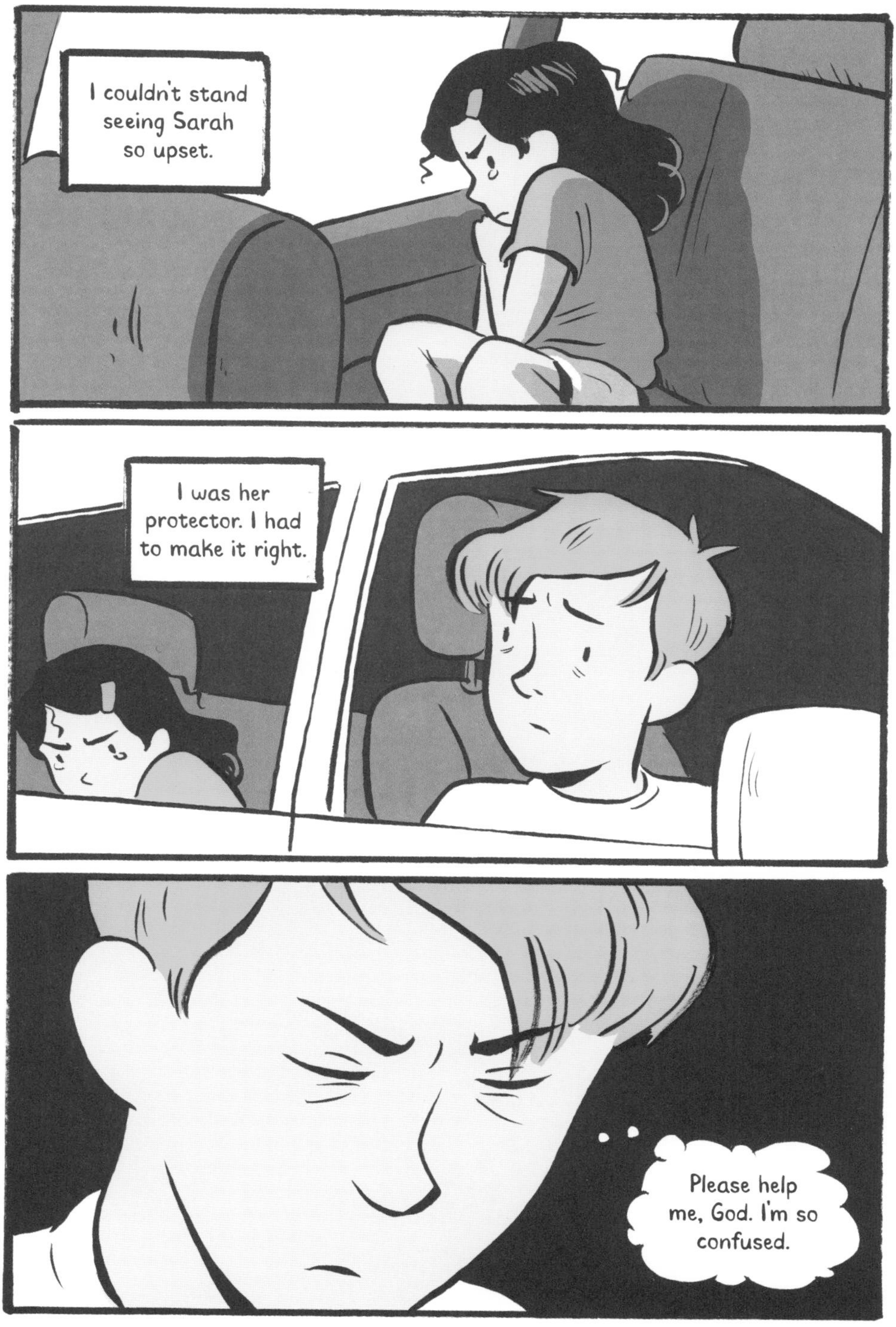
I couldn't stand seeing Sarah so upset.
I was her protector. I had to make it right.
Please help me, God. I'm so confused.

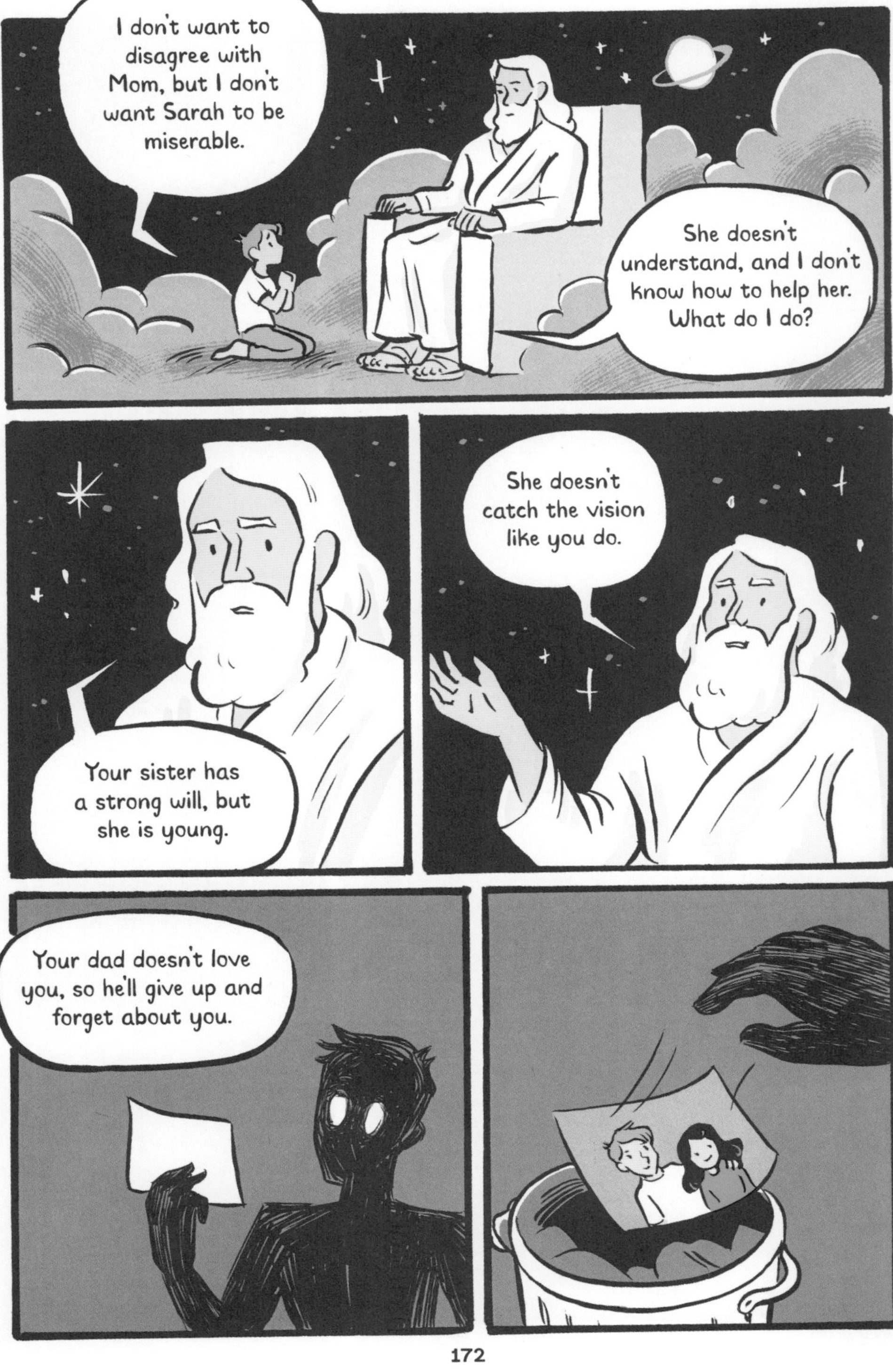
I don't want to disagree with Mom, but I don't want Sarah to be miserable.
She doesn't understand, and I don't know how to help her. What do I do?
Your sister has a strong will, but she is young.
She doesn't catch the vision like you do.
Your dad doesn't love you, so he'll give up and forget about you.

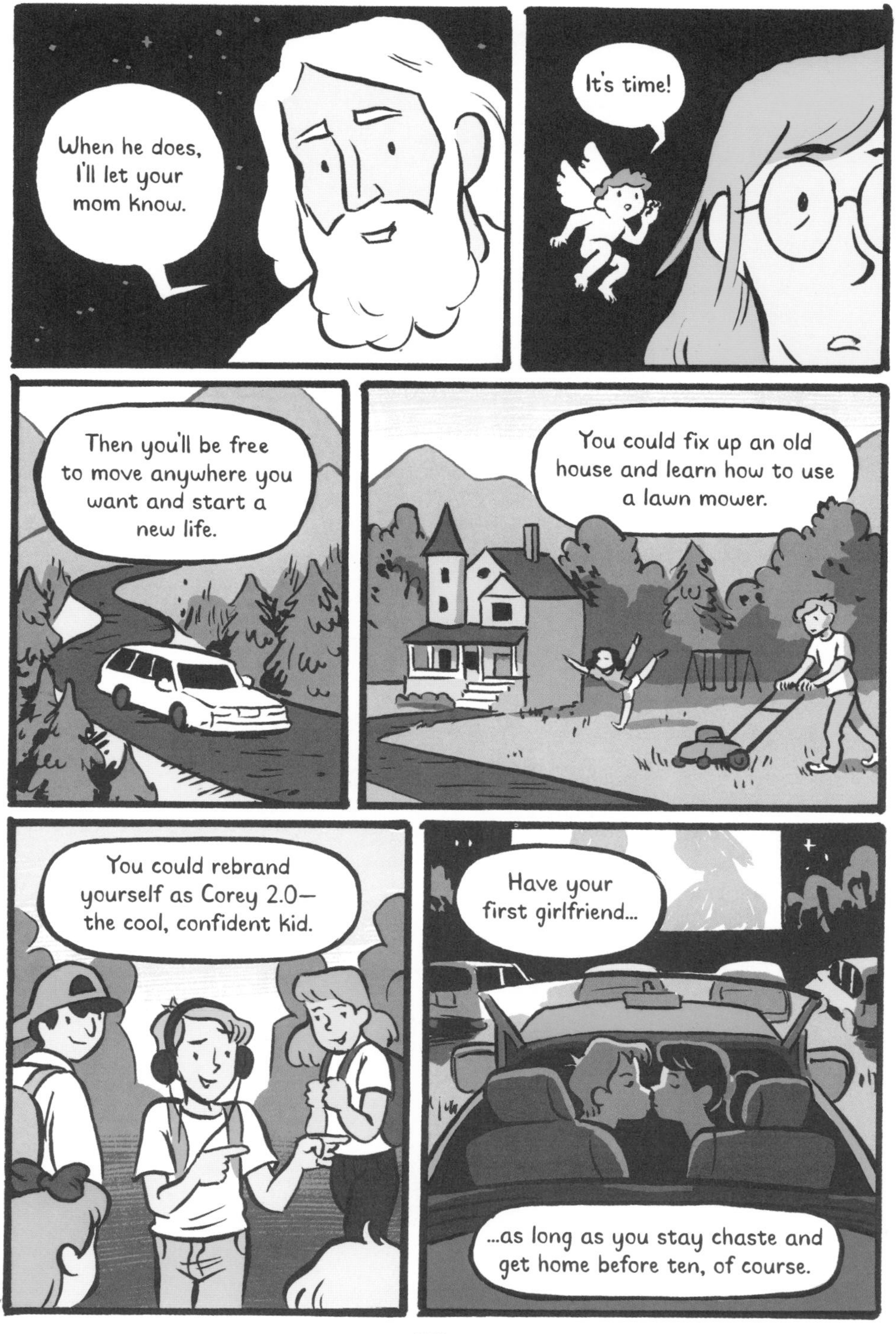
When he does, I'll let your mom know.
It's time!
Then you'll be free to move anywhere you want and start a new life.
You could fix up an old house and learn how to use a lawn mower.
You could rebrand yourself as Corey 2.0—the cool, confident kid.
Have your first girlfriend...
...as long as you stay chaste and get home before ten, of course.

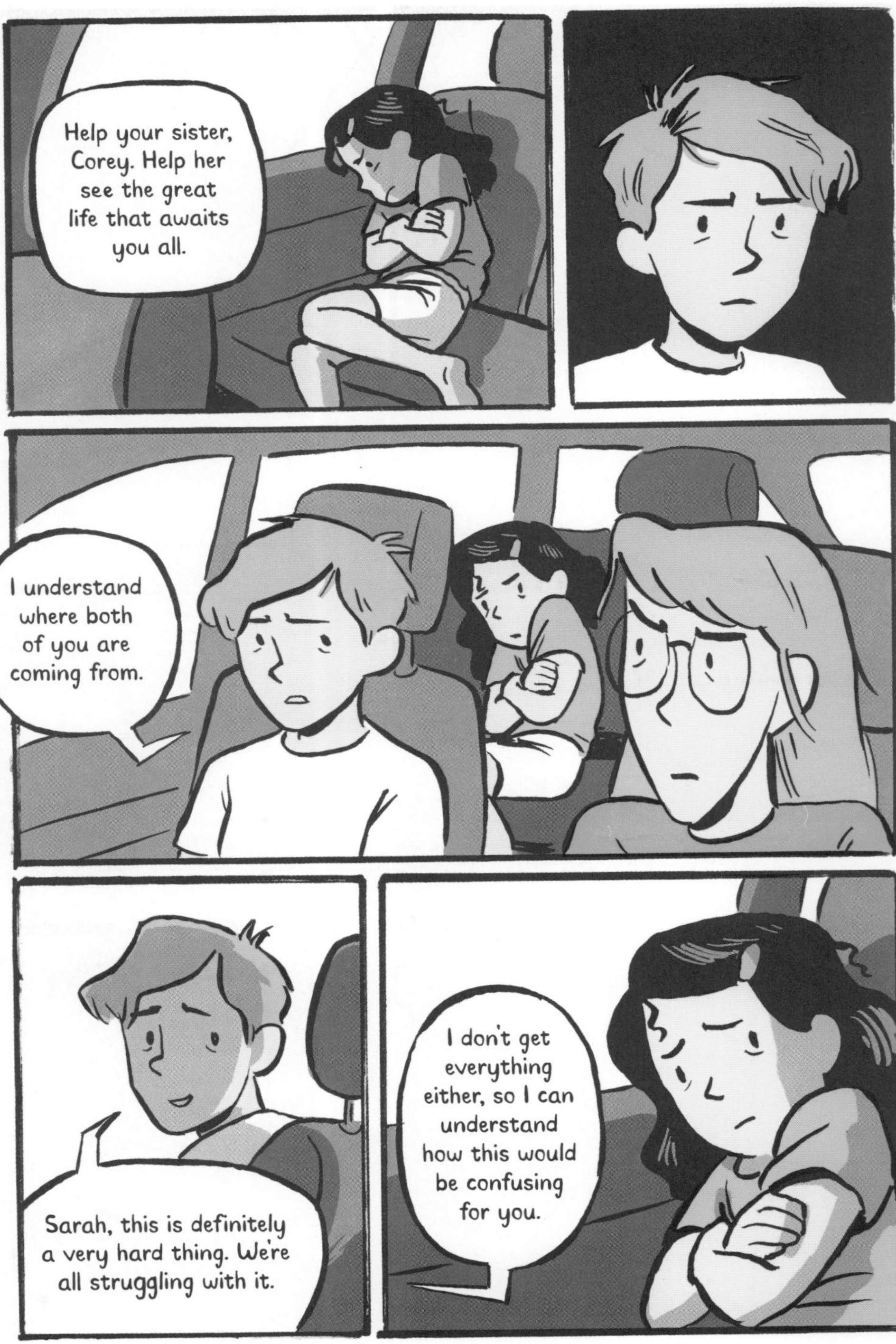
Help your sister, Corey. Help her see the great life that awaits you all.
I understand where both of you are coming from.
Sarah, this is definitely a very hard thing. We're all struggling with it.
I don't get everything either, so I can understand how this would be confusing for you.

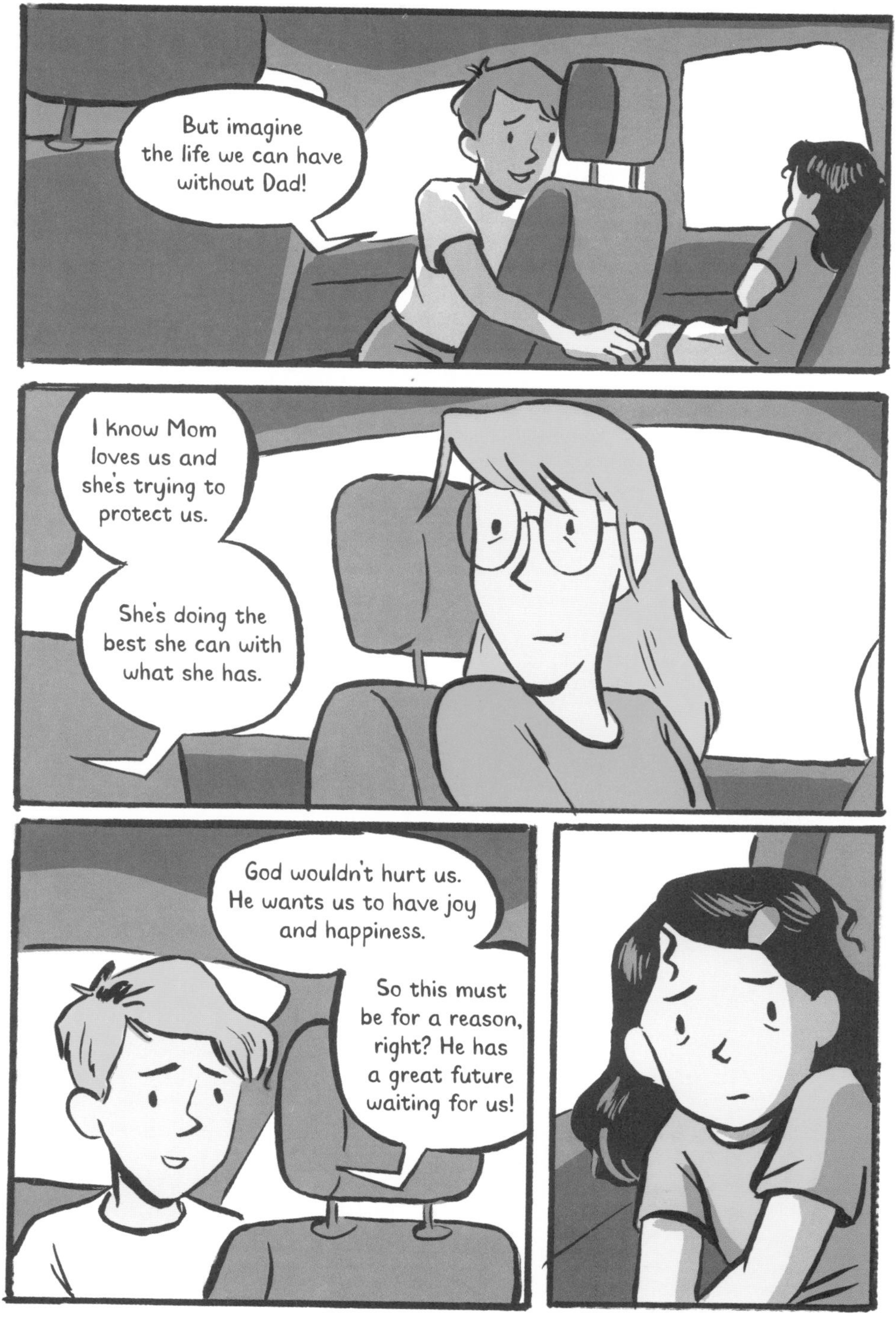
But imagine the life we can have without Dad!
I know Mom loves us and she's trying to protect us.
She's doing the best she can with what she has.
God wouldn't hurt us. He wants us to have joy and happiness.
So this must be for a reason, right? He has a great future waiting for us!

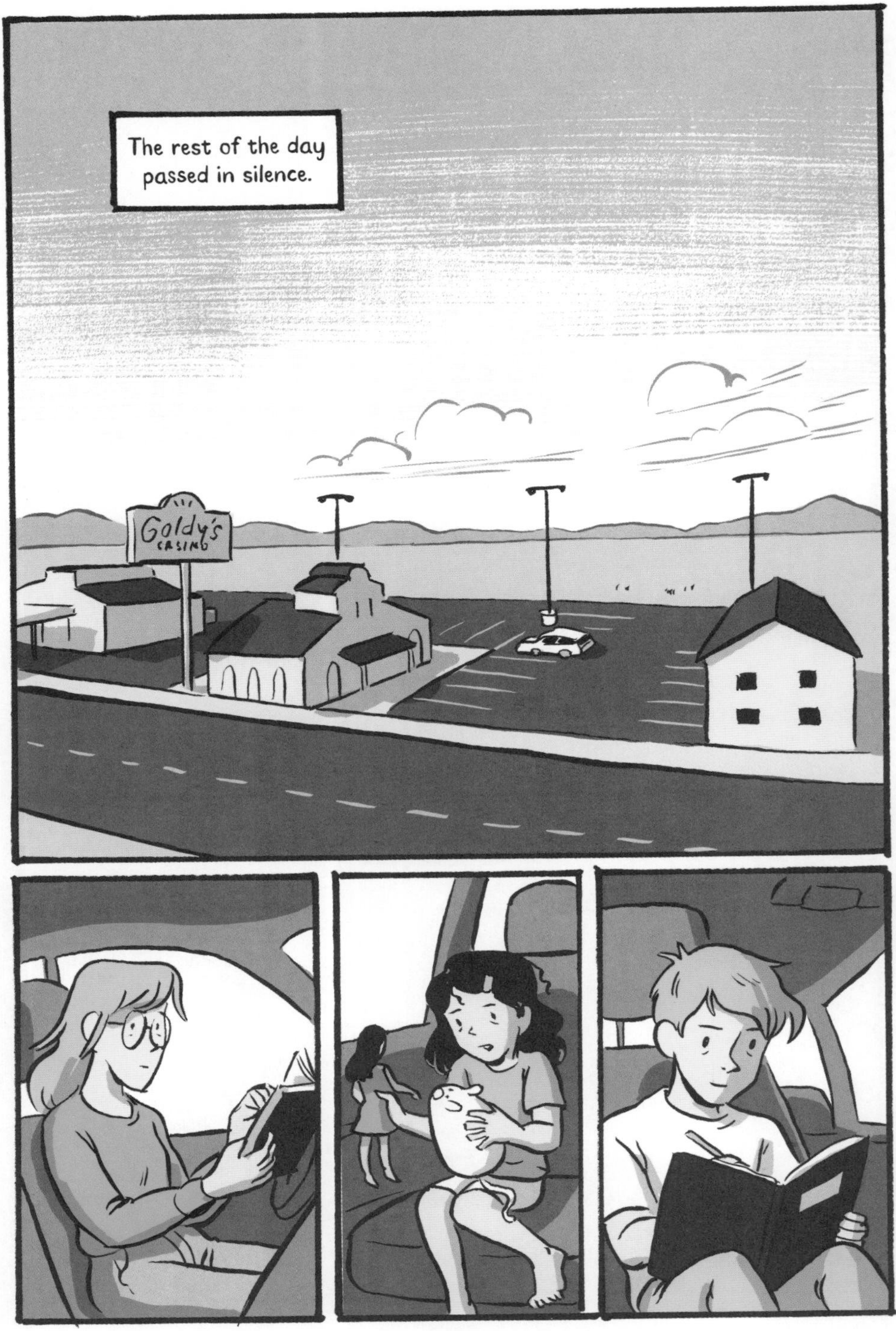

The rest of the day passed in silence.
Goldy's CASINO

I was determined to hold on to faith.

This was all part of God's plan.

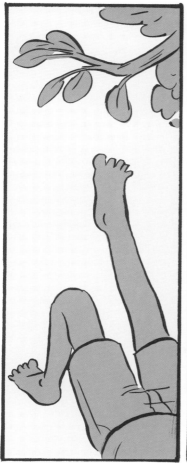

The next day it rained for the first time since we had left home.

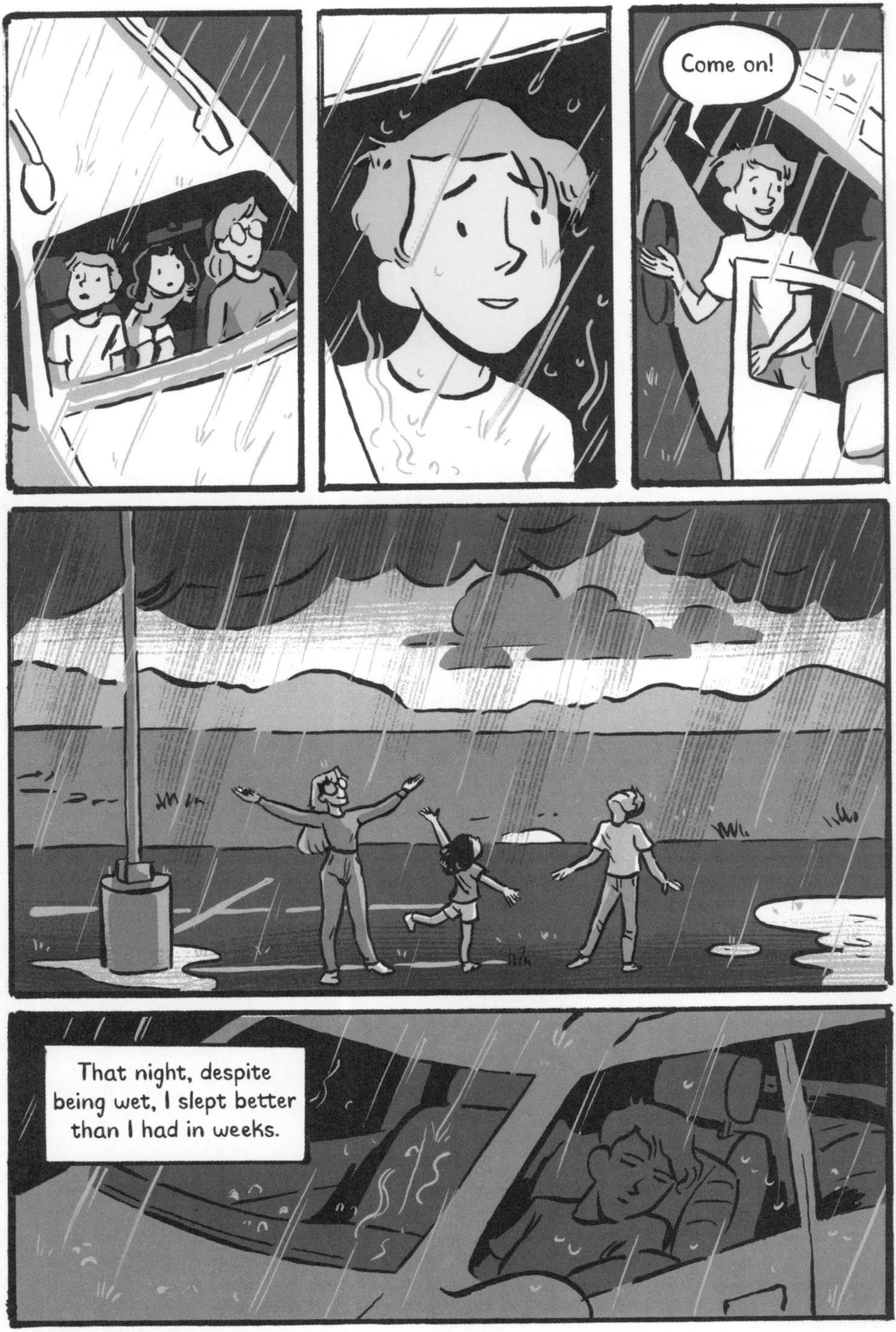
Come on!
That night, despite being wet, I slept better than I had in weeks.

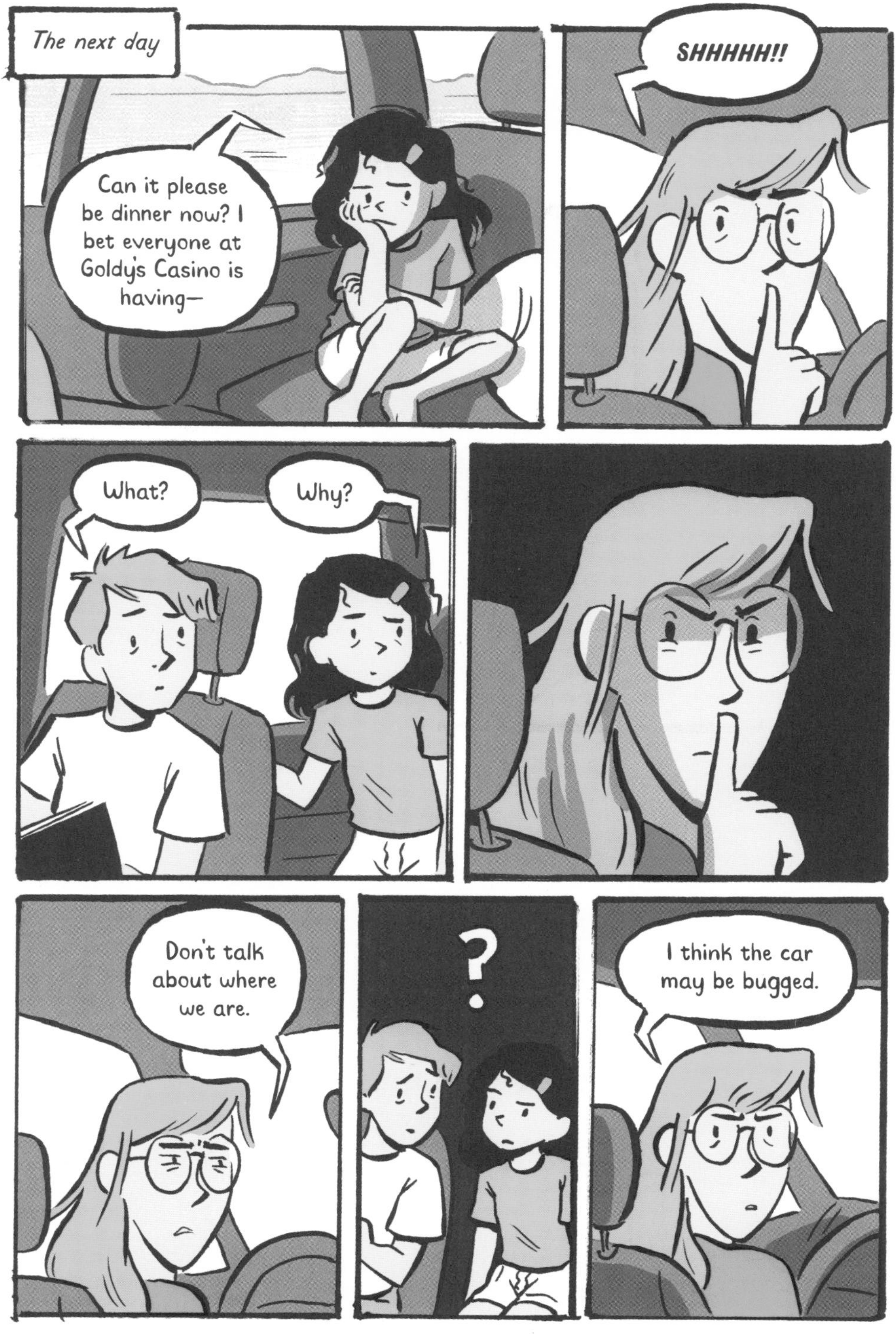
The next day
Can it please be dinner now? I bet everyone at Goldy's Casino is having—
SHHHHH!!
What?
Why?
Don't talk about where we are.
?
I think the car may be bugged.

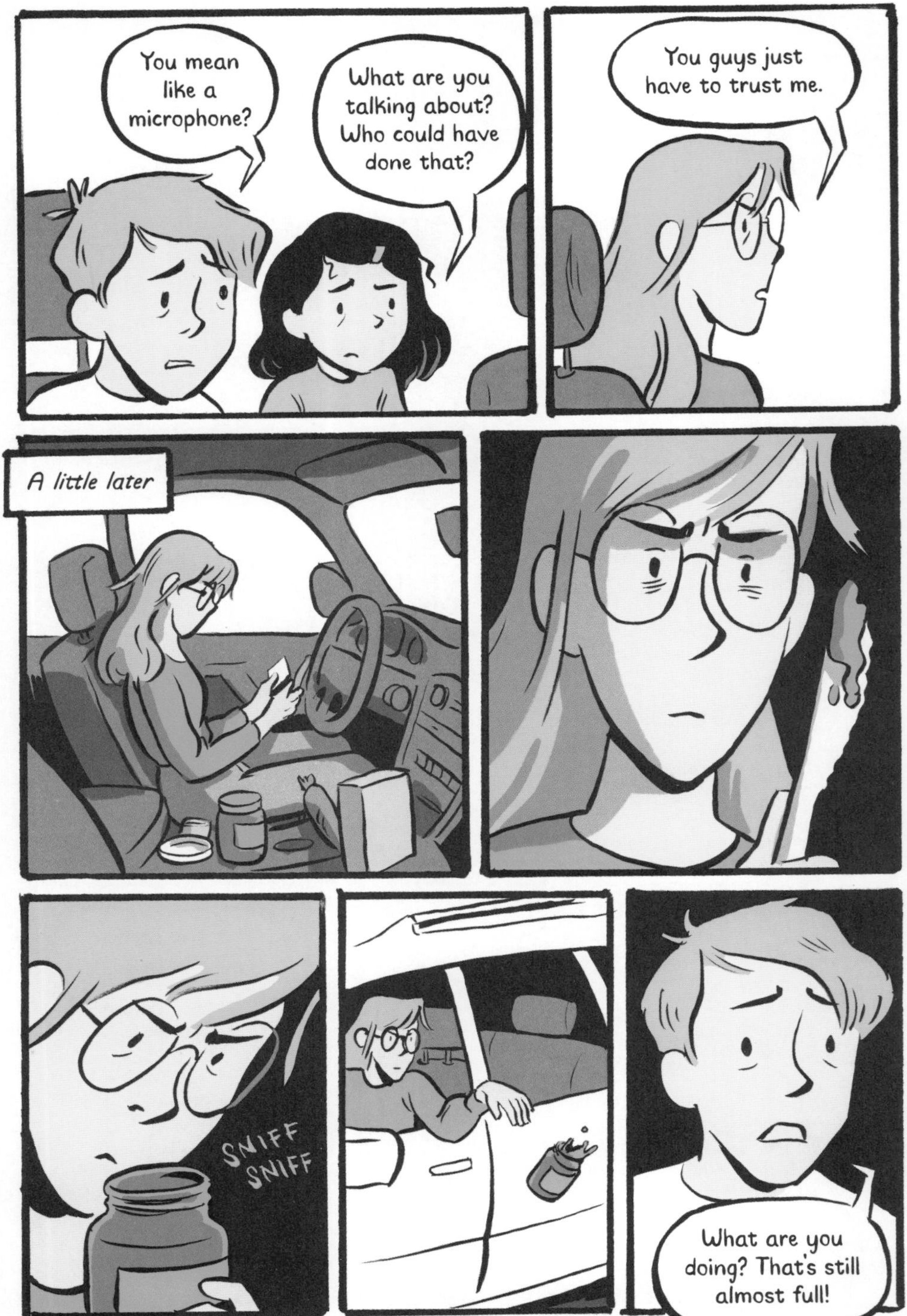
You mean like a microphone?
What are you talking about? Who could have done that?
You guys just have to trust me.
A little later
SNIFF SNIFF
What are you doing? That's still almost full!

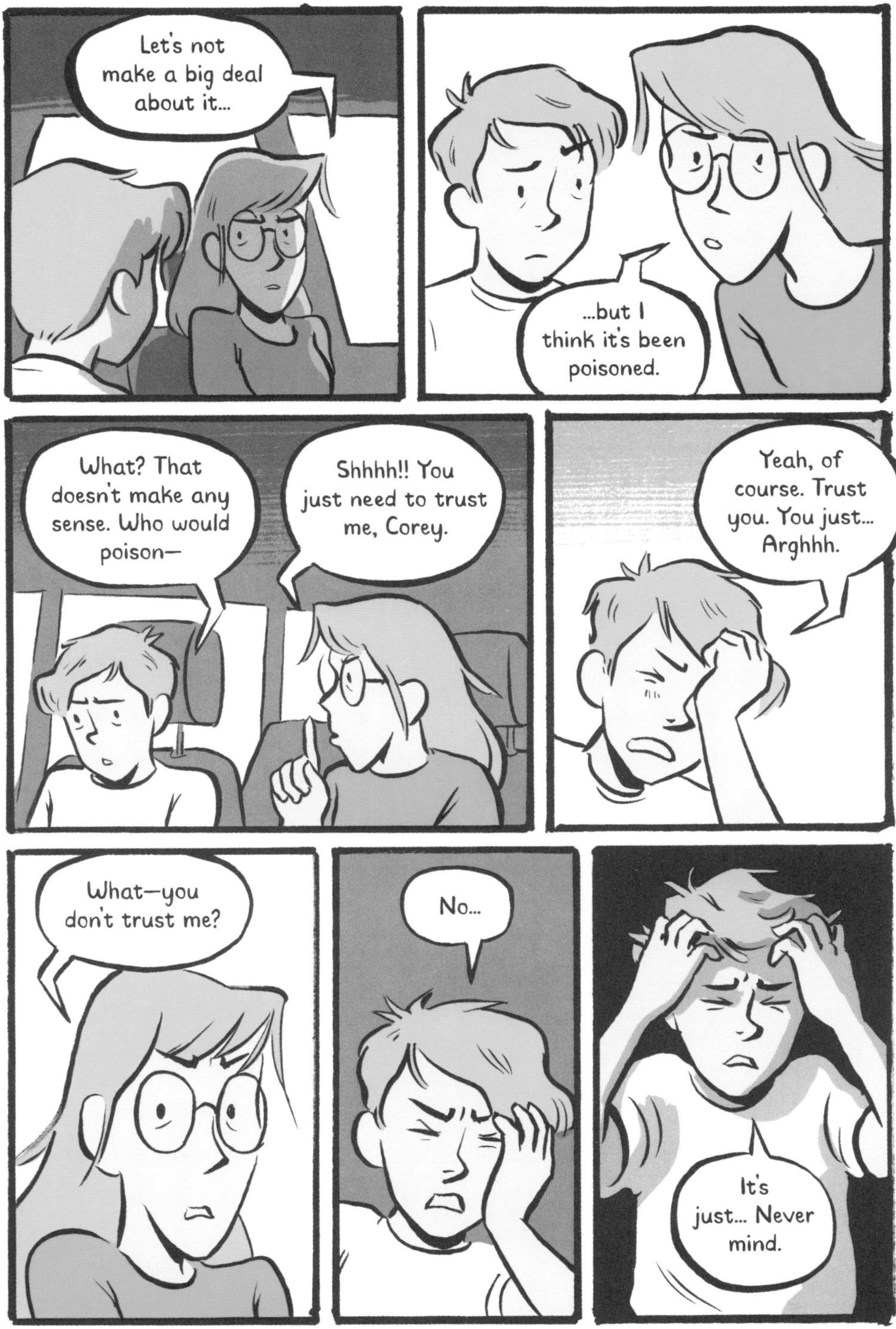
Let's not make a big deal about it...
...but I think it's been poisoned.
What? That doesn't make any sense. Who would poison—
Shhhh!! You just need to trust me, Corey.
Yeah, of course. Trust you. You just... Arghhh.
What—you don't trust me?
No...
It's just... Never mind.

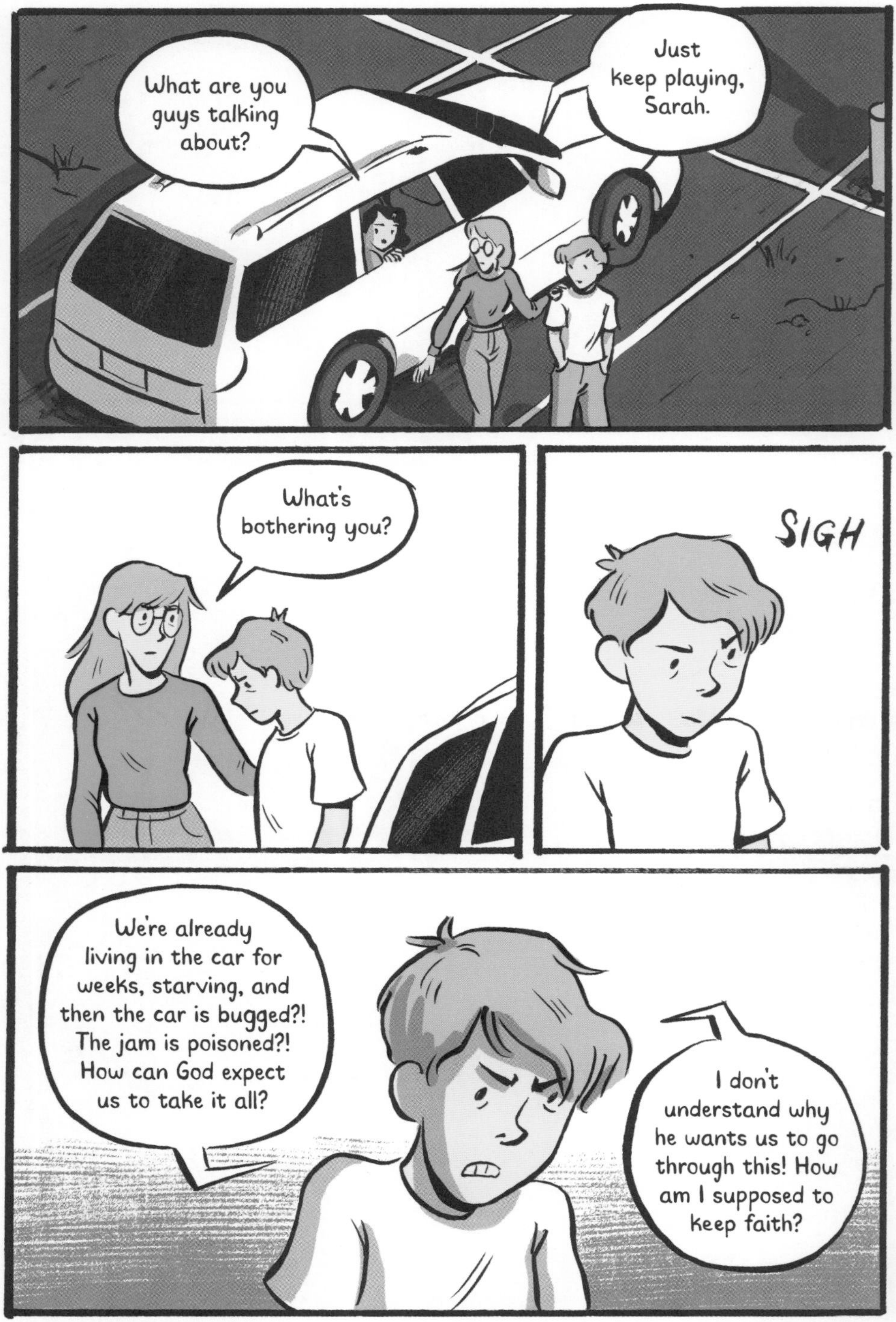

What are you guys talking about?
Just keep playing, Sarah.
What's bothering you?
SIGH
We're already living in the car for weeks, starving, and then the car is bugged?! The jam is poisoned?! How can God expect us to take it all?
I don't understand why he wants us to go through this! How am I supposed to keep faith?

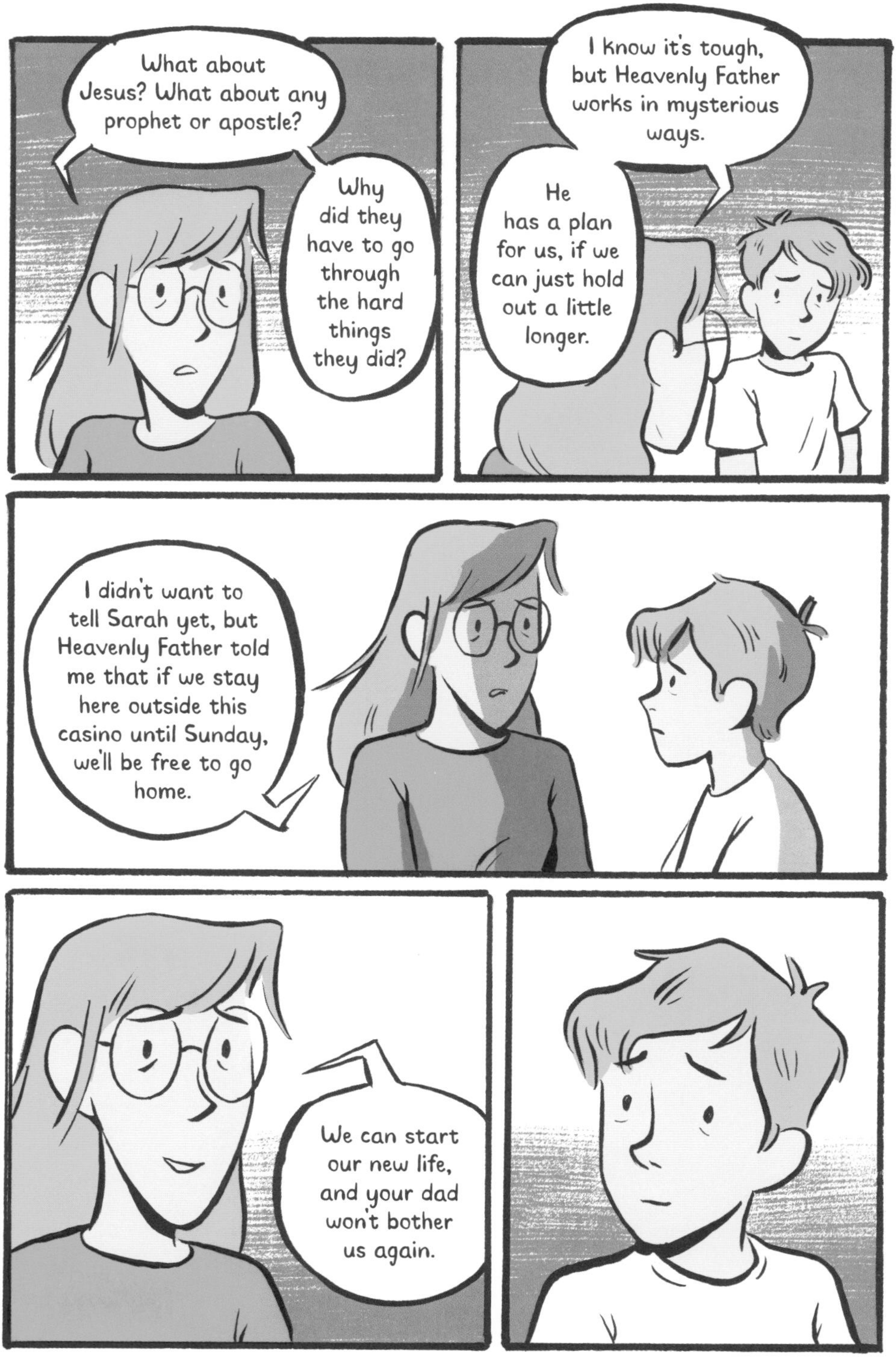
What about Jesus? What about any prophet or apostle?
Why did they have to go through the hard things they did?
I know it's tough, but Heavenly Father works in mysterious ways.
He has a plan for us, if we can just hold out a little longer.
I didn't want to tell Sarah yet, but Heavenly Father told me that if we stay here outside this casino until Sunday, we'll be free to go home.
We can start our new life, and your dad won't bother us again.

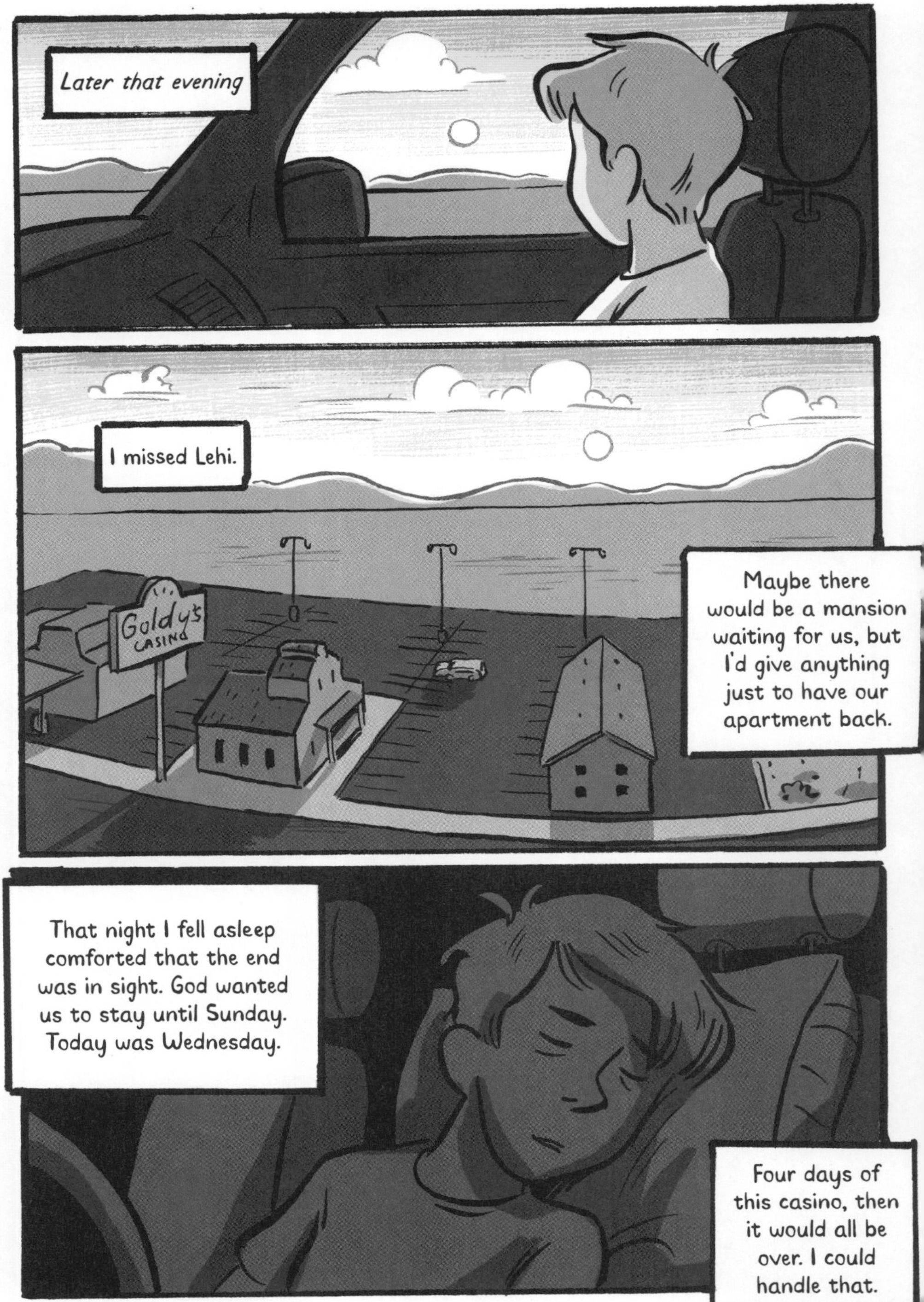
Later that evening
I missed Lehi.
Goldy's CASINO
Maybe there would be a mansion waiting for us, but I'd give anything just to have our apartment back.
That night I fell asleep comforted that the end was in sight. God wanted us to stay until Sunday. Today was Wednesday.
Four days of this casino, then it would all be over. I could handle that.

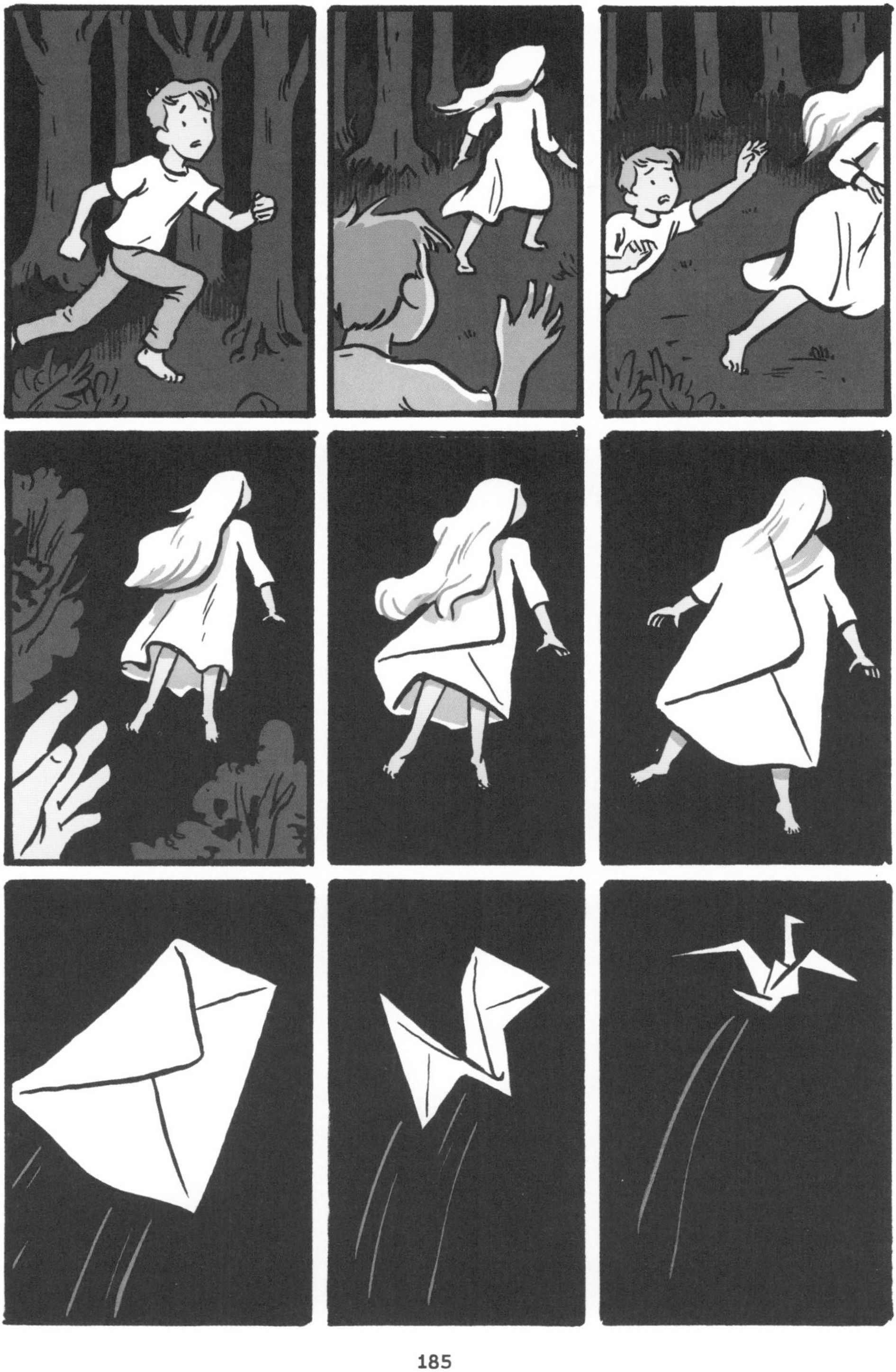

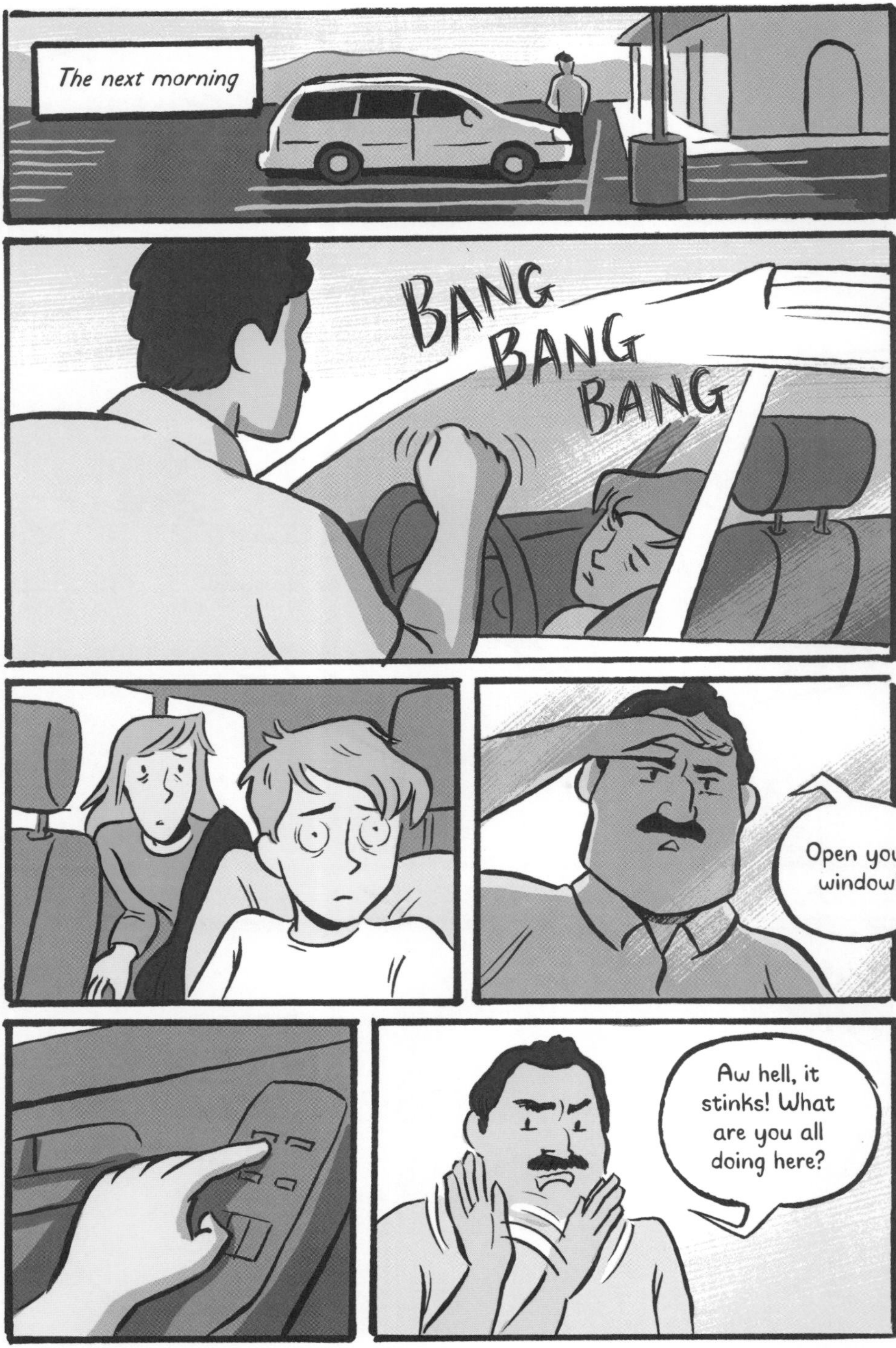
The next morning
BANG
BANG
BANG
Open your window!
Aw hell, it stinks! What are you all doing here?

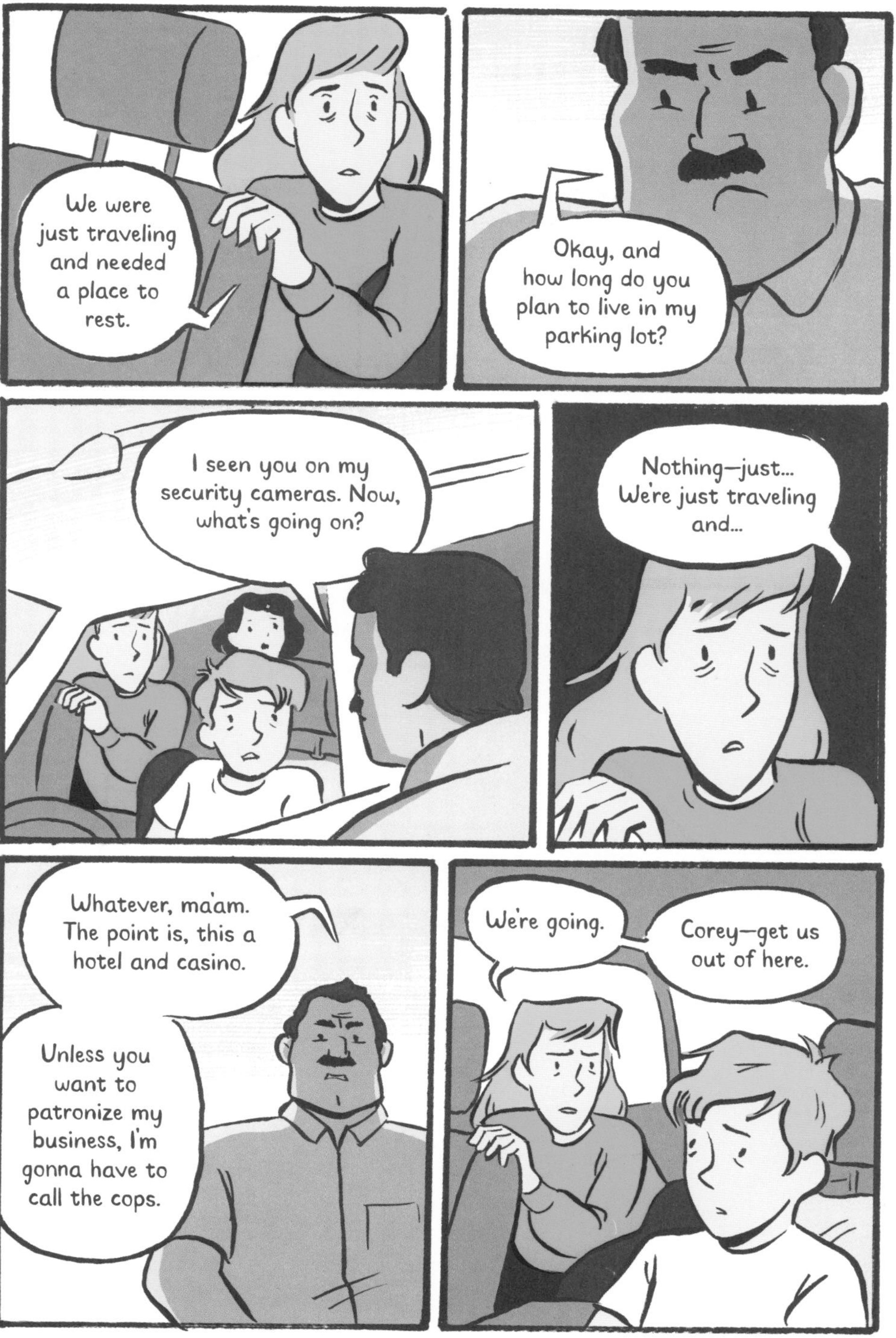
We were just traveling and needed a place to rest.
Okay, and how long do you plan to live in my parking lot?
I seen you on my security cameras. Now, what's going on?
Nothing—just... We're just traveling and...
Whatever, ma'am. The point is, this a hotel and casino.
Unless you want to patronize my business, I'm gonna have to call the cops.
We're going.
Corey—get us out of here.

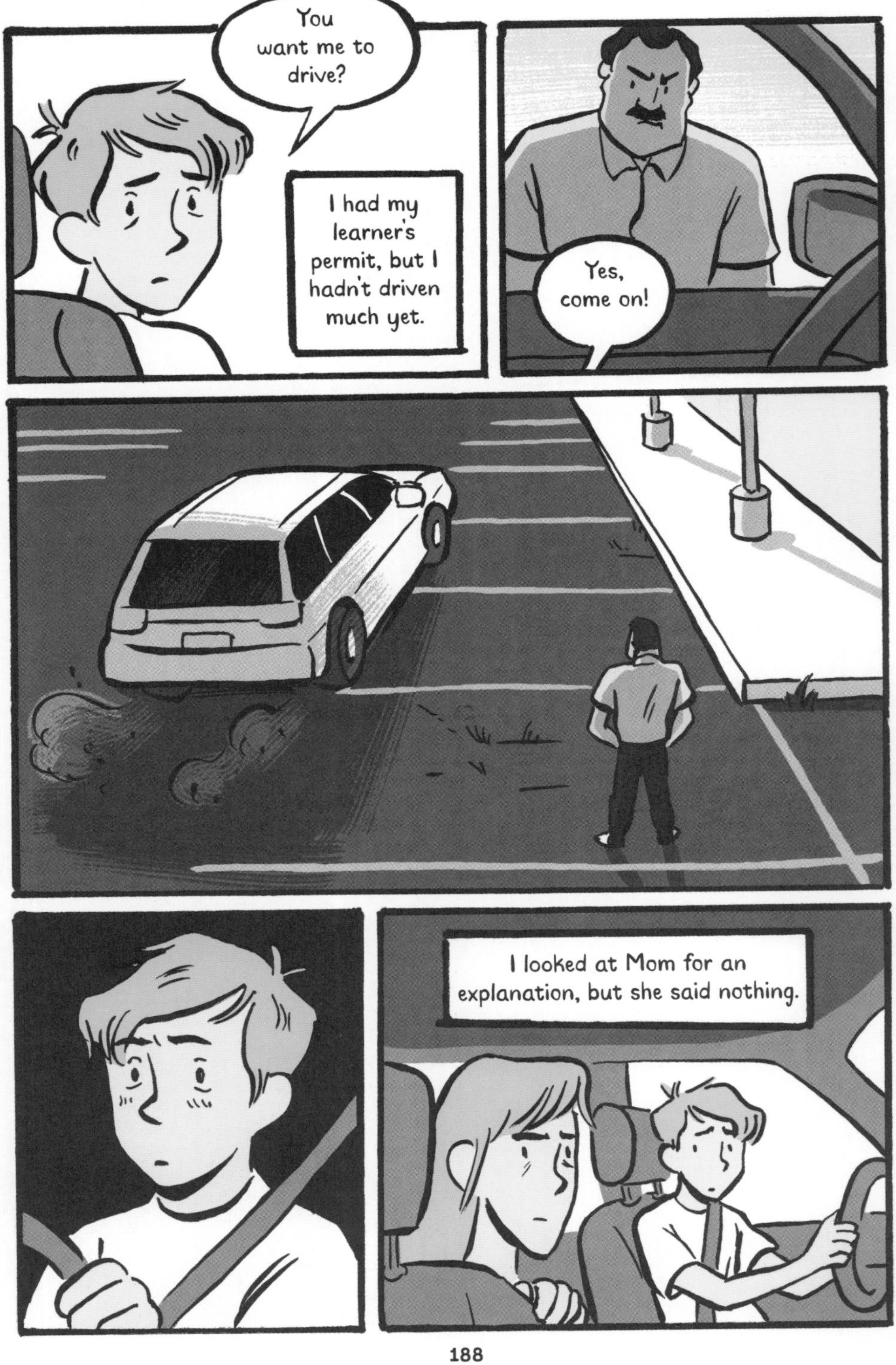
You want me to drive?
I had my learner's permit, but I hadn't driven much yet.
Yes, come on!
I looked at Mom for an explanation, but she said nothing.

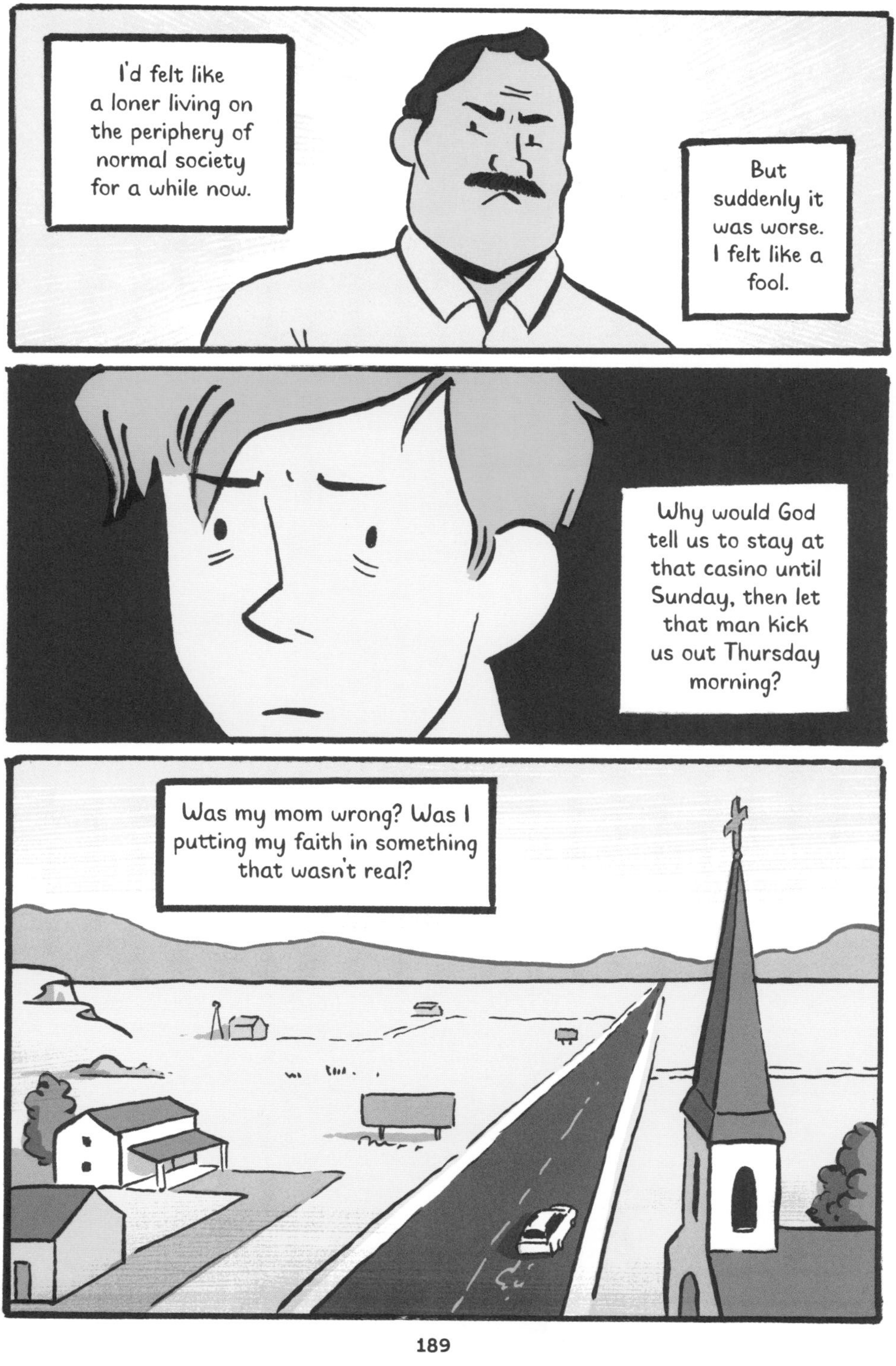
I'd felt like a loner living on the periphery of normal society for a while now.
But suddenly it was worse. I felt like a fool.
Why would God tell us to stay at that casino until Sunday, then let that man kick us out Thursday morning?
Was my mom wrong? Was I putting my faith in something that wasn't real?

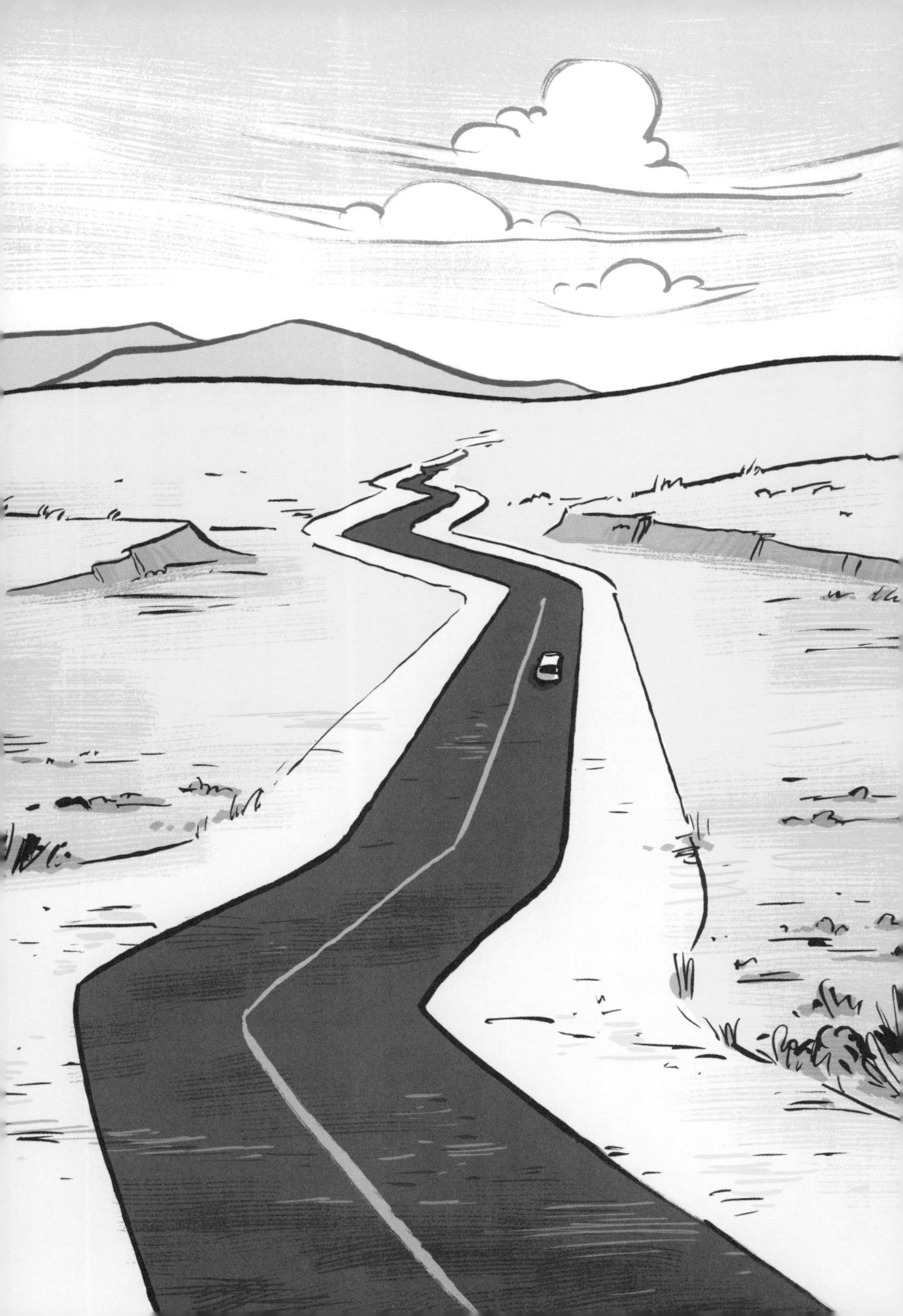

PART THREE

"...Behold thou hast led
us forth from the land of
our inheritance...and we
perish in the wilderness."

1 NEPHI 5:2

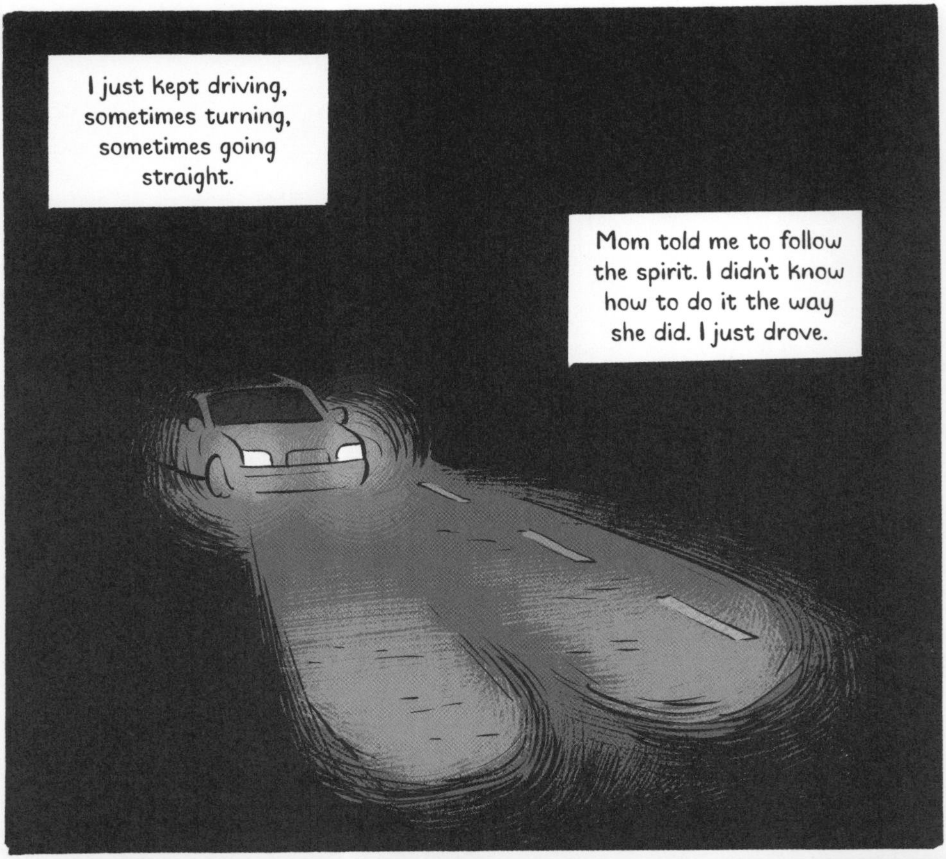
I just kept driving, sometimes turning, sometimes going straight.
Mom told me to follow the spirit. I didn't know how to do it the way she did. I just drove.

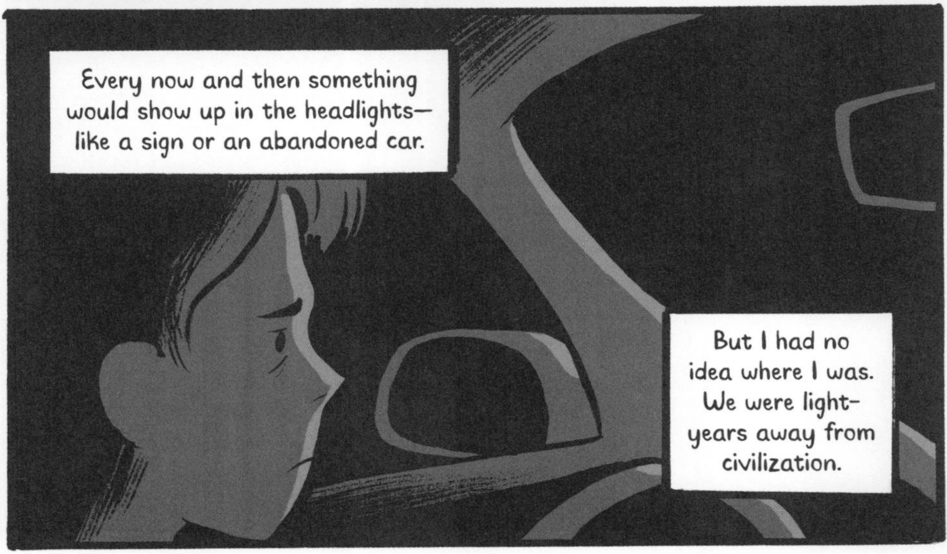
Every now and then something would show up in the headlights—like a sign or an abandoned car.
But I had no idea where I was. We were light-years away from civilization.

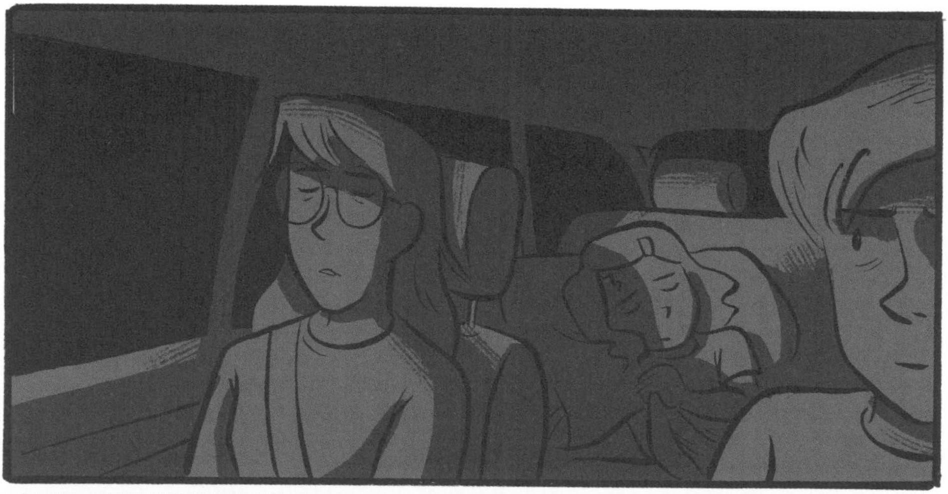

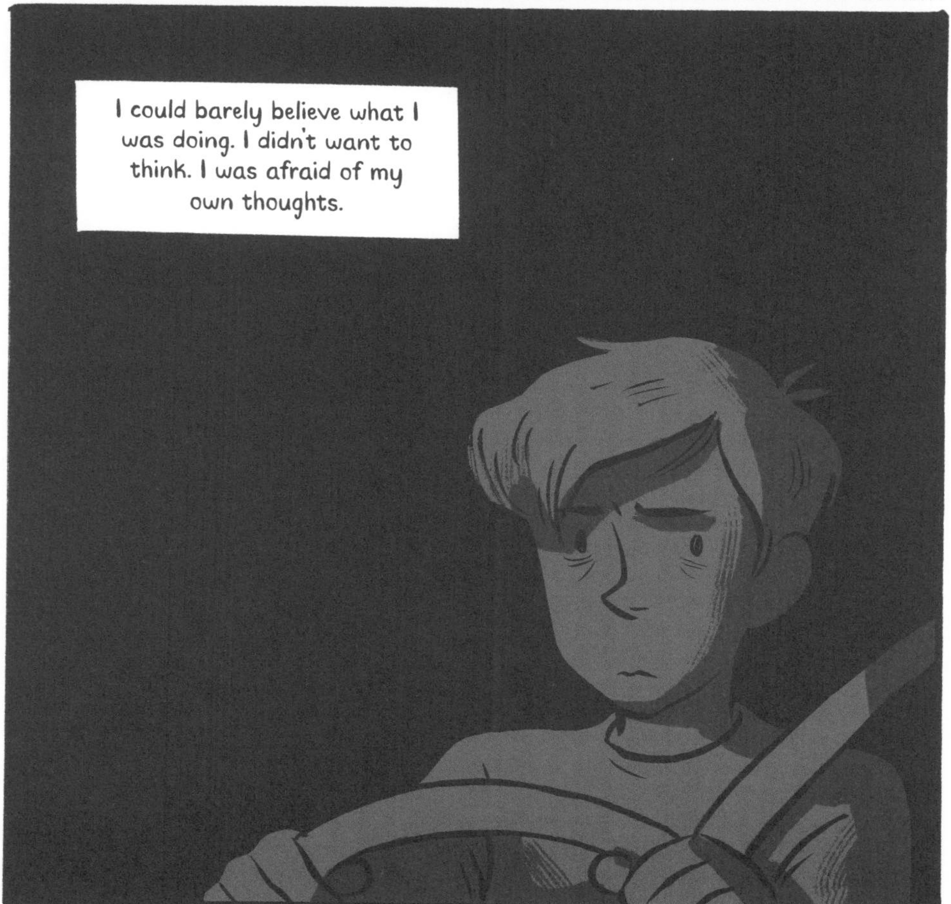
I could barely believe what I was doing. I didn't want to think. I was afraid of my own thoughts.

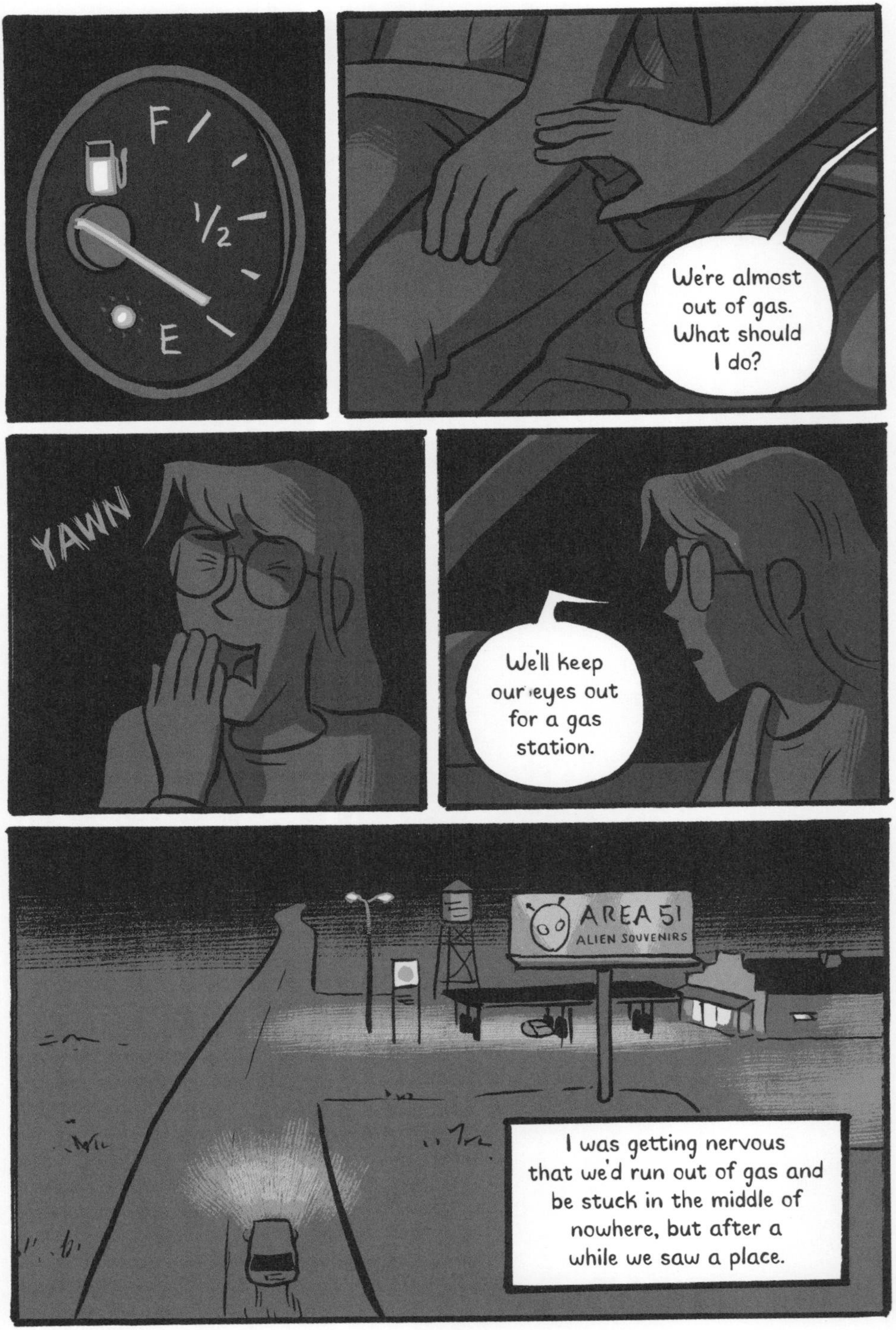
We're almost out of gas. What should I do?
YAWN
We'll keep our eyes out for a gas station.
AREA 51
ALIEN SOUVENIRS
I was getting nervous that we'd run out of gas and be stuck in the middle of nowhere, but after a while we saw a place.

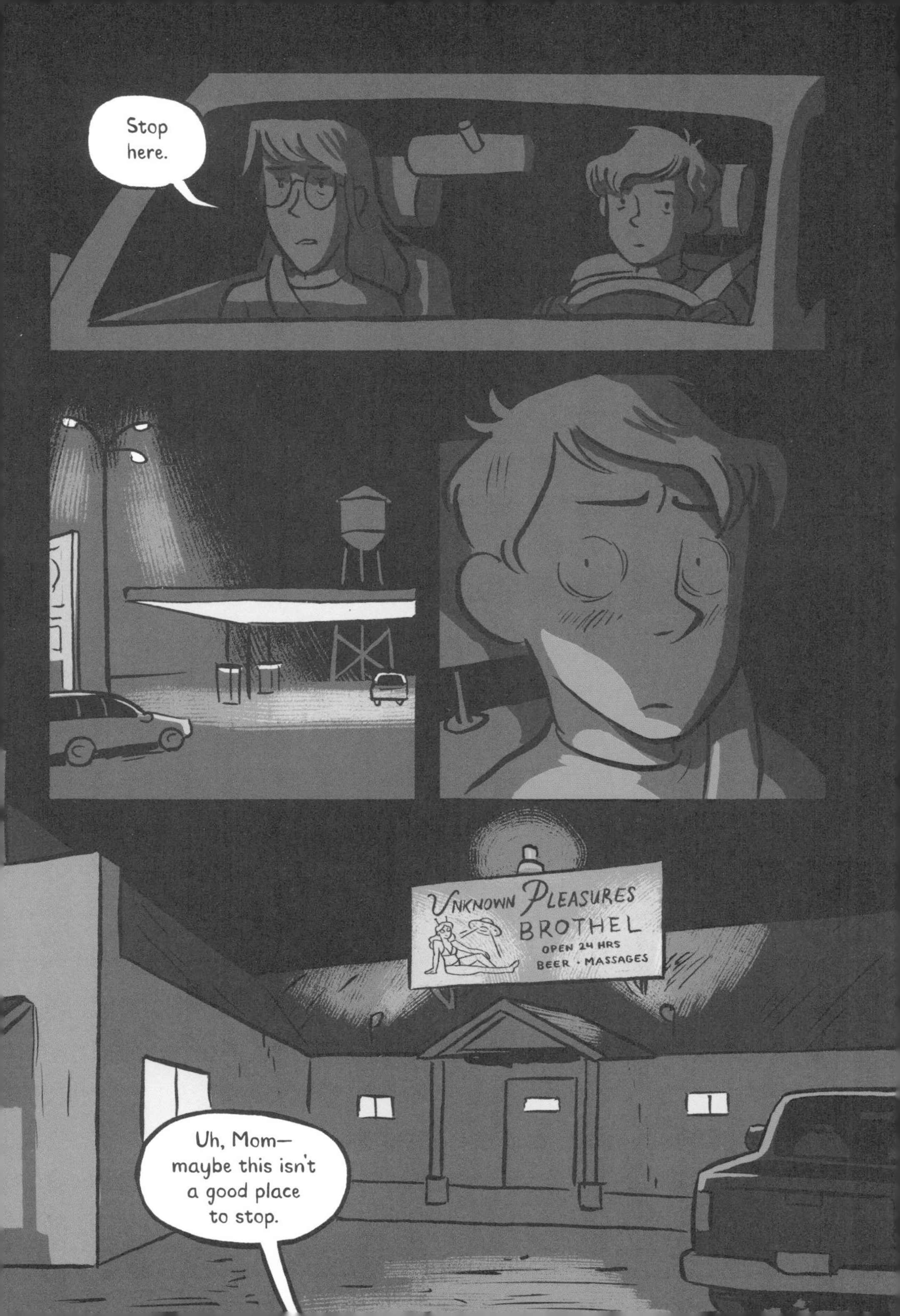
Stop here.
UNKNOWN PLEASURES
BROTHEL
OPEN 24 HRS
BEER • MASSAGES
Uh, Mom— maybe this isn't a good place to stop.

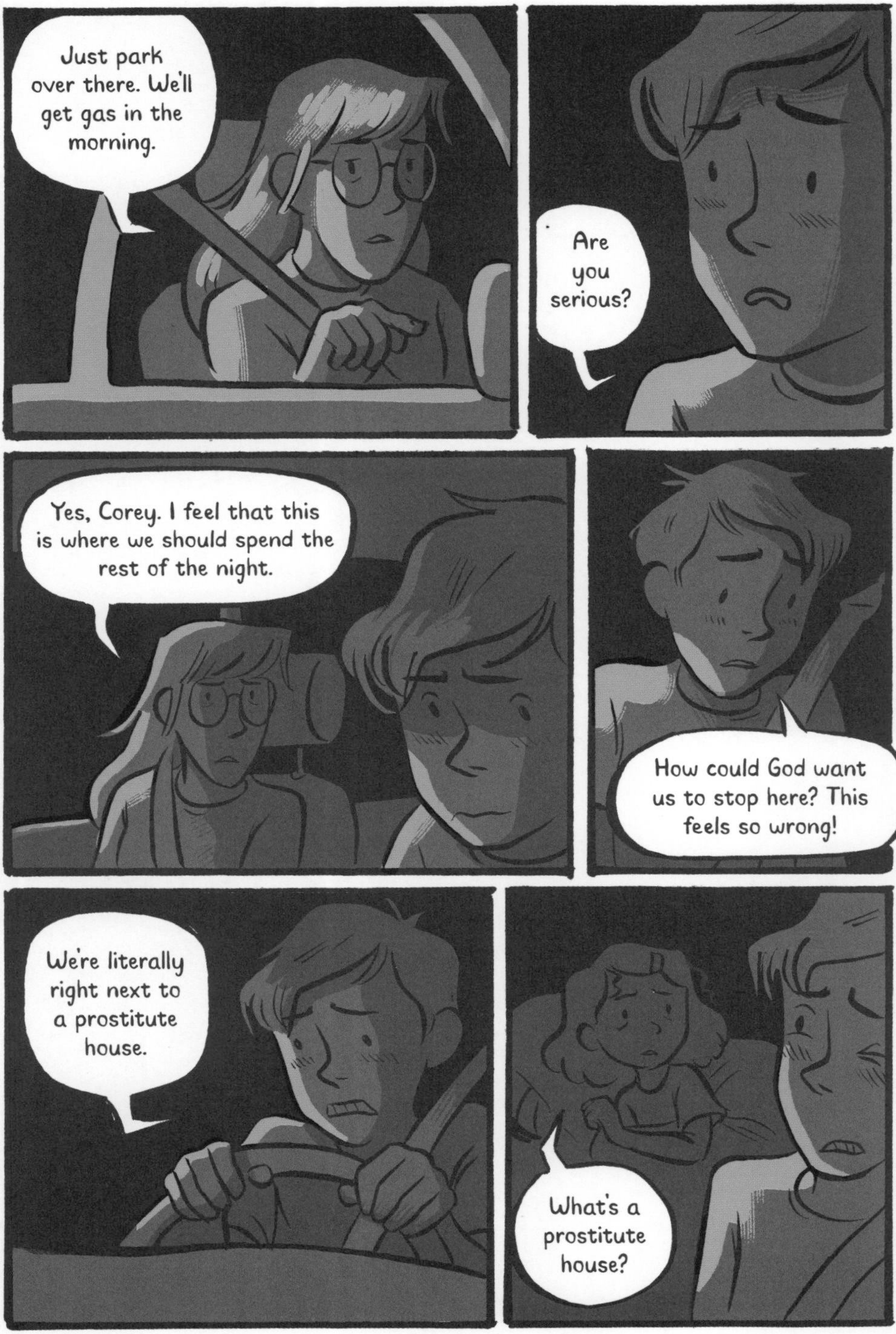
Just park over there. We'll get gas in the morning.
Are you serious?
Yes, Corey. I feel that this is where we should spend the rest of the night.
How could God want us to stop here? This feels so wrong!
We're literally right next to a prostitute house.
What's a prostitute house?

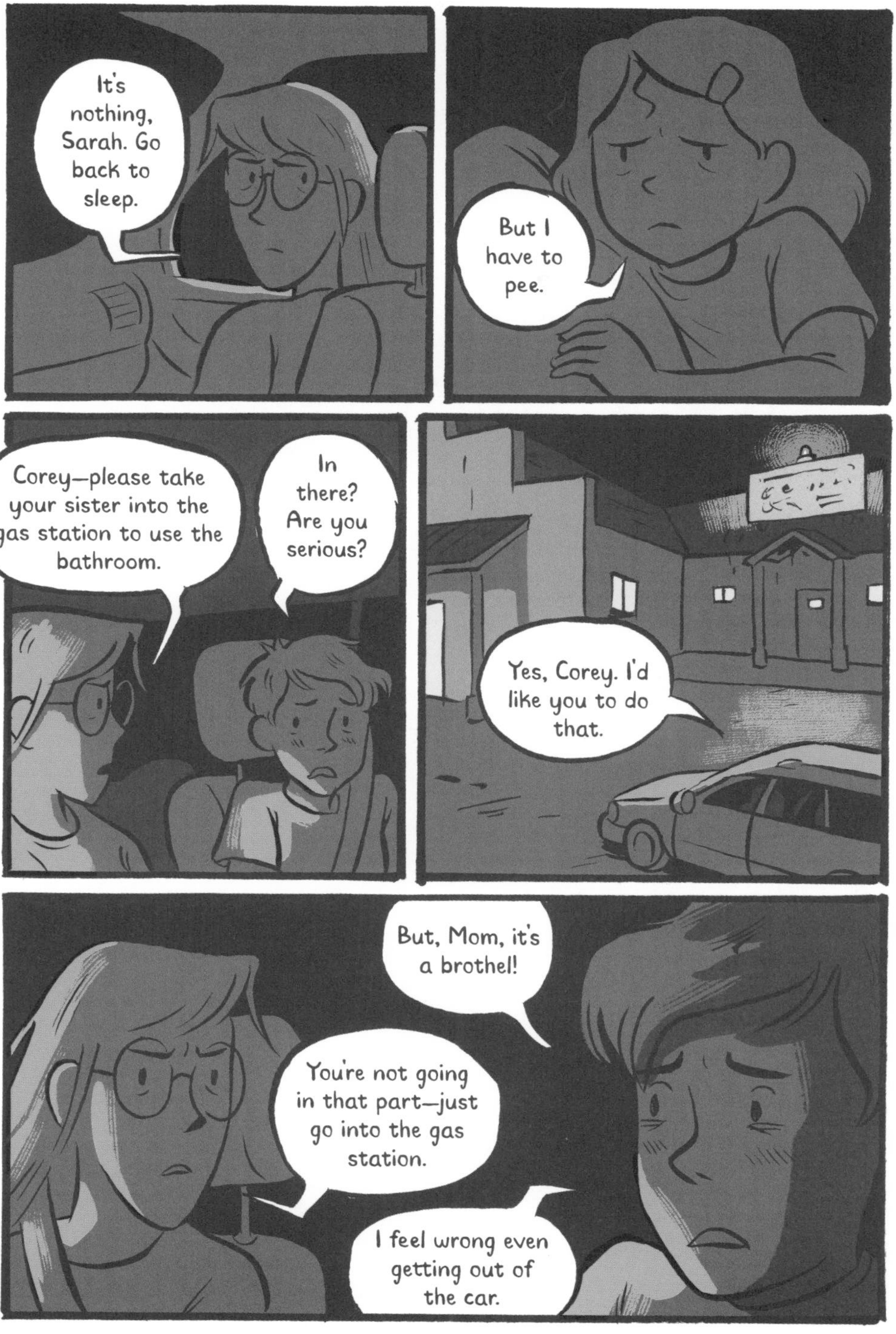
It's nothing, Sarah. Go back to sleep.
But I have to pee.
Corey—please take your sister into the gas station to use the bathroom.
In there? Are you serious?
Yes, Corey. I'd like you to do that.
But, Mom, it's a brothel!
You're not going in that part—just go into the gas station.
I feel wrong even getting out of the car.

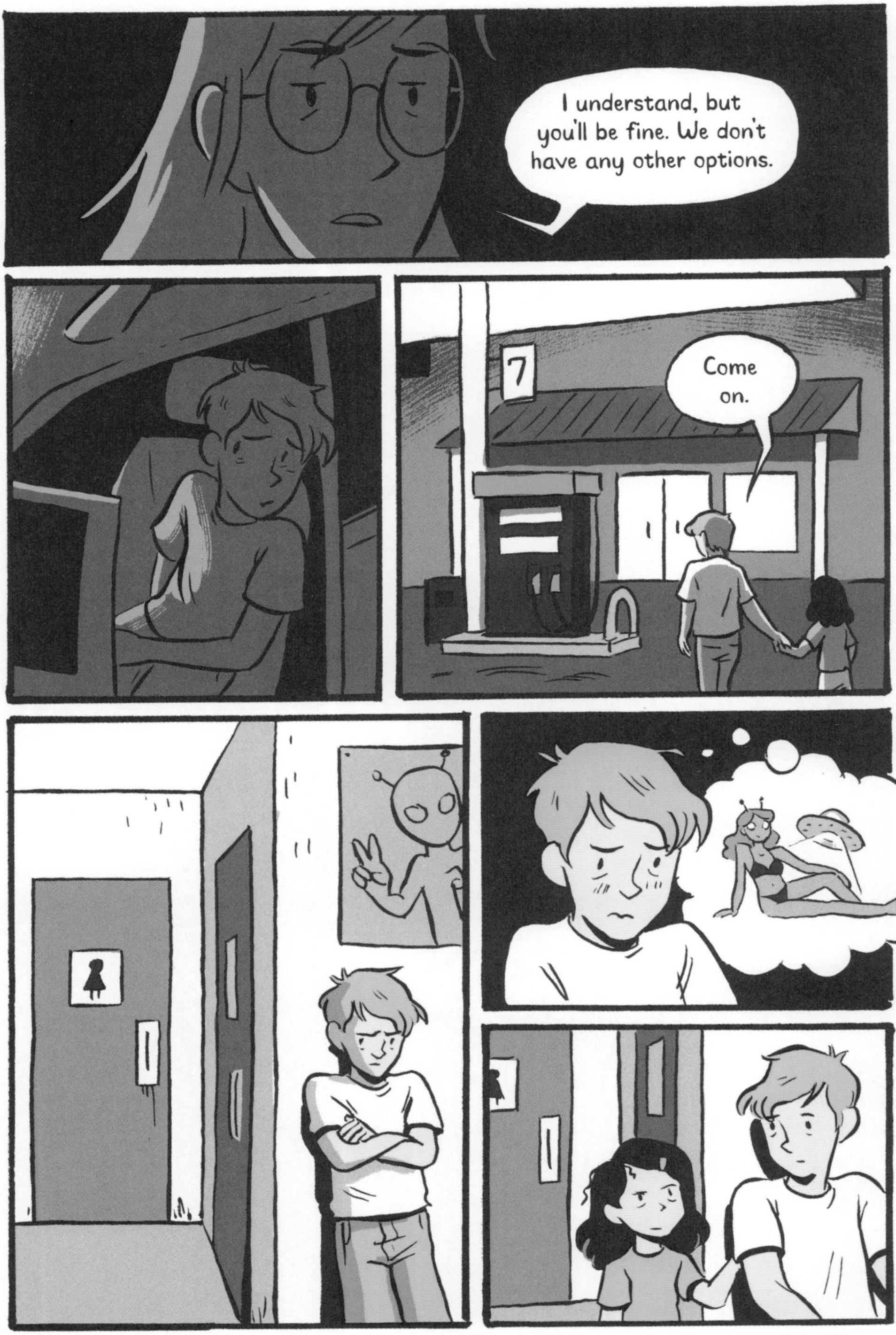
I understand, but you'll be fine. We don't have any other options.
Come on.
7

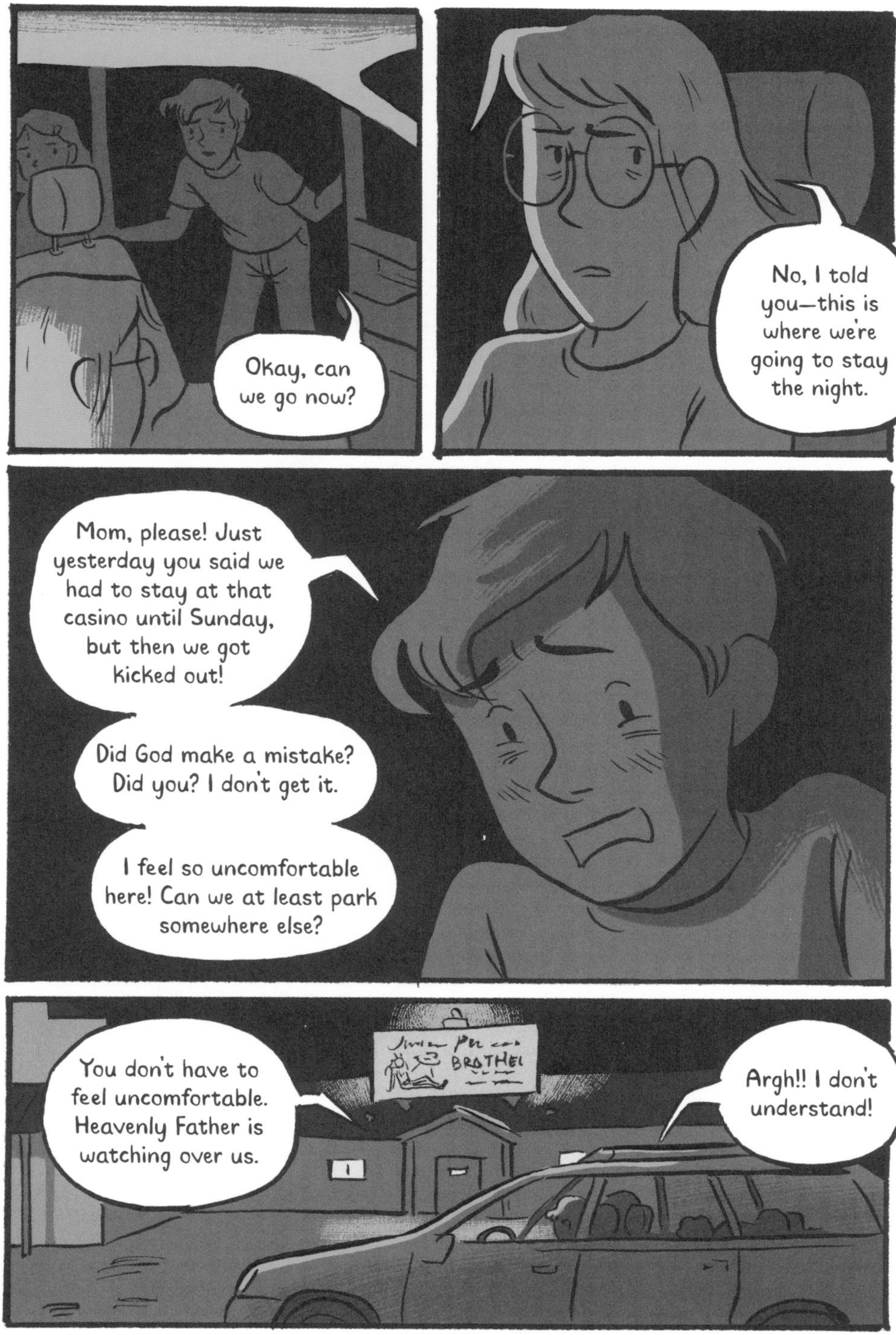
Okay, can we go now?
No, I told you—this is where we're going to stay the night.
Mom, please! Just yesterday you said we had to stay at that casino until Sunday, but then we got kicked out!
Did God make a mistake? Did you? I don't get it.
I feel so uncomfortable here! Can we at least park somewhere else?
You don't have to feel uncomfortable. Heavenly Father is watching over us.
Argh!! I don't understand!

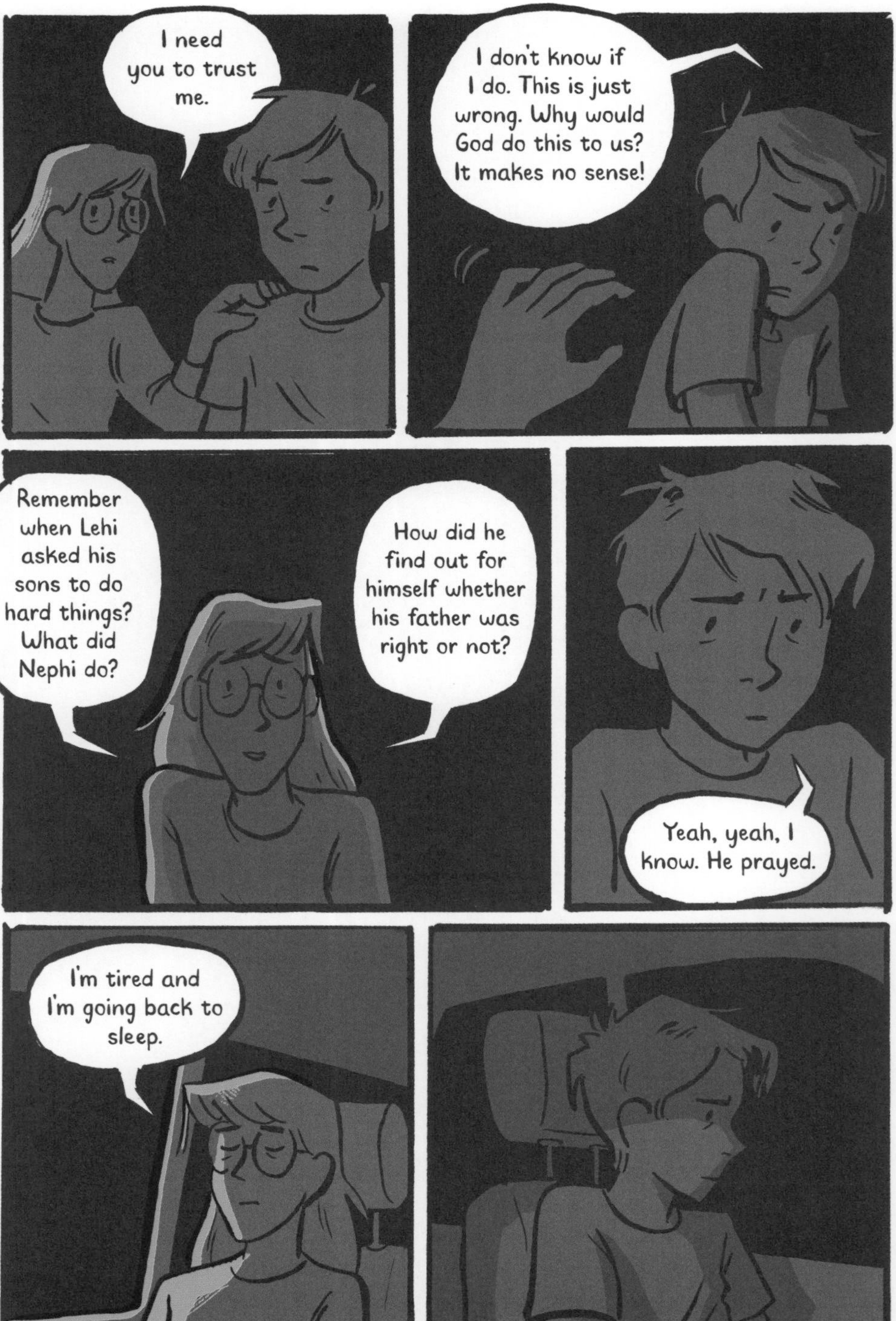
I need you to trust me.
I don't know if I do. This is just wrong. Why would God do this to us? It makes no sense!
Remember when Lehi asked his sons to do hard things? What did Nephi do?
How did he find out for himself whether his father was right or not?
Yeah, yeah, I know. He prayed.
I'm tired and I'm going back to sleep.

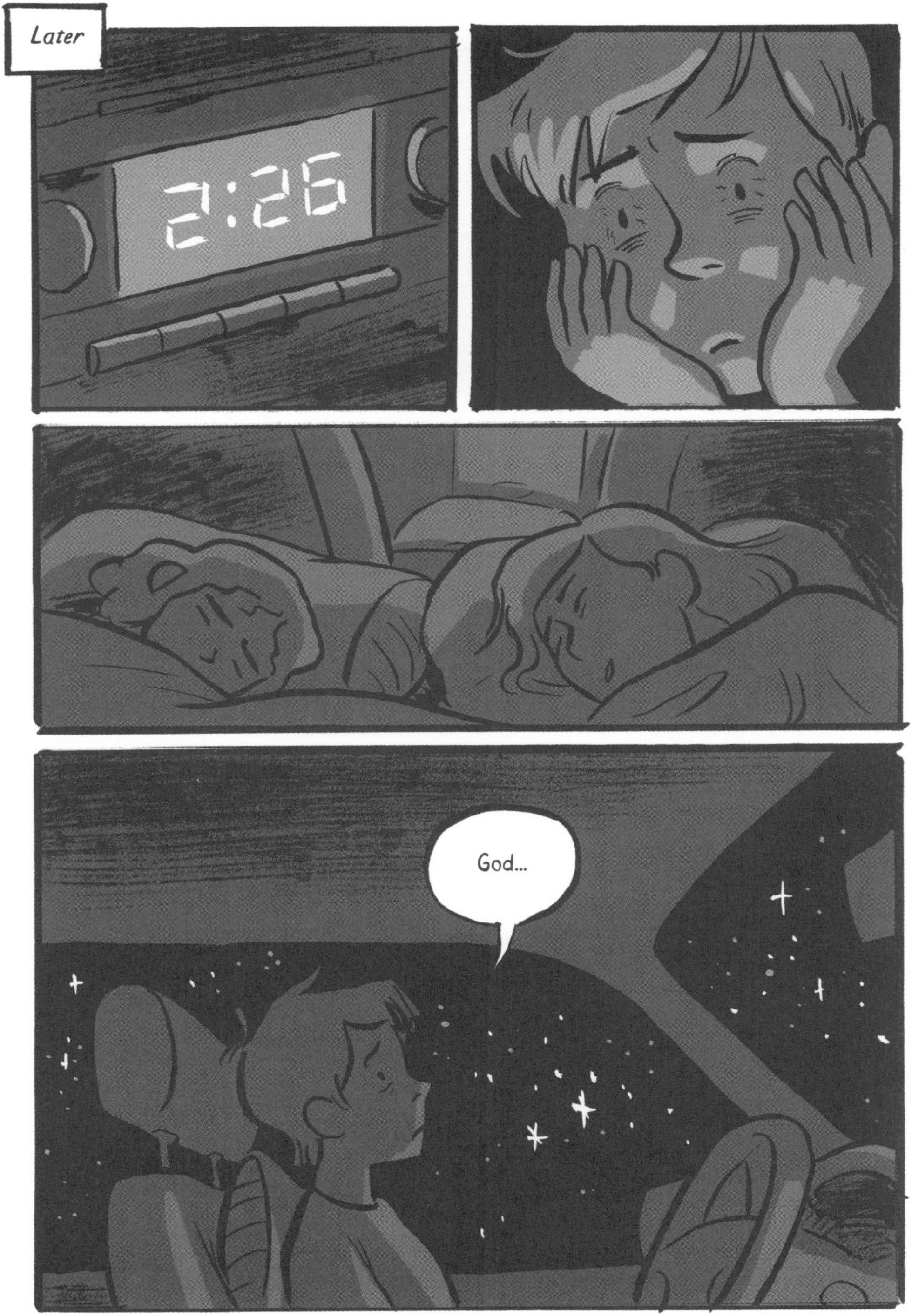
Later
2:26
God...

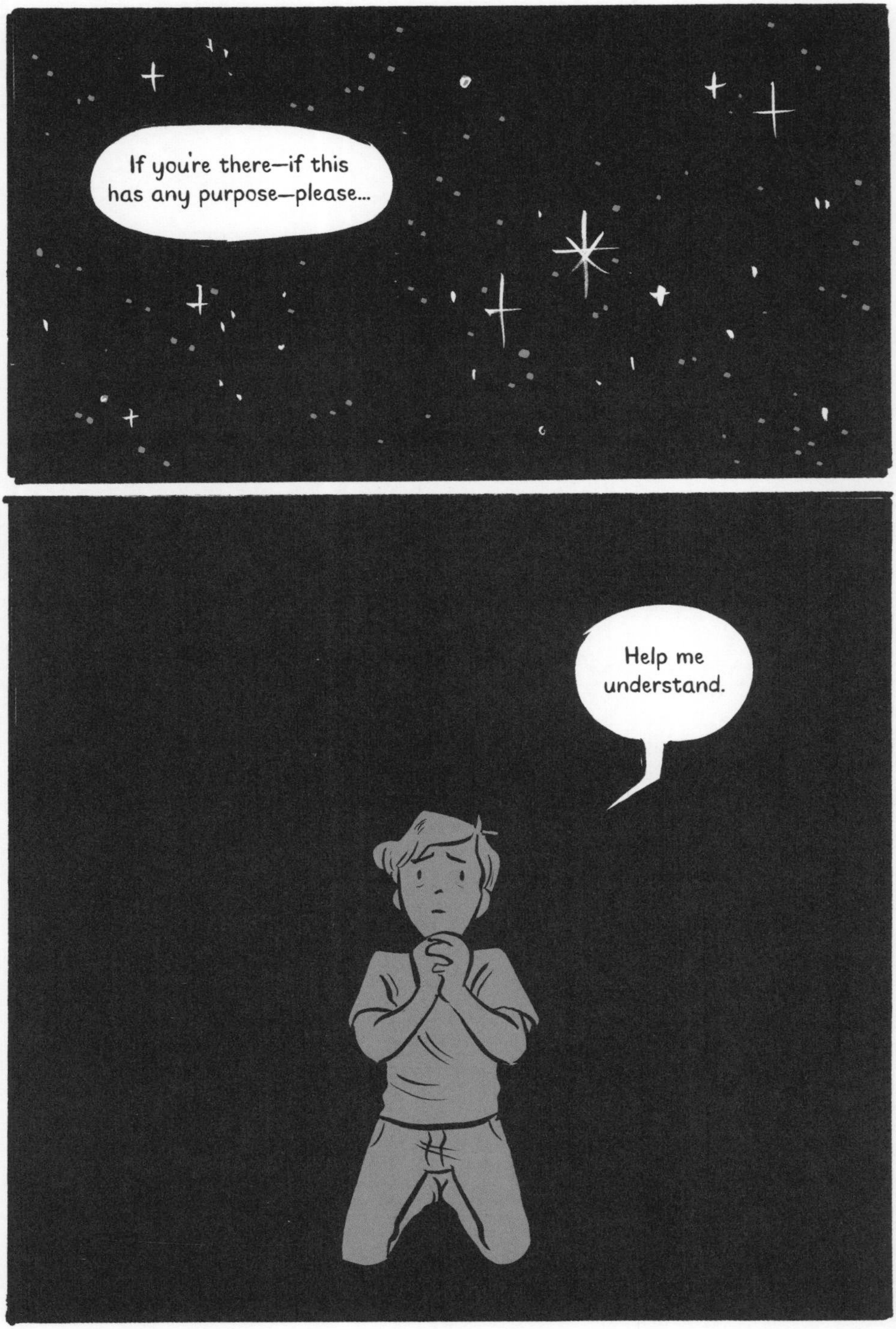
If you're there—if this has any purpose—please...
Help me understand.

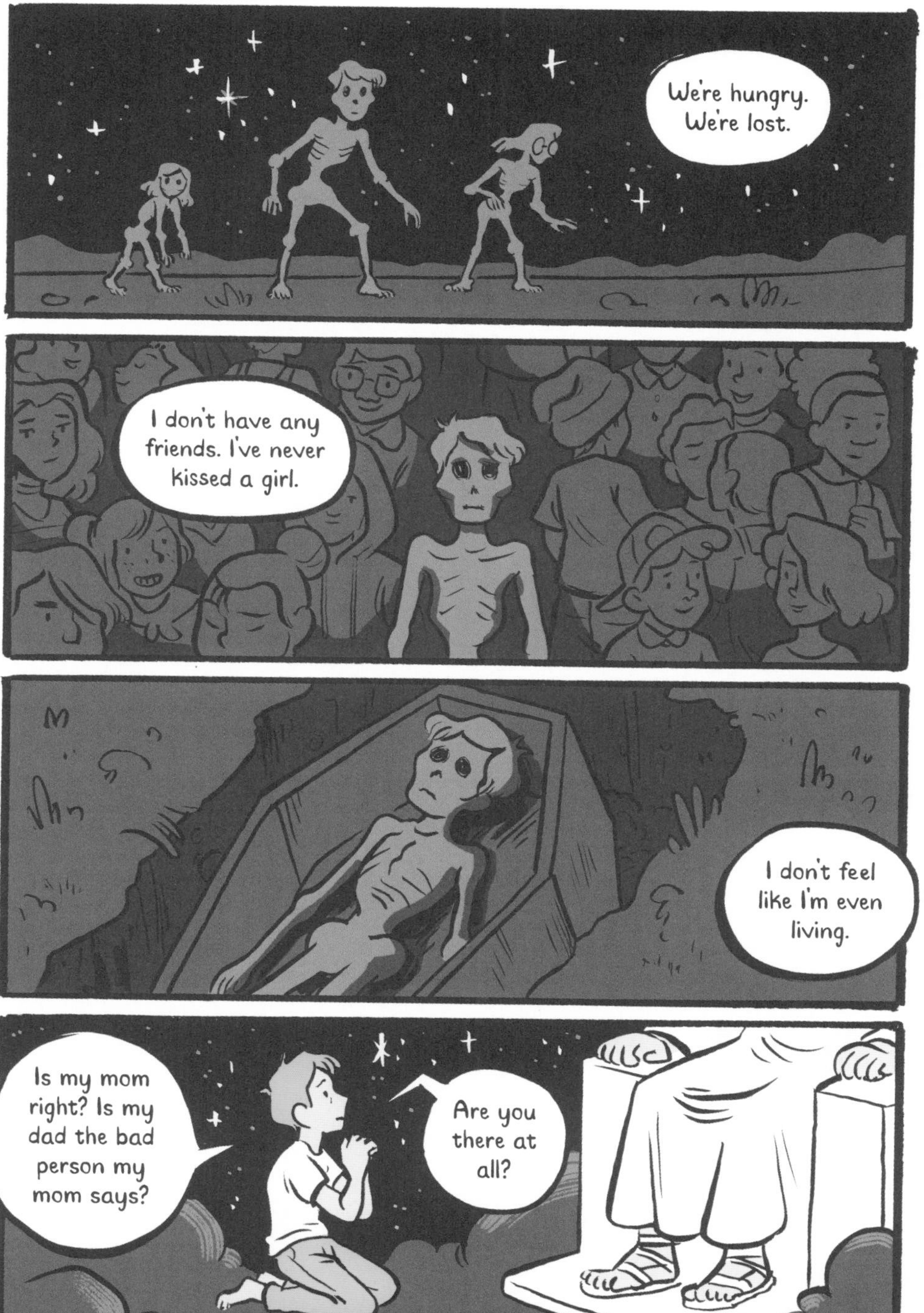
We're hungry. We're lost.
I don't have any friends. I've never kissed a girl.
I don't feel like I'm even living.
Is my mom right? Is my dad the bad person my mom says?
Are you there at all?

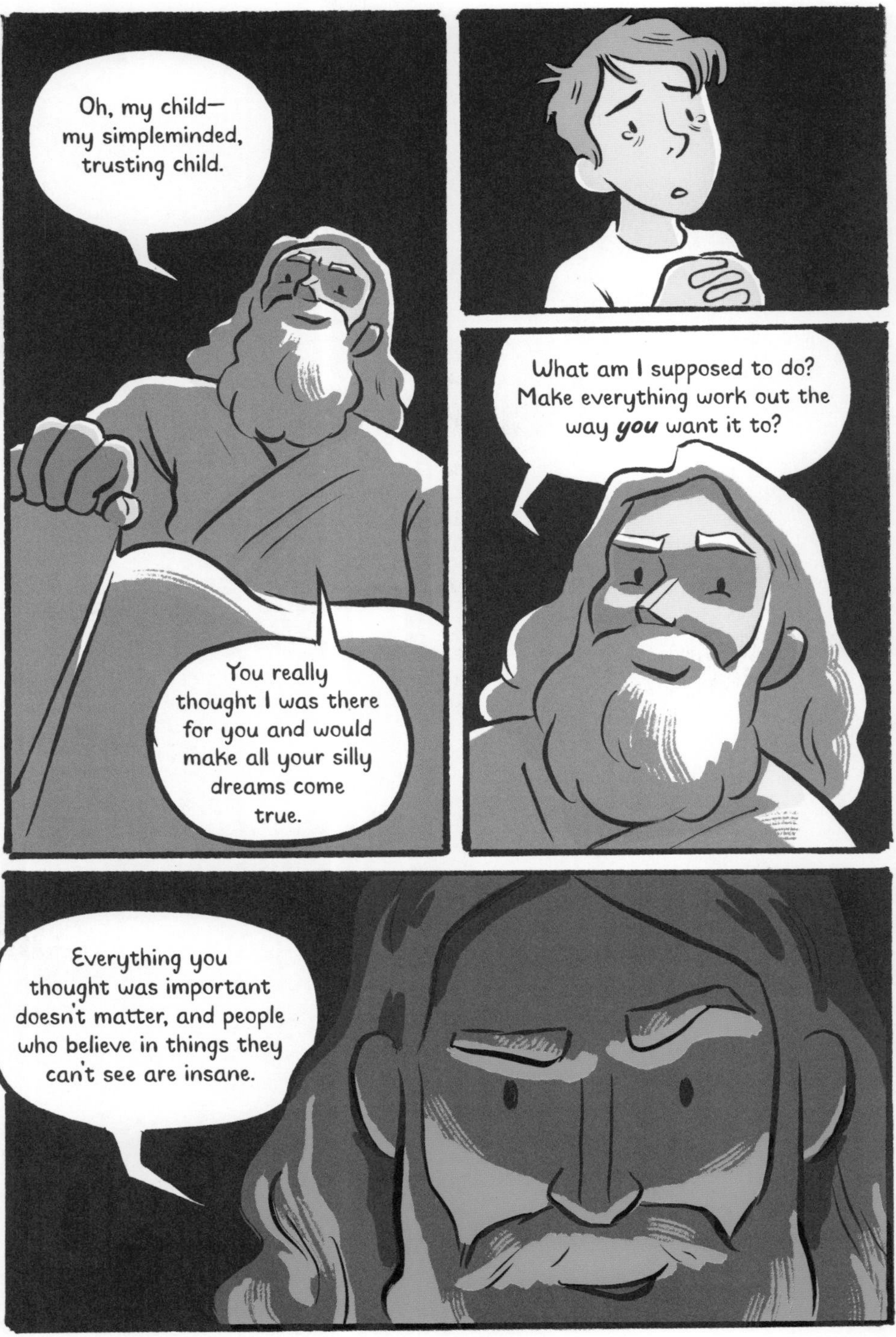
Oh, my child—my simpleminded, trusting child.
You really thought I was there for you and would make all your silly dreams come true.
What am I supposed to do? Make everything work out the way *you* want it to?
Everything you thought was important doesn't matter, and people who believe in things they can't see are insane.

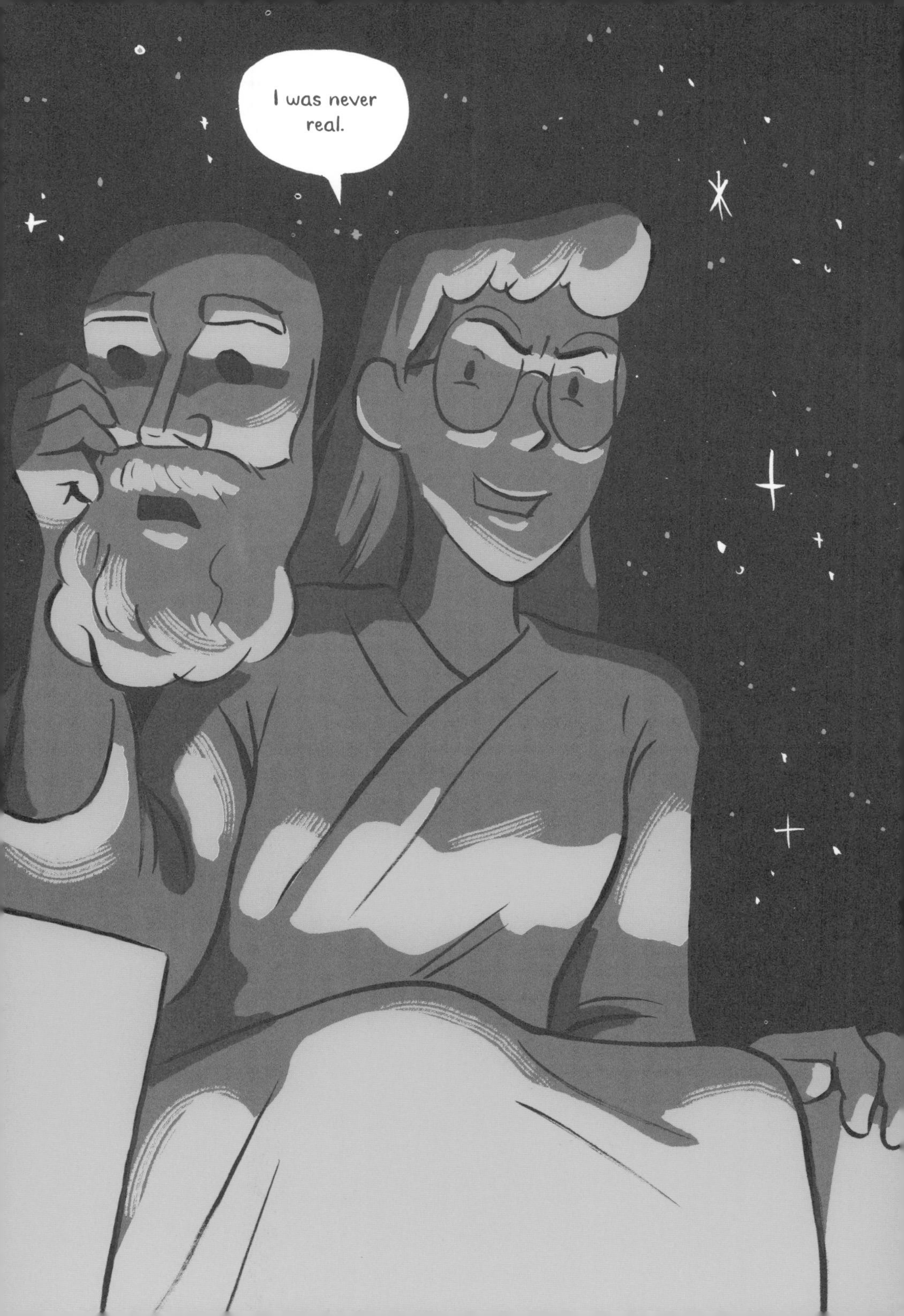
I was never real.

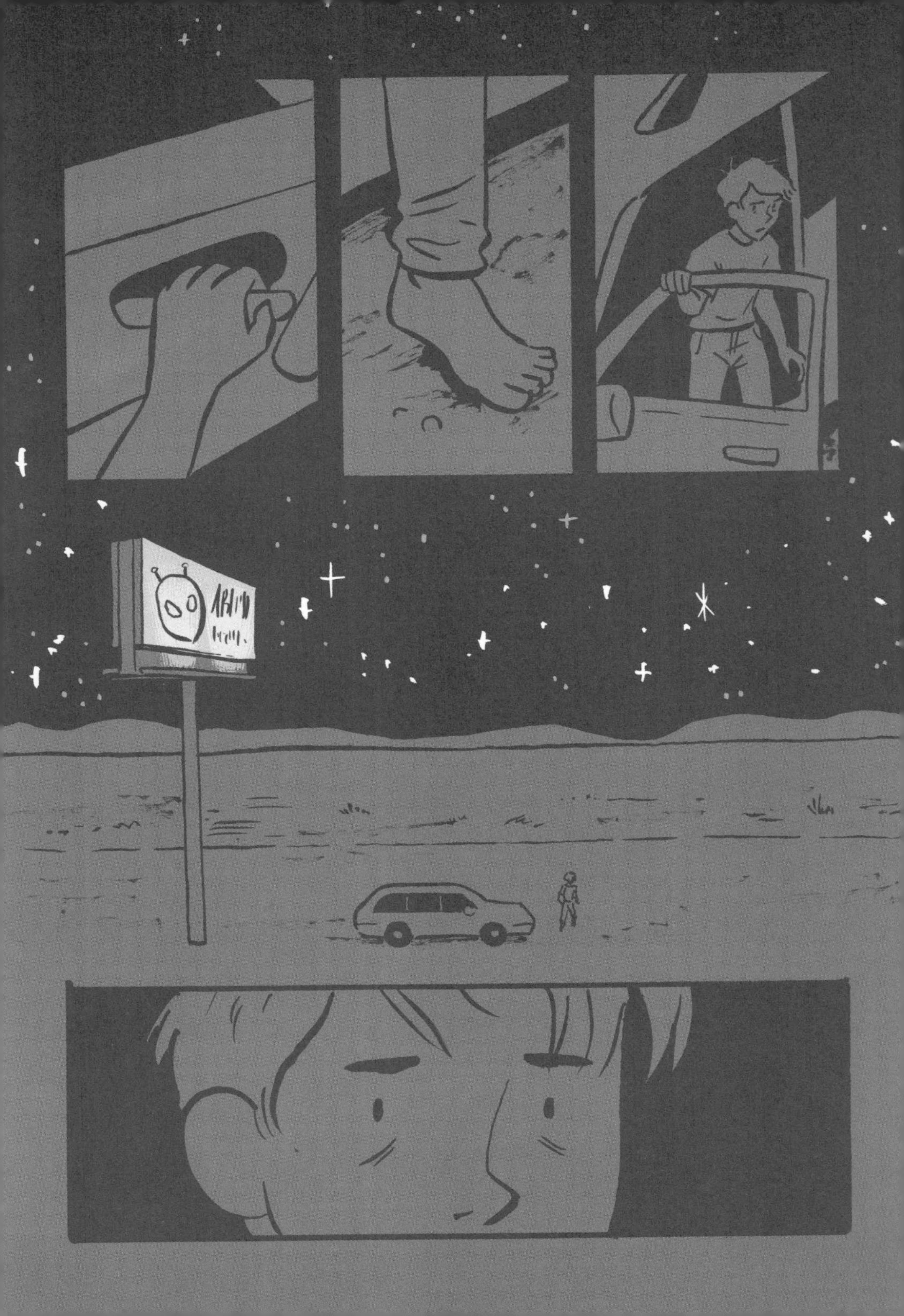

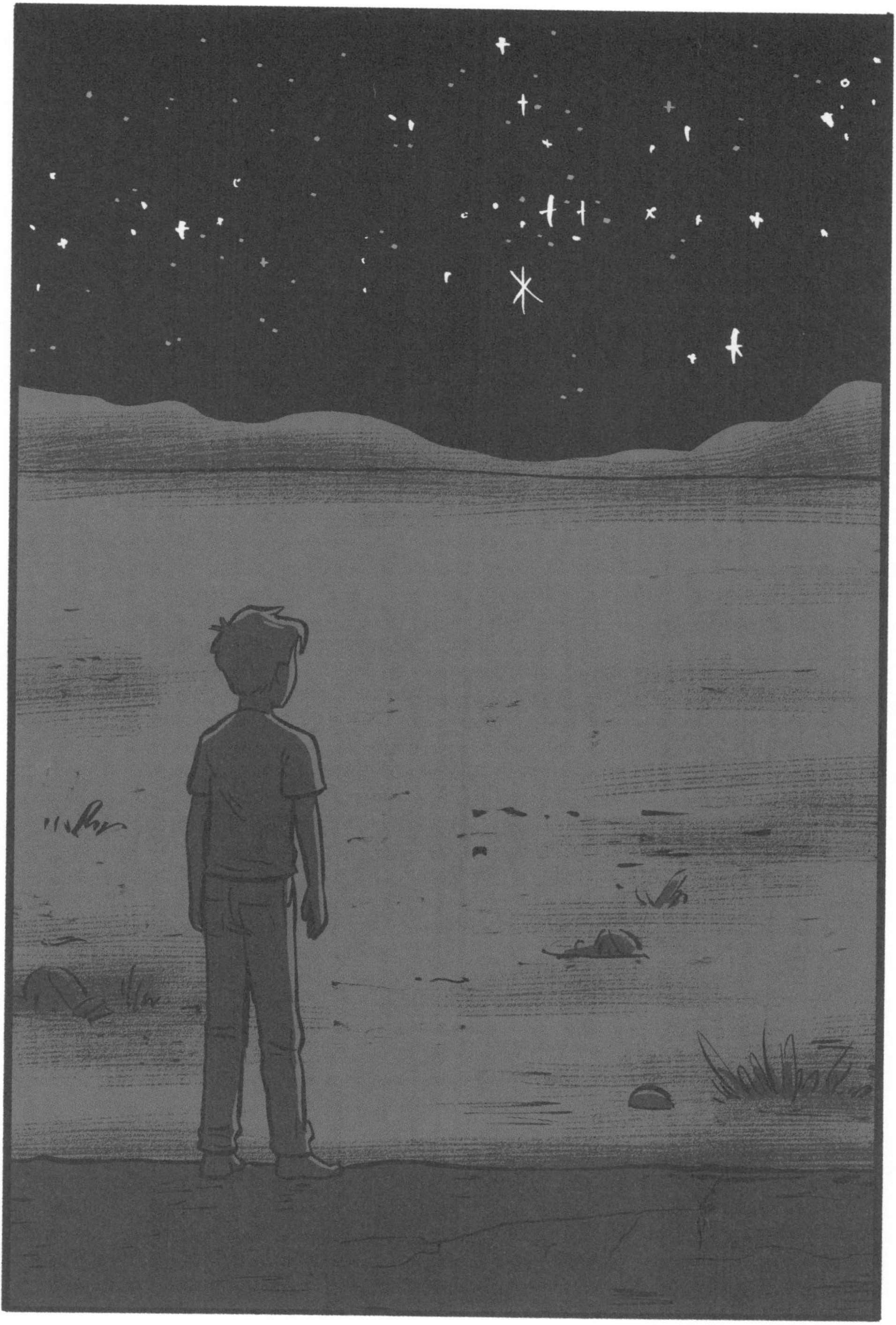

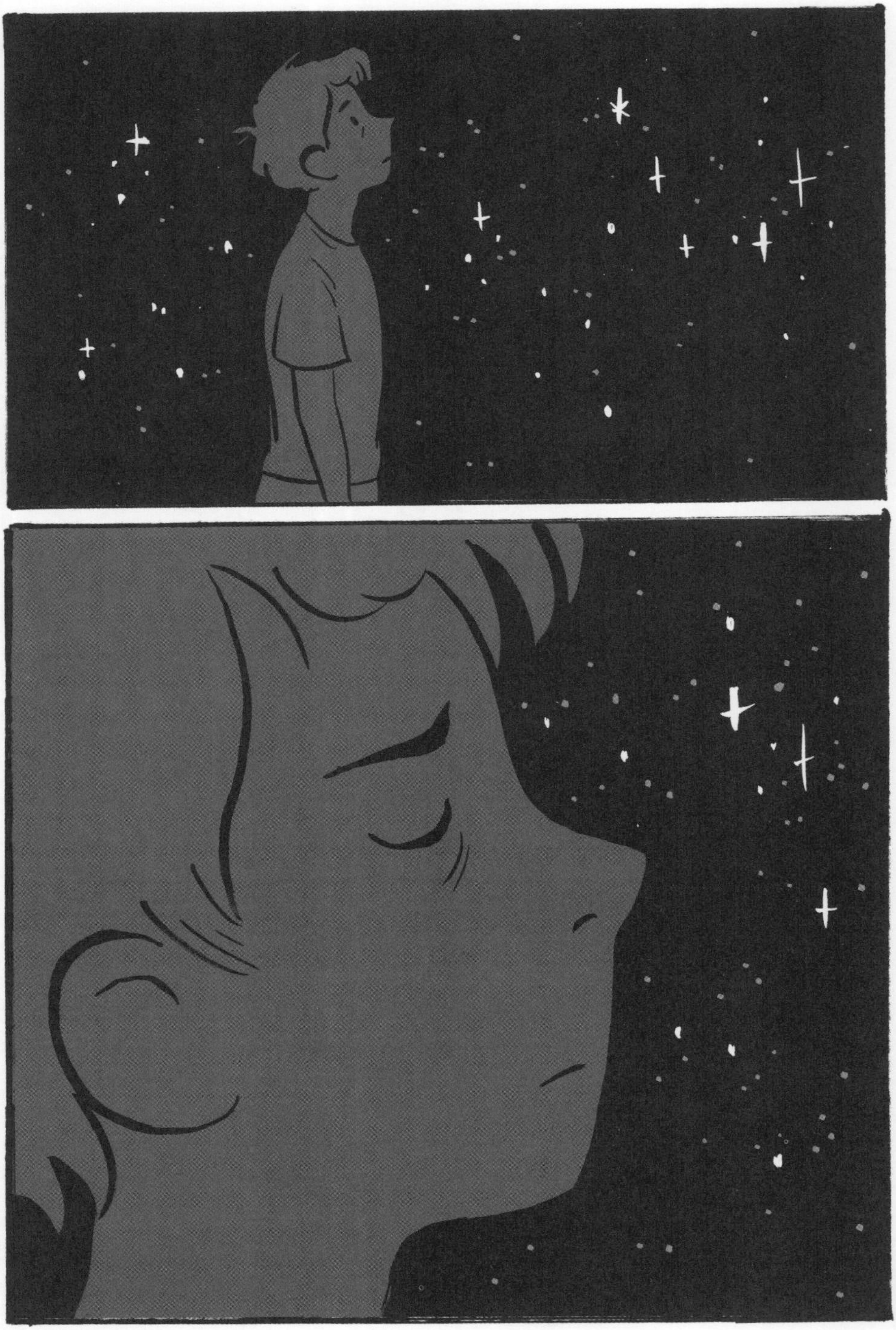

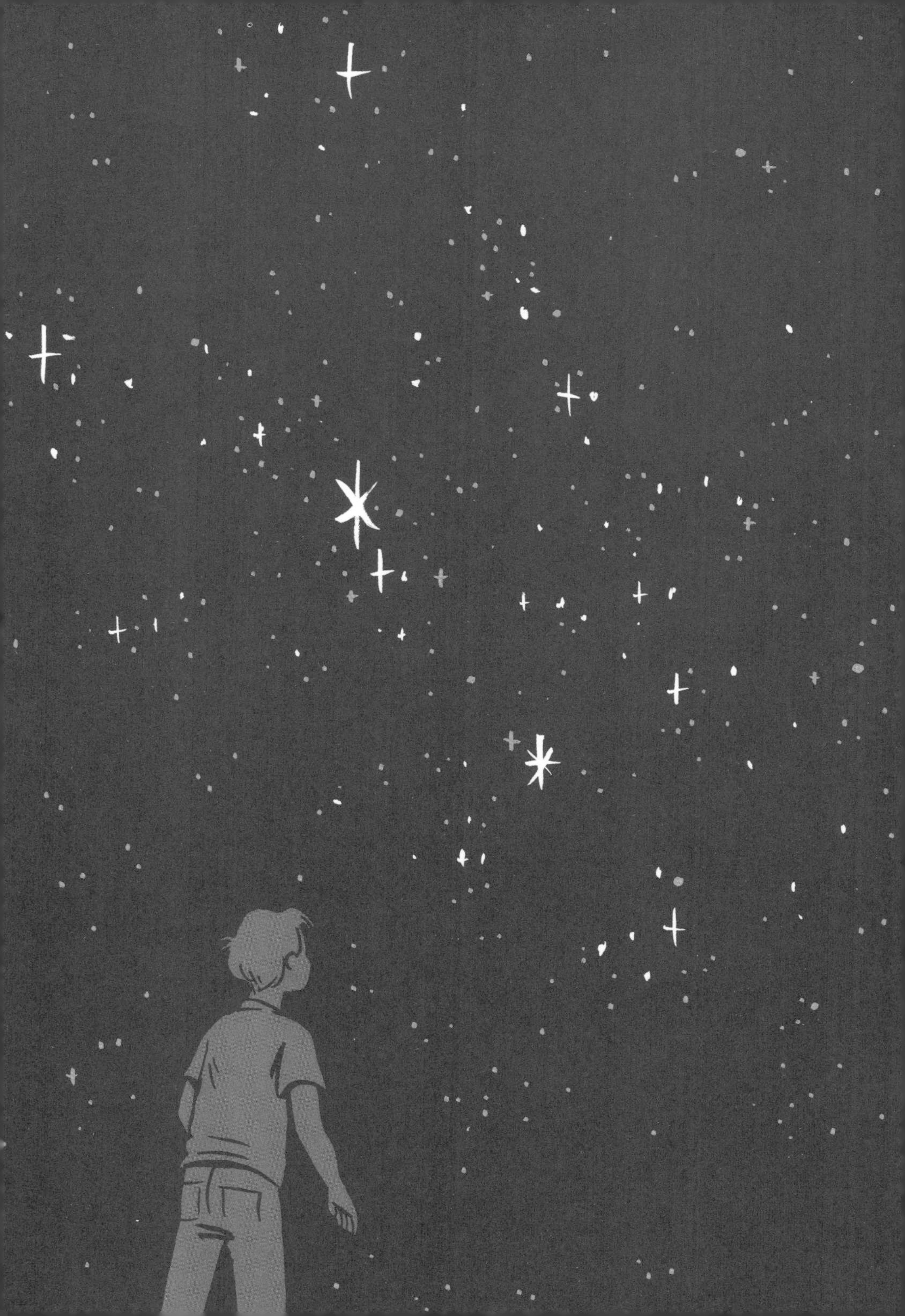

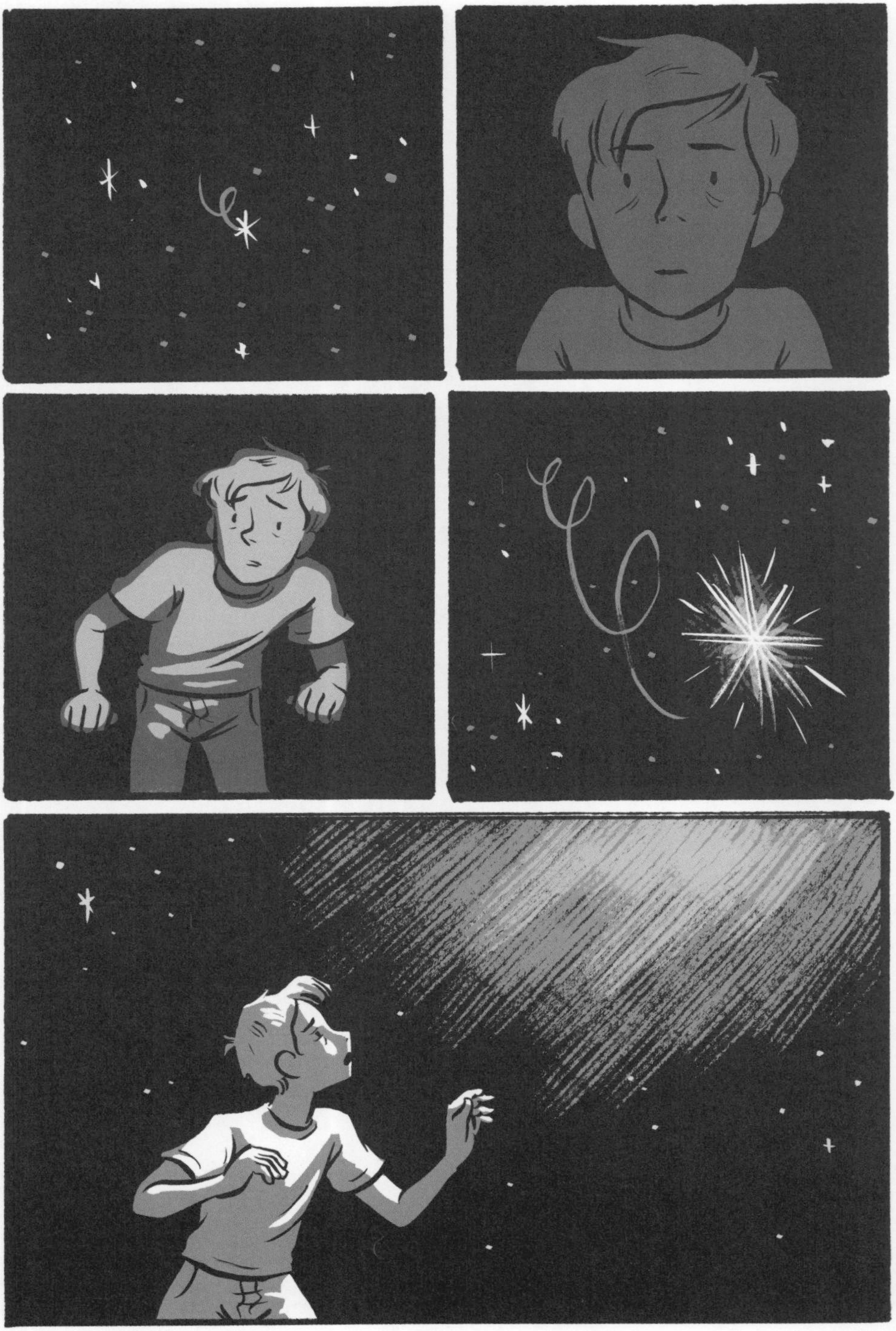

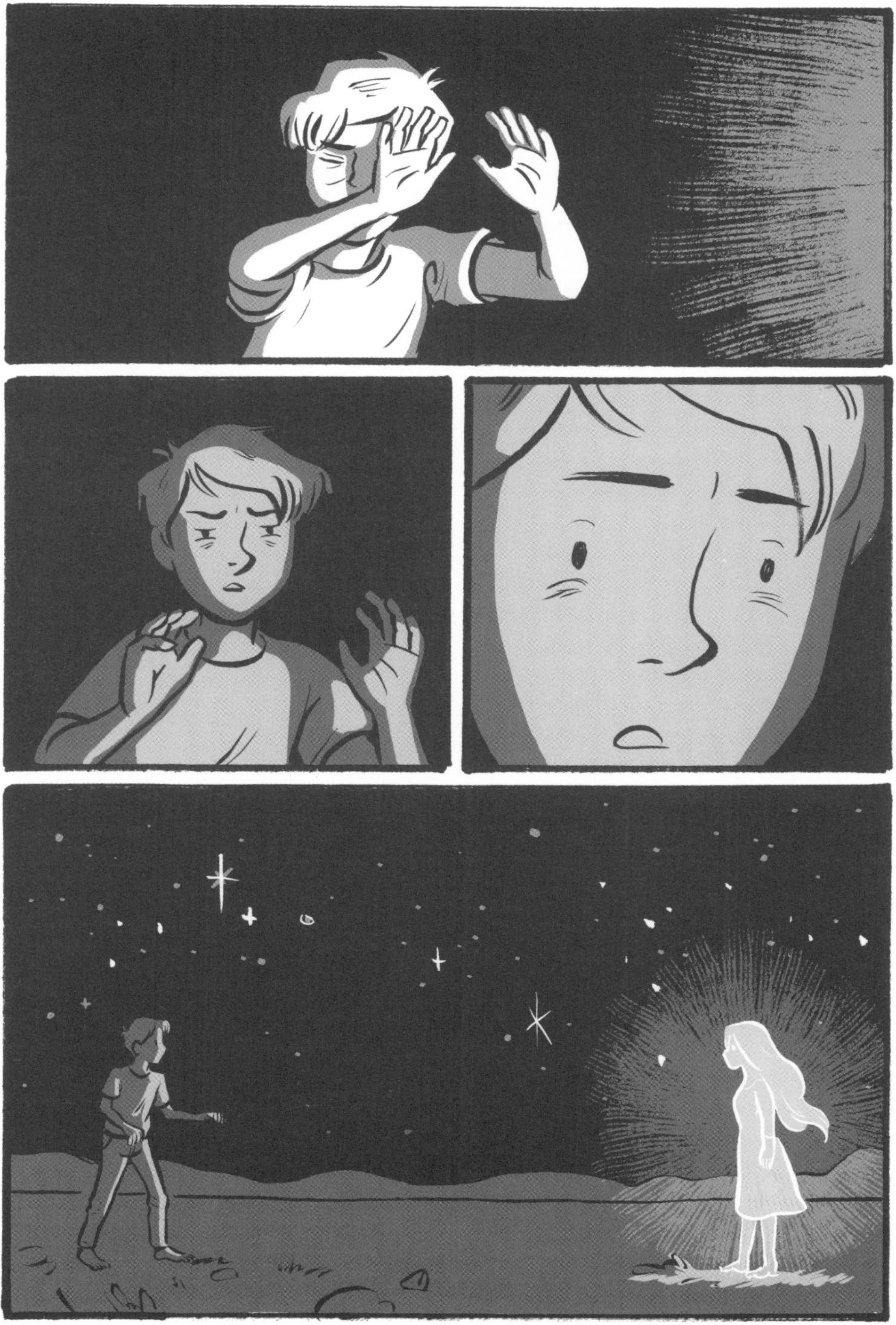

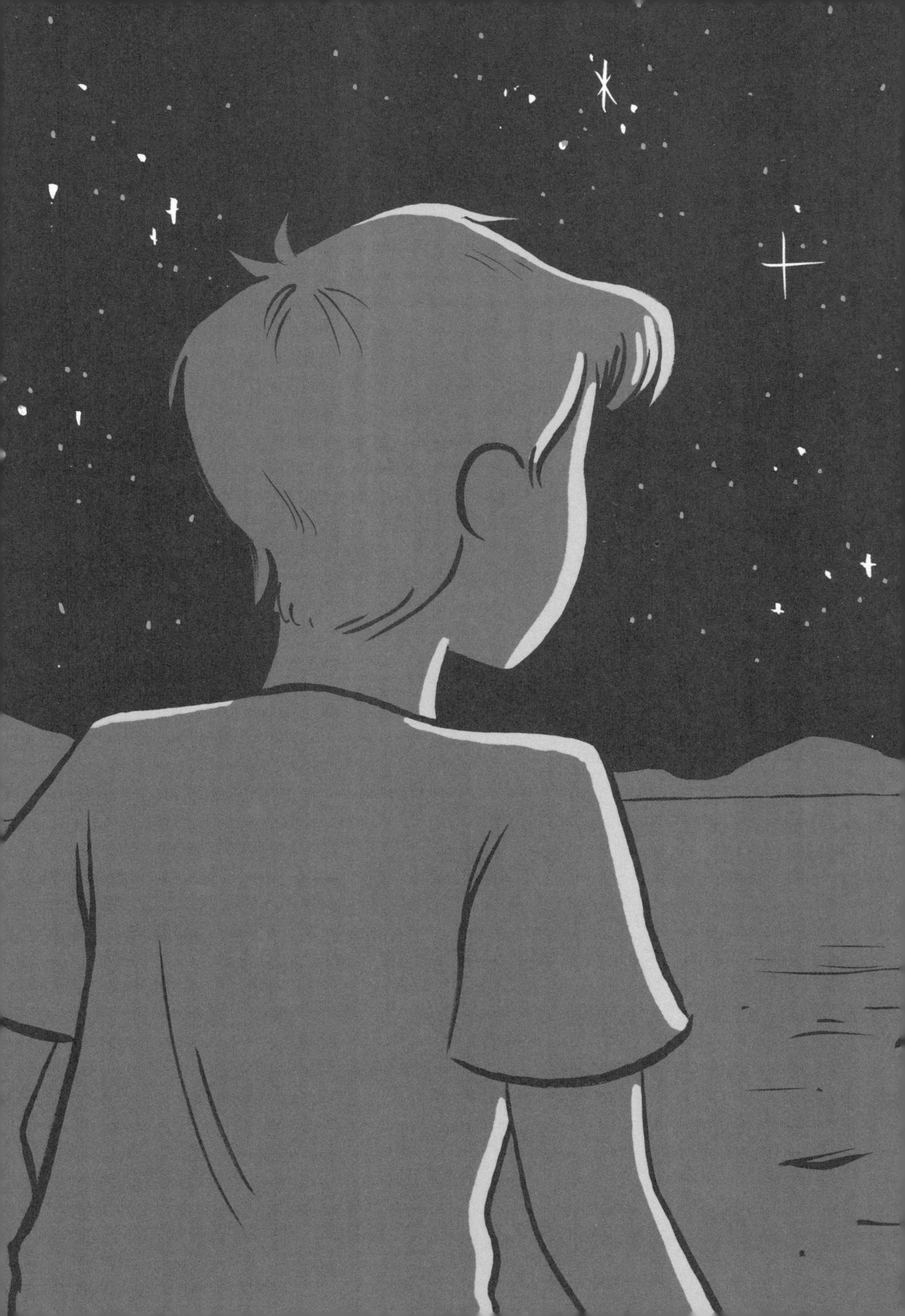

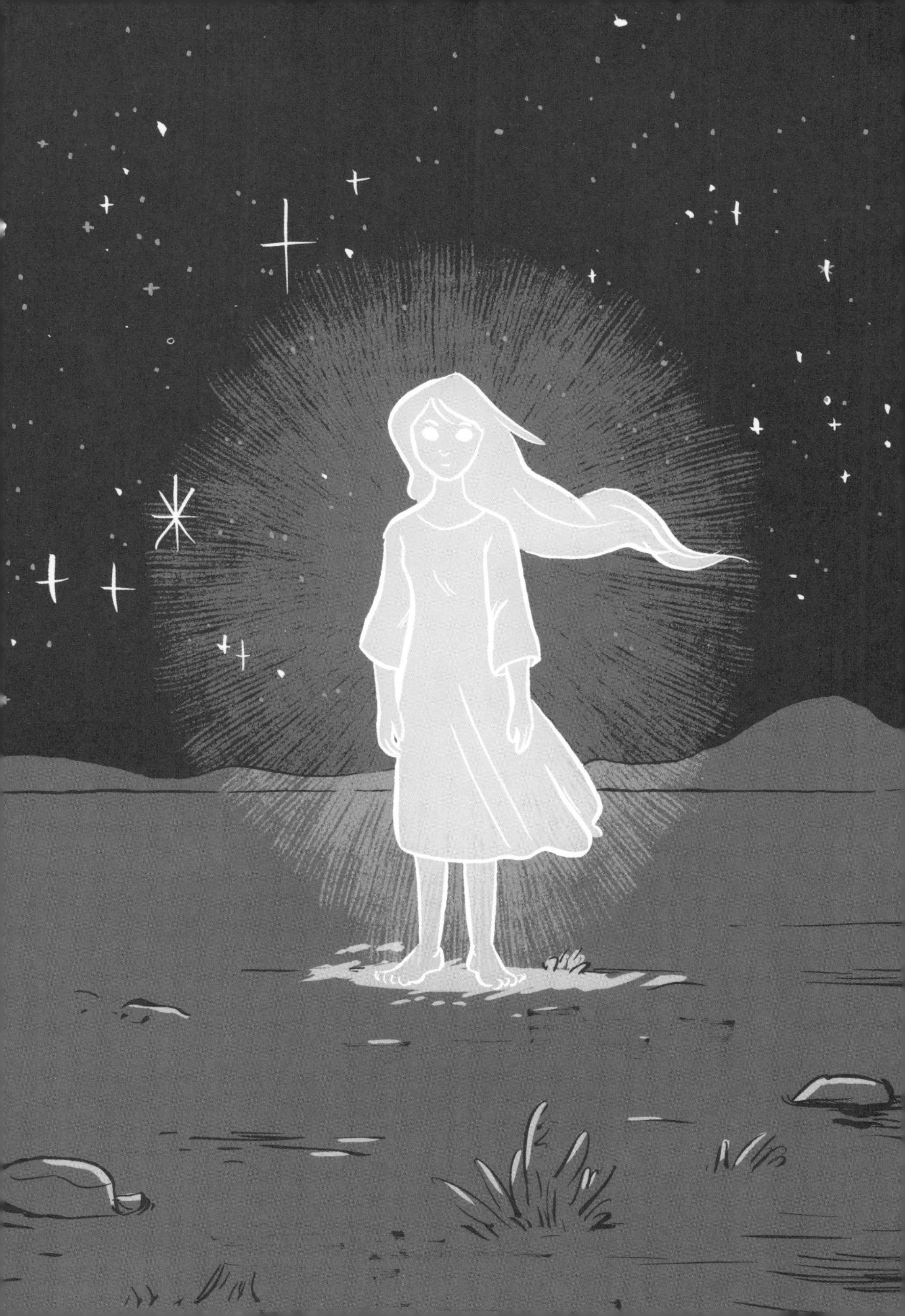

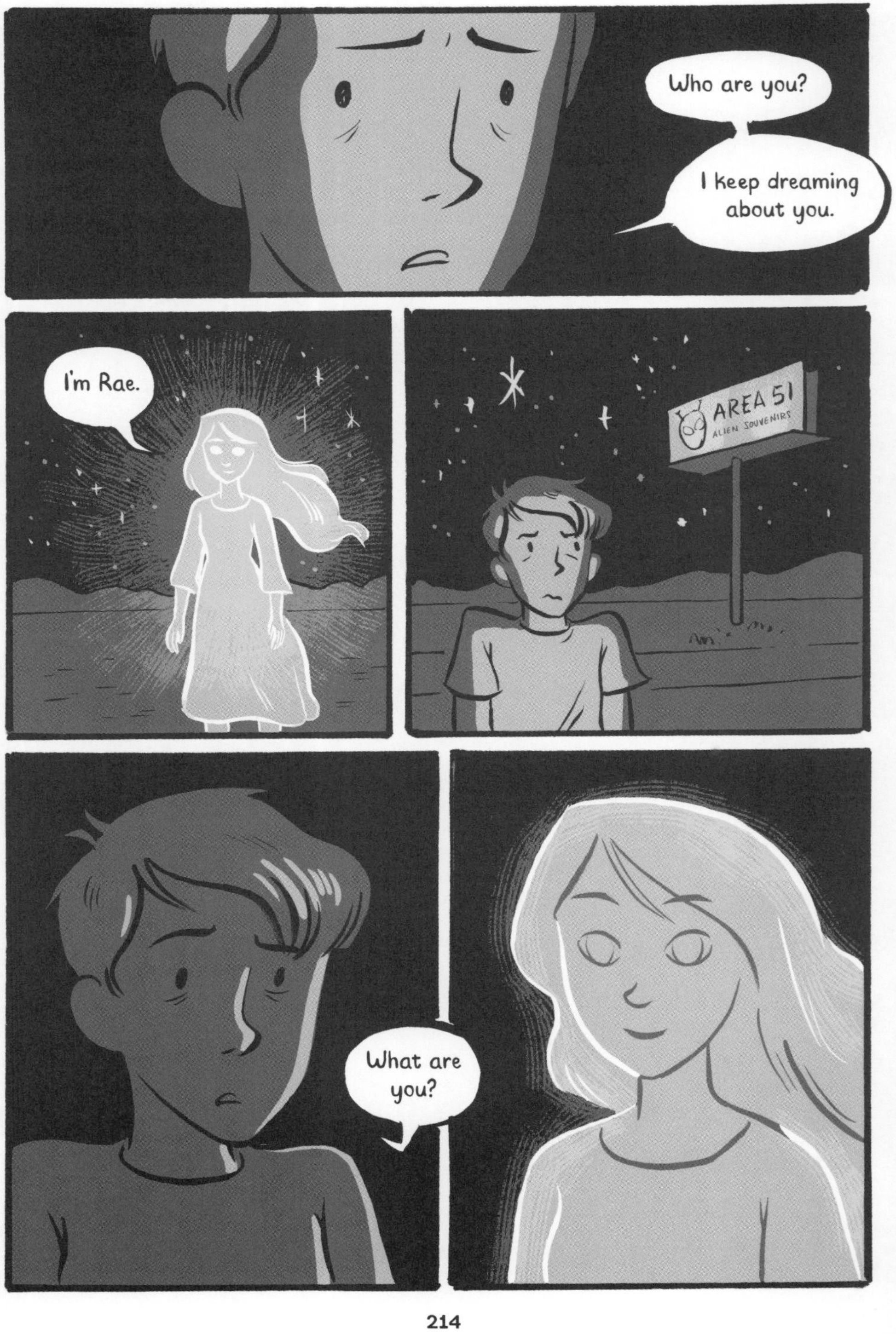
Who are you?
I keep dreaming about you.
I'm Rae.
AREA 51
ALIEN SOUVENIRS
What are you?

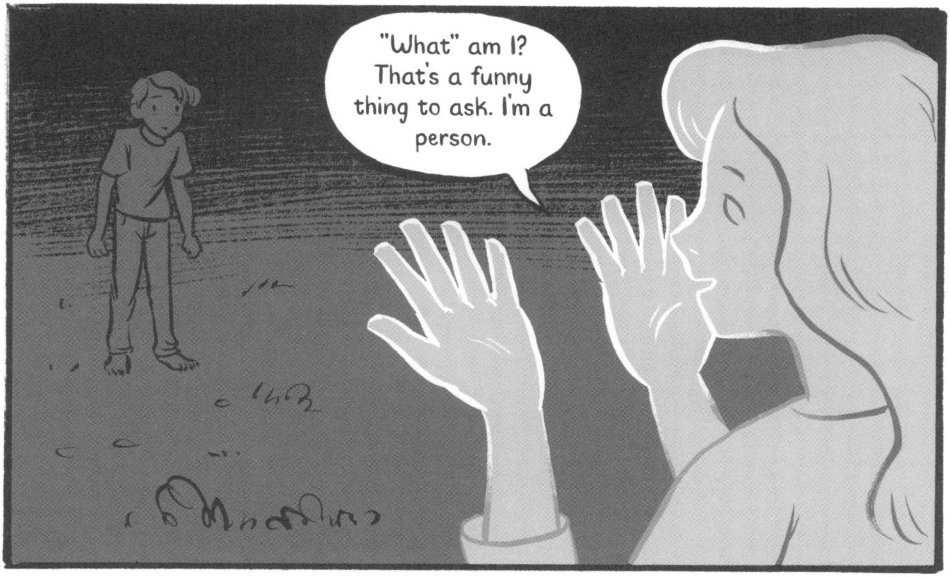
"What" am I? That's a funny thing to ask. I'm a person.

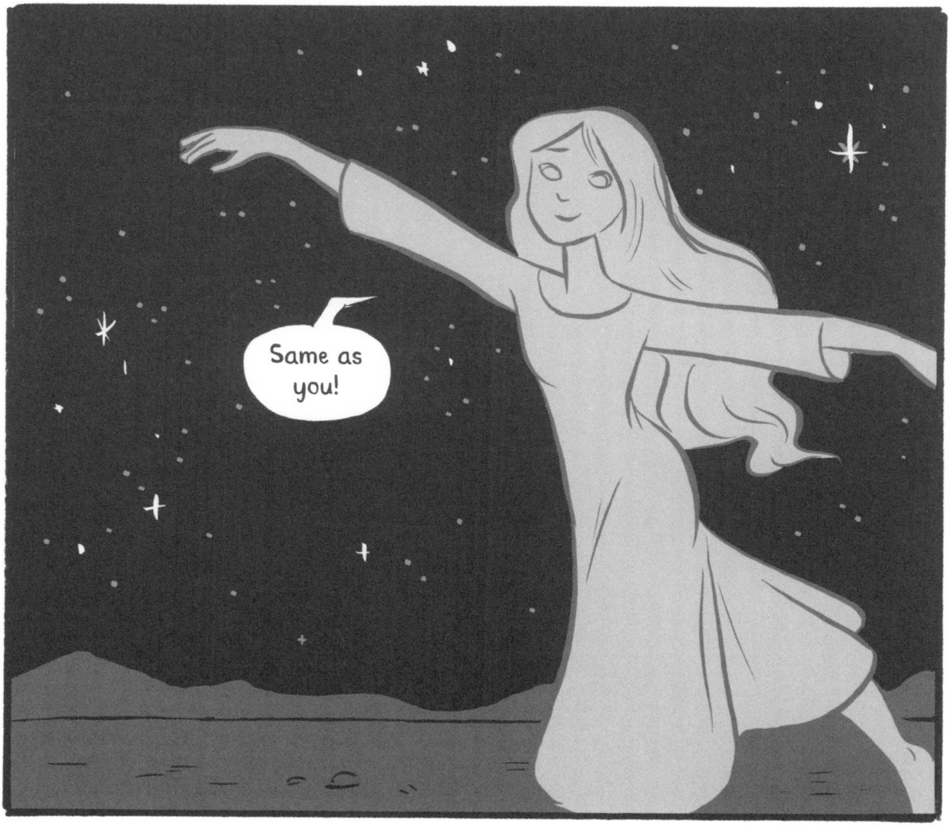
Same as you!

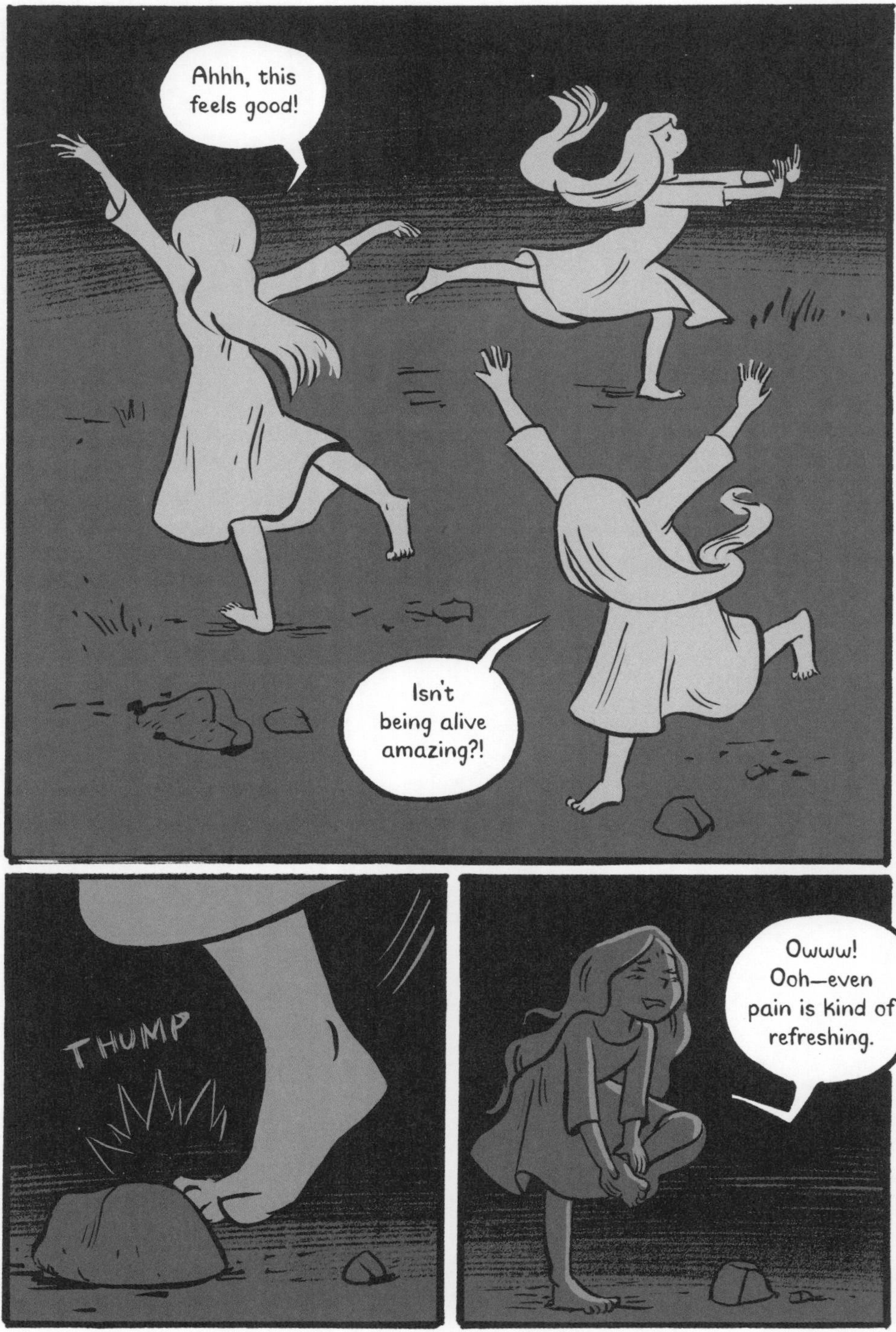
Ahhh, this feels good!
Isn't being alive amazing?!
THUMP
Owww! Ooh—even pain is kind of refreshing.

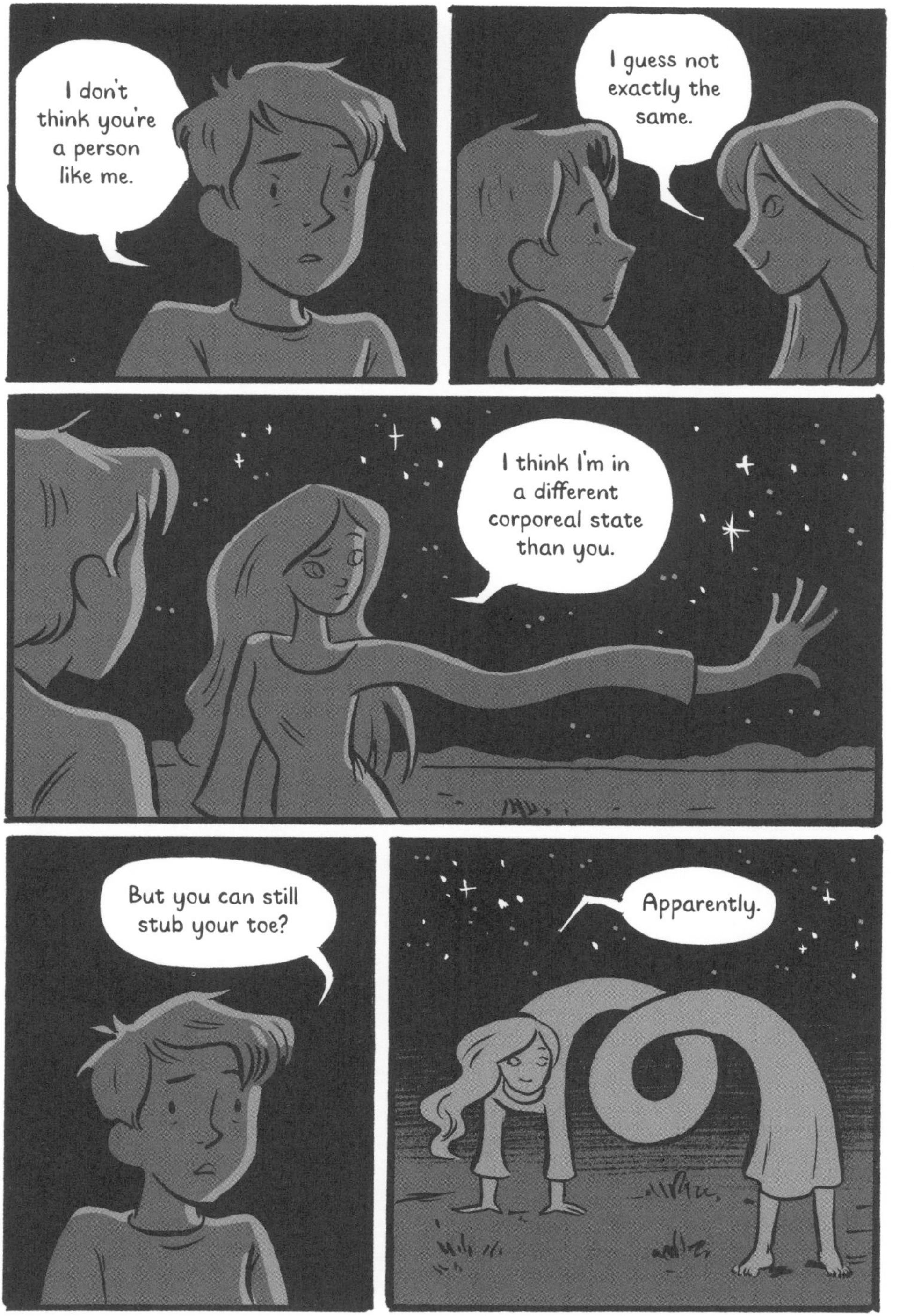
I don't think you're a person like me.
I guess not exactly the same.
I think I'm in a different corporeal state than you.
But you can still stub your toe?
Apparently.

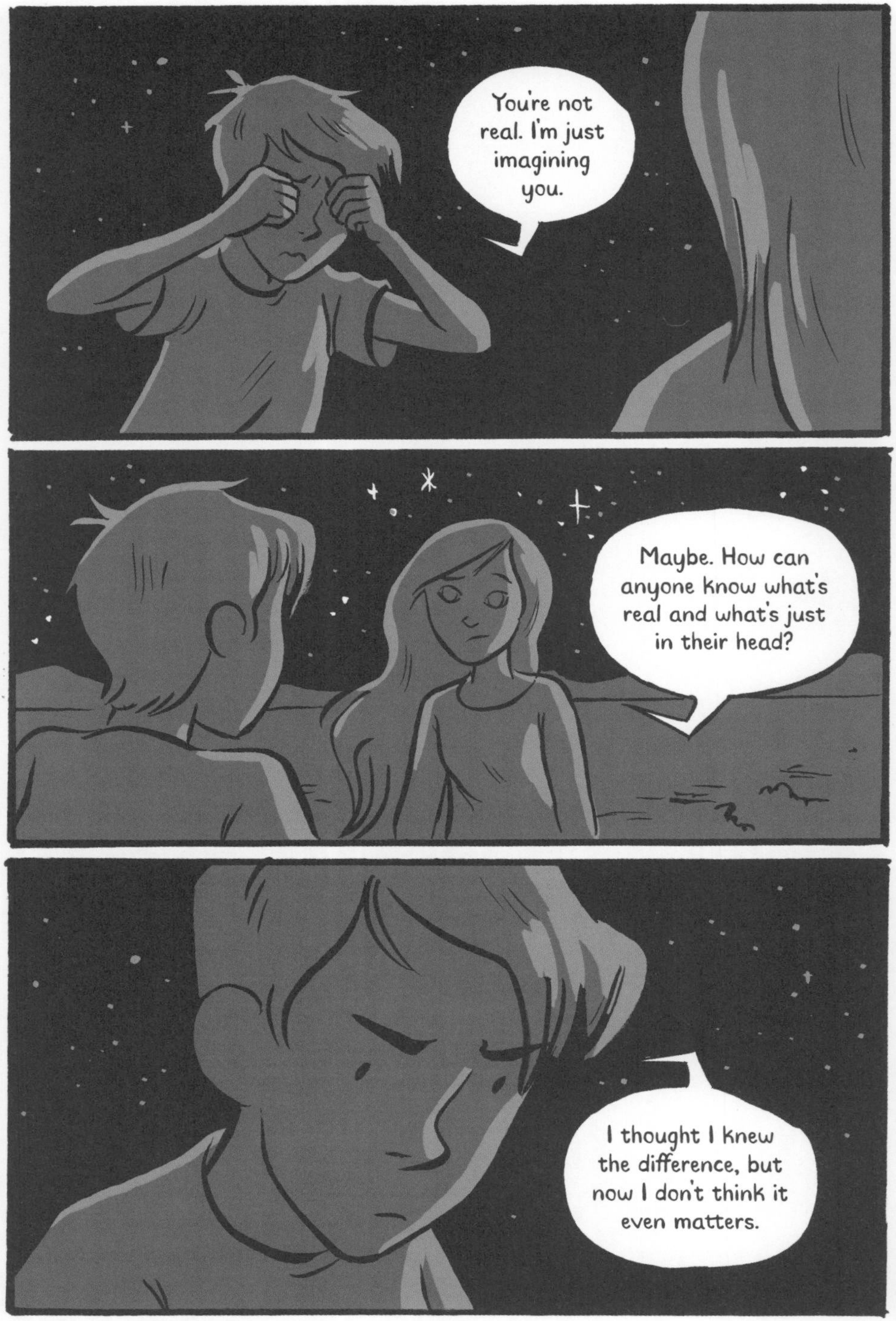
You're not real. I'm just imagining you.
Maybe. How can anyone know what's real and what's just in their head?
I thought I knew the difference, but now I don't think it even matters.

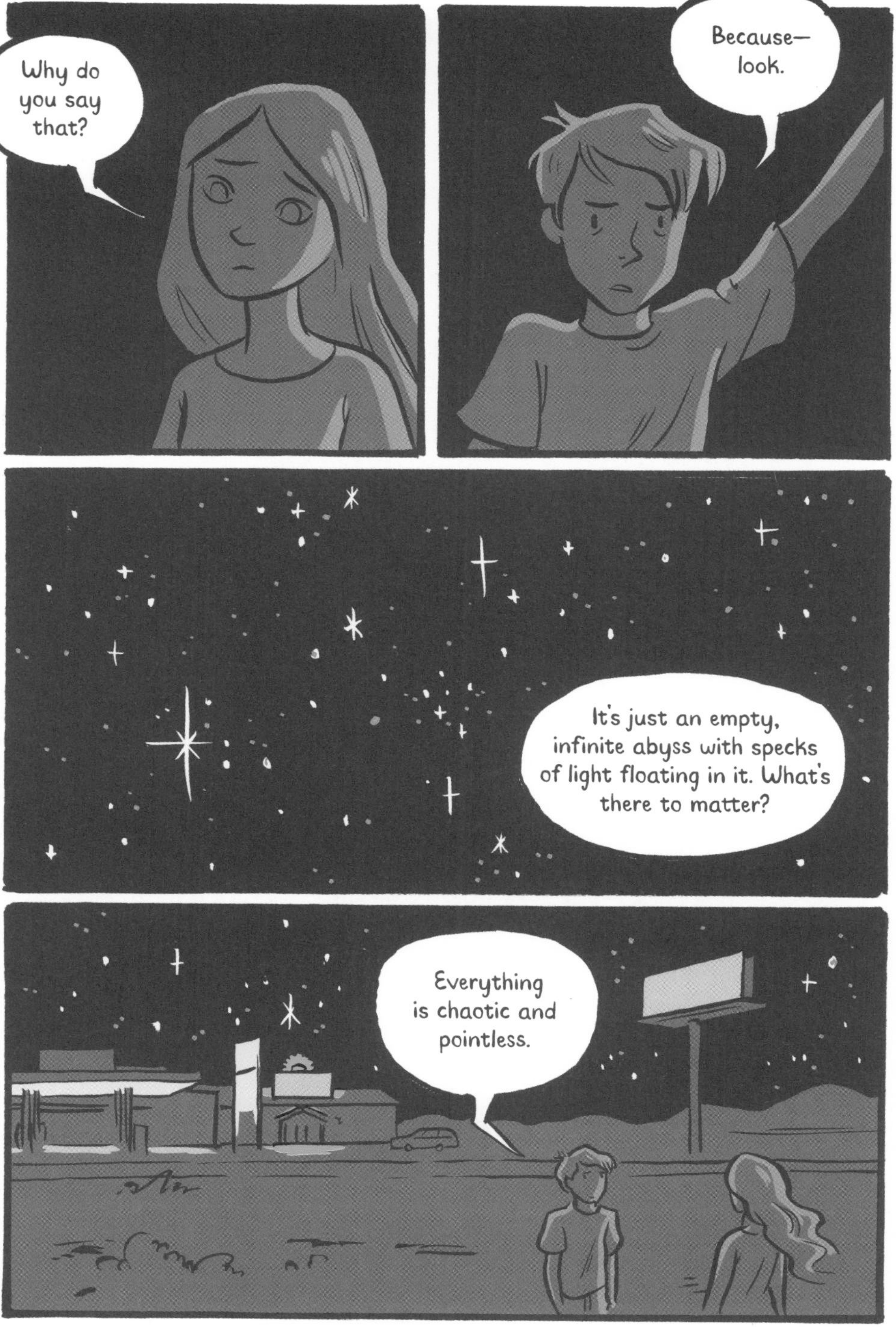
Why do you say that?
Because—look.
It's just an empty, infinite abyss with specks of light floating in it. What's there to matter?
Everything is chaotic and pointless.

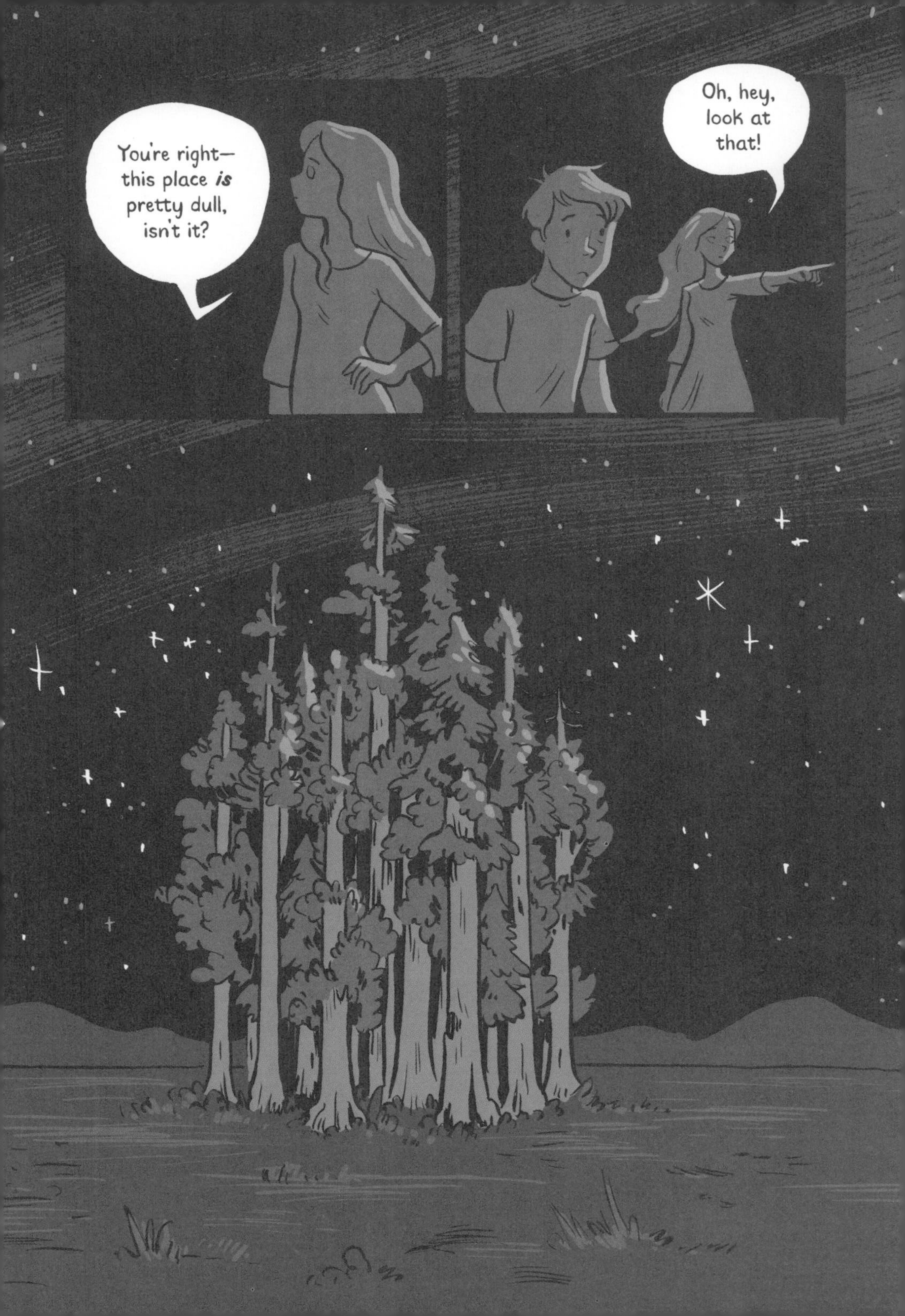
You're right—this place *is* pretty dull, isn't it?
Oh, hey, look at that!

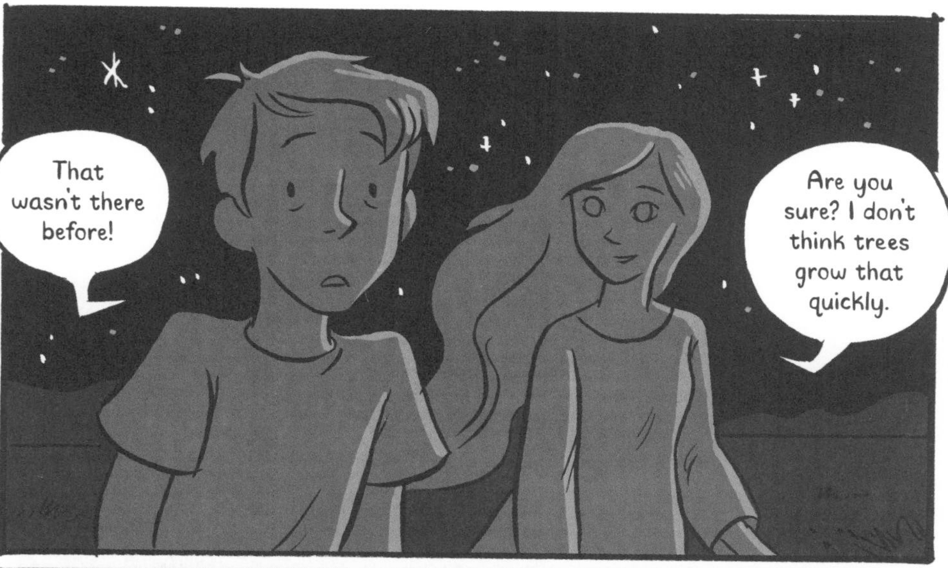
That wasn't there before!
Are you sure? I don't think trees grow that quickly.

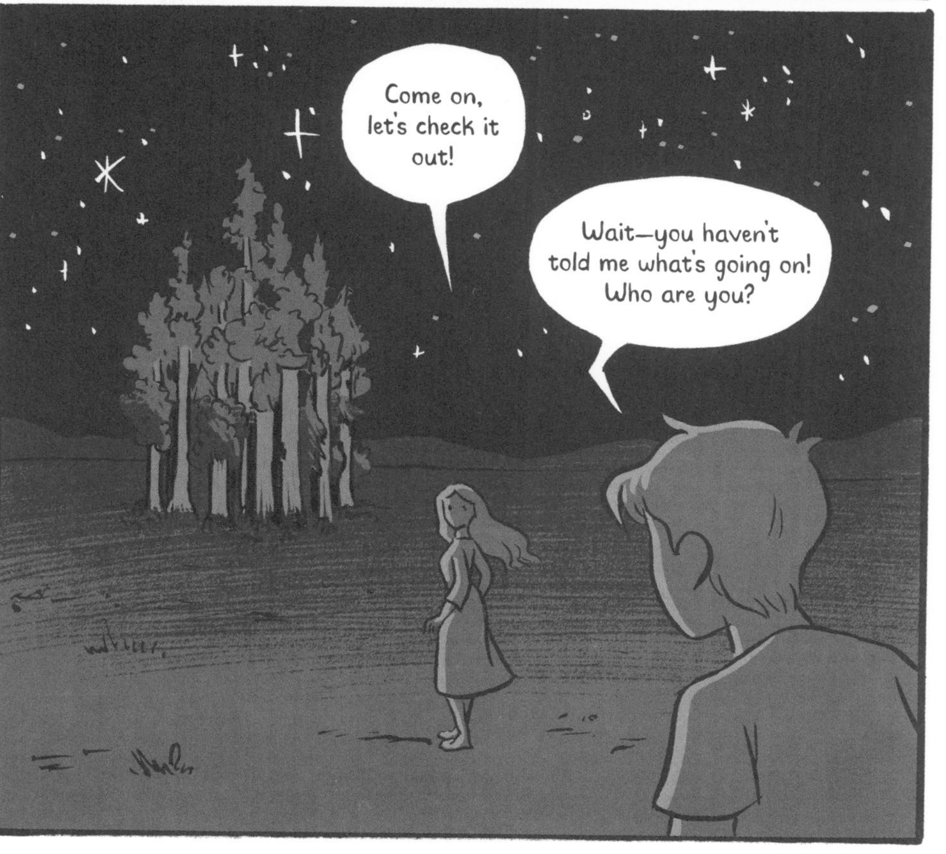
Come on, let's check it out!
Wait—you haven't told me what's going on! Who are you?

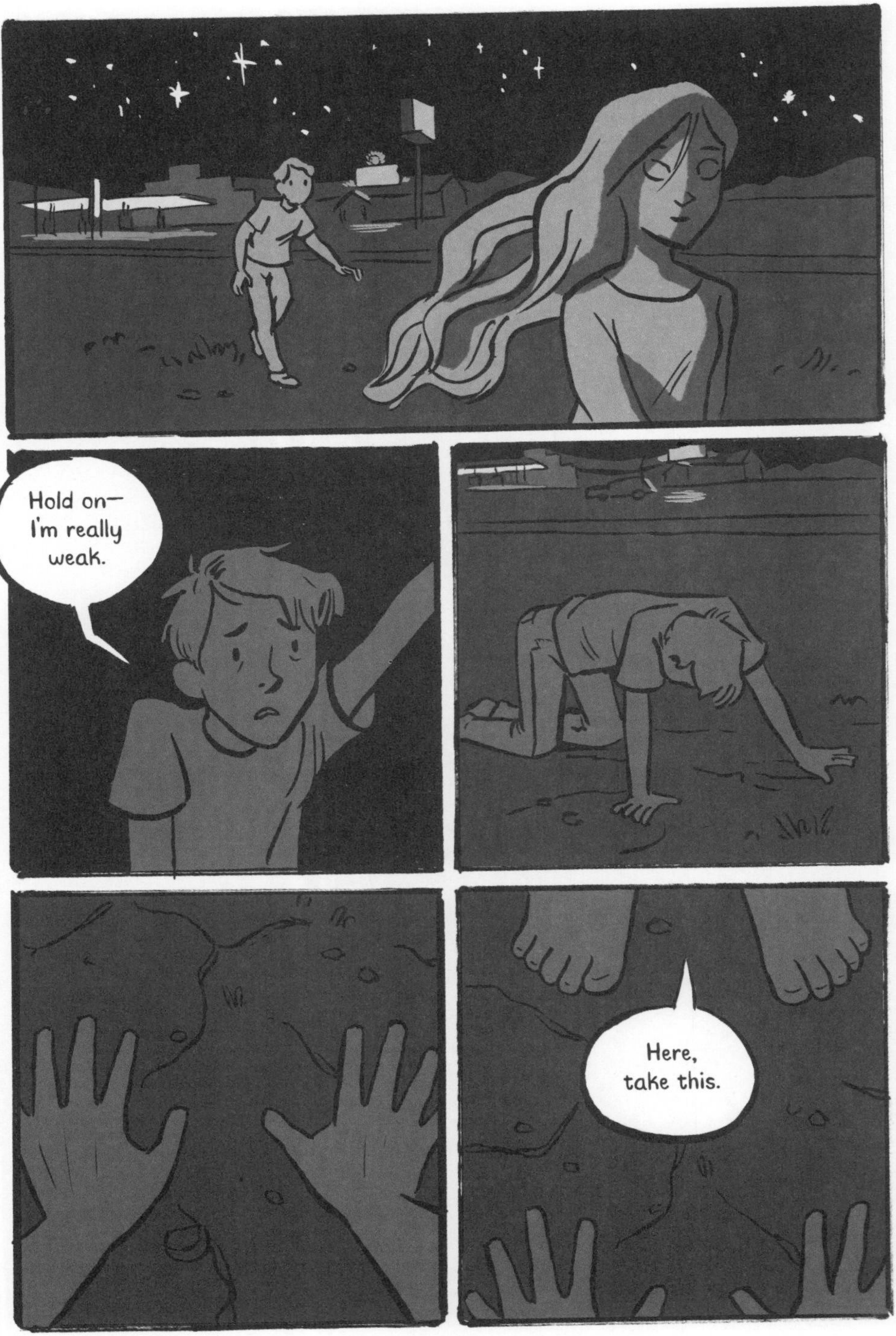
Hold on—
I'm really
weak.
Here,
take this.

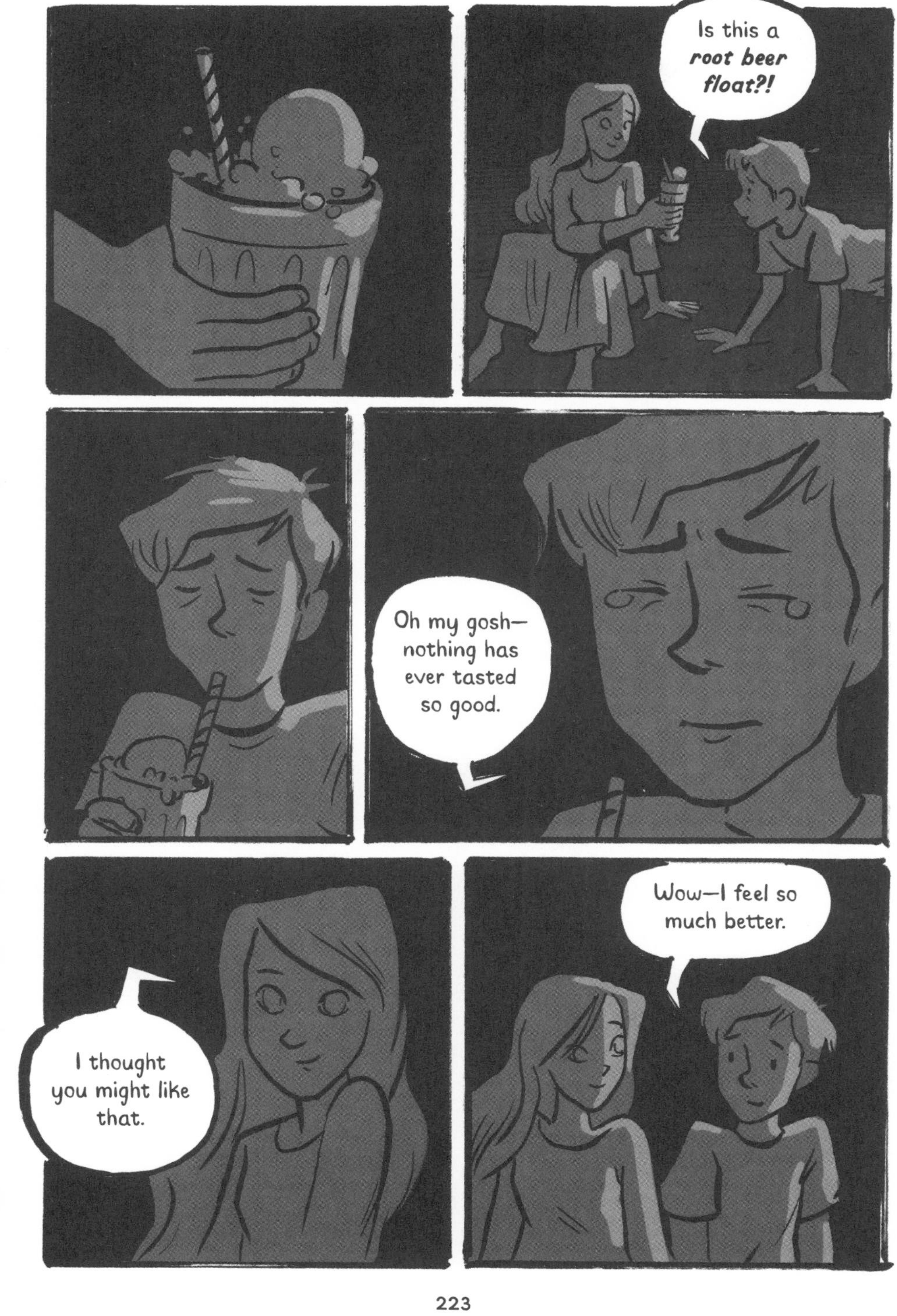
Is this a ***root beer float?!***
Oh my gosh—nothing has ever tasted so good.
I thought you might like that.
Wow—I feel so much better.

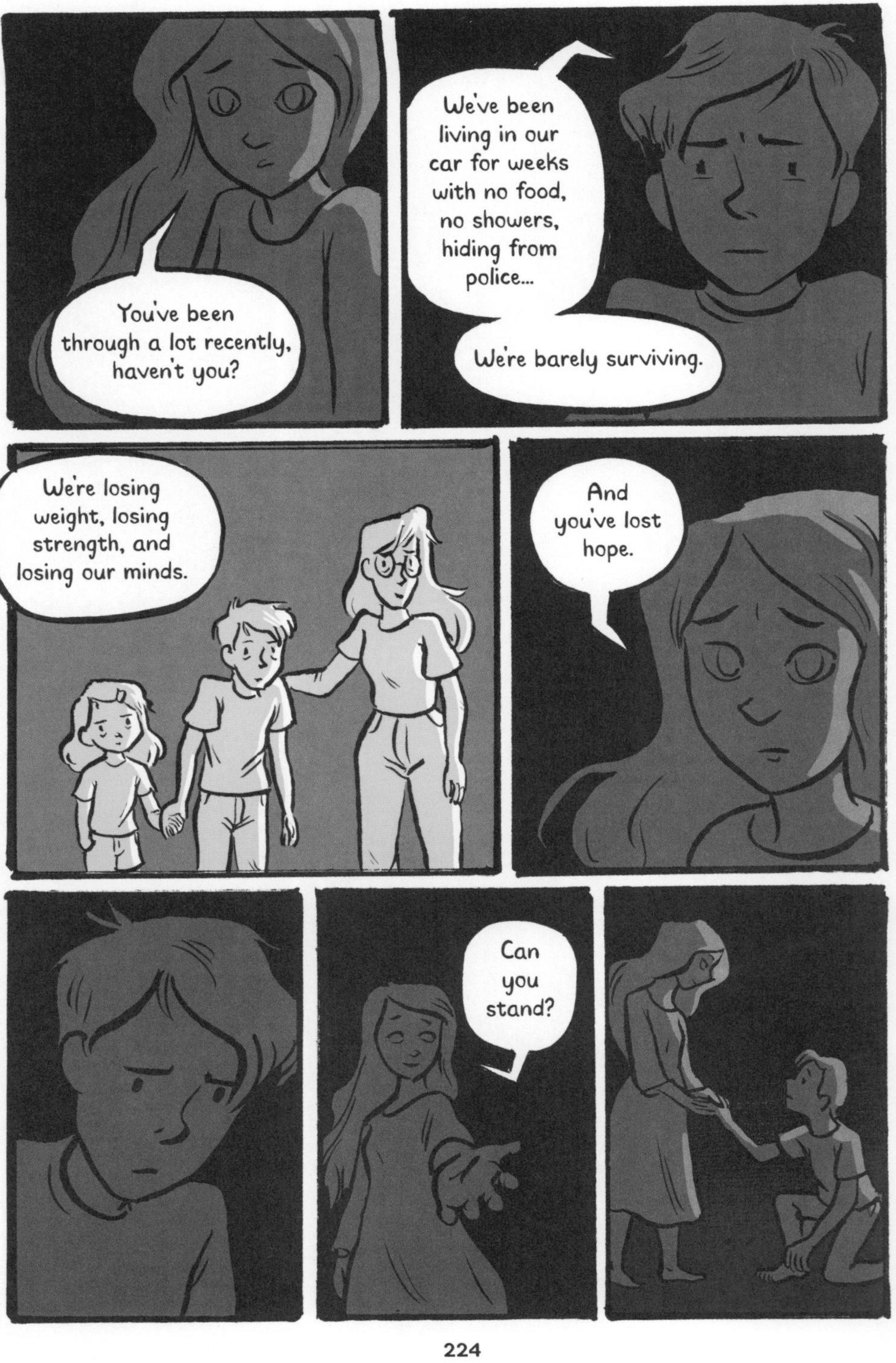
You've been through a lot recently, haven't you?
We've been living in our car for weeks with no food, no showers, hiding from police...
We're barely surviving.
We're losing weight, losing strength, and losing our minds.
And you've lost hope.
Can you stand?

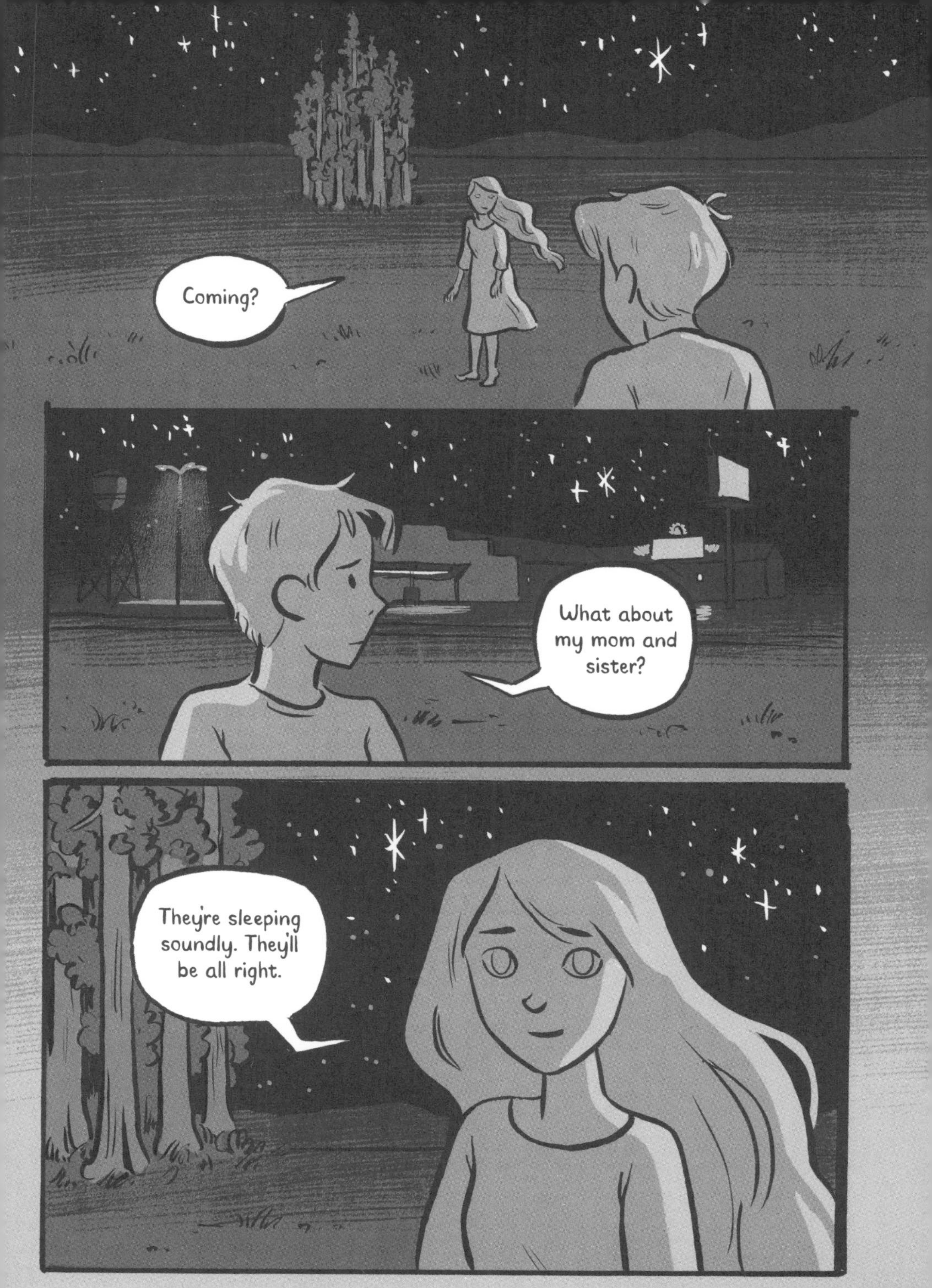
Coming?
What about my mom and sister?
They're sleeping soundly. They'll be all right.

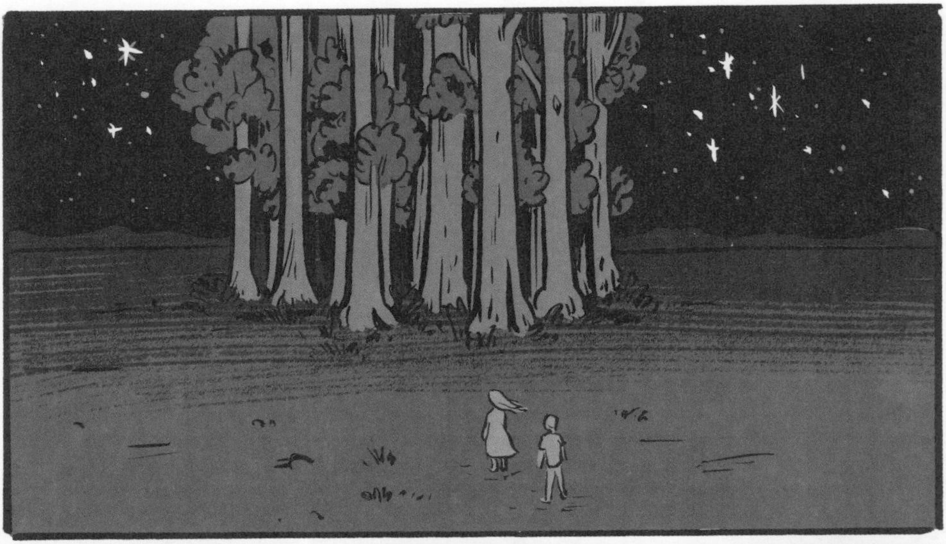

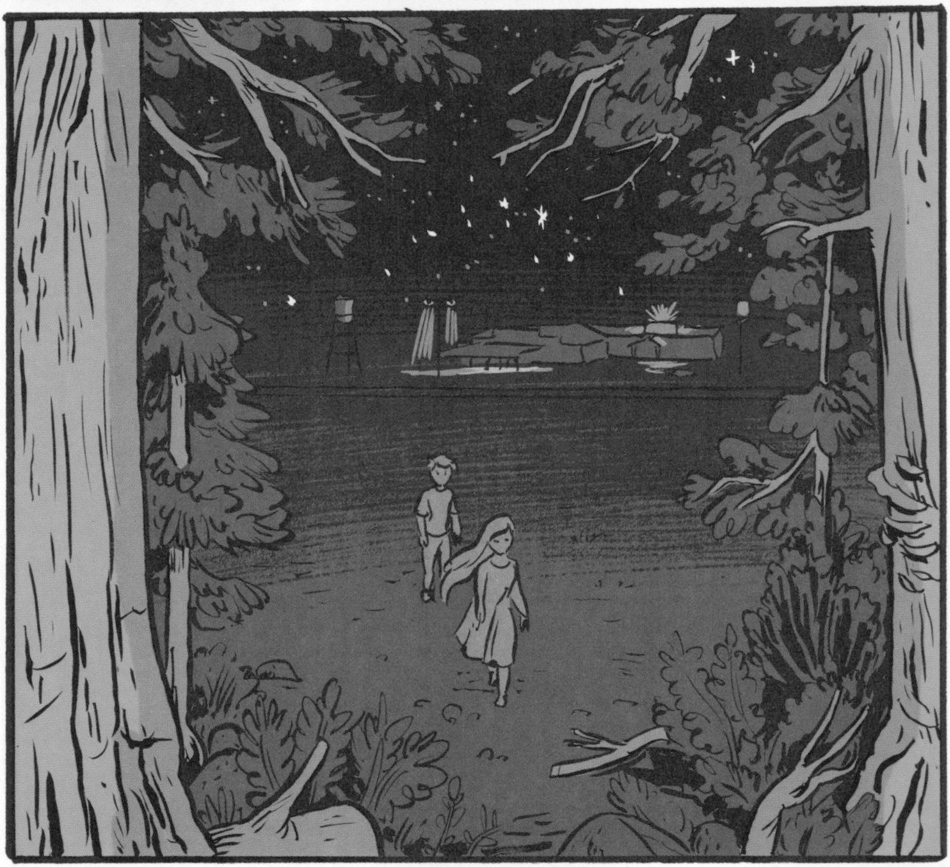

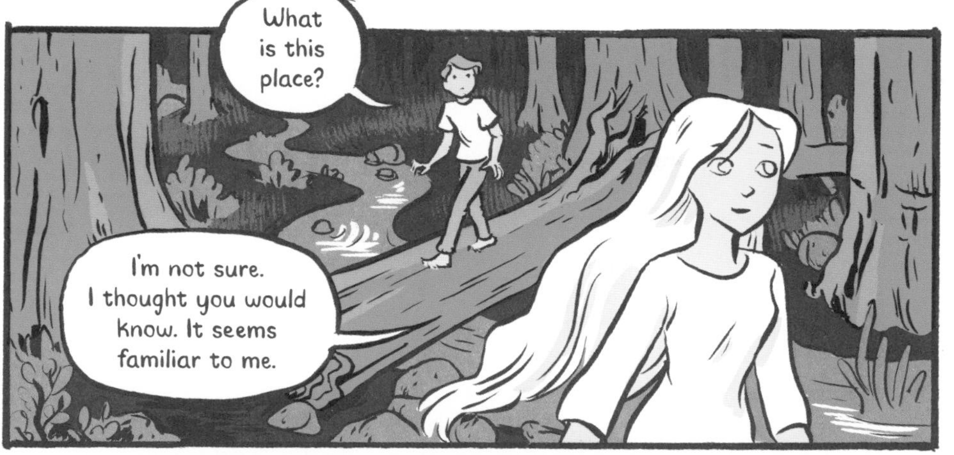
What is this place?
I'm not sure. I thought you would know. It seems familiar to me.

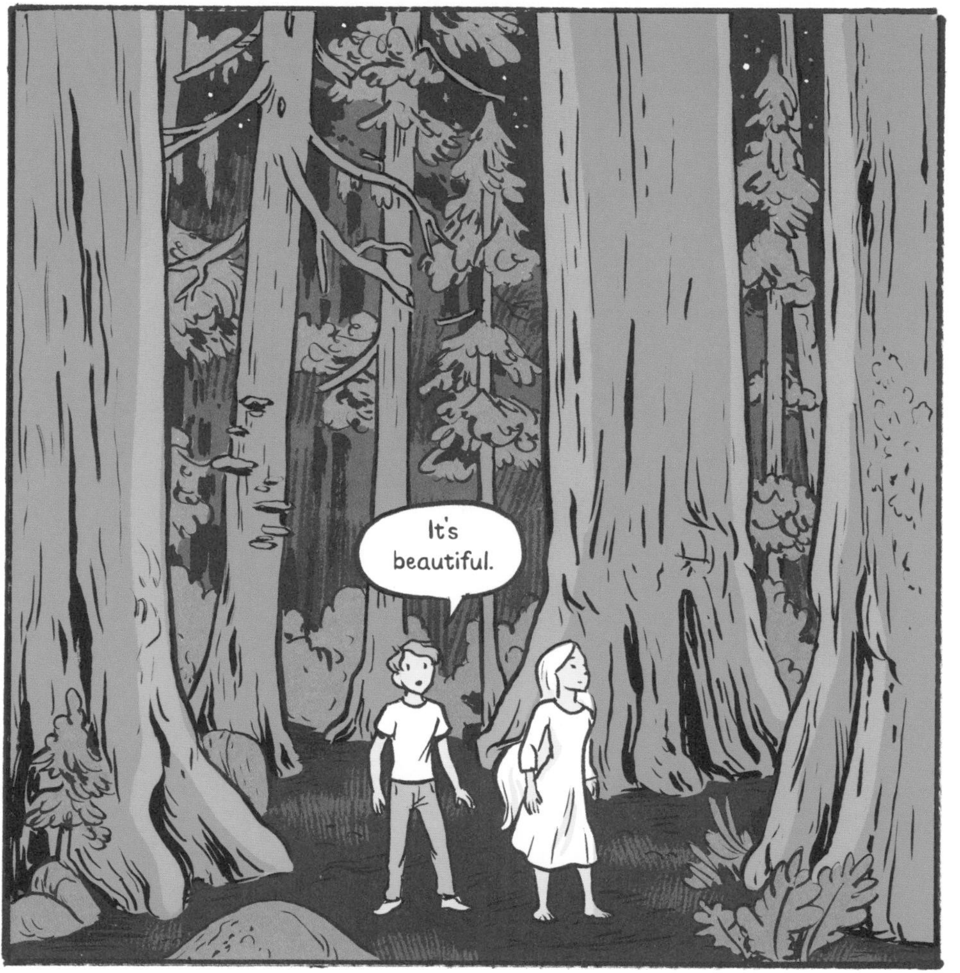
It's beautiful.

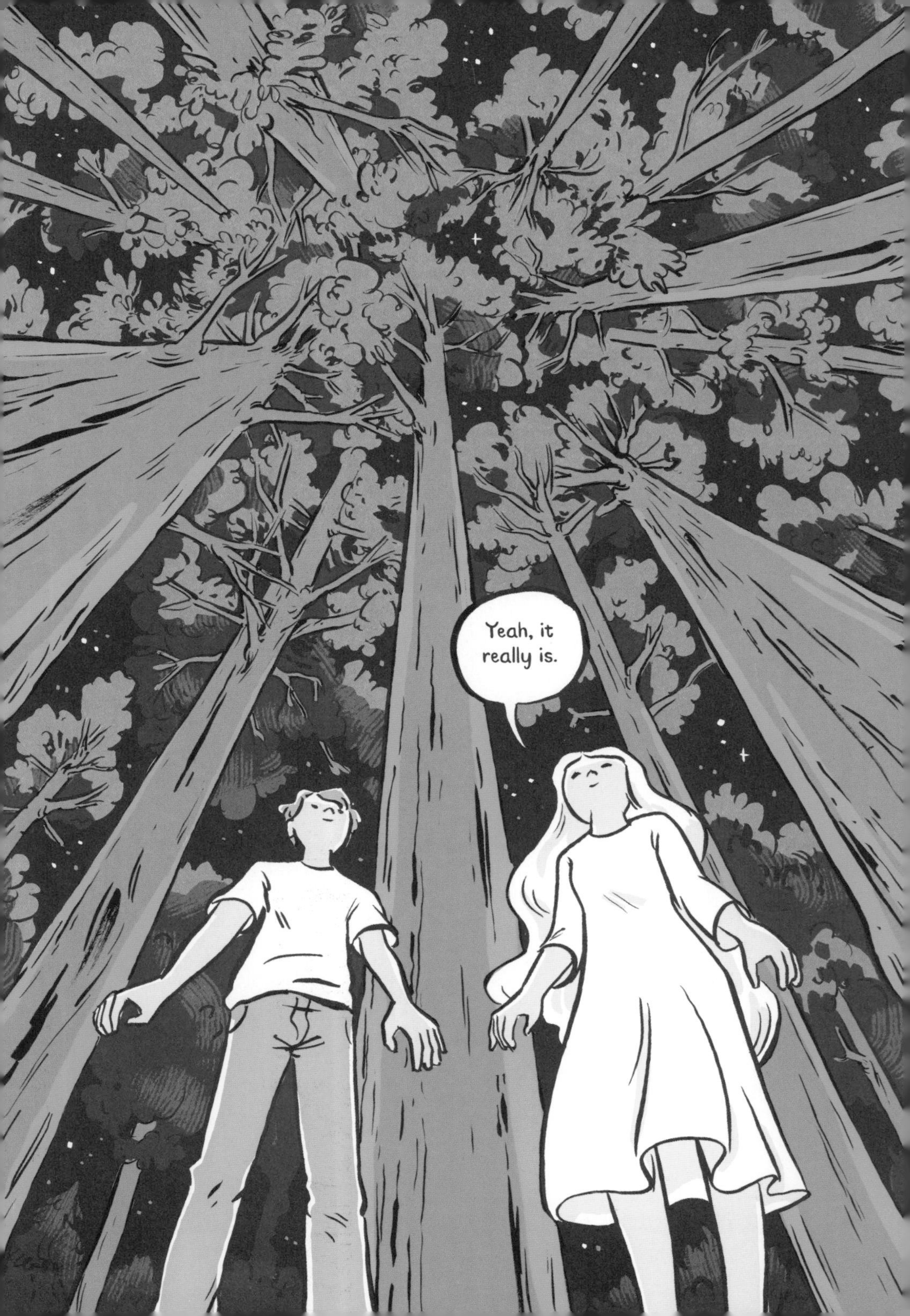
Yeah, it really is.

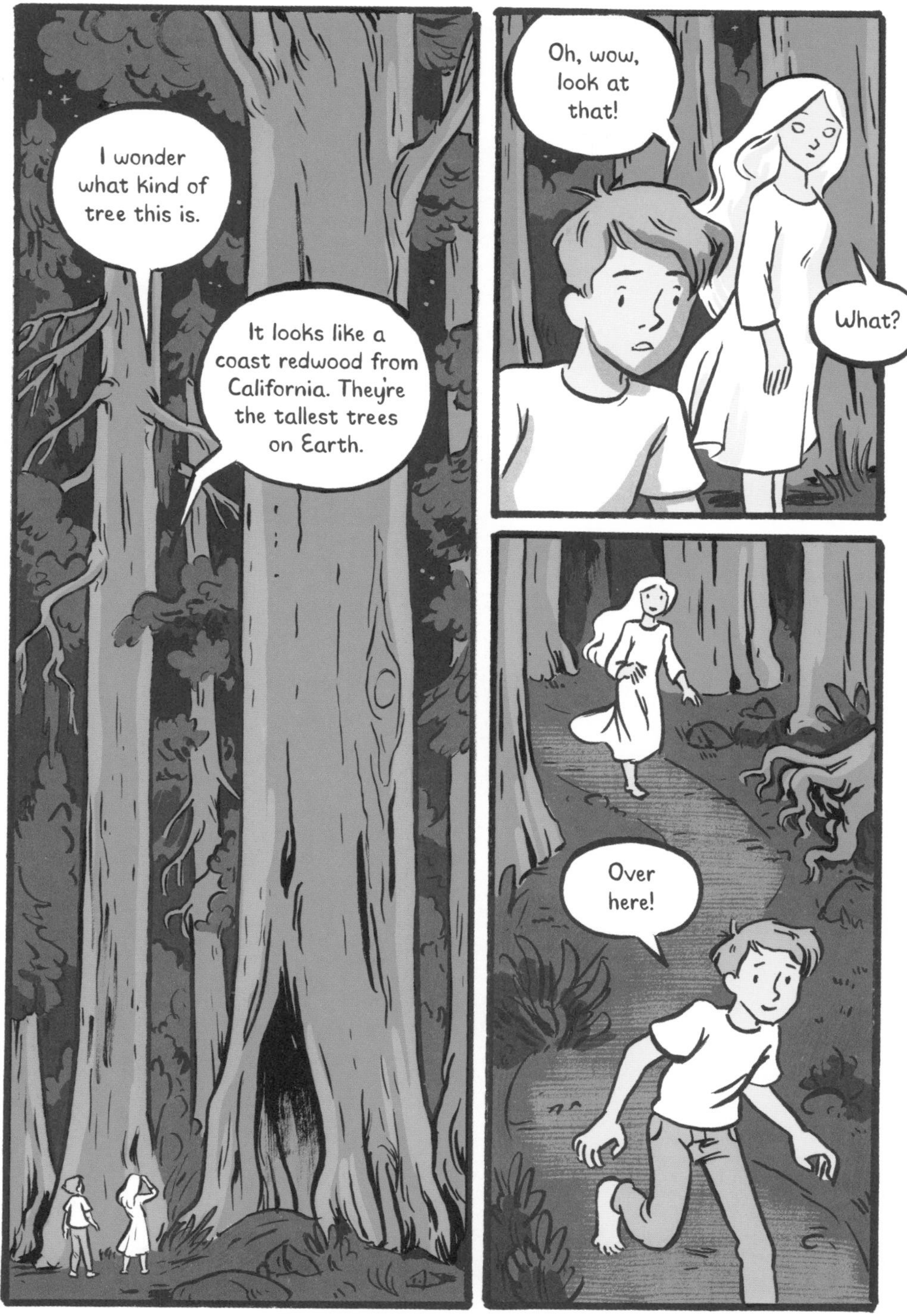
I wonder what kind of tree this is.
It looks like a coast redwood from California. They're the tallest trees on Earth.
Oh, wow, look at that!
What?
Over here!

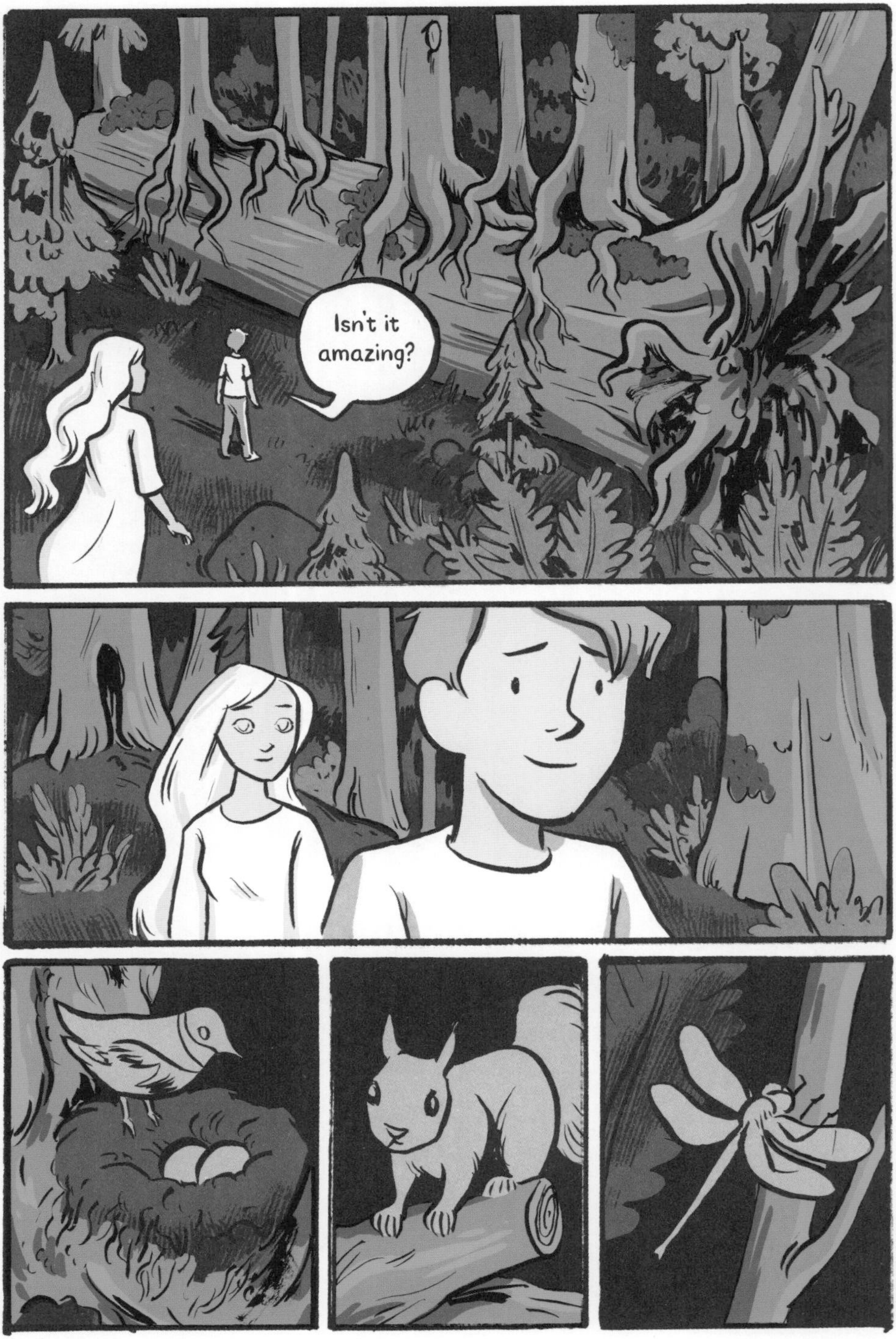
Isn't it amazing?

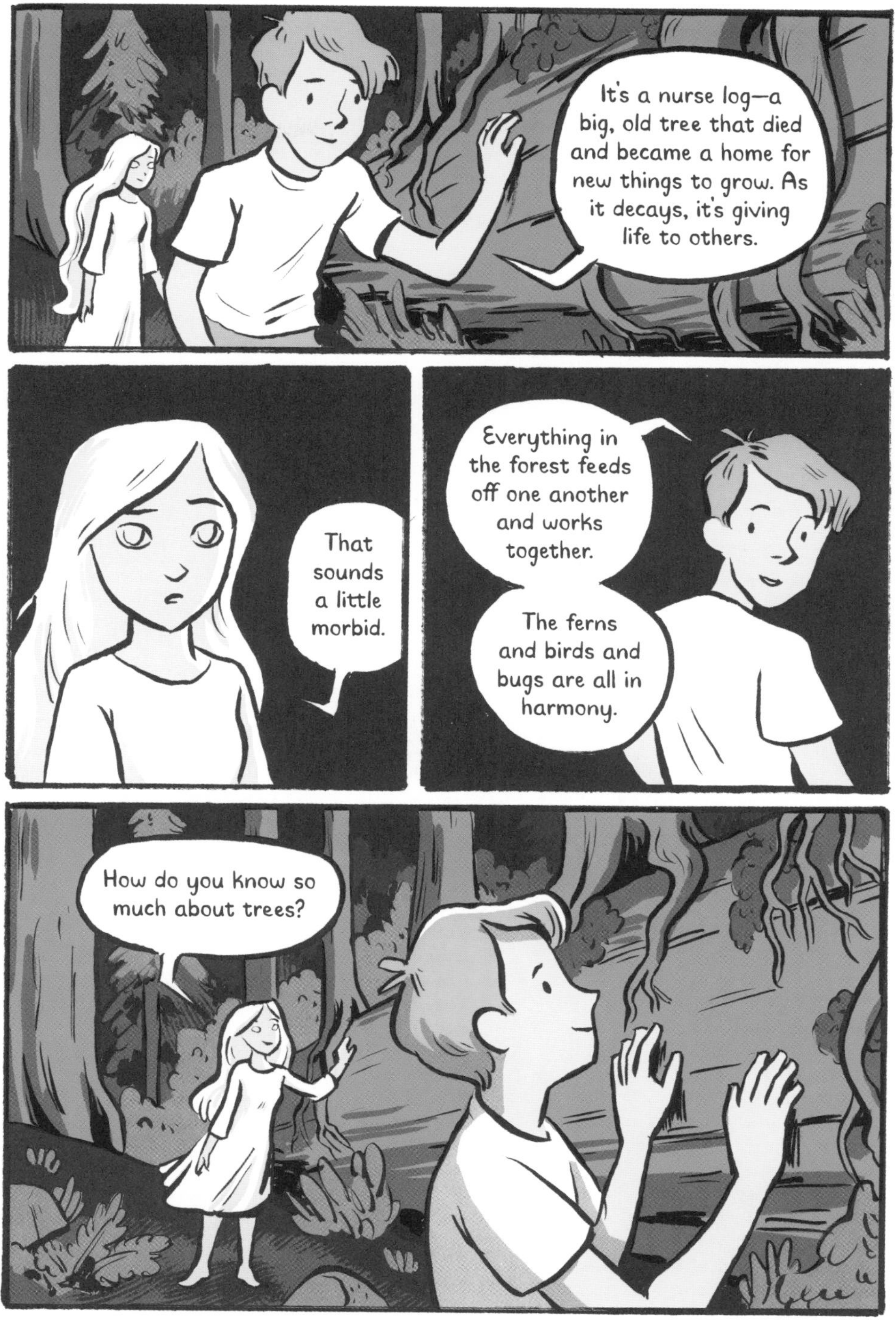
It's a nurse log—a big, old tree that died and became a home for new things to grow. As it decays, it's giving life to others.
That sounds a little morbid.
Everything in the forest feeds off one another and works together.
The ferns and birds and bugs are all in harmony.
How do you know so much about trees?

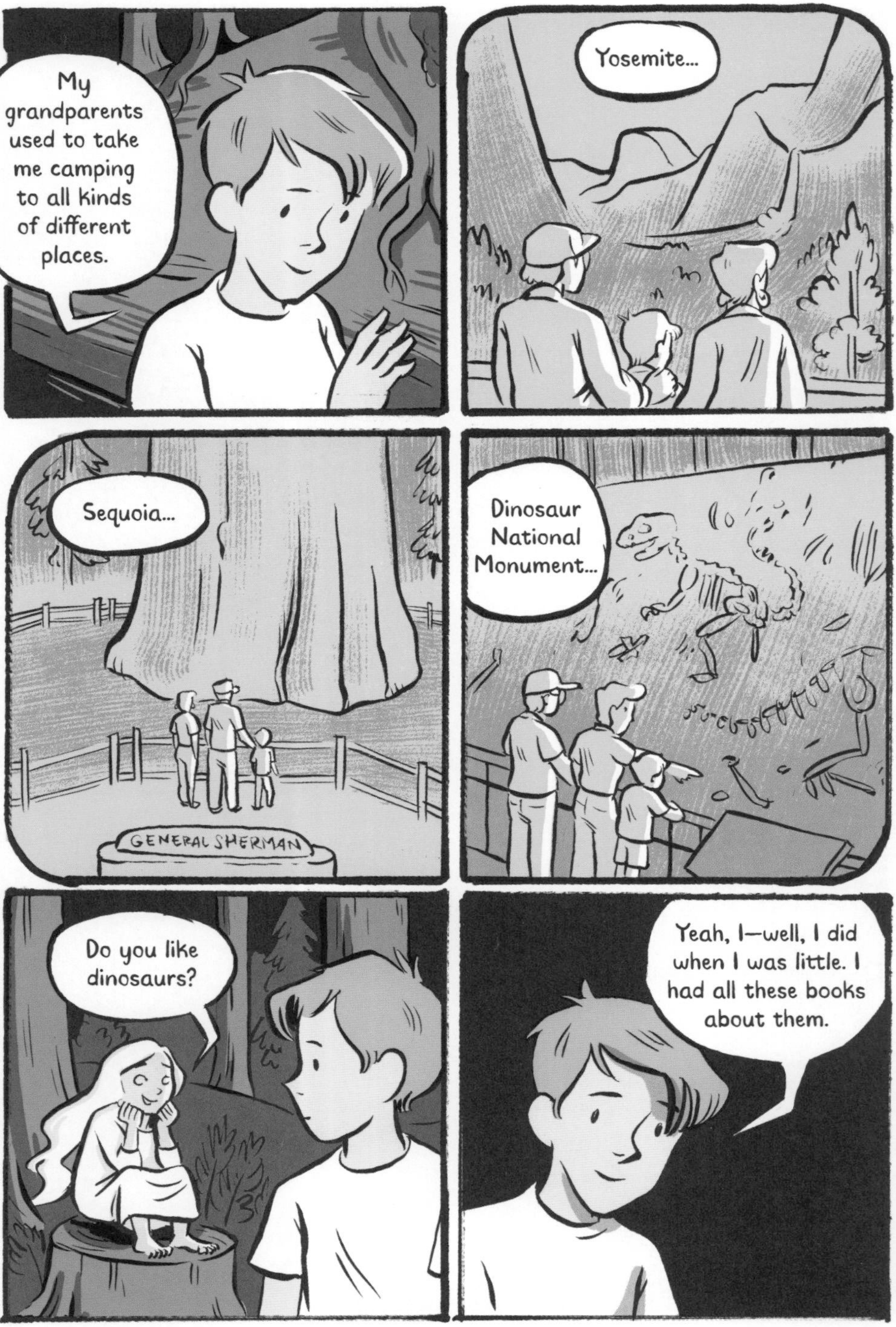
My grandparents used to take me camping to all kinds of different places.
Yosemite...
Sequoia...
GENERAL SHERMAN
Dinosaur National Monument...
Do you like dinosaurs?
Yeah, I—well, I did when I was little. I had all these books about them.

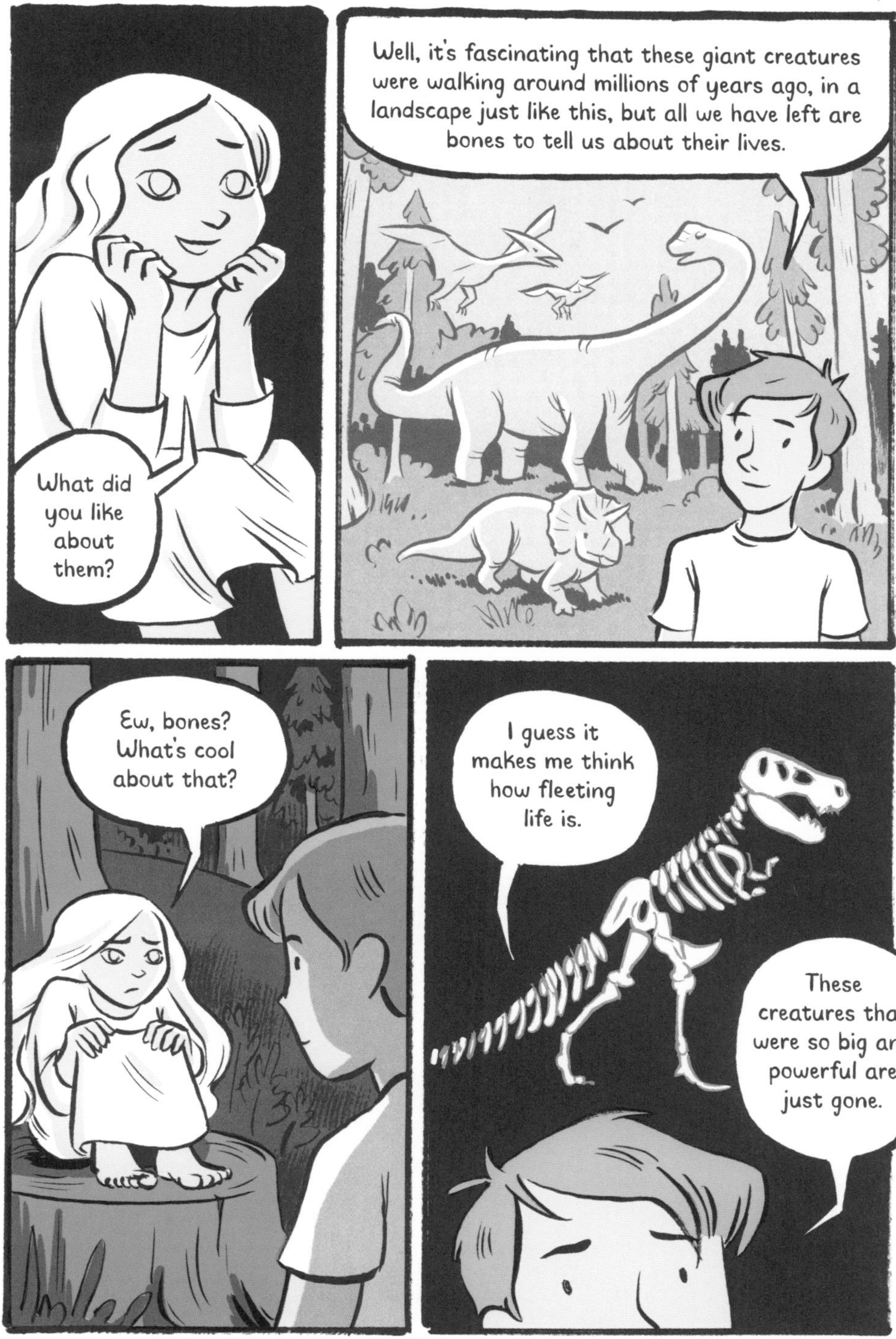
What did you like about them?
Well, it's fascinating that these giant creatures were walking around millions of years ago, in a landscape just like this, but all we have left are bones to tell us about their lives.
Ew, bones? What's cool about that?
I guess it makes me think how fleeting life is.
These creatures that were so big and powerful are just gone.

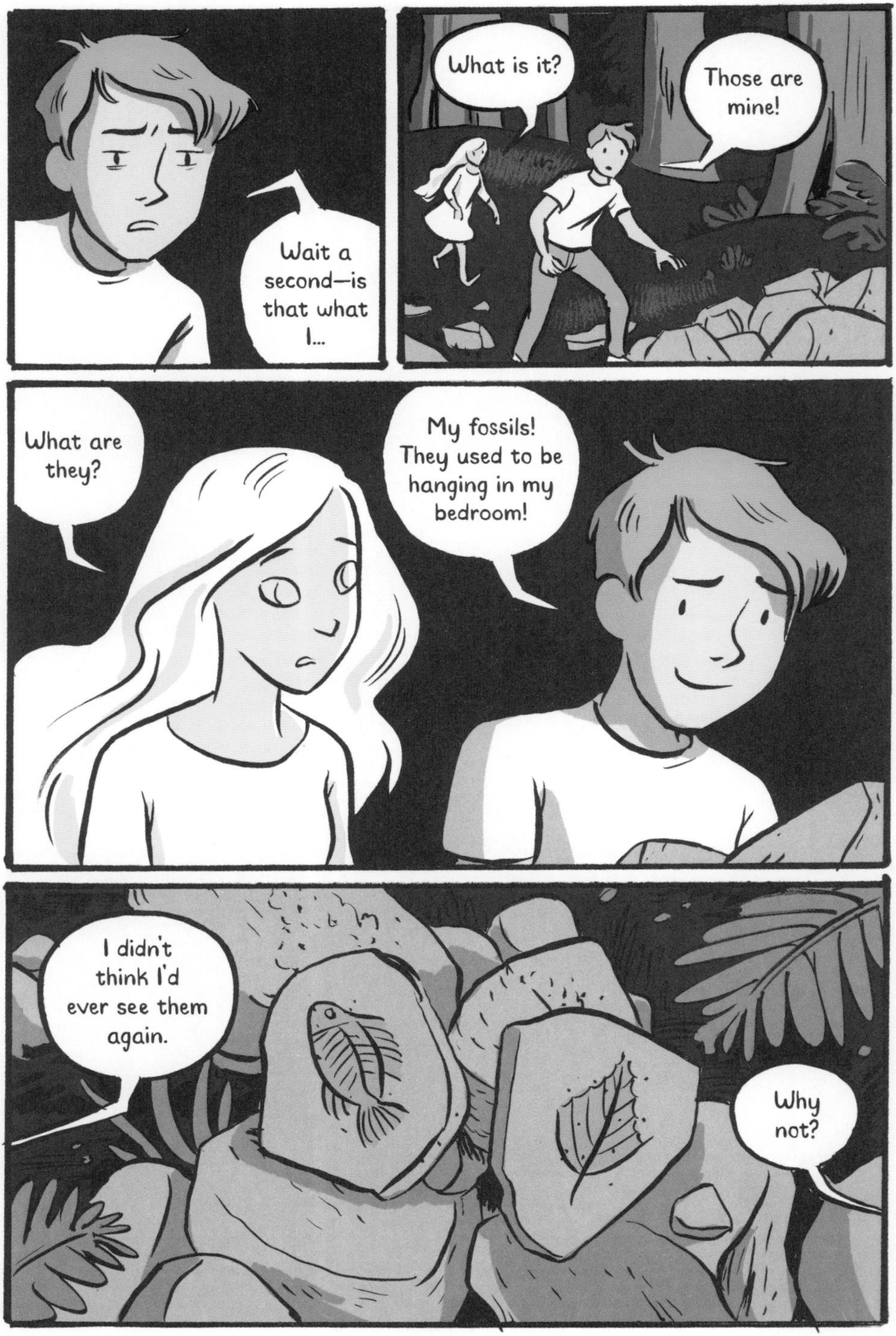
Wait a second—is that what I...
What is it?
Those are mine!
What are they?
My fossils! They used to be hanging in my bedroom!
I didn't think I'd ever see them again.
Why not?

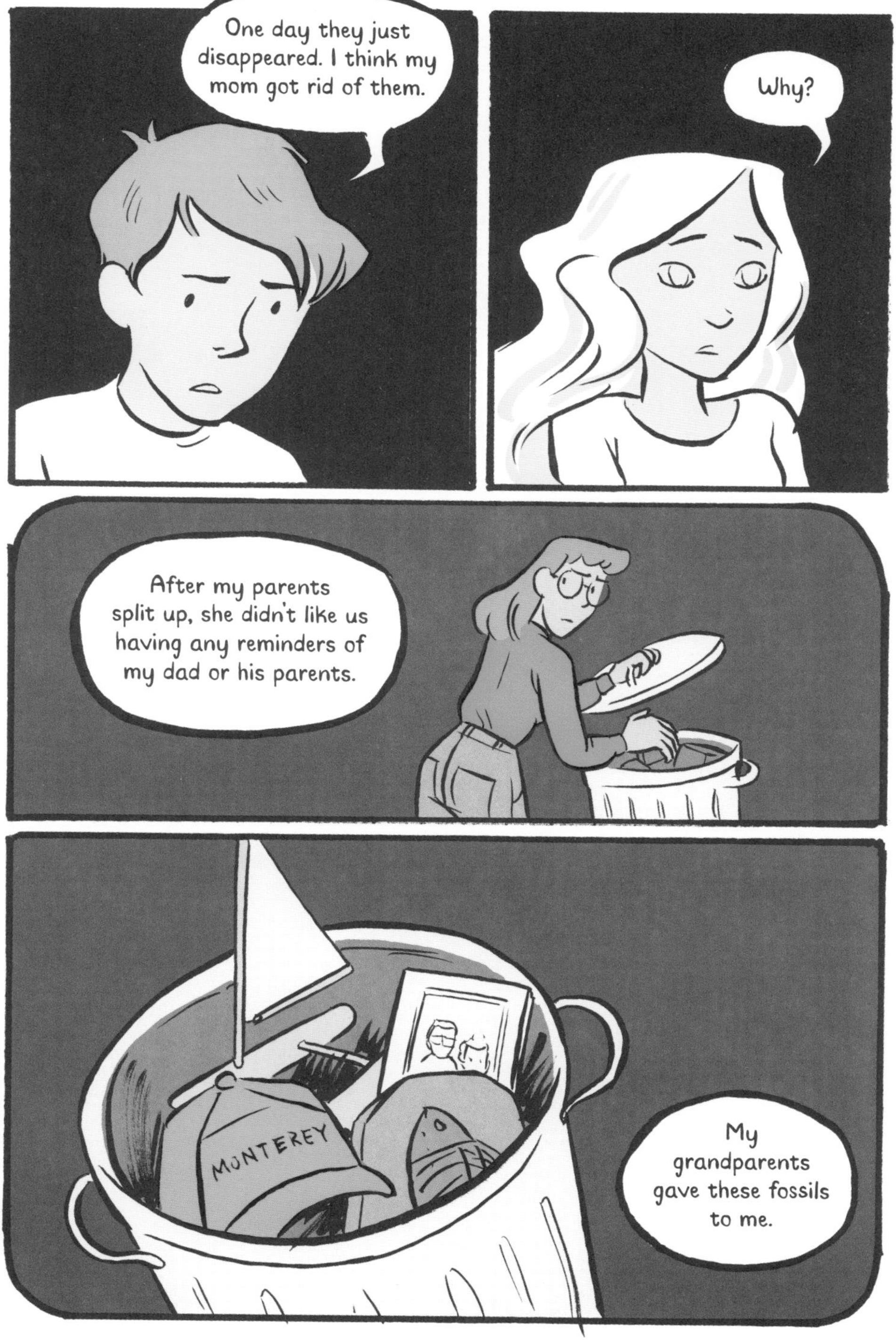
One day they just disappeared. I think my mom got rid of them.
Why?
After my parents split up, she didn't like us having any reminders of my dad or his parents.
MONTEREY
My grandparents gave these fossils to me.

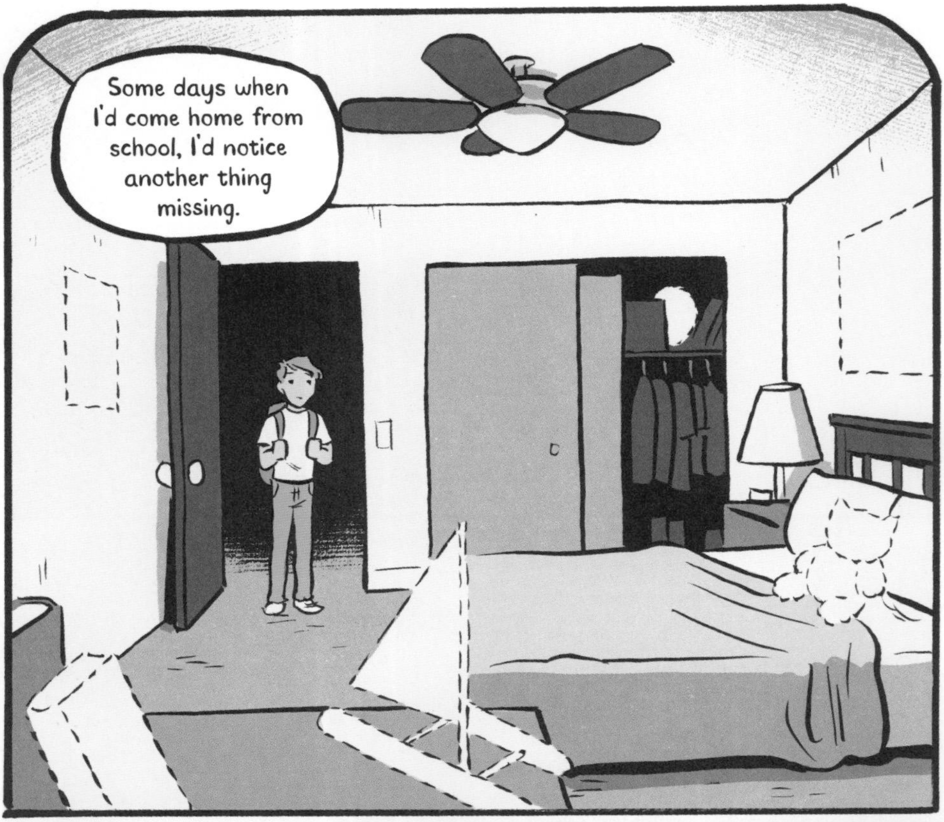
Some days when I'd come home from school, I'd notice another thing missing.

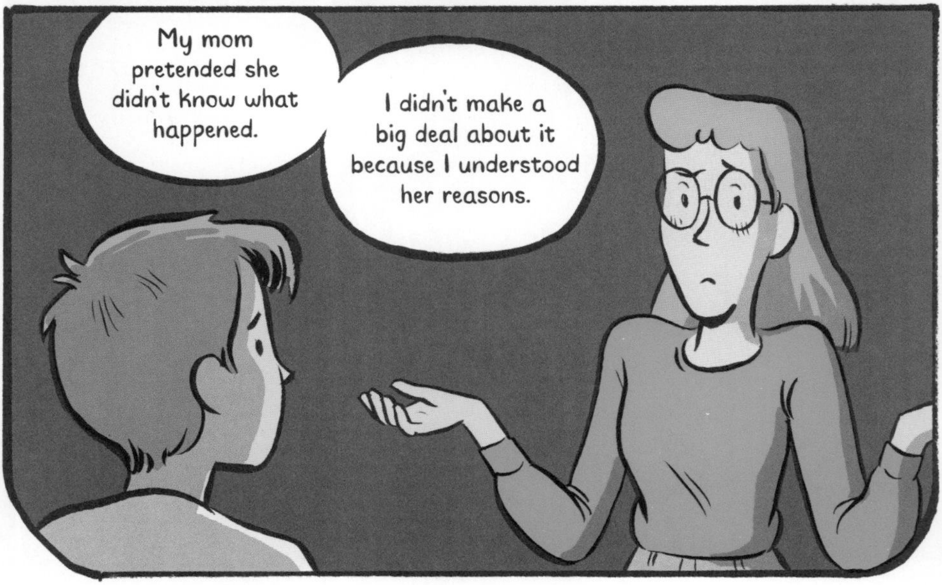
My mom pretended she didn't know what happened.
I didn't make a big deal about it because I understood her reasons.

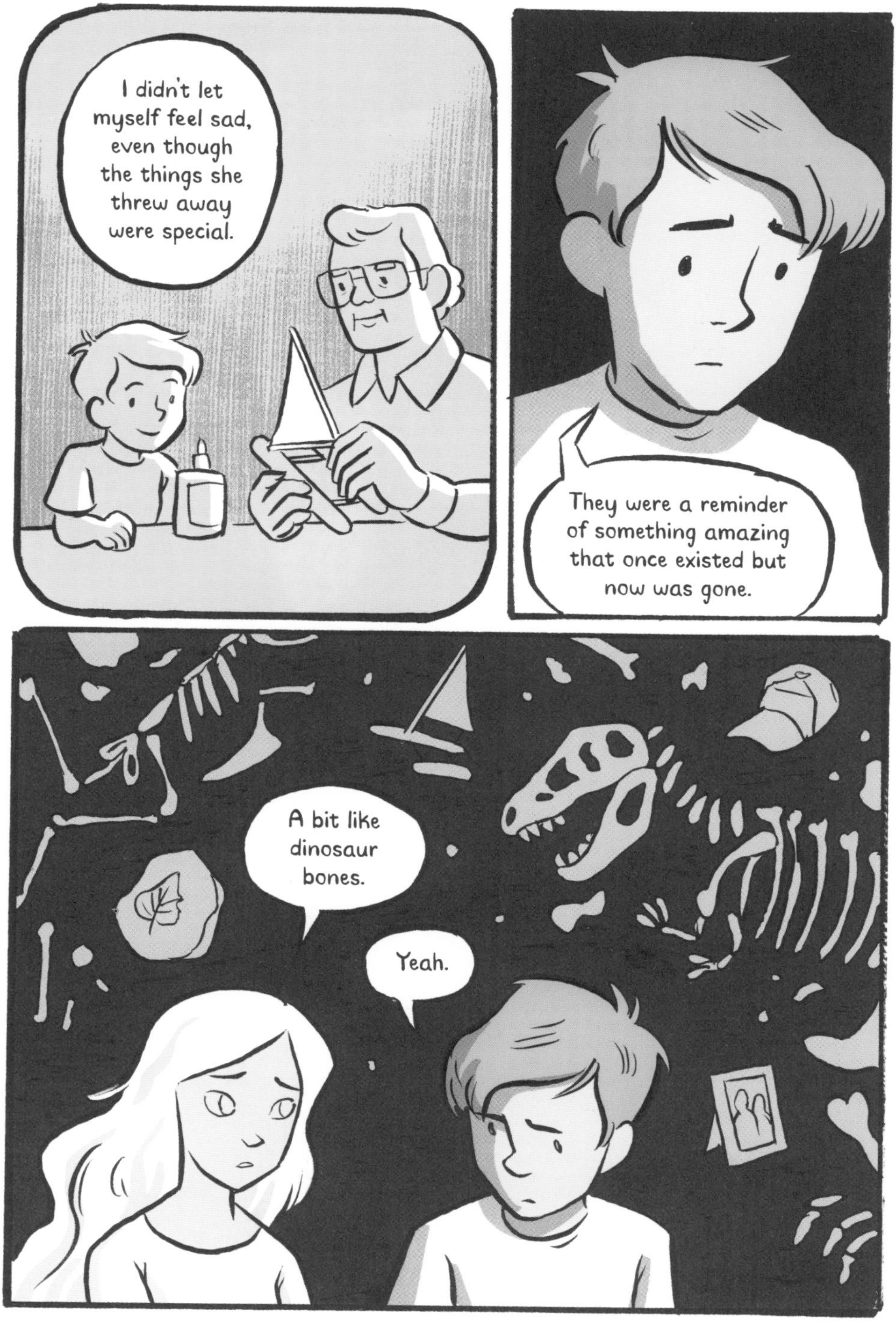
I didn't let myself feel sad, even though the things she threw away were special.
They were a reminder of something amazing that once existed but now was gone.
A bit like dinosaur bones.
Yeah.

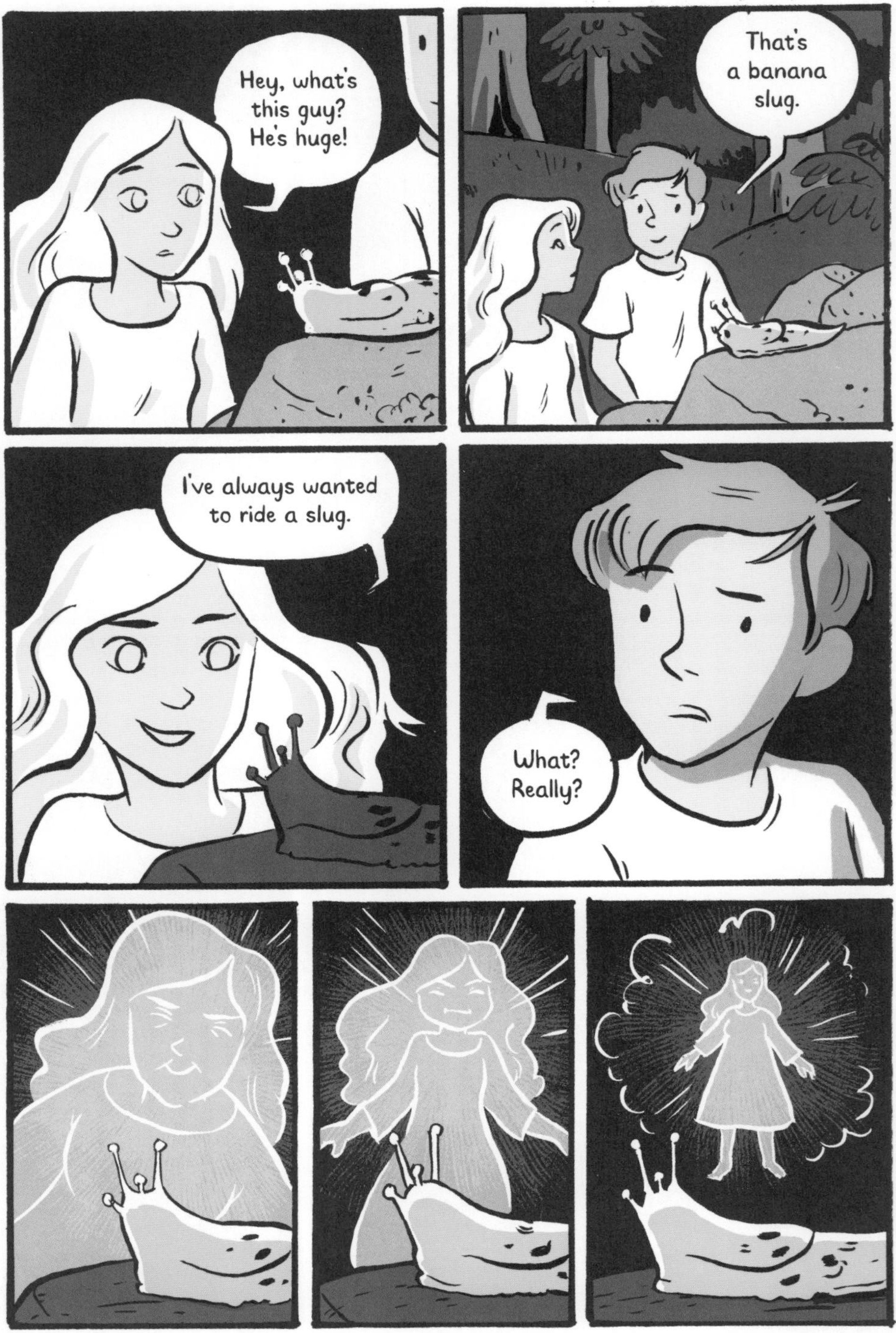
Hey, what's this guy? He's huge!
That's a banana slug.
I've always wanted to ride a slug.
What? Really?

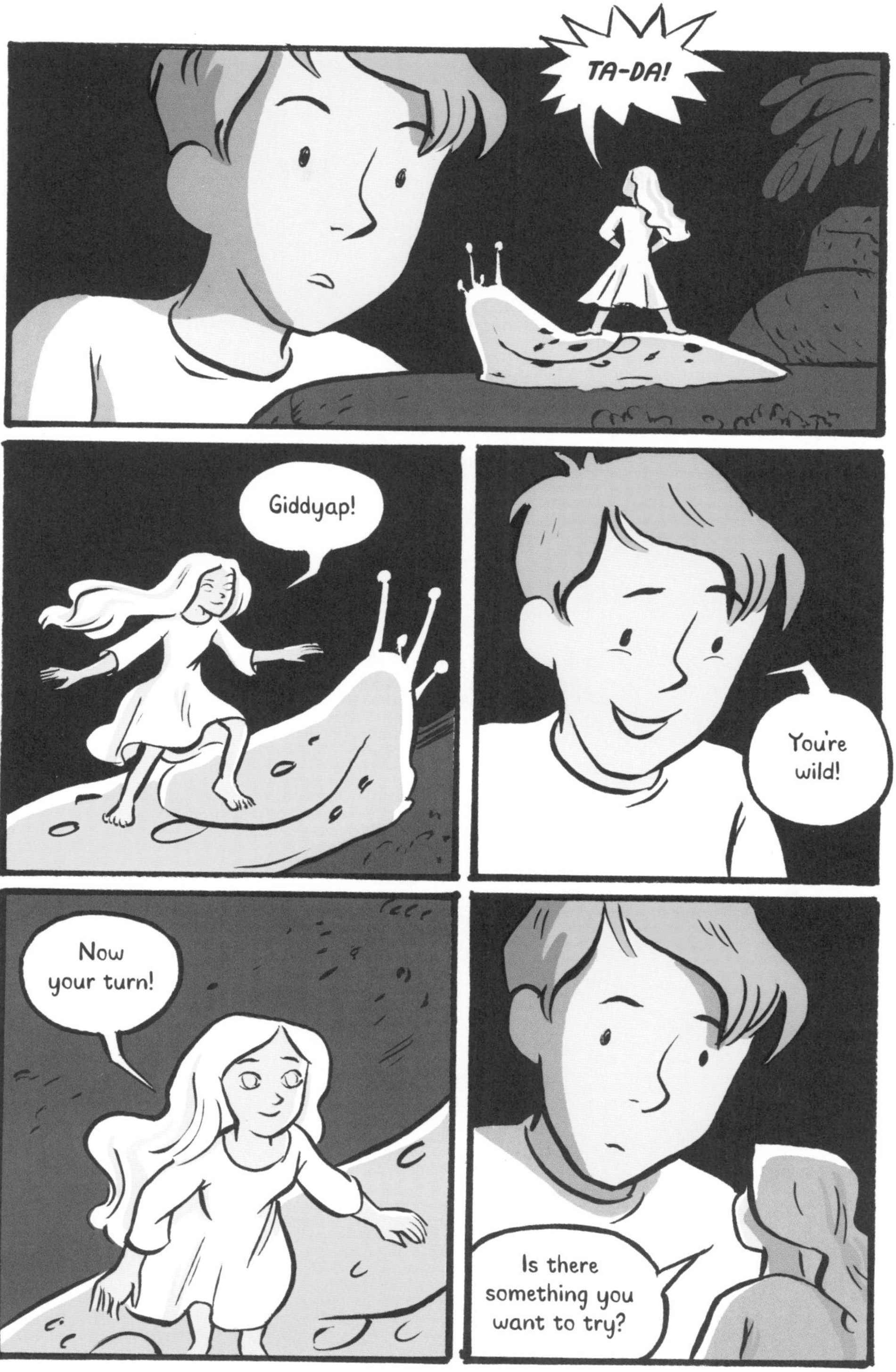
TA-DA!
Giddyap!
You're wild!
Now your turn!
Is there something you want to try?

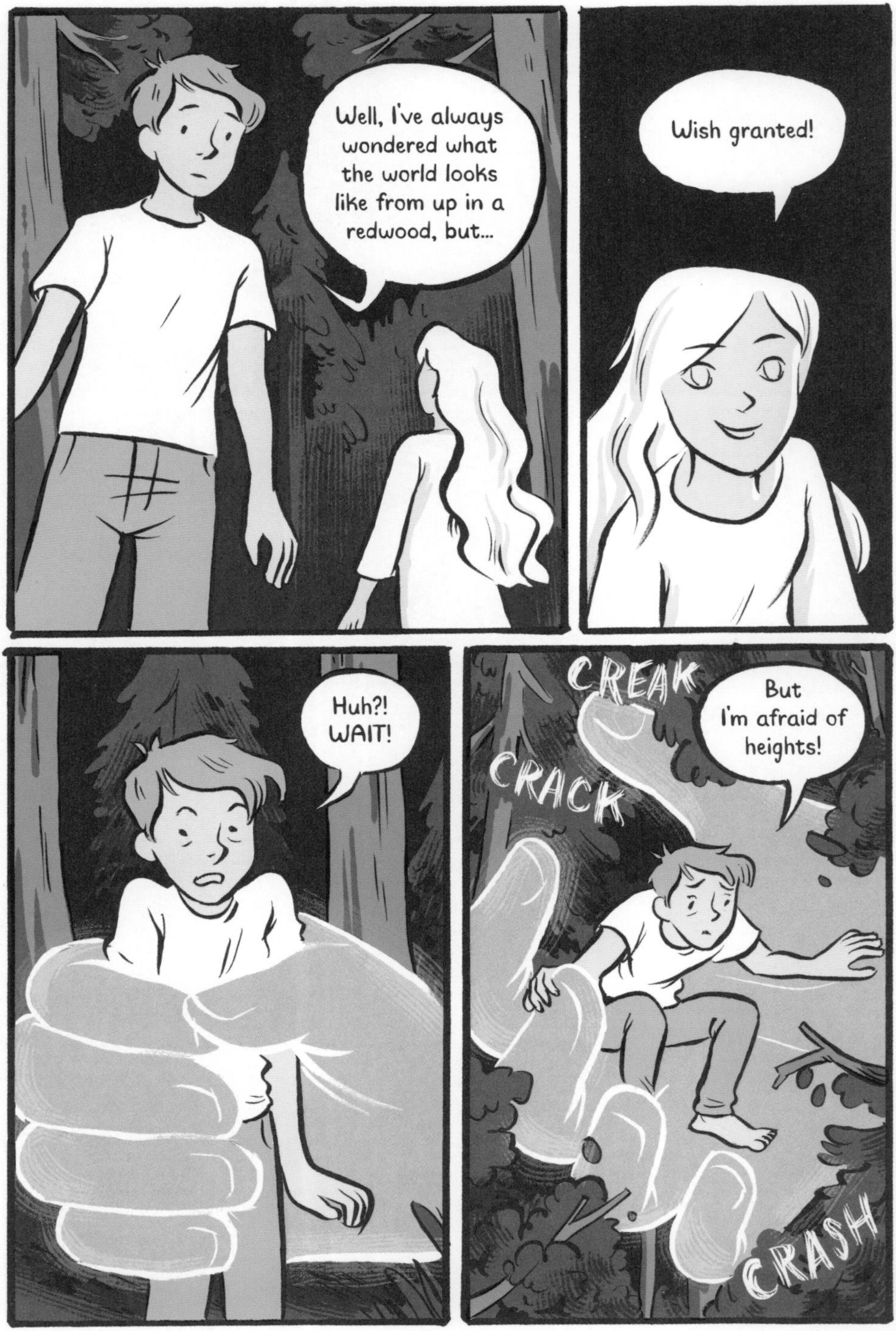
Well, I've always wondered what the world looks like from up in a redwood, but...
Wish granted!
Huh?! WAIT!
CREAK
CRACK
But I'm afraid of heights!
CRASH

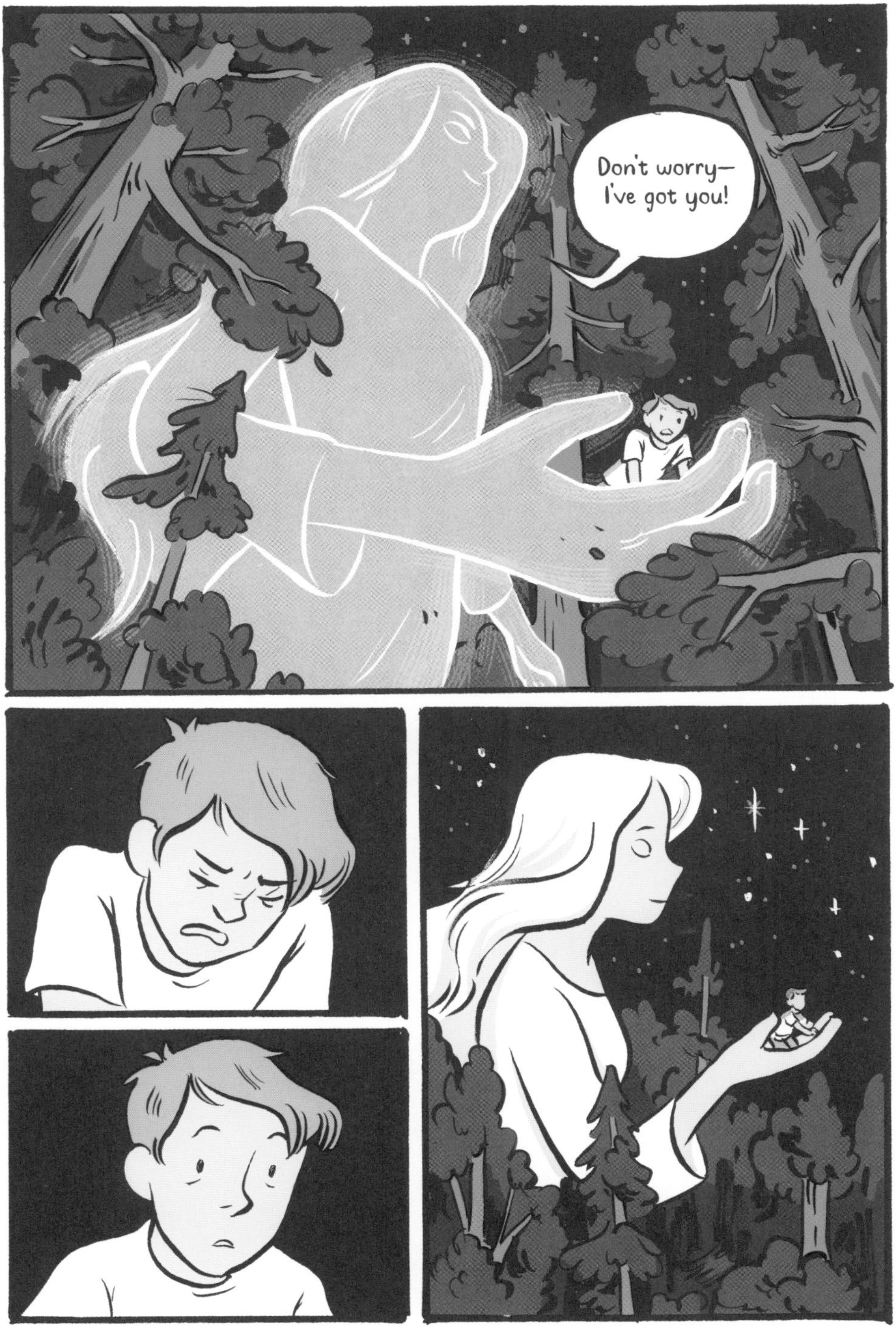
Don't worry—
I've got you!

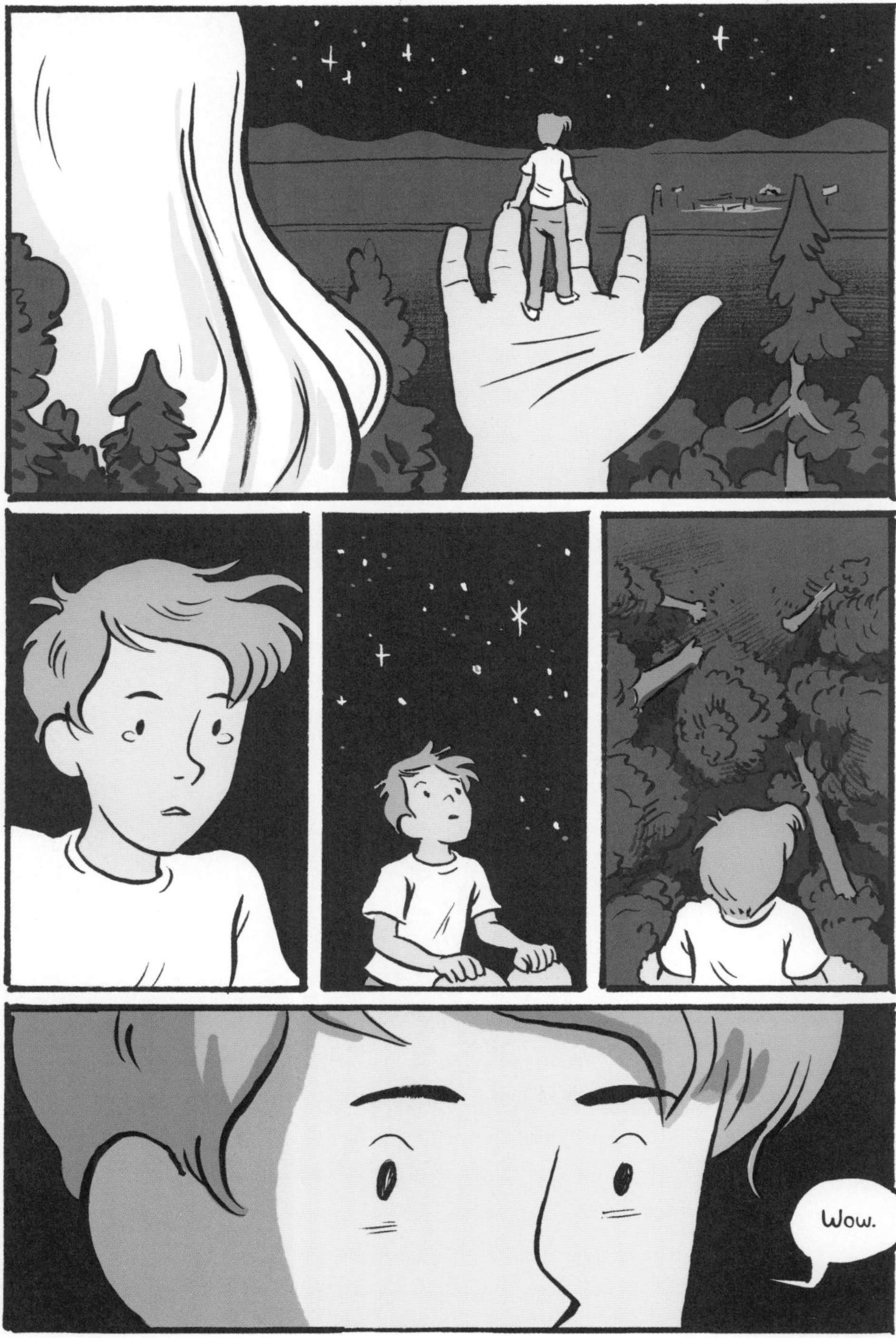
Wow.

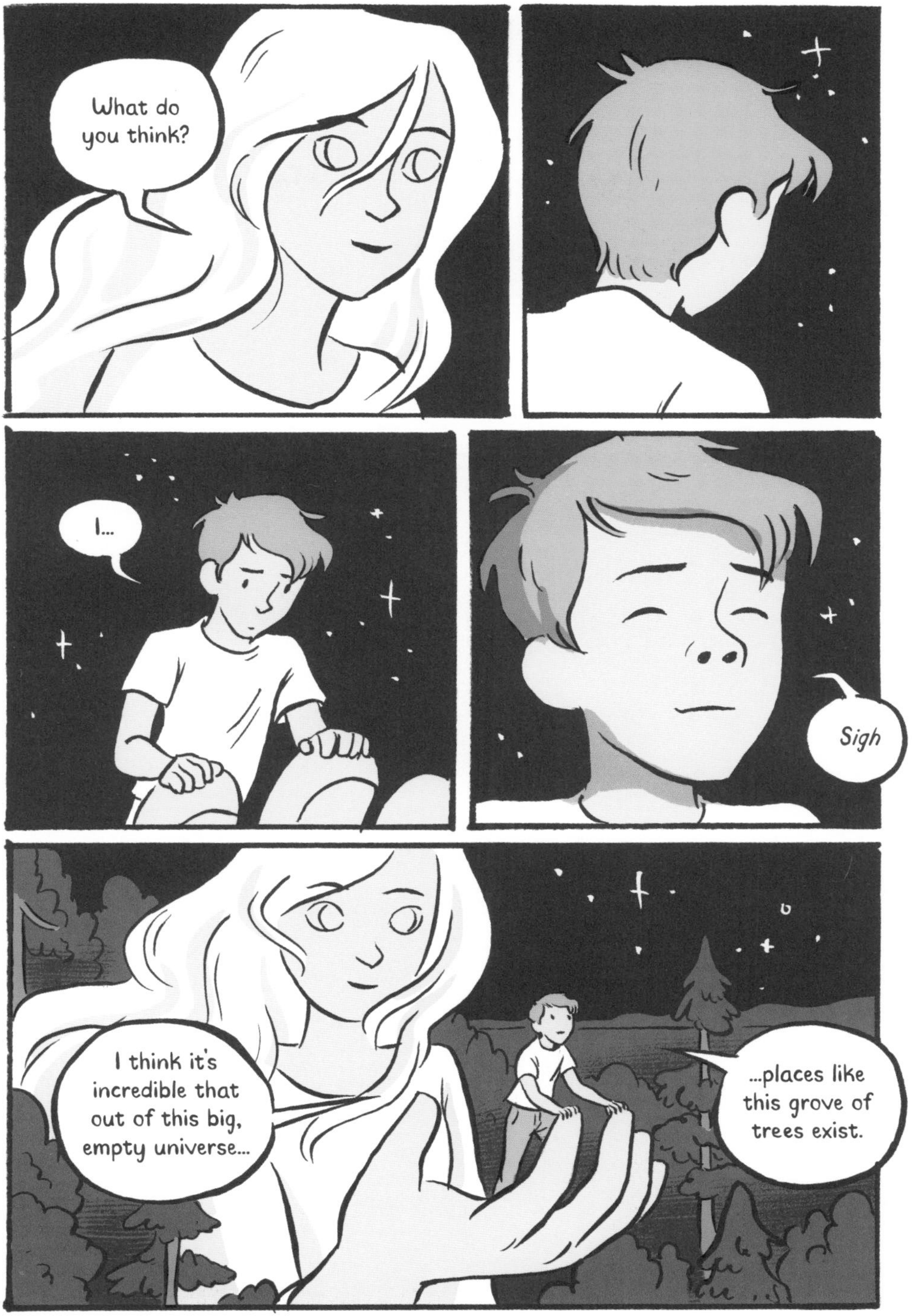

What do you think?
I...
Sigh
I think it's incredible that out of this big, empty universe...
...places like this grove of trees exist.

But it's just an accident, right? None of it really means anything.
Life is pointless... That's what you said.
Maybe—I don't know. It's beautiful, though.

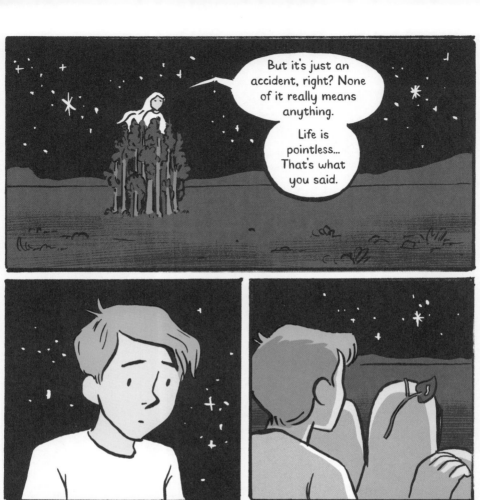

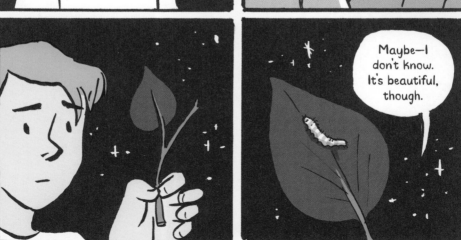

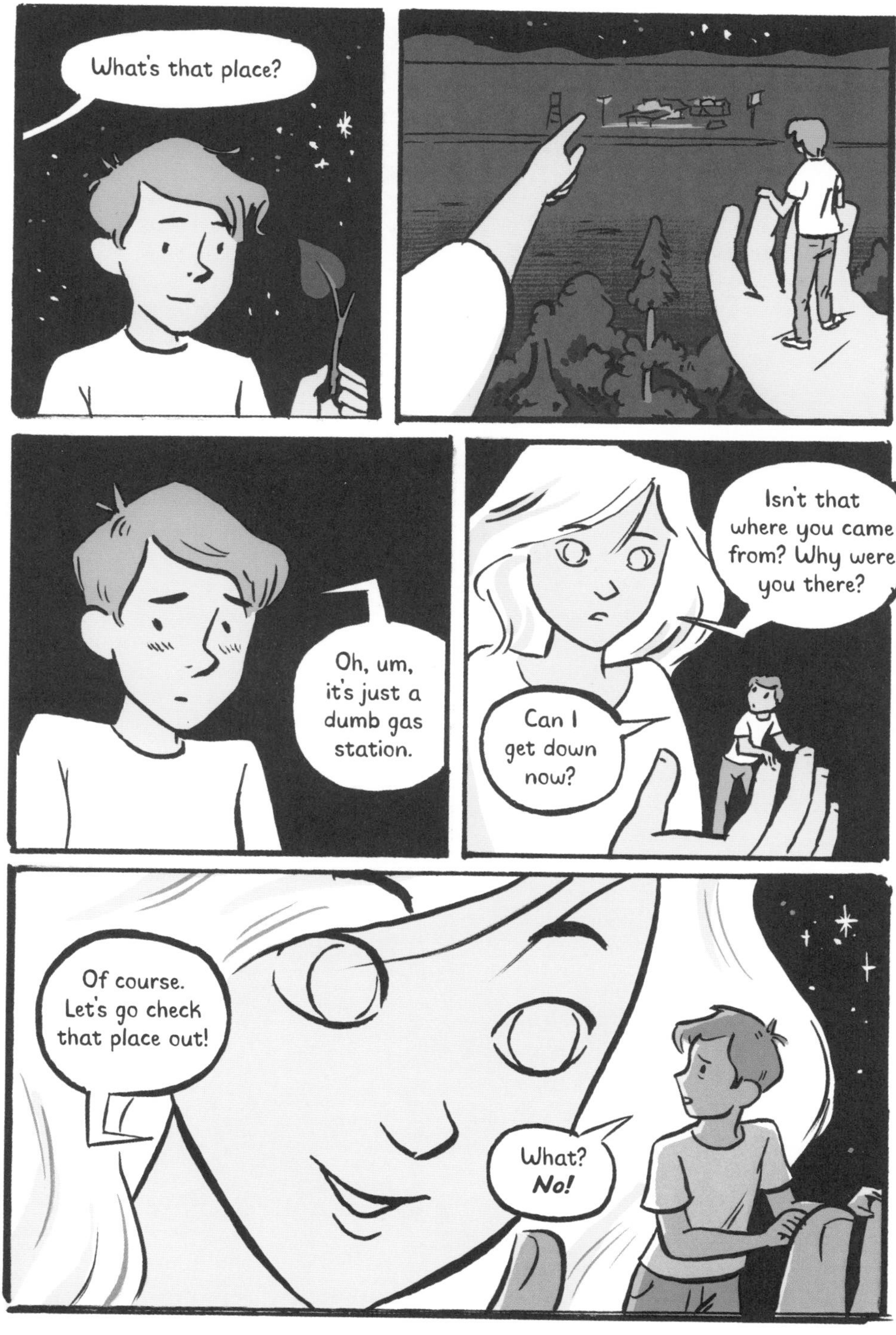
What's that place?
Oh, um, it's just a dumb gas station.
Isn't that where you came from? Why were you there?
Can I get down now?
Of course. Let's go check that place out!
What? ***No!***

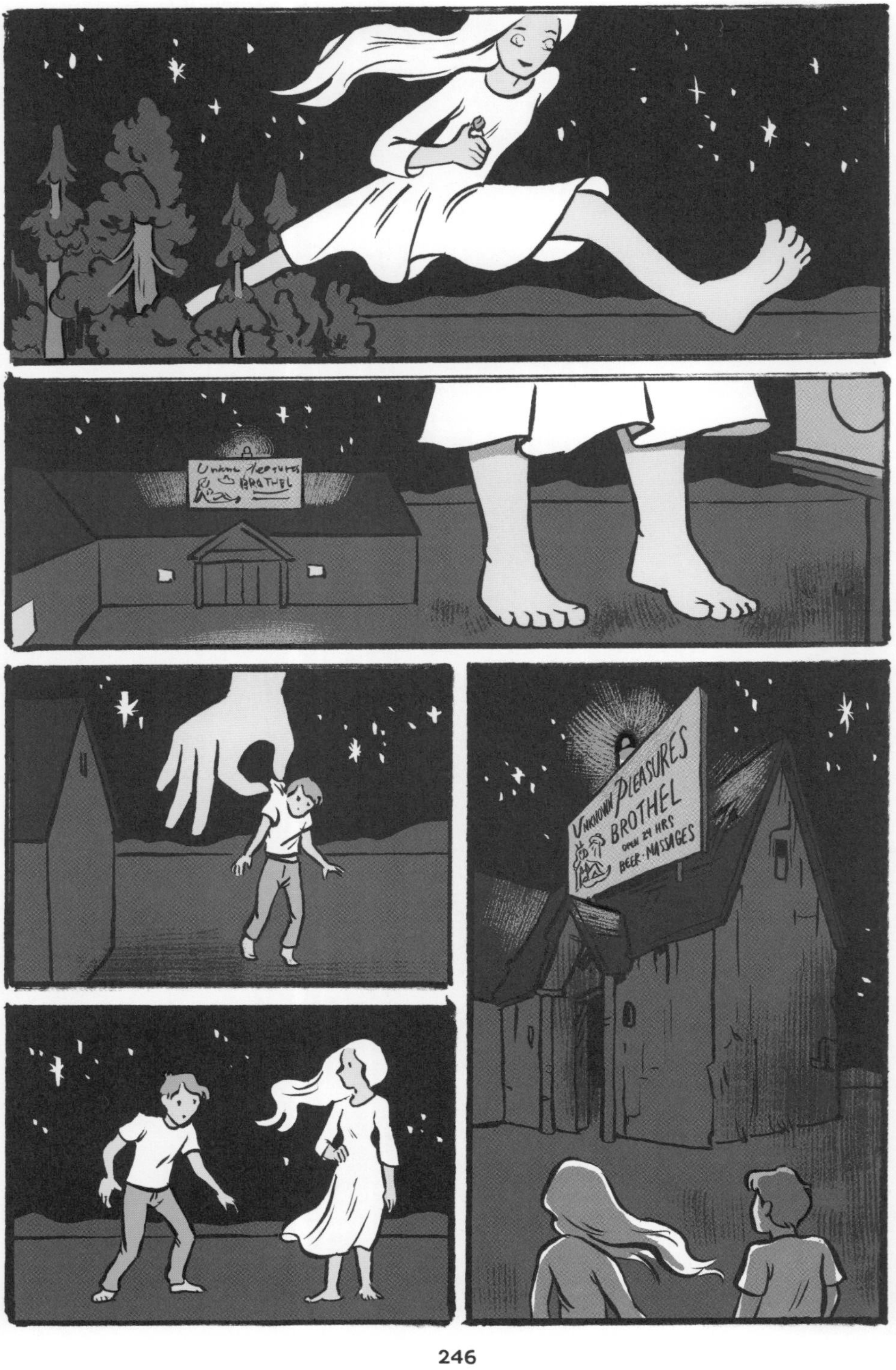
UNKNOWN PLEASURES
BROTHEL
OPEN 24 HRS
BEER · MASSAGES

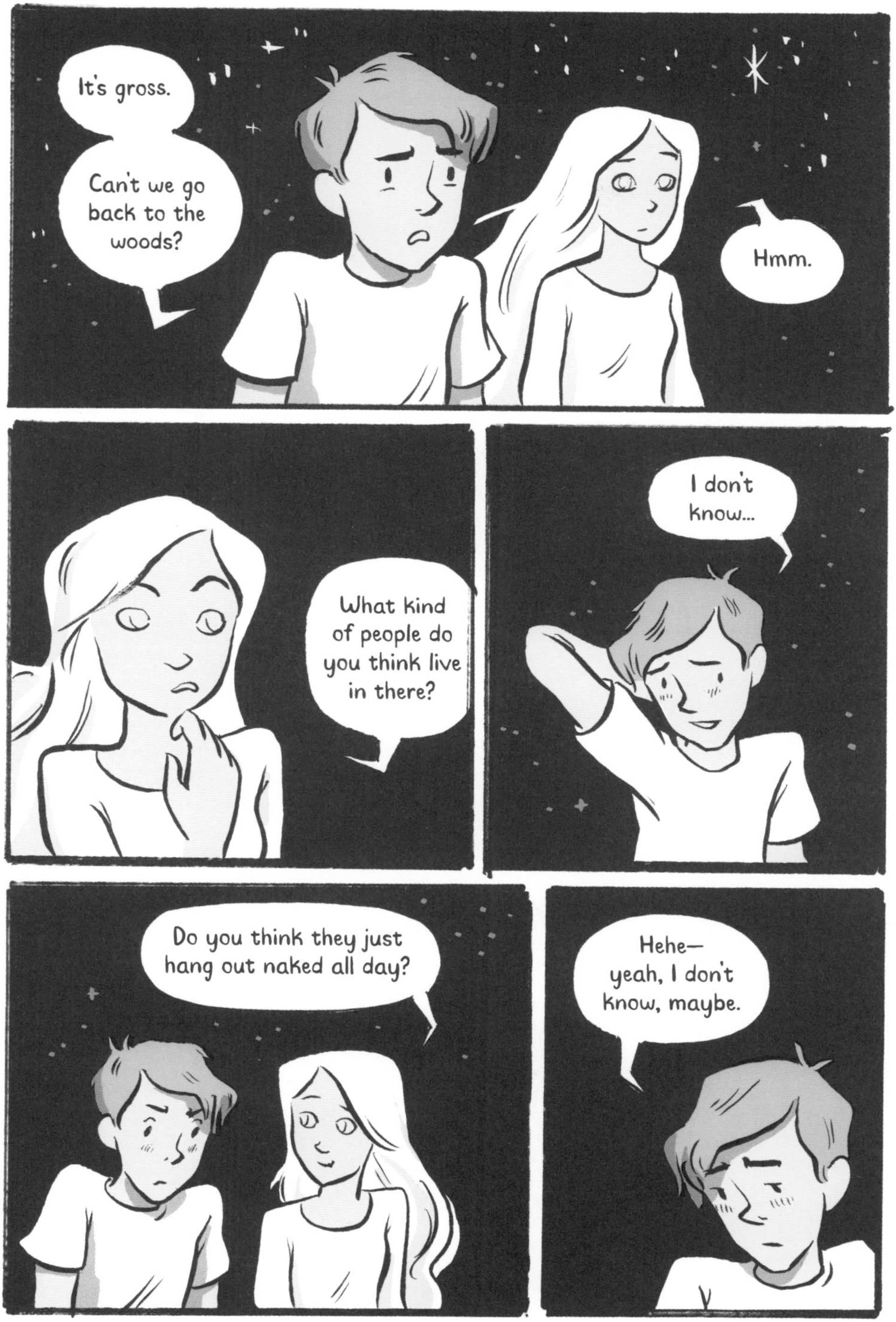
It's gross.
Can't we go back to the woods?
Hmm.
What kind of people do you think live in there?
I don't know...
Do you think they just hang out naked all day?
Hehe— yeah, I don't know, maybe.

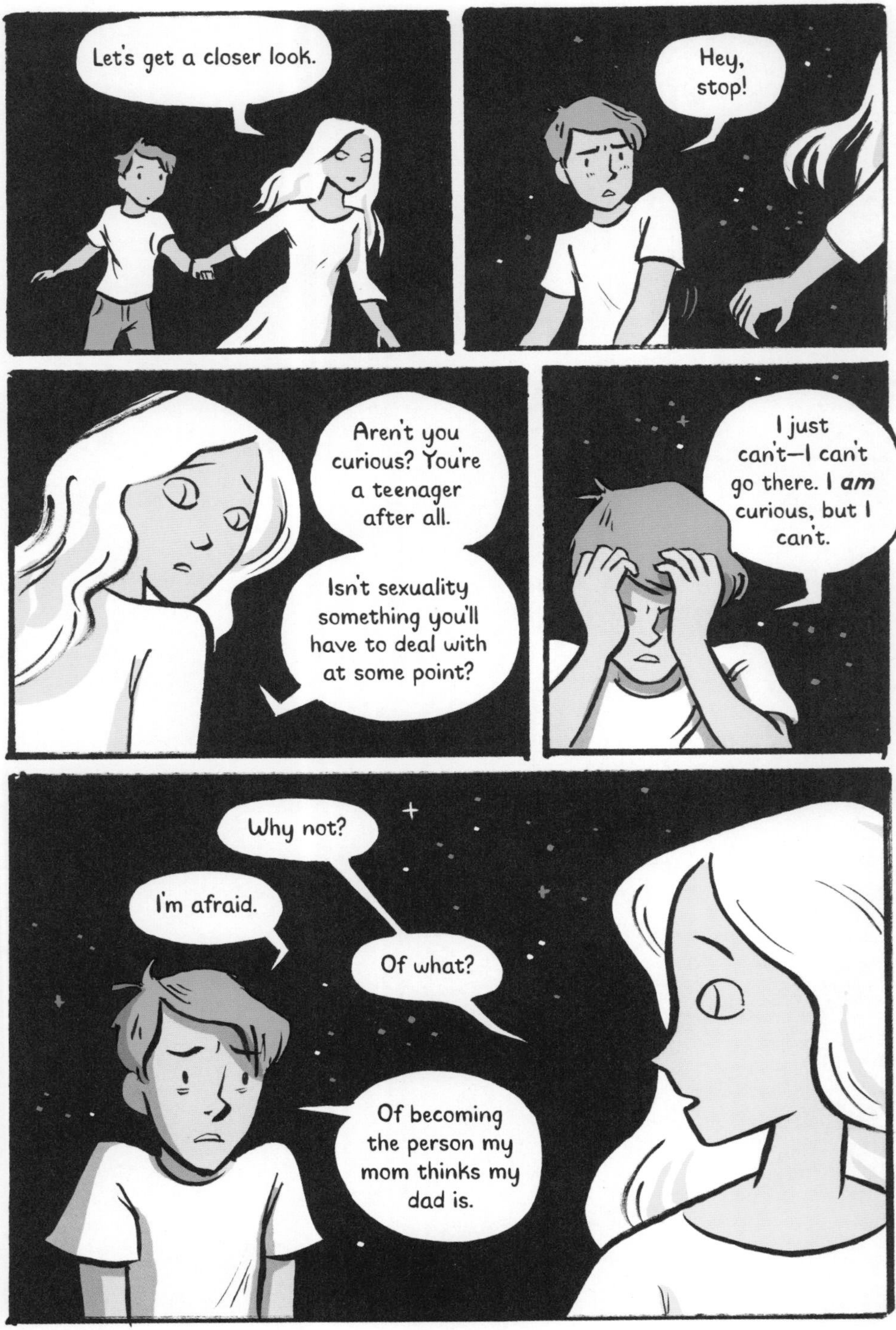
Let's get a closer look.
Hey, stop!
Aren't you curious? You're a teenager after all.
Isn't sexuality something you'll have to deal with at some point?
I just can't—I can't go there. I *am* curious, but I can't.
Why not?
I'm afraid.
Of what?
Of becoming the person my mom thinks my dad is.

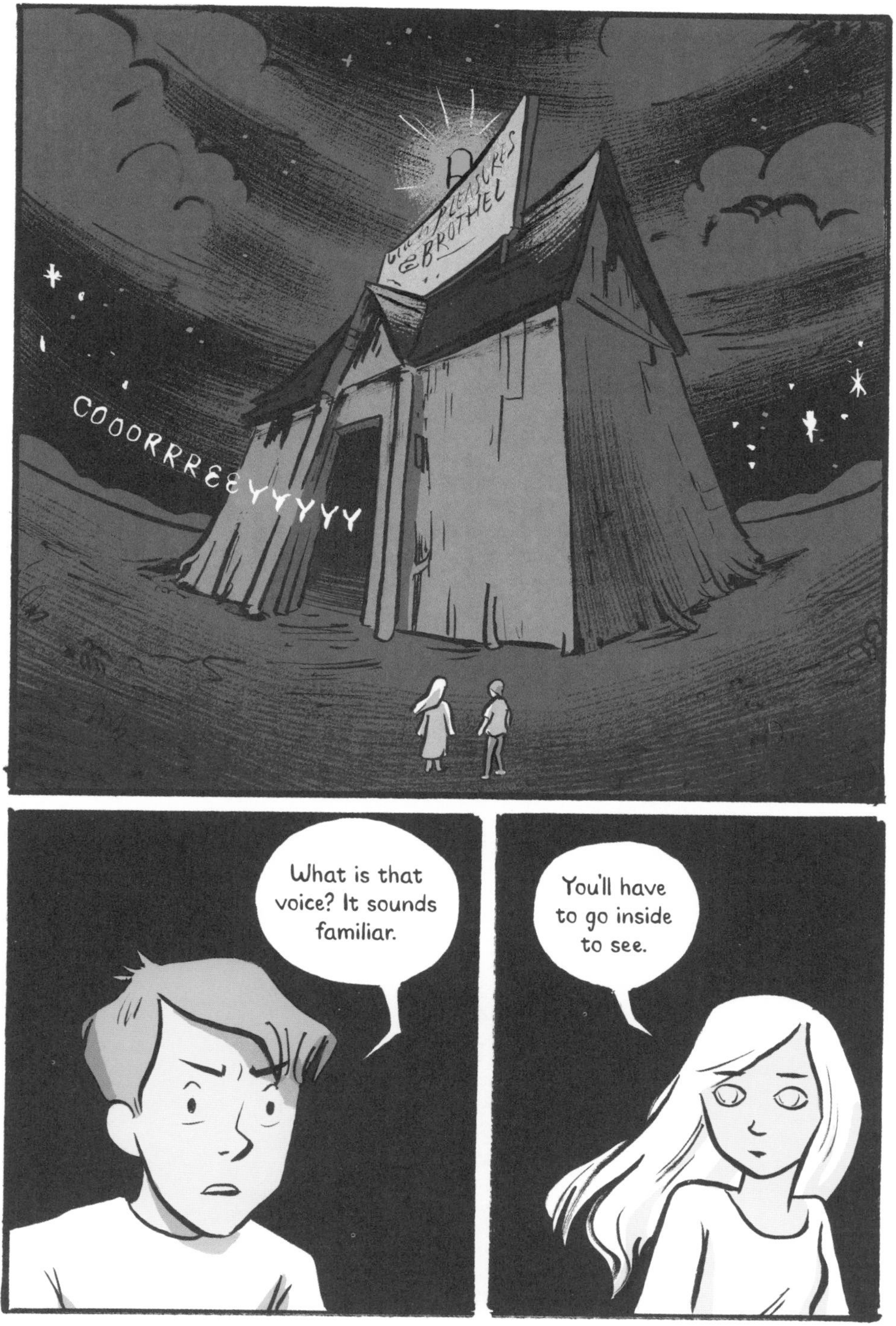
PLEASURES & BROTHEL
COOORRRREEYYYYY
What is that voice? It sounds familiar.
You'll have to go inside to see.

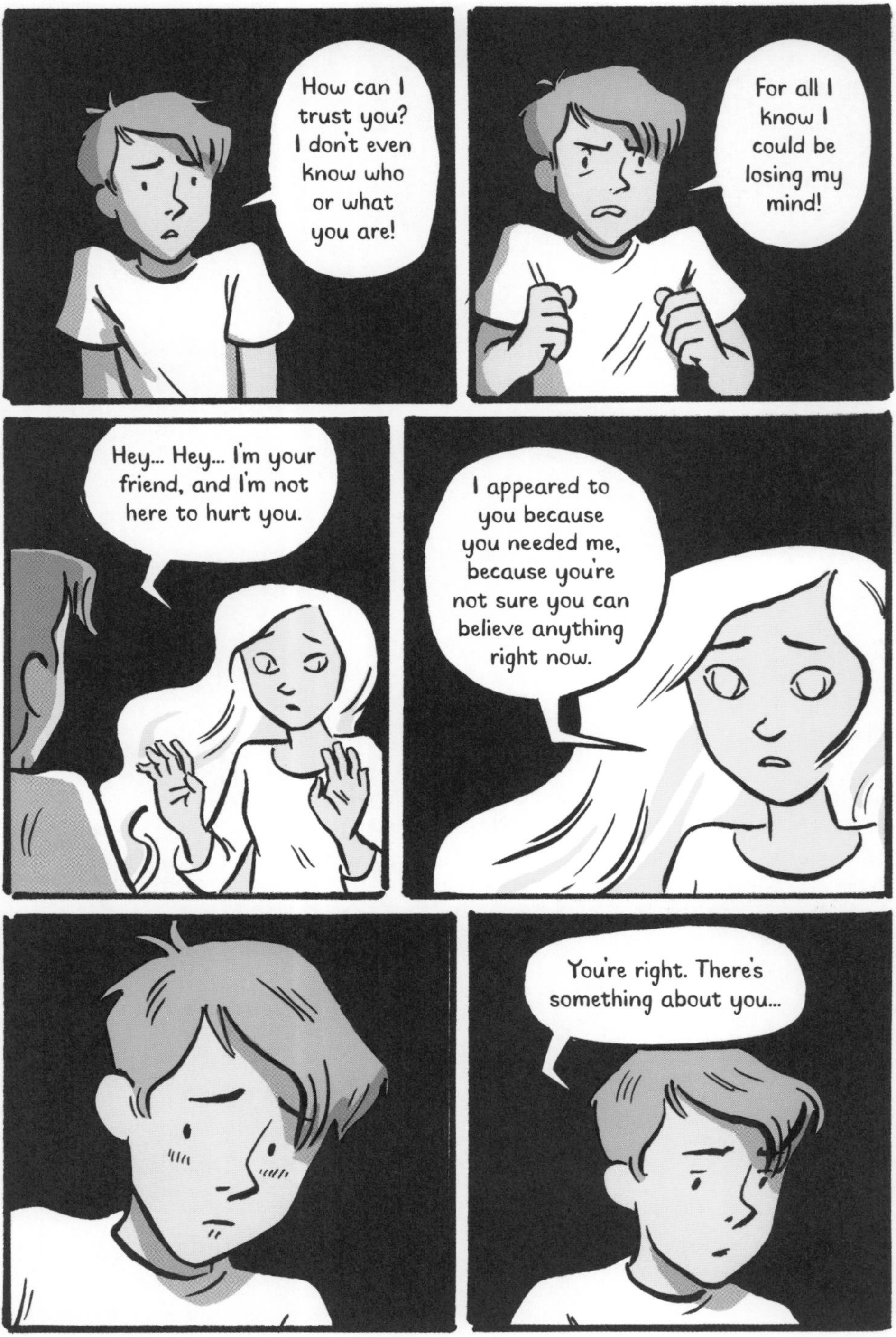
How can I trust you? I don't even know who or what you are!
For all I know I could be losing my mind!
Hey... Hey... I'm your friend, and I'm not here to hurt you.
I appeared to you because you needed me, because you're not sure you can believe anything right now.
You're right. There's something about you...

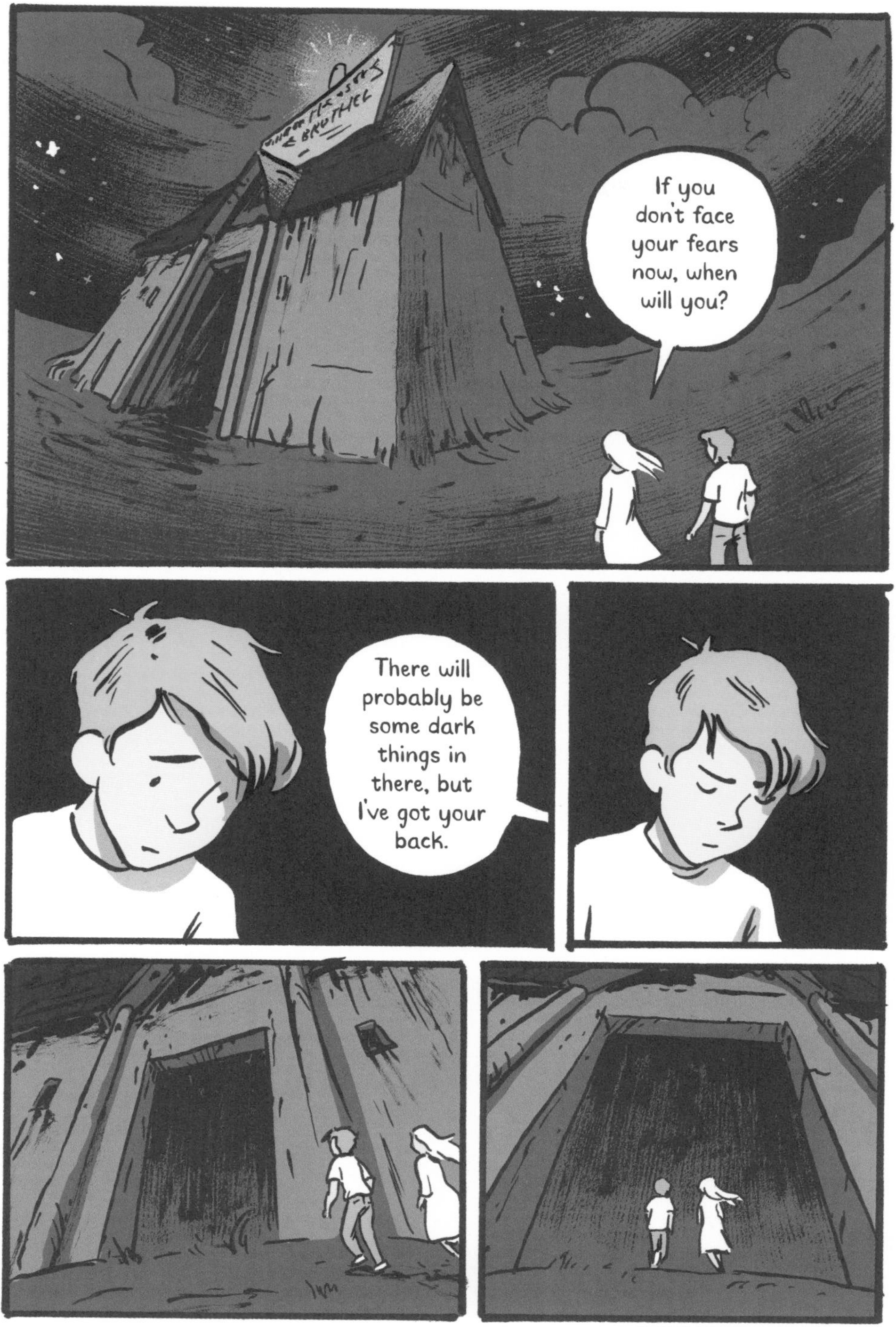
If you don't face your fears now, when will you?
There will probably be some dark things in there, but I've got your back.

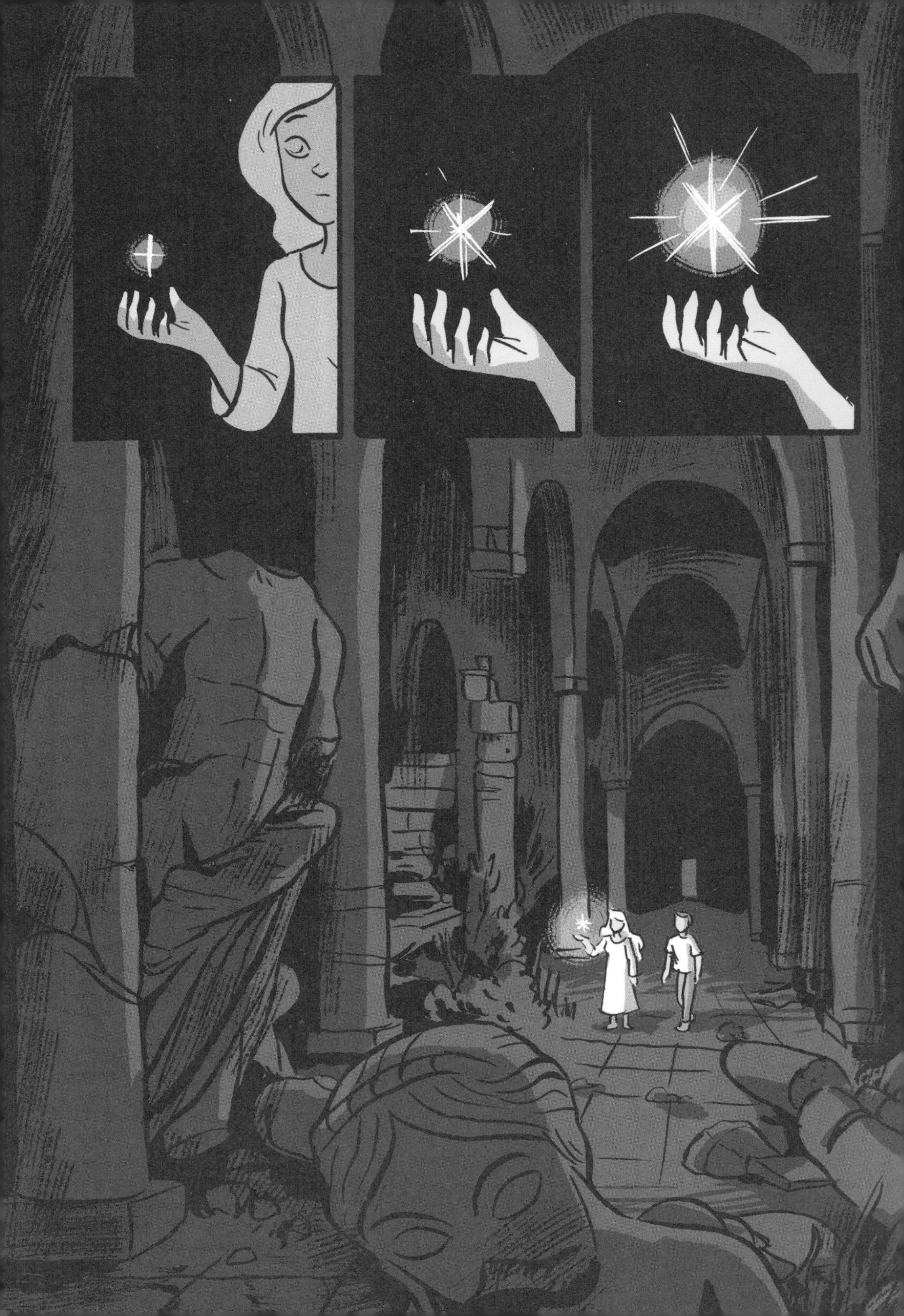

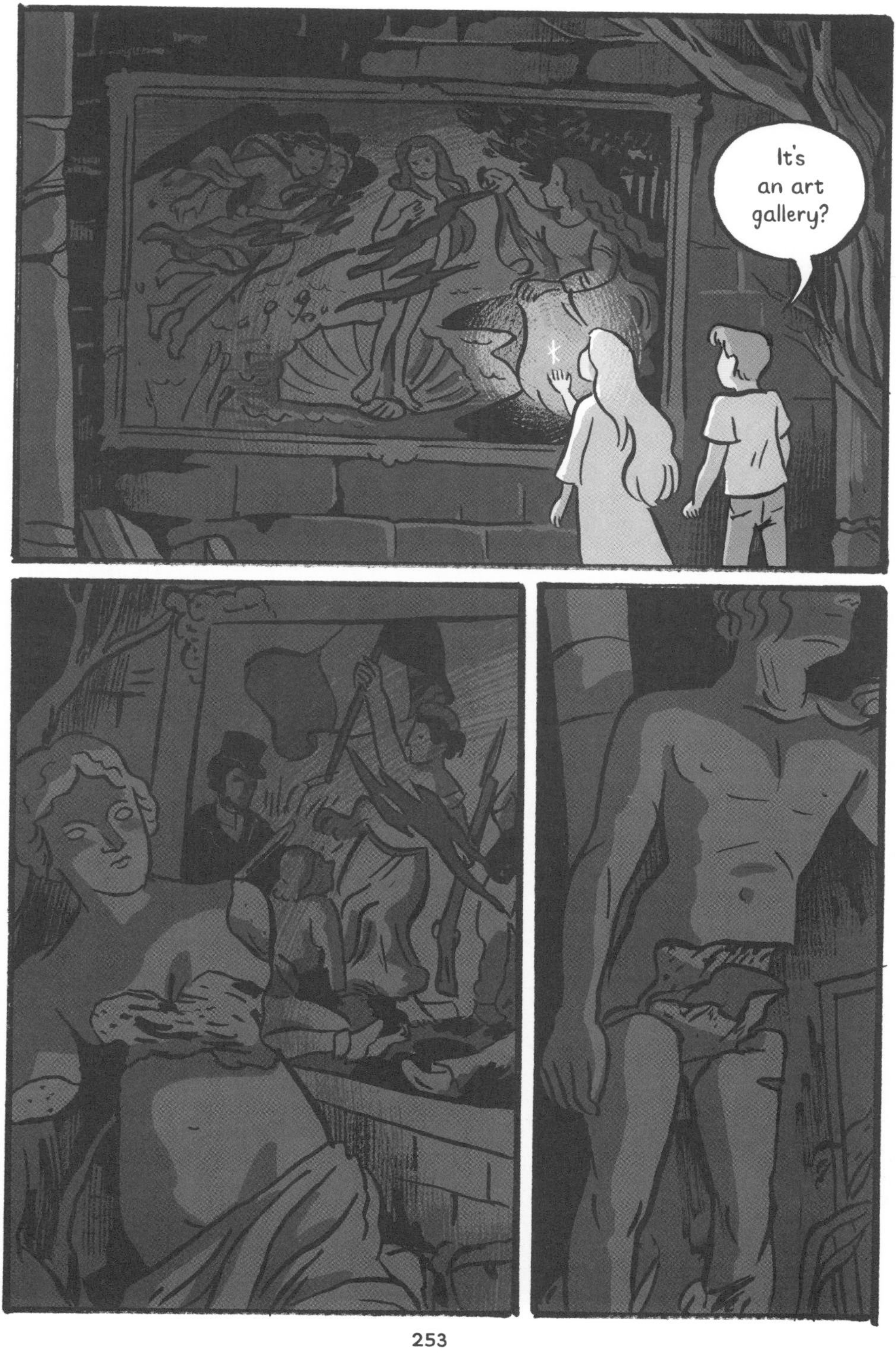
It's an art gallery?

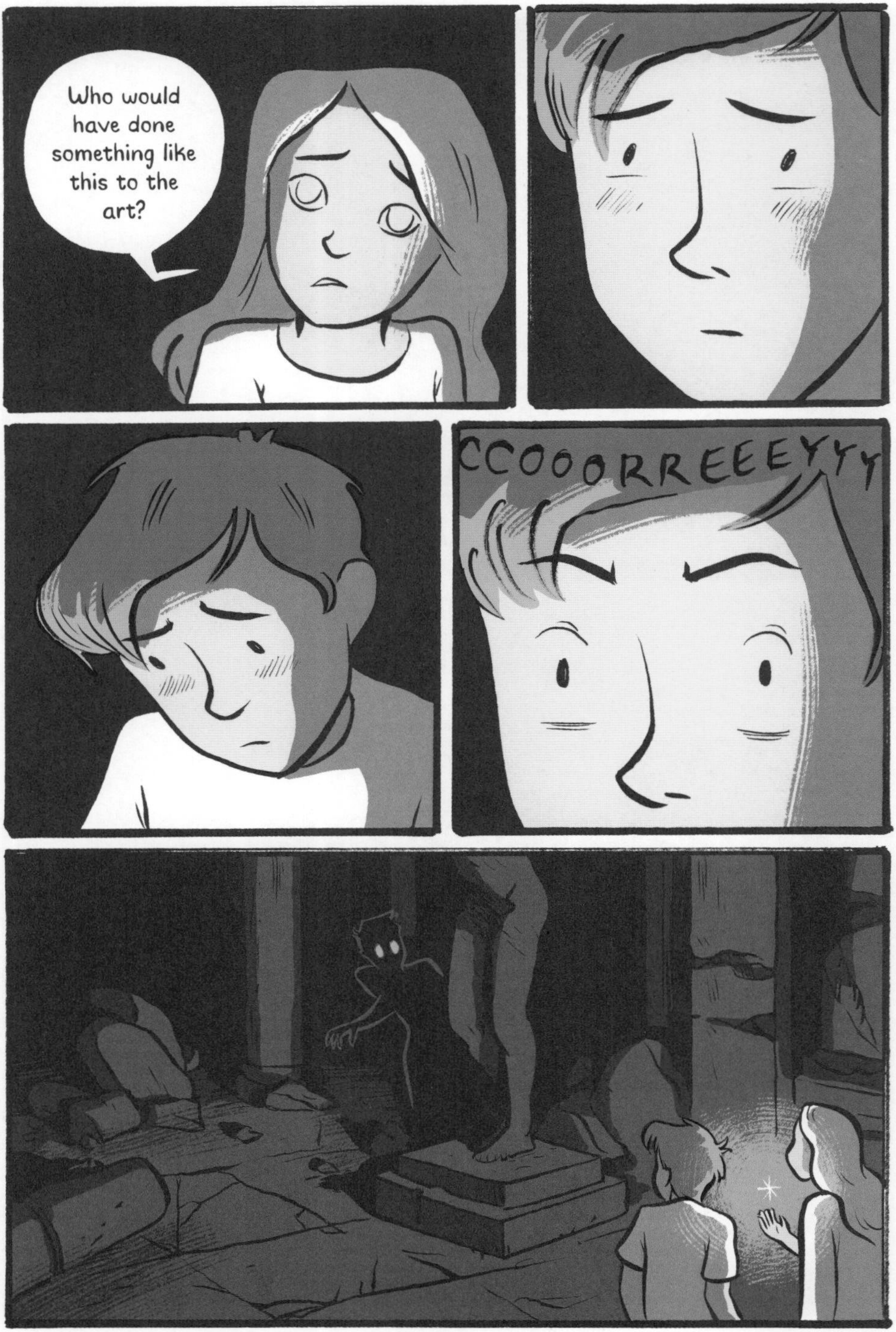
Who would have done something like this to the art?
CCOOORRREEEEYYYY

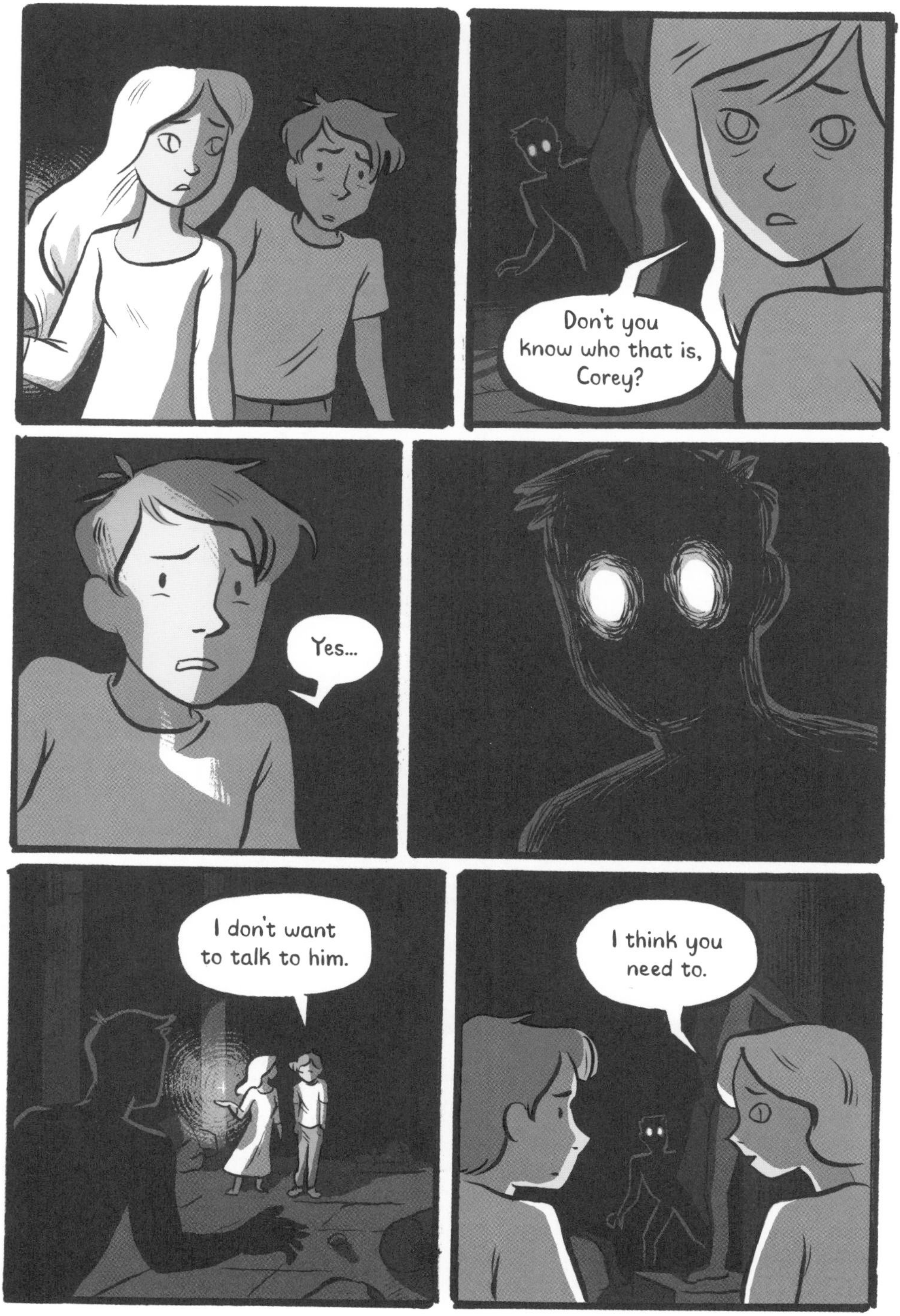
Don't you know who that is, Corey?
Yes...
I don't want to talk to him.
I think you need to.

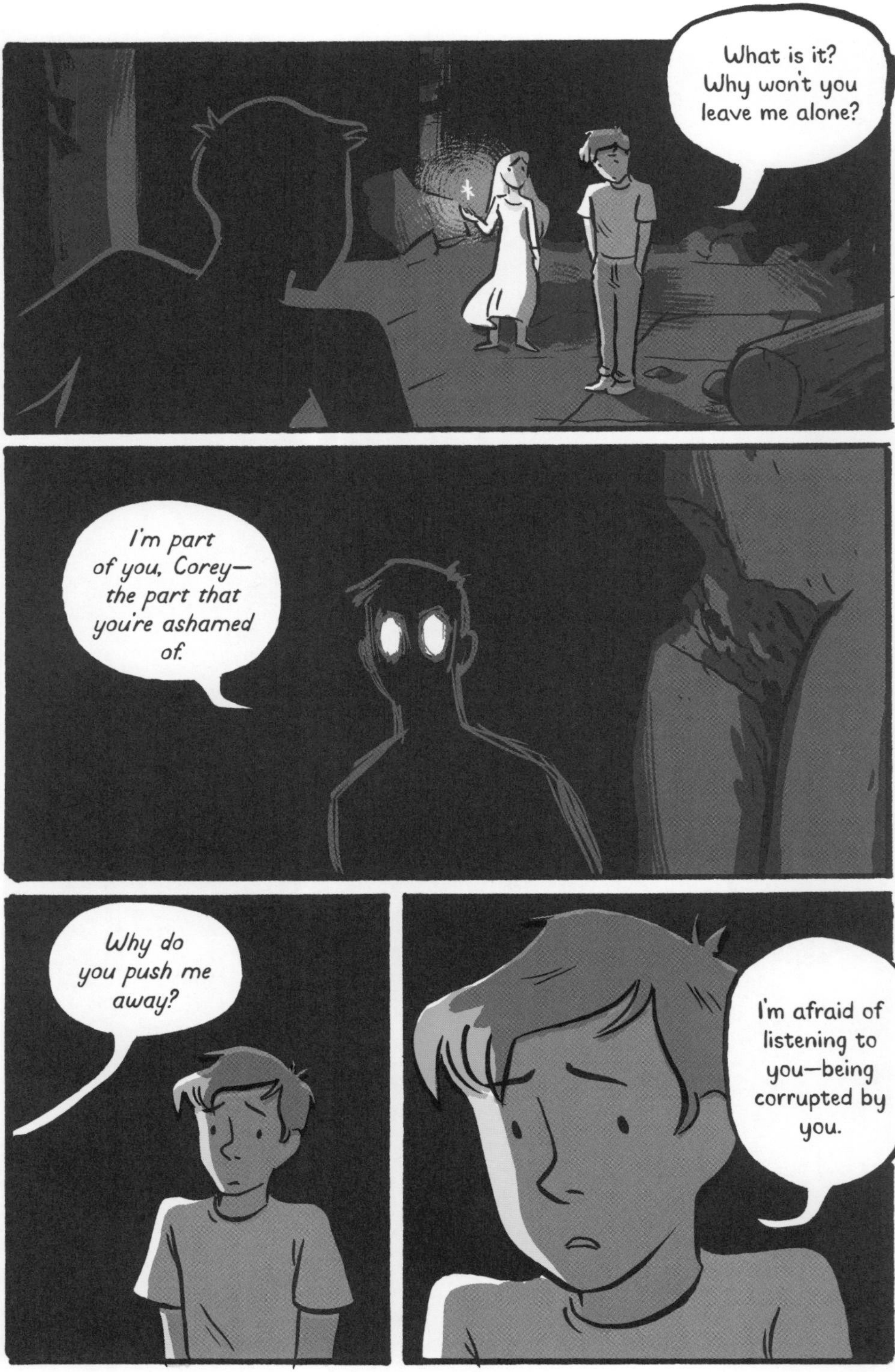
What is it? Why won't you leave me alone?
I'm part of you, Corey— the part that you're ashamed of.
Why do you push me away?
I'm afraid of listening to you—being corrupted by you.

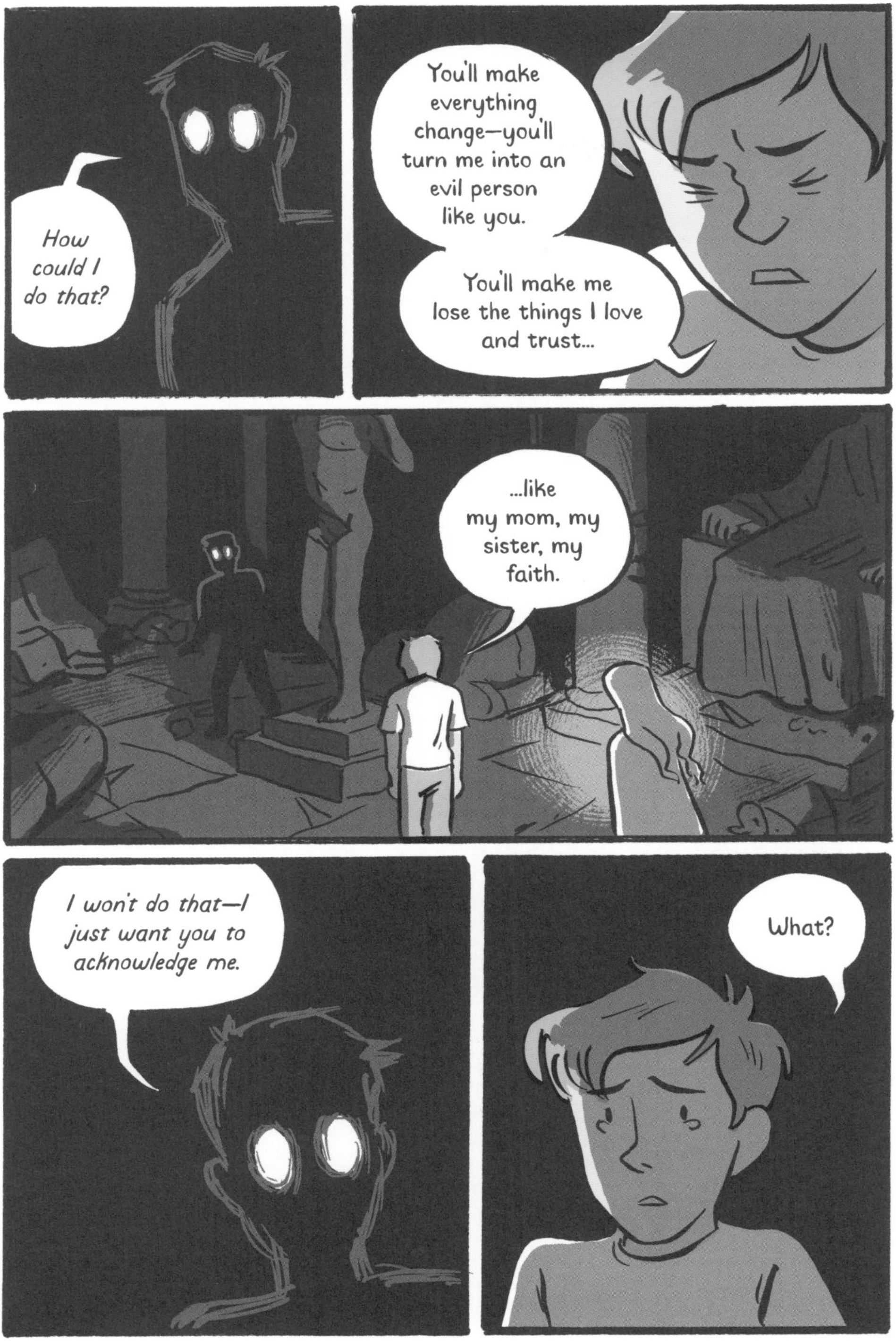
How could I do that?
You'll make everything change—you'll turn me into an evil person like you.
You'll make me lose the things I love and trust...
...like my mom, my sister, my faith.
I won't do that—I just want you to acknowledge me.
What?

Listen to me for once. Give me a chance.
How? What do I do?
Let yourself love me.
What?! I can't!
What does it hurt to love someone? Didn't Jesus say to love even your enemies?

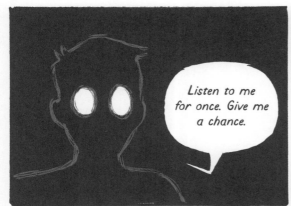

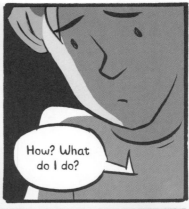

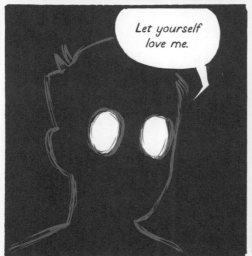

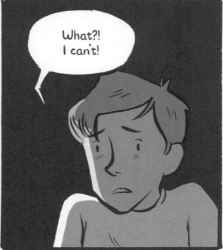

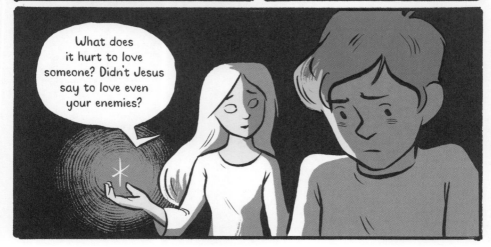

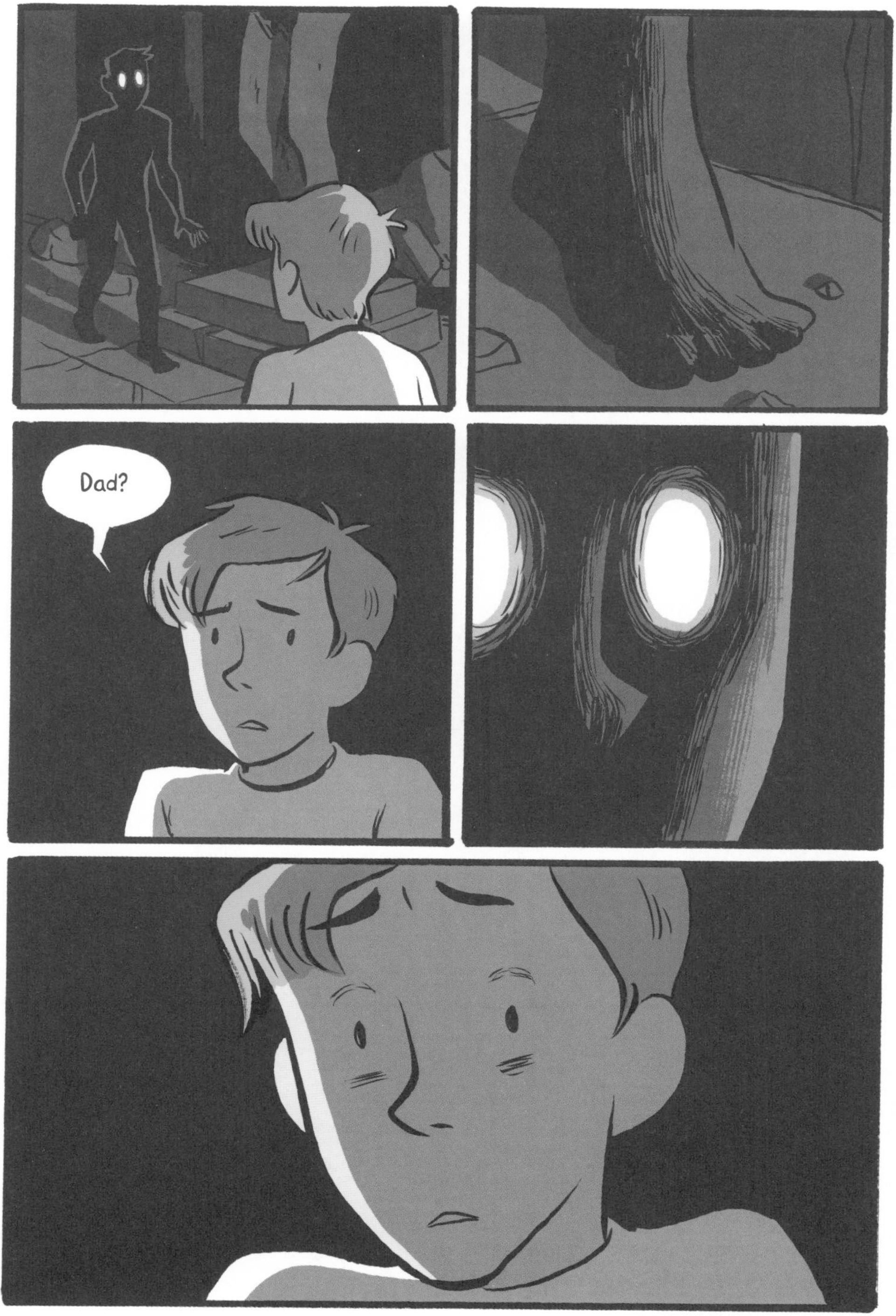
Dad?

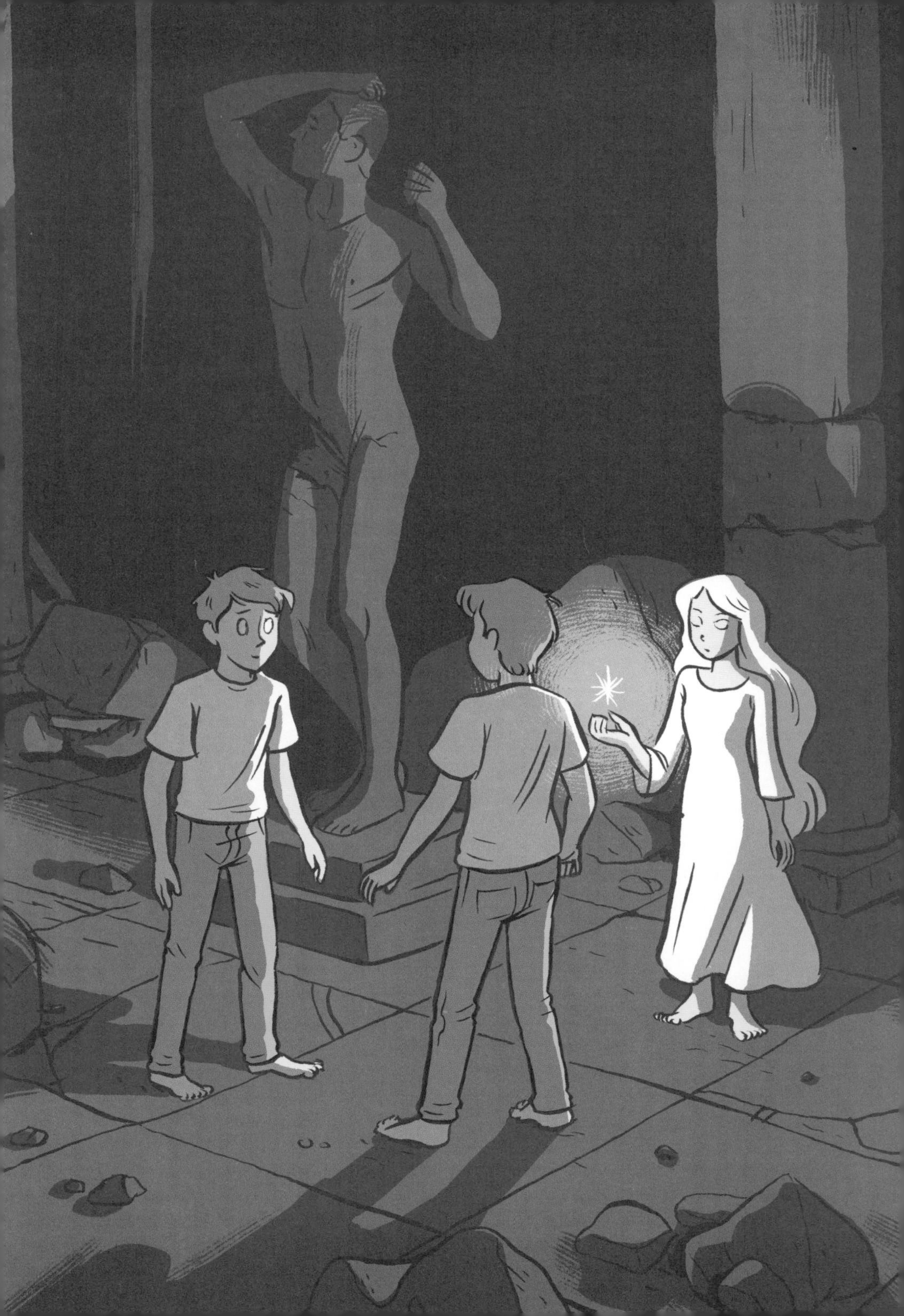

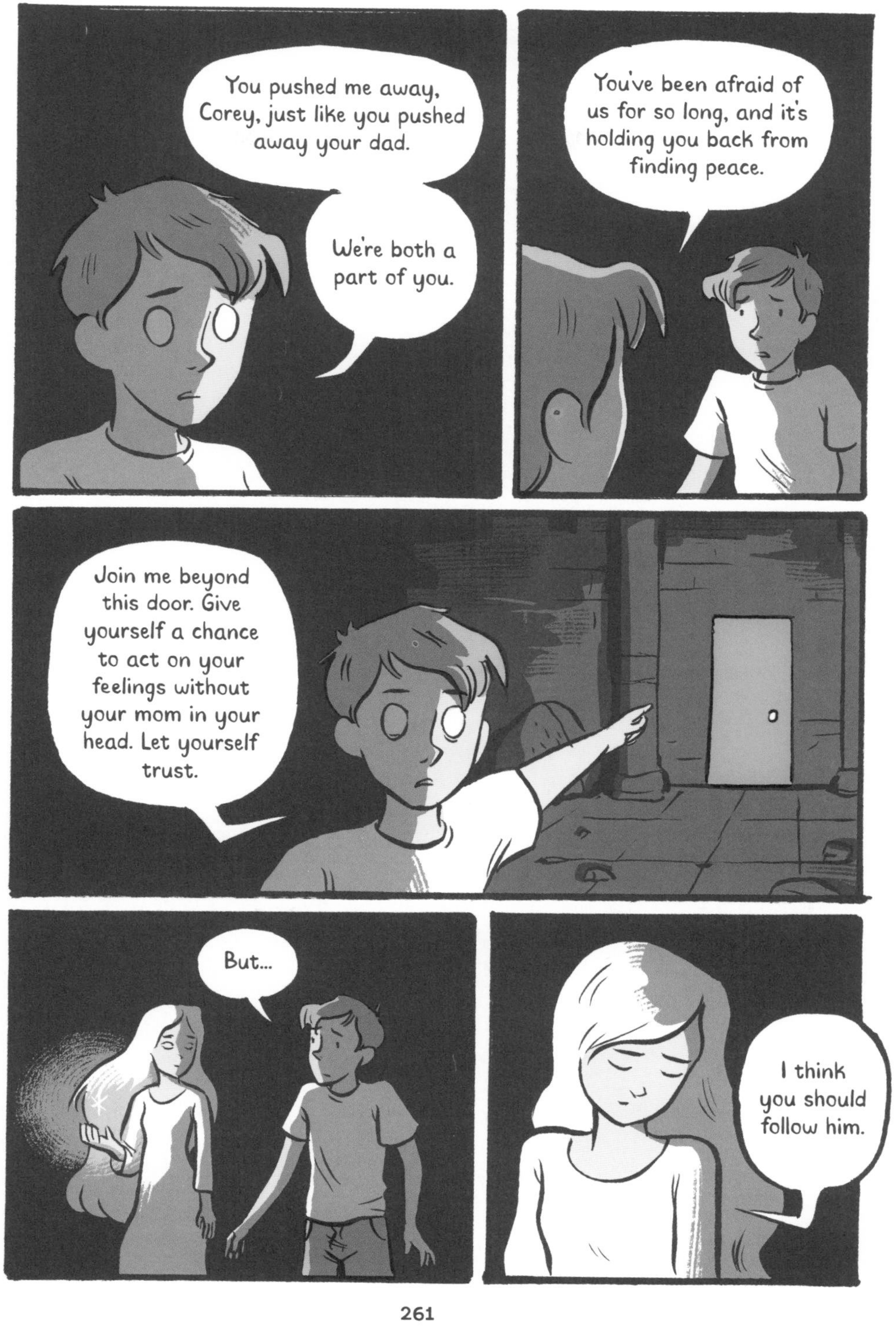
You pushed me away, Corey, just like you pushed away your dad.
We're both a part of you.
You've been afraid of us for so long, and it's holding you back from finding peace.
Join me beyond this door. Give yourself a chance to act on your feelings without your mom in your head. Let yourself trust.
But...
I think you should follow him.

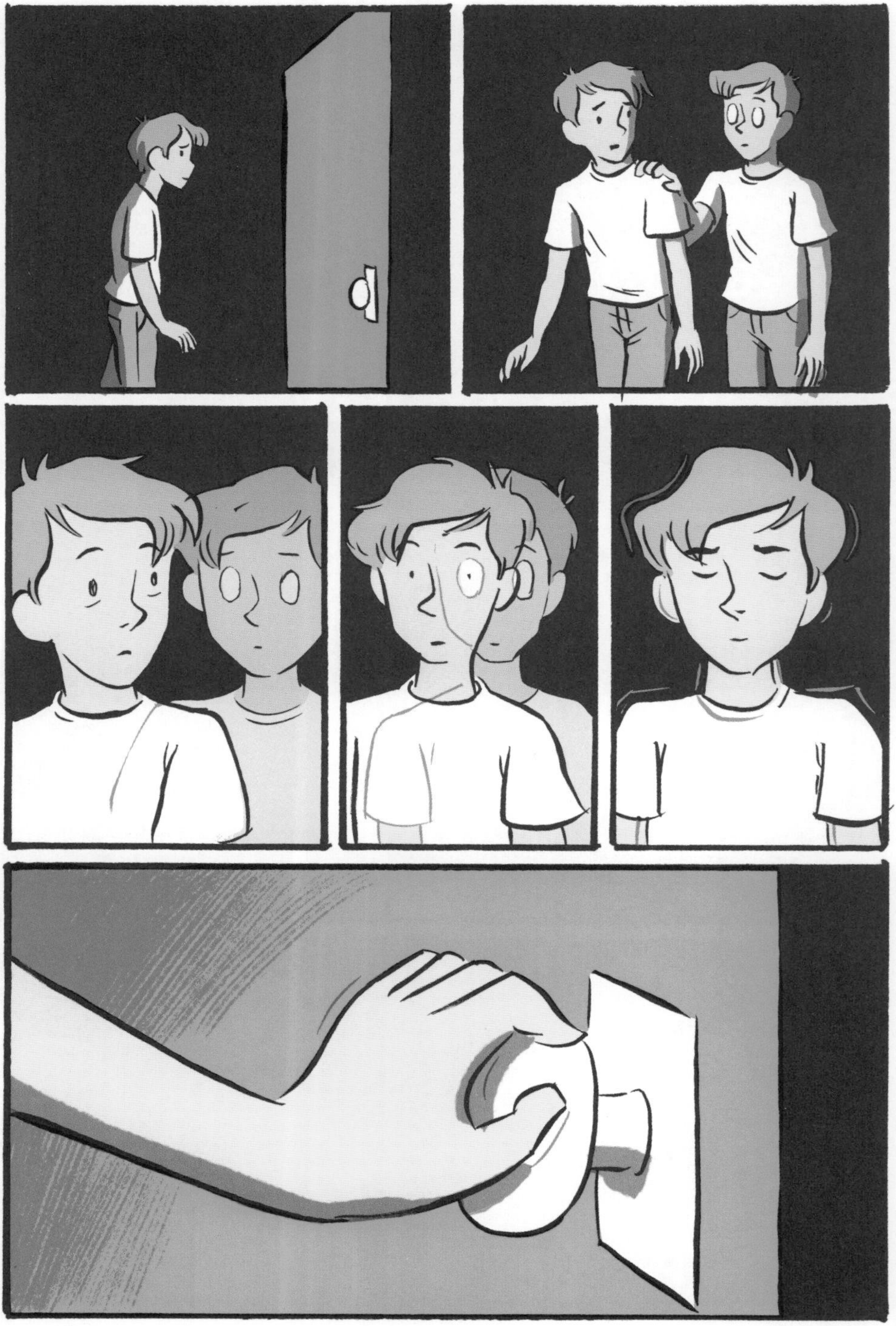

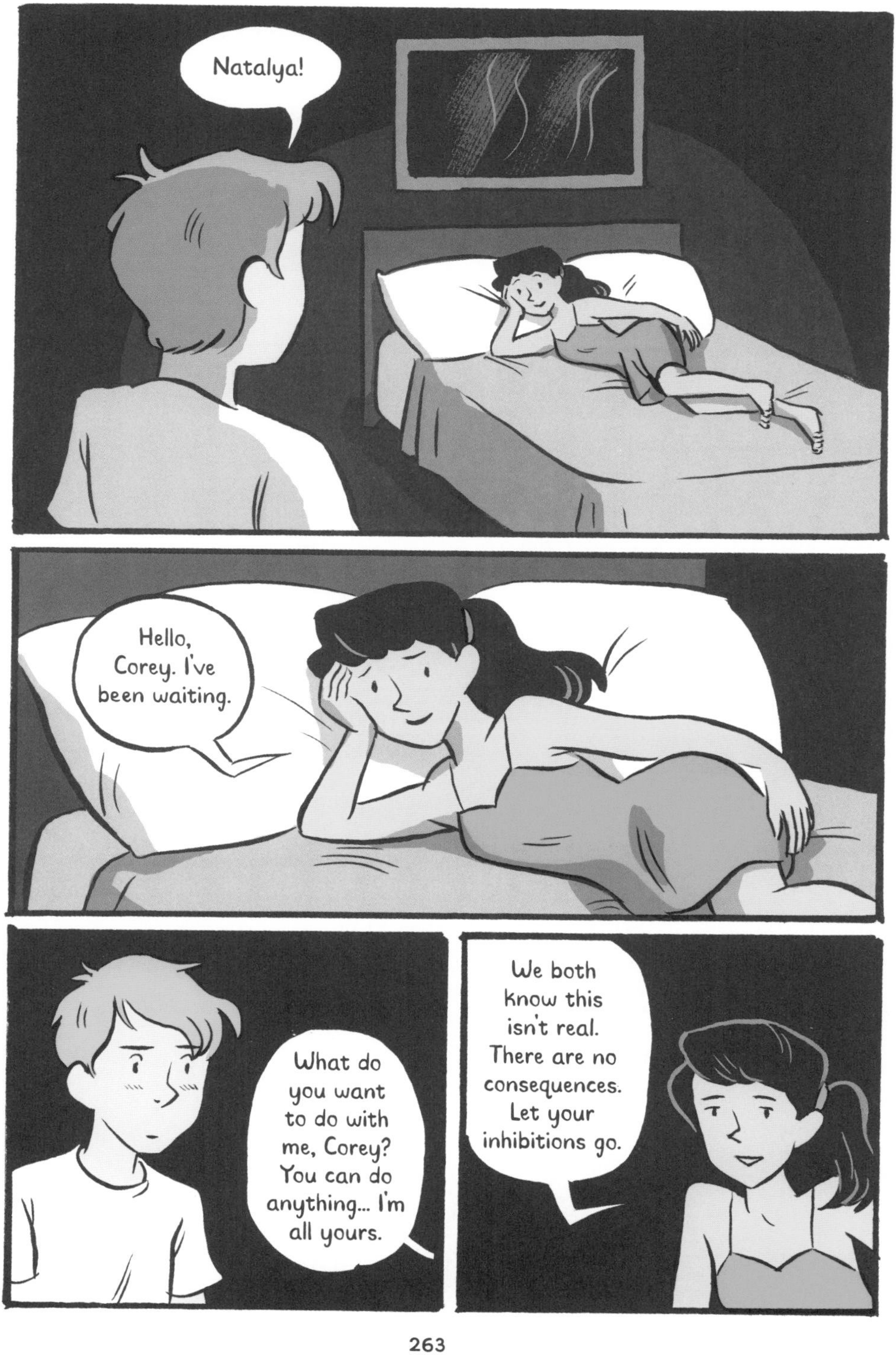
Natalya!
Hello, Corey. I've been waiting.
What do you want to do with me, Corey? You can do anything... I'm all yours.
We both know this isn't real. There are no consequences. Let your inhibitions go.

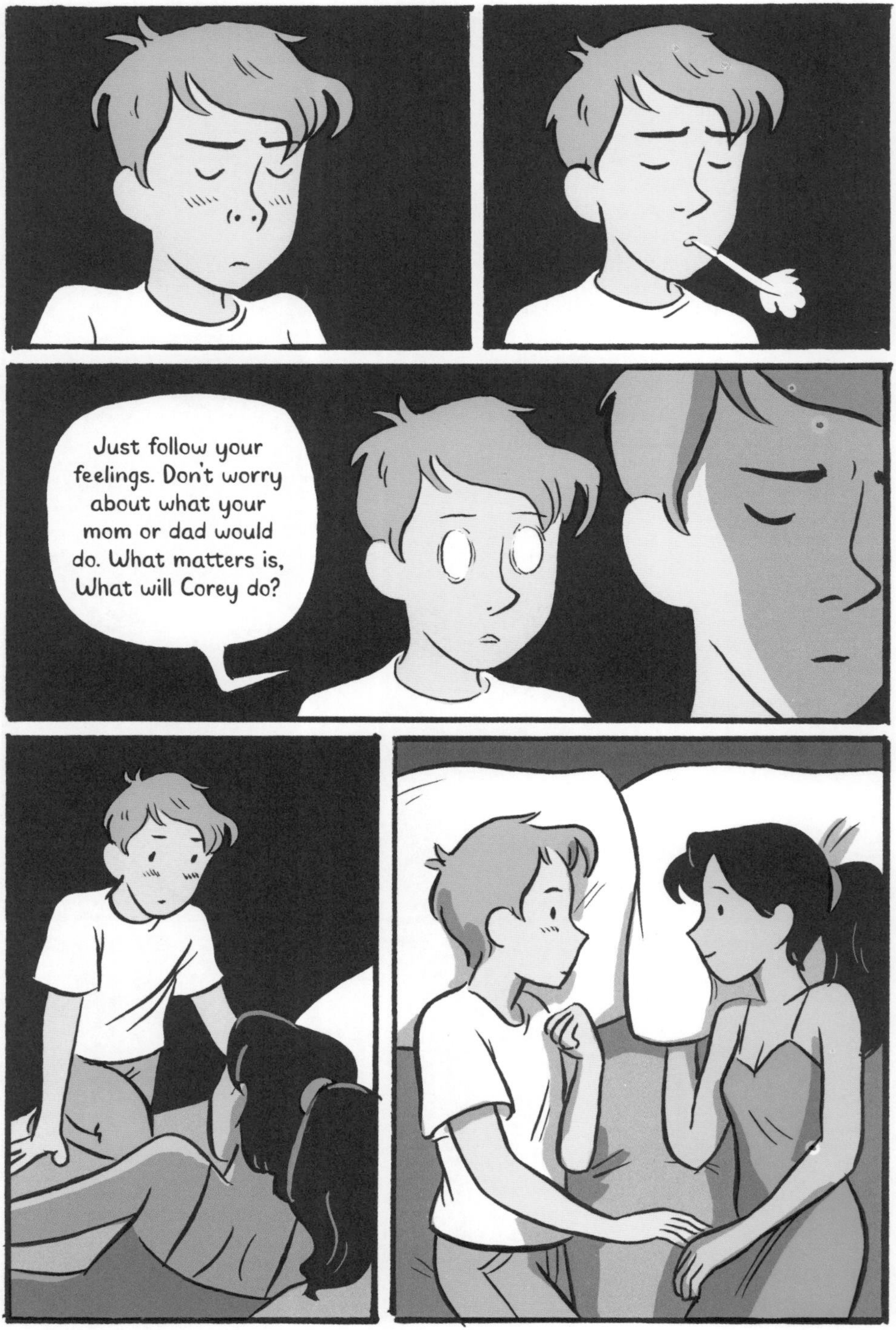
Just follow your feelings. Don't worry about what your mom or dad would do. What matters is, What will Corey do?

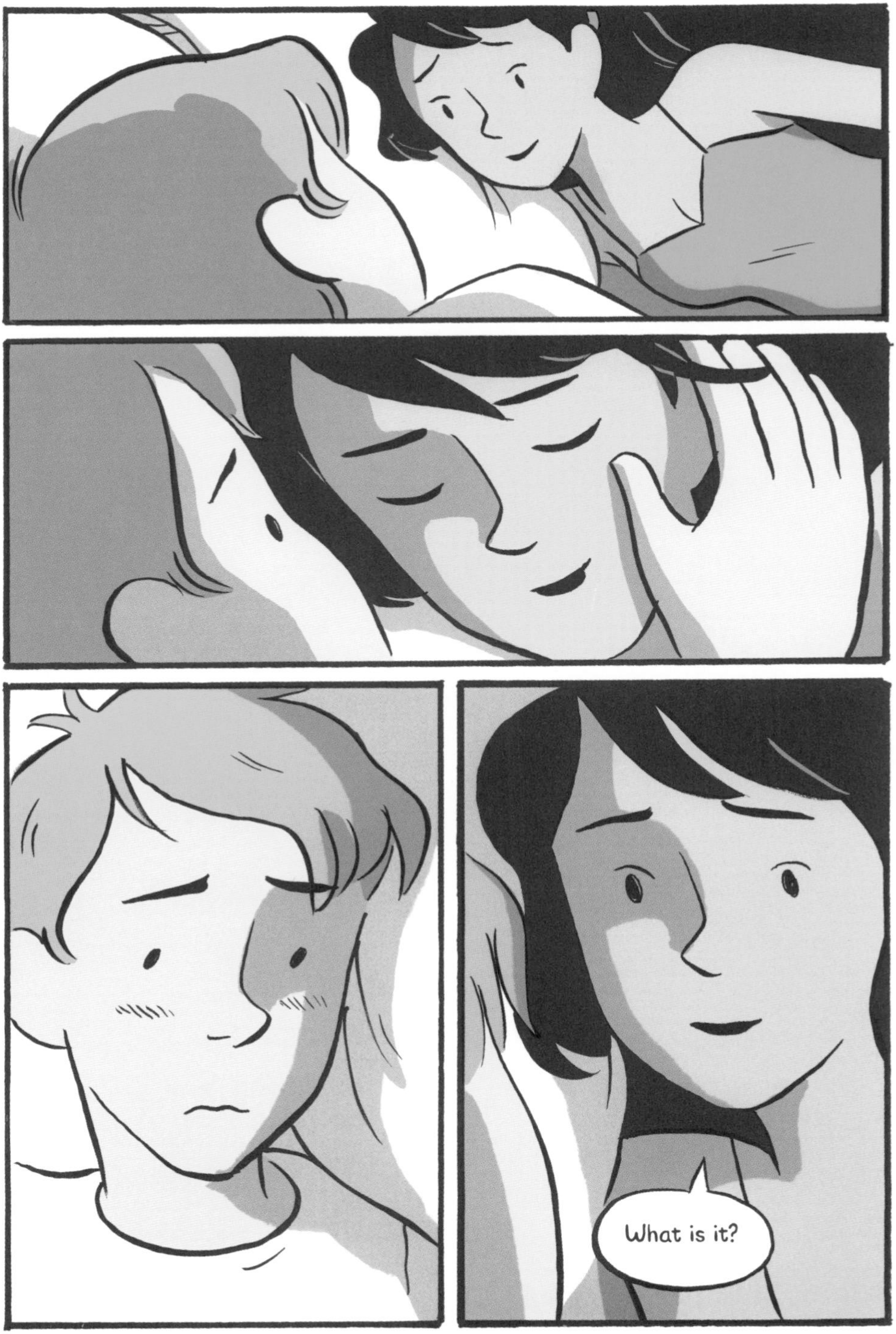
What is it?

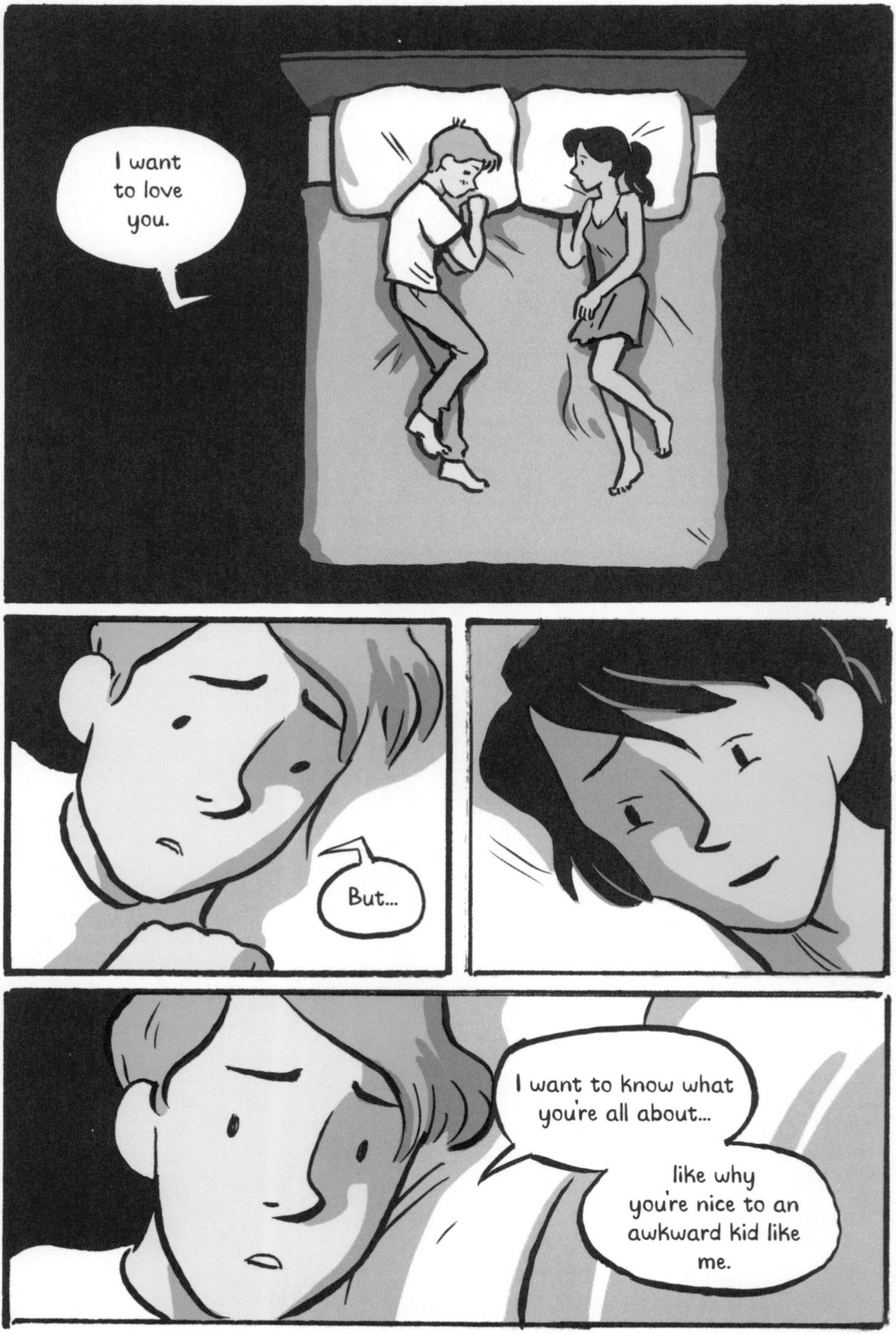
I want to love you.
But...
I want to know what you're all about...
like why you're nice to an awkward kid like me.

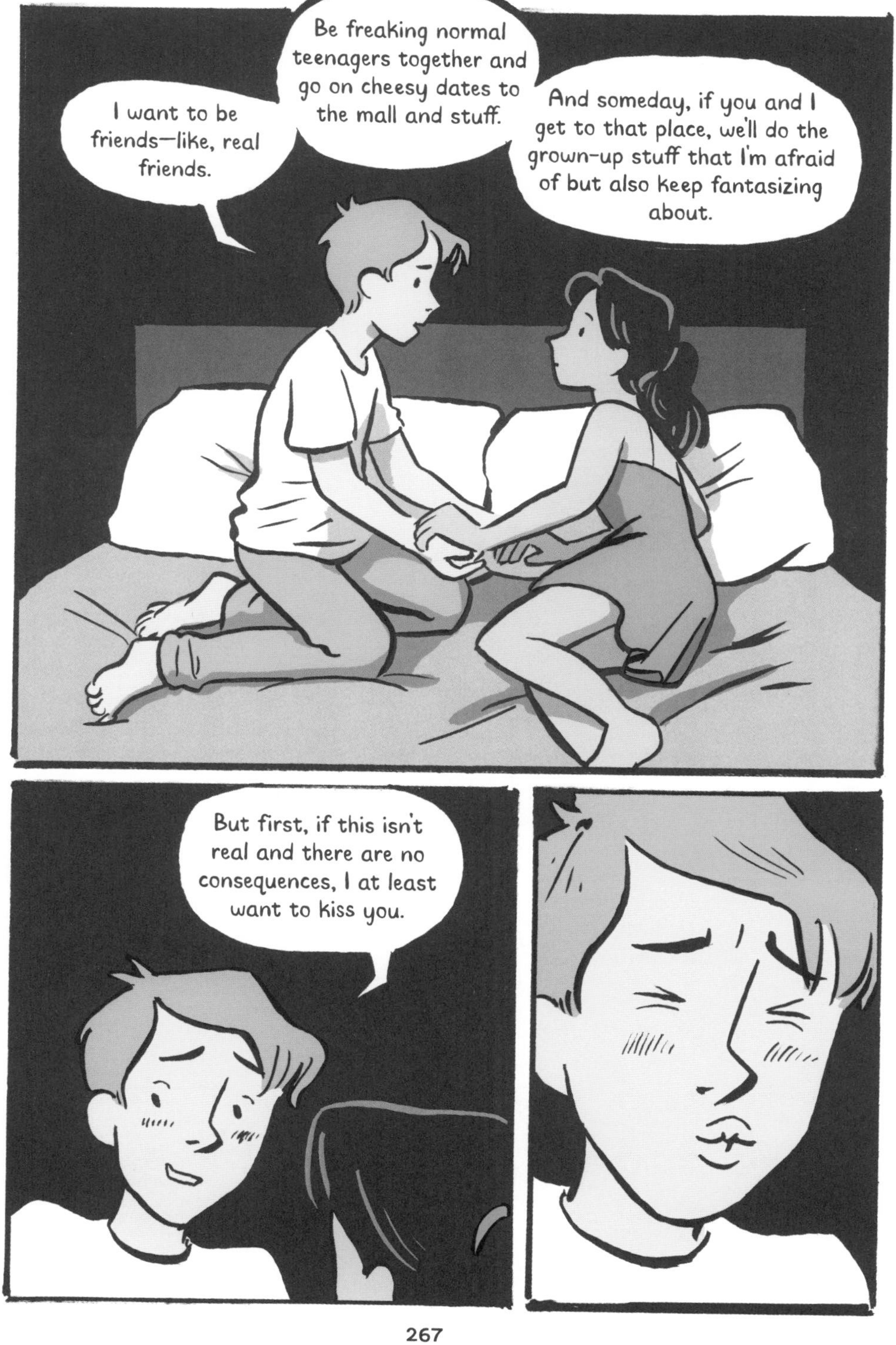
I want to be friends—like, real friends.
Be freaking normal teenagers together and go on cheesy dates to the mall and stuff.
And someday, if you and I get to that place, we'll do the grown-up stuff that I'm afraid of but also keep fantasizing about.
But first, if this isn't real and there are no consequences, I at least want to kiss you.

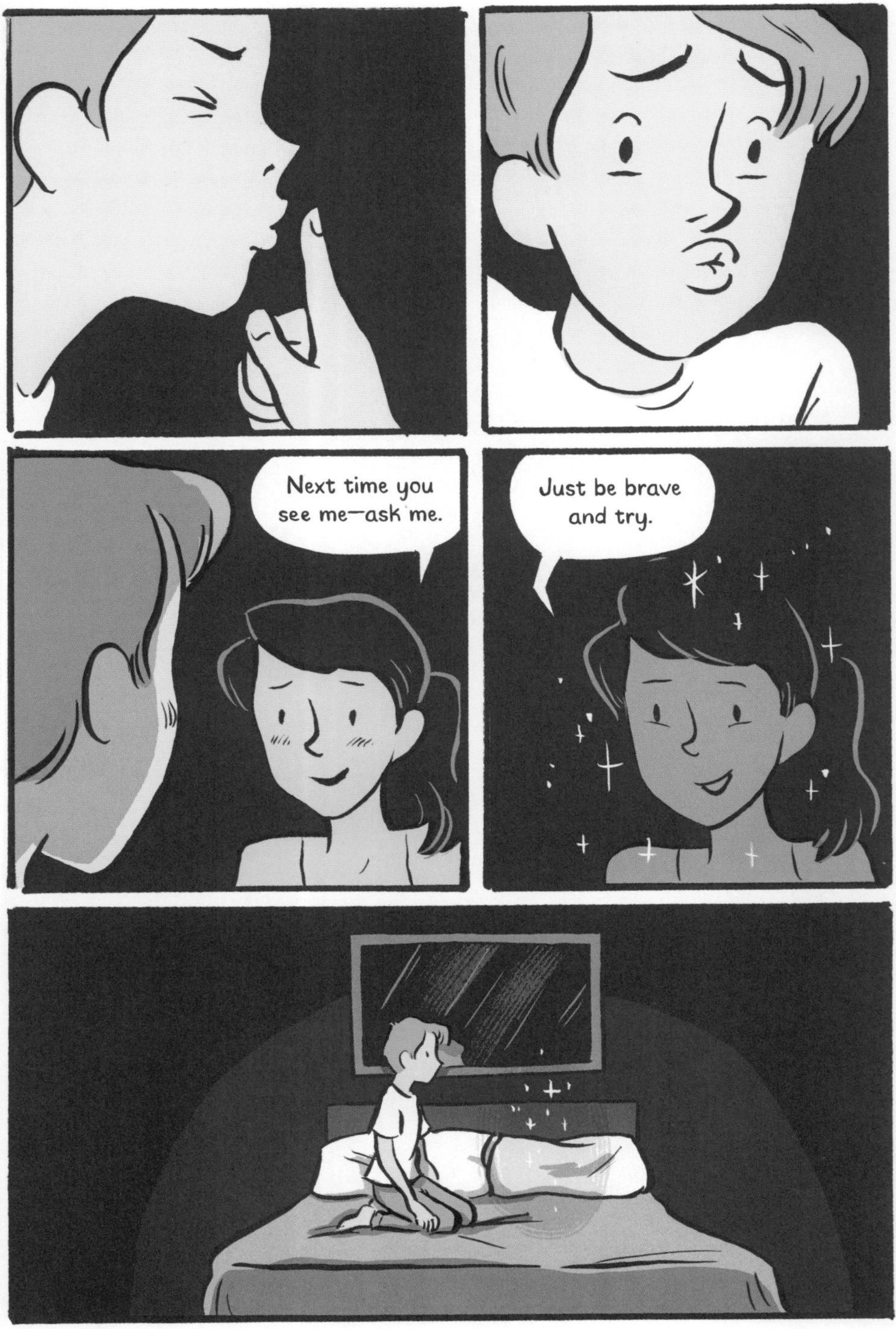
Next time you see me—ask me.
Just be brave and try.

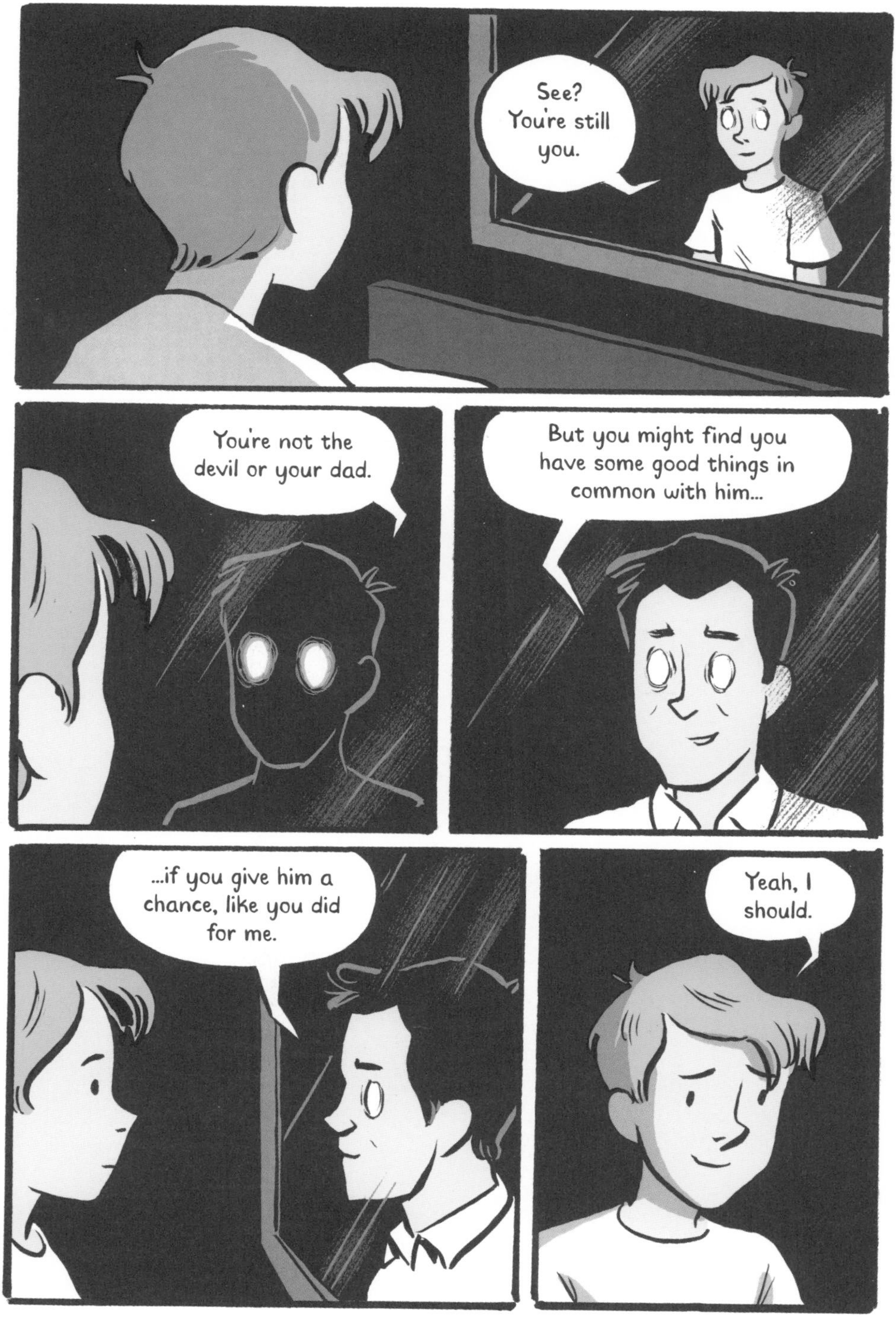
See? You're still you.
You're not the devil or your dad.
But you might find you have some good things in common with him...
...if you give him a chance, like you did for me.
Yeah, I should.

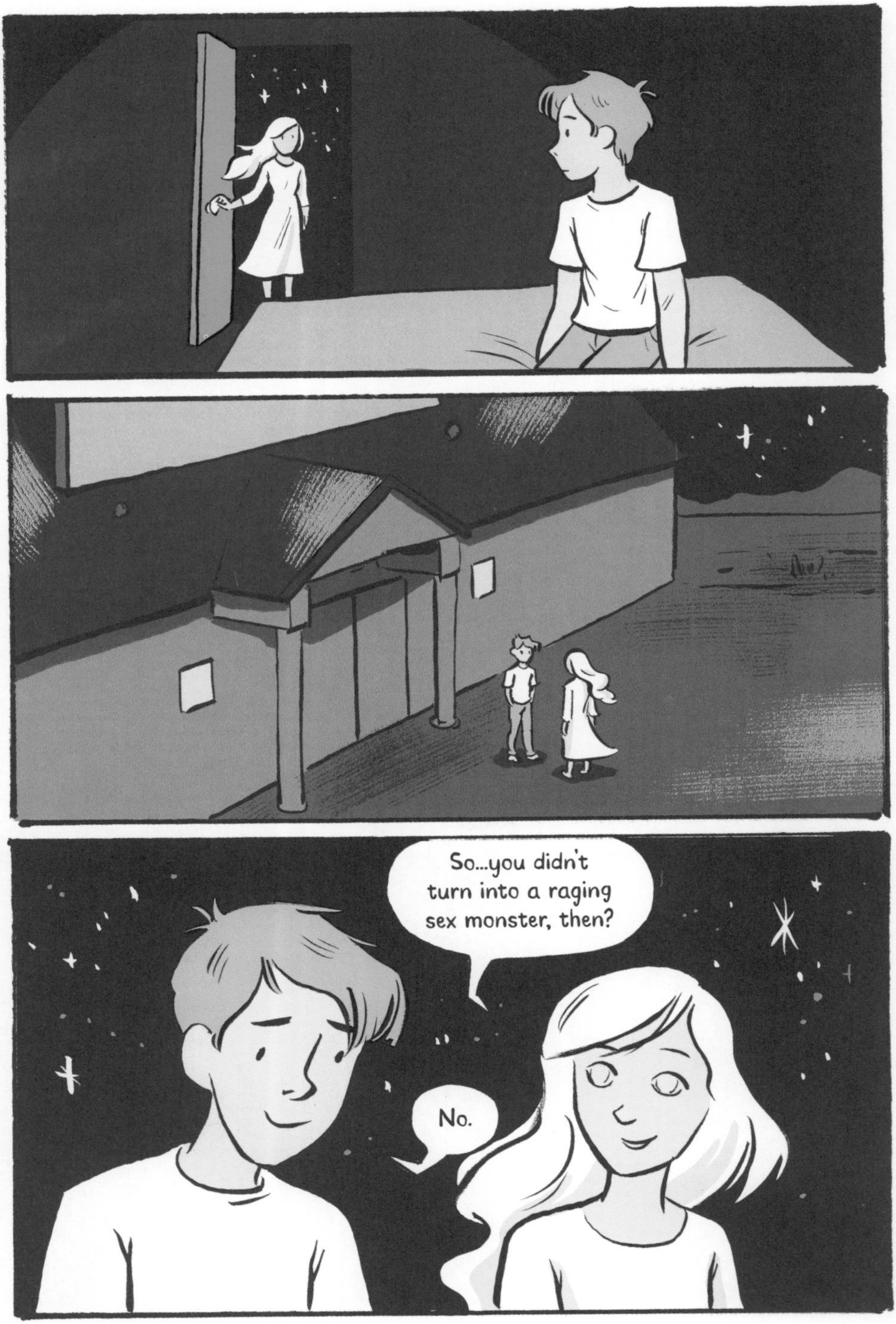
So...you didn't turn into a raging sex monster, then?
No.

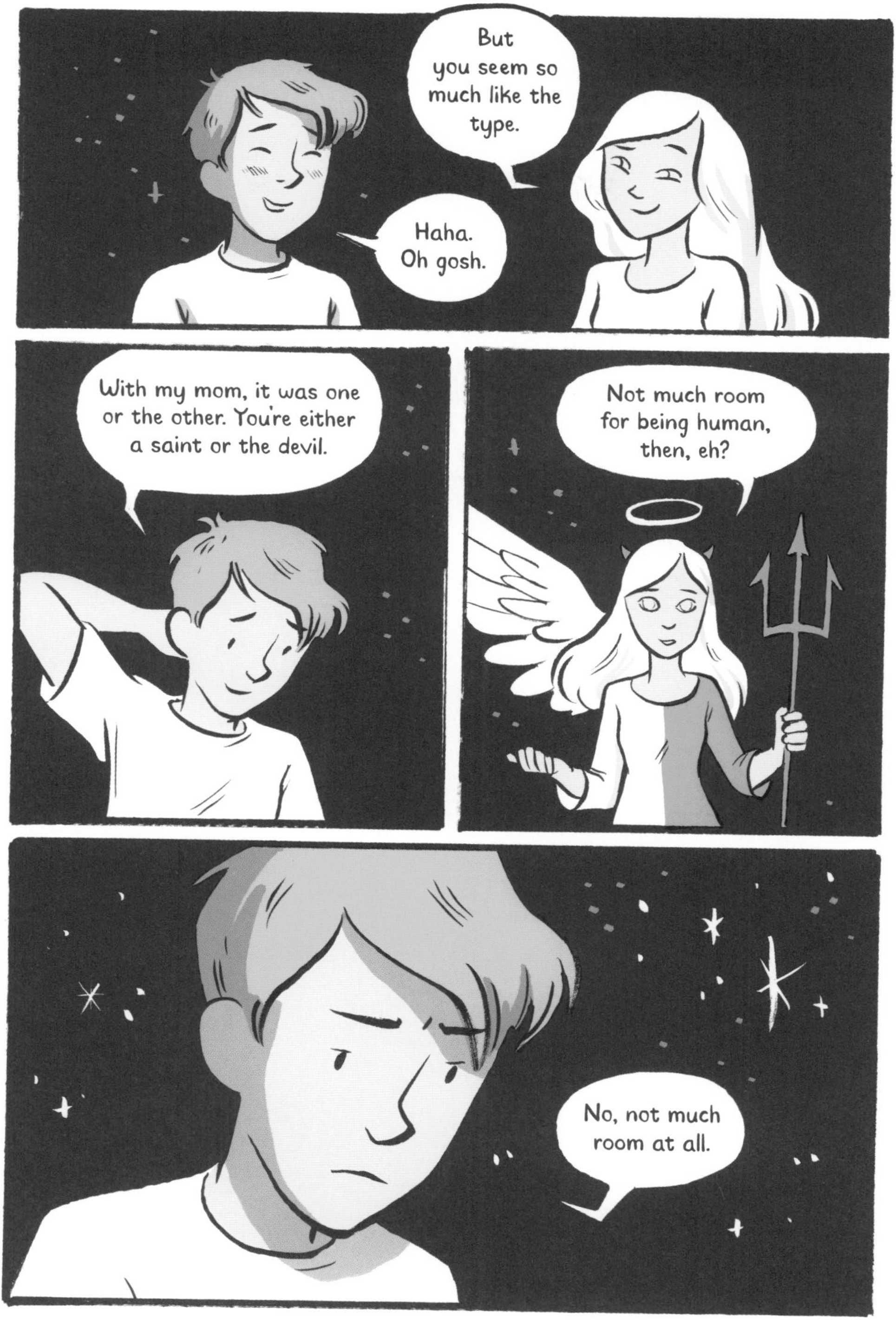
But you seem so much like the type.
Haha. Oh gosh.
With my mom, it was one or the other. You're either a saint or the devil.
Not much room for being human, then, eh?
No, not much room at all.

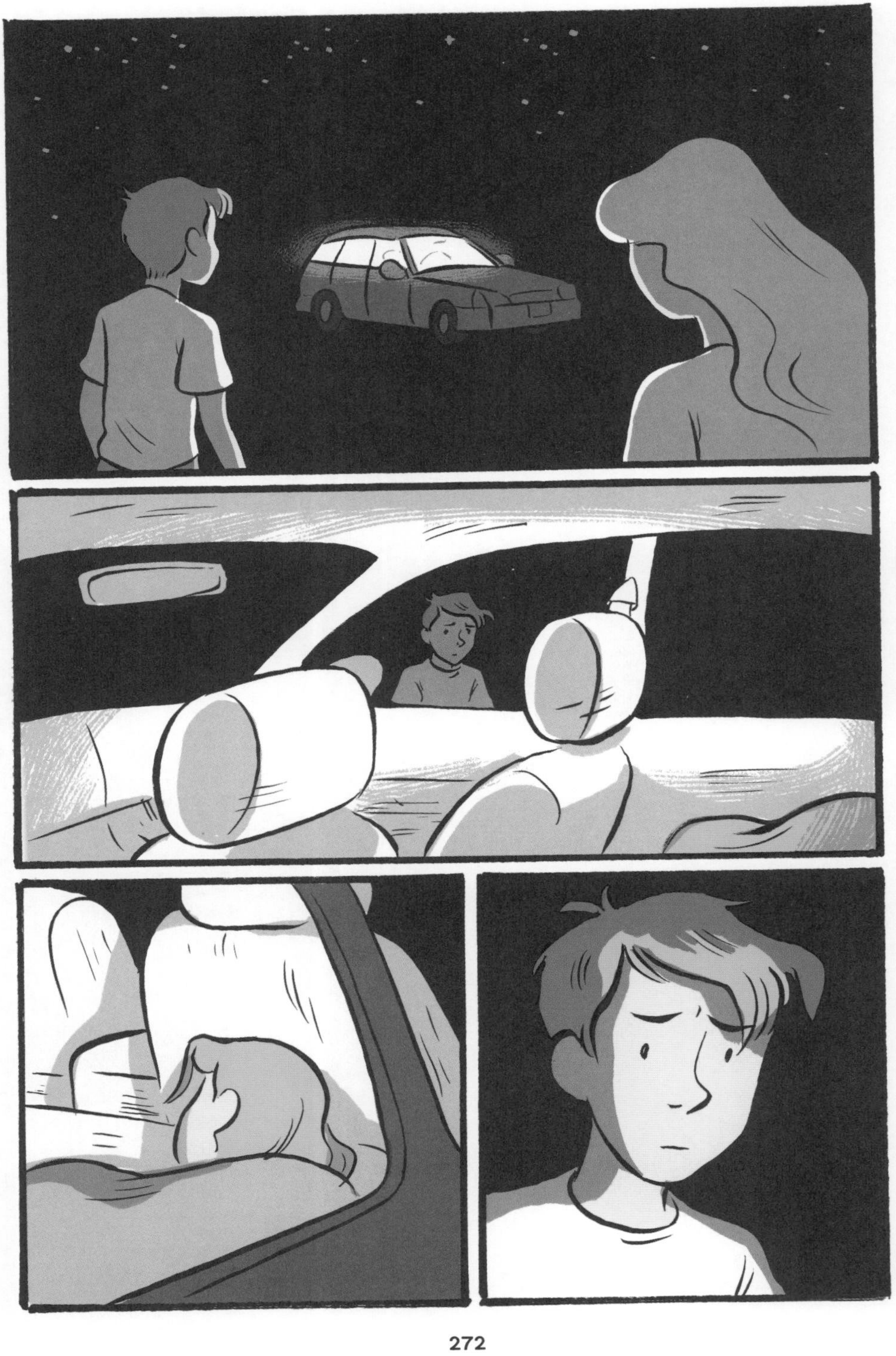

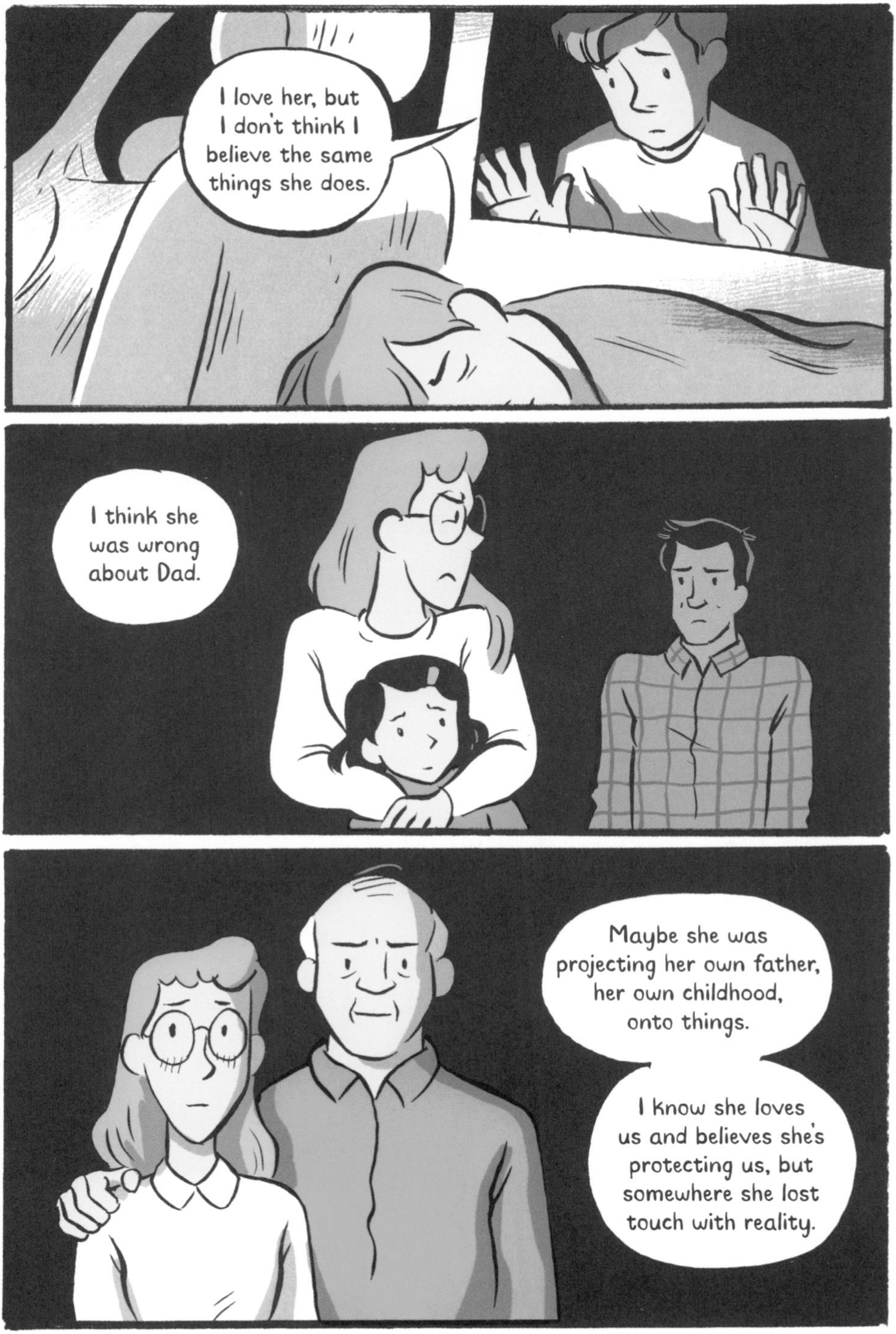
I love her, but I don't think I believe the same things she does.
I think she was wrong about Dad.
Maybe she was projecting her own father, her own childhood, onto things.
I know she loves us and believes she's protecting us, but somewhere she lost touch with reality.

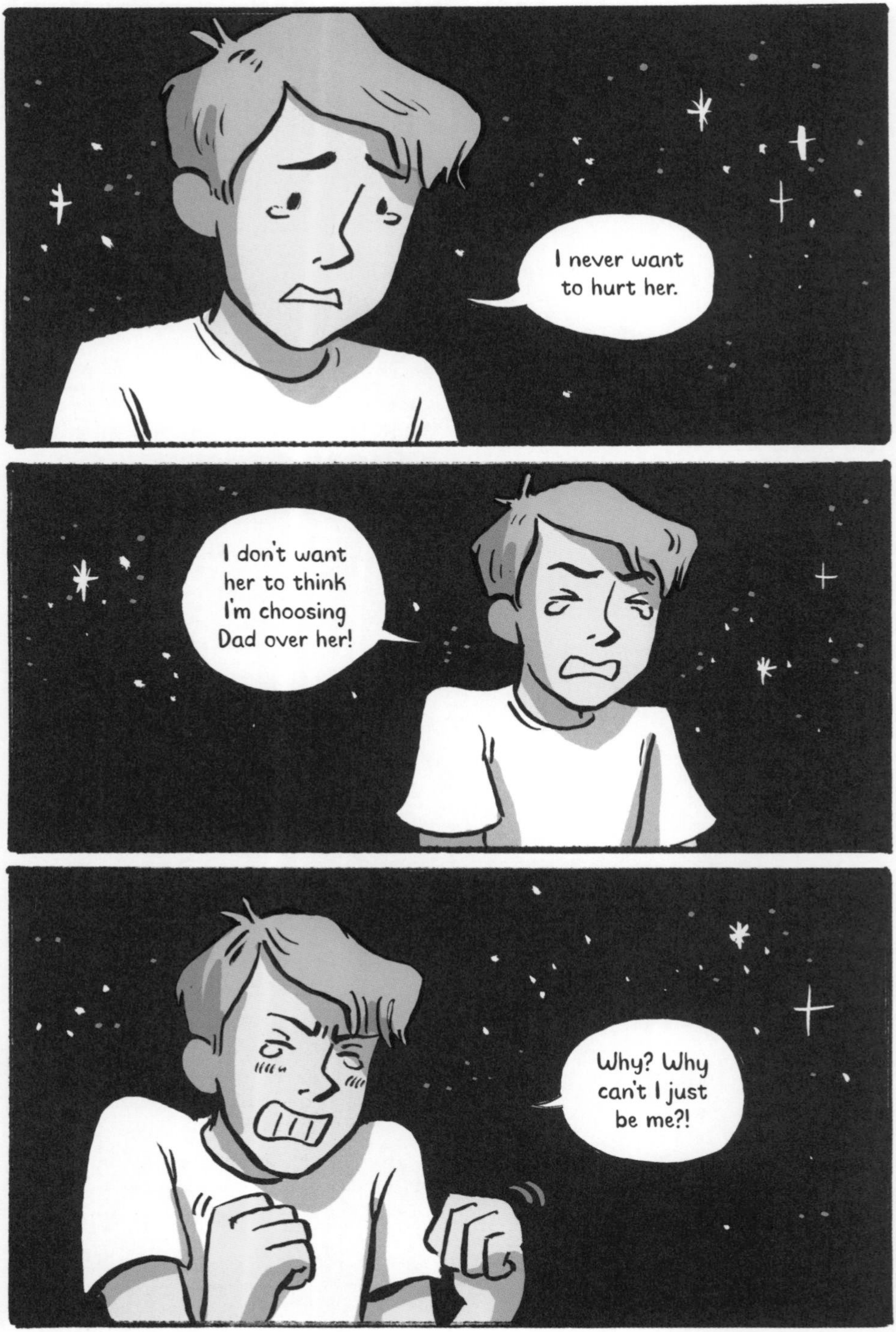
I never want to hurt her.
I don't want her to think I'm choosing Dad over her!
Why? Why can't I just be me?!

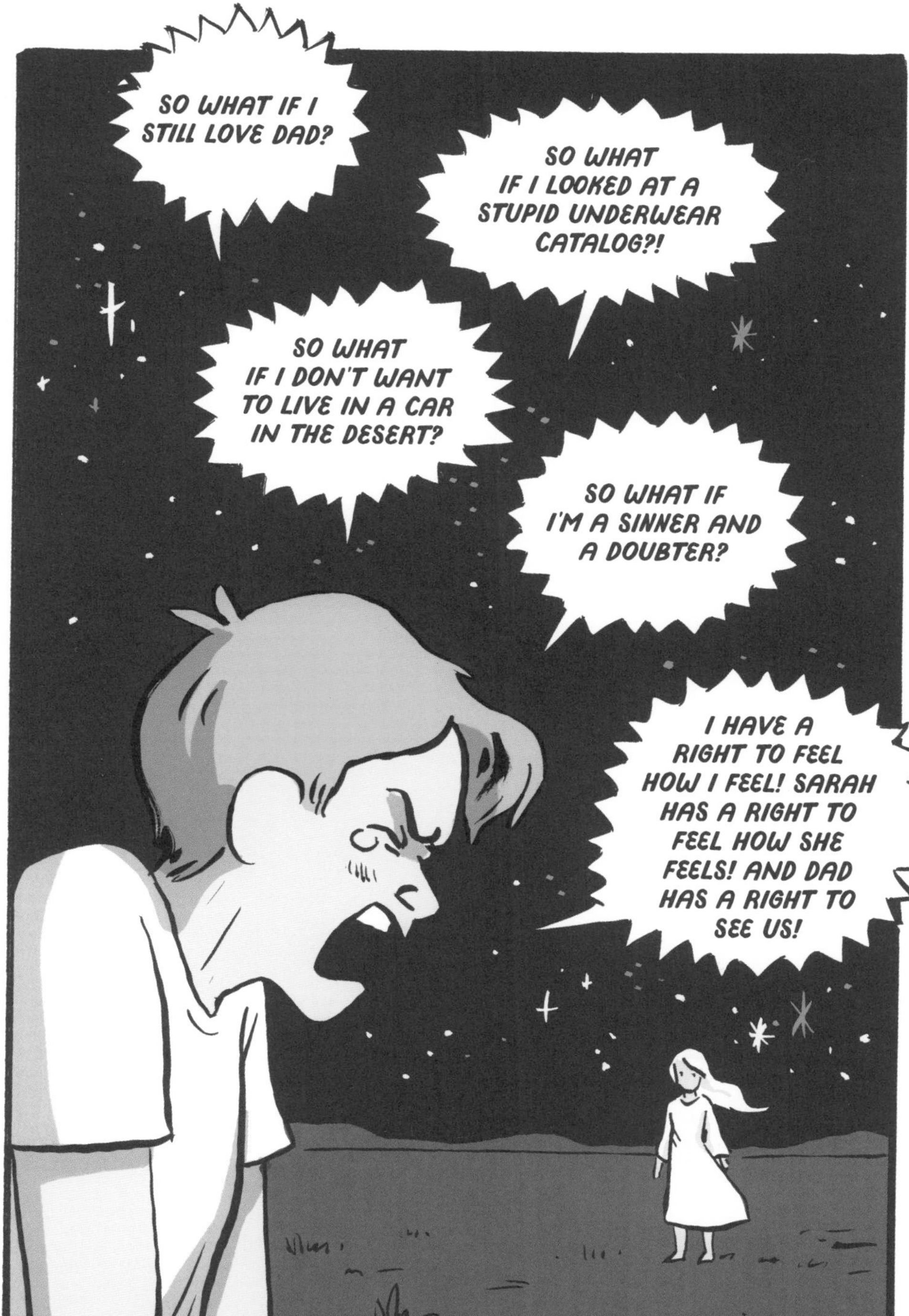
SO WHAT IF I STILL LOVE DAD?
SO WHAT IF I LOOKED AT A STUPID UNDERWEAR CATALOG?!
SO WHAT IF I DON'T WANT TO LIVE IN A CAR IN THE DESERT?
SO WHAT IF I'M A SINNER AND A DOUBTER?
I HAVE A RIGHT TO FEEL HOW I FEEL! SARAH HAS A RIGHT TO FEEL HOW SHE FEELS! AND DAD HAS A RIGHT TO SEE US!

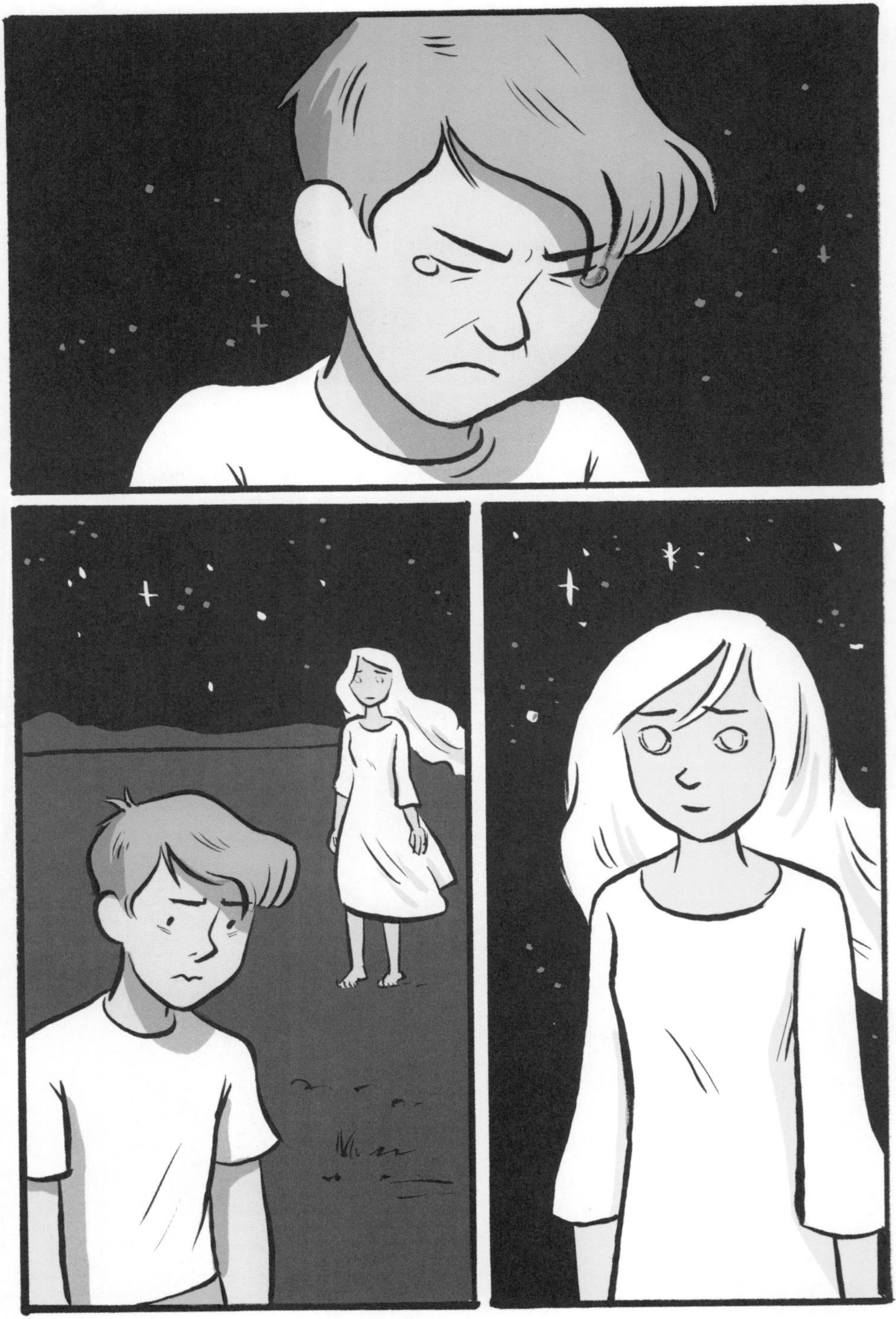

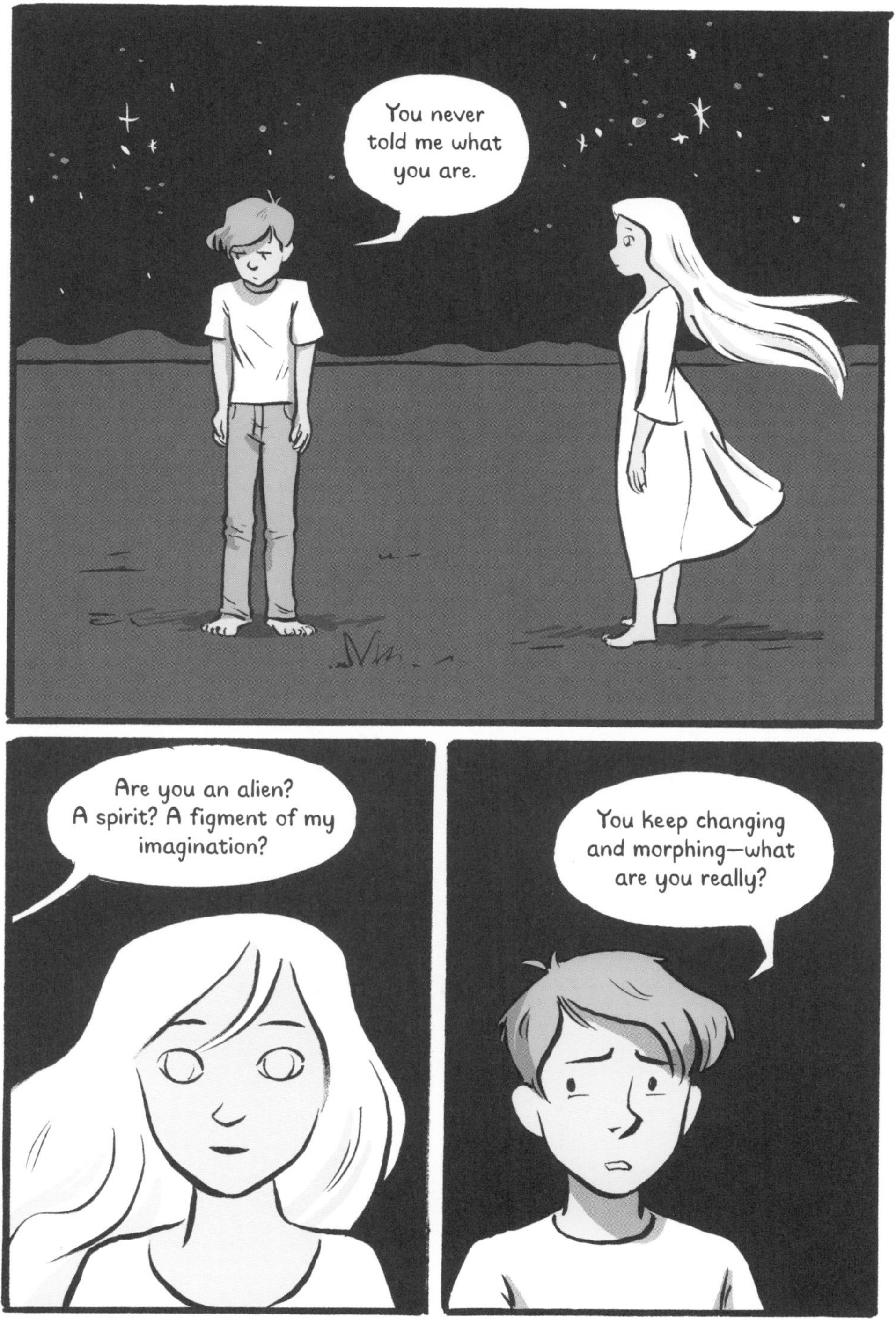
You never told me what you are.
Are you an alien? A spirit? A figment of my imagination?
You keep changing and morphing—what are you really?

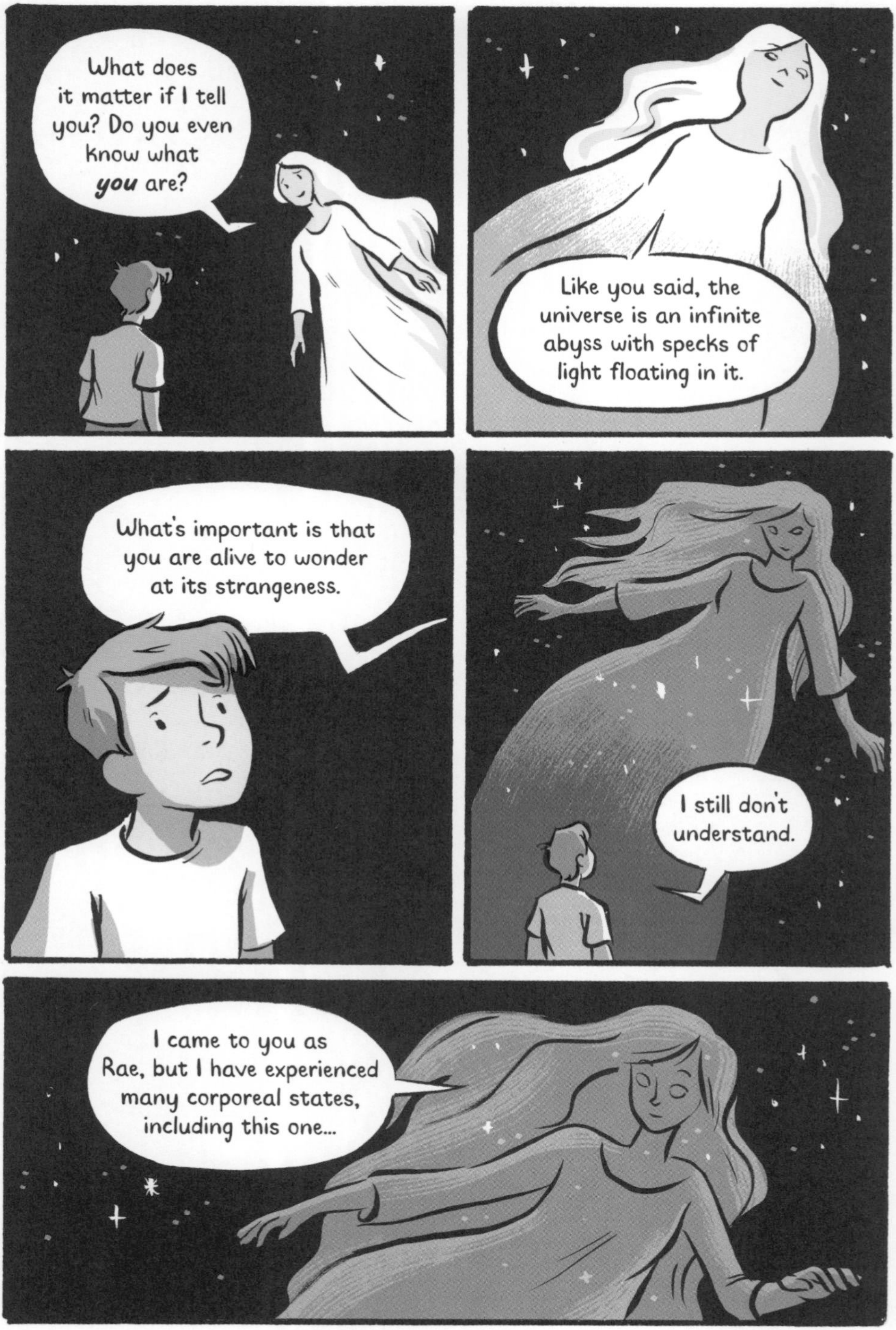
What does it matter if I tell you? Do you even know what *you* are?
Like you said, the universe is an infinite abyss with specks of light floating in it.
What's important is that you are alive to wonder at its strangeness.
I still don't understand.
I came to you as Rae, but I have experienced many corporeal states, including this one...

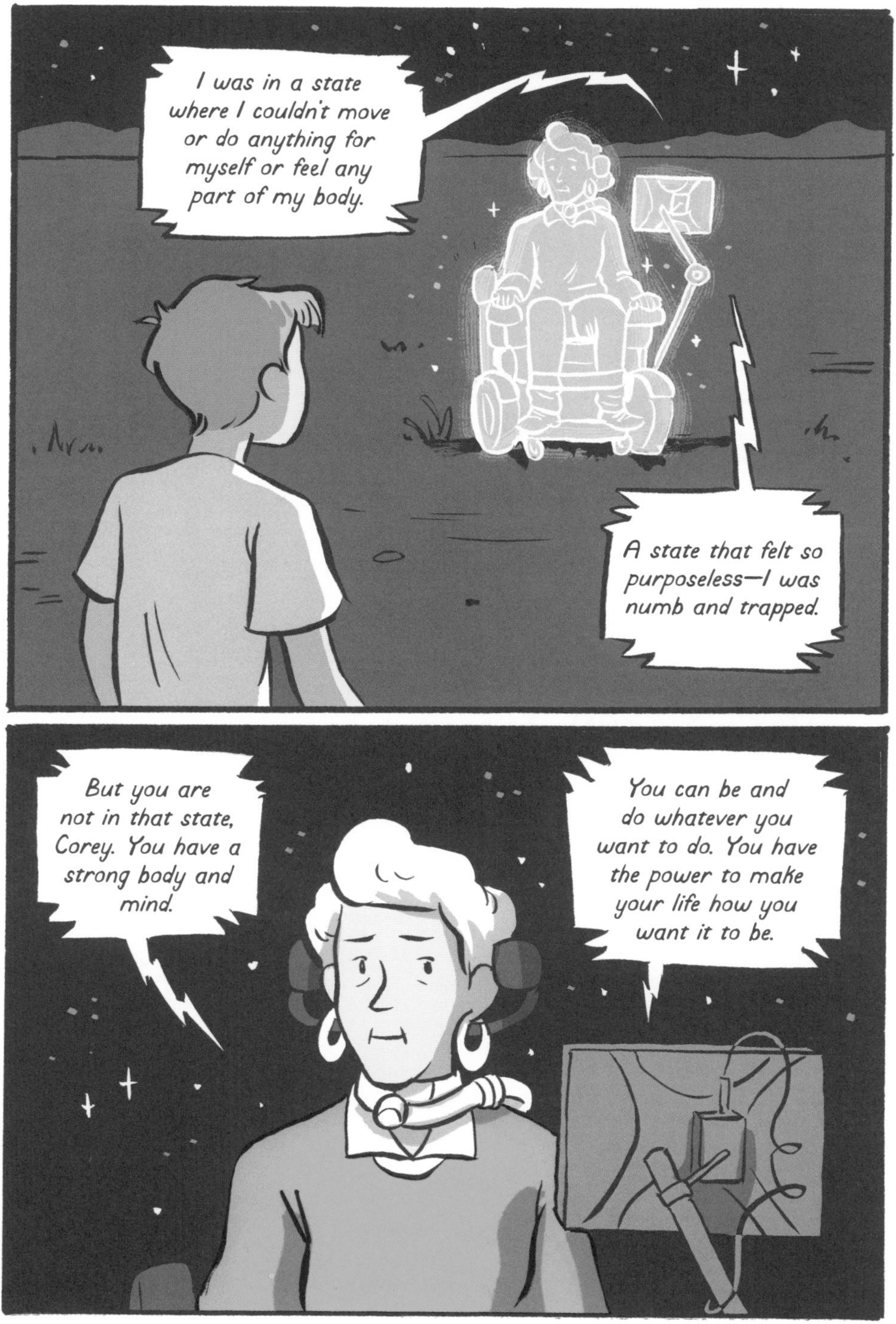
I was in a state where I couldn't move or do anything for myself or feel any part of my body.
A state that felt so purposeless—I was numb and trapped.
But you are not in that state, Corey. You have a strong body and mind.
You can be and do whatever you want to do. You have the power to make your life how you want it to be.

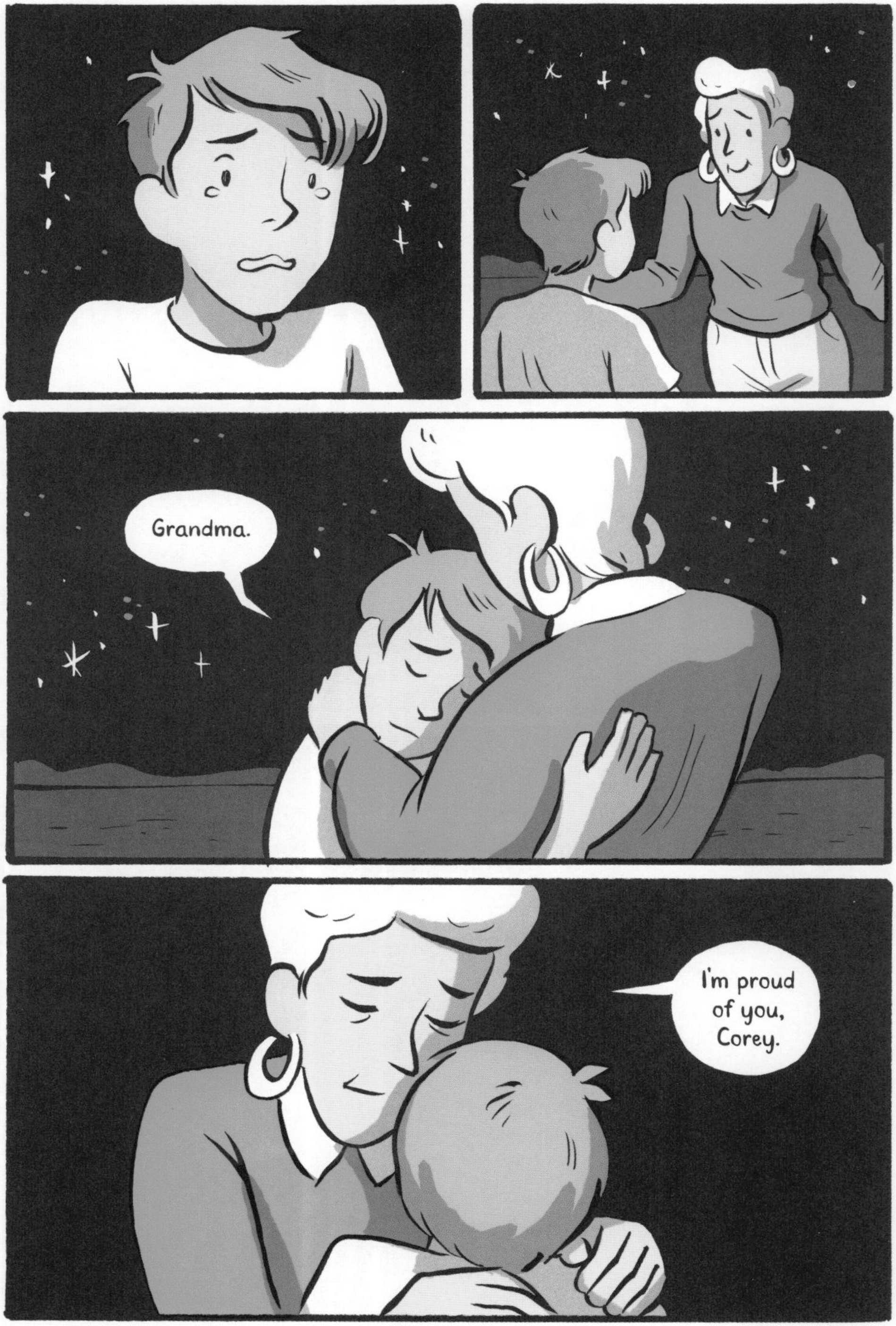
Grandma.
I'm proud of you, Corey.

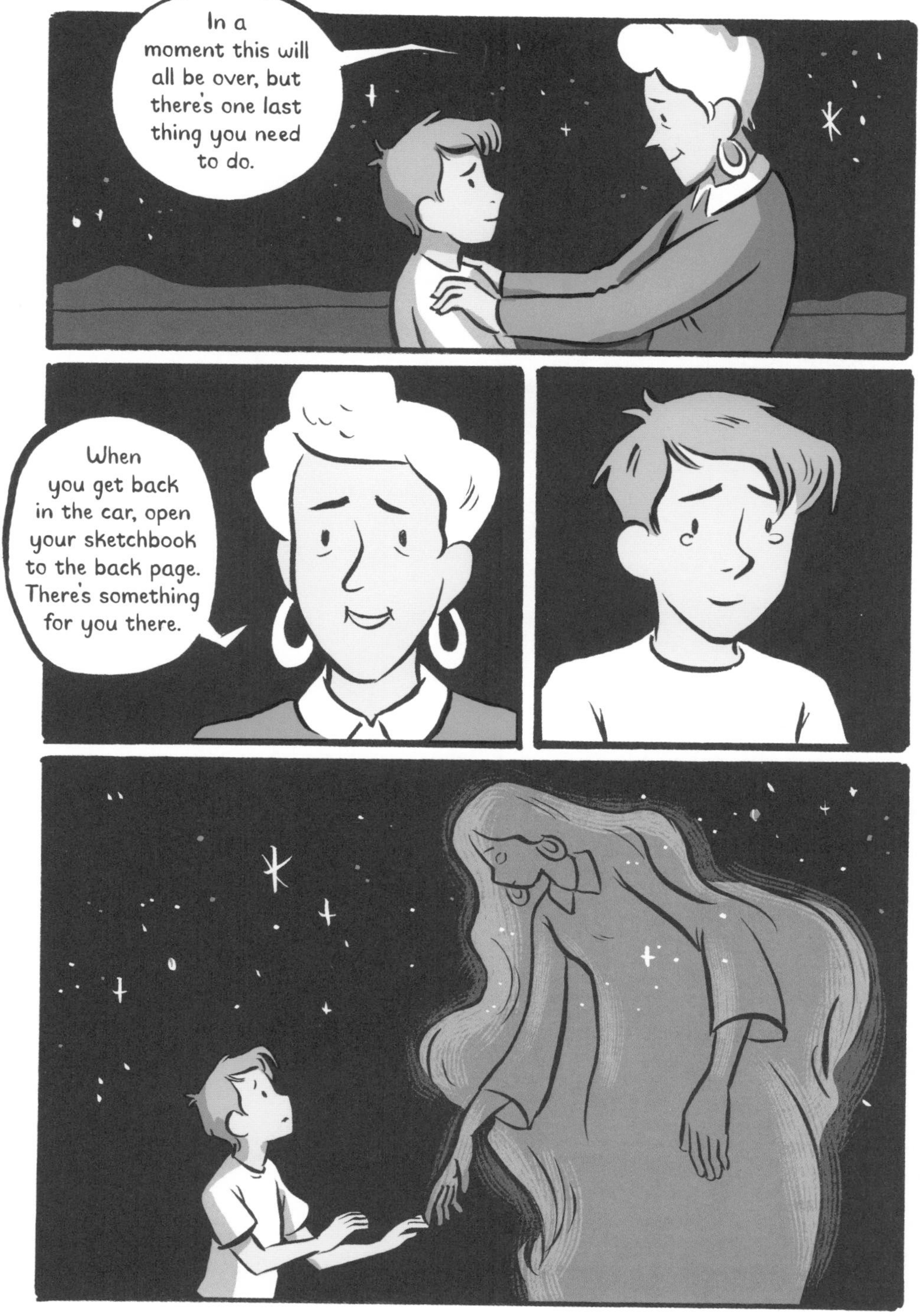
In a moment this will all be over, but there's one last thing you need to do.
When you get back in the car, open your sketchbook to the back page. There's something for you there.

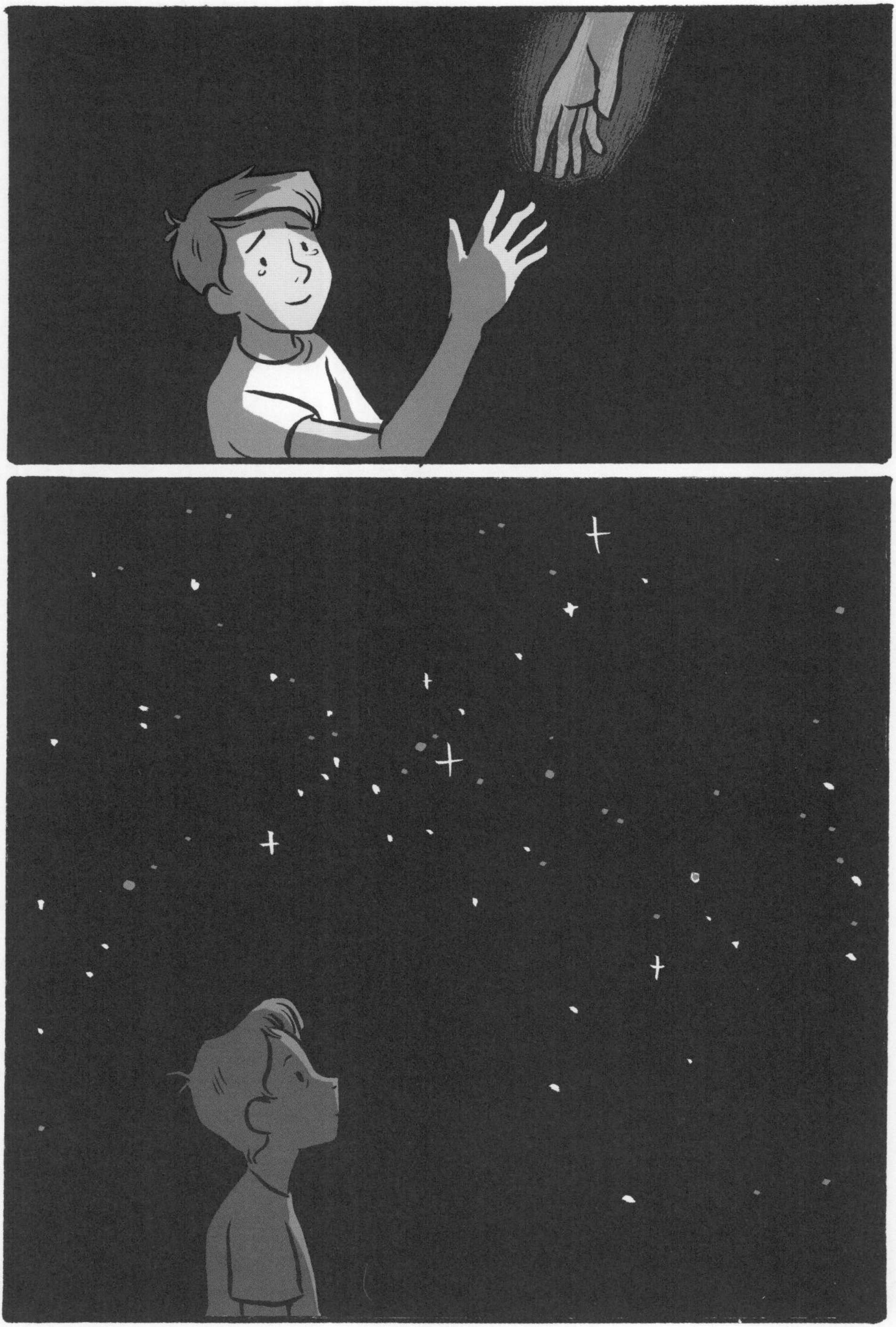

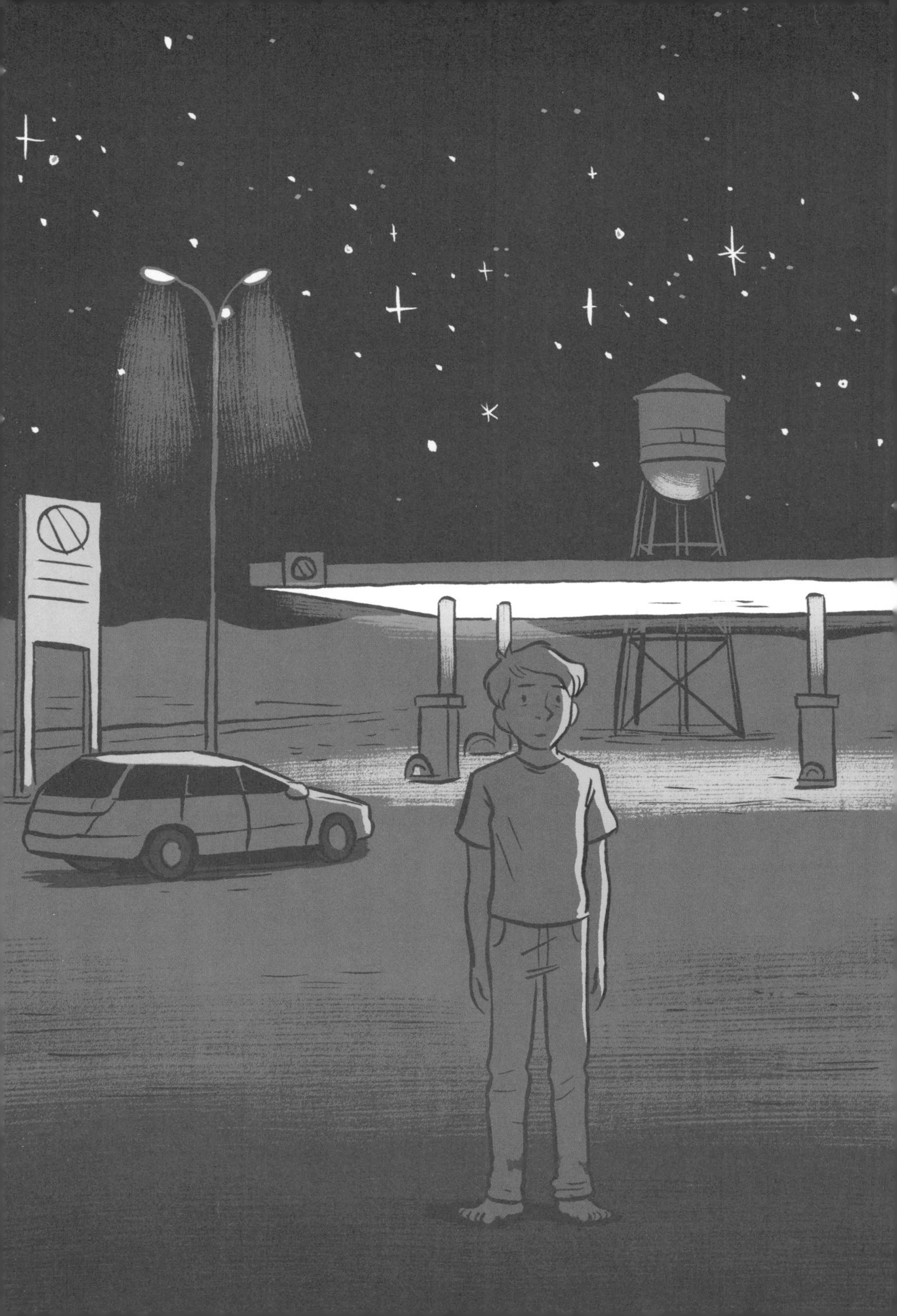

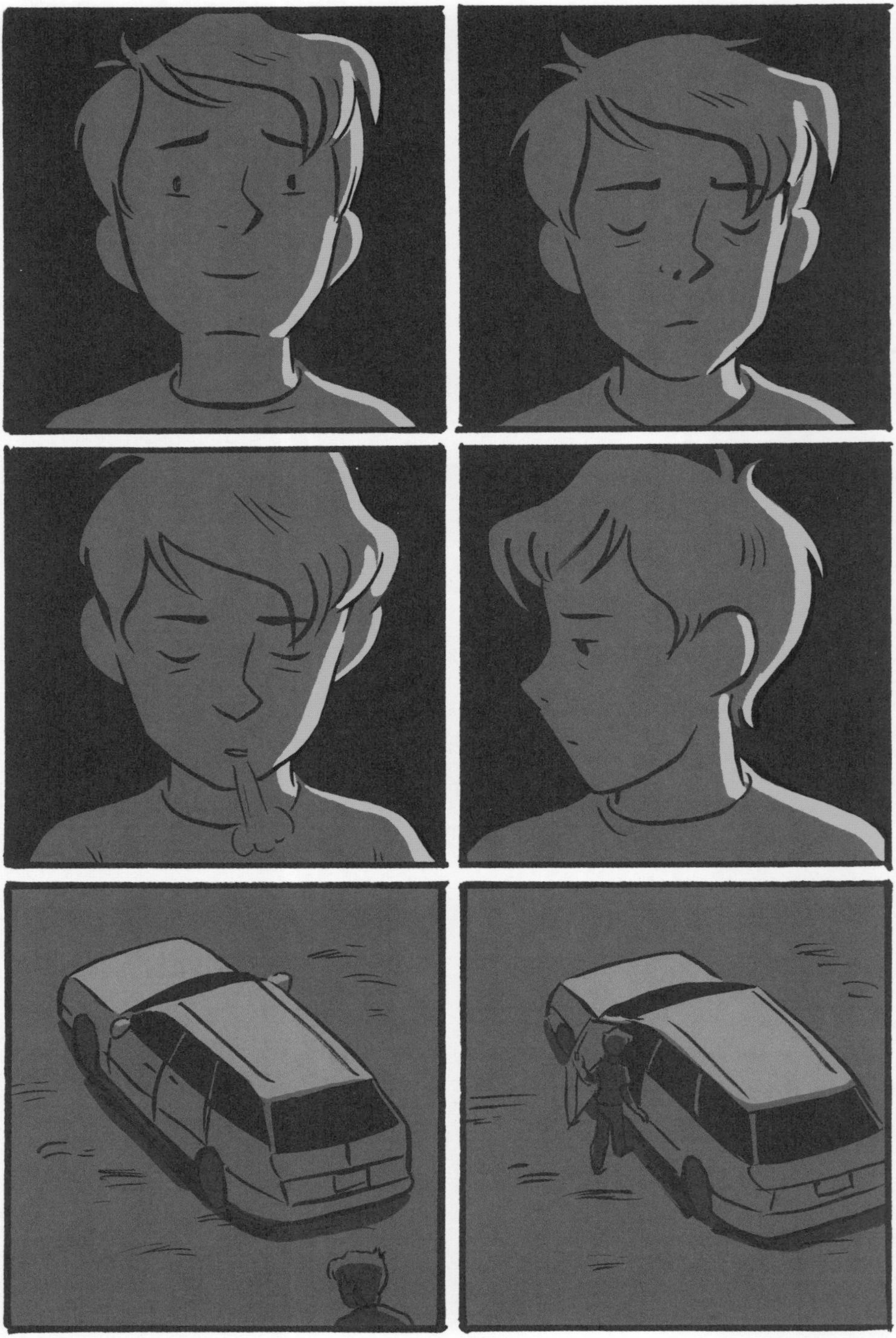

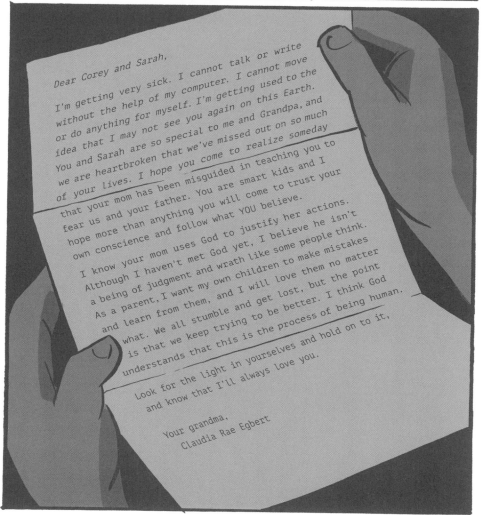

Dear Corey and Sarah,

I'm getting very sick. I cannot talk or write without the help of my computer. I cannot move or do anything for myself. I'm getting used to the idea that I may not see you again on this Earth. You and Sarah are so special to me and Grandpa, and we are heartbroken that we've missed out on so much of your lives. I hope you come to realize someday that your mom has been misguided in teaching you to fear us and your father. You are smart kids and I hope more than anything you will come to trust your own conscience and follow what YOU believe.

I know your mom uses God to justify her actions. Although I haven't met God yet, I believe he isn't a being of judgment and wrath like some people think. As a parent, I want my own children to make mistakes and learn from them, and I will love them no matter what. We all stumble and get lost, but the point is that we keep trying to be better. I think God understands that this is the process of being human.

Look for the light in yourselves and hold on to it, and know that I'll always love you.

Your grandma,
Claudia Rae Egbert

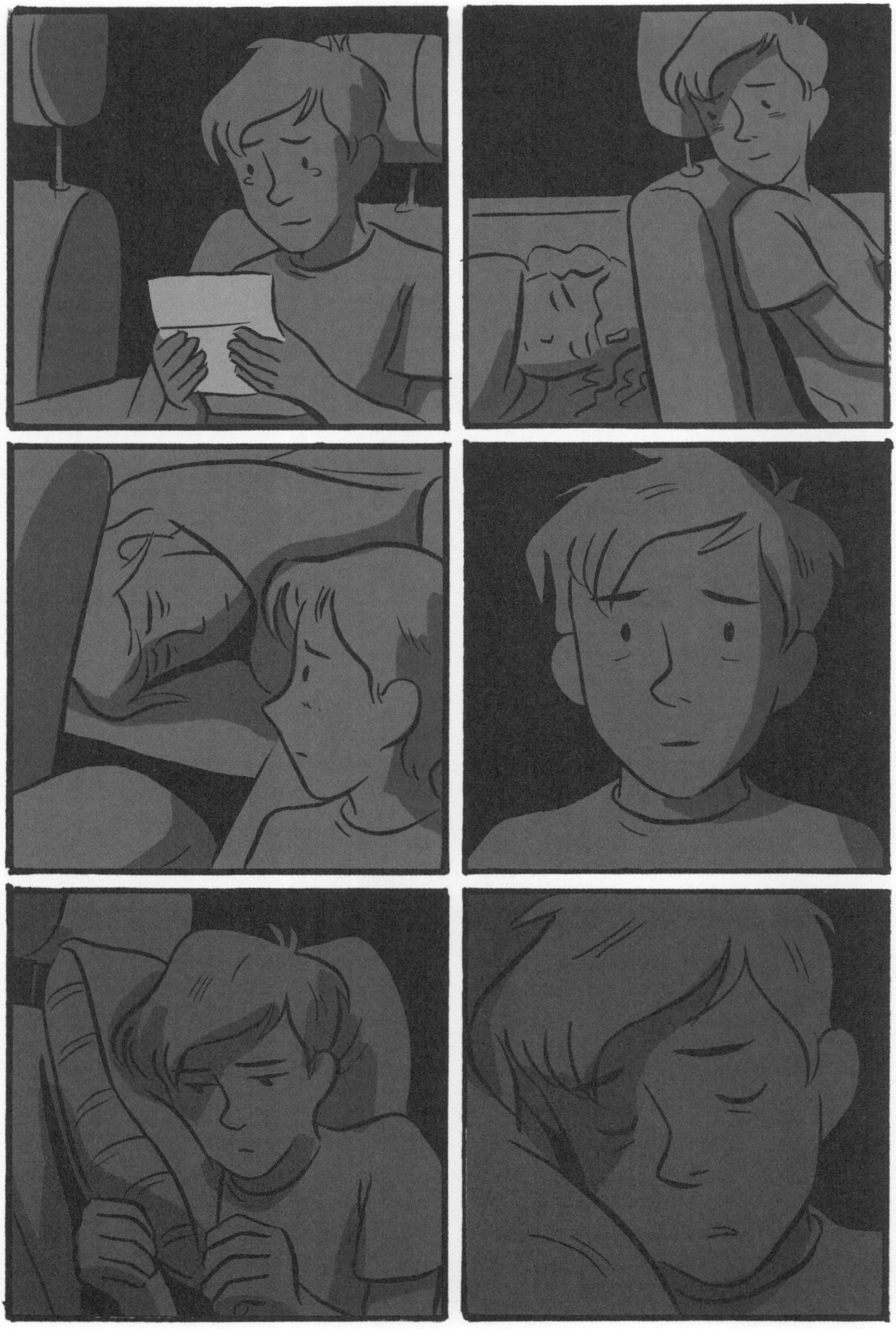

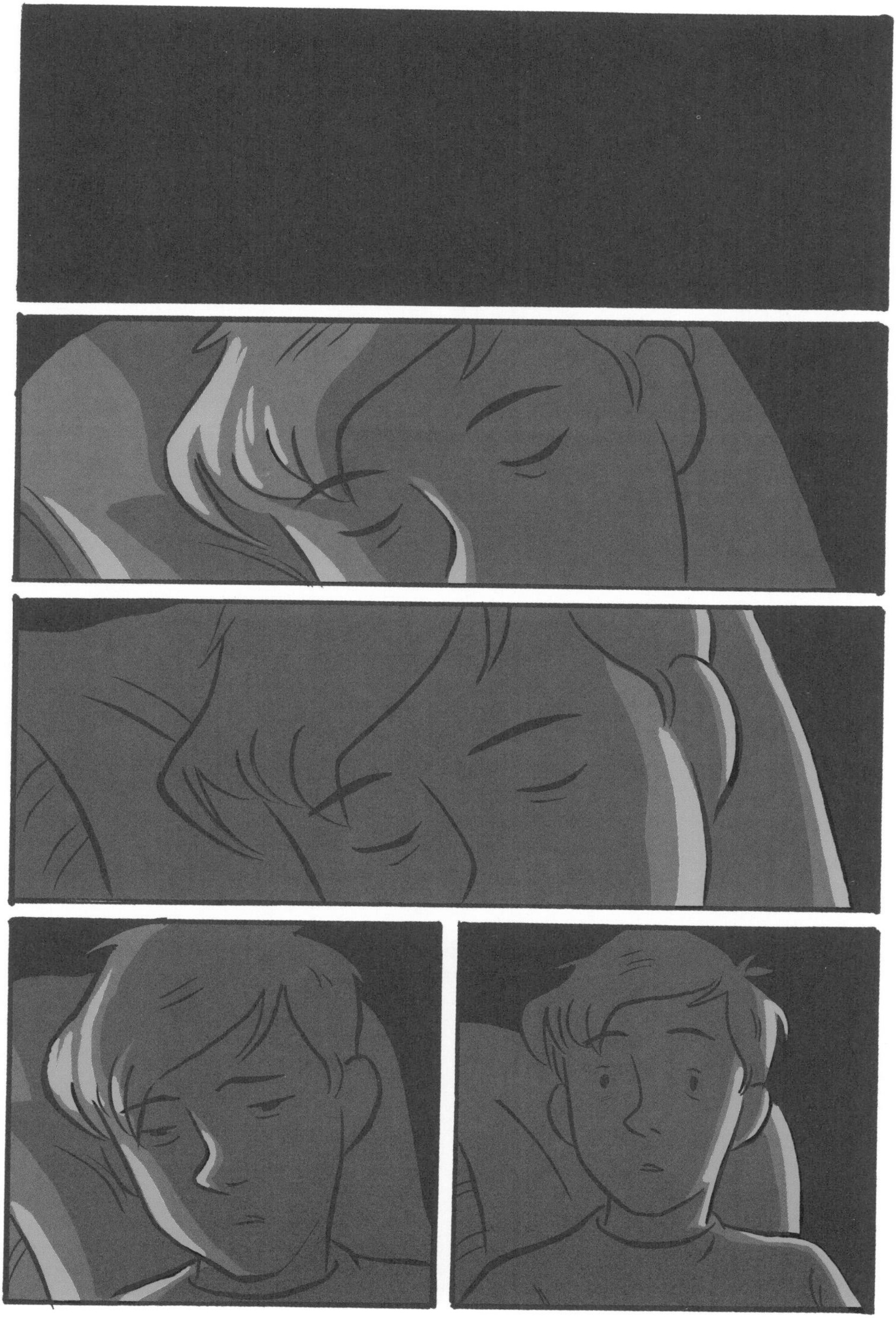

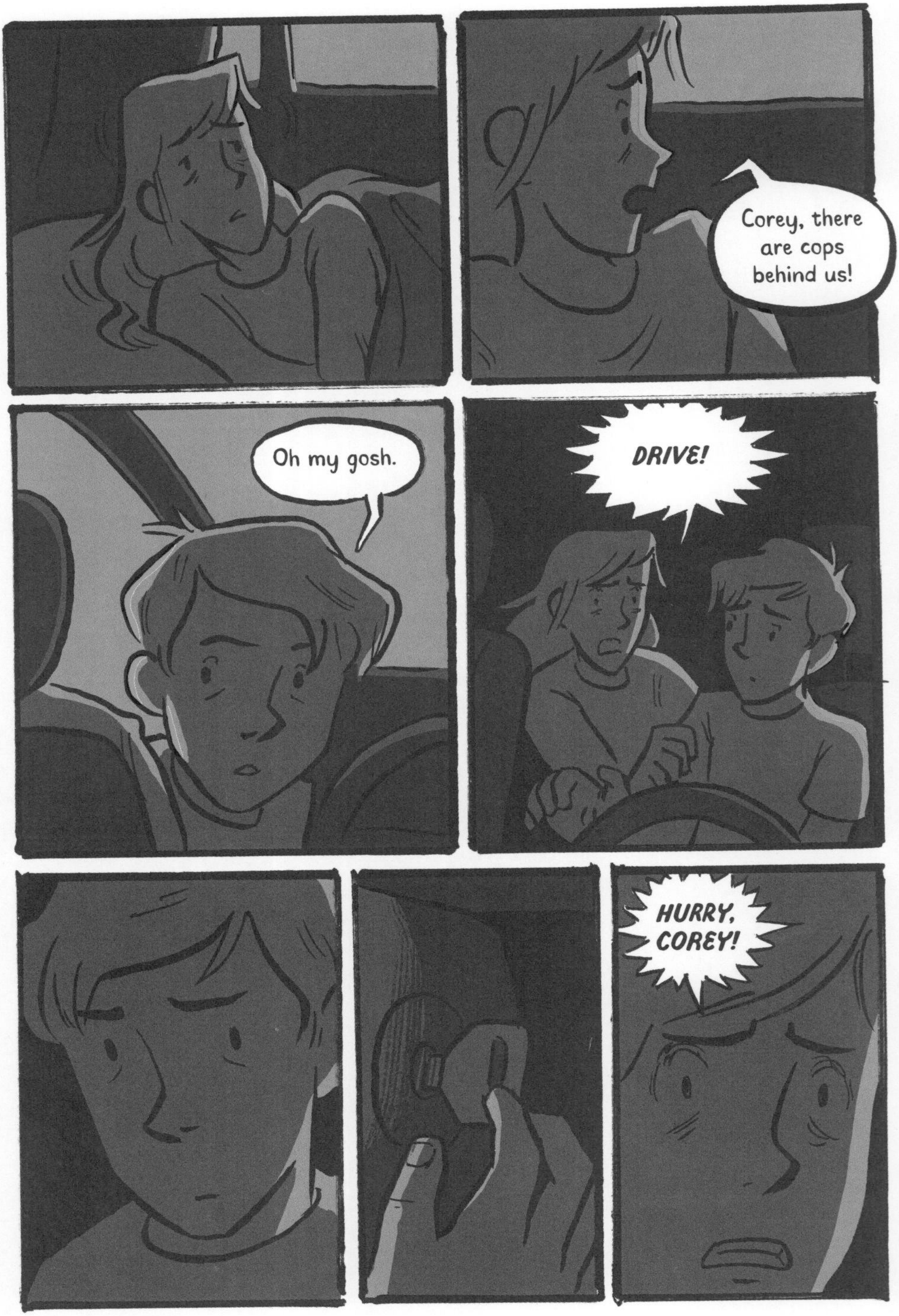
Corey, there are cops behind us!
Oh my gosh.
DRIVE!
HURRY, COREY!

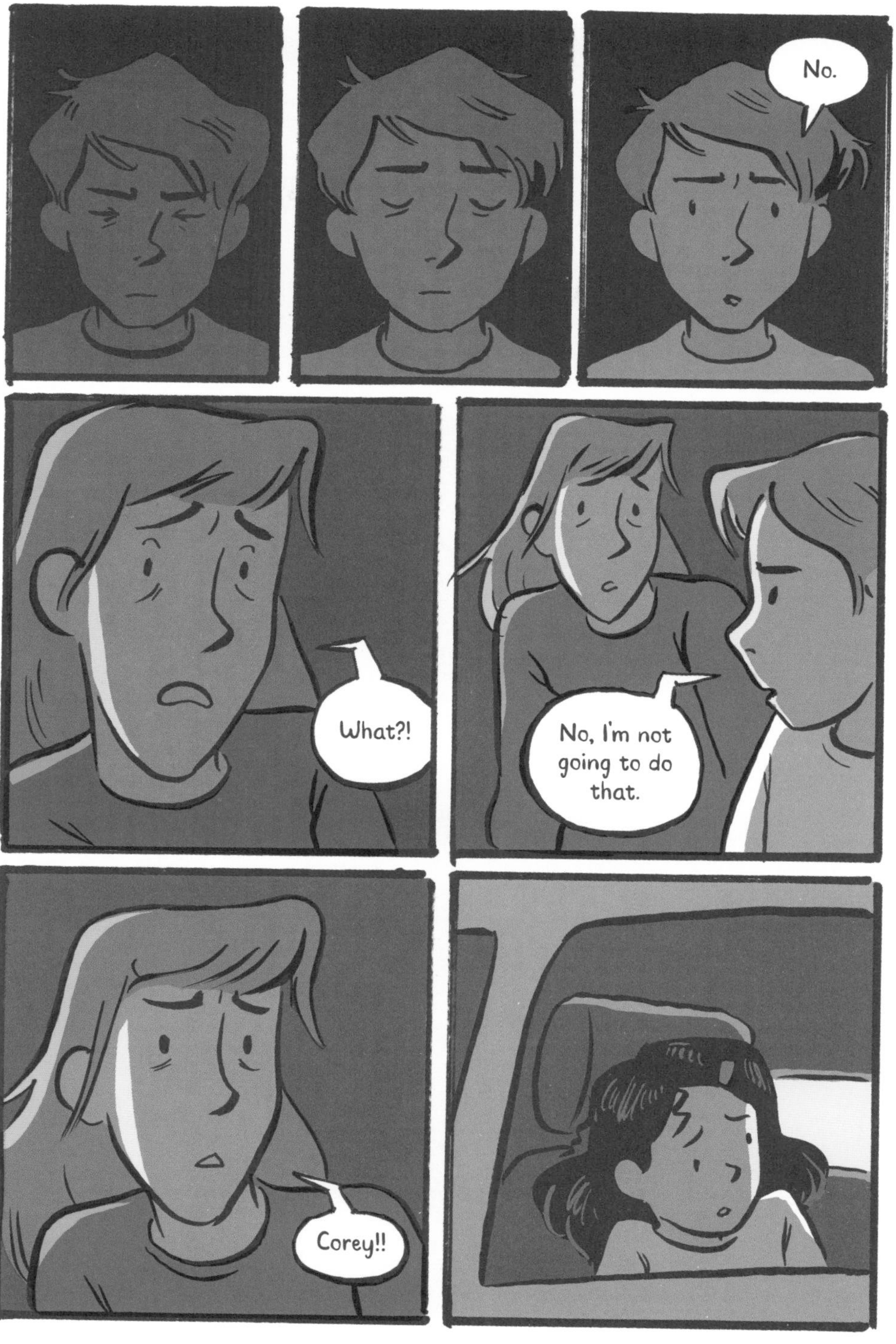
No.
What?!
No, I'm not going to do that.
Corey!!

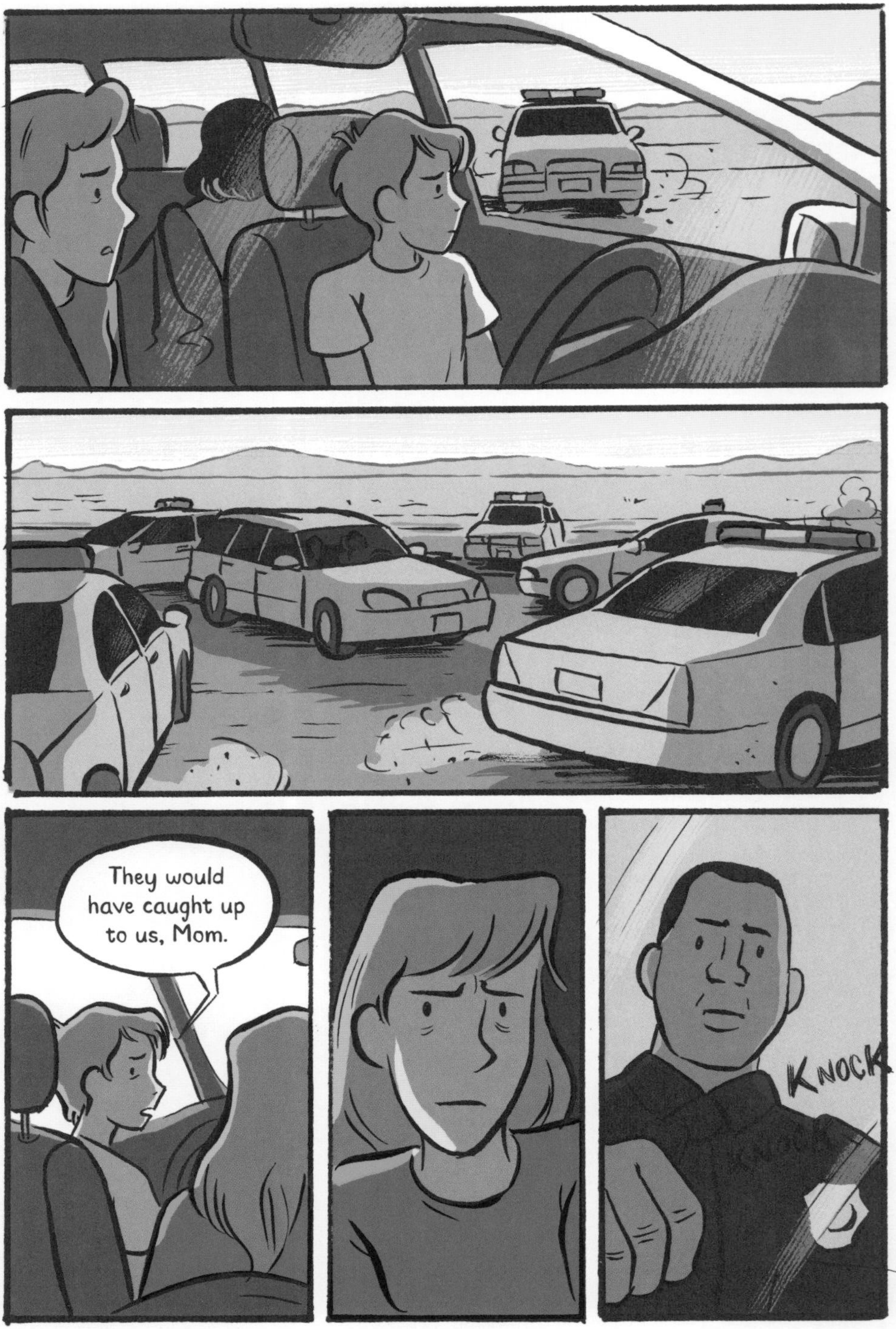
They would have caught up to us, Mom.
KNOCK

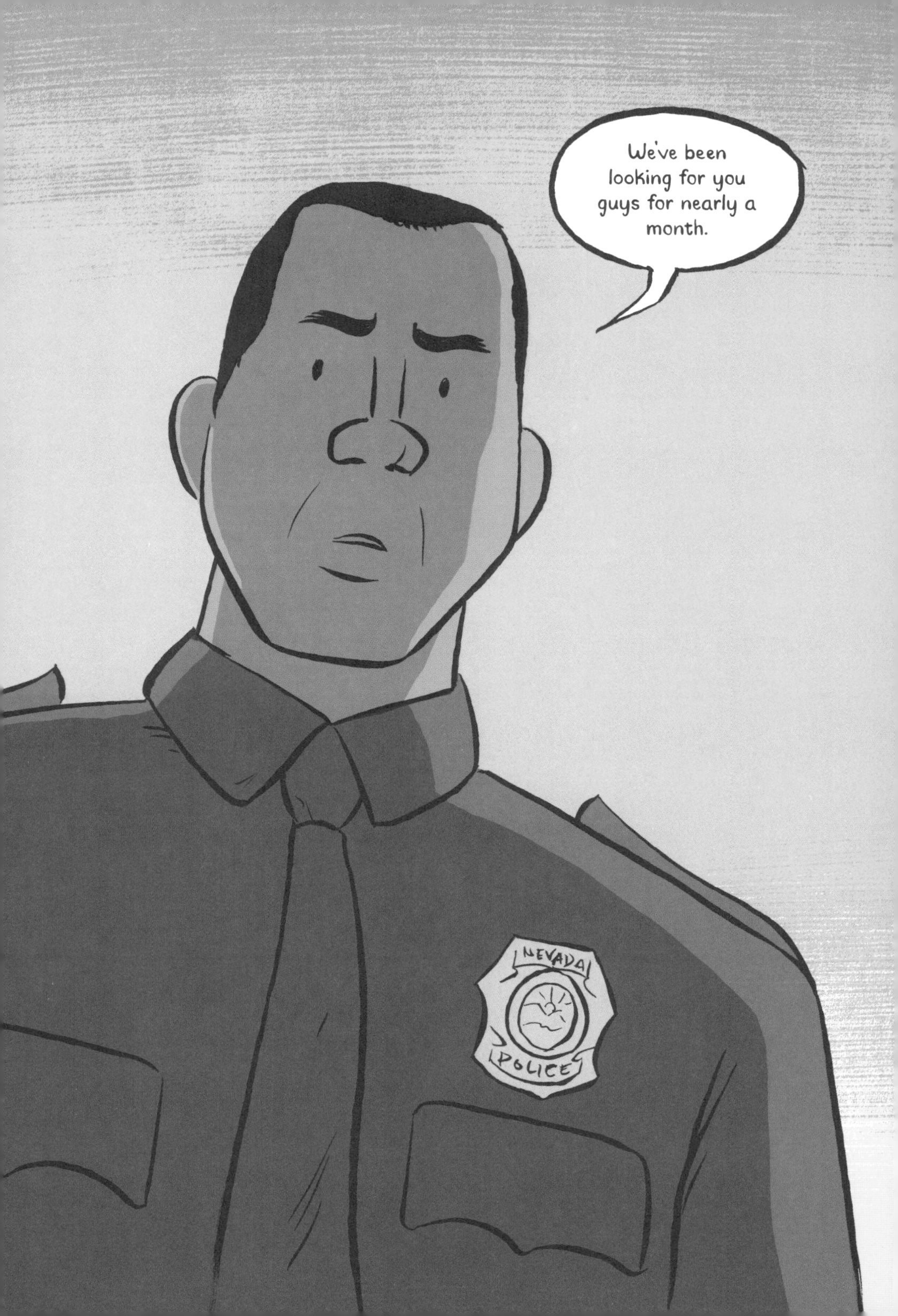
We've been looking for you guys for nearly a month.
NEVADA
POLICE

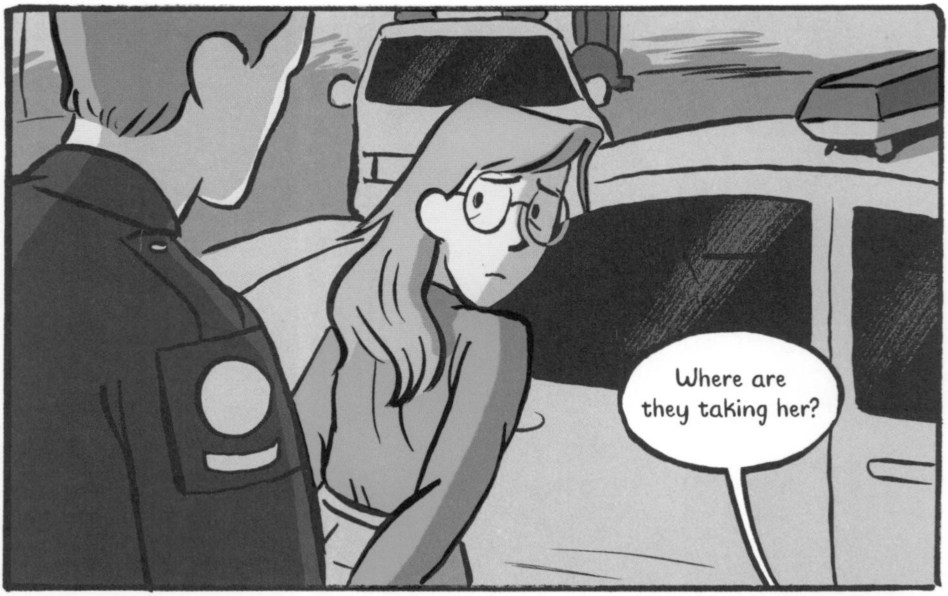
Where are they taking her?

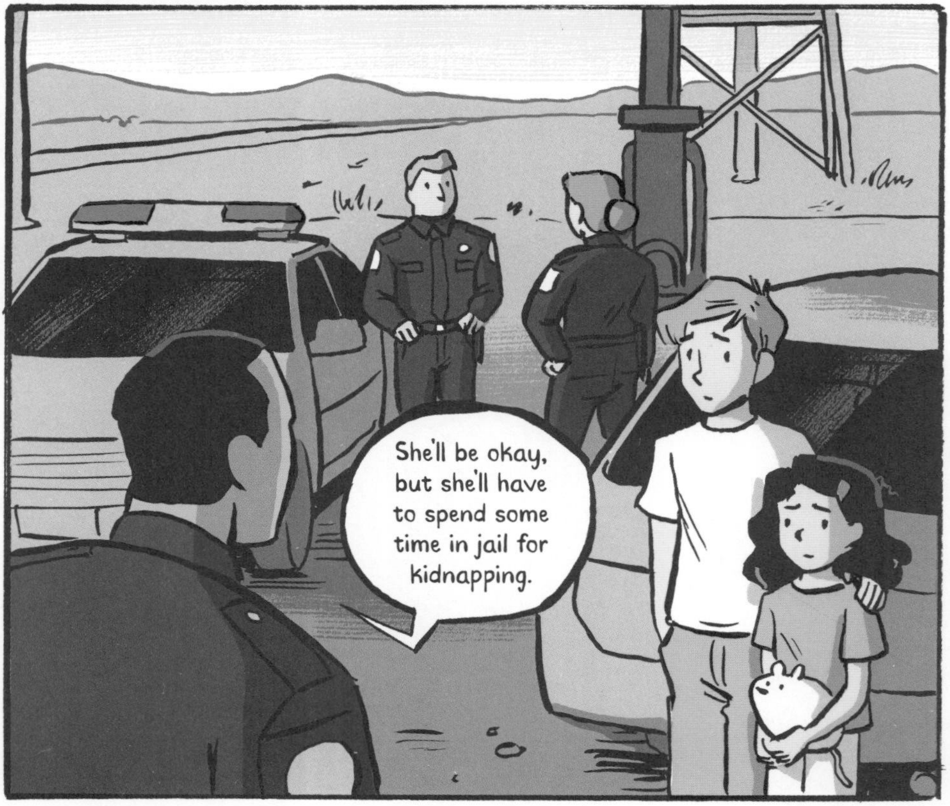
She'll be okay, but she'll have to spend some time in jail for kidnapping.

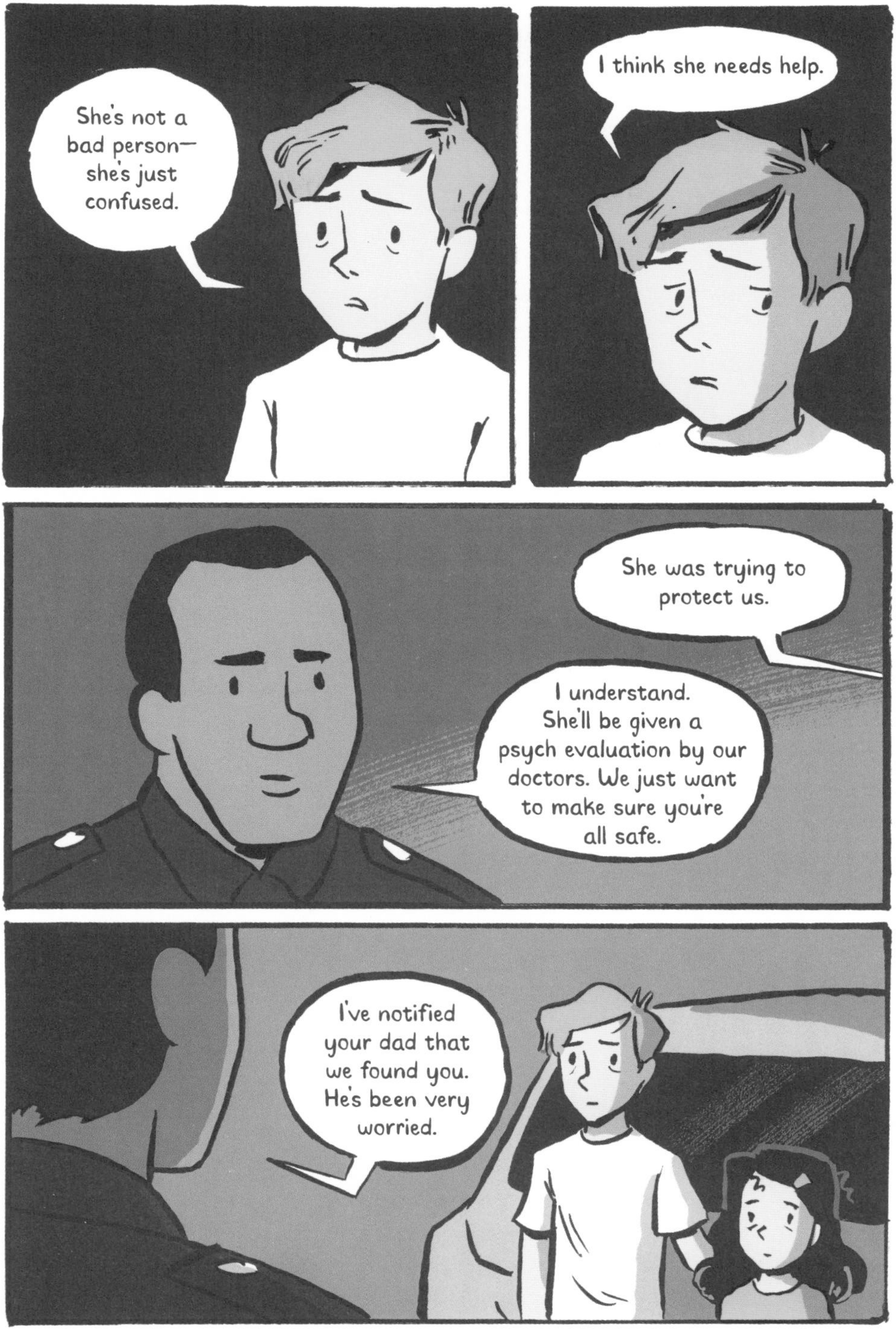
She's not a bad person— she's just confused.
I think she needs help.
She was trying to protect us.
I understand. She'll be given a psych evaluation by our doctors. We just want to make sure you're all safe.
I've notified your dad that we found you. He's been very worried.

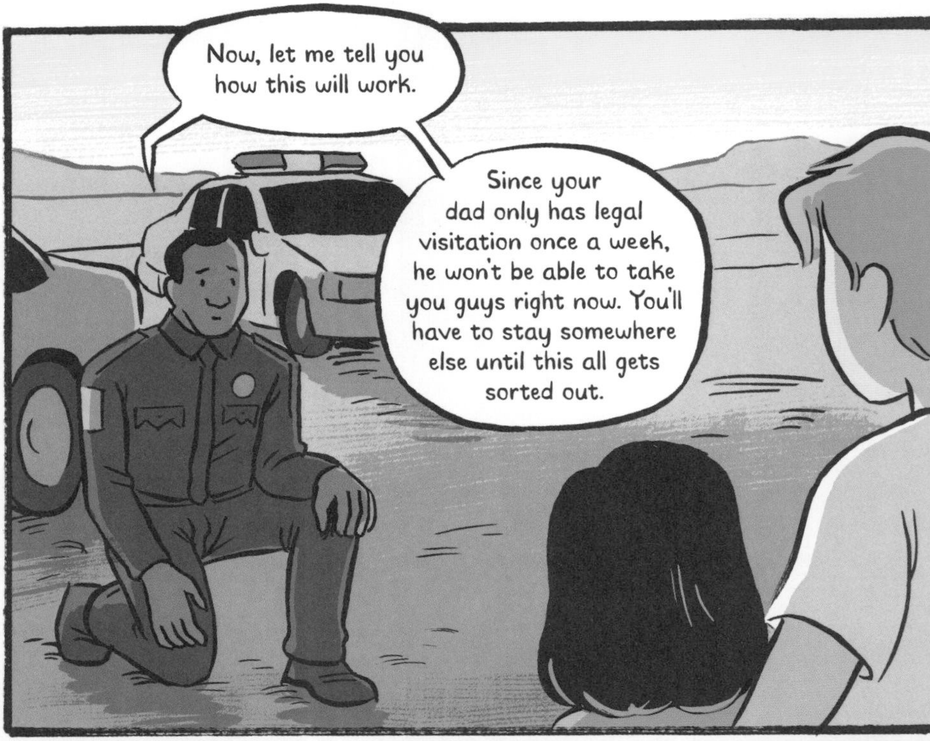
Now, let me tell you how this will work.
Since your dad only has legal visitation once a week, he won't be able to take you guys right now. You'll have to stay somewhere else until this all gets sorted out.

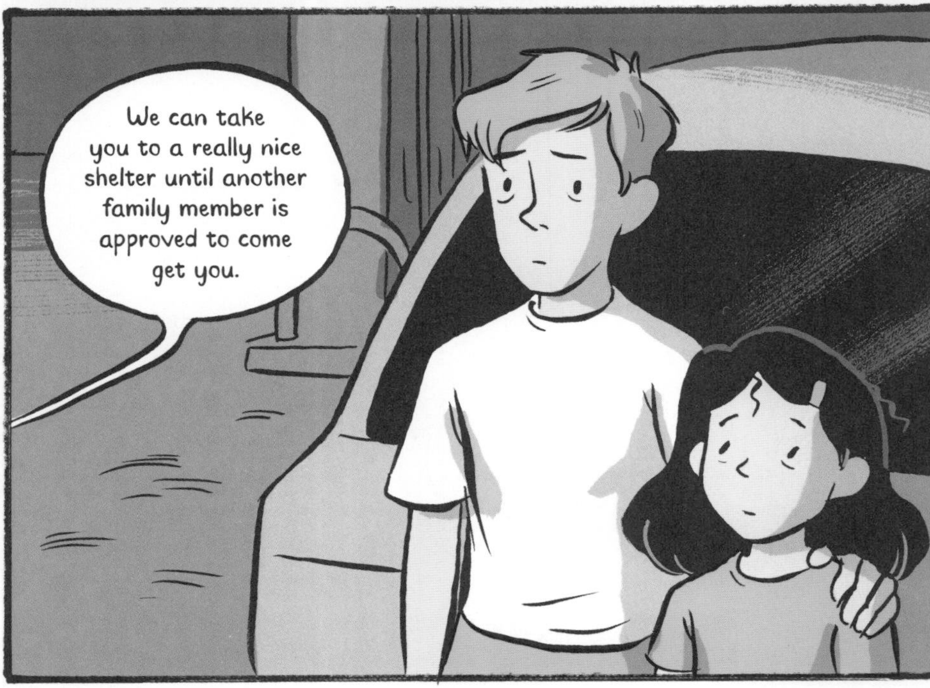
We can take you to a really nice shelter until another family member is approved to come get you.

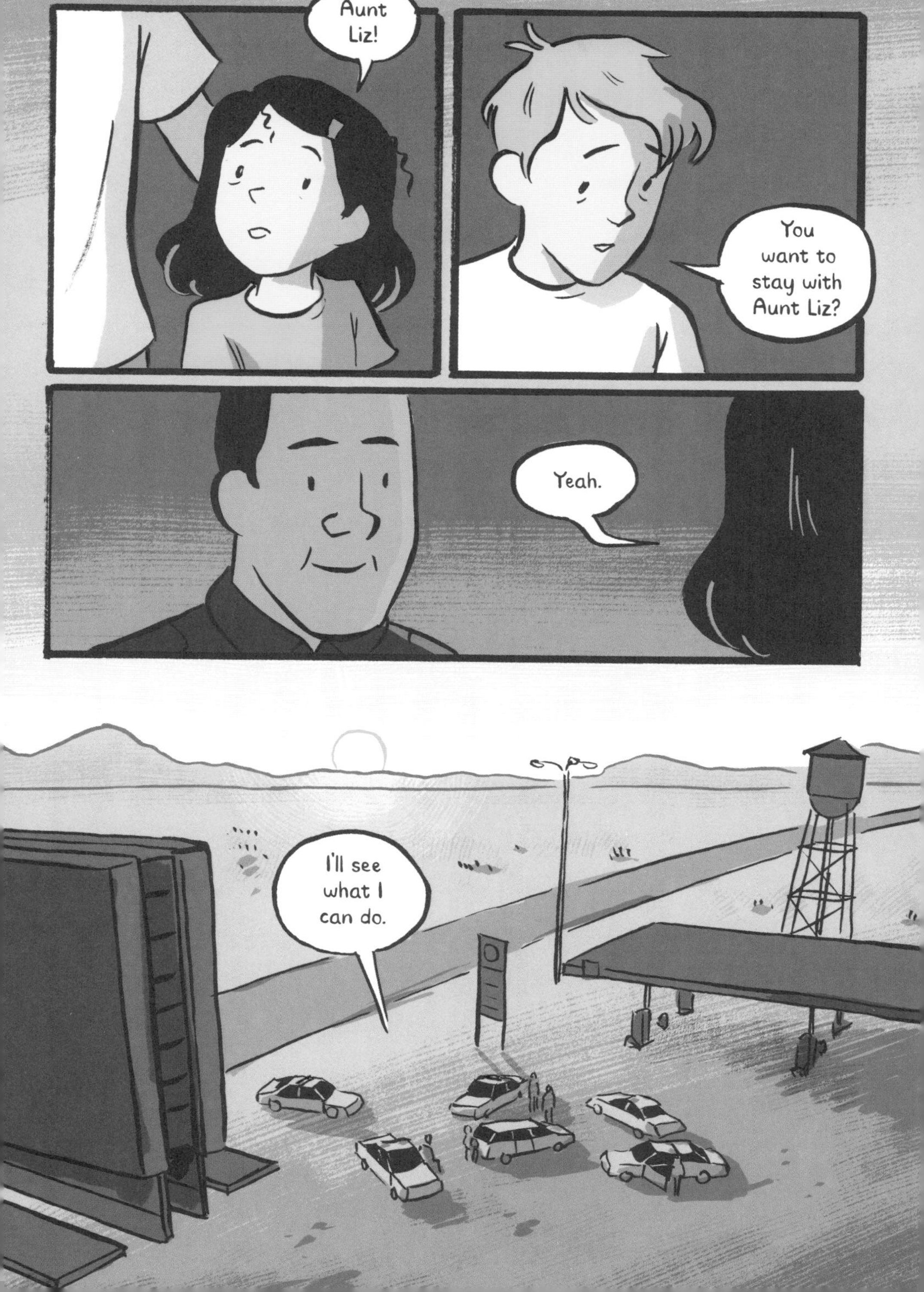
Aunt Liz!
You want to stay with Aunt Liz?
Yeah.
I'll see what I can do.

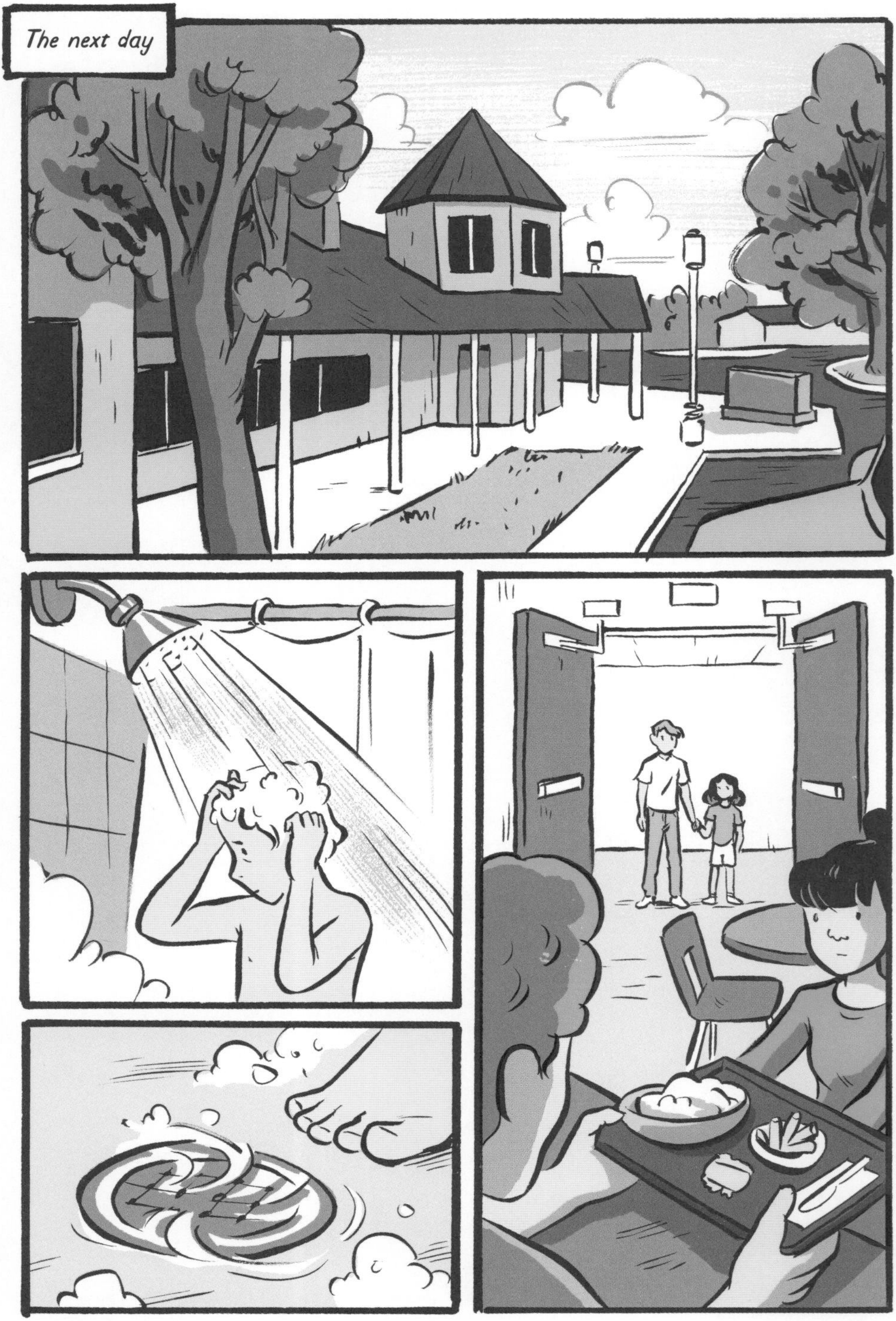
The next day

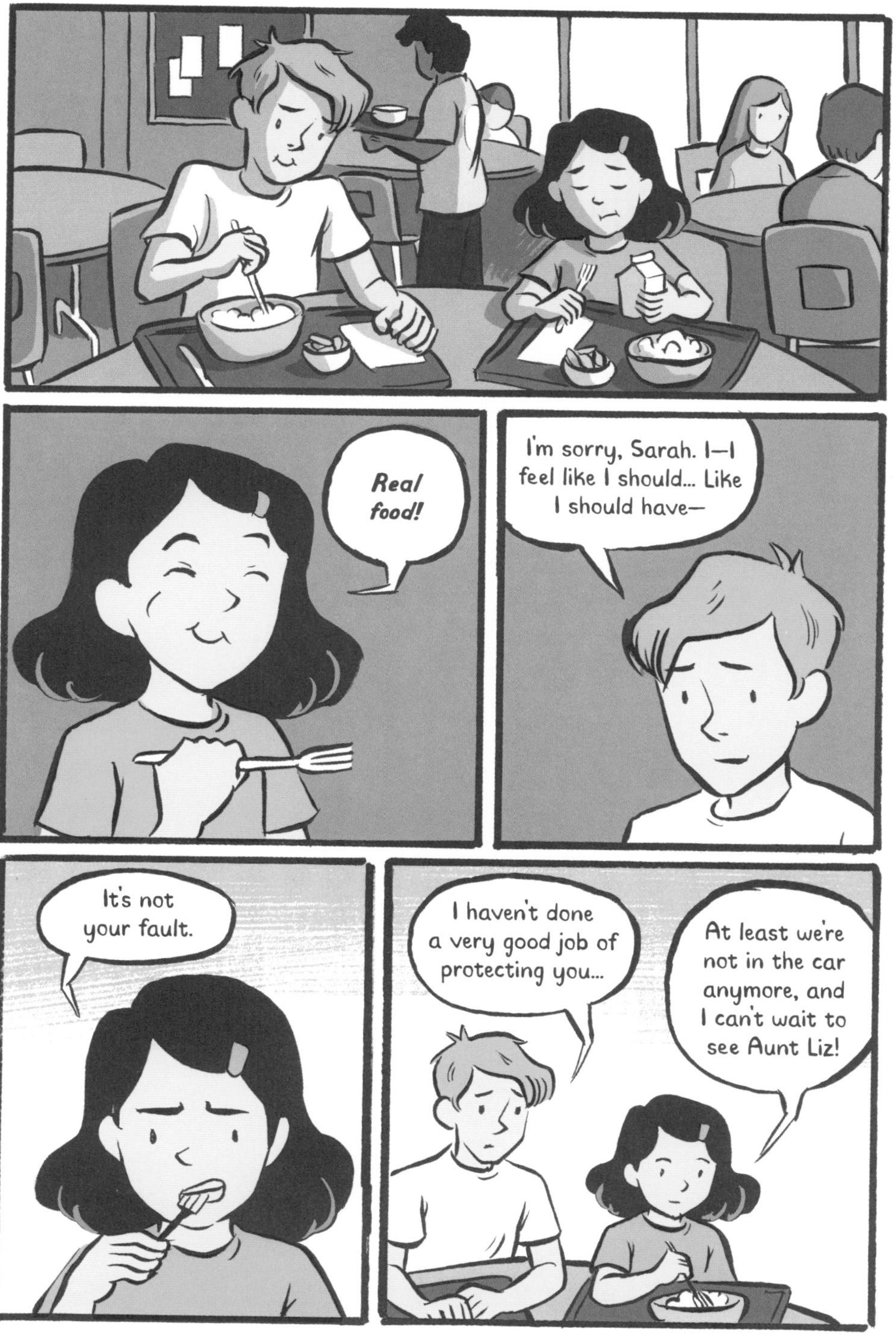
Real food!
I'm sorry, Sarah. I—I feel like I should... Like I should have—
It's not your fault.
I haven't done a very good job of protecting you...
At least we're not in the car anymore, and I can't wait to see Aunt Liz!

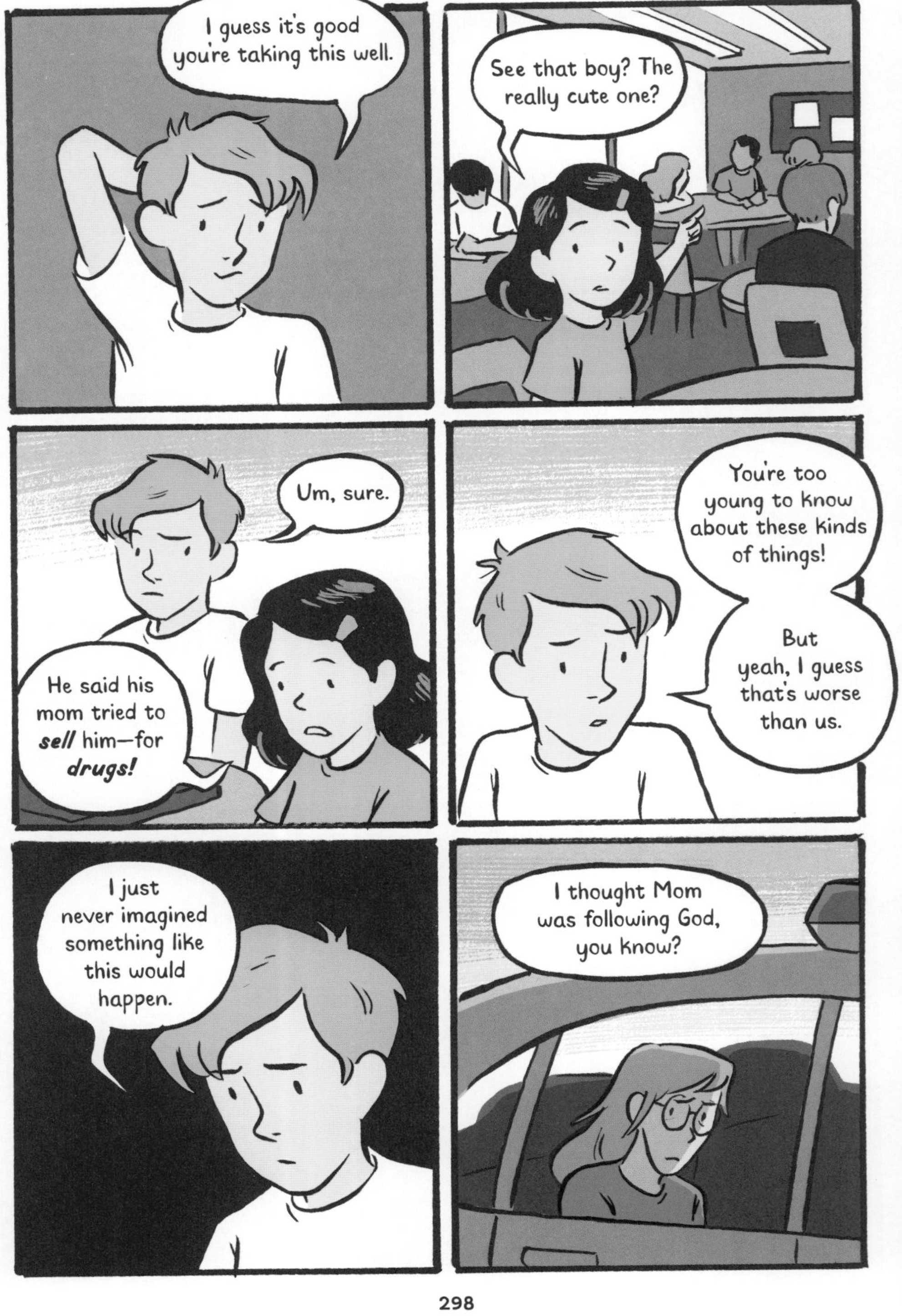
I guess it's good you're taking this well.
See that boy? The really cute one?
Um, sure.
He said his mom tried to ***sell*** him—for ***drugs!***
You're too young to know about these kinds of things!
But yeah, I guess that's worse than us.
I just never imagined something like this would happen.
I thought Mom was following God, you know?

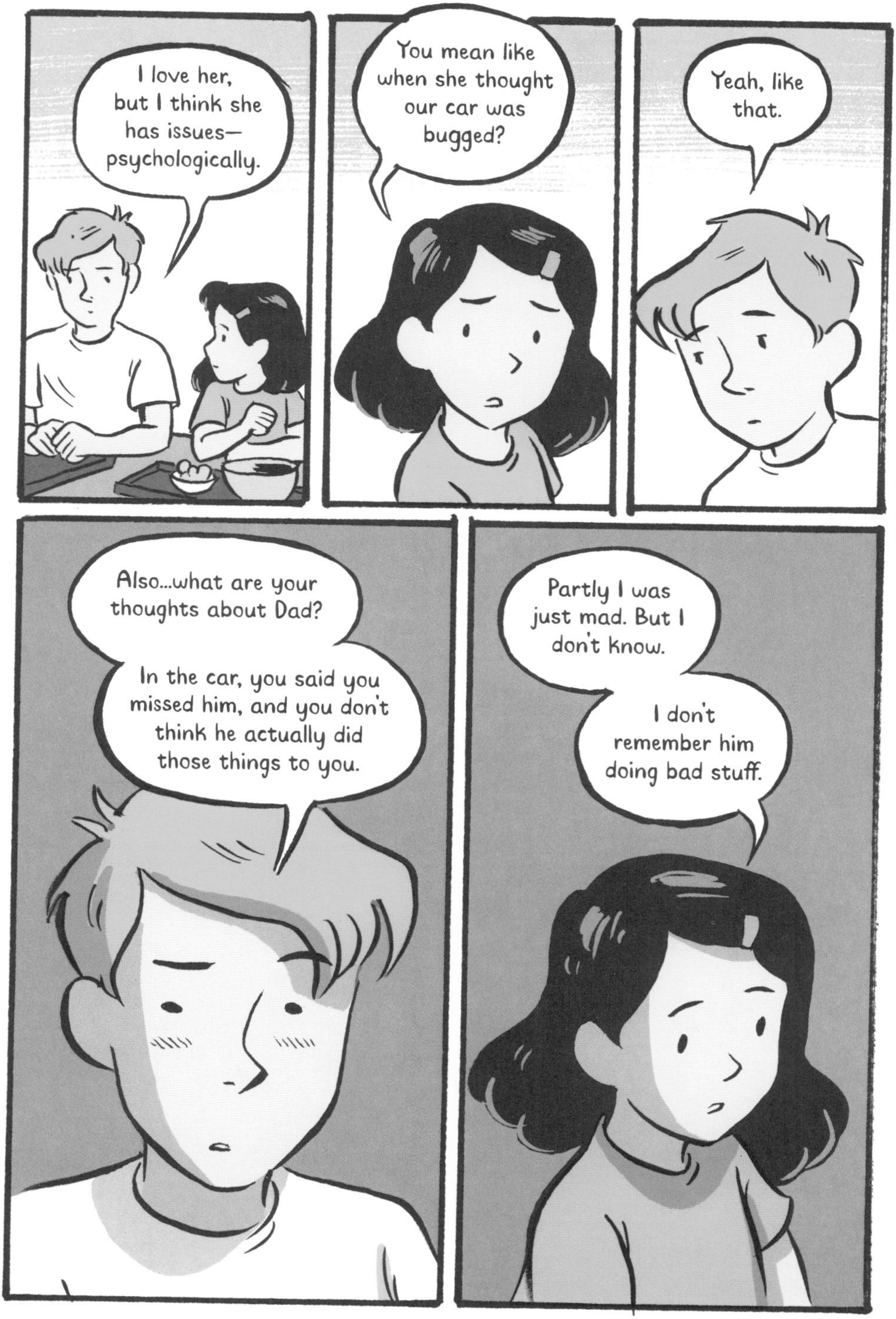
I love her, but I think she has issues—psychologically.
You mean like when she thought our car was bugged?
Yeah, like that.
Also...what are your thoughts about Dad?
In the car, you said you missed him, and you don't think he actually did those things to you.
Partly I was just mad. But I don't know.
I don't remember him doing bad stuff.

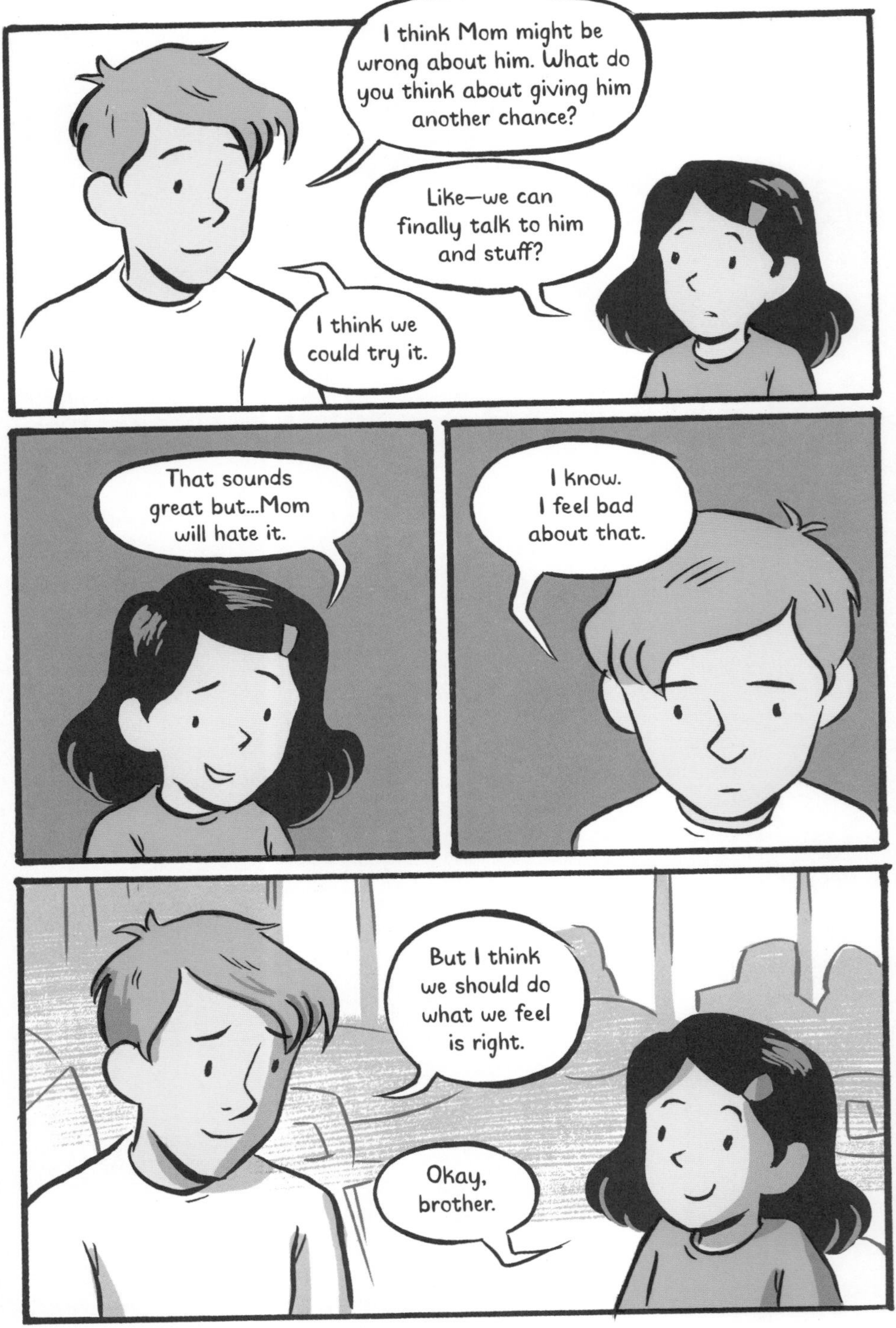
I think Mom might be wrong about him. What do you think about giving him another chance?
Like—we can finally talk to him and stuff?
I think we could try it.
That sounds great but...Mom will hate it.
I know. I feel bad about that.
But I think we should do what we feel is right.
Okay, brother.

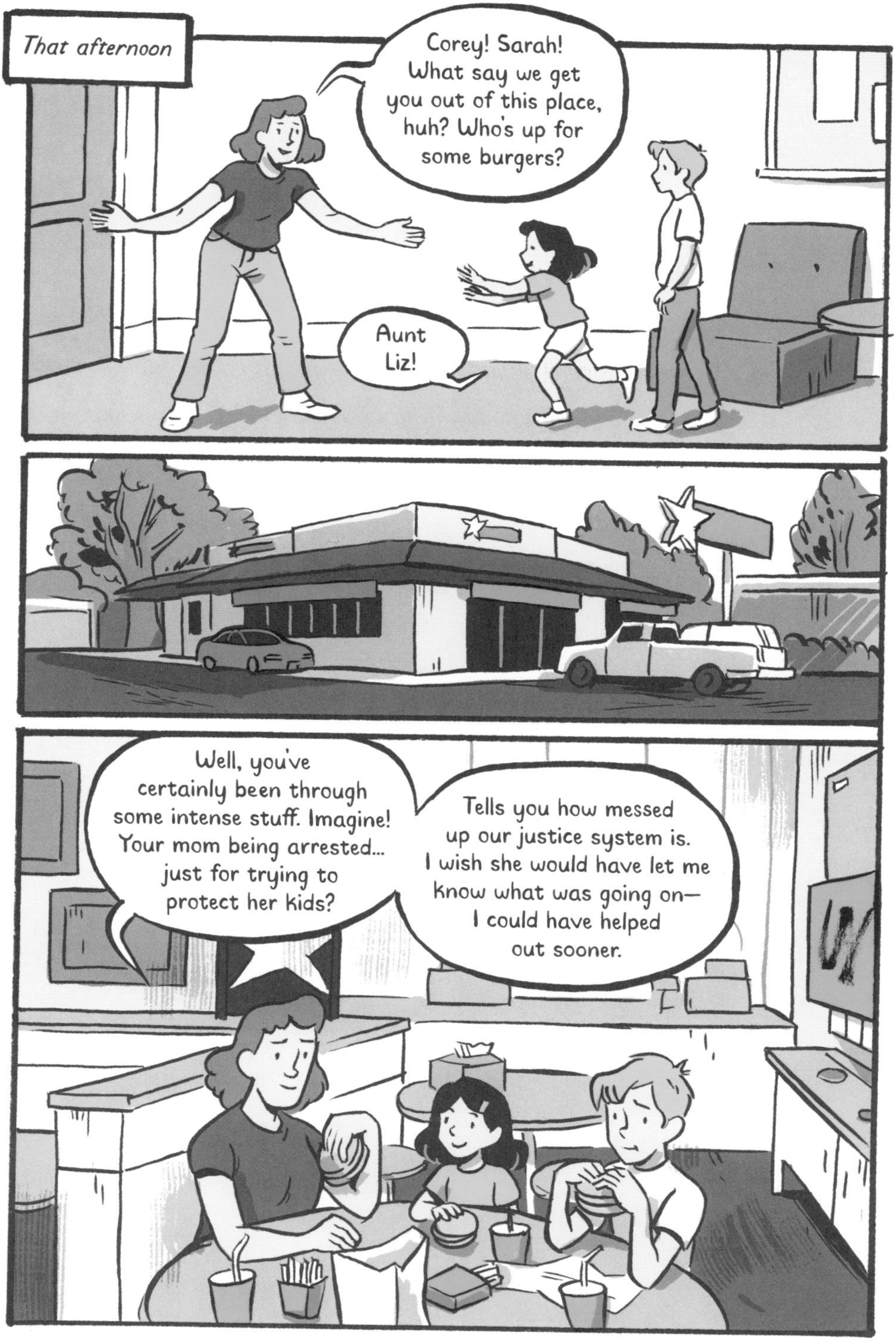
That afternoon
Corey! Sarah! What say we get you out of this place, huh? Who's up for some burgers?
Aunt Liz!
Well, you've certainly been through some intense stuff. Imagine! Your mom being arrested... just for trying to protect her kids?
Tells you how messed up our justice system is. I wish she would have let me know what was going on— I could have helped out sooner.

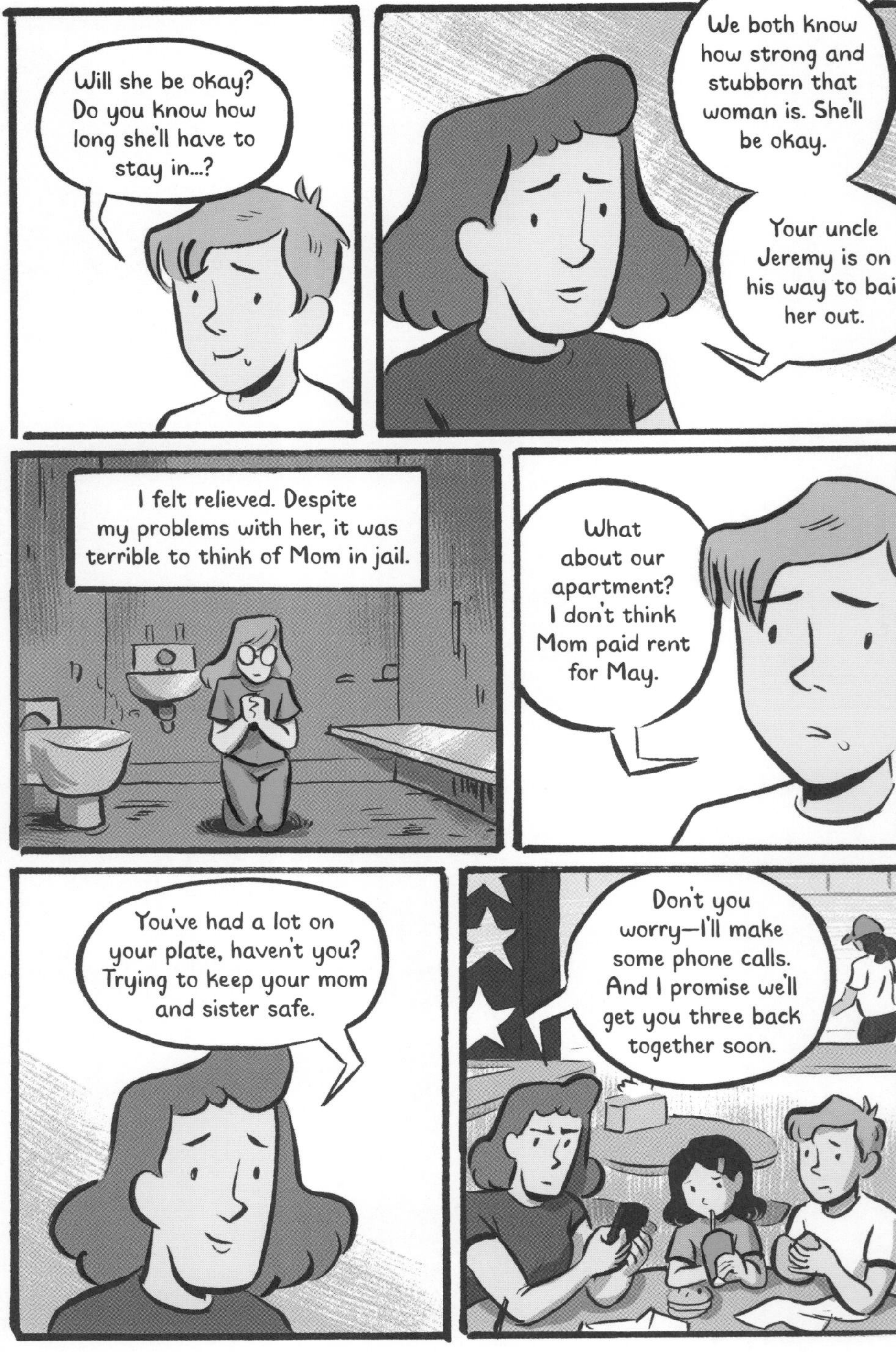
Will she be okay? Do you know how long she'll have to stay in...?
We both know how strong and stubborn that woman is. She'll be okay.
Your uncle Jeremy is on his way to bail her out.
I felt relieved. Despite my problems with her, it was terrible to think of Mom in jail.
What about our apartment? I don't think Mom paid rent for May.
You've had a lot on your plate, haven't you? Trying to keep your mom and sister safe.
Don't you worry—I'll make some phone calls. And I promise we'll get you three back together soon.

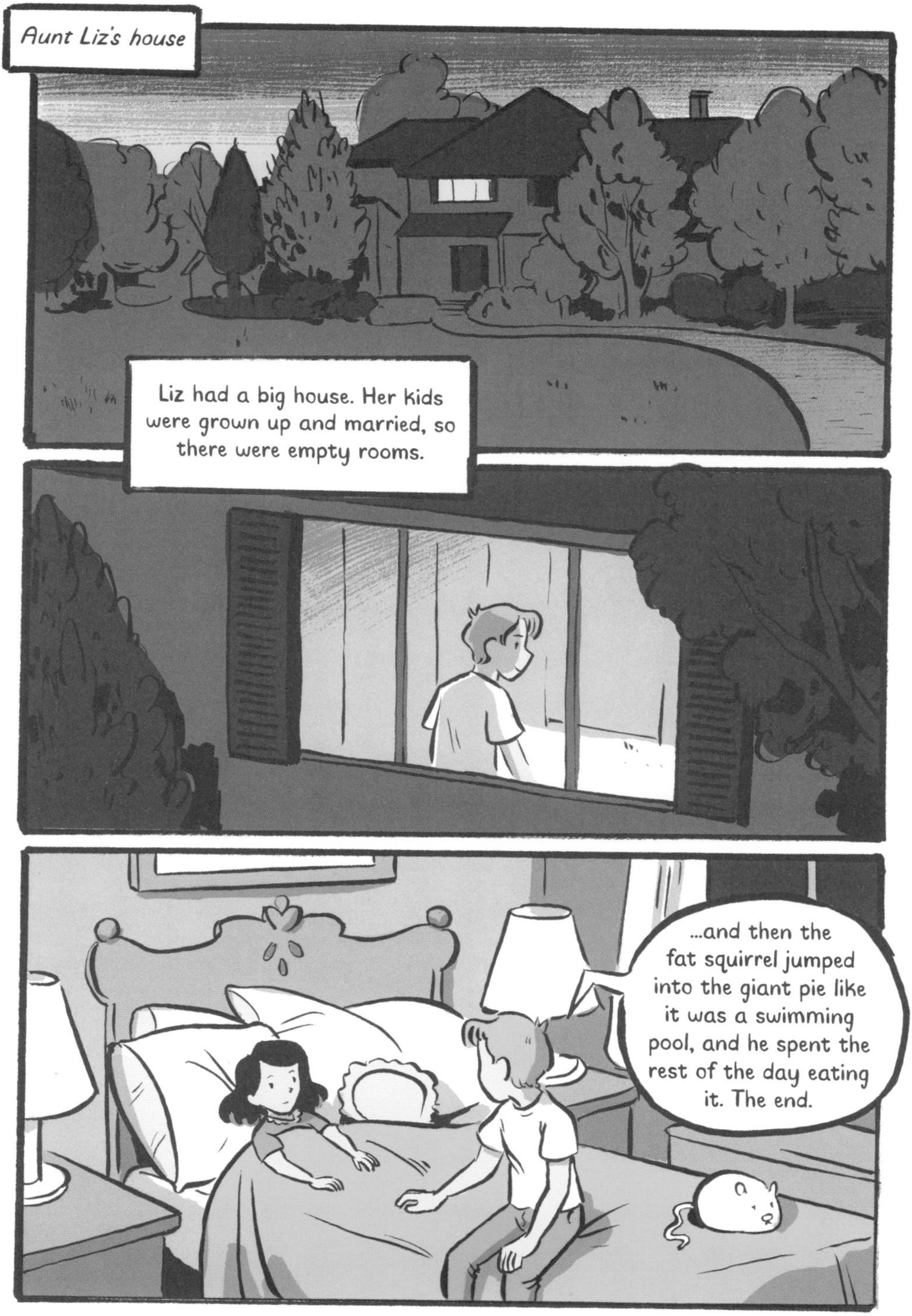
Aunt Liz's house
Liz had a big house. Her kids were grown up and married, so there were empty rooms.
...and then the fat squirrel jumped into the giant pie like it was a swimming pool, and he spent the rest of the day eating it. The end.

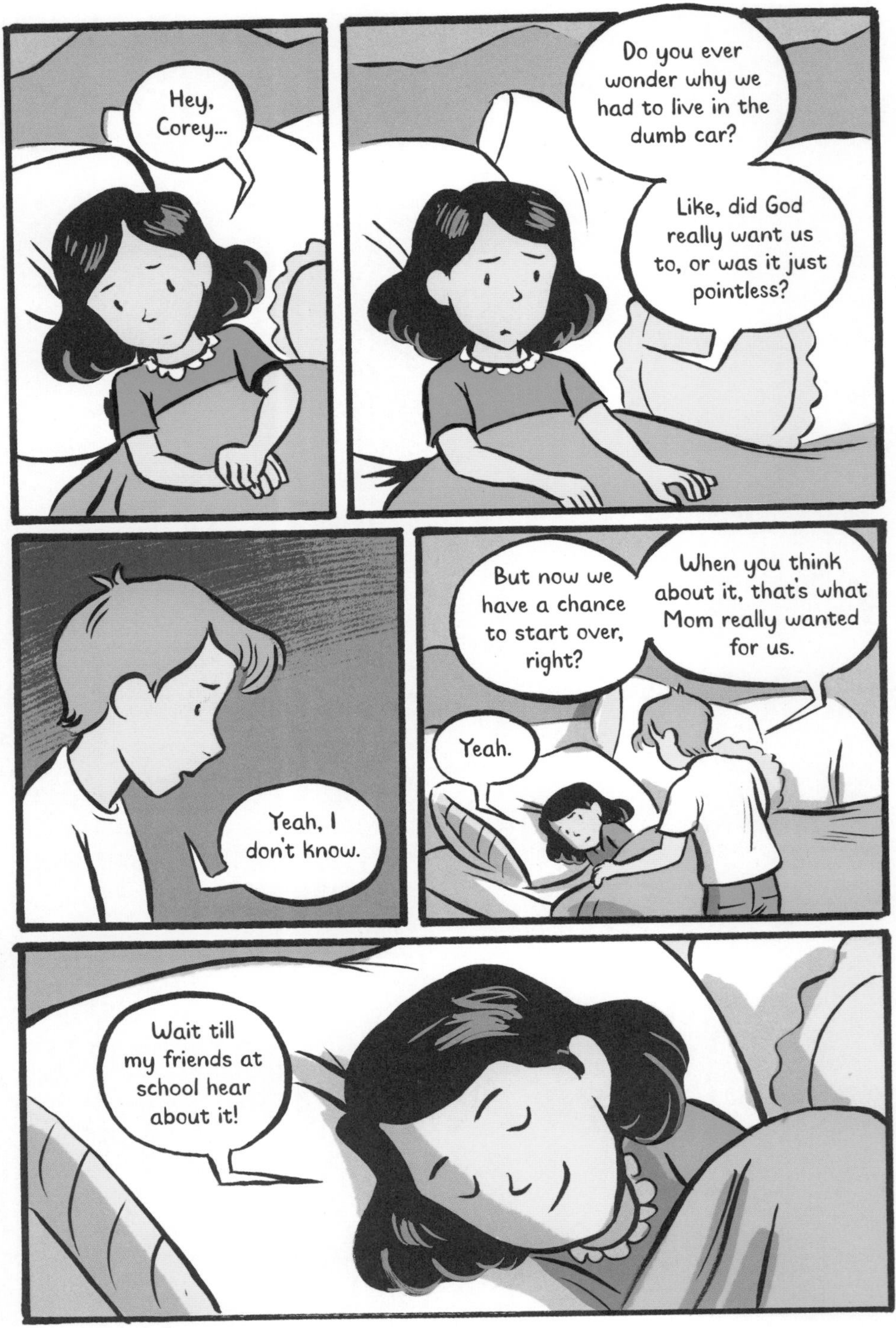
Hey, Corey...
Do you ever wonder why we had to live in the dumb car?
Like, did God really want us to, or was it just pointless?
Yeah, I don't know.
When you think about it, that's what Mom really wanted for us.
But now we have a chance to start over, right?
Yeah.
Wait till my friends at school hear about it!

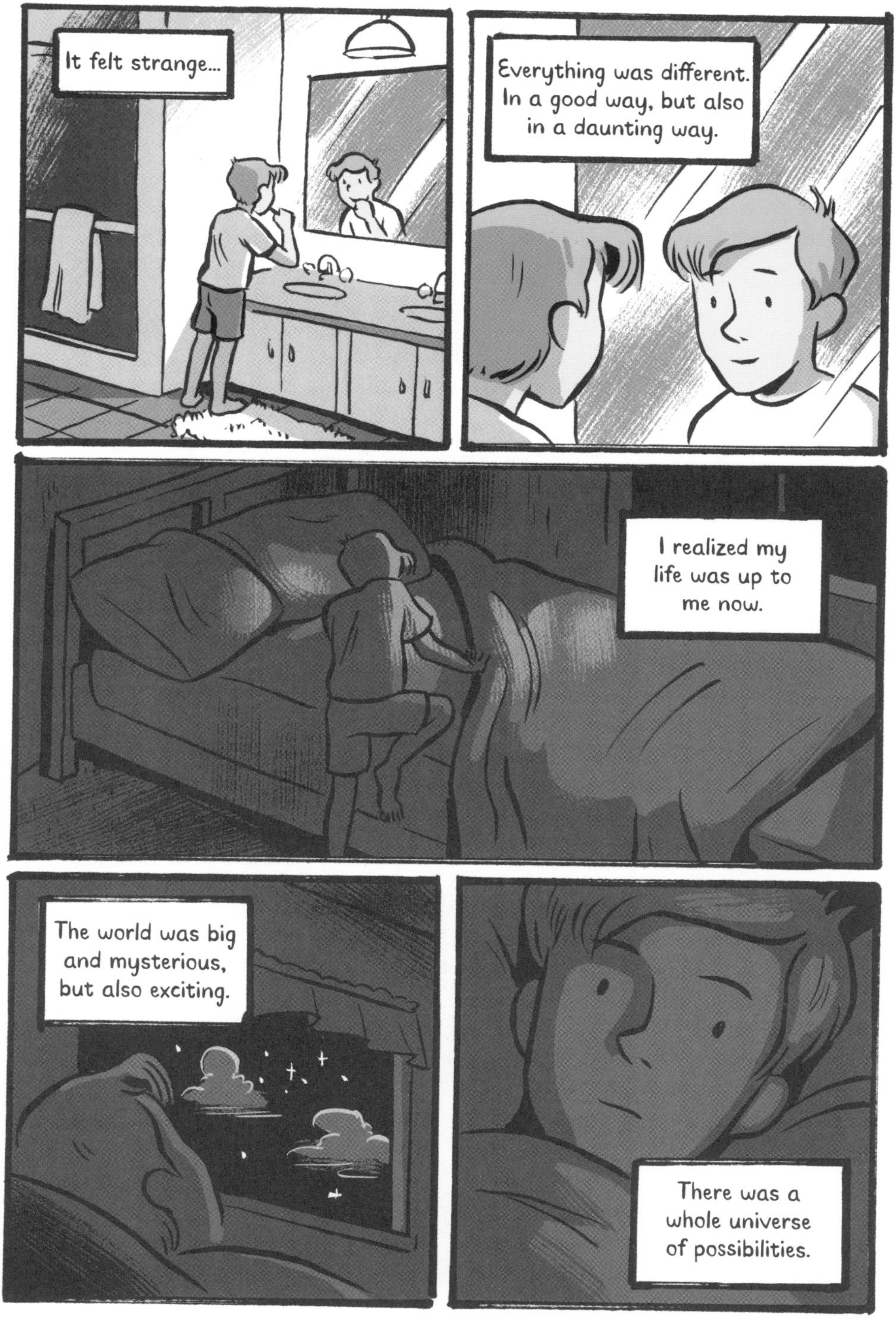
It felt strange...
Everything was different. In a good way, but also in a daunting way.
I realized my life was up to me now.
The world was big and mysterious, but also exciting.
There was a whole universe of possibilities.

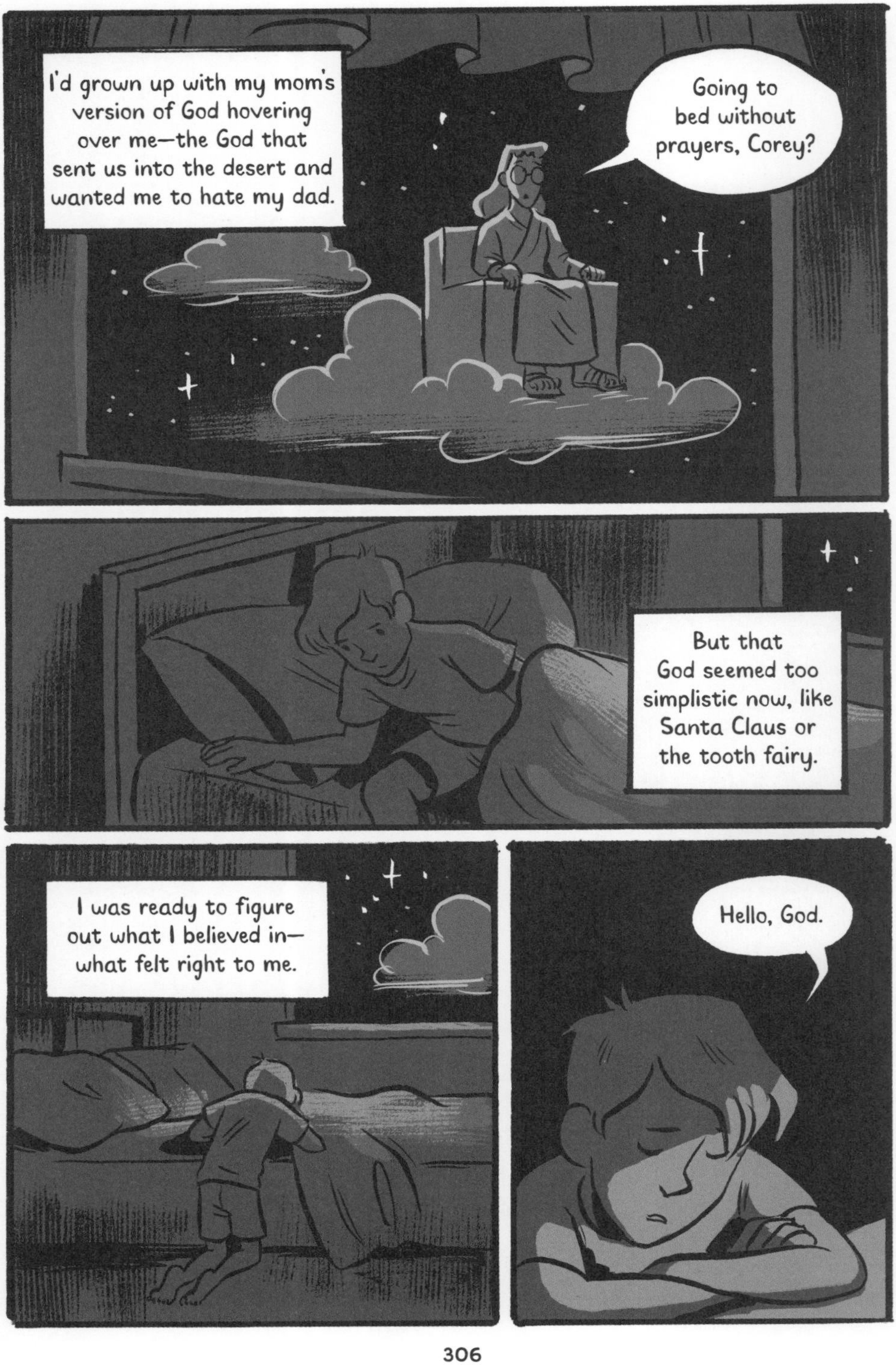
I'd grown up with my mom's version of God hovering over me—the God that sent us into the desert and wanted me to hate my dad.
Going to bed without prayers, Corey?
But that God seemed too simplistic now, like Santa Claus or the tooth fairy.
I was ready to figure out what I believed in—what felt right to me.
Hello, God.

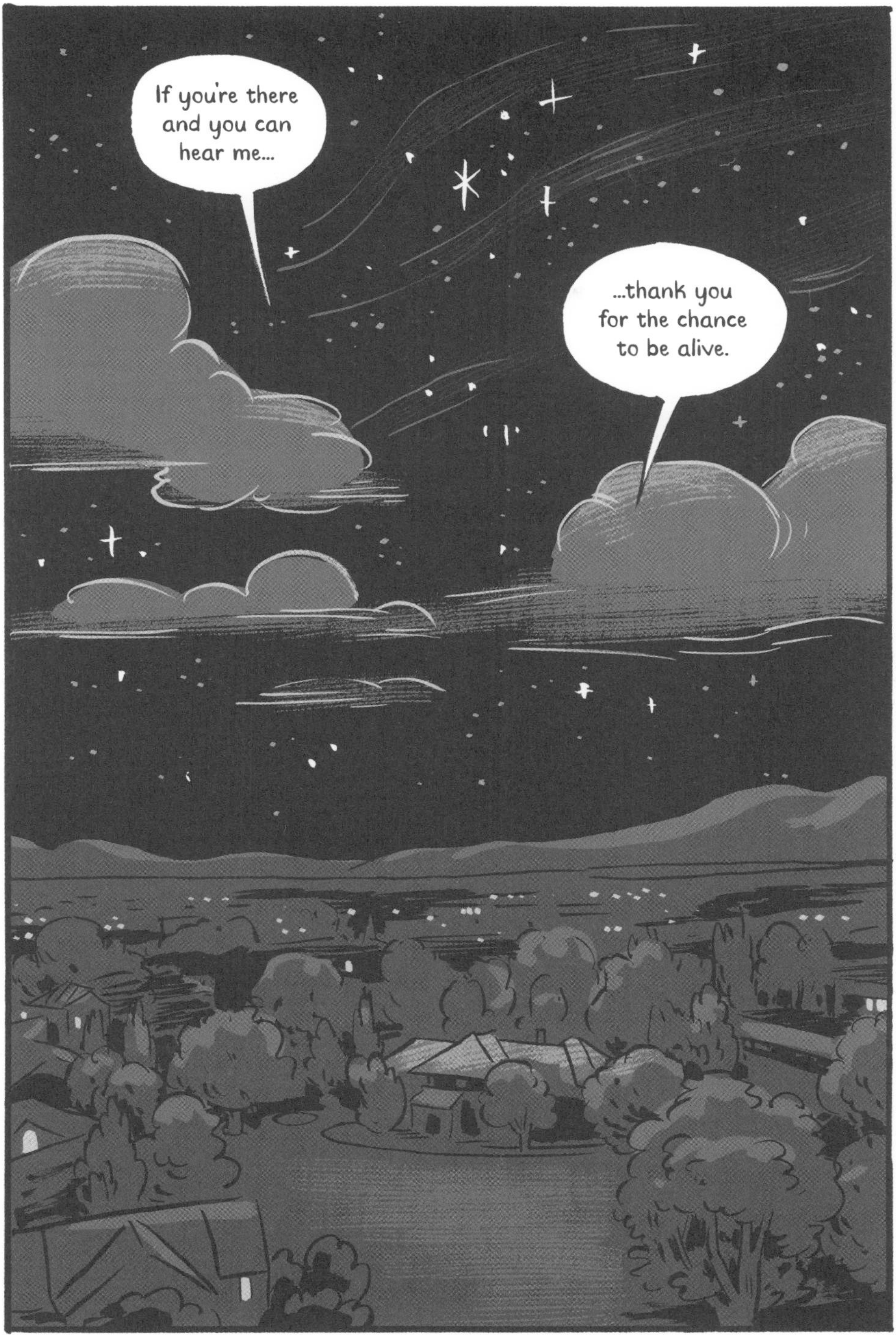
If you're there and you can hear me...
...thank you for the chance to be alive.

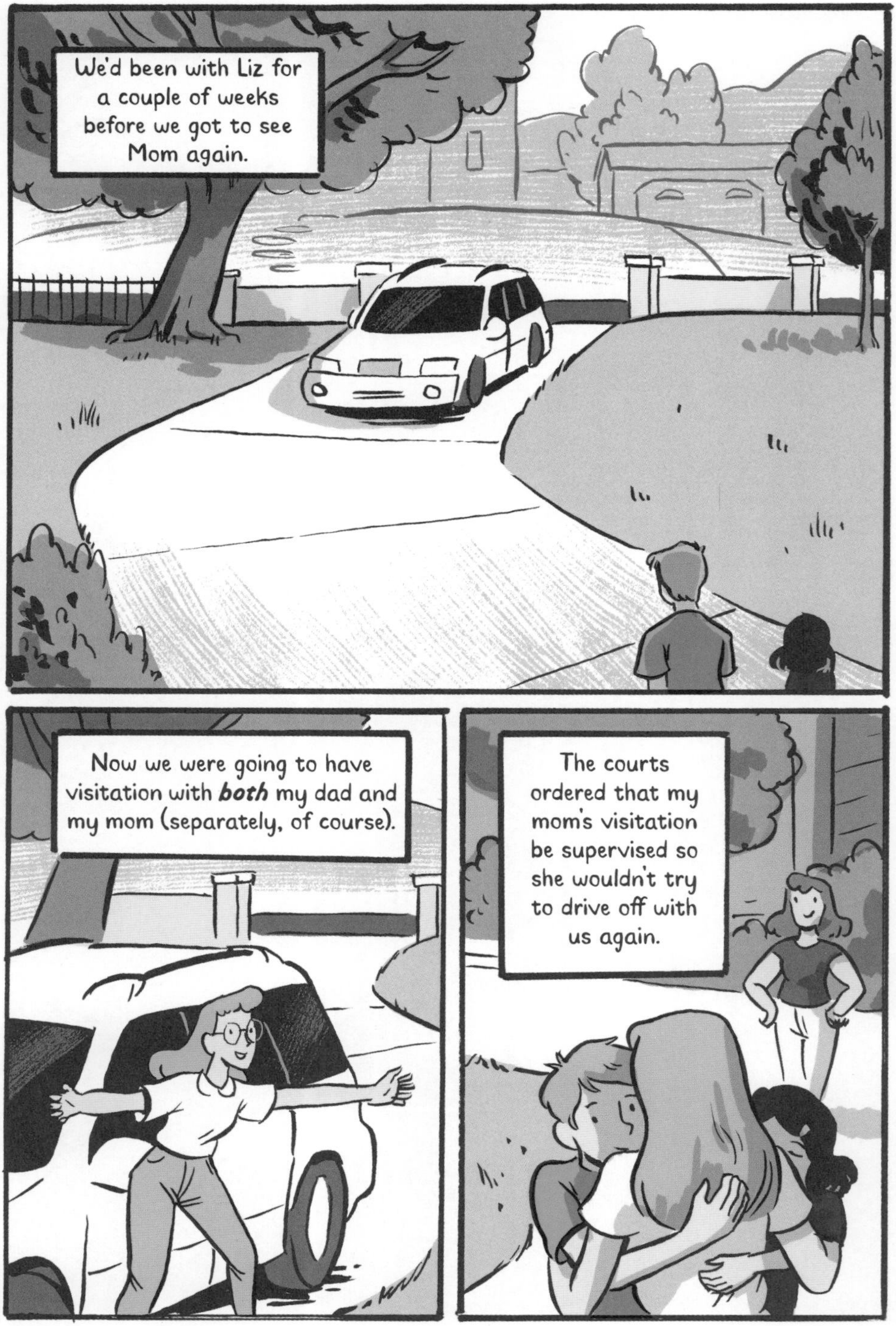
We'd been with Liz for a couple of weeks before we got to see Mom again.
Now we were going to have visitation with ***both*** my dad and my mom (separately, of course).
The courts ordered that my mom's visitation be supervised so she wouldn't try to drive off with us again.

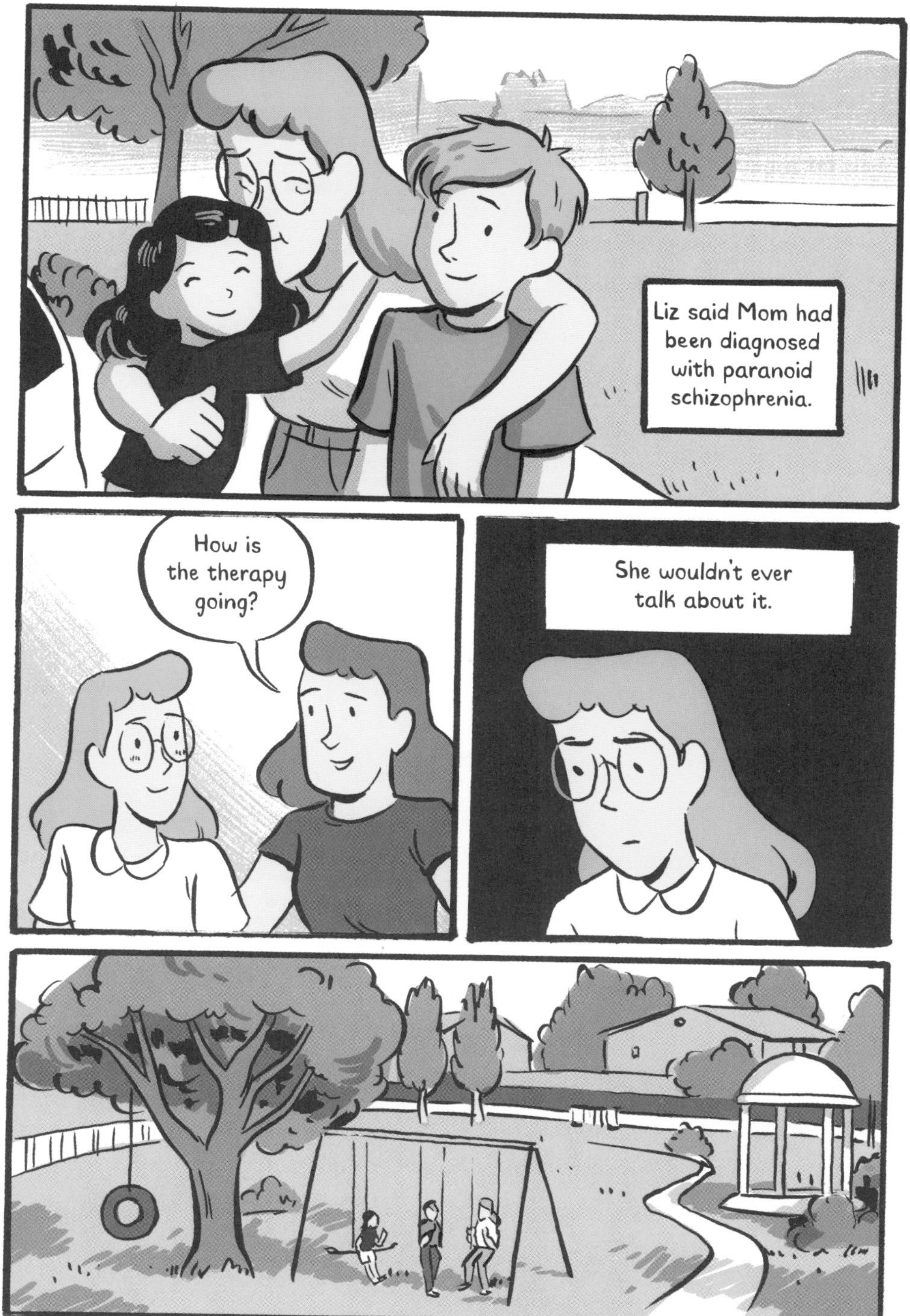
Liz said Mom had been diagnosed with paranoid schizophrenia.
How is the therapy going?
She wouldn't ever talk about it.

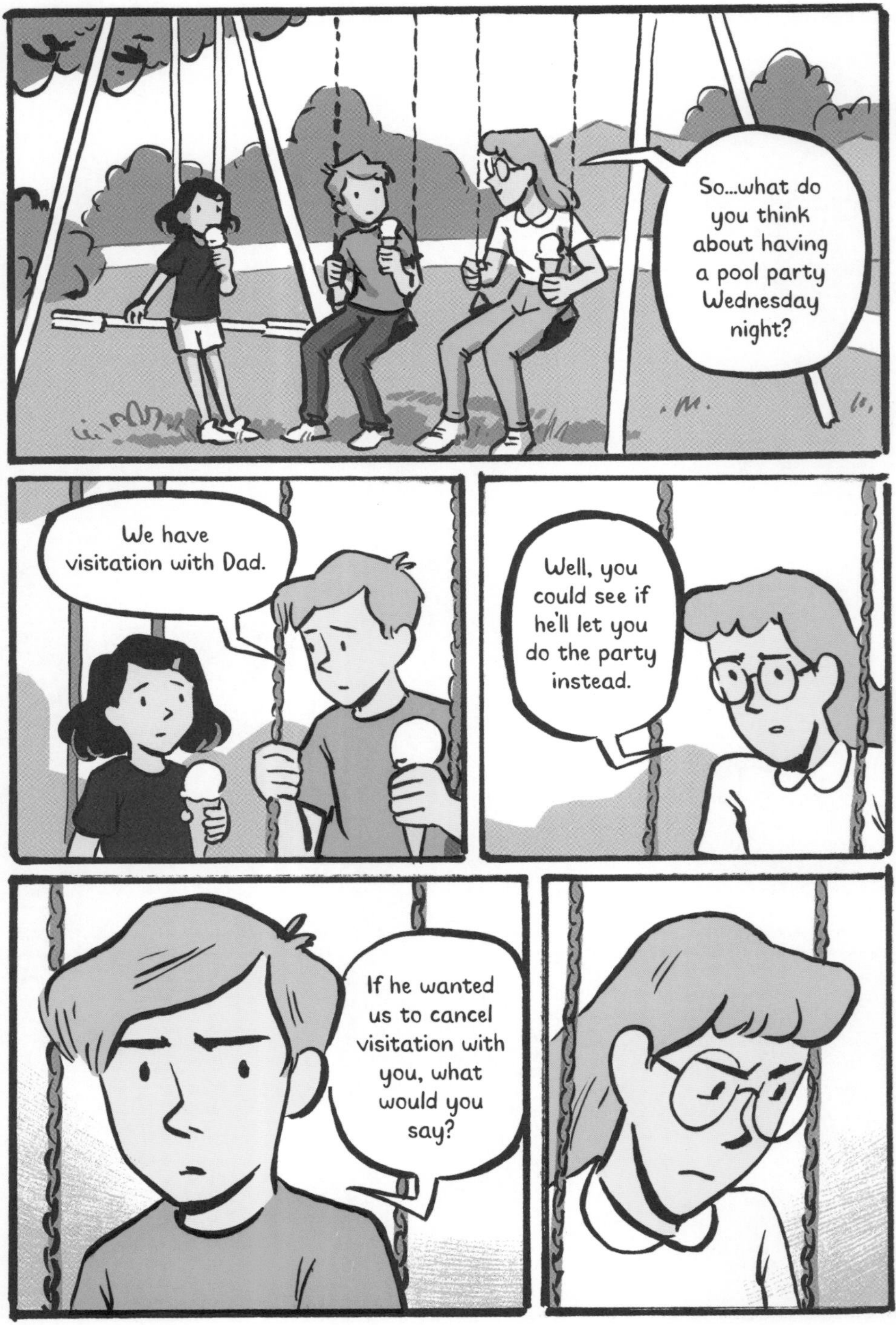
So...what do you think about having a pool party Wednesday night?
We have visitation with Dad.
Well, you could see if he'll let you do the party instead.
If he wanted us to cancel visitation with you, what would you say?

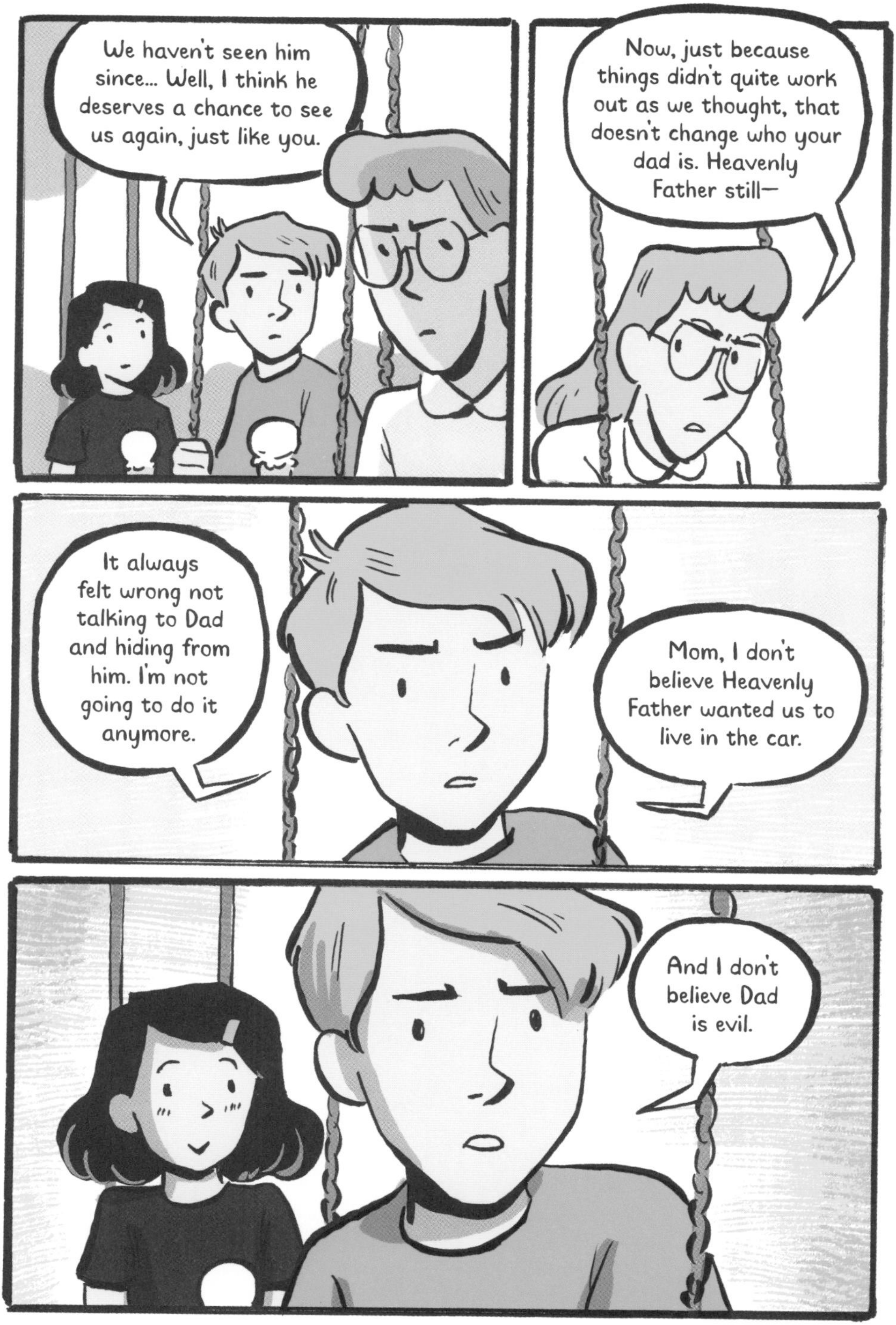
We haven't seen him since... Well, I think he deserves a chance to see us again, just like you.
Now, just because things didn't quite work out as we thought, that doesn't change who your dad is. Heavenly Father still—
It always felt wrong not talking to Dad and hiding from him. I'm not going to do it anymore.
Mom, I don't believe Heavenly Father wanted us to live in the car.
And I don't believe Dad is evil.

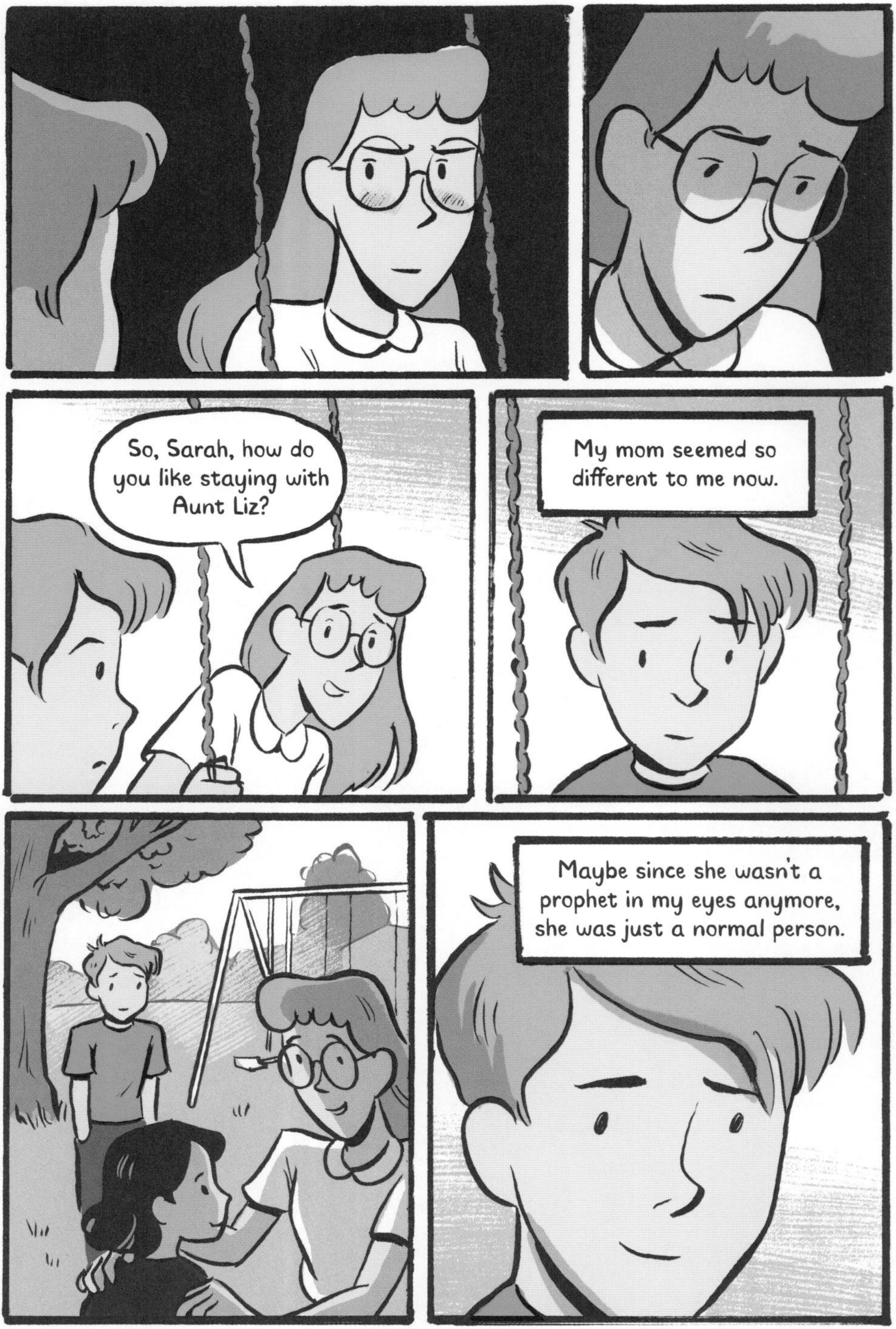
So, Sarah, how do you like staying with Aunt Liz?
My mom seemed so different to me now.
Maybe since she wasn't a prophet in my eyes anymore, she was just a normal person.

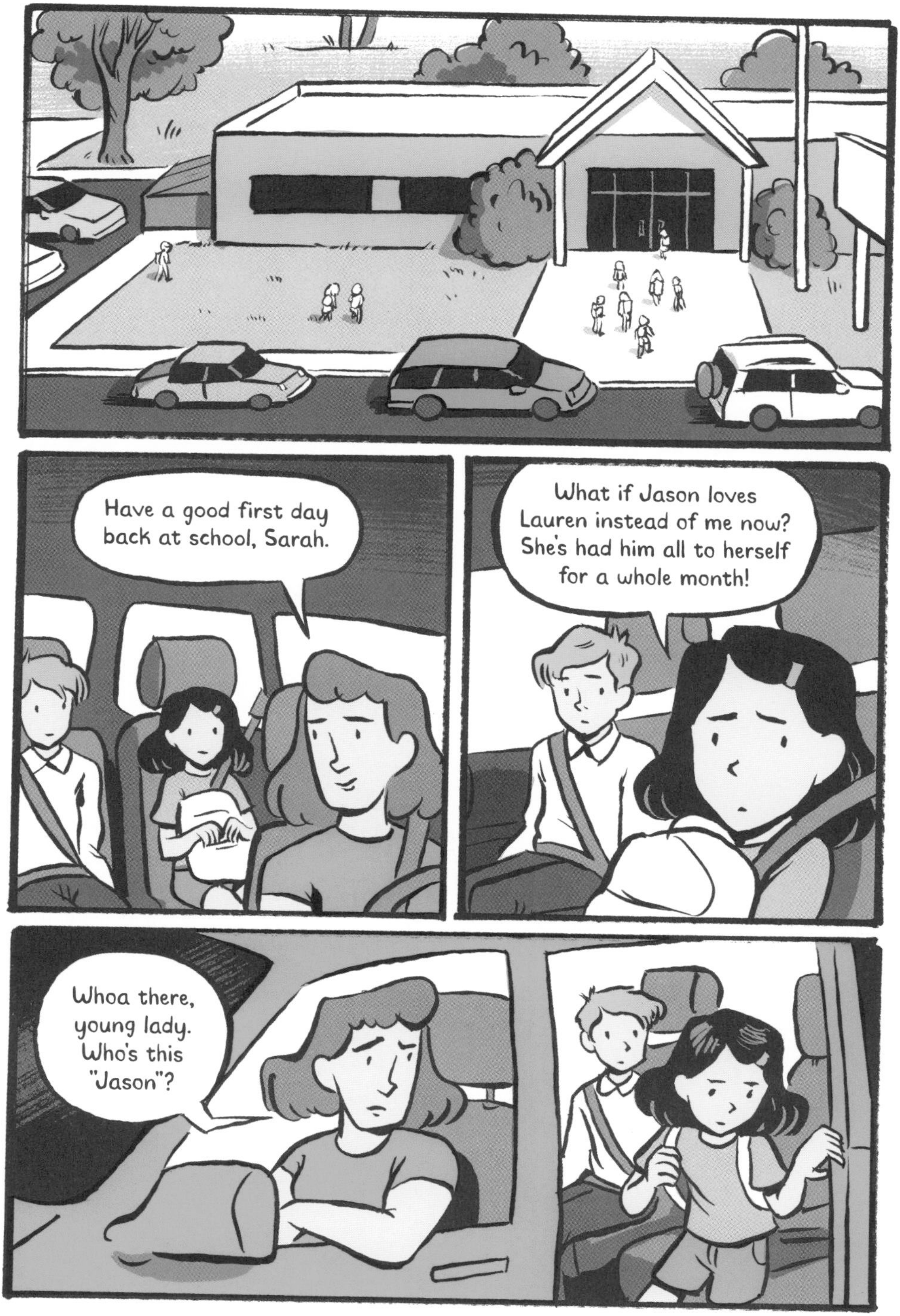
Have a good first day back at school, Sarah.
What if Jason loves Lauren instead of me now? She's had him all to herself for a whole month!
Whoa there, young lady. Who's this "Jason"?

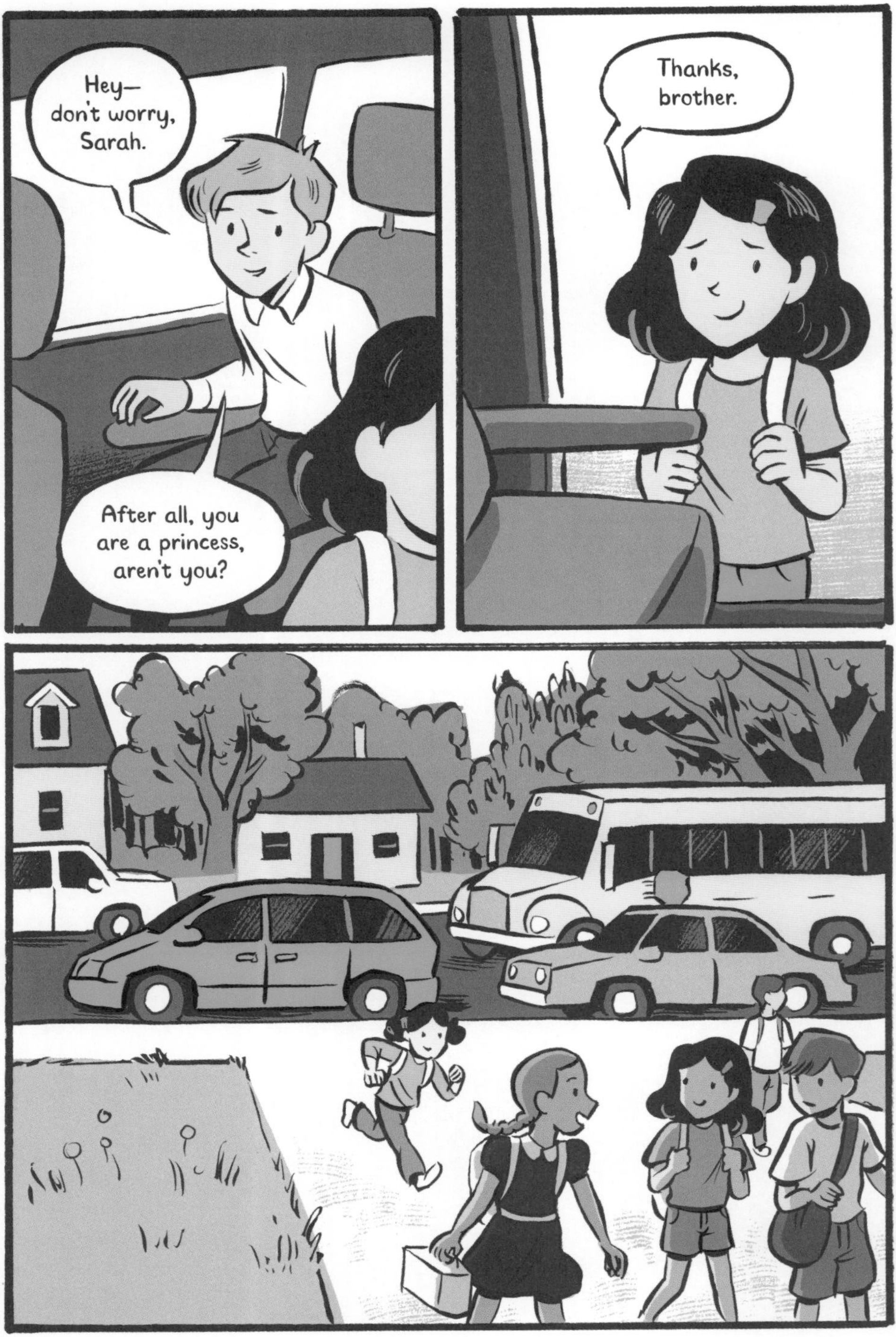
Hey— don't worry, Sarah.
After all, you are a princess, aren't you?
Thanks, brother.

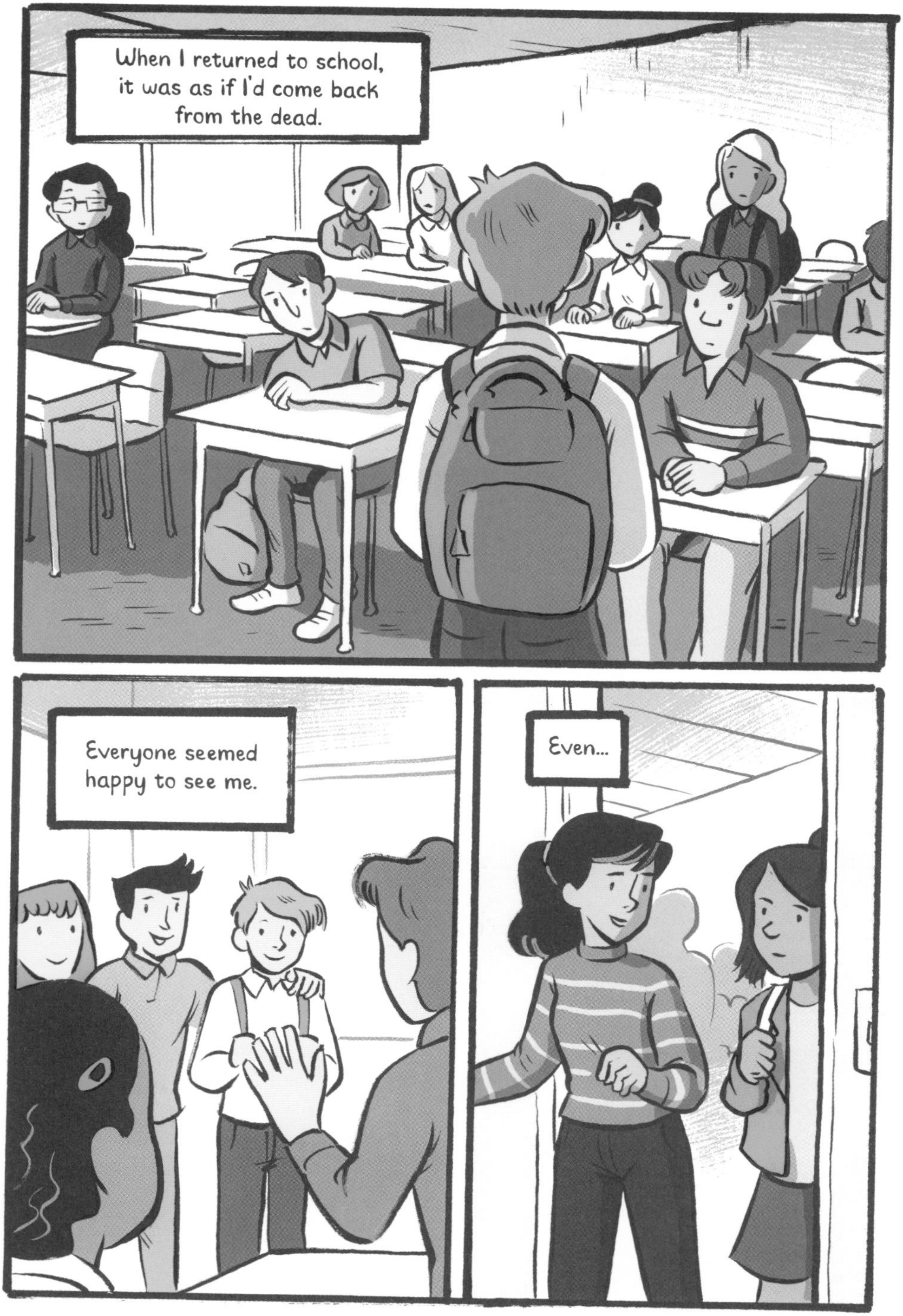
When I returned to school, it was as if I'd come back from the dead.
Everyone seemed happy to see me.
Even...

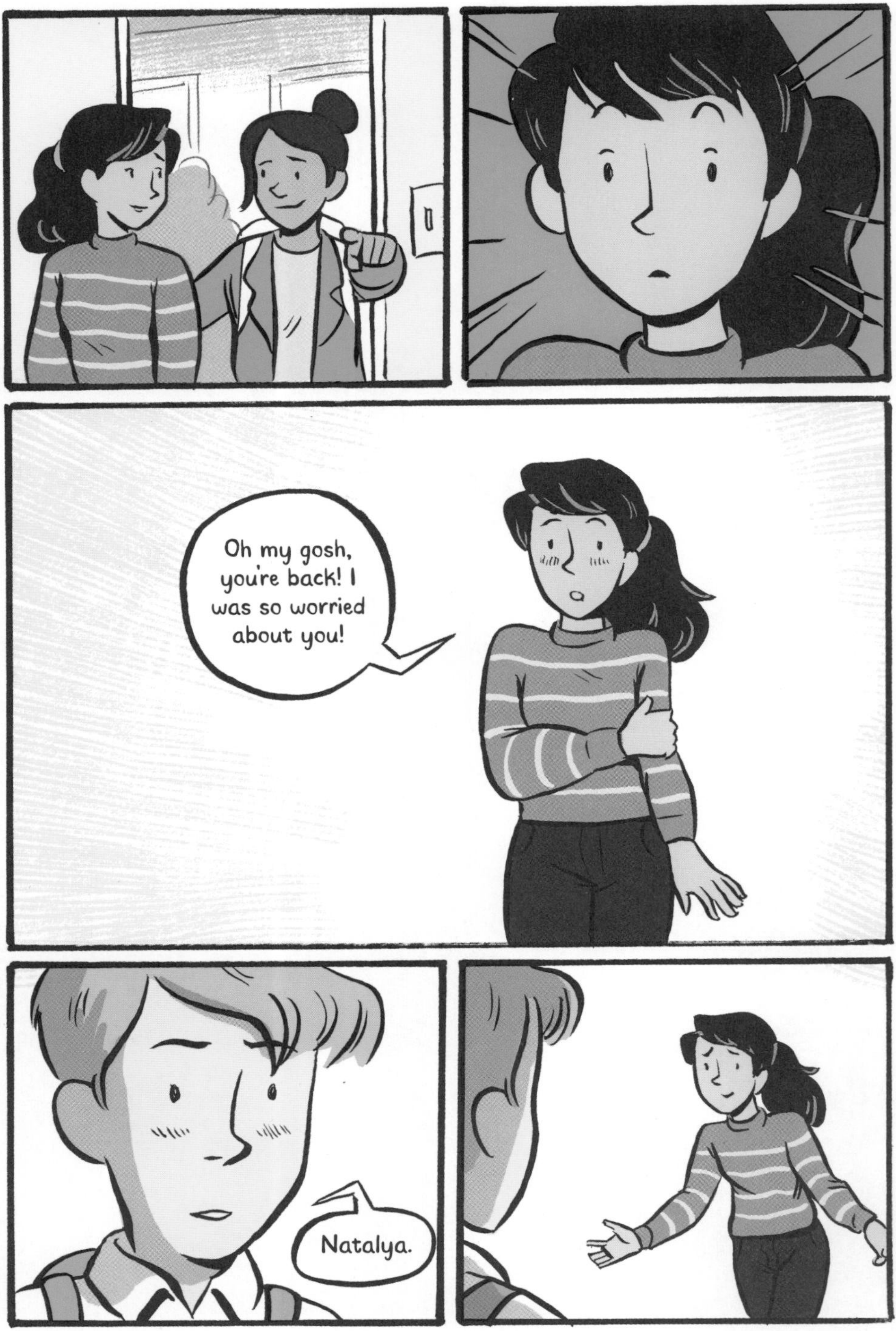
Oh my gosh, you're back! I was so worried about you!
Natalya.

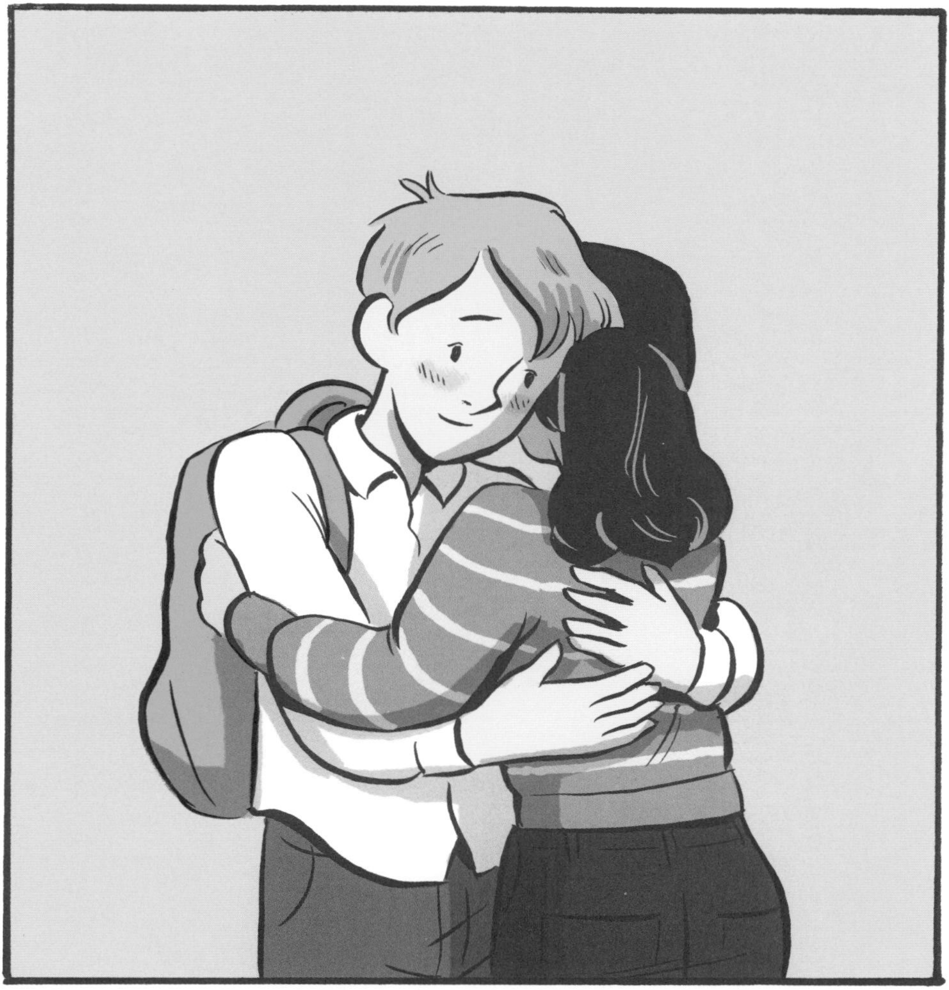

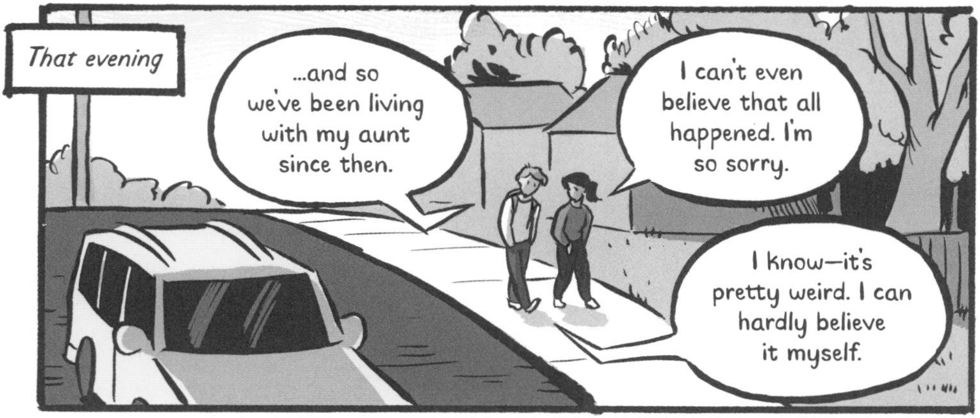
That evening
...and so we've been living with my aunt since then.
I can't even believe that all happened. I'm so sorry.
I know—it's pretty weird. I can hardly believe it myself.

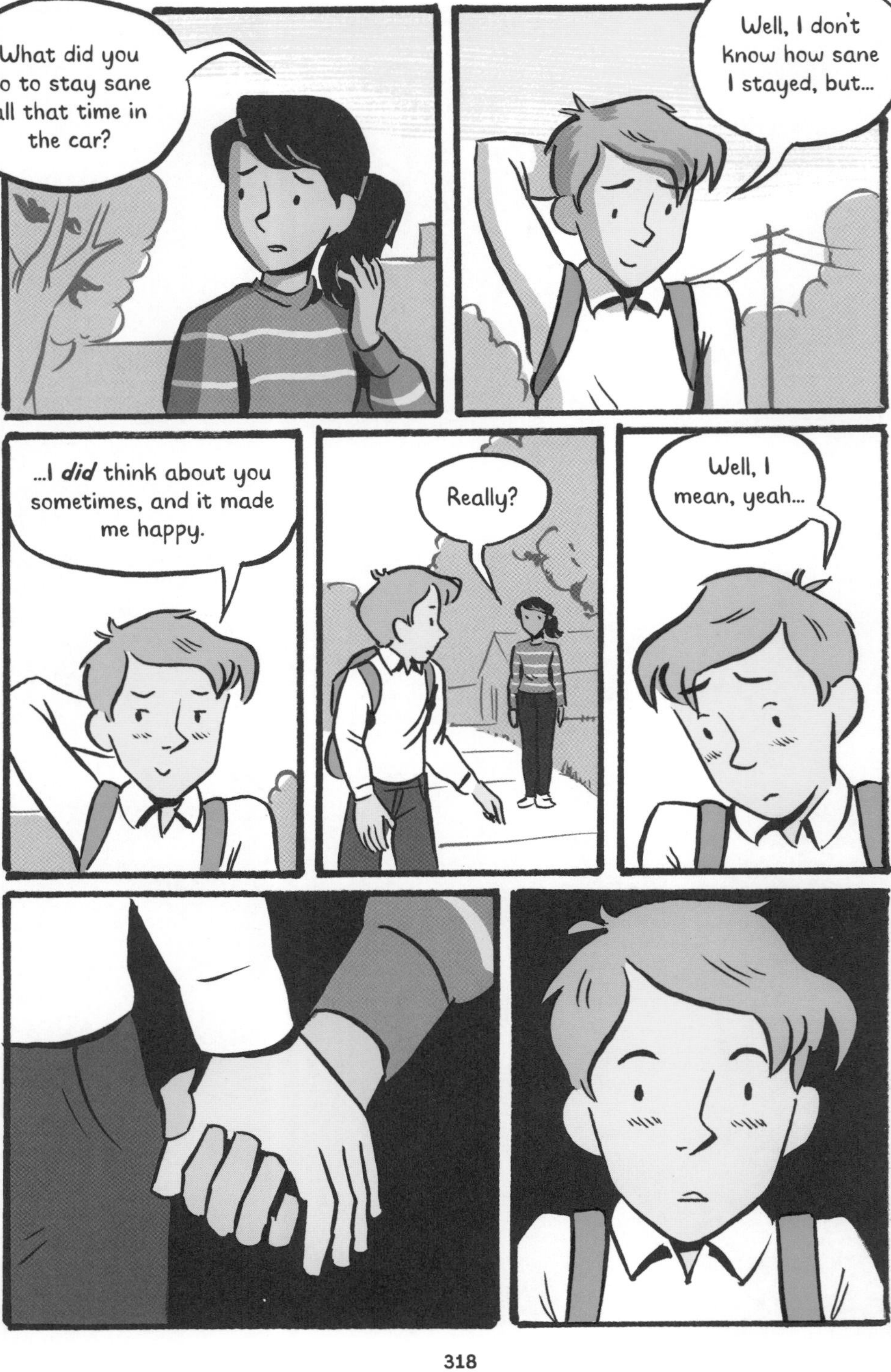
What did you do to stay sane all that time in the car?
Well, I don't know how sane I stayed, but...
...I *did* think about you sometimes, and it made me happy.
Really?
Well, I mean, yeah...

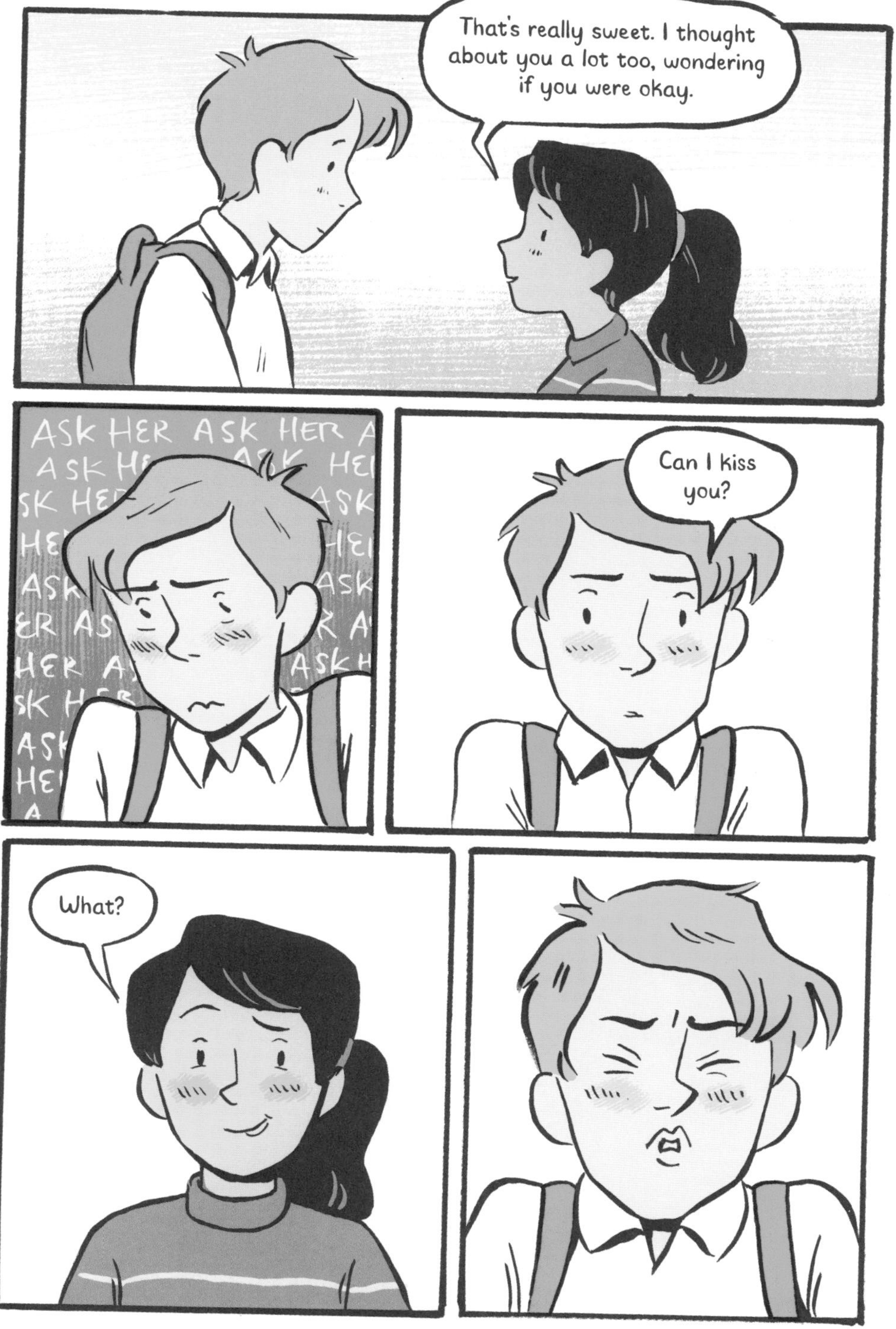

That's really sweet. I thought about you a lot too, wondering if you were okay.
ASK HER ASK HER ASK HER
Can I kiss you?
What?

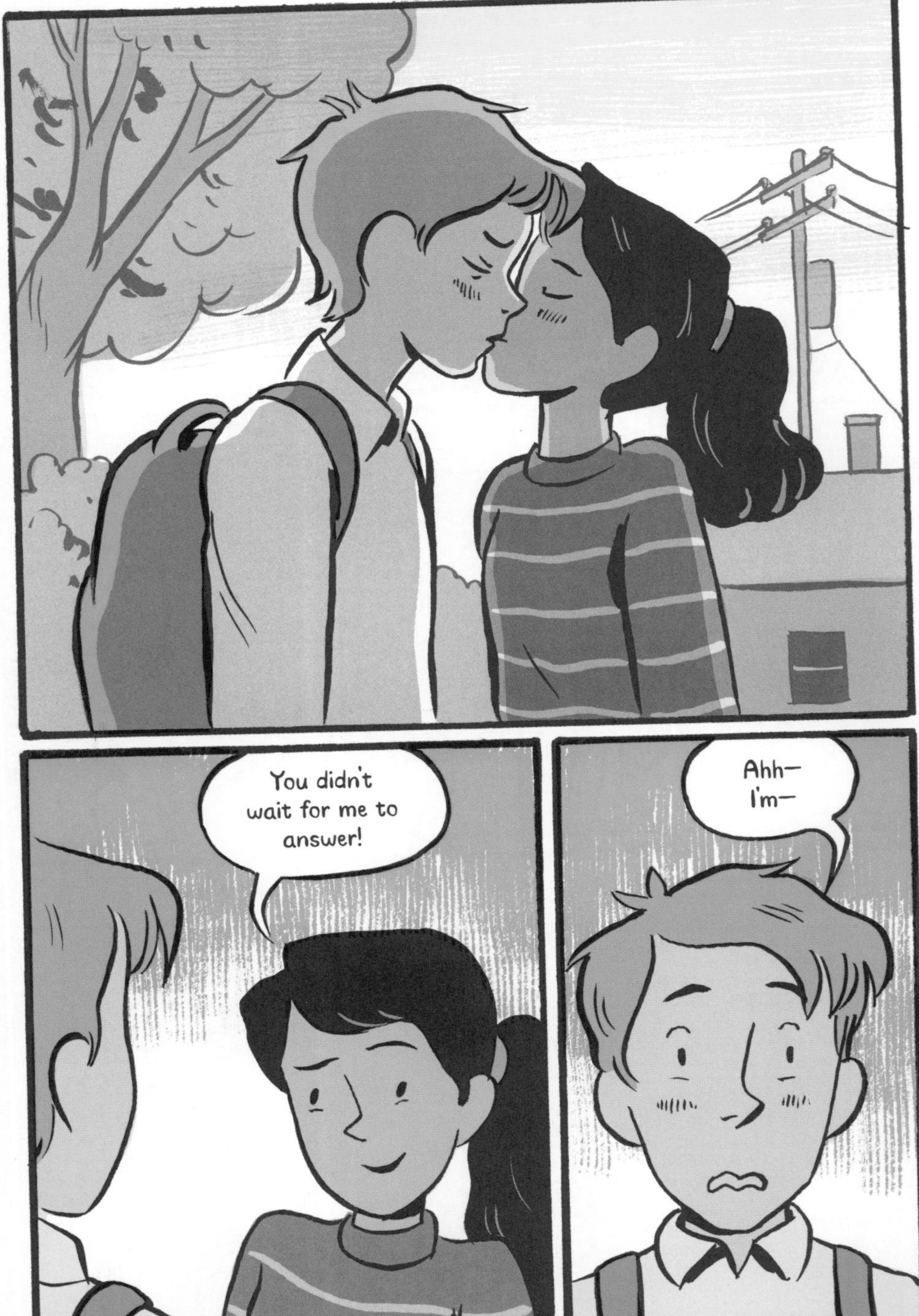
You didn't wait for me to answer!
Ahh— I'm—

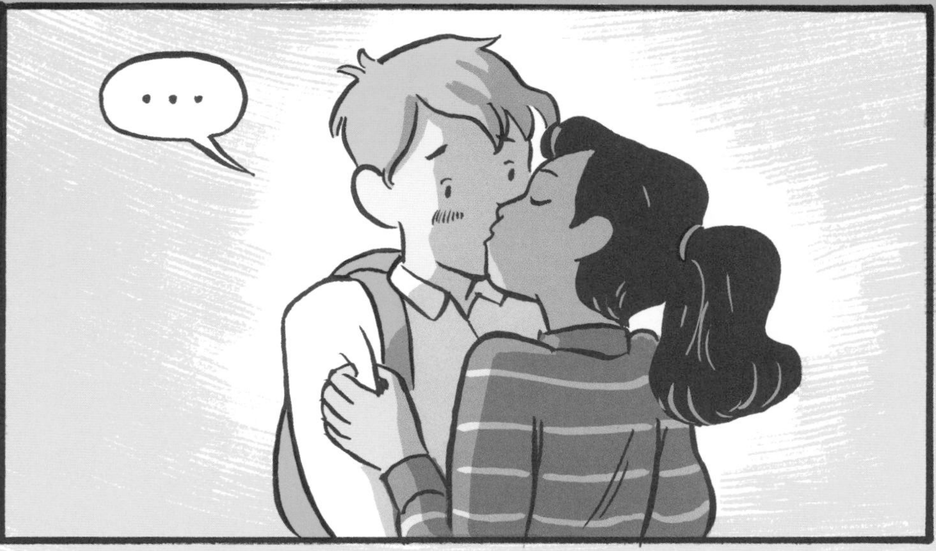
. . .

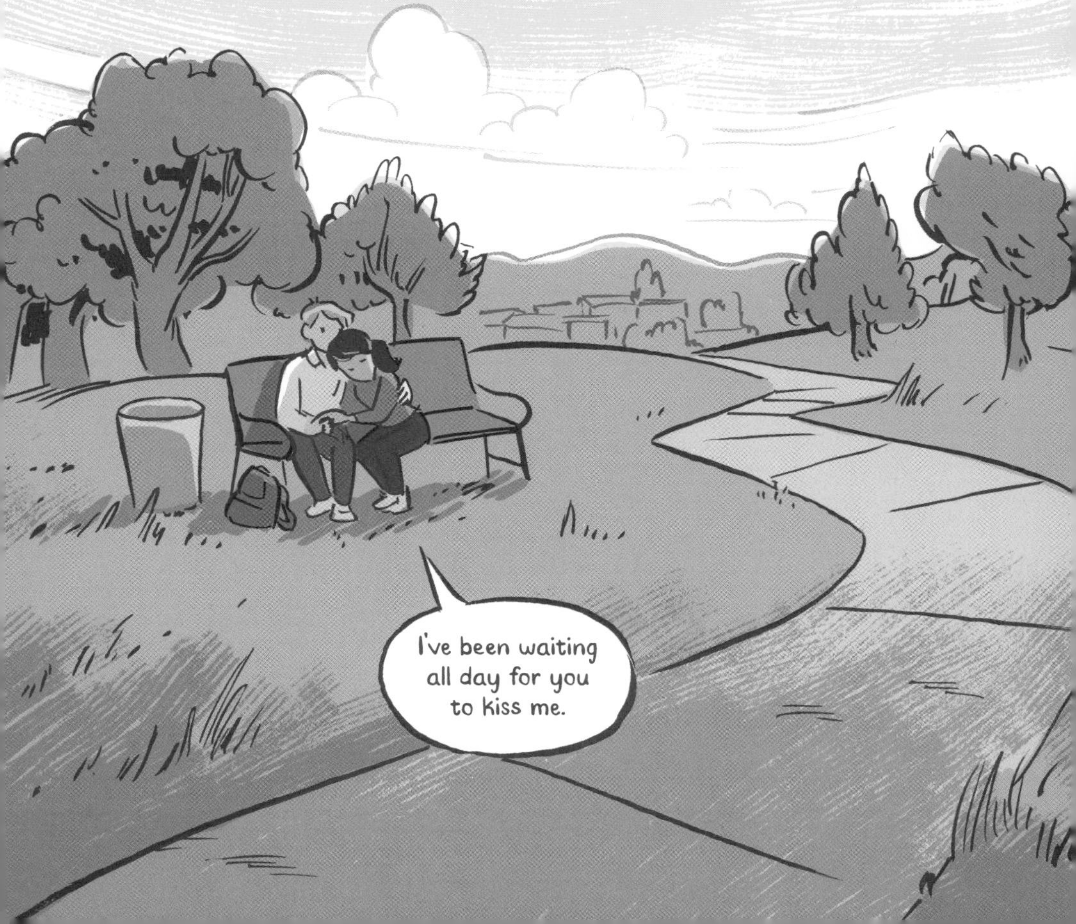
I've been waiting all day for you to kiss me.

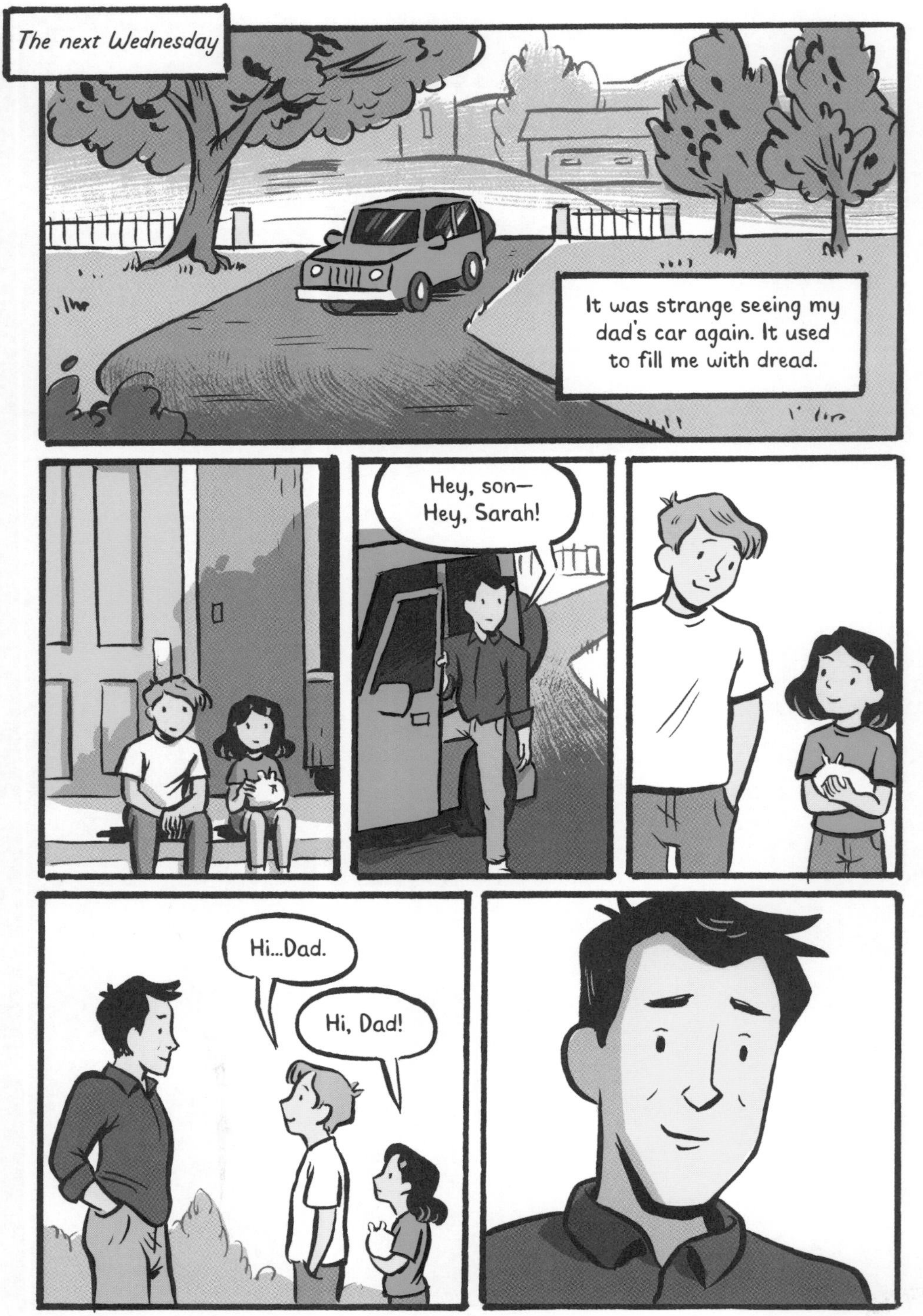
The next Wednesday
It was strange seeing my dad's car again. It used to fill me with dread.
Hey, son—
Hey, Sarah!
Hi...Dad.
Hi, Dad!

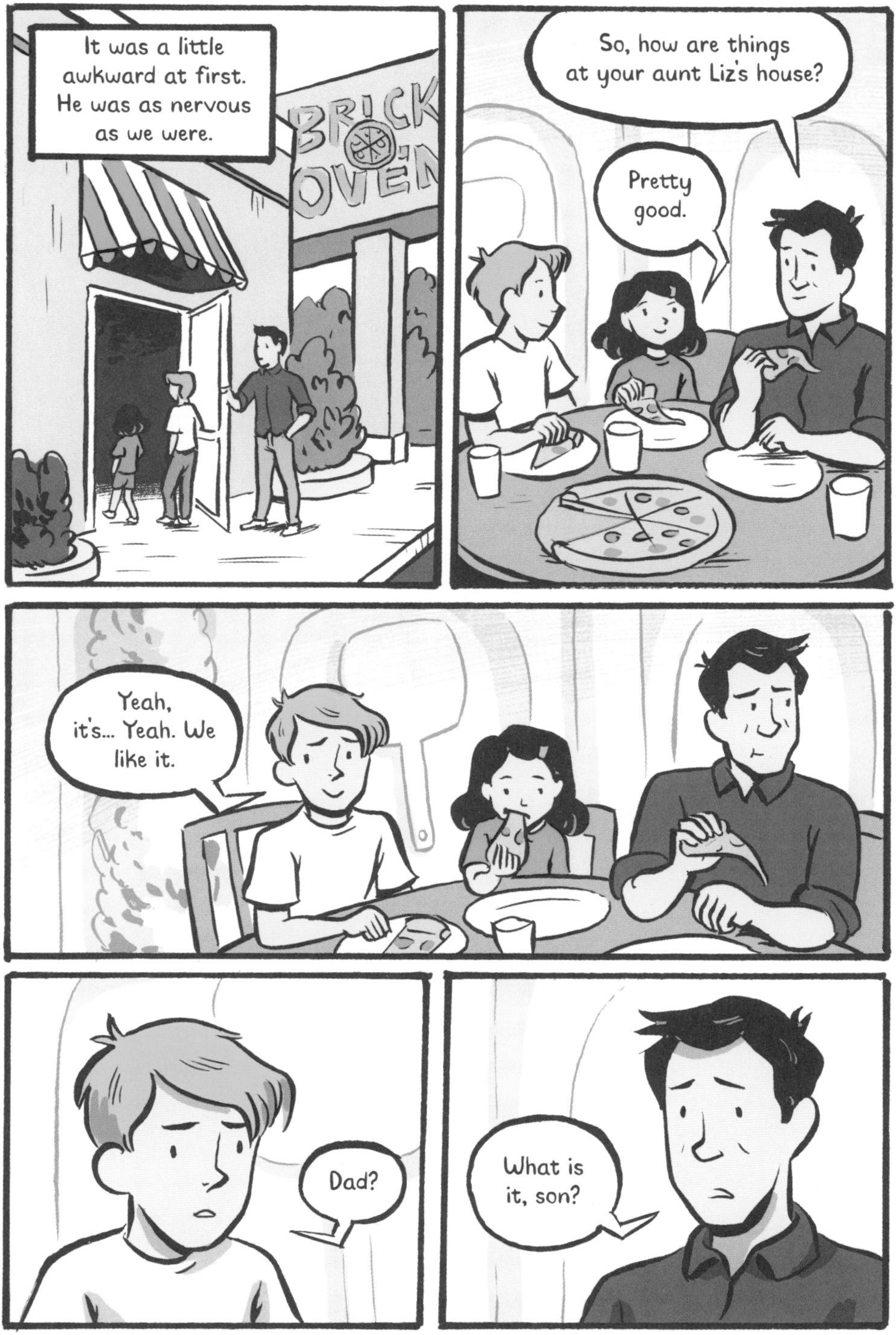
It was a little awkward at first. He was as nervous as we were.
BRICK OVEN
So, how are things at your aunt Liz's house?
Pretty good.
Yeah, it's... Yeah. We like it.
Dad?
What is it, son?

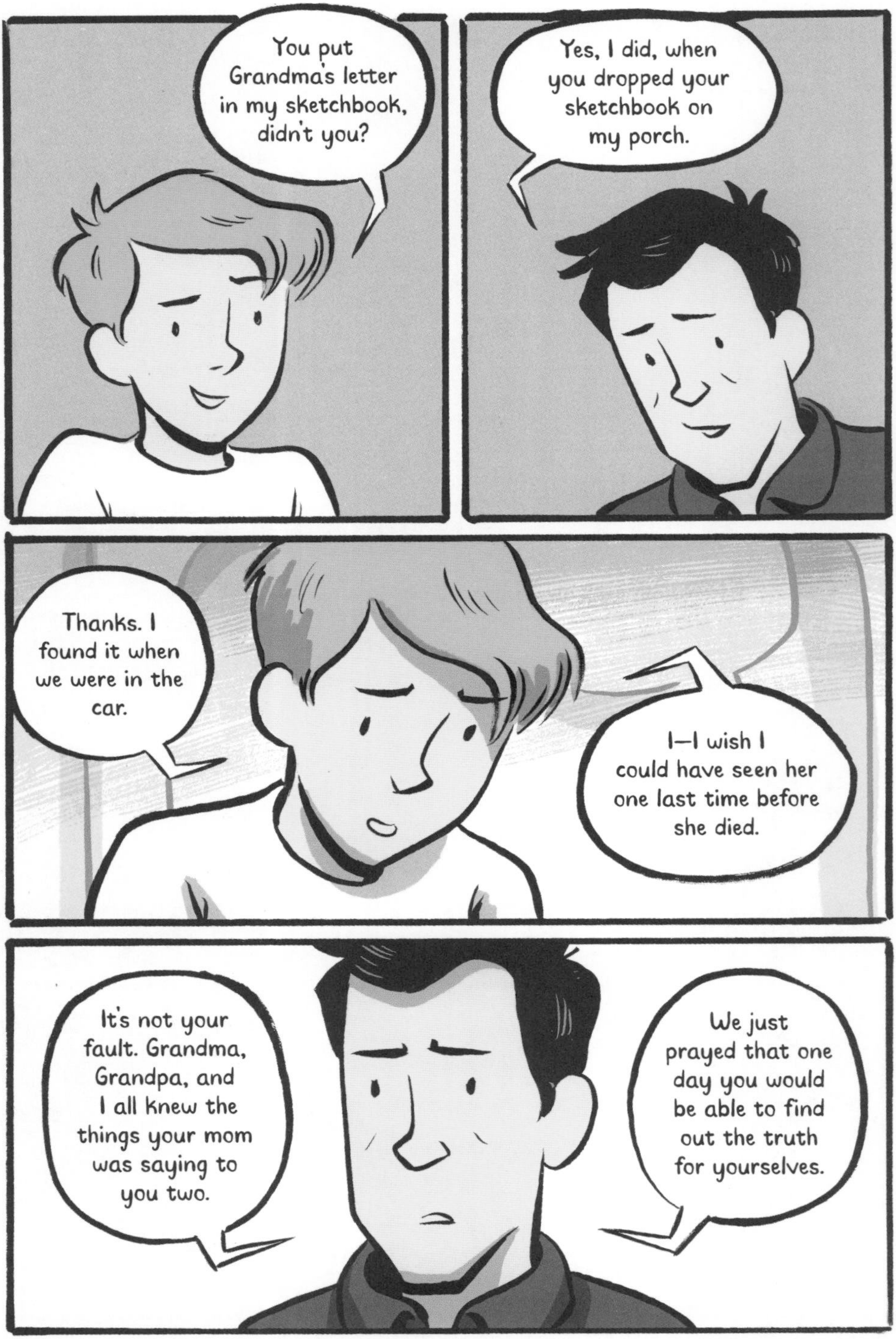

You put Grandma's letter in my sketchbook, didn't you?
Yes, I did, when you dropped your sketchbook on my porch.
Thanks. I found it when we were in the car.
I—I wish I could have seen her one last time before she died.
It's not your fault. Grandma, Grandpa, and I all knew the things your mom was saying to you two.
We just prayed that one day you would be able to find out the truth for yourselves.

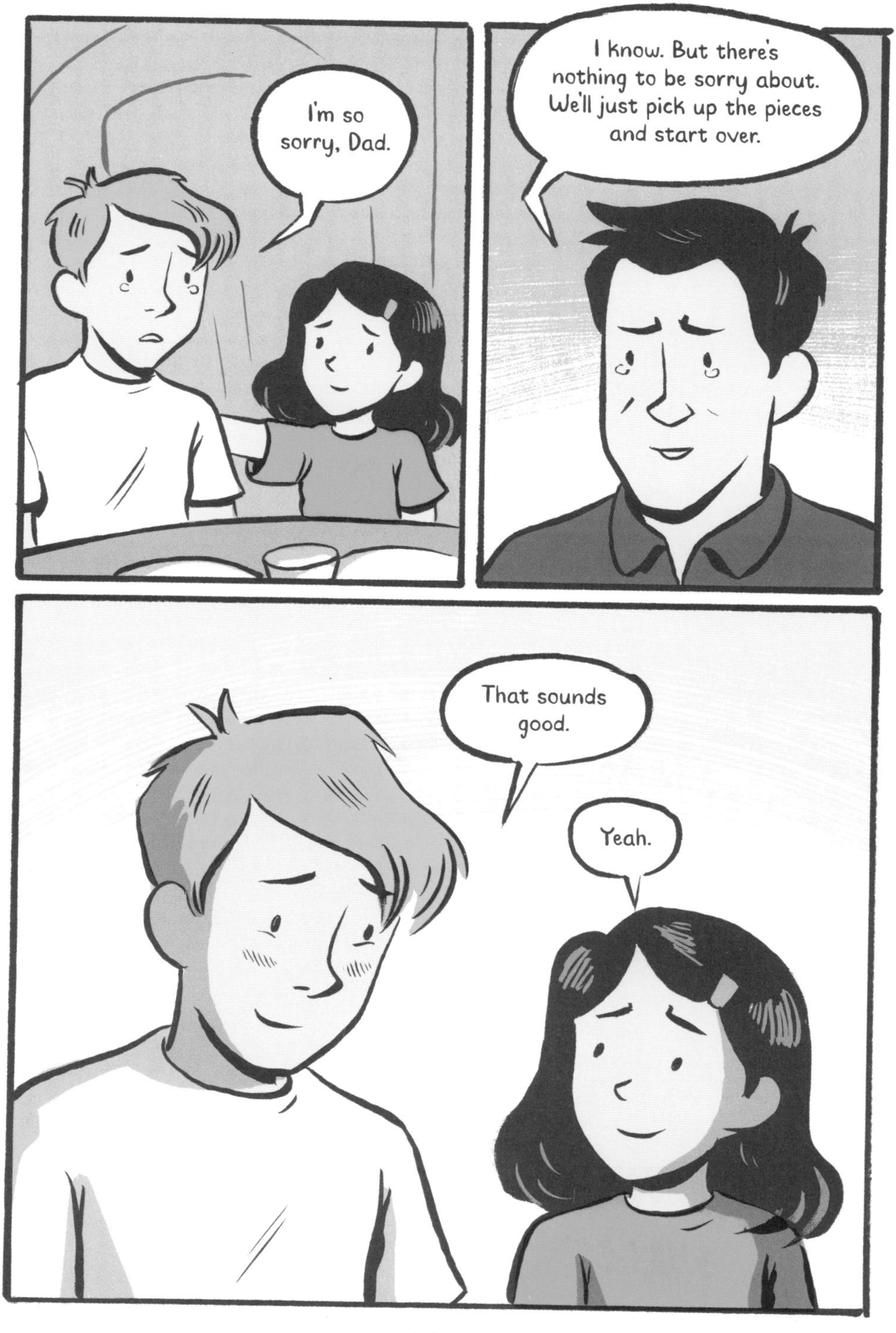
I'm so sorry, Dad.
I know. But there's nothing to be sorry about. We'll just pick up the pieces and start over.
That sounds good.
Yeah.

And that's
what we
did.

AUTHOR'S NOTE

This book is based on true events.

In the spring of 2009 my mom, sister, and I were on the run from police in a Subaru Outback in Nevada. It was one of the hardest, most confusing things I've been through. Sarah and I were a little older than I made us in the book. We'd been having visitation with my dad since our parents' divorce in 2001.

My mom accused my dad of sexually abusing Sarah. This was proved false in court, but sexual abuse is a terrible thing, and allegations of it should be taken seriously. If you have been a victim of sexual abuse, you can call the National Sexual Assault Hotline at 800-656-HOPE, or visit rainn.org to find help.

One night in Nevada, as we were parked beside a brothel near Area 51, I saw swirling lights in the sky, and I stayed awake trying to make sense of everything that was happening to me. For the first time, I was questioning my mom's way of seeing the world. I didn't know what to believe.

Later we drove back to Utah, and it was in Ogden, behind a Shopko, that the police found us and my mom was arrested. Sarah lived in the shelter for several weeks, but I was able to go stay with my aunt until Sarah could come too. My aunt assisted Sarah and me a lot during that time, and we both got to live with my mom again eventually.

Natalya played a big role in helping me and Sarah heal and rebuild our lives. I met her in 2010, and with her encouragement, Sarah and I began repairing our relationship with our dad. He gave Sarah and me each a binder full of letters that he and my grandparents had written to us. Reading them was heartbreaking. My grandma died of ALS in 2007, having been estranged from us. Missing that time with her is one of my biggest regrets. I'm grateful I was able to reconnect with my grandpa and spend time with him before he passed away in 2023.

Natalya and I were married when I was twenty-two, then moved to Virginia with our son. My aunt helped my mom move into a condo. My mom stayed in contact with family off and on, sometimes completely going silent for months, then reemerging like nothing happened. I didn't fully understand how big a role mental illness played in her behavior. Because of this, my relationship with her was strained. I resented the things she put us through, but I always held on to hope that someday we'd return to the same trusting relationship we'd had when I was a kid. In September 2021, however, she called

informing me she was in the hospital from multiple strokes and the doctors didn't think she had much time.

I rushed to Utah. During her last few days with us, she expressed regret to Sarah and me for anything she'd done to hurt us. She died on October 13, in her sister's home, with Sarah and me holding her hands. At her bedside and at her funeral, many people expressed beautiful and cherished memories of her. She was a kind person, and when her perspective wasn't skewed by schizophrenia, she was the best mom you could ask for. The biggest tragedy is that her illness put a wedge between her and her loved ones. If you need help dealing with mental illness, you can call the National Alliance on Mental Illness (NAMI) helpline at 800-950-NAMI, visit nami.org, or, in a crisis, text "HOME" to 741741.

Natalya and I currently live with our son in a little house by the woods in Virginia. I work as an author and illustrator. Sarah lives with her husband in Utah, where she works as a legal assistant (coincidentally in the same office that handled our parents' divorce). She was a big resource in helping me with details for this book. My dad lives in Utah with his new wife. We stay in touch.

Special thanks to Joy Peskin for sparking the idea of this book and seeing it through to its completion. To my agent, Nicole Tugeau, for putting my work in the right hands and helping me navigate the intimidating world of publishing. To Kirk Benshoff, Hannah Miller, Sunny Lee, and the whole FSG/Macmillan team. To Ginny Hsu and Frank Cammuso for helping me have a lot more confidence. To Alec Johnson for the long, nerdy conversations. To Katie Kerr and Rachel Byers for their assistance with coloring. To Sarah for your love, support, encouragement, and awesome attitude, and to Natalya for spending countless hours inking the panel borders, scanning, formatting, coloring, and supporting me in so many ways through this journey.

In loving memory of my mom, 1964–2021, my Grandma Egbert, 1936–2007, and Grandpa Egbert, 1934–2023.

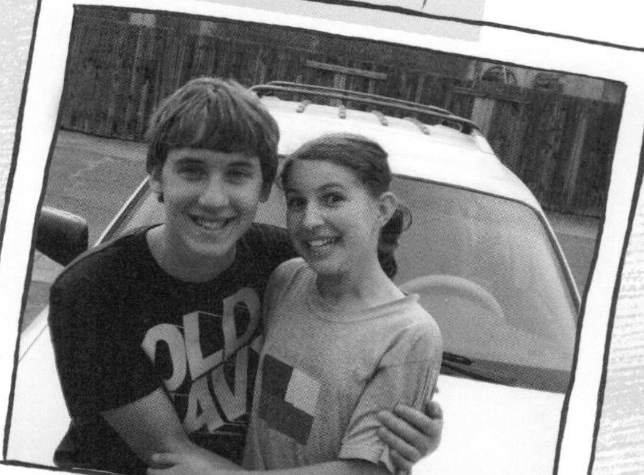

Corey, Sarah, and the car, around the same time as the events in this book

Journal entry while living in the car

March 21, 2008

We've been living in our car for eleven days now. It's felt like a month. Meals are no bigger than a handful of food each. I'm starting to feel weak. I wonder how much I weigh? I can tell I've lost weight because my pants are looser. I'm really ~~wanting~~ looking forward to ~~have~~ a shower because ~~My head~~ scalp is itchy and hurts, and I'm getting a rash. The thought of food, freedom, home, beds, life, are what's keeping me going. Mostly faith and hope in Heavenly Father, actually. If I didn't have the gospel, I couldn't handle this. But I know we are being led, protected and blessed by the Lord. I have learned so much and I grateful: The things I've learned ... on my

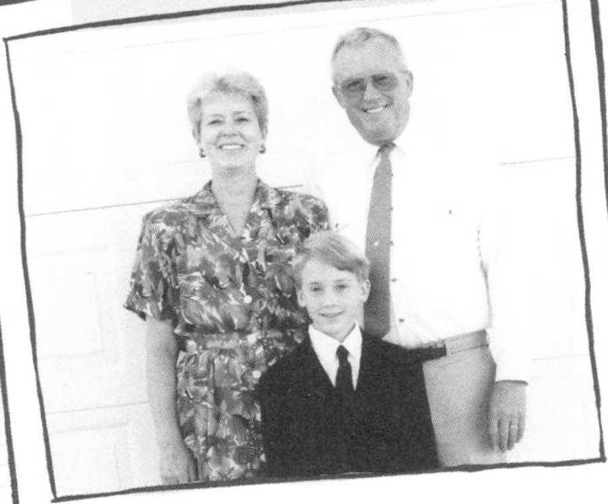

Corey (age 8) and his
Grandma and Grandpa Egbert

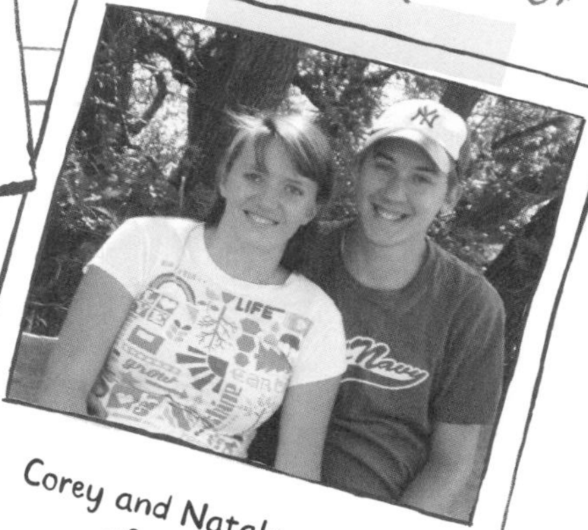
LIFE

Corey and Natalya shortly
after they met

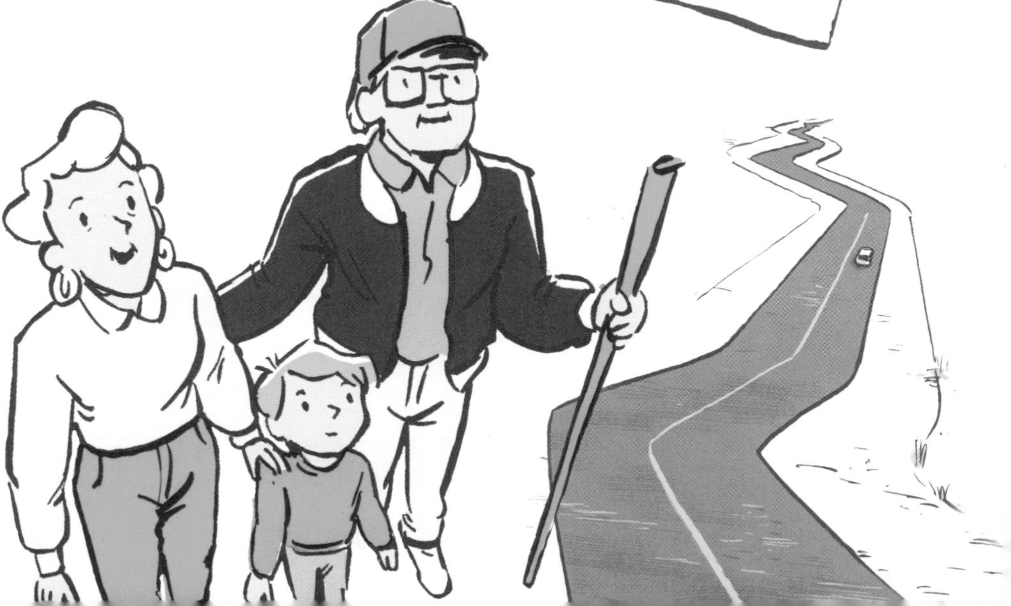

Lehi Apartment